Praise for *Black against Empire*

"There have been at least a half dozen books and films by former Panthers, or about them, over the last decade. *Black against Empire,* however, is unique among them in the scope and depth of its scholarship."
—Héctor Tobar, *Los Angeles Times Book Review*

"Vivid renderings of scene . . . make comprehensible both the movement and the times."
—*Publishers Weekly* STARRED REVIEW

"The first comprehensive history of the Party."
—Fredrick Harris, *London Review of Books*

"A comprehensive and compelling history of the Black Panther Party. As close to complete as one text can possibly be, it is the book I would recommend to anyone wanting to read just one book about the Black Panthers."
—Ron Jacobs, *CounterPunch*

"Twelve years of archival research helped the authors produce this first comprehensive book on the Black Panther Party, its members, its leaders, and its resistance to the politics of the American government."
—*Los Angeles Magazine*

"Lets you understand what happened—and why."
—*American History*

"*Black against Empire* breaks new scholarly ground in providing the first comprehensive history of the Black Panther Party. . . . [It] represents a significant contribution in restoring the integrity of Black Panther Party activists who fought for social justice, and shows how the history of racism in America sparked mental anguish and torment among black peoples, who resisted in the best ways they knew how."
—Jeremy Kuzmarov, *History News Network*

"A welcome addition to the literature about the Oakland-born organization that spread across the country like a prairie fire in the aftermath of the assassination of Martin Luther King Jr. in April 1968 and that altered the consciousness of African Americans."
—Jonah Raskin, *San Francisco Chronicle*

"Immediately assumed a central and critical spot within the Panther canon. . . . As authoritative, respectful, and complete a record of the Black Panther Party's workings as we are likely to get."
—Mark Reynolds, *PopMatters*

"A riveting and thoughtful narrative of the Party's formation and ideational evolution. . . . *Black against Empire* is essential reading for those looking to understand the rise and fall of movements for social change."
—Mary Potorti, *Confluence*

"A bracingly narrated, voluminously researched history of the Black Panther Party. It plumbs rare archives and provides trenchant analysis of how and why the Panthers tapped the historical moment and emerged as a potent force."
—Christopher D. Cook, *Progressive*

"The first high-quality history of the Black Panther Party. . . . For the first time, one can read, in a single volume, a well-researched history that explains the origins of the Panthers in the context of Oakland neighborhood politics and the group's transformation into a social service organization. For that reason alone, the book will become a classic in the growing black power scholarship."
—Fabio Rojas, *American Historical Review*

"This meticulously researched history explores the combination of revolutionary commitment and historical circumstance that enabled the emergence of the Black Panther Party. Because they do not shy away from the contradictions that animated this movement, Joshua Bloom and Waldo Martin pose crucial questions about the genesis, rise, and decline of the BPP that are as relevant to young generations of activists as they are to those who came of age during that era."
—Angela Y. Davis, Distinguished Professor Emerita, History of
　　Consciousness, University of California, Santa Cruz

"This is the book we've all been waiting for: the first complete history of the Black Panther Party, devoid of the hype, the nonsense, the one-dimensional heroes and villains, the myths, or the tunnel vision that has limited scholarly and popular treatments across the ideological spectrum."
—Robin D. G. Kelley, Gary B. Nash Professor of American History,
　　University of California, Los Angeles

"This is, by a wide margin, the most detailed, analytically sophisticated, and balanced account of the Black Panther Party yet written. Anyone who hopes to understand the group and its impact on American culture and politics will need to read this book."
—Doug McAdam, Ray Lyman Wilbur Professor of Sociology,
　　Stanford University

"Impressive. . . . *Black against Empire* does a brilliant job of revealing how prominent figures in American (indeed global) public, social, and intellectual life were touched by the Party's influence."
—Joyce M. Bell, *Social Forces*

"Future historians of the Panthers and American radicalism will find *Black against Empire* a foundational text."
—Michan Connor, *Southern California Quarterly*

THE GEORGE GUND FOUNDATION
IMPRINT IN AFRICAN AMERICAN STUDIES

The George Gund Foundation has endowed
this imprint to advance understanding of
the history, culture, and current issues
of African Americans.

The publisher gratefully acknowledges the generous support of the African American Studies Endowment Fund of the University of California Press Foundation, which was established by a major gift from the George Gund Foundation.

Black against Empire

Black against Empire

The History and Politics
of the Black Panther Party

WITH A NEW PREFACE

Joshua Bloom
and Waldo E. Martin, Jr.

UNIVERSITY OF CALIFORNIA PRESS

University of California Press, one of the most distinguished university presses in the United States, enriches lives around the world by advancing scholarship in the humanities, social sciences, and natural sciences. Its activities are supported by the UC Press Foundation and by philanthropic contributions from individuals and institutions. For more information, visit www.ucpress.edu.

University of California Press
Oakland, California

ISBN 978-0-520-29328-1 (paper)
ISBN 978-0-520-96645-1 (ebook)

The Library of Congress has cataloged an earlier edition of this book as follows:

Library of Congress Cataloging-in-Publication Data

Bloom, Joshua.
    Black against empire : the history and politics of
the Black Panther Party / Joshua Bloom and Waldo E.
Martin, Jr.
        p. cm.
    Includes bibliographical references and index.
    ISBN 978-0-520-27185-2 (cloth : alk. paper)
    1. Black Panther Party—History.   2. African
Americans—Politics and government—20th century.
3. African Americans—Civil rights—History—20th century.
4. Civil rights movements—United States—History—20th
century.   5. United States—Race relations—History—20th
century.   6. United States—Race relations—Political
aspects—History—20th century. I. Martin, Waldo E.,
1951–. II. Title.
    E185.615.B5574   2013
    322.4'20973—dc23   2012021279

Manufactured in the United States of America

24 23 22 21 20 19 18 17
10 9 8 7 6 5 4 3

To
Hana, Mikhayla, Julius, Theodore, Eva, Emila, and Kian;
Jetta, Coral, and Kayla
and
Che Patrice Lumumba, Darryl, Dassine, Dorian, Ericka,
Fred Jr., Jaime, Joju Younghi, Maceo, Mai, Malik Nkrumah
Stagolee, Patrice, Romaine, Tupac, and all the cubs (here
and gone)
and

young revolutionaries everywhere.

When in the course of human events, it becomes necessary for one people to disolve the political bonds which have connected them with another, and to assume among the powers of the earth, the separate and equal station to which the laws of nature and nature's god entitled them, a decent respect to the opinions of mankind requires that they should declare the causes which impel them to separation.

We hold these truths to be self-evident, that all men are created equal, that they are endowed by their creator with certain unalienable rights, that among these are life, liberty and the pursuit of happiness. That to secure these rights, governments are instituted among men, deriving their just powers from the consent of the governed; *that whenever any form of government becomes destructive of these ends, it is the right of the people to alter or to abolish it, and to institute new government, laying its foundation on such principles and organizing its powers in such form, as to them shall seem most likely to effect their safety and happiness.*

Prudence, indeed, will dictate that governments long established should not be changed for light and transient causes; and accordingly all experience hath shewn, that mankind are more disposed to suffer, while evils are sufferable, than to right themselves by abolishing the forms to which they are accustomed. *But when a long train of abuses and usurpations, pursuing invariably the same object evinces a design to reduce them under absolute despotism, it is their right, it is their duty, to throw off such government, and to provide new guards for their future security.*

—Declaration of Independence, July 4, 1776, as excerpted in the Black Panther Party's original Ten Point Program, *Black Panther,* May 15, 1967

Contents

Figures follow pages 160 and 322

Figures

Preface to the 2016 Edition

How do you fight white supremacy in the era of "color blindness"?

In the early morning of April 1, in North Richmond, California, Deputy Sheriff Mel Brunkhorst shot Denzil Dowell, black and unarmed, in the back and head as he ran away. Dowell was left bleeding without medical attention and died lying in the street. His mother proclaimed, "The police murdered my son." After thirty minutes of deliberation the coroner's inquest found "justifiable homicide," and the state declined to investigate further or to try Brunkhorst for any crime. The year was 1967. We would not know Denzil Dowell's name if not for the Black Panther Party.

By the time of Dowell's death, the Civil Rights Movement had valiantly dismantled legal segregation. But whites maintained many forms of racial privilege. Most black people continued to live impoverished, in segregated communities, excluded from the middle class. Black people enjoyed little electoral representation, little access to elite higher education. And black communities were mostly policed by whites—often brutally. Politicians worked within, and sometimes intentionally leveraged, these institutionalized racial divides to win and maintain power.

Traditional civil rights organizations had little to offer Dowell's family. Many movement activists had come to recognize the limits of civil rights politics three years earlier when President Lyndon Johnson had tricked his "allies" from the movement into participating in a faux negotiation while he seated the exclusionary white Mississippi delegation at the Democratic National Convention in Atlantic City, New Jersey. As with many politicians, Johnson's power rested, in part, on racist political institutions immune to the pressures of civil rights action. With redress unavailable from traditional civil rights organizations, the Dowell family sought assistance from the Black Panther Party.

Soon, hundreds of black people were joining Black Panther Party rallies in North Richmond demanding justice for Denzil Dowell. At that time still a small group of young activists based in nearby Oakland, the Black Panther Party frontally challenged containment policing and the legitimacy of the American state with its anti-imperialist politics and armed self-defense against the police. The virulent repression it drew exposed the brutality of American rule in black communities. In the late 1960s the Party grew exponentially, catalyzing a wide movement for black liberation and eclipsing traditional civil rights organizations in activity, influence, funding, and notoriety.

We wrote this book because we wanted to learn how the Black Panther Party mobilized so many people to take severe personal risks to fight racism. Like Max Weber, we believe the questions that motivate social research are always informed by social and political commitments and that the objectivity of social science inheres in the rigor of research and analysis. Some would prefer we had instead produced a study of the personalities of the Party leaders and their flawed judgments or the crimes of the small remnants of the Party in Oakland after it unraveled in the 1970s. Those stories have been told before, and we recount them here. But first and foremost, this book is dedicated to making sense of the politics of the Black Panther Party.

Our analysis shows how the Black Panther Party mobilized so many people to fight white supremacy and capitalist exploitation. The Party generated an escalating cycle of insurgency by linking disruptive actions to community programs as part of a coherent anti-imperialist politics. In the late 1960s this politics forged common cause with a wide array of domestic and international constituencies. The Black Panther Party sustained disruption as a source of power by leveraging broad political cleavages to draw widespread black, antiwar, and international support in resistance to repression. The Party became repressible only once the state made sweeping concessions to its allies—namely affirmative action, repeal of the draft, and international diplomatic reconciliation.

We see our findings as especially important in the contrasts and similarities they illuminate with the political practices of the Civil Rights

Movement. These suggest important lessons about the fight against white supremacy today.

As racial progress has proceeded in the fifty years since the formation of the Black Panther Party, so have the forces of racial retrenchment. Whites have fought mightily to maintain their racial advantages. Political leaders—from Richard Nixon in the Panther era to Bill Clinton in the 1990s and Donald Trump today—have used racial division as a source of power. Despite the absence of formal racial subordination, the election of a black president, and broad proclamations of a postracial era, racial inequality has expanded in recent decades. Since 1970 the prison population of the United States has quintupled. Black people suffer seven times the rate of incarceration of whites. Young black men are twenty-one times more likely than young white men to be killed by police. As Michelle Alexander observes in *The New Jim Crow*, there are more black people under carceral control today than there were slaves in 1850. By 2000 the median white family owned ten times the assets of the median black family. Today, a decade and a half later, the median white family owns almost twenty times the assets of the median black family.

In the past several years, graphic video footage of police killings of unarmed black people has called attention to the persistent inhumanity of "color-blind" racism. Activists have rallied around these cases to some effect. Like the Black Panther Party, #BlackLivesMatter and other contemporary activists have coupled confrontational tactics with community organizing and sought to challenge racism by mobilizing against police brutality. And again, today antiracist activists face repression including state surveillance, arrests, and coordinated public vilification. As in the 1960s, the forces of racial retrenchment are eager to move on without disturbing the basic arrangements of white privilege.

Unfortunately, antiracist activists today cannot dismantle the new Jim Crow by emulating the specific practices of the Civil Rights Movement. The law now purports to protect black people's citizenship rights. Unlike segregated lunch counters in 1960, police brutality cannot be directly defied with a sit-in. Bodily integrating public institutions is no longer illegal. Neither can antiracist activists today dismantle the new Jim Crow by emulating the specific practices of the Black Panther Party. Armed resistance to police brutality would be broadly construed as terrorist activity.

Indeed, each generation must make its own history, under new conditions, in new ways. Rather than emulating the specifics, we believe that developing effective antiracist practices today requires emulating the general political dynamic common to both the Civil Rights Movement and the Black Panther Party. History shows how difficult it is to frontally challenge white supremacy in the face of coordinated repression. Yet it also reveals important lessons about how contemporary antiracist activists might sustain such a challenge.

Our findings suggest that dismantling the new Jim Crow will require insurgent practices that not only make business as usual impossible but do so in a way that is difficult to repress. Historically, antiracist insurgents have built followings and influence by drawing wide support in resistance to repression. In particular, antiracist insurgents sustained disruption as a source of power by advancing practices whose repression graphically exposed the brutality of racism. This was true of the sit-ins, the Freedom Rides, Selma, and the other civil rights campaigns in the early 1960s. This was true of Ferguson in 2014. And perhaps especially, this was true of the practices of the Black Panther Party in the late 1960s and early 1970s analyzed in this book.

In our view, only by developing such practices will contemporary activists drive the dynamics of mobilization rather than simply respond to external events. Only then will #BlackLivesMatter draw the breadth of allied support in resistance to repression achieved by the Black Panther Party. Only then will the movement command, rather than being held subject to, the media's inclinations. Only then will contemporary activists be able to sustain disruption as a source of power. Such insurgent practices are the source of democracy, the best hope for dismantling white supremacy, and the pathway toward creating an egalitarian society.

Joshua Bloom, Pittsburgh, Pennsylvania
Waldo E. Martin, Jr., Berkeley, California

Introduction

The Panthers shut out the pack of zealous reporters and kept the door locked all day, but now the hallway was empty. Huey Newton and two comrades casually walked from the luxury suite down to the lobby and slipped out of the Hong Kong Hilton. Their official escort took them straight across the border, and after a short flight, they exited the plane in Beijing, where they were greeted by cheering throngs.[1]

It was late September 1971, and U.S. national security adviser Henry Kissinger had just visited China a couple months earlier. The United States was proposing a visit to China by President Nixon himself and looking toward normalization of diplomatic relations. The Chinese leaders held varied views of these prospects and had not yet revealed whether they would accept a visit from Nixon.

But the Chinese government had been in frequent communication with the Black Panther Party, had hosted a Panther delegation a year earlier, and had personally invited Huey Newton, the Party's leader, to visit. With Nixon attempting to arrange a visit, Newton decided to accept the invitation and beat Nixon to China.[2]

When Zhou Enlai, the Chinese premier, greeted Newton in Beijing, Newton took Zhou's right hand between both his own hands. Zhou clasped Newton's wrist with his left hand, and the two men looked deeply into each other's eyes. Newton presented a formal petition requesting that China "negotiate with . . . Nixon for the freedom of the oppressed peoples of the world." Then the two sat down for a private meeting.[3] On National Day, the October 1 anniversary of the founding of the People's Republic of China, Premier Zhou honored the Panthers as national guests. Tens of thousands of Chinese gathered in Tiananmen Square, waving red flags and applauding the Panthers. Revolutionary theater groups, folk dancers, acrobats, and the revolutionary ballet performed. Huge red banners declared, "Peoples of the World, Unite to destroy the American aggressors and their lackeys."[4] At the official state dinner, first lady Jiang Qing sat with the Panthers.[5] A *New York Times* editorial encouraged Nixon "to think positively about Communist China and to ignore such potential sources of friction as the honors shown to Black Panther leader Huey Newton."[6]

FORBIDDEN HISTORY

In Oakland, California, in late 1966, community college students Bobby Seale and Huey Newton took up arms and declared themselves part of a global revolution against American imperialism. Unlike civil rights activists who advocated for full citizenship rights within the United States, their Black Panther Party rejected the legitimacy of the U.S. government. The Panthers saw black communities in the United States as a colony and the police as an occupying army. In a foundational 1967 essay, Newton wrote, "Because black people desire to determine their own destiny, they are constantly inflicted with brutality from the occupying army, embodied in the police department. There is a great similarity between the occupying army in Southeast Asia and the occupation of our communities by the racist police."[7]

As late as February 1968, the Black Panther Party was still a small local organization. But that year, everything changed. By December, the Party had opened offices in twenty cities, from Los Angeles to New York. In the face of numerous armed conflicts with police and virulent direct repression by the state, young black people embraced the revolutionary vision of the Party, and by 1970, the Party had opened offices in sixty-eight cities from Winston-Salem to Omaha and Seattle.[8] The Black Panther Party had become the center of a revolutionary movement in the United States.[9]

Readers today may have difficulty imagining a revolution in the United States. But in the late 1960s, many thousands of young black people, despite the potentially fatal outcome of their actions, joined the Black Panther Party and dedicated their lives to revolutionary struggle. Many more approved of their efforts. A joint report by the Federal

Bureau of Investigation (FBI), the Central Intelligence Agency, Defense Intelligence Committee, and National Security Agency expressed grave concern about wide support for the Party among young blacks, noting that "43 per cent of blacks under 21 years of age [have] . . . a great respect for the [Black Panther Party]."[10] Students for a Democratic Society, the leading antiwar and draft resistance organization, declared the Black Panther Party the "vanguard in our common struggles against capitalism and imperialism."[11] FBI director J. Edgar Hoover famously declared, "The Black Panther Party, without question, represents the greatest threat to the internal security of the country."[12]

As the Black Panthers drew young blacks to their revolutionary program, the Party became the strongest link between the domestic Black Liberation Struggle and global opponents of American imperialism. The North Vietnamese—at war with the United States—sent letters home to the families of American prisoners of war (POWs) through the Black Panther Party and discussed releasing POWs in exchange for the release of Panthers from U.S. jails. Cuba offered political asylum to Black Panthers and began developing a military training ground for them. Algeria—then the center of Pan-Africanism and a world hub of anti-imperialism that hosted embassies for most postcolonial governments and independence movements—granted the Panthers national diplomatic status and an embassy building of their own, where the Panthers headquartered their International Section under the leadership of Eldridge and Kathleen Cleaver.

But by the time of Newton's trip to China, the Black Panther Party had begun to unravel. In the early 1970s, the Party rapidly declined. By mid-1972, it was basically a local Oakland community organization once again. An award-winning elementary school and a brief local renaissance in the mid-1970s notwithstanding, the Party suffered a long and painful demise, formally closing its last office in 1982.

Not since the Civil War almost a hundred and fifty years ago have so many people taken up arms in revolutionary struggle in the United States. Of course, the number of people who took up arms for the Union and Confederate causes and the number of people killed in the Civil War are orders of magnitude larger than the numbers who have engaged in any armed political struggle in the United States since. Some political organizations that embraced revolutionary ideologies yet eschewed armed confrontation with the state may have garnered larger followings than the Black Panther Party did. But in the general absence of armed revolution in the United States since 1865, the thousands of Black Panthers—who dedicated their lives to a political program involving armed resistance to state authority—stand alone.

Why in the late 1960s—in contrast to the Civil Rights Movement's nonviolent action and demands for African Americans' full participation in U.S. society and despite severe personal risks—did so many young people dedicate their lives to the Black Panther Party and embrace armed revolution? Why, after a few years of explosive growth, did the Party so quickly unravel? And why has no similar movement developed since?

Most obvious explanations do not stand up to the evidence. Some believe the Party was a creation of the media. But most of the media attention came after the Party's rapid spread. Some assert that the Party's success was just a product of the times. But many other black political organizations, some with similar ideologies, sought to mobilize people at the same time, and none succeeded like the Panthers. Others contend that this or that Panther leader was an unrivaled organizer and that by the force of his or her efforts, the Party was able to recruit its vast following. But most of the new recruits to the Black Panthers came to the Party asking to join, not the other way around. One common view is that the Party collapsed because it could not withstand the government's repression, but the year of greatest repression, 1969, was also the year of the Party's greatest growth.[13]

While much has been written on aspects of the Black Panther Party, none of the accounts to date have offered a rigorous overarching analysis of the Party's evolution and impact. Most writers have looked at a small slice of the Party's temporal and geographic scope, providing limited historical context. Party sympathizers are as guilty of such reduction as its detractors are. Commentators reduce the Party to its community service programs or to armed confrontation with the police. They claim the Panthers espoused narrowly Marxist or black nationalist ideology. They maintain that Huey Newton was a genius or that he was overly philosophical, or that he was a criminal. They say the Party's power came from organizing young blacks from the urban ghettos or that its influence stemmed from its ability to draw broad support from a range of allies. To some people, the Party was a locus of cutting-edge debate on gender politics, and they applaud its embrace of women's and gay liberation; to others, it was sexist and patriarchal.

Occasionally, commentators have even suggested that the Black Panther Party was all of these things. But no one has made sense of the relationship among the parts, situated the varying practices of the

Party in time and place, and adequately traced the evolution of the Party's politics. As Pulitzer Prize–winning historian David Garrow recently pointed out in an extensive review of historical works on the Panthers, no one has yet offered a serious analysis of how the political practices of the Black Panther Party changed during its history or why people were drawn to participate at each juncture of its evolution. "Panther scholarship," Garrow observes, "would benefit immensely from a detailed and comprehensive narrative history that gives special care to how rapidly the [Black Panther Party] evolved through a succession of extremely fundamental changes. . . . Far too much of what has been written about the [Party] fails to specify expressly which period of Panther history is being addressed or characterized, and interpretive clarity, and accuracy, will benefit greatly from a far more explicit appreciation and identification of the major turning points in the [Black Panther Party's] eventually tragic evolution."[14]

Writing in the *New York Times* in 1994, sociologist Robert Blauner commented, "Because of the political mine fields," the "complex and textured social history that the Panthers deserve" has not yet been written and "may be 10 or 15 years in the future."[15] More than forty years have passed since the heyday of the Black Panther Party, and almost twenty years have passed since Blauner's writing, but to date, despite comment by a diversity of writers, no one has presented an adequate or comprehensive history.[16]

As a popular adage suggests, "History is written by the victors."[17] Writing a history that transcends preconceptions is challenging. It takes time and perspective and endless sifting through often-contradictory evidence to test competing explanations and weigh the importance of divergent forces. But the lack of an overarching history of the Panthers and their politics, despite the abundance of writing on various aspects of the Party, is unusual. We suspect that the long absence of an adequate history is due, in part, to the character of state repression of the Party. Aimed specifically at vilifying the Black Panther Party, state repression powerfully shaped public understandings and blurred the outlines of the history.

The federal government and local police forces across the nation responded to the Panthers with an unparalleled campaign of repression and vilification. They fed defamatory stories to the press. They wiretapped Panther offices around the country. They hired dozens of informants to infiltrate Panther chapters. Often, they put aside all pretense and simply raided Panther establishments, guns blazing. In one case, in

Chicago in December 1969, equipped with an informant's map of the apartment, police and federal agents assassinated a prominent Panther leader in his bed while he slept, shooting him in the head at point-blank range.[18]

In attacking the Black Panthers as enemies of the state, federal agents sought to repress not just the Party as an organization but the political possibility it represented. The FBI's Counterintelligence Program (COINTELPRO) sought to vilify the Black Panthers and "prevent [the Party and similar] black nationalist groups and leaders from gaining respectability by discrediting them."[19]

FBI director J. Edgar Hoover emphasized time and again, in different ways, that "one of our primary aims in counterintelligence as it concerns the BPP is to keep this group isolated from the moderate black and white community which may support it."[20] Federal agents sought "to create factionalism" among Party leaders and between the Panthers and other black political organizations.[21] FBI operatives forged documents and paid provocateurs to promote violent conflicts between Black Panther leaders—as well as between the Party and other black nationalist organizations—and congratulated themselves when these conflicts yielded the killing of Panthers. And COINTELPRO sought to lead the Party into unsupportable action, "creating opposition to the BPP on the part of the majority of the residents of the ghetto areas."[22] For example, agent provocateurs on the government payroll supplied explosives to Panther members and sought to incite them to blow up public buildings, and they promoted kangaroo courts encouraging Panther members to torture suspected informants.[23]

One school of commentators simply took up Hoover's program of vilification, portraying the Party as criminals and obscuring and minimizing its politics. In an influential article in 1978, Kate Coleman and Paul Avery made a series of allegations about personal misdeeds and criminal actions by Panthers in the 1970s, after the Party had lost influence as a national and international political organization: "Black Panthers have committed a series of violent crimes over the last several years. . . . There appears to be no political explanation for it; the Party is no longer under siege by the police, and this is not self-defense. It seems to be nothing but senseless criminality, directed in most cases at other blacks."[24]

David Horowitz wrote a series of essays in 1994 building on these allegations, treating them as the totality of what was important or interesting about the Panthers and describing the Black Panthers as "an organized street gang."[25] Hugh Pearson, in consultation with Horowitz, then wrote *The Shadow of the Panther,* a full-length book version of the story Horowitz had developed, telling the history of the Black Panther Party through the alleged crimes and personal misdeeds of Huey Newton.[26] The major newspapers celebrated the book as a respectable history of the Party and its politics. The *New York Times* called the book "a richly detailed portrait of a movement" and named it one of its Notable Books of the Year 1994.[27]

The storm of criminal allegations touted as movement history effectively advanced J. Edgar Hoover's program of vilifying the Party and shrouding its politics. While many of the criminal allegations that Horowitz and his colleagues made about Huey Newton and other Panther leaders were thinly supported and almost none were verified in court, these treatments also omit and obscure the thousands of people who dedicated their lives to the Panther revolution, their reasons for doing so, and the political dynamics of their participation, their actions, and the consequences.

Hoover's program aimed to drive a wedge between the Party and its nonblack allies. Today, the popular misconception persists that the Black Panther Party was separatist, or antiwhite. Many current internet postings mischaracterize the Party in this way.[28] In fact, the Party was deeply antiracist and strongly committed to interracial coalitions. Even some newspapers got the basic story wrong, such as the *Providence Journal-Bulletin,* whose editorial board characterized the Party as an "organization based on racial hostility . . . a mirror image of the Ku Klux Klan."[29] Such misconceptions have also taken root among some of today's young activists seeking to emulate the historical example of the Black Panthers, such as the so-called New Black Panther Party, darling of Fox News, which while claiming to carry on the legacy of the original Black Panthers, preaches separatism and racial hate.

Another influential line of attack—the argument that the Panthers primarily advanced "black macho" rather than a broader liberation politics—has also done more to obscure than to illuminate the history of the Party. Michelle Wallace first popularized this argument in her influential 1978 book *Black Macho and the Myth of Superwoman,* in which she denigrates the role of Angela Davis and other revolutionary black women as "do-it-for-your-man" selfless subservience to misogyny in the name of black liberation.[30] As June Jordan commented in a 1979 review, *Black Macho* is "a divisive, fractious tract devoid of hope and dream, devoid even of competent scholarship for the subject so glibly undertaken."[31] Yet the argument gained traction, perhaps in part because it built upon a kernel of truth. Stewarding a predominantly male organization in the beginning, some Black Panthers indeed asserted an aggressive black masculinity. But by misrepresenting this black masculinism as the totality of the Party's politics, Wallace and her ilk distorted and defamed the Party. They erased the women who soon constituted a majority of the Panther membership and devalued the considerable struggles Panther women and men undertook to advance gender and sexual liberation within and through the Party, often progressing well in advance of the wider society.

If J. Edgar Hoover were alive today, he would undoubtedly take great pride in the persistence of the factionalism he sought to create among the Panthers. Fights that erupted between Panther factions as the Party lost its national and international political influence in the 1970s have long outlived the organization. Decades later, former Black Panther leaders continue to condemn each other virulently in public. These disputes distract from the politics of the Black Panthers in their heyday and sustain the Party's public vilification.

But in recent decades, the history of the Black Panther Party has proven irrepressible. Memoirs by former Black Panthers, as well as scholarly books, edited collections, articles, doctoral dissertations, and master's theses, have chipped away at public fallacies, clearing obscurity and uncovering the history of the Party piece by piece. Memoirs by, and biographies of, Black Panther activists who served in various parts of the country, and some who were national leaders—including David Hilliard, Elbert "Big Man" Howard, Assata Shakur, Geronimo Pratt, Elaine Brown, Safiya Bukhari, Stokely Carmichael, Marshall "Eddie" Conway, Flores Forbes, Evans Hopkins, Mumia Abu-Jamal, Steve McCutchen, Robert Hillary King, Huey P. Newton, Afeni Shakur, and Johnny Spain—provide personal perspectives and rich accounts of life in the Party. Edited collections by Kathleen Cleaver and George Katsiaficas, Judson Jeffries, Charles Jones, Yohuru Williams and Jama Lazerow, and countless journal articles, fill out the story of local chapters in cities across the country and develop thematic insights across them. Books on the Panthers by Paul Alkebulan, Curtis Austin, Christian Davenport, Donna Murch, Jane Rhodes, as well as more general recent books that contain significant discussions of the Panthers, build analytic perspective.[32] A new generation of scholars has provided rigorous treatments of myriad facets of the Party's history, producing the extraordinary number of ninety dissertations and master's theses—most written in the last decade—analyzing specific aspects of the Party's history, such as the sickle-cell-anemia programs, the multiracial alliances of the Chicago Panthers, or the artwork of Black Panther minister of culture Emory Douglas.[33]

These previous treatments are invaluable, and the depth of our analysis is much richer for them. But despite the strength of many of these contributions, none has presented a complete picture of the Black Panther Party, or an adequate analysis of its politics. Pinning down history is always complex. The vociferous efforts of the federal government to vilify the Panthers, and the legacy of factional dispute, made the history of the Black Panther Party nearly impenetrable.

HOW WE WROTE THIS BOOK

What is unique and historically important about the Black Panther Party is specifically its politics. So in seeking to uncover the history of the Black Panther Party, we have sought to analyze the Party's *political* history. In an early proposal for the book in 2000, we elaborated a method of "strategic genealogy" to conduct this analysis. Rather than center our analysis on particular individuals or on dissection of the Party's organization, we uncovered the political dynamics of the Party by studying the evolution of its political practices.[34]

We could not have written this book without the insight we gained talking with former Panthers, especially David Hilliard, former Black Panther chief of staff, and Kathleen Cleaver, former Black Panther communications secretary. We also benefited from getting to know almost all of the other living former leaders of the Black Panther Party, and together with our students, we spoke with many regional leaders, rank-and-file members of the Party, and important Party allies, including Bobby Seale, Elaine Brown, Ericka Huggins, Angela Davis, Emory Douglas, Billy X Jennings, Mumia Abu-Jamal, Geronimo ji Jaga (Pratt), Richard Aoki, Kumasi Aguila, Alex Papillon, Melvin Newton, John Seale, Tom Hayden, and dozens of others. The hundreds of hours we spent talking about the Party and working with former members on related historical projects provided invaluable insight into life inside the Party and the crucial concerns of the leadership at various junctures.

When we began the project in the late 1990s, we conducted formal interviews with Bobby Seale and a range of others, expecting that these conversations would be the main source of data for the project. But the more interviews we conducted, the clearer the limits of that medium became. Retrospective accounts decades after the fact—with memories shaped by intervening events, interests, and hearsay—are highly contradictory. So although we did rely extensively on conversations with historical actors to test our analysis and push our understanding, we have avoided using retrospective interviews as a principal source of evidence, preferring to consult documentary or recorded evidence that was temporally proximate to the events. In the end, what made it possible to uncover this history was a vast wealth of primary sources, including many thousands of firsthand accounts of historical events offered by participants shortly after they occurred.

We conducted much of the research through the Social Movements Project at the Institute for the Study of Social Change at the University of California, Berkeley, which we codirected from 2000 to 2005. We benefited greatly from the assistance of dozens of graduate and undergraduate research assistants. Several of our graduate research assistants and advisees have gone on to complete dissertations and publish their own books on aspects of the Party history (see our acknowledgments). We early consulted the range of primary sources on the Party already available in archives at Stanford University, the University of California, Berkeley, Howard University, the University of Wisconsin–Madison, the Schomburg Center for Research in Black Culture, the New Haven Museum and Historical Society, and the Oakland Public Library; in articles in the black press, underground press, and mainstream press; and in government documents. In addition, we developed two new archival sources in the course of producing this book.

In our first major archival project, we assembled the only near-complete collection of the Party's own newspaper, the *Black Panther*. This collection includes every issue published during the Party's heyday from 1967 to 1971, and 520 of the 537 issues published overall. Chockfull of Party members' firsthand accounts of unfolding events and programmatic statements by Party leaders, the *Black Panther* offers the most comprehensive documentation of the ideas, actions, and projections of the Party day to day, week to week. Under our editorial direction, the Alexander Street Press digitized this collection, made the text searchable, and published the documents online as part of its Black Thought and Culture collection, in collaboration with Huey Newton's widow, Fredrika Newton, and the Huey P. Newton Foundation.[35]

In our second major archival project, we collaborated with the H. K. Yuen family to recover, preserve, and index (a good portion of) the H. K. Yuen collection, which contains thousands of fliers and pamphlets and over thirty thousand hours of audio recordings on the Panthers and other social movements in the Bay Area from the 1960s and 1970s. As a doctoral student at Berkeley, in 1964, H. K. Yuen began collecting every movement flier and pamphlet circulated on the Berkeley campus, and he recorded every meeting and rally in the Bay Area that he could. Yuen dropped out of school and made a career of this collection for almost two decades. He also set up an apparatus to record almost all shows about social movements broadcast on Bay Area radio stations. Working with his son, Eddie Yuen, we recovered this extensive collection from boxes overflowing the Yuen family basement and then preserved and indexed the contents and facilitated donation of the collection, which auditors value at several million dollars, to the Bancroft Library at the University of California, Berkeley.

This collaborative work thus resulted from a series of joint scholarly projects led by Bloom. As first author, Bloom did the lion's share of the research, writing, and analysis. As coauthor, Martin contributed substantially to the research, writing, and analysis. In the end, each author contributed crucially to all phases of the making of this book.

BLACK AGAINST EMPIRE

Civil rights activists nonviolently defied Jim Crow, demanding full citizenship rights. Their insurgent Civil Rights Movement of the early 1960s dismantled legal segregation and expanded black enfranchisement in the United States. The 1964 Civil Rights Act and 1965 Voting Rights Act codified their inspiring victories. But once there was little legal segregation left to defy, the insurgent Civil Rights Movement fell apart.[36]

In the late 1960s, the Student Nonviolent Coordinating Committee and Congress of Racial Equality, two organizations that led much of the nonviolent civil disobedience, imploded. The Southern Christian Leadership Conference declined. But the broader vision of black liberation that had motivated civil rights activists remained salient. Many black people, having won a measure of political incorporation, organized to win electoral political power. Many sought economic advancement. Moderate civil rights organizations, such as the National Association for the Advancement of Colored People and the Urban League, turned their attention to the hard work of civil rights enforcement. Countless activists continued to chip away at racial discrimination in jobs, education, and housing.

For many blacks, the Civil Rights Movement's victories proved limited, even illusory. Especially for young urban blacks in the North and West, little improved. The wartime jobs that drew the black migration had ended, much remaining industry fled to the suburbs along with white residents, and many blacks lived isolated in poor urban ghettos with little access to decent employment or higher education and with minimal political influence. Municipal police and fire departments in cities with large black populations employed few if any blacks. And many cities developed containment policing practices—designed to isolate violence in black ghettos rather than to keep ghetto residents safe. Although black people were formally full citizens, most remained ghettoized, impoverished, and politically subordinated, with few channels for redress.

Starting in 1966, young blacks in cities across the country took up the call for "Black Power!" The Black Power ferment posed a question: how would black people in America win not only formal citizenship rights but actual economic and political power? Dozens of organizations sprang up seeking to attain Black Power in different ways. More a question than an answer, *Black Power* meant widely different things to different people. Despite the belief among many young blacks that their mobilization as black people was the key, no one knew *how* to mobilize effectively.[37]

Into this vacuum, Huey Newton and Bobby Seale advanced a black anti-imperialist politics that powerfully challenged the status quo yet was difficult to repress. Drawing on the nationalist ideas of Malcolm X, Newton and Seale declared the Black Panther Party steward of the black community—its legitimate political representative—standing in revolutionary opposition to the oppressive "power structure." But unlike many black nationalists, the Panthers made common cause with the domestic antiwar movement and anti-imperialist movements abroad. The Panthers argued that black people constituted a "colony in the mother country." With an unpopular imperial war under way in Vietnam, popular anti-imperialist movements agitating internationally, and a crisis of legitimacy brewing in the Democratic Party, they posited a single worldwide struggle against imperialism encompassing Vietnamese resistance against the United States, draft resistance against military service, and their own struggle to liberate the black community. In the face of brutal repression, the Black Panther Party forged powerful alliances, drawing widespread support not only from moderate blacks but also from many nonblacks, as well as from anti-imperialist governments and movements around the globe.

The Black Panthers' crucial political innovation was not only ideational but practical. At the center of their politics was the practice of armed self-defense against the police. While revolutionary ideas could be easily ignored, widespread confrontations between young armed black people and the police could not. The Panthers' politics of armed self-defense gave them political leverage, forcibly contesting the legitimacy of the American political regime. In late 1968, Bobby Seale and David Hilliard shifted the Party's focus to organizing community programs such as free breakfasts for children. In 1969, every Panther chapter organized community services, and these programs soon became the staple activity for Party members nationwide. By that summer, the Party estimated it was feeding ten thousand children free breakfast every day. The Black Panther Party's community programs gave members meaningful daily activities, strengthened black community support, burnished Party credibility in the eyes of allies, and vividly exposed the inadequacy of the federal government's concurrent War on Poverty. Community programs concretely advanced the politics the Panthers stood for: they were feeding hungry children when the vastly wealthier and more powerful U.S. government was allowing children to starve. The more the state sought to repress the Panthers, the more the Party's allies mobilized in its defense. The Black Panther Party quickly became a major national and international political force.

Individuals created the Black Panther Party. Without their specific efforts and actions, the Party would not have come about, and there is little reason to believe that a powerful black anti-imperialist movement would have developed in the late 1960s. Yet the Black Panther Party was also specific to its times. The times did not make the Black Panther Party, but the specific practices of the Black Panthers became influential precisely because of the political context. Without the success of the insurgent Civil Rights Movement, and without its limitations, the Black Power ferment from which the Black Panther Party emerged would not have existed. Without widespread exclusion of black people from political representation, good jobs, government employment, quality education, and the middle class, most black people would have opposed the Panthers' politics. Without the Vietnam War draft and the crisis of legitimacy in the Democratic Party, few nonblack allies would have mobilized resistance to state repression of the Party. Without powerful anti-imperialist allies abroad, the Panthers would have been deprived of both resources and credibility.

It was not simply what the Black Panthers did—but what they did in the conditions in which they found themselves—that proved so consequential. They created a movement with the power to challenge established social relations and yet—given the political context—very difficult to repress. Once the Black Panther Party developed, until the conditions under which it thrived abated, some form of revolutionary anti-imperialism would necessarily persist. Had government hiring and university enrollment remained inaccessible to blacks, had black electoral representation not expanded, had affirmative action programs never proliferated, had the military draft not been scaled back and then repealed, and had revolutionary governments abroad not normalized relations with the United States, revolutionary black anti-imperialism would still be a powerful force in the United States today. While the Black Panther Party might have been repressible as an organization, the politics the Panthers created were irrepressible so long as the conditions in which they thrived persisted.

From 1968 through 1970, the Black Panther Party made it impossible for the U.S. government to maintain business as usual, and it helped create a far-reaching crisis in U.S. society. The state responded to the destabilizing crisis with social concessions such as municipal hiring of blacks and the repeal of the military draft. Because history is so complex, we cannot isolate all influences and precisely predict what would have happened if Huey Newton, Bobby Seale, and many others had not created the Black Panther Party. But we do know that without the Black Panther Party, we would now live in a very different world.

The parts of this book analyze in turn the major phases of the political development of the Black Panther Party. Part 1, "Organizing Rage," analyzes the period through May of 1967, tracing the Party's development of its ideology of black anti-imperialism and its preliminary tactic of policing the police. Part 2, "Baptism in Blood," analyzes the Party's rise to national influence through 1968, during which time it reinvented the politics of armed self-defense, championed black community self-determination, and promoted armed resistance to the state.

Part 3, "Resilience," and part 4, "Revolution Has Come!" analyze the period through 1969 and 1970 when the Party was at the height of its power, proliferating community service programs and continuing to expand armed resistance in the face of the state's intensified repression. We unpack the dynamics of repression and response in three cities—Los Angeles, Chicago, and New Haven—showing how the Panthers attracted support from multiracial allies at home and from revolutionary movements and governments abroad and explaining why Black Panther insurgent practices were irrepressible.

Part 5, "Concessions and Unraveling," analyzes the demise of the Black Panther Party in the 1970s, showing how state concessions and broad political transformations undercut the Party's resilience. During this period, the Black Panthers divided along ideological lines, with neither side able to sustain the politics that had driven the Party's development.

The concluding chapter sums up our findings and explores their implications for three broader contemporary debates about the history of the Black Liberation Struggle and about social movements generally. Finally, we consider the history of the Black Panther Party in light of Antonio Gramsci's theory of revolution, illuminating the political dynamics by which social movements become revolutionary and explaining why there is no revolutionary movement in the United States today.

PART ONE

Organizing Rage

This is the genius of Huey Newton, of being able to TAP this VAST RESERVOIR of revolutionary potential. I mean, street niggers, you dig it? Niggers who been BAD, niggers who weren't scared, because they ain't never knew what to be scared was, because they been down in these ghettos and they knew to live they had to fight; and so they been able to do that. But I mean to really TAP it, to really TAP IT, to ORGANIZE it, and to direct it into an onslaught, a sortie against the power structure, this is the genius of Huey Newton, this is what Huey Newton did. Huey Newton was able to go down, and to take the nigger on the street and relate to him, understand what was going on inside of him, what he was thinking, and then implement that into an organization, into a PROGRAM and a PLATFORM, you dig it? Into the BLACK PANTHER PARTY—and then let it spread like wildfire across this country.

—Alprentice "Bunchy" Carter, leader of the Slauson gang and
   founder of the Los Angeles chapter of the Black Panther Party

1

Huey and Bobby

On February 17, 1942, in Monroe, Louisiana, Huey P. Newton was born, the seventh and youngest child of Walter and Armelia Newton. Walter Newton was a paragon of responsibility. He held down two jobs at any given time, working in the gravel pit, the carbon plant, sugarcane mills, sawmills, and eventually as a brakeman for the Union Saw Mill Company. On Sundays, he served as the minister at the Bethel Baptist Church in Monroe, where he and his family lived. He preached as the spirit moved him, often promising to address his parishioners on a particular topic, then improvising an inspirational sermon salient to the moment. The rest of the time he spent with his family, the joy and purpose of his life.[1]

Armelia Johnson liked to say that she married young and finished growing up with her children. She was only seventeen when she gave birth to her first child. The others soon followed. Unlike most black women in the South in the 1930s and 1940s, Armelia stayed at home, raising her children, seeing them through life's challenges, and relishing life's humor.[2] The Newton family saw Armelia's not working as a domestic servant for whites as an act of rebellion.

Walter Newton often used to say, "You can take a killing but you can't take a beating." On one occasion, Walter Newton got into an argument with a younger white man for whom he worked about a detail of the job. The white man told him that when a "colored" disputed his word, he whipped him. Walter Newton replied that no man whipped him unless he was a better man, and he doubted that the white man qualified. The man was shocked at this uncharacteristic response and backed down.[3]

This was just one of many times that Walter Newton defied whites in ways that often got blacks in the South lynched. He developed a reputation for being "crazy," so whites steered clear of him, gaining him powerful respect among blacks. Newton's ability to challenge whites and stay alive is something of a mystery. One factor, according to Huey Newton, may have been his mixed race. Walter Newton's father was a white man who had raped his black mother. Thus, local whites knew his father, cousins, aunts, and blood relatives, and while they might not have hesitated to kill a black person, they may have been reluctant to shed his white family's blood.[4]

The Newtons moved to Oakland in 1945, following the path of many black families migrating from the South to the cities of the North and West to fill the jobs in the shipyards and industries that opened up with the onset of World War II. When the war ended, many blacks were laid off as wartime industry waned, and soldiers returning from the war created a labor surplus. Both new and expanded black communities in cities across the country rapidly sank into poverty. While the Newtons were better off than many of the black families they knew, they were poor, with seven children to feed, and often ate cush, a dish made of fried cornbread, several times a day. Making payments on the family's bills became Walter Newton's constant preoccupation.

The Newton family was on the edge, and Huey looked to his older brothers for survival strategies. Each coped with ghetto life in a different way. Walter Newton Jr., the oldest, became a hustler, working outside legal channels to keep poverty at bay. He always dressed sharp, and he drove a nice car. Everyone in the neighborhood called him "Sonny Man." Lee Edward gained a reputation as a street fighter before joining the military. He knew how "to persist in the face of bad odds, always to look an adversary straight in the eye, and to keep moving forward."[5] Melvin Newton took a different path. He became a bookworm, went to college, and eventually taught sociology at Oakland's Merritt College.

Huey P. Newton became all of these things—hustler, fighter, and scholar. From his oldest brothers, Lee Edward and "Sonny Man," he mastered the ways of the street and learned how to fight. Through his teen years, Huey fought constantly.[6] Unlike Melvin, Huey was not a bookworm. For years he rebelled at school. By the time he entered the eleventh grade, he still could not read, and his teachers often told him he was unintelligent. But outside of school, he had been learning how to think. With Melvin, he memorized and analyzed poetry. When a counselor in his high school told him he was "not college material," Huey decided to prove him wrong. Over the next two years, through intense focus and will, he taught himself to read, graduated high school, and in 1959, enrolled in Merritt College.[7]

By the time Huey Newton became involved in the Afro-American Association at Merritt, he could debate theory as well as any of his peers. Yet he had a side that most of the budding intellectuals around him lacked; he knew the street. He could understand and relate to the plight of the swelling ranks of unemployed, the "brothers on the block" who lived outside the law. Newton's street knowledge helped put him through college, as he covered his bills through theft and fraud. But when Newton was caught, he used his book knowledge to study the law and defend himself in court, impressing the jury and defeating several misdemeanor charges.

In 1962, at a rally at Merritt College opposing the U.S. blockade of Cuba, Newton's political life took a leap forward: there, he met fellow student Bobby Seale, with whom he would eventually found the Black Panther Party. The rally featured Donald Warden, leader of the Afro-American Association. Warden praised Cuba's Fidel Castro and voiced opposition to domestic civil rights organizations. After the speeches, an informal debate began among the students, during which Newton convinced Seale that the U.S. policy in Cuba was wrong and also made him question mainstream civil rights organizations. Newton impressed Seale with his command of the argument presented by E. Franklin Frazier in *Black Bourgeoisie,* a scathing critique of the black middle class that he had read with Warden. Seale soon joined Warden's group.[8]

More than five years older than Newton, Bobby Seale was born in Dallas, Texas, on October 22, 1936, the oldest of three siblings, and raised in Oakland.[9] His father worked as a carpenter, and his mother also worked, sometimes as a caterer. Besides teaching Bobby how to build things and how to hunt and fish, Bobby's father also taught him about injustice, often beating him badly for no apparent reason.

The arbitrary beatings filled Bobby with a rage for which he had few outlets. They also meant he had little to fear from fights; he had already tasted the worst. Rather than become a bully himself, from an early age, Bobby started to stand up for the little guy. When his family first moved to Oakland, a local bully pushed his little sister Betty off the swing. Despite being outnumbered in new territory, Bobby knocked the bully out of the swing and then told all the kids they could share the swing.[10] Bobby had a penchant for taking on bullies, even when he had little hope of winning, once challenging a neighborhood kid twice his size who was cheating the smaller kids in marbles, and was often beaten to the ground.[11]

When he was fifteen, Bobby became close to a loner named Steve Brumfield. Steve told Bobby that the white man had stolen the land from the American Indians. The two of them escaped the pettiness and injustices at school and home by emulating Lakota warriors, running through the Berkeley hills for hours every day, dressed in moccasins and beads, and fighting each other for sport. Bobby used metalworking skills he learned in a vocational program at Berkeley High School to make large knives and tomahawks that the two carried wherever they went. When they were not practicing fighting, they climbed trees and dreamed of moving to South Dakota, marrying American Indian women, and living off the land. Bobby had never felt happier. He quickly became fast and strong, and soon the bullies tried to stay out of his way.[12]

But after high school, Steve joined the military and Bobby, lonely once again, drifted from city to city, job to job, and woman to woman. When things got hard, he ended up back at home with his parents. No longer willing to be pushed around by his father—and now perfectly able to defend himself—he joined the U.S. Air Force. While further developing his metalworking skills and mastering the use of firearms, he learned to contain and channel his rage, turning his explosive temper into cold calculation. When three soldiers refused to pay back a debt and threatened to beat Bobby if he mentioned the matter again, he suppressed his instinct to fight and bade his time. Later that week, Bobby attacked the main perpetrator when his defenses were down, nearly killing him with a pipe.[13]

Huey and Bobby both had their first serious political experiences with Donald Warden in the Afro-American Association. Warden had founded the all-black study group while he was a student at Boalt Law School at the University of California, Berkeley, creating a space for in-depth discussion of books by black authors such as W. E. B. Du Bois, Ralph Ellison, Booker T. Washington, and James Baldwin. Warden asserted a black nationalist perspective inspired by Malcolm X, emphasizing racial pride and embracing a transcontinental black identity rooted in Africa. Warden believed in the virtues of black capitalism, arguing that black people "must develop our own planned businesses where efficiency, thrift and sacrifice are stressed." Feisty and charismatic, Warden challenged students and professors alike, debated groups such as the Young Socialist Alliance, and gave public lectures on black history and culture. Willing to debate anyone, Warden made a strong impression on fellow students, and became an important intellectual influence on many of the future leaders of the Black Liberation Movement.[14]

In addition to Newton and Seale, association members included Leslie and Jim Lacy, Cedric Robinson, Richard Thorne, Ernest Allen, and Ron Everett, who later changed his name to Ron Karenga, founded the black cultural nationalist organization US, and created the holiday Kwanza. Warden also became a mentor to James Brown in 1964, and through him, helped influence the politicization of soul music.[15]

The Afro-American Association produced local radio shows debating the concerns of Black America, regularly mobilized street-corner rallies preaching racial consciousness to unemployed blacks, and sponsored conferences entitled Mind of the Ghetto. At a September 1963 conference at McClymonds High School in Oakland, Cassius Clay, the future heavyweight boxing champion who would change his name to Muhammad Ali and have his title stripped for resisting the draft, was the featured speaker.[16]

But Newton was a man of action, and he grew dissatisfied with Warden's teaching. Newton felt that Warden was heavy on the talk but ultimately could not be counted on. In Newton's view, Warden "offered the community solutions that solved nothing," and he also doubted that much could be accomplished through black capitalism. Soon he split from Warden in search of a new path.[17]

RAGE

When Malcolm X was assassinated on February 21, 1965, Bobby's rage overflowed. He gathered six bricks from his mother's garden, broke them in half, and stood in wait at the corner, hurling bricks at the cars of any whites he saw passing by. "I'll make my own self into a motherfucking Malcolm X," he swore, "and if they want to kill me, they'll have to kill me."[18]

By then the civil rights juggernaut had run its course. Throughout the early 1960s, in campaign after campaign, the Civil Rights Movement successfully tore down the Jim Crow system of legal segregation. Activists crossed the color line with their bodies, drawing brutal repression from local white authorities and forcing the federal government to intervene—politically, legally, and militarily. But by the summer of 1964, the limits of civil rights political practice were becoming clear, particularly at the Democratic Convention in Atlantic City.

As late as 1964, the Democratic Party in Mississippi excluded blacks, all too often doling out violence or death to blacks who attempted to register to vote. In the Freedom Summer campaign that year, leading civil rights organizations developed a parallel political party, the Mississippi Freedom Democratic Party (MFDP), that included blacks as well as nonblacks and began registering blacks to vote. Three of the Freedom Summer activists—James Chaney, Michael Schwerner, and Andrew Goodman—were kidnapped, mutilated, and killed. Undaunted, the campaign continued. The MFDP held a state convention in Jackson in early August and selected sixty-eight delegates to attend the upcoming Democratic National Convention in Atlantic City, New Jersey.[19]

President Johnson was determined to maintain white southern support and worked to undermine the MFDP. On August 12, Mississippi's Democratic governor, Paul B. Johnson, told the all-white Dixiecrat delegation that President Johnson had personally promised him not to seat the MFDP. The president refused to discuss the MFDP with civil rights leaders and instructed FBI director Hoover to monitor the renegade party closely and provide regular updates on its activities to the White House.

It became clear by the start of the convention that the MFDP would not win outright support in the Credentials Committee to seat its delegation in Atlantic City. But MFDP leaders hoped that a strong minority report from the committee would bring the issue to an open vote on the floor and that, under the pressure of public scrutiny, convention delegates would at least vote to seat both delegations.

On August 22, after intensive one-on-one lobbying of the state delegations, the MFDP presented its case to the Credentials Committee. Fannie Lou Hamer's testimony about the consequences of her efforts with the Student Nonviolent Coordinating Committee (SNCC) to register Mississippi blacks vote—in which she described how she was fired from her job and beaten in jail by black prisoners under orders of the police—caught the nation's attention:

> The first Negro began to beat, and I was beat until I was exhausted. . . . After the first Negro . . . was exhausted, the State Highway Patrolman ordered the second Negro to take the blackjack. The second Negro began to beat . . . I began to scream, and one white man got up and began to beat me on my head and tell me to "hush." One white man—my dress had worked up high—he walked over and pulled my dress down and he pulled my dress

back, back up. . . . All of this is on account we want to register, to become first-class citizens, and if the Freedom Democratic Party is not seated now, I question America.[20]

The television audience responded almost instantly. Phones started to ring, and the delegates began receiving telegrams urging them to support the MFDP. Quickly, President Johnson called a press conference, and Hamer's testimony was cut off so that the president's statement could be broadcast.

Behind the scenes, the president's staff twisted the arms of Credentials Committee members while soon-to-be vice president Hubert Humphrey called a meeting at the Pageant Motel across the street from the convention with Fannie Lou Hamer, Bob Moses, and the other MFDP leaders to discuss a compromise. Humphrey told them that the MFDP delegation would not be seated but that educated professionals from the delegation—Aaron Henry of the National Association for the Advancement of Colored People (NAACP) and white minister Ed King—would be given seats alongside the official all-white Mississippi delegation. Ms. Hamer would not be part of any official delegation. "The President will not allow that illiterate woman to speak from the floor of the convention," said Humphrey.[21]

The MFDP had not been consulted in the compromise offer, and the delegates rejected the proposal on the spot. Then someone knocked on the meeting room door and announced, "It's over!" The MFDP leaders turned on the TV to see Minnesota attorney general Walter Mondale, head of the Democratic Party committee appointed to resolve the MFDP challenge, announcing that the MFDP had accepted the "compromise." Apparently, the Democratic Party leadership had timed the introduction of the issue on the convention floor to coincide with the MFDP leaders' meeting with Humphrey across the street so that the leaders could not voice any opposition. Feeling deeply betrayed, SNCC and MFDP leader Bob Moses stormed out of the room, slamming the door in Hubert Humphrey's face.[22]

Civil rights mobilization played a central role in defeating legal segregation, and the Voting Rights Act of 1965 enfranchised southern blacks. But for blacks outside the South, neither generated political gains or significant economic concessions. Even in its heyday in the early 1960s, the Civil Rights Movement never significantly challenged de facto, or customary, economic and political exclusion in the black ghettos of the North and West. As de jure, or legal, segregation was defeated in the South, economic and political empowerment lagged, civil rights strategies lost their punch, and black activists across the country looked for other solutions. Many, including Newton and Seale, turned to Malcolm X.

In December 1964, after the Atlantic City convention, Malcolm X spoke at the Williams Institutional CME Church in Harlem on the same stage with Fannie Lou Hamer. In sharp contrast to the nonviolent tactics of the Civil Rights Movement, Malcolm X suggested that black activists take up the revolutionary activities of the anticolonial Mau Mau rebels in Kenya:

> In my opinion, not only in Mississippi and Alabama, but right here in New York City, you and I can best learn how to get real freedom by studying how Kenyatta brought it to his people in Kenya, and how Odinga helped him, and the excellent job that was done by the Mau Mau freedom fighters. In fact, that's what we need in Mississippi. In Mississippi we need a Mau Mau. In Alabama we need a Mau Mau. In Georgia we need a Mau Mau. Right here in Harlem, in New York City, we need a Mau Mau. . . . We *need* a Mau Mau. If they don't want to deal with the Mississippi Freedom Democratic Party, then we'll give them something else to deal with. If they don't want to deal with the Student Nonviolent [Coordinating] Committee, then we have to give them an alternative.[23]

Malcolm X developed a form of revolutionary black nationalism as a minister in the Nation of Islam (NOI). Maintaining a central focus on a black nationalist identity as advocated by the NOI, he came to see black liberation as part of the global struggle against Western imperialism—a stance that posed a challenge not only to the integrationist politics of the Civil Rights Movement but also to the NOI's tradition of abstaining from political controversy.

> Uncle Sam's hands are dripping with blood, dripping with the blood of the black man in this country. He's the earth's number-one hypocrite. He has the audacity—yes, he has—imagine him posing as the leader of the free world. The free world!—and you over here singing 'We Shall Overcome.' Expand the civil-rights struggle to the level of human rights, take it into the United Nations, where our African brothers can throw their weight on our side, where our Latin-American brothers can throw their weight on our side, and where 800 million Chinamen are sitting there waiting to throw their weight on our side.[24]

When he continued to strike this tone in public statements, becoming increasingly politically outspoken and controversial, his mentor Elijah Muhammad expelled Malcolm X from the NOI.

Malcolm X's words resonated with many young blacks, especially those in the ghettos who had not seen the Civil Rights Movement bring any noticeable change in their condition. He also spoke to the activists who felt betrayed by President Johnson and the federal government and were sick of turning the other cheek: "And now you're facing a situation where the young Negro's coming up," Malcolm X declared. "They don't want to hear that 'turn-the-other-cheek' stuff, no. . . . There's a new deal coming. There's new thinking coming in. There's new strategy coming in. It'll be Molotov cocktails this month, hand grenades next month, and something else next month. It'll be ballots, or it'll be bullets. It'll be liberty, or it will be death. The only difference about this kind of death—it'll be reciprocal."[25]

In the 1960s, most black families—like the Newtons and the Seales—faced the peril of poverty. After migrating to the cities of the North and West to meet the demand for wartime jobs, thousands of black workers were left empty-handed when the war ended and the jobs evaporated. Many of the jobs that did remain followed whites fleeing to the suburbs—leaving sprawling black ghettos in their wake. Living in substandard housing and subjected to inferior and overcrowded schools, blacks were largely denied their rightful share of political power and economic opportunity. As unemployment increased, so did crime, and white urban politicians responded with strategies of containment, beefing up police patrols and attacking crime through force. While President Johnson's Civil Rights Act and the supposed redress of black grievances were widely touted as success stories, the poverty, political exclusion, police brutality, and desperation of ghetto life had only intensified. As a result, many young urban blacks rejected civil rights politics as ineffectual and were drawn to the revolutionary nationalism of Malcolm X.

When Malcolm X was gunned down in the Audubon Ballroom in Harlem in February 1965, he came to symbolize the struggle for black liberation—everything the Civil Rights Movement promised but could not deliver. In the words of historian William L. Van Deburg, Malcolm's "impassioned rhetoric was 'street smart'—it had almost visceral appeal to a young, black, economically distressed constituency. Before his assassination, Malcolm constantly urged this constituency to question the validity of their schoolbook- and media-inspired faith in an integrated American Dream. Many responded." After his death, Malcolm's influence expanded dramatically. "He came to be far more than a martyr for the militant, separatist faith. He became a Black

Power paradigm—the archetype, reference point, and spiritual adviser in absentia for a generation of Afro-American activists."[26]

In August 1965, six months after Malcolm X died, the Watts neighborhood in Los Angeles exploded in one of the largest urban rebellions in U.S. history. Black migrants had begun moving into Watts in the 1920s, creating a black island in a sea of white towns such as South Gate, Lynwood, Compton, and Bell (Compton did have one black resident in 1930). Home-lending regulations excluded blacks from obtaining mortgages to buy houses in white neighborhoods. By 1945, Watts was 80 percent black.[27] Through the 1950s, the black migration continued, and more blacks migrated to California than to any other state. During this decade, the black population of New York City increased almost two and a half times, and Detroit's black population tripled—while Black L.A. grew eightfold. Meanwhile, white residents fled in droves for the suburbs, taking capital and employment opportunities with them.[28]

Tensions between Watts residents and the police ran high. While the vast majority of Watts residents in 1965 were black, only 4 percent of the sworn personnel of the Los Angeles Police Department and 6 percent of the Los Angeles County Sheriff's Department were black.[29] Police Chief William Parker used analyses of crime data to develop and justify a policy that explicitly targeted Watts and other black neighborhoods for heavy police coverage, including intrusive techniques such as routine frisking of people on the street. "I don't think you can throw the genes out of the question when you discuss the behavior patterns of people," Parker wrote in 1957.[30] Officers on the force called their nightsticks "nigger-knockers." Residents of one of the most highly patrolled precincts called their area "little Mississippi." The local NAACP reported, "Negroes in Los Angeles never know where or at what hour may come blows from the guardians of the law who are supposed to protect them." One activist recalled, "You just had to be black and moving to be shot by the police."[31]

Between January 1962 and July 1965, Los Angeles law enforcement officers (mostly police but also sheriff's deputies, highway patrol personnel, and others) killed at least sixty-five people. Of the sixty-five homicides by police that the Los Angeles coroner's office investigated during this period, sixty-four were ruled justifiable homicides. These included twenty-seven cases in which the victim was shot in the back by law officers, twenty-five in which the victim was unarmed, twenty-three in which the victim was suspected of a nonviolent crime, and four in which the victim was not suspected of any crime at the time of the shooting. The only case that the coroner's inquest ruled to be unjustified homicide was one in which "two officers, 'playing cops and robbers' in a Long Beach Police Station shot a newspaperman."[32]

The incident that sparked the Watts rebellion was a traffic stop. Twenty-one-year-old Marquette Frye was driving his 1955 Buick along 116th Street near his family's house at 6 P.M. on August 11, 1965, when he was pulled over by a California Highway Patrol officer. His younger brother Ronald Frye, the only passenger, had just been discharged from the U.S. Air Force. A crowd gathered, including Marquette's mother, Rena. More police arrived. Soon a crowd of more than two hundred had gathered, and the onlookers became agitated as the police reportedly slapped Rena Frye, beat her with a blackjack, and twisted her arm behind her back.[33]

Watts exploded. On August 12, at 9:30 P.M., a group identifying itself as "followers of Malcolm X" arrived on Avalon Boulevard shouting "Let's burn . . . baby, burn!" The next day, at 3:30 P.M., the Emergency Control Center journal recorded "6 male Negroes firing rifles at helicopter from vehicle, 109th & Avalon." Governor Edmund "Pat" Brown cut short an aerial tour of South Los Angeles because of "sniper fire." Delta Airlines rerouted flights over the city because rebels were "shooting at planes."[34]

By the second day of the rebellion, according to the *Los Angeles Times,* more than seven thousand people were looting stores, in particular stealing guns, machetes, and other weapons. Rebels were filling glass bottles with gasoline and hurling Molotov cocktails at cars and stores, setting them on fire. Many were also firing shots at police. Fire trucks and ambulances that attempted to enter the area were also attacked.[35]

During the heat of battle, Police Chief Parker declared, "This situation is very much like fighting the Viet Cong. . . . We haven't the slightest idea when this can be brought under control." One rebel standing on the corner of Avalon and Imperial made a different reference to Vietnam, telling an interviewer, "I've got my 'stuff' [gun] ready, I'm not going to die in Vietnam, whitey has been kicking ass too long."[36]

As the fires still burned, the local CBS radio station reported, "This was not a riot. It was an insurrection against all authority. . . . If it had gone much further it would have become civil war." The *CBS Reports* TV broadcast in December 1965 called it a "virtual civil insurrection probably unmatched since" the Civil War. Scholars David O. Sears and John B. McConahay noted that the "legally constituted authority . . . was overthrown." Sociologist Robert Blauner saw the rebellions as "a preliminary if primitive form of mass rebellion against a colonial status."[37]

The rebellion spread out over 46.5 square miles. All told, 34 people—almost all black—were killed, many by police, and more than 1,032 were wounded; 3,952 people were arrested. The rebellion caused more than $40 million in property damage to over six hundred buildings, completely destroying two hundred of them.[38]

Full of rage at ghetto conditions, chafing against police repression, and frustrated with a civil rights politics unable to redress their situation, the Watts rebels sought to take matters into their own hands, forcefully rejecting the old-guard civil rights leadership. Following the rebellion, Martin Luther King Jr. went to Watts to bring his vision of an integrated society and the tactics of nonviolence. On August 18, he spoke to a meeting of five hundred people at the Westminster Neighborhood Association. He began his appeal in rolling cadence: "All over America . . . the Negroes must join hands . . . " "And burn!" shouted a member of the audience. Throughout the evening, the audience repeatedly challenged and ridiculed King's appeal. Nonviolent activist and comedian Dick Gregory fared even worse in Watts. While the rebellion still flared, he borrowed a bullhorn from the police so that he could speak to the rebels. He attempted to calm them and pleaded "Go home!" The crowd did not respond kindly. A gunman in the crowd shot Gregory in the leg. The politics of nonviolence were failing.[39]

Commenting on the wave of urban rebellions and the rejection of civil rights strategies by disenchanted and dispossessed blacks, Paul Jacobs and Saul Landau observed, "The masses of poor Negroes remain an unorganized minority in swelling urban ghettos, and neither SNCC nor any other group has found a form of political organization that can convert the energy of the slums into political power."[40]

ARMCHAIR REVOLUTIONARIES

In Oakland in 1964, far away from Fannie Lou Hamer and the convention battles in Atlantic City, Huey Newton stabbed a man named Odell Lee with a steak knife at a party. At his trial, he claimed he had done so in self-defense, but the all-white jury was not convinced, and he spent six months in jail, mostly in solitary confinement because he would not obey orders from the guards. Newton later recalled finding a new sense of freedom in prison. The guards could lock up his body, but they could not cage his mind. Newton emerged from jail eager to embrace the new political ideas and organizations developing in Oakland.[41]

Newton soon reconnected with Seale, and the two joined the Soul Students Advisory Council (SSAC), founded by Ernie Allen. The council was a front group for the Revolutionary Action Movement (RAM), an anti-imperialist and Marxist black nationalist organization based in Philadelphia. Allen had collaborated with Newton and Seale in Warden's Afro-American Association when he was a student at Merritt College. After transferring to the University of California, Berkeley, Allen had traveled to Cuba in 1964 on a trip sponsored by the Progressive Labor Party. The contingent also included other radical black students from Detroit and around the country. In Cuba, Allen and the others met Max Stanford, the leader of RAM, who was there visiting his mentor Robert F. Williams, a pioneering advocate of armed black self-defense. Williams had moved to Cuba after local authorities—in collusion with the Ku Klux Klan and backed by the FBI—forced him to flee North Carolina.[42] Allen got to know Stanford and Williams in Cuba, and through his intense conversations and debates with them, he found a way to move beyond the limits of Warden's Afro-American Association, embracing the idea that U.S. blacks could win their freedom by participating in a global revolution against imperialism. By the time he returned to the United States, Allen was committed to organizing a chapter of RAM in California.[43]

Ernie Allen, his brother Doug, Kenny Freeman (Mamadou Lumumba), and others began to build several front groups for RAM in the Bay Area. One project was *Soulbook: The Revolutionary Journal of the Black World,* a beautifully presented quarterly magazine of cultural criticism and political theory whose content ranged from essays on the significance of John Coltrane to analyses of the writings of Frantz Fanon. Both poetry and black revolutionary nationalist artwork graced the magazine.[44]

Virtual Murrell, Alex Papillon, Isaac Moore, and other friends of Newton and Seale at Merritt also joined the SSAC and helped launch a campaign to create courses in Afro-American studies at the college. The Merritt student body was predominantly black, and there was a large demand for such courses. The demand for Afro-American studies cut across intrablack differences and garnered support from many black individuals and organizations. The administration put up resistance, but hundreds of students turned out for meetings and protests, and the administration slowly began making concessions, including development of a black studies curriculum.[45]

Working with RAM exposed Newton and Seale to a new world of writings and ideas. Both had been strongly influenced by the thinking of Malcolm X and the readings in the Afro-American Association. But unlike the association, RAM was a revolutionary nationalist organization with a strong socialist and anti-imperialist bent. Guided by the political ideas of Robert F. Williams, RAM exposed Newton and Seale to the key writings of revolutionary nationalism, and they were particularly attracted to the writings of Frantz Fanon, Mao Zedong, and Che Guevara, as well as RAM's own publications on revolutionary black nationalism, including articles by Max Stanford and Robert Williams.[46]

The Revolutionary Action Movement advanced a pivotal idea that would become central to the politics of the Black Panther Party. Drawing on a line of thought reaching back at least to the mid-1940s and the black anticolonialism of W. E. B. Du Bois, Paul Robeson, and Alpheus Hunton, RAM argued that Black America was essentially a colony and framed the struggle against racism by blacks in the United States as part of the global anti-imperialist struggle against colonialism.[47] Max Stanford defined the politics of revolutionary black nationalism this way in 1965: "We are revolutionary black nationalist, not based on ideas of national superiority, but striving for justice and liberation of all the oppressed peoples of the world. . . . There can be no liberty as long as black people are oppressed and the peoples of Africa, Asia and Latin America are oppressed by Yankee imperialism and neo-colonialism. After four hundred years of oppression, we realize that slavery, racism and imperialism are all interrelated and that liberty and justice for all cannot exist peacefully with imperialism."[48]

The politics of RAM connected the struggles of black Americans with liberation struggles abroad. Whereas black soldiers returning from World War II helped catalyze the Civil Rights Movement by arguing that if they could die fighting for their country, then they should be considered full citizens upon their return, RAM insisted that blacks were not full citizens in the United States. RAM viewed Black America as an independent nation that had been colonized at home. Because black Americans were colonial subjects rather than citizens, RAM argued, they owed no allegiance to the U.S. government and thus should not fight in the Vietnam War.

On July 4, 1965, RAM wrote an open statement to the Vietnamese National Liberation Front declaring the independence of Black America from the United States and asserting its solidarity with the Vietnamese struggle against American imperialism.[49] In a separate statement that day, RAM addressed blacks in the military, arguing that if they should be fighting against anyone, it should be the U.S. government for the liberation of Black America: "Why should we go 'anywhere' to fight for the racist U.S. government, only to return home and be faced with murder, rape, castration, and extermination? How can the racist U.S. government talk about 'freeing' anyone, when the U.S. government practices racism against Black Americans every day? If the U.S. government says it cannot protect us from local and national racists, then let your battle assignment be against those who are abusing your children, wives, mothers, fathers, sisters, brothers, and loved ones."[50]

RAM and its front group the SSAC identified a common cause between blacks and the Vietnamese, and they were on the cutting edge of early opposition to the Vietnam War. Before there was any significant draft resistance, they criticized the draft and organized a campaign "to oppose the drafting of black men" into the military, holding rallies for the cause, including one at Merritt College on April 26, 1966, featuring local organizers Alex Papillon and Mark Comfort.[51]

Through its honorary chair-in-exile, Robert F. Williams, RAM began building relationships with anti-imperialist leaders around the world. Williams had served as president of the local NAACP chapter in Monroe, North Carolina. As Jim Crow came under growing attack by the Civil Rights Movement, the Ku Klux Klan, with the support of the local white government, increasingly relied on violence to protect racial segregation. With no support from the federal government, Williams turned to the skills he had learned as a private first class in the Marine Corps to turn the tide, arming himself and other members of his NAACP chapter. Williams and the Monroe NAACP fought several armed battles in self-defense against whites. In 1961, facing dubious criminal charges and threatened by a lynch mob that promised to kill him for his activities, Williams fled North Carolina.[52]

Williams found asylum in Cuba and soon met Mao Zedong in China. Mao was deeply impressed with Williams and saw common cause in the struggle for black liberation in the United States and the global struggle against imperialism. In 1963, Mao articulated this position in an essay he wrote at Williams's behest, asking the people of the world to recognize the Black Liberation Struggle in the United States as part of the global struggle against imperialism.[53]

Robert Williams's life exemplified a different approach to politics than that of RAM, and Williams's memoir, *Negroes with Guns,* greatly influenced Newton.[54] Newton was deeply impressed by Williams's courage in standing up to the lynch mobs, but he was not sure how to apply this political approach to the ghettos of the North and West. He wanted to organize poor blacks. He wanted to mobilize the "brothers on the block," the unemployed black men seen on every street of the ghetto, the black underclass. These were the people who faced the brutality of the expanding urban police departments. And many were the same folks who had rioted in Watts. RAM claimed to be talking for them, but it was not reaching them or moving them to action. Newton did not yet know how to mobilize these "brothers on the block," but given what he knew of his brother Sonny Man, he believed that they would understand armed self-defense—that they would understand the language of the gun.[55]

The Revolutionary Action Movement led the way in developing revolutionary black nationalist thought in the United States in the 1960s, but the group's practical application of these ideas was limited. RAM leaders fashioned themselves as revolutionaries: They read socialist and anti-imperialist texts and raised the possibility of urban guerilla warfare. Some evidence indicates that RAM members attempted to implement these ideas, but most of them were intellectuals like Huey's brother Melvin.[56] They rarely emphasized practical action, and when they did, they oriented their efforts toward students. Huey soon became dissatisfied with the group's inability to appeal to the "brothers on the block" and sought new ways to meld theory with on-the-ground action.

Huey and Bobby wanted to challenge police brutality directly, and they found some inspiration in the activities of Mark Comfort and Curtis Lee Baker, talented young organizers who had emerged from traditional civil rights organizations in Oakland.[57] Comfort and Baker had begun appealing to young African Americans with militant style— adopting black outfits and berets in early 1966—and with challenges to police brutality.[58] In February 1965, Comfort organized a protest "to put a stop to police beating innocent people." A crowd of more than two hundred—mostly high school students—encircled the Oakland Hall of Justice, urging Governor Pat Brown to "make a full scale investigation" of police brutality.[59] That August, Baker and others demanded that the Oakland City Council keep white policemen out of black neighborhoods.[60] During that summer, Comfort organized citizen patrols to monitor the actions of the police and document incidents of brutality. When people were arrested, he followed them to the jail and bailed them out. He soon abandoned the tactic, though, because it was too costly.[61]

On Thursday night, March 17, 1966, at approximately 9 P.M., Newton and Seale and a friend they called "Weasel" were walking on Telegraph Avenue in Berkeley, just north of Oakland, headed toward the University of California campus. The street was a small bohemian mecca, with students, hippies, and young people congregating and milling about in the restaurants, cafes, bars, and shops. With encouragement from Huey and Weasel, Bobby stood on a chair outside the Forum restaurant near the corner of Telegraph and Haste and began to recite Ronald Stone's black antiwar poem "Uncle Sammy Call Me Fulla Lucifer":

> You school my naïve heart to sing
> red-white-and-blue-stars-and-stripes songs and to pledge eternal
>   allegiance to all things blue, true,
> blue-eyed blond, blond-haired, white chalk white skin with U.S.A.
>   tattooed all over. . . .
> I will not serve.[62]

The poem struck a chord. The war was escalating, and many students felt conflicted, scared, and angry about the draft. A crowd began to gather. Soon more than twenty-five people were cheering Bobby on and asking him to recite the poem again. George Williamson, an off-duty police officer, pushed into the crowd and grabbed Seale. A scuffle broke out. More police arrived. Newton and Seale were both arrested for disturbing the peace.[63] Virtual Murrell withdrew $50 from the SSAC treasury and bailed them out.[64]

A few weeks later, Newton and Seale saw a policeman pushing around a black man for no apparent reason. The officer arrested the man and took him to the station. Following Mark Comfort's example, Newton and Seale went to the station and bailed the man out using money from the SSAC treasury.[65] The brother started to cry, and it touched Bobby deeply. Bobby was fed up with "armchair intellectualizing" and wanted to stand up against the police, recalling, "I was filled with a staunch belief of the need for brotherhood and revolution and rebellion against the racist system."[66]

Huey and Bobby were ready to take meaningful, on-the-ground action. Seeking to emulate Robert Williams's defiant stance, Newton proposed that the SSAC organize a rally for Malcolm X's birthday in May 1966 and wear loaded guns in the spirit of his call for armed self-defense. Newton believed that this would attract the "brothers on the block" to participate. Seale supported Newton's proposal, but Kenny Freeman and the other RAM leaders flatly rejected it.[67]

Perhaps feeling threatened, Freeman and other RAM leaders suggested that Newton and Seale had misused money from the SSAC treasury. That was the last straw. Already frustrated with the failure of the
local RAM leadership to stand up to police brutality, the organization's
lack of support during the fray on Telegraph Avenue, and its inability to
organize brothers on the block, Bobby and Huey confronted Freeman
and the others and then left the SSAC.[68]

EPIPHANY

In the summer of 1966, Seale was hired to run a youth work program
at the North Oakland Neighborhood Anti-Poverty Center funded by
the federal War on Poverty. Through his role as a social service pro-
vider, he came to understand even more clearly the economic and social
needs of black youth. Beyond delivering services, Bobby brought his
revolutionary nationalist theory to the job and used the opportunity
to push up against the ideological bias in the government program.
Rather than merely guiding young blacks into a government-prescribed
path, he used his authority to help them stand up against oppressive
authority, particularly against police brutality. One day Seale's boss
instructed him to take a group of young black men and women on
a tour of the local police station. When the group arrived, the police
officers pulled out notepads and pencils and started to interview the
teenagers about the character of gangs in the neighborhood. Seale protested, instructing his group to remain silent and announcing that his
program would not be used as a spy network to inform on people in
the community. The officers claimed that they simply wanted to foster
better relations with the community. In response, Seale turned the conversation around, creating an opportunity for the teenagers to describe
their experiences with police brutality in the neighborhood.

It was the first time the young people had had the opportunity to
look white police officers in the eye and express their anger and frustration. One teenager berated the police for an incident in which several
officers had thrown a woman down and beaten her in the head with
billy clubs. "Say you!" said a sixteen-year-old girl, pointing at a policeman. "You don't have to treat him like that," Seale said to the girl. "I'll
treat him like I want to, because they done treated me so bad," she
replied. Bobby sat back as the girl grilled the officer about whether he
had received proper psychiatric treatment. The officer turned red and
started to shake. "The way you're shaking now," she said, "the way

you're shaking now and carrying on, you must be guilty of a whole lot! And I haven't got no weapon or nothin.'"[69]

The poverty program provided a paycheck, some skills, and an opportunity to work with young people. But Newton and Seale were still searching for a way to galvanize the rage of the "brothers on the block." They wanted to mobilize the ghetto the way that the Civil Rights Movement had mobilized blacks in the South. They dreamt of creating an unstoppable force that would transform the urban landscape forever. The problem was now clear to Huey and Bobby, but they did not yet have a solution.

Huey and Bobby were not the only ones looking for answers. Within a year of the Watts rebellion, the younger generation of black liberation activists had widely rejected the goals of integration and the tactics of nonviolence. On June 5, 1966, James Meredith, the first black student to gain admission to the University of Mississippi, was shot on his solo march from Memphis to Jackson. Civil rights leaders Martin Luther King Jr. and Stokely Carmichael flew to Memphis to take up his march, and they were soon joined by black liberation activists from around the country as well as many local blacks. As the march proceeded, a split began to emerge between the old-guard civil rights leaders represented by King and the younger wing represented by Carmichael. The younger activists wanted the march to be a blacks-only event, and they also wanted the Deacons of Defense—a militant black organization that promoted armed self-defense—to provide protection for the marchers. These were significant departures from the civil rights integrationist frame and nonviolent tactics.[70]

As the march made its way to Greenwood, Mississippi, Carmichael and a group of activists were arrested and held in jail for six hours. Upon their release, Carmichael announced to a rally of supporters, "This is the twenty-seventh time I have been arrested. I ain't going to jail no more. What we gonna start saying now is 'Black Power.'" Willie Ricks, a SNCC activist, took up the phrase and called it out: "What do you want?" The crowd replied, "Black Power!"[71] The phrase caught on like wildfire. The old-guard civil rights leaders soon acknowledged the shift. King even appealed to the government for help: "The government has got to give me some victories if I'm gonna keep people nonviolent. . . . I know I'm gonna stay nonviolent no matter what happens. But a lot of people are getting hurt and bitter, and they can't see it that way anymore."[72]

Black Power was not so much an answer as a new way of framing the quest for black liberation. No one knew quite what Black Power was or how to achieve it. But the younger generation of black activists put their minds and energies to figuring it out.

By 1966, racial tensions were rising in Oakland. Mayor John Reading called the City Council to his office for a special meeting to warn its members that if communication between the city government and low-income blacks did not improve, Oakland would become "another Watts."[73] Amory Bradford, a Johnson administration official sent to Oakland in 1966 to develop a federal plan for reducing racial tensions, reported, "Experts sent by the President to survey conditions in other ghettos picked Oakland as one of those most likely to be the next Watts."[74] Another visiting white official described Oakland as a "powder keg."[75] One Economic Development Administration outreach flier widely distributed in west Oakland in 1966 read:

LET'S TALK ABOUT PROBLEMS

Eugene R. Foley,
U.S. Department of Commerce,
President Johnson's Troubleshooter,
wants to talk to you to prevent a Watts
in Oakland.[76]

That fall, word spread that Oakland police officers had beaten a black girl during the arrest of her brother. A large crowd of disgruntled youths began to gather. They soon "laid siege" to a ten-block area on East 14th Street, smashing windows, attacking cars, and throwing gasoline bombs. Sixty police officers arrived on the scene and arrested twelve people.[77]

On September 27, 1966, sixteen-year-old Matthew Johnson was pulled over by police in Hunters Point, a black neighborhood across the bay in San Francisco. Johnson and his friends had stolen a car and were cruising around the neighborhood. When police pulled them over, the teens panicked and fled. Matthew Johnson was shot in the back by police and was left bleeding on the ground for more than an hour. By the time ambulances arrived, he was dead. The neighborhood erupted in a rebellion that went on for several days. Using bricks and Molotov cocktails, rebels damaged or destroyed thirty-one police cars and ten fire department vehicles. The police arrested 146 people, injuring 42, 10 of them with gunshots.[78]

The situation was unbearable. Newton and Seale would tolerate no more police brutality and were fed up with the disorganized and impotent attempts of the black community to resist. They were determined to find a solution.[79] Newton soon experienced an epiphany sparked by an article he read in the August 1966 edition of the West Coast SNCC newspaper, the *Movement*, about the Community Alert Patrol (CAP) in Watts. "Brother Lennie" and "Brother Crook," two activists from Watts, organized CAP after the rebellion in 1965 to prevent further police brutality. CAP members monitored the police, driving around the black neighborhoods of Watts with notepads and pencils, documenting police activities. In August 1966, CAP began displaying a Black Panther logo on its patrol vehicles—inspired by SNCC's use of the Panther symbol when helping to organize an independent black political party in Lowndes County, Alabama. CAP was not left alone to carry out its activities, however; it was vulnerable to harassment and abuse by the police. One frustrated CAP member commented on the police harassment to a *Movement* reporter: "There's only one way to stop all this," he said, "and that's to get out our guns and start shooting."[80]

Newton had been studying law at Merritt College and San Francisco State College, and he also read on his own at the North Oakland Service Center law library. He discovered that California law permitted people to carry loaded guns in public as long as the weapons were not concealed. He studied California gun law inside and out, finding that it was illegal to keep rifles loaded in a moving vehicle and that parolees could carry a rifle but not a handgun. In California, he learned, citizens had the right to observe an officer carrying out his or her duty as long as they stood a reasonable distance away.[81]

Newton had finally hit upon a way to stand up to the police and organize the "brothers on the block." He would organize patrols like the CAP in Watts. But he and his comrades would carry loaded guns.

THE BLACK PANTHER

Following the September 27 killing of Matthew Johnson, the UC Berkeley chapter of Students for a Democratic Society decided to hold a conference on Black Power and invited Stokely Carmichael, SNCC chairperson and the leading national proponent of Black Power, to be the keynote speaker. Because of the timing of the Conference on Black Power and Its Challenges, scheduled for October 29 in Berkeley, it immediately became an explosive political issue for the campus and in state politics. Republican Ronald Reagan was running a highly polarizing campaign against Democratic incumbent Edmund Brown for governor of California, and the election was coming up in early November. Given the contentious national debate on Black Power and Carmichael's stature, the conference threatened to become an election issue. The campus administration decided to deny the campus chapter of SDS permission to hold the event.

The move echoed recent battles between students and the administration over students' rights in the Free Speech Movement. Soon, a raging battle arose on campus over whether SDS would be allowed to hold the conference. Wary of further escalation, the university capitulated.[82] In response, Ronald Reagan criticized the conference publicly: "We cannot have the university campus used as a base to foment riots from." Reagan sent Stokely Carmichael a telegram urging him to stay out of California. He then challenged Governor Brown to cosign his telegram. The governor refused, saying that he did not want to dignify Carmichael's cause. Nevertheless, Governor Brown made public statements similar to Reagan's. "I wish Stokely Carmichael would stay out of California. I wish he'd not come in here at all. I think he's caused nothing but trouble," the governor told a crowd at the University of California, Santa Barbara. Californians, he pronounced, "don't want black power." The day before the conference, Governor Brown made a surprise appearance in Oakland to meet with the Alameda County sheriff to assure that "the peace of this community will be protected." Reagan quipped sarcastically, "I'm happy to see he has hurried north like a man of action."[83]

In addition to Carmichael, speakers scheduled for the conference included Ivanhoe Donaldson, the New York director of SNCC; Brother Lennie, leader of the Watts Community Alert Patrol; Mark Comfort, leader of the Oakland Direct Action Project; Ron Karenga; James Bevel from the Southern Christian Leadership Conference; Mike Parker and Mike Smith from SDS; Mike Miller and Clay Carson from SNCC; Terry Cannon, editor of the *Movement* newspaper; Elijah Turner, an Oakland organizer; and Barbara Arthur, a student at UC Berkeley.[84]

The controversy stoked interest in the conference, not only among students but also among local black activists. Huey and Bobby's former mentor Donald Warden and members of RAM such as Doug Allen spoke out against the "racist" university administration for attempting to bar the conference. On Saturday October 29, people flooded the Greek Theatre to listen to the speakers. By midafternoon, more than three thousand people had packed into the open-air theater, with students standing in the aisles, sitting on the stage, and spread out on the grass hill above the theater to hear the speeches.[85] It is not clear whether Huey and Bobby participated in the conference, but they certainly heard about it.

The podium was black with big red letters identifying SDS. Behind the podium, a large banner, three feet wide and fifty feet long, read "Black Power and Its Challenges." Ivanhoe Donaldson introduced Carmichael, emphasizing Carmichael's leadership against the war and drawing an analogy between the struggle of blacks in American cities and the struggle of the Vietnamese against imperialism: "The Vietnamese are fighting the same establishment that the brothers in Oakland, Chicago and Watts are fighting." Carmichael approached the podium wearing a dark suit, white shirt, and dark tie. He straightened his shirt, adjusted the microphone, and looked out at the predominantly white student audience.[86]

"It's a privilege and an honor to be in the white intellectual ghetto of the West," Carmichael began, making common cause with the students. But the familiarity was brief. "White America cannot condemn herself," Carmichael told the students, "so black people have done it— you stand condemned. . . . Move on over, or we're going to move on over you." Carmichael talked about the limitations of integrationism and the need for Black Power in international terms. "In order for America to really live on a basic principle of human relationships, a new society must be born. Racism must die. The economic exploitation by this country of nonwhite people around the world must also die."[87]

Carmichael focused most of his speech on the question of Vietnam. "The war in Vietnam is an illegal and immoral war," he argued. He compared the plight of black people in America with the plight of the Vietnamese: "Any time a black man leaves the country where he can't vote to supposedly deliver the vote to somebody else, he's a black mercenary. Any time a black man leaves this country, gets shot in Vietnam on foreign ground, and returns home and you won't give him a burial place in his own homeland, he's a black mercenary. Even if I were to believe the lies of [President] Johnson," said Carmichael, "if I were to believe his lies that we are fighting to give democracy to the people in Vietnam, as a black man in this country, I wouldn't fight to give this to anybody."[88]

Carmichael also criticized the student peace movement and argued that if peace activists wanted to be relevant to most people, they needed to start organizing to resist the draft:

The peace movement has been a failure because it hasn't gotten off the college campuses where everybody has a⸱2S [draft deferment] and is not afraid of being drafted anyway. The problem is how you can move out of that into the white ghettos of this country and articulate a position for those white youth who do not want to go. . . . [SNCC is] the most militant organization for peace or civil rights or human rights against the war in Vietnam in this country today. There isn't one organization that has begun to meet our stand on the war in Vietnam. We not only say we are against the war in Vietnam; we are against the draft. . . . There is a higher law than the law of a racist named [Secretary of Defense] McNamara; there is a higher law than the law of a fool named [Secretary of State] Rusk; there is a higher law than the law of a buffoon named Johnson. It's the law of each of us. We will not allow them to make us hired killers. We will not kill anybody that they say kill. And if we decide to kill, we are going to decide who to kill.[89]

The conference program featured the symbol of a black panther from the Lowndes County Freedom Organization (LCFO) that Carmichael was publicizing. The LCFO was part of a new effort by local blacks and SNCC to build an independent political party outside of the exclusive white Democratic Party, marking a departure from its strategy of mobilizing civil disobedience against Jim Crow segregation in the early 1960s. Lowndes County was 80 percent black, yet in early 1966, despite the 1965 passage of the Voting Rights Act, there was still not a single black person registered to vote in Lowndes County. So on May 3, 1966, with SNCC's help, the LCFO convened and nominated candidates for sheriff, tax assessor, coroner, and school board and encouraged blacks to register to vote. As blacks registered, white resistance intensified. At one SNCC rally, a deputy sheriff fired into the crowd, shooting two civil rights workers and killing one, Carmichael's friend Jonathan Daniels, a white ministerial student.

Because so many whites in Lowndes were illiterate, the ballot featured a drawing of a party mascot. The all-white Democratic Party featured a white rooster and the slogan White Supremacy/For the Right. The LCFO selected the black panther as its symbol to signify a fierce black political challenge. In a June 1966 interview, John Hulett, the chairman of the LCFO, explained the symbol of the panther: "The black panther is an animal that when it is pressured it moves back until it is cornered, then it comes out fighting for life or death. We felt we had been pushed back long enough and that it was time for Negroes to come out and take over."[90]

In late August 1966, SNCC had organized a rally at the Mt. Morris

Presbyterian Church in New York City to promote the newly formed Harlem branch of the Black Panther Party. The speakers included Carmichael; William Epton, the head of the Harlem branch of the Progressive Labor Party; and Max Stanford, the leader of RAM, who identified himself at the time as the head of the Harlem branch of the Black Panther Party. Black Panther members came dressed in uniforms of black pants and shirts displaying the panther emblem. In front of a cheering crowd of 250, Carmichael called on blacks to unite with people of color in Vietnam and throughout the world. He also spoke in favor of armed self-defense for blacks. "If the police and the federal government won't protect us," said Carmichael, "we must protect ourselves." Both he and Stanford spoke in favor of the recent wave of ghetto rebellions. The United States, Stanford suggested, "could be brought down to its knees with a rag and some gasoline and a bottle."[91]

In September 1966, Carmichael wrote that organizing had begun under the black panther symbol across the country, in the North as well as the South—including independent efforts in Los Angeles, New York, Philadelphia, and New Jersey. "A man needs a black panther on his side when he and his family must endure—as hundreds of Alabamans have endured—loss of job, eviction, starvation and sometimes death for political activity," Carmichael explained. "He may also need a gun and SNCC reaffirms the right of black men everywhere to defend themselves when threatened or attacked."[92]

The Black Power conference and the symbol of the black panther captured the attention of Kenny Freeman, Doug Allen, Ernie Allen, and the West Coast members of RAM. At this time, RAM's political analysis was fairly close to that of SNCC and Carmichael. Like the New York branch of RAM, the West Coast members were drawn to Carmichael's charisma and the defiant symbol of the black panther, and they were impressed by his organizing efforts in Lowndes County. They followed the example of Max Stanford and the New York RAM and formed the Black Panther Party of Northern California.

Not only did the program for the October 1966 Berkeley Black Power conference feature the black panther logo of the Lowndes County Freedom Organization in recognition of Carmichael's work there, but two days before the conference, activists distributed a pamphlet and fliers about the Lowndes County Black Panther Party on the Berkeley campus.[93]

Huey Newton was among those to take notice of the bold logo and courageous organizing. Writing several years later, Newton recalled,

"I had read a pamphlet about voter registration in [Alabama], how the people in Lowndes County had armed themselves against Establishment violence. Their political group, called the Lowndes County Freedom Organization, had a black panther for its symbol. A few days later, while Bobby and I were rapping, I suggested that we use the panther as our symbol."[94]

Like the West Coast members of RAM with whom they had worked in the Soul Students Advisory Council, Newton and Seale decided to form a chapter of the Black Panther Party. But guided by Newton's epiphany, they took their party in a different direction that would have long-term political consequences.[95]

2

Policing the Police

One night in early 1967, Huey Newton, Bobby Seale, and Little (Lil')
Bobby Hutton, the first recruit to their Black Panther Party for Self-
Defense, were cruising around north Oakland in Seale's 1954 Chevy.
Newton was at the wheel. They saw a police car patrolling the area
and decided to monitor it. As Bobby Seale later recounted the incident, Newton sped up to within a short residential block behind the car
and kept that distance.[1] When the officer turned right, Newton turned
right. When the officer turned left, Newton turned left. Newton was
armed with a shotgun, Seale with a .45 caliber handgun, and Hutton
with an M-1 rifle. A law book sat on the back seat.

After they had followed the police car for a while, the officer pulled
the patrol car to the curb and stopped at the corner. There was a
stop sign at the corner, so Newton pulled up to the intersection and
stopped next to the police car. The three men looked over at the officer. Seale held Newton's shotgun while he drove, and both the shotgun
and Hutton's M-1 were plainly visible through the window. The officer looked back. After a pause, Newton stepped gently on the gas and
rounded the corner to the right in front of the officer. As Newton completed the turn, the officer flashed his high beams. Newton kept driving
without changing speed. The officer stepped on the gas and pulled out
after him. Seale could see the flashing red lights, but Newton kept moving. He told Seale, "I'm not going to stop 'till he puts his damn siren on
because a flashing red light really don't mean nothin', anything could

be a flashing red light." At this point, the car headed north on Dover Street behind Merritt College. Newton took a left on 58th Street and headed down the block, passing Merritt's track field. The officer turned on his siren, and Newton pulled over, coming to a stop across the street from the back door of the college.

As soon as Newton pulled over, the officer stopped and burst out of his car, hollering, "What the goddam hell you niggers doing with them goddam guns? Who in the goddam hell you niggers think you are? Get out of that goddam car. Get out of that goddam car with them goddam guns." At this point, students who had just finished their evening classes at the predominantly black school began filing out the back door, and they stopped to watch. Many residents of the homes along the street looked out their windows.

The officer approached the car, screaming, "Get out of that car!" Newton said, "You ain't putting anybody under arrest. Who the hell you think you are?" At this point, the officer pulled open the car door and shouted, "I said get out of the goddam car and bring them goddam guns out of there." The officer stuck his head in the car, reached across Newton, and grabbed the barrel of the shotgun Seale was holding. Seale pulled back on the shotgun. Newton grabbed the officer by the collar and slammed his head up into the roof of the car. He then swiveled in his seat, kicked the officer in the stomach, and pushed him out of the car.

Newton took the shotgun from Seale, leapt out of the car, and jacked a round of ammunition into the chamber. He shouted, "Now, who in the hell do you think you are, you big rednecked bastard, you rotten fascist swine, you bigoted racist? You come into my car, trying to brutalize me and take my property away from me. Go for your gun and you're a dead pig." The officer lifted his hands away from his gun while Seale and Hutton jumped out of the passenger side of the car. Seale pulled back the hammer on his .45. The officer backed away from Newton toward his car, where he radioed for backup.

People streamed out of their houses; more students streamed out of Merritt. Seale and Newton beckoned people to come out and observe the police. A sizable crowd soon coalesced. Seale called the police "racist dogs, pigs." He explained to the crowd that police were "occupying our community like a foreign troop that occupies territory" and that "Black people are tired of it."[2]

Several more police cars arrived, and an officer walked up to Newton and demanded, "Let me see that weapon!"

Newton said, "Let you see my weapon? You haven't placed me under arrest."

The officer insisted: "Well, you just let me see the weapon, I have a right to see the weapon."

Newton refused. "Ain't you ever heard of the Fourteenth Amendment of the Constitution of the United States? Don't you know you don't remove nobody's property without due process of law? What's the matter with you? You're supposed to be people enforcing the law, and here you are, ready to violate my constitutional rights. You can't see my gun. You can't have my gun. The only way you're gonna get it from me is to try to take it."

Another officer walked up to Seale and shouted, "Come over here by the car."

Seale said: "I ain't going no goddam place. Who the hell you think you are? You ain't placed me under arrest."

"But I have a right to take you over to the car," the officer replied loudly.

Seale responded, "You don't have no right to move me from one spot to another. You just got through telling me I wasn't under arrest, so I'm not moving nowhere, I'm staying right here."

The officer then demanded that Seale hand over his gun, and Seale refused. Newton, Seale, and Hutton would not submit to the police. Citing local ordinances as well as the Second Amendment to the Constitution, they asserted their right to bear arms as long as the guns were not concealed. The standoff threatened to escalate. But after tense deliberations, the police lieutenant told the other officers he did not see sufficient grounds for arrest. After looking around, one of the officers noticed that the license plate on Seale's Chevy was attached with a coat hanger. He then wrote Seale a ticket for not having the license plate securely fastened to his vehicle.

The police soon left, and the excited crowd gathered around Newton and Seale to hear what had happened. The men described their organization, the Black Panther Party for Self-Defense. The next day, several community members who had witnessed the event joined the Party.

Bobby Seale provided the first guns for the Black Panther Party for Self-Defense from his personal collection: a .30–30 Winchester rifle and a shotgun. Even before his time in the military, Seale had been around guns, mostly when hunting with his father. Once new recruits began joining the Party, obtaining more firearms became a priority. Newton and Seale approached Richard Aoki, a Japanese American radical who they knew had an impressive collection of guns. A small and energetic man with a big smile, a dirty mouth, and a generous sense of humor, Aoki was a dedicated revolutionary committed to Third World liberation. He was pleased to help the Black Panthers get started and donated two guns to the Party in support of their revolutionary cause, an M-1 Garand rifle and a 9mm pistol, both weapons designed for the military.[3]

Newton and Seale needed to raise money to purchase more guns for their Party. Newton got the idea to sell Mao Zedong's Little Red Book on the Berkeley campus to raise money—a small but influential book of quotations by the chairman of the Chinese Communist Party that was receiving a lot of news coverage. They went to Chinatown in San Francisco and bought the books at thirty cents apiece and then sold them on the Berkeley campus for a dollar. Soon they raised enough money to buy a .357 Magnum (a pistol designed for law enforcement officers) from Aoki and a High Standard shotgun at the local department store.[4]

Over the course of several months patrolling the police, Newton and Seale gained a small following. Bobby got Huey a job at the War on Poverty youth program where he worked, and the two used a portion of their paychecks to rent an office on Grove Street and 56th in north Oakland near Merritt College.[5] In early 1967, the Black Panther Party for Self-Defense had only a handful of members. The organization had received no coverage in the press and was known only by those with whom the Party had direct contact, or through word of mouth. By February, this began to change.

That January, Eldridge Cleaver, a writer for *Ramparts* magazine—an independent Catholic magazine that had become an influential voice of opposition to the Vietnam War—had recently moved to San Francisco and joined forces with playwright Marvin Jackman, poet Ed Bullins, and singer Willie Dale to found Black House, a cultural center for the burgeoning Black Power movement in the Bay Area. Along with the RAM-affiliated Black Panther Party of Northern California run by Kenny Freeman, Doug Allen, Ernie Allen, and Roy Ballard, they decided to organize a memorial for Malcolm X on the two-year anniversary of his death, February 21, 1967. The idea came out of Cleaver's plan to create a new organization that represented the true legacy of Malcolm X and to name it after the group he had started before his death, the Organization for Afro-American Unity. Cleaver's idea was to bring Betty Shabazz, Malcolm X's widow, to the Bay Area as the keynote speaker at the memorial conference to legitimize the new organization. Cleaver was new to the area, and the group appointed Roy Ballard as coordinator of the event.[6]

A number of the organizers feared that Betty Shabazz could become a target like her husband, so Roy Ballard asked Bobby Seale if the Black Panther Party for Self-Defense would speak at the conference and provide an armed escort for Shabazz. After consulting with Newton, Seale agreed, and arranged to meet Shabazz at the San Francisco Airport. In the early afternoon of February 21, eight members of Newton and Seale's Black Panther Party for Self-Defense, dressed in uniform—waist-length leather jackets, powder blue shirts, and black berets cocked to the right—met up with Roy Ballard, Kenny Freeman, and several other members of the RAM-affiliated group.

At 3:05 P.M., the Black Panther contingent, led by Newton, entered the lobby of the San Francisco Airport displaying shotguns and pistols. The airport security chief, George Nessel, and his armed deputies confronted them and ordered them to wait outside the building. Newton refused. Nessel acquiesced, telling the press later that the Panthers were "quite hip on the law."[7] The Panthers made their way in military fashion to American Airlines gate 47, where Shabazz was scheduled to arrive. According to one eyewitness, "Each one, like clockwork, set themselves up at various stations at the arrival gate and waited, rifles in hand."[8]

From the airport, the Panthers escorted Shabazz to the office of *Ramparts* magazine for an interview with Eldridge Cleaver. There, the group had another, more intense confrontation with law enforcement. Chuck Banks, an aggressive reporter from KGO-TV, tried to push his way through the Panther bodyguard. When he tried to push aside Huey Newton, Newton grabbed his collar and pushed him back against the wall. Police officers reacted, several flipping loose the little straps that held their pistols in their holsters. One started shouting at Newton, who stopped and stared at the cop. Seale tried to get Newton to leave. Newton ignored him and walked right up to the cop. "What's the matter," Newton said, "you got an itchy finger?"

The cop made no reply and simply stared Newton in the eye, keeping his hand on his gun and taking his measure. The other officers called out for the cop to cool it, but he kept staring at Newton. "O.K. you big fat racist pig, draw your gun," Newton challenged. The cop made no move. Newton shouted "Draw it, you cowardly dog!" He pumped a round into the shotgun chamber.

The other officers spread out, stepping away from the line of fire. Finally, the cop gave up, sighing heavily and hanging his head. Newton laughed in his face as the remaining Panthers dispersed. Shabazz had already been whisked away by other Panthers while Newton occupied the attention of the police.

Witnessing Newton stand his ground with the police, back them down, and call them cowards, Eldridge Cleaver was filled with jubilation. "Work out soul brother!" his mind screamed, "You're the baddest motherfucker I've ever seen."[9]

Cleaver was as unimpressed by Ballard and the RAM group as he was impressed by Huey Newton and the Black Panther Party for Self-Defense. He decided then that he would give his full support to Huey Newton as the legitimate heir to the legacy of Malcolm X. Word quickly spread about Huey Newton's stand against the police, and about the bold new Black Power organization, the Black Panther Party for Self-Defense.

The Panthers' patrols of police sparked interest in the community, but still Huey and Bobby's following remained small. Newton was very conscious that black people were excluded from power and that the government did not represent their interests. He knew that many blacks in Oakland saw the police as oppressive. Newton hoped that by standing up to the police, he would be able to organize blacks to build political power. But even though his actions won respect, not many people were ready to join the Black Panther Party.

DENZIL DOWELL

Six weeks later, at 3:50 A.M. on Monday April 1, 1967, all this changed. George Dowell and several neighbors from North Richmond, an unincorporated all-black community near Oakland, heard ten gunshots. Sometime after 5:00 A.M., George came upon his older brother Denzil Dowell lying in the street, shot in the back and head.[10] Police from the county sheriff's department were there, but no ambulance had been called. Something did not seem right. Why had no one called an ambulance? George rushed home to tell his mother and father that their son, Denzil Dowell, a twenty-two-year-old construction laborer, was dead.

When the newspaper came out that day, the Contra Costa sheriff's office reported that deputy sheriffs Mel Brunkhorst and Kenneth Gibson had arrived at the scene at 4:50 A.M. on a tip from an unidentified caller about a burglary in progress. They claimed that when they arrived, Denzil Dowell and another man ran from the back of a liquor store and refused to stop when ordered to halt. Brunkhorst fired one blast from a shotgun, striking Dowell and killing him. The other man escaped.[11]

For the Dowells, the official explanation did not add up, and community members helped the family investigate. The Dowells knew Mel Brunkhorst. He had issued citations to Denzil in the past, and on occasion, Brunkhorst had threatened to kill Dowell. The more they probed, the more contradictory the facts appeared. There was no sign of entry, forced or otherwise, at Bill's Liquors, the store Dowell had allegedly been robbing. Further, the police had reported that Dowell had not only run but also jumped two fences to get away before being shot down. But Dowell had a bad hip, a limp, and the family claimed that he could not run, let alone jump fences. When the coroner released his report, community skepticism only grew. The report stated that Dowell had bled to death, yet there had been no pool of blood where Dowell was found. There was a pool of blood, however, twenty yards away from the site where police claimed Dowell died. The report also listed six bullet holes, apparently confirming neighbors' reports of hearing multiple shots. A doctor who worked on the case told the family that judging from the way the bullets had entered Dowell's body, Dowell had been shot with his hands raised. Bullet holes in nearby walls also suggested alternate trajectories and a different story. The family demanded to have the clothes Dowell wore when he was shot and to be allowed to take pictures of the corpse to verify how many times he had been shot. The county refused. Mrs. Dowell publicly announced, "I believe the police murdered my son."[12]

The city of Richmond, a few miles north of Oakland, had been the site of several major shipyards during World War II. Many blacks migrated to the area for wartime jobs but found themselves unemployed and underemployed during the postwar demobilization and deindustrialization. Much of the postwar black community lived in ghettos consisting of public housing units built by the federal government during the war. North Richmond, a town of six thousand people stuck between a garbage dump and the toxic-fume-producing Chevron Oil refinery, was almost entirely black. As an unincorporated area, the community received no public services from the city. Instead, North Richmond came under the jurisdiction of Contra Costa County, including the Contra Costa County Sheriff's Department. Extremely isolated, the area had only three streets on which to enter or exit. On occasion, county police blocked those streets, sealing off the entire area.[13]

Two weeks before Christmas 1966, just a few months before Denzil Dowell died, two unarmed black men had been shot and killed in North Richmond. Bullet holes in their armpits showed that they had been shot with their hands raised. It was rumored that police were responsible. A black woman from the neighborhood had also been brutally beaten by police.[14] Denzil Dowell's killing added insult to injury. A white jury took little time deciding that the killing of unarmed Dowell was "justifiable homicide" because the police officers on the scene had suspected that he was in the act of committing a felony. Outraged, the black community demanded justice.

The Dowell family supported a petition drive demanding the suspension of officer Brunkhorst and a full investigation of Denzil's death. Almost one-fourth of the North Richmond community signed on— twelve hundred people in all. Yet county officials refused to investigate. For many, this was the last straw.[15]

Paralleling black anger about police brutality nationally, the rage in North Richmond over Dowell's killing was palpable. With no sympathetic response from local government, the situation appeared headed in a clear direction: toward riot. Mark Comfort knew the Dowell family and understood how high the stakes were. As North Richmond threatened to boil over, instead of organizing a sit-in or prevailing upon the traditional civil rights organizations to act, he drove down to 56th Street and Grove in Oakland to see Huey Newton and Bobby Seale.

Ruby Dowell, Denzil's sister, called a meeting at Neighborhood House, a community center in North Richmond, to discuss the situation. Newton and Seale attended.[16] The meeting was emotional. Mrs. Dowell was still very angry, but she was also despondent and scared. Alongside her husband, who remained in the background during much of the crisis, she had worked so hard to survive in North Richmond, to support her family, and to raise her children. Now, her son Denzil had been taken from her by the very police sworn to protect him. Her appeals to the authorities had been treated with indifference at best.[17] Who was she to look to? How could she find justice?

Newton and Seale calmly maintained that only through armed self-defense could the black community find security. They asked lots of questions about the case and tried to understand what had actually happened the night Denzil Dowell was killed. George Dowell immediately saw in the Panthers the first glimmer of hope for finding justice for his brother. "I was really impressed. They made me feel like they were really interested in the people, and they knew what they were doing. . . . When I listened to Huey and Bobby talk, I could tell that they were talking from their hearts. A person can tell when another person is telling the truth and that's what all our people been waiting to hear."[18]

The next day the Panthers began their own investigation into the killing of Denzil Dowell. Newton, Seale, and a few Party members started to spend time in North Richmond, talking with George Dowell and the younger generation on the street, and sitting with Mrs. Dowell in her home. They spoke with the neighbors and other community members, sought out witnesses, talked with the coroner's office, and spoke to forensic experts.[19] They decided to do whatever they could to find justice for Denzil Dowell.

The Panthers' first confrontation with police in North Richmond was unplanned. Newton observed, "Policemen were constantly coming to Mrs. Dowell's house and treating her like dirt. They would knock on the door, walk in, and search the premises any time they wanted." One Sunday in April 1967, Newton was at the house when they came. "When Mrs. Dowell answered the knock, a policeman pushed his way in, asking questions. I grabbed my shotgun and stepped in front of her, telling him either to produce a search warrant or leave. He stood for a minute, shocked, then ran out to his car and drove off."[20] Given recent events, many locals felt vulnerable to police attack, and word about the Panthers spread rapidly throughout North Richmond.

On the following Sunday, April 16, community members met at George Dowell's home to discuss his brother's death. Talk soon turned to a recent rash of student beatings by teachers at the local Walter Helms Junior High School—yet another example of institutional brutality. One student's mother asked the Panthers for help. The Panthers had stated publicly that they were there for the community's protection, and now they were being asked to deliver. The next day, three carloads of mothers of students at Walter Helms went to the school accompanied by a carload of armed Panthers.

When the lunch bell rang, the mothers entered the school and proceeded to patrol the hallways. The Panthers remained outside in case any problems arose. The mothers informed the principal that they were there to ensure their children's safety and protect them from brutal treatment by school officials. "We're concerned citizens," they told him, "and we'll whip your ass and anyone else's that we hear of slapping our children around."[21]

School officials called the police, and an officer soon arrived. Upon hearing about the angry parents inside, he demanded to know what was going on. Five of the Panthers sitting in their car outside the school were openly armed, four with shotguns and one with an M-1. According to Seale, when the officer saw the guns, he began to stutter. He asked what all the guns were for, and Newton told him that he and his companions were members of the Black Panther Party and that the guns belonged to them. The officer asked for his driver's license, and Newton obliged. When he saw Newton's name, he went to his car and radioed for reinforcements. Another police car soon arrived, but there was nothing the police could do. The Panthers were acting within the law, and apparently the police did not want to inflame the situation further. The mothers patrolled the hallways until the end of the lunch period.[22]

The next morning Newton received a call. Mrs. Dowell and other community members had scheduled a meeting in Richmond with a representative of the county district attorney to discuss the Dowell case. The caller asked if the Panthers would come. Newton was skeptical about whether anything could be accomplished, but to satisfy the Dowells, he took a group of Panthers to the meeting. Little progress was made with the DA, so the entire group of Panthers and community members went to see County Sheriff Walter F. Young in Martinez.

Sheriff Young was cordial and polite, but he remained unyielding. Young maintained that because Dowell had been in the act of committing a felony when Brunkhorst shot him, the killing was legally justified. While claiming he had the best interests of the North Richmond community at heart, Young insisted he would neither suspend Brunkhorst nor modify the department's policy on when to shoot and when not to shoot potential suspects. An undersheriff added, "If you want the policy changed, you should go to the legislature."[23]

The Dowells had held out hope that local officials would eventually help them find justice. The meeting in Martinez left no doubt that they would have to find another approach.[24]

Seale and Newton quickly organized a street-corner rally to talk with community members about Denzil Dowell's case and explain their program, especially their position on community self-defense. They had organized street-corner rallies in the past in both Oakland and San Francisco, and the sight of armed and uniformed Black Panthers had always caught people's attention, often getting them to listen to the Panther political program.

Most of North Richmond had no sidewalks. But there was one corner in front of a liquor store at Third and Chesley that did, and Newton and Seale planned a rally there for Saturday April 22. At 5 P.M. that day, fifteen Panthers showed up in uniform, most of them armed and lined up on each corner, north, south, east, and west. In this way, they effectively claimed the corner and unofficially declared it a Panther zone.

A small crowd started to gather. Seale began talking about the Dowell case. The Panthers had always attracted attention when they organized street discussions, but the response this day reached another level. If Denzil Dowell could be killed by police with impunity, so could any young person in the neighborhood. The crowd soon swelled. While the police scared many in the community, here was a group of young black men, organized and disciplined, openly displaying guns and speaking their minds. Cars stopped, and traffic began backing up. Soon over 150 people had gathered.

A police car arrived and took a post across the street from the crowd; the officer casually smoked as he observed the rally. Seale pointed out the officer, declaring that he and everyone else who had gathered would continue exercising their right to free speech. No "pig," he shouted, would stop them. Four Panthers quickly surrounded the officer: Reginald Forte carrying a 9mm pistol, Warren Tucker with a .38 pistol hanging at his side, one Panther with a .357 Magnum, and another unarmed. The officer quickly started up his car and drove away.

When the time came for Newton to speak, he talked about the need to organize and to use guns to defend the community from racist attacks. He explained that the community had to organize to patrol the police to keep them in line; everyone would have to get guns to protect their homes, even the elderly. As the rally progressed, another policeman arrived. A number of cars pulled out of the way to let his car through, but one man refused to move, and the officer got stuck in the swelling traffic jam and had to stay there in his car observing the rally until it ended.[25]

The rally was a tremendous success. Community members had been searching for ways of doing something about Denzil Dowell's killing, and the Panthers had shown them a way. This was indeed what Newton and Seale had been looking for: a way to mobilize the black community by showing people they could take issues into their own hands. The Panthers called a second rally for April 29, the following Saturday. This time, they planned to shut off a whole section of the street.

Newton and Seale had captured the community's imagination, and others began chipping in to help organize the next rally. Eldridge Cleaver, who had been impressed with Newton during the confrontation with police at *Ramparts,* helped Newton and Seale publicize the rally, in the process creating the Party's first newspaper. Emory Douglas, a student at San Francisco City College and a new Panther member, contributed his graphic arts expertise. The paper immediately became a key Party tool, running for over a decade with an international distribution and, at its height, a circulation in the hundreds of thousands. The first issue was simply two mimeographed sheets stapled together.

On April 25, 1967, the paper hit the streets, its masthead reading *"The Black Panther—Black Community News Service* Volume 1 Number 1." The headline was "Why Was Denzil Dowell Killed?" The paper explained the facts of the case from the Panthers' perspective. It also explained the Party's political position and announced the North Richmond rally for the coming Saturday: "So we'll know what to do and how to do it." Three thousand copies were printed, and kids from the North Richmond neighborhood helped distribute the paper door-to-door on foot and on bicycle.[26]

The rally got under way at 1:30 P.M. outside the home of a Dowell relative at 1717 Second Street in North Richmond. The Panthers showed up armed and in uniform and closed off the street. Word had spread and almost four hundred people of all ages came. Many working-class and poor black people from North Richmond were there. They wanted to know how to get some measure of justice for Denzil Dowell and in turn how to protect themselves and their community from police attacks. People lined both sides of the block. Some elderly residents brought lawn chairs to sit in while they listened. Some of the younger generation climbed on cars.

Several police cars arrived on the scene, but the reception they received was even less friendly than that at the previous rally, so they kept their distance. A Contra Costa County helicopter patrolled above. According to a sheriff's spokesman, the department took no other action because the Panthers broke no laws and, as required, displayed their weapons openly.

Newton, Seale, and Cleaver all spoke, proclaiming that the community would not get justice from the government, nor from its arm, the police. In outlining the Party's program, they emphasized that black people would never be safe and secure if they depended on the police to protect them. The police were part of the problem, extensions of the oppressive power structure. Black people would be safe only if they took the situation into their own hands and defended themselves. At one point, Newton explained what kinds of guns people should buy. He pointed to Panther John Sloan stationed on a rooftop. Sloan did a weapons demonstration, and people cheered wildly.

That day, something startling occurred that had never happened at any other Panther event. Neighbors showed up with their own guns. Some of these people had seen the armed Panthers at the previous rally and decided to bring their guns this time as a gesture of support and solidarity. Others, seeing the Panthers for the first time, went home to get their guns and returned. One young woman who had been sitting in her car got out and held up her M-1 for everyone to see. The Panthers passed out applications to join their party, and over three hundred people filled them out. According to FBI informant Earl Anthony, he "had never seen Black men command the respect of the people the way that Huey Newton and Bobby Seale did that day."[27]

SACRAMENTO

As the Black Panthers' strategy of armed self-defense became more and more effective at mobilizing members of the black community, the Panthers attracted even greater attention among authorities, who took steps to stop them. The Oakland Police Department circulated internal memos identifying Party members and describing their vehicles.[28] Assemblyman Donald Mulford, a Republican from Piedmont, the predominantly white and affluent suburb of Oakland, took particular notice.

On April 5, 1967, six weeks after the Black Panther Party's well-publicized confrontation with police while escorting Betty Shabazz, Assemblyman Mulford introduced a bill, AB 1591, in the California legislature proposing to outlaw the carrying of loaded firearms in public.[29] In response to the "increasing incidence of organized groups and individuals publicly arming themselves," Mulford argued, "it is imperative that this statute take effect immediately." If signed into law, the act would criminalize armed patrols of police and the open display of guns at "self-defense" rallies in the black community—effectively outlawing the Black Panther strategy.[30]

The day after the Panthers' big rally in North Richmond, the *San Francisco Chronicle* carried an extended piece on the Party. Concluding with a discussion of Mulford's bill, the article noted, "The bill is scheduled to go before the Assembly Committee on Criminal Procedure in Sacramento Tuesday. Whether the Black Panthers will show up for the hearing is problematical."[31] Newton and Seale had already considered traveling to Sacramento to look for ways to challenge the police brutality that led to the killing of Denzil Dowell. When Newton saw the article and Mulford's intent to undermine the party, he called Seale over to his house. He told Seale that it was to be expected that the state would change the law to stop them. Indeed, there was little they could do to stop the state from changing the law.

Had the Mulford Act gone to a vote several months earlier, even at the time of the Malcolm X memorial, it might have spelled the end of the Black Panther Party by forcing the Panthers to stop their armed patrols of the police. But now, after the rallies in North Richmond, everything was different. Newton and Seale had effectively challenged police brutality and government neglect. They had organized the rage of a black community into a potent political force. Newton decided to raise the encounter to a higher level: he would send an armed delegation to the state capitol.

On Tuesday morning May 2, 1967, thirty Black Panthers put on their uniforms, picked up their guns, and headed to Sacramento. Seale led the delegation of twenty-four men and six women, which included Emory Douglas, Lil' Bobby Hutton, Mark Comfort, Ruby Dowell, and George Dowell. Hutton carried a High Standard 12-gauge shotgun, Tucker had a .357 Magnum, and eighteen of the other men were also armed. The women were not armed. Eldridge Cleaver also went to Sacramento that day, but not as part of the delegation. *Ramparts* magazine had assigned him to cover the Panther action with the understanding that he would not take part. Consistent with their Oakland patrols, the Panthers planned to remain firmly within the laws restricting gun use. They would take care, for example, to keep their guns aimed only up or down, not to point them at anyone, an action that could be construed as displaying a weapon in a threatening manner. Newton instructed the group not to shoot unless fired upon.[32]

When the Panthers arrived at the capitol building in Sacramento, they got out of their cars heavily armed, and Seale began asking bystanders how to find the assembly chambers. Right away, several TV cameramen took notice and ran up to the delegation to begin filming.[33]

By the time the delegation arrived outside the California State Assembly chambers on the second floor, a swarm of reporters had gathered around them, taking pictures and asking questions. Assembly sessions are open to the public, but the public is not allowed on the assembly floor. When the Panthers reached the door to the assembly floor, several of the reporters barged into the assembly to get a better picture of the Panthers as they entered. Seale and about twelve of the Panthers followed.[34] According to the *San Francisco Chronicle*, "Assembly Speaker Pro-Tem Carlos Bee (Dem-Hayward) who was facing the door saw only a gaggle of news and television cameramen in what seemed to be a stampede. Angrily he shouted for the sergeant-at-arms, Tony Beard, to remove the intruding photographers."[35]

One of the guards said to the Panthers, "This is not where you're supposed to be. This is not where you're supposed to be." While they were trying to decide whether to stay on the assembly floor or go upstairs, a police officer came up behind Bobby Hutton and grabbed the gun out of his hand. Hutton started shouting at the officer and chasing him to try to get his gun back, and the Panthers followed him out into the hallway. Assemblyman Mulford wasted no time in lobbying for his legislation. He quickly rose to inform his colleagues that reporters were not the only ones who had been on the assembly floor. "A serious incident has just occurred," he explained, "People with weapons forced their way into this chamber and were ejected."[36]

When the Panthers entered the hallway, the state police surrounded them and then grabbed them and took their weapons. Seale started to shout, "Wait a minute, now wait a minute! Am I under arrest? Am I under arrest?! Take your hands off me if I am not under arrest! If I am under arrest, I will come. If I am not, don't put your hands on me." Seale demanded the guns back and a chance to publicly read the Party's statement. As the police pushed the Panthers into an elevator, Seale shouted, "Is this the way the racist government works, won't let a man exercise his constitutional rights?" Once downstairs, the police reviewed the situation, decided the Panthers had broken no laws, and returned their guns.[37]

Having now captured the attention of many reporters, Seale read the Panther statement in front of the press. With much of California and the country watching, he read Black Panther Executive Mandate #1:

> The Black Panther Party for Self-Defense calls upon the American people in general and the Black people in particular to take careful note of the racist California Legislature which is now considering legislation aimed at keeping the Black people disarmed and powerless at the very same time that racist police agencies throughout the country are intensifying the terror, brutality, murder, and repression of Black people. . . . The enslavement

of Black people from the very beginning of this country, the genocide practiced on the American Indians and the confining of the survivors on res-
ervations, the savage lynching of thousands of Black men and women, the
dropping of atomic bombs on Hiroshima and Nagasaki, and now the cowardly massacre in Vietnam, all testify to the fact that toward people of color
the racist power structure of America has but one policy: repression, genocide, terror, and the big stick. . . . The Black Panther Party for Self-Defense
believes that the time has come for Black people to arm themselves against
this terror before it is too late. The pending Mulford Act brings the hour of
doom one step nearer. A people who have suffered so much for so long at
the hands of a racist society, must draw the line somewhere. We believe that
the Black communities of America must rise up as one man to halt the pro-
gression of a trend that leads inevitably to their total destruction.[38]

With the group now released and his companions again with their
guns again in tow, Seale read the statement to the press several times.
The members of the Party delegation then walked down the capitol
steps, across the lawn, and back to their cars. But as they walked across
the lawn, they passed a picnicking group of thirty youngsters from the
Valley View Intermediate School in Pleasant Hill who were receiving
a visit from Governor Ronald Reagan. News of the Panthers had not
reached Reagan yet, and the sight of these armed black men ambling
by the picnic unnerved him. He hastily deserted the youngsters from
Valley View and hightailed it to the security of his offices. Shortly after
the Panthers got in their cars and headed back toward Oakland, a contingent of police armed with riot guns and pistols appeared on their
tail, accompanied by reporters.[39]

As soon as the Panthers pulled into a service station, the police surrounded them. A couple of officers came up behind Panther Sherman
Forte and grabbed his hands, forcing them behind his back. When
Seale asked if Forte was under arrest, the officers answered that he
was, and Seale told Forte to take the arrest. With cameramen captur-
ing the scene for national TV, the police then searched and arrested
the remainder of the group on what appeared to be makeshift charges.
Seale was originally arrested for carrying a concealed pistol, when in
fact he openly displayed the pistol in a holster on his hip. Television
footage caught officers looking for illegal weapons and comparing the
length of Panther shotguns to their own. To one officer's charge, a
Panther explained, "That ain't no sawed off, that's a riot gun, just like
yours." Officers booked several of the Panthers on an obscure Fish and
Game Code violation that prohibited loaded guns in a vehicle.[40]

Nineteen young adults and five juveniles were arrested. But this group included not only armed Panthers but also Eldridge Cleaver, covering the event for *Ramparts* and carrying only a camera, as well as an anonymous black woman from Sacramento, unknown to the Panthers, who happened to be buying gas at the time. At the police station, officials changed the charges to conspiracy to invade the assembly chambers, a felony.[41] Seale and Comfort were bailed out that evening and returned with Newton for a court hearing and press conference the following day.[42]

Extensive press coverage boosted the party's profile exponentially. The *San Francisco Chronicle* alone printed at least twelve stories on the Panther "invasion" of the state capitol that week.[43] The event and its aftermath received extensive coverage in the country's major dailies in early May, from the *New York Times* and *Washington Post* to the *Chicago Tribune,* as well as widespread television coverage. The Party soon became the topic of discussion in innumerable political circles. In particular, it became a hot topic in the left alternative press, garnering extensive coverage in *Ramparts* and the *Movement*. The event also prompted more thorough investigative coverage, including a massive story in the *New York Times Magazine*.[44]

The Panthers graphically introduced the public to a new vision of black politics. Like the leaders of the earlier Civil Rights Movement, the Panthers continued to focus on black liberation. Yet, rather than appeal for a fair share of the American pie, the Panthers portrayed the black community as a colony within America and the police as an "army of occupation" from which blacks sought liberation.[45] In their view, the racist power structure was the common enemy of all those engaged in freedom struggles.

Newton and Seale were not deeply concerned when the Mulford Act passed. They believed that their Sacramento action would loudly proclaim the power of their vision to the world and that many young blacks would join them. And they were right.[46]

The Sacramento protest attracted a wider movement audience and established the Black Panther Party as a new model for political struggle. Soon students at San Francisco State College and the University of California, Berkeley flocked to Panther rallies by the thousands. Countless numbers of young blacks—looking for a way to join the "Movement," or just to channel their anger at the oppressive conditions in which they lived—now had a political organization they could call their own. Twenty-two-year-old Billy John Carr, once a star athlete at Berkeley High School who now constantly struggled to support his wife and child, joined the Party immediately after the Sacramento protest. He explained his decision to the *New York Times:* "As far as I'm concerned it's beautiful that we finally got an organization that don't walk around singing. I'm not for all this talking stuff. When things start happening I'll be ready to die if that's necessary and it's important that we have somebody around to organize us."[47]

The Panthers knew that they were on to something historically significant. They could feel themselves becoming a viable model for black liberation. Emory Douglas recalled, "It was like being a part of a movement you had seen on TV, and now being able to share and participate in that movement . . . it brought a sense of pride."[48] George Dowell, who had joined in the Sacramento action, explained later to a reporter:

> We are tired of police brutality. We want something done about it. If they won't do something we will. I know going to the Capitol was a big step and the Panthers made the first step. If we hadn't done that first step our people would still be wishing. The Panthers took the first [step] in my brother's investigation and [were] the first to show the world that black people need protection and that we never had it. That's why we are arming to protect ourselves. We are just tired of living like this. We want freedom now. I hope it won't come to bloodshed but if it does and if I die, I'll know I did my part. That's a good feeling because up till now there haven't been too many men or women that could say that.[49]

By the end of May, the Black Panther Party had a burgeoning membership dedicated to a revolutionary program. And yet the tactic Newton and Seale used to build the organization had been outlawed.

PART TWO

Baptism in Blood

The master's room was wide open. The master's room was
brilliantly lighted, and the master was there, very calm . . .
and our people stopped dead . . . it was the master . . . I went
in. "It's you," he said, very calm. It was I, even I, and I told
him so, the good slave, the faithful slave, the slave of slaves,
and suddenly his eyes were like two cockroaches, frightened
in the rainy season . . . I struck, and the blood spurted; that
is the only baptism that I remember today.

—Aimé Césaire excerpted in Frantz Fanon, *Wretched of the Earth,*
    Black Panther Party booklist

3

The Correct Handling of a Revolution

The Black Panther leadership found itself in a most ironic situation after Sacramento. On the strength of their tactic of policing the police, the Panthers had thrust themselves into the center of the movement debate about how to define Black Power and what direction the Black Liberation Struggle should take now that the civil rights insurgency had run its course. At the same time, the tactics so key to the Panther's effectiveness had been taken from them. How would the Black Panthers continue to mobilize the "brothers on the block" without the legal option of publicly arming themselves? And how would they pay for their mounting legal costs, such as the bail payments and lawyers' fees stemming from the Sacramento incident?

In the summer of 1967, this problem kept Newton up at night, posing both a political puzzle and a personal dilemma. How would he respond if a police officer attempted to abuse or brutalize him? Before California enacted the Mulford Act and restricted the Black Panther Party's right to bear arms in public, the response had been clear. On countless occasions, Newton had pulled out his law book and insisted, by section and point, that he be accorded his full legal rights under the law. When an officer refused to accord him these rights, he made it clear that he would accept an arrest peacefully but that he would take the officer to court for false arrest. But if an officer attempted to go outside the law and abuse or brutalize him in any way, Newton was armed, as was his legal right, and he made it clear that he would not hesitate to use his weapon in self-defense.

In all of the Black Panther Party's confrontations with police, not a single shot had been fired. But now that this tactic had been outlawed, what would Newton do—what would a *Panther* do?

THE LEGITIMATE REPRESENTATIVES OF THE BLACK COMMUNITY

In the summer months of 1967 following the Sacramento action, Huey Newton published a series of essays in the *Black Panther* newspaper in which he explored ways to transcend the tactic of legally armed patrols of police. In "Fear and Doubt," "The Functional Definition of Politics," "In Defense of Self-Defense" (a two-part essay), and "The Correct Handling of a Revolution," he articulates a new politics. Drawing upon the writings of Malcolm X, Mao Zedong, and the psychiatrist Frantz Fanon, who participated in the Algerian revolution, Newton expands on the Revolutionary Action Movement's identification of the black community as a colony within the American empire. He links both the conditions and the struggle for liberation in the black community to anticolonial struggles around the world, not only in Africa but also in Vietnam and elsewhere.

From there, Newton departs from RAM, seeking to define a politics that, like the tactic of legally armed patrols of police, would speak to and mobilize the "brothers on the block." He develops his argument in four parts, first applying Frantz Fanon's theory of the psychology of colonization and liberation struggle to the ghettos of the United States, then extending the analogy to identify the police as an occupying force, interpreting U.S urban riots as protopolitical resistance to this occupation, and asserting the role of the Black Panther Party as the legitimate representative of the black community—the vanguard party—in the struggle for Black Power.

Newton lays out the first part of his argument in "Fear and Doubt," where he analyzes the psychological dimensions of ghettoization, specifically on black *men*. He applies the theory developed by Fanon during the Algerian Revolution to the concrete and particular experience of blackness in the American ghetto in the mid-1960s, analyzing how black men experience ghetto life.[1] The essay describes the way in which society denies black men their humanity. Yet, Newton writes, the black man blames himself for his inferior position in society, finding himself in a double bind. On the one hand, he believes he is inherently inferior, that he lacks the "innate ability" to advance himself. On the other hand, he wants to believe that he is not innately inferior but then blames himself for being lethargic and not trying hard enough. "Society responds to him as a thing, beast, nonentity, something to be ignored or stepped on. He is asked to respect laws that do not respect him. He is asked to digest a code of ethics that act upon him but not for him. He is confused and in a constant state of rage, of shame and doubt. This psychological set permeates all his interpersonal relationships." This dynamic permeates all aspects of black men's lives in America, Newton says, from processing their hair to pursuing fancy cars, from attending ghetto schools to being unemployed and fathering illegitimate children in an attempt to demonstrate masculinity.

While a number of Black Power organizations at the time were reading Fanon and interpreting the psychological dimensions of racial oppression in the United States, Newton's innovation is to focus on the police as a brutal and illegitimate occupying force, the immediate barrier to self-determination. In this second part of his argument, presented in "The Functional Definition of Politics," Newton writes, "Because black people desire to determine their own destiny, they are constantly inflicted with brutality from the occupying army, embodied in the police department. There is a great similarity between the occupying army in Southeast Asia and the occupation of our communities by the racist police. The armies are there not to protect the people of South Vietnam, but to brutalize and oppress them for the interests of the selfish imperial power."[2]

By this time, the Panthers were no longer using the law to monitor the police and bear arms in self-defense; these tactics had been outlawed. Now, Newton seeks to take the issue of police abuse of power to a broader political level. He identifies the police as representatives of the oppressive imperial power, an occupying force with no legitimate role in the black community.

In the third part of his argument for a new politics, Newton identifies the urban riots, such as the rebellion in Watts, as protopolitical resistance to this occupation and proposes that by arming and organizing the ghetto, black people can obtain power, channeling these protopolitics into an organized military force. In "In Defense of Self-Defense," he writes,

> We are continuing to function in petty, futile ways, divided, confused, fighting among ourselves, we are still in the elementary stage of throwing rocks, sticks, empty wine bottles and beer cans at racist cops who lie in wait for a chance to murder unarmed Black people. The racist cops have worked out a system for suppressing these spontaneous rebellions that flare up from the anger, frustration, and desperation of the masses of black people. We

can no longer afford the dubious luxury of the terrible casualties wantonly inflicted upon us by the cops during these spontaneous rebellions. . . . We must organize and unite to combat by long resistance the brutal force used against us daily, the power structure depends upon the use of force without retaliation. . . . There is a world of difference between 30 million unarmed, submissive black people and 30 million black people armed with freedom and defense guns and the strategic methods of liberation.[3]

This argument marks a critical step in Newton's thinking. Here he does not simply pinpoint the juncture of conflict between the police and the ghettos, but he identifies the riots as a protopolitical resistance to, and rebellion against, this colonial relationship. Yet unlike many Black Power advocates, Newton does not celebrate the riots. He argues that they represent an infantile approach, an unsophisticated spontaneous reaction incapable of meeting the interests and needs from which they arise. In his essay, Newton elaborates on this rebellious protopolitics. No longer able to pursue the tactic of policing the police legally, he argues for expressing these riotous tendencies of political resistance by arming and organizing Black America into a coherent military force.

Newton points out that military and political power are inextricably linked: without military power, there can be no political power. "Politics is war without bloodshed," and "war is politics with bloodshed." He criticizes black politics as toothless and thus powerless. Only by developing a force with real destructive capacity can black people obtain political power:

> When black people send a representative, he is somewhat absurd because he represents no political power. He does not represent land power because we do not own any land. He does not represent economic or industrial power because black people do not own the means of production. The only way he can become political is to represent what is commonly called a military power—which the Black Panther Party for Self-Defense calls Self-Defense Power. Black People can develop Self-Defense Power by arming themselves from house to house, block to block, community to community, throughout the nation. Then we will choose a political representative and he will state to the power structure the desires of the black masses. If the desires are not met, the power structure will receive a political consequence. We will make it economically nonprofitable for the power structure to go on with its oppressive ways. We will then negotiate as equals. There will be a balance between the people who are economically powerful and the people who are potentially economically destructive.[4]

Finally, in an essay written in late July, less than three months after the Black Panther action in Sacramento, Newton asserts the role of the

Black Panther Party for Self-Defense as a vanguard party, the legitimate representative of the black community in its struggle for Black Power. He adapts this idea from RAM and, indirectly, from Mao and the Chinese revolution. But RAM had tried to assume this key role as an underground organization and had not succeeded in making its theory the basis for widespread politics. Newton, in exploring how to turn the riotous energy of the ghetto into an organized military—and thus political—force, departs from RAM and articulates a concept of a vanguard party with the practical capacity to build Black Power in the United States. In his seminal essay "On the Correct Handling of a Revolution," he writes,

> The Vanguard Party must provide leadership for the people. It must teach the correct strategic methods of prolonged resistance through literature and activities. If the activities of the party are respected by the people, the people will follow the example. This is the primary job of the party. . . . When the people learn that it is no longer advantageous for them to resist by going to the streets in large numbers, and when they see the advantage in the activities of the guerilla warfare method, they will quickly follow this example. But first, they must respect the party which is transmitting this message. . . . The vanguard party is never underground in the beginning of its existence, because this would limit its effectiveness and educational process. How can you teach a people if the people do not know and respect you?[5]

In this way, Newton was able to reinvent the politics of armed self-defense after the passage of the Mulford Act. He believed that black people were ready to fight the police. By organizing this capacity for armed resistance, he sought to build political power and gain leverage to redress the wrongs against black people and meet their needs. At least at the beginning, Newton sought to organize this capacity for armed resistance aboveground—that is, legally.

Newton's conception of the vanguard party was important because of the way he envisioned the party's relationship to the people. He did not simply want to educate the people but also saw the importance of winning their respect.[6] While approvingly citing Mao Zedong's dictum that "power grows out of the barrel of a gun," Newton understood that the respect and loyalty of the community were about much more than that. He knew that the black community would look to and respect the Black Panther Party only if the people believed that the Party's main concern was their needs and interests.

Thus Newton sought not only to organize the rage of the ghetto into a military force but also to assert its role in the vanguard of Black

Power by championing solutions to the pressing needs of the black community: decent housing, employment, education, and freedom. Starting
with the second issue of the *Black Panther,* on May 15, 1967 (less than
two weeks after the Sacramento incident), every one of the newspaper's
537 issues contained the Party's ten-point platform and program, titled
"What We Want Now! What We Believe," which emphasized the Party's
commitment to advancing a revolution that addressed the needs and
interests of the black community.

The platform and program emphasized the nationalist character of
the Party as a steward of black people's interests. The Party was not
just about armed action; it was the legitimate voice of black people, and
as such, it intended to take care of the broad range of the community's needs. The platform drew heavily from the ten-point platform that
Malcolm X crafted for Elijah Muhammad's Nation of Islam, published
in August 1963. However, it emulated Malcolm X's nationalism without the Islamic flavor. For example, Malcolm X's ten-point program
included the following points under "What the Muslims Want":

> [1.] We want freedom. We want a full and complete freedom. . . . [4.] We
> want territory to] establish a separate state. [5.] We want freedom for all
> Believers of Islam now held in federal prisons. We want freedom for all black
> men and women now under death sentence in innumerable prisons in the
> North as well as the South. [6.] We want an immediate end to the police bru-
> tality and mob attacks against the so-called Negro throughout the United
> States. [7.] We demand not only equal justice under the laws of the United
> States, but equal employment opportunities—NOW! [8.] We want the gov-
> ernment of the United States to exempt our people from ALL taxation as
> long as we are deprived of equal justice under the laws of the land. [9.] We
> want all black children educated, taught and trained by their own teachers.[7]

Using this program as a model, the Black Panthers developed their
famous Ten Point Program. Most previous accounts present a version
written in October 1968 as the original and claim it was first distributed in October 1966, but that is incorrect. The Black Panther Party's
original Ten Point Program, first publicized in May 1967, read:

> WHAT WE WANT NOW! WHAT WE BELIEVE
>
> To those poor souls who don't know Black history, the beliefs and desires of
> the Black Panther Party for Self Defense may seem unreasonable. To Black
> people, the ten points covered are absolutely essential to survival. We have
> listened to the riot producing words "these things take time" for 400 years.
> The Black Panther Party knows what Black people want and need. Black
> unity and self defense will make these demands a reality.

WHAT WE WANT

1. We want freedom. We want power to determine the destiny of our Black community.
2. We want full employment for our people.
3. We want an end to the robbery by the White man of our Black community.
4. We want decent housing, fit for shelter [of] human beings.
5. We want education for our people that exposes the true nature of this decadent American society. We want education that teaches us our true history and our role in the present day society.
6. We want all Black men to be exempt from military service.
7. We want an immediate end to *police brutality* and *murder* of Black people.
8. We want freedom for all Black men held in federal, state, county, and city prisons and jails.
9. We want all Black people when brought to trial to be tried in court by a jury of their peer group or people from their Black communities. As defined by the constitution of the United States.
10. We want land, bread, housing, education, clothing, justice and peace.

WHAT WE BELIEVE

1. We believe that Black people will not be free until we are able to determine our destiny.
2. We believe that the federal government is responsible and obligated to give every man employment or a guaranteed income. We believe that if the White American business men will not give full employment, then the means of production should be taken from the business men and placed in the community so that the people of the community can organize and employ all of its people and give a high standard of living.
3. We believe that this racist government has robbed us and now we are demanding the overdue debt of forty acres and two mules. Forty acres and two mules was promised 100 years ago as retribution for slave labor and mass murder of Black people. We will accept the payment in currency which will be distributed to our many communities: the Germans are now aiding the Jews in Israel for the genocide of the Jewish people. The Germans murdered 6,000,000 Jews. The American racist has taken part in the slaughter of over 50,000,000 Black people; therefore, we feel that this is a modest demand that we make.
4. We believe that if the White landlords will not give decent housing to our Black community, then the housing and the land should be made into cooperatives so that our community, with government aid, can build and make decent housing for its people.

5. We believe in an educational system that will give to our people a knowledge of self. If a man does not have knowledge of himself and his position in society and the world, then he has little chance to relate to anything else.

6. We believe that Black people should not be forced to fight in the military service to defend a racist government that does not protect us. We will not fight and kill other people of color in the world who, like Black people, are being victimized by the White racist government of America. We will protect ourselves from the force and violence of the racist police and the racist military, by whatever means necessary.

7. We believe we can end police brutality in our Black community by organizing Black *self defense* groups that are dedicated to defending our Black community from racist police oppression and brutality. The Second Amendment of the Constitution of the United States gives us a right to bear arms. We therefore believe that all Black people should arm themselves for *self defense.*

8. We believe that all Black people should be released from the many jails and prisons because they have not received a fair and impartial trial.

9. We believe that the courts should follow the United States Constitution so that Black people will receive fair trials. The 14th amendment of the U.S. Constitution gives a man a right to be tried by his peer group. A peer is a person from a similar economic, social, religious, geographical, environmental, historical and racial background. To do this the court will be forced to select a jury from the Black community from which the Black defendant came. We have been, and are being tried by all White juries that have no understanding of the "average reasoning man" of the Black community.

10. When in the course of human events, it becomes necessary for one people to dissolve the political bonds which have connected them with another, and to assume among the powers of the earth, the separate and equal station to which the laws of nature and nature's god entitle them, a decent respect to the opinions of mankind requires that they should declare the causes which impel them to separation. We hold these truths to be self-evident, that all men are created equal, that they are endowed by their creator with certain inalienable rights, that among these are life, liberty and the pursuit of happiness. That to secure these rights, governments are instituted among men, deriving their just powers from the consent of the governed,—that *whenever any form of government becomes destructive of these ends, it is the right of people to alter or to abolish it, and to institute new government, laying its foundation on such principles and organizing its powers in such form as to them shall seem most likely to effect their safety and happiness.* Prudence, indeed, will dictate that governments long established should not be changed for light and transient causes; and accordingly all experience hath shewn, that mankind are more disposed to suffer, while evils are sufferable, than to right themselves

by abolishing the forms to which they are accustomed. *But when a long train of abuses and usurpations, pursuing invariably the same object, evinces a design to reduce them under absolute despotism, it is their right, it is their duty, to throw off such government, and to provide new guards for their future security.*[8]

Above the Ten Point Program, under the headline "Minister of Defense," the *Black Panther* carried a photo of Huey that serves to announce to the world that the vanguard of Black Power had arrived. In the photo, Huey is seated and facing the camera. His forehead, nose, and left cheekbone are well illuminated, whereas the right side of his face is obscured in shadow, capped by the trademark black beret tilted at a precise angle to cover the top of his right ear. His slacks, shoes, and leather jacket are also black, his pressed shirt light colored—the standard Black Panther uniform. He sits comfortably but alert, his feet positioned, ready to stand. Behind him is the ornate fan of the wicker throne in which he sits. A handful of live ammunition sits in a small pile on the ground near the butt of the rifle he holds in his right hand. Like the zebra-skin rugs on the floor and the two shields behind him, the tall black spear in his left hand suggests Africa. The photo announces Huey as leader and defender of the black colony in the white motherland America.

ENGAGING THE LEFT

Beyond rethinking the political ideology of the Party, during the summer of 1967, the Black Panthers forged important new relations with the broader Left. Newton was both an intellectual and a man of action. He could analyze the precise emotional dynamics in a confrontation with the police and know just how to push and how far. He could see the implications of his actions in the moment while considering their potential for broad political resonance. But he was not much of a public relations man. He had a high-pitched voice and hated public speaking. And he was too intensely focused on the crux of the issue to worry about advertising. Newton could envision and take exemplary action, but he was not particularly talented at broadcasting these actions to the world. Bobby Seale was a much more skillful public speaker, and a true organizational craftsman, keeping the Party running day to day. Seale proved time and again, as he had in Sacramento, that he had great integrity and could stand up without wavering in the face of intense pressure. But he was not much of a public relations man either.

Newton's vanguard politics called for putting the Party front and center in the public eye. In the summer of 1967, Eldridge Cleaver turned out to have just the flamboyant edge the Party needed.

After Sacramento, the Panthers faced the legal challenges of raising bail and hiring lawyers. Such challenges had been an important part of the daily work of the earlier insurgent Civil Rights Movement and were not unfamiliar to the Panthers. But until this point, legal challenges had been only a peripheral concern of the Black Panther Party for Self-Defense. Now, facing the courts became central. Although it was perfectly legal for the Panthers to enter the state capitol bearing arms, a fact that the state police acknowledged at the time, officials later charged members of the Black Panther delegation with "conspiracy to disrupt the assembly," a felony.

Eldridge and Beverly

Eldridge Cleaver was among those arrested with the Black Panther entourage in Sacramento. In the months following the Sacramento action, the Panthers' newfound fame allowed Cleaver to draw upon his connections with *Ramparts* and the broader Left to raise money to help the Party pay its legal bills stemming from Sacramento.

Leroy Eldridge Cleaver was born on August 31, 1935, in Wabbaseka, Arkansas, the son of Leroy Cleaver, a waiter and nightclub piano player, and Thelma Hattie Robinson Cleaver, an elementary school teacher.[9] Like many black families from the South, Cleaver's family had migrated west for work during World War II. The Cleavers settled in Los Angeles, where Cleaver soon became involved in petty crime. He went to jail several times, and in 1954, at the age of nineteen, was sent to Soledad State Prison as an adult for two and a half years for possession of marijuana. The Civil Rights Movement was heating up then, and Cleaver became politicized, spending an increasing amount of time with a group of black inmates who "were in vociferous rebellion against what we perceived as a continuation of slavery."[10]

Unmarried, Cleaver was denied conjugal visits and soon became lonely and thought often of women. "In prison," Cleaver later wrote, "those things withheld from and denied to the prisoner become precisely what he wants most of all." He tore a photo of a woman out of *Esquire* magazine and pinned it to the wall of his cell, deciding that this was his bride and that he would fall in love and lavish all his affections on her. One day he returned to his cell to find the picture torn from the wall by a guard and the pieces dumped in the toilet. When he confronted the guard, the guard said, "Get yourself a colored girl for a pinup—no white women—and I'll let her stay up."[11]

Soon after the incident, Cleaver heard the news about the murder of Emmett Till. In 1955, Till, a black fourteen-year-old from Chicago visiting relatives in Mississippi, whistled at a white woman. That night, local whites kidnapped him from his relatives' house and beat him brutally. They fastened a large metal fan around his neck with barbed wire, shot him in the head, and dumped his mutilated corpse in the Tallahatchie River. Witnesses identified the murderers, but the accused men were exonerated after only an hour of deliberation by an all-white male jury. After the case was tried (and could not be appealed), the murderers publicly confessed that they had killed Till for flirting with a white woman.[12]

Cleaver came across a picture of the white woman that Till had flirted with in a magazine and found her attractive. He saw himself in Till's shoes, and it distressed him. "It intensified my frustrations," Cleaver later explained, "to know that I was indoctrinated to see the white woman as more beautiful and desirable than my own black woman." Cleaver's emotional turmoil about his attraction to white women was not unusual. While white men often took liberties with black women, a black man who flirted even mildly with a white woman was considered to be making the gravest violation of white supremacy, one that was all too often punished by death. In this context, it is not surprising that many black men associated a sexual desire for white women with a desire to be recognized as human and free.

Fanon graphically described the psychological dimensions of this type of desire:

> Out of the blackest part of my soul, across the zebra striping of my mind, surges this desire to be suddenly *white*. I wish to be acknowledged not as *black* but as *white*. Now . . . who but a white woman can do this for me? By loving me she proves that I am worthy of white love. I am loved like a white man. I am a white man. Her love takes me onto the noble road that leads to total realization. . . . I marry white culture, white beauty, white whiteness. When my restless hands caress those white breasts, they grasp white civilization and dignity and make them mine.[13]

Cleaver's confrontation with the guard and his attraction to the white woman in the Till case shook him to the core and sent him in search of answers. He had many conversations with other inmates and studied books such as Richard Wright's *Native Son*. Through further studies, Cleaver earned his high school diploma—reading Karl Marx, Rousseau, Thomas Paine, Voltaire, W. E. B. Du Bois, Bakunin, Lenin, and Machiavelli—before his release in 1957.[14]

But Cleaver was still in turmoil, and within less than a year, he was arrested again, this time for assault with intent to kill. He was sentenced to two to fourteen years in prison. At this point, he turned to the Nation of Islam and also began to write.[15] Eight years later, he was still in prison, and still writing, but the mood of the country had changed. The Civil Rights Movement had fought Jim Crow and won. The antiwar movement was building. When Cleaver's hero Malcolm X was assassinated in 1965, he swore to take up Malcolm X's fight. He committed himself to the struggle for the liberation of black people and to the strengthening of the association that Malcolm X had founded shortly before his death—the Organization of Afro-American Unity.

From prison, Cleaver began writing letters to progressive lawyers he saw mentioned in the newspaper in hopes of finding legal support. In an issue of the *Sun Reporter,* a black community newspaper in San Francisco, Cleaver came across a story about Beverly Axelrod, a young white civil rights lawyer. The story featured a photo of Axelrod with one of her clients, a large black man who participated in 1964 protests on Cadillac Row to win black employment. Cleaver learned everything he could about Axelrod and then wrote her a letter calculated to win her support. It did.[16] Axelrod visited Cleaver several times, and the two began to exchange letters. Soon their letters became romantic.[17]

In his letters to Beverly, Eldridge wrote of the sense of hope and humanity that he found in her affection. But he also expressed a rawness, a lack of apology. As he wrote, he seemed to take off the mask obscuring his true identity. Finding legitimate love and support from a white woman seemed to confirm his humanity. He no longer had to play at being timid or to make himself appear insignificant in the world:

> I was 22 when I came to prison and of course I have changed tremendously over the years. But I always had a strong sense of myself and in the last few years I felt I was losing my identity. There was a deadness in my body that eluded me, as though I could not exactly locate its site. . . . since encountering you, I feel life strength flowing back into that spot. . . . I may even swagger a little, and, as I read in a book somewhere, "push myself forward like a train."

NOW TURN THE RECORD OVER AND PLAY THE OTHER SIDE

I have tried to mislead you. I am not humble at all. I have no humility and I do not fear you in the least. If I pretend to be shy, if I appear to hesitate, it is only a sham to deceive. By playing the humble part, I sucker my fellow men in and seduce them of their trust. And then, if it suits my advantage, I lower the boom—mercilessly. I lied when I stated that I had no sense of myself. . . . My vanity is as vast as the scope of a dream, my heart is that of a tyrant, my arm is the arm of the Executioner. . . . I wish to be the Voice of Doom itself. I am angry at the insurgents of Watts. They have pulled the covers off me and revealed to all what potential may lie behind my Tom Smile.[18]

Beverly responded in kind:

I know you little and I know you much, but whichever way it goes, I accept you. Your manhood comes through in a thousand ways, rare and wonderful. I'm out in the world, with an infinity of choices. You don't have to wonder if I'm grasping at something because I have no real measuring stick. I accept you.

About the other side of the record: Did you really think I didn't know? Another facet of the crystal might be an apter term. I have a few facets myself. I do not fear you, I know you will not hurt me. Your hatred is large, but not nearly so vast as you sometimes imagine; it can be used, but it can also be soothed and softened.[19]

In this reply, Beverly expresses more than personal love and acceptance. She embraces Cleaver's humanity, and in doing so, expresses her own. She not only accepts Cleaver's rage, but suggests it can be softened. She sees herself as righting the racial wrongs he has suffered. By validating his humanity, she is standing up to the racism that denied it. Like Cleaver's, her love is political as well as personal. As a civil rights lawyer, she dedicates her life to fighting for justice. In loving Cleaver and validating his humanity, she seeks to challenge the social injustices that deny him his humanity.

Eldridge understood that Beverly needed him as much as he needed her. He was aware that Beverly wanted to see her love of him as politically righteous. He saw their romance as politically transformative rather than simply individual, and appealed to Beverly in these terms:

It is not that we are making each other up and it is not ourselves alone who are involved in what is happening to us. It is really a complex movement taking place of which we are mere parts. We represent historical forces and it is really these forces that are coalescing and moving toward each other. And it is not a fraud, forced out of desperation. We live in a disoriented, deranged social structure, and we have transcended its barriers in our own ways and have stepped psychologically outside its madness and repressions.[20]

Beverly took a keen interest in Eldridge's writings, and because prison authorities prohibited Cleaver from distributing his essays, she smuggled the manuscripts out of prison, hidden inside legal documents. She brought them to Edward Keating, the publisher of *Ramparts,* who was impressed by Cleaver's work.[21] He shared Cleaver's writings with luminaries such as Norman Mailer and Norman Podhoretz, who in turn praised the work. Amid these successes, Cleaver, still in prison, asked Axelrod to marry him.[22] By the time Cleaver was released on parole in December 1966, having spent nine years in the penitentiary, he had a job as a writer at *Ramparts,* a publisher for his book—and a fiancée.[23] The book, *Soul on Ice,* a collection of Cleaver's prison writings, was published in February 1968 and became an instant sensation, selling more than a million copies within months and eventually several million.[24]

The mid-1960s in the United States were a time of intense exploration of questions of race and sexuality. As Jim Crow crumbled, people increasingly challenged the boundaries of racial segregation, including the powerful taboos against interracial sex. In finding legitimate love from Beverly Axelrod, a white woman, Cleaver saw a powerful form of redemption: refusing to play Uncle Tom, he was able to be his "terrible" true masculine self. In entering into this relationship, Cleaver considered himself to be striking a fatal blow to white supremacy. *Soul on Ice* also depicts the relationship as a means for Axelrod to help transform society. Not only does she help him find "liberation" in his portrayal, she gets to be "a rebel, a revolutionary"—a different kind of white woman.[25] Through her romance with him, Beverly realizes her particular humanity, crossing over the line from participating in the oppressive system to becoming a revolutionary. More generally, Cleaver's writings suggest that by embracing each other and sharing the commitment to destroy the oppressive system, black and white revolutionaries could realize their humanity.

Parts of *Soul on Ice* are deeply misogynist and sexist—a disturbing aspect of the text that received insufficient attention amid its initial embrace by a primarily masculinist literary establishment. In the essay "On Becoming," Cleaver claimed that after the Till murder, when he was back on the street, he had become a rapist, first practicing on black women and then repeatedly raping white women "as an insurrectionary act." "It delighted me," wrote Cleaver, "that I was defying and trampling upon the white man's law, upon his system of values, and that I was defiling his women." Upon his return to prison, Cleaver wrote, he became deeply ashamed and believed that he had gone astray "not so much from the white man's law as from being human."[26] While it is impossible to measure Cleaver's sincerity, this is the story with which Cleaver presented himself to the world—and the story sold.

Now a well-known author, Cleaver cultivated a growing coterie of Left-Progressive friends and supporters, notably in the Bay Area. Unlike most other black nationalist organizations, the Panthers embraced cross-racial politics. In practical terms, Cleaver played a crucial role in helping the Party forge powerful alliances with nonblack individuals and organizations.

By the time of the action in Sacramento, Cleaver was becoming increasingly involved in Panther activities. As the Panthers' needs for legal assistance and financial support grew, Cleaver's connections to Beverly Axelrod and *Ramparts* became increasingly important. Cleaver was still on parole and had made a point of attending the Sacramento action as a reporter rather than a Party member. At the time of his arrest, he was unarmed, carrying only a camera. Still newly out of prison, Cleaver now faced a revocation of parole because of his arrest in Sacramento. Axelrod represented Cleaver in court, arguing that Cleaver had been arrested with the other Panthers only because he was black. To support her argument, she pointed out that a black woman from Sacramento with no affiliation with the Black Panthers had also been arrested because she happened to be black and happened to be in the same place at the same time.[27] The district attorney acknowledged that Cleaver had been carrying only a camera and dropped the charges against him.[28]

The Black Panther

As the Panthers reached out to communicate with members, recruit new members, and garner support and funds for their cause, they developed the *Black Panther* newspaper as a key tool of their revolution. Cleaver's connections were very helpful in this endeavor. From the start, the newspaper served as a unique and dynamic voice of the Black Liberation Struggle. Rank-and-file Black Panthers did most of the work on the paper, including the writing and layout. But especially in the newspaper's early period, Cleaver's friends provided critical technical support, helping with editing and publishing.

Three days after the Sacramento action, Huey and Bobby began to work with Cleaver on the second issue of the Party's paper, which would be its first full-format edition.[29] They laid out the paper at Beverly Axelrod's house in San Francisco. The cover included a postcard that Beverly contributed featuring a woodblock picture of a fat pig with the headline, "Support Your Local Police." Eldridge and Barbara Arthur, an undergraduate at the University of California, wrote articles, and the Panthers called in a radical white photographer who brought over his cameras and tripods to take the pictures for the issue. For the photo shoots, Eldridge brought in the zebra-skin rug, rattan chair, and African shields and composed the famous picture of Huey Newton on his wicker throne. The photographer also shot an unidentified Black Panther woman in a similar scene. She stands in striking profile with a hood covering most of her face, a heavy rifle grasped in her right hand.[30]

Campus Rallies

The Panthers also reached out to students on college campuses. As soon as Bobby Seale was released on bail from the arrest in Sacramento, Peter Camejo of the Young Socialist Alliance at the University of California, Berkeley, scheduled an event on campus to set the record straight about the Black Panther Party's political positions.[31] Twelve Panthers came to campus on May 10, 1967, and Bobby Seale was the featured speaker. Seale asked, "Why don't cops who patrol our community live in our community? I don't think there would be so much police brutality if they had to go and sleep there." The audience of several thousand, composed mostly of white students, clapped loudly. Seale emphasized that the Black Panther Party was not racist. "You've been told that the Black Panthers . . . make no bones about hating whites," said Seale. "That's a bare-faced lie. We don't hate nobody because of color. We hate oppression."[32]

Seale explained the Panther's anticolonialist politics: "We're going to arm ourselves and protect ourselves from white racist cops. White cops are occupying our community like foreign troops. They're there to hurt us and brutalize us, and we got to arm ourselves because they're shooting us up already." Barbara Arthur, a fellow student of many of those in the crowd, announced, "I represent the women's department of the Party. We believe that an education system which still teaches and preaches that white is right, black is wrong" is itself wrong. Reminding the students about the Denzil Dowell case, she added, "[When] black men are armed, racist cops are going to take a second thought before harassing a black man."[33]

On Friday, May 5, the Black Panthers held a rally at San Francisco State College to raise bail money for the Sacramento arrestees, drawing heavily on support from the burgeoning Black Power Left. Cleaver's friend and renowned black nationalist poet LeRoi Jones (soon known as Amiri Baraka) was the keynote speaker. He praised the Black Panthers while calling the police "killers" and President Johnson a "mass murderer." Jones urged black people to arm themselves: "You'd better get yourself a gun if you want to survive the white man's wrath. Those white policemen aren't here to protect you, they're here to kill you." Playwright Ed Bullins also spoke and called black people a "captive nation."[34]

Setting the Terms of White Support

On May 3, the day after the Sacramento action, Newton went on the radio and made a plea for bail support. The Panthers needed $5,000, 10 percent of the $50,000 bail, to get the Party members back on the street.[35] The Party had to compete for funds with other Black Power and left-wing organizations. As the Black Panthers sought to attract support from the broader universe of left-wing activists, largely through Cleaver's networks, they also strove to define the character of these relationships. The Panthers' reach was expanding rapidly. Radical groups lined up to help the Black Panthers with their legal defense, including the *Ramparts*-affiliated Community for a New Politics (CNP), the Communist Party, and the Socialist Workers Party.[36] Representatives of these groups—including Roscoe Proctor, a black member of the Communist Party; Peter Camejo and Bob Himmel from the Socialist Workers Party; and Bob Avakian from the CNP—formed the Black Panther Legal Defense Committee and assisted in the defense of the Black Panthers arrested in Sacramento. By mid-July, however, the committee had fallen apart. Avakian, who worked as a researcher at *Ramparts,* continued to work with the Party. But as the Legal Defense Committee fell apart, the Black Panthers cut off formal ties with the Communist Party and the Socialist Workers Party, publicly condemning the patronizing attitudes of some on the white Left.

Eldridge Cleaver wrote a scathing critique in the Panther newspaper titled "White 'Mother Country' Radicals." In the article, Cleaver noted that whites had historically played an important role in black independence struggles internationally, particularly in supplying guns, money, and information. He argued that white radicals in America, however, had failed to live up to this standard, instead acting as if they "are the smartest" and attempting to dominate Black Power politics. Cleaver then defined the kind of relationship the Black Panther Party sought with radical whites—one in which they would offer material contributions, information, and skills. Reflecting the black demand for self-determination dating back at least to the nineteenth-century roots of the Black Liberation Struggle, Cleaver explained that whites must learn to listen to blacks and follow black leadership. Whites would not be allowed to run the show in the Party; their role had to be subordinate. The Black Panthers intended to direct their own Party. The Party lauded Bob Avakian as an acceptable voice of radical White America, perhaps because of his supportive role in the Legal Defense Committee. The *Black Panther* published an article by Avakian echoing Cleaver's critique, endorsing the idea that white radicals in America had a duty to support the black revolution. The paper also contained photos of Avakian posing with a pistol.[37]

LONG HOT SUMMER

More than any other group at the time, the Black Panther Party was highly attuned to the wave of ghetto rebellions. Following Sacramento, as envisioned in Newton's theoretical writings, the Panthers sought to position their Party as the vanguard of this black revolt, aiming to shape its raw energy into a powerful, organized, revolutionary force. In mid-June 1967, Bobby Seale published an article about the urban rebellions in the *Black Panther* called "The Coming Long Hot Summer." Seale predicted that the rebellions would expand explosively, creating the impetus for a black revolution:

> Since July 18, 1964, the Harlem "riots," there have been some fifty rebellions in the black communities throughout the nation. These fifty rebellions include the most recent rebellions of black people that have occurred within the last few weeks, some ten or fifteen. If one would look closely, and check this three year history, he will find that in damn near every rebellion a racist cop was involved in the starting of that rebellion. And these same pig cops, under orders from the racist government, will probably cause 50 or more rebellions to occur the rest of this year alone, by inflicting brutality or murdering some black person within the confines of one of our black communities. Black people will defend themselves at all costs. They will learn the correct tactics to use in dealing with the racist cops. . . . The racist *military*

police force occupies our community just like the foreign American troops in Vietnam. But to inform you dog racists controlling this rotten government and for you to let your pig cops know you ain't just causing a "long hot summer", you're causing a Black Revolution.[38]

In the summer of 1967, the wave of rebellion did in fact swell. Through the early summer, most local rebellions were small, like the Hunters Point riot in San Francisco in response to the killing of Matthew Johnson by police the previous year. None had anything like the scope or destructive capacity of the Watts rebellion in 1965. Yet in black communities throughout the country, small rebellions continued to erupt, often triggered by incidents of police brutality. Then came Newark, and Detroit.

Newark

In 1967, the black community in Newark, New Jersey, was emblematic of the ghetto isolation and containment from which rebellions grew. At that time, Newark was the thirtieth largest city in the United States, with a population of four hundred thousand. As blacks migrated to Newark in the late 1950s and early 1960s, whites deserted the city; in 1960, Newark was still 65 percent white, but by 1967, it was more than 52 percent black and 10 percent Cuban and Puerto Rican. Yet whites maintained near-total political control. From Mayor Hugh Addonizio to seven of nine city council representatives and seven of nine board of education members, the city leadership was almost entirely white. Whites also dominated the city commissions. The police were almost all Italian American. Almost all of those the police arrested, though, were black. Tensions between the black community and the police had escalated to the point that the mayor had handed over responsibility for investigating charges of police brutality to the Federal Bureau of Investigation. The FBI heard only cases that involved a violation of federal civil rights. While apparently taking the mayor off the hot seat, this move effectively shut down all channels for redress.

Very few black families, fewer than 13 percent, owned their own homes. Black residents had minimal access to education. Newark's per capita expenditures on education were significantly lower than those in the surrounding areas, and 70 percent of the children in the Newark public school system were black. Almost half of Newark's black children did not finish high school. In 1960, more than half of the city's adult blacks had less than an eighth-grade education, and 12 percent were unemployed. Newark had the highest rates of crime, venereal disease, substandard housing, maternal mortality, and tuberculosis in the country.[39] Organized crime was rampant. Most people convicted of crimes were black, and the majority of the victims were also black. Like the city government, organized crime—the operation, the money and power—was run by Italian Americans.

On Wednesday July 12, three weeks after the publication of Bobby Seale's article predicting a spread of urban rebellions, John Smith, a black cab driver, was pulled over by Newark police officers John DeSimone and Vito Pontrelli.[40] Just across the street from the police station, residents from the high-rise towers of the Reverend William P. Hayes Public Housing Projects watched as the policemen dragged Smith, apparently beaten too badly to walk, across the pavement and into the station. By 10:00 P.M., a crowd had gathered outside the police station, mostly comprised of housing project residents and cab drivers, who had been notified over their radios.

The police and "community leaders" asked the crowd to disperse. Then someone lit a match. In a small arc, two glass bottles full of liquid capped with burning rags passed over the crowd. Shattering against the wall of the police station, the Molotov cocktails burst into balls of flame. Frenzied police officers scrambled out of the station. Local officials from the Congress of Racial Equality (CORE) tried to calm the crowd and persuade people to march to city hall, but some in the crowd hurled stones and later broke the windows of several liquor stores and set a car on fire. The police put on riot helmets and moved to disperse the crowd.

The next day, representatives of a variety of Black Power groups met to discuss what to do about the clashes with police. They decided to call a "police brutality protest rally" for early that evening in front of the Fourth Precinct Station. The media started to gather. At 7:00 P.M., James Threatt, the black director of the Human Rights Commission announced that the mayor had decided to form a citizens committee to investigate the Smith incident and that a black policeman was being promoted to the rank of captain. Someone shouted "Black Power!" and people started to throw rocks.

Police moved to disperse the crowd, which began looting and setting more fires. There were not enough officers to contain the rebellion, so the police concentrated on a two-mile stretch of the commercial district on Springfield Avenue. The rebellion grew. The mayor called in help from the state police and the National Guard.

Law enforcement did a lot of shooting during the weekend. They shot looters and also fired at random into crowds, hitting uninvolved bystanders on the sidelines and even some in their homes. They also shot up businesses that placed "Black Owned" signs in the windows. Countless people were wounded. Twenty-three were killed, twenty-one of them black, including two children, six women, and a seventy-three-year-old man.

LeRoi Jones was among those beaten and arrested by Newark's police. "Again and again . . . we have sought to plead through the reference of progressive humanism . . . again and again our complaints have been denied by an unfeeling, ignorant, graft-ridden, racist government . . . [Now] we will govern ourselves or no one will govern Newark, New Jersey."[41]

On July 20, the Black Panthers devoted an issue of their newspaper to the Newark rebellion. Front-page headlines read "The Significance of the Black Liberation Struggle in Newark" and "Police Slaughter Black People." The cover photograph showed three police officers pinning down a black man, his face pressed into the sidewalk. The caption read,

> How can any black man in his right mind look at this picture in racist dog America and not understand what is happening? It's obvious that the brother on the ground is the underdog and that the arrogant Gestapo dogs on top have the advantage. What is the essential difference between the man on the bottom and the pigs on top? The gun. If the brother had had his piece with him, it is obvious that the pigs would have had to deal with him in a different way. And the brother may have gotten something down—that is, if he knew how to shoot straight.[42]

Lower on the page was a picture of a rifle under huge type reading, "Guns Baby Guns."

The paper featured a two-page centerfold with a photographic montage of the Newark rebellion. Each of the sixteen pictures emphasized the violent clash between heavily armed government officers and neighborhood blacks. Pictures of bloodied and brutalized black men and women accompanied a large photo of several blacks lying face down on the concrete with armed officers standing over them as other officers hold back a crowd. Another photo showed a military jeep packed with officers carrying machine guns driving past a burned-out building. The caption read, "Vietnam? Dominican Republic? The Congo? No!!! Racist NEWARK, U.S.A." In another shot, an officer crouched behind a jeep taking aim with his rifle. The caption: "Vicious, mad, raving, racist dog, sniping at colonized black people as though at a foreign enemy." One photo showed a crowd of unarmed black men yelling at soldiers over the points of their bayonets. The caption read, "America's black colonial subjects show contempt and a total lack of fear of the racist dog occupying troops." In the center of the page were the words "Racists call it 'rioting', but actually it's a political conse-quence on the part of black people who have been denied freedom, justice and equality."[43]

Detroit

On July 23, 1967, three days after the *Black Panther* issue on the Newark rebellions, Detroit exploded in the largest urban rebellion in the United States in the twentieth century. Most discussions of the Detroit rebellions, as well as the other urban rebellions of 1967, draw extensively on the analysis by the Kerner Commission, appointed by President Johnson to investigate the incident.[44] The commission report portrayed the rebellions as apolitical, spontaneous reactions to poor conditions rather than signs of a broader struggle over social power. As journalist Andrew Kopkind observed, though, "The Kerner Commission was designed not to study questions, but to state them, not to conduct investigations but to accept them, not to formulate policy but to confirm it." Kopkind argued that the report's shallow lip service to the core problem of racism bolstered rather than challenged structural racism. "Failure to analyze in any way the 'white racism' asserted by the commissioners in the report's summary," argued Kopkind, "transformed that critical category into a cheap slogan. And overall, the Report's mindless attention to documenting conventional perceptions and drowning them in conventional wisdom made meaningless the commissioners' demands for social reconstruction."[45]

The 120 social scientists and investigators hired by the Kerner Commission, working under the guidance of Research Director Robert Shellow, provided a much more perceptive political analysis of the rebellions that the commission never published. In the concluding chapter of the analysis, "America on the Brink: White Racism and Black Rebellion," the social scientists argued that racism pervaded all U.S. institutions and that blacks "feel it is legitimate and necessary to use violence against the social order. A truly revolutionary spirit has begun to take hold . . . an unwillingness to compromise or wait any longer, to risk death rather than have their people continue in a subordinate status." Shellow and his team were subsequently fired, and their analysis was removed from the report.[46] Powerful evidence supported the Shellow team's view that many black people in Detroit saw the unrest as political action—that is, as a rebellion. In the Campbell-Schumann survey several months after the incident, 56 percent of the black respondents in Detroit characterized the incident as a "rebellion or revolution," whereas only 19 percent characterized it as a "riot."[47]

In the Detroit uprising, rebels not only looted but also turned to more serious insurrectionary tactics, such as arson and sniping. Unlike looting—which offers rebels instant material benefit—these activities subjected rebels to significant risk while offering no instant material benefit, thus suggesting a challenge to the social order. According to police, 552 buildings were destroyed or damaged by fires started by the rebels. Some 7,231 rebels were arrested, more than twice as many as in the Watts uprising and four times more than in Newark. By the end of the Detroit rebellion, 43 people had been killed, 33 of them black. Ten whites were also killed, a number of them government officials.[48]

As with other urban uprisings, the Detroit rebellion did not spring out of the blue. Strong racial polarization had existed in Detroit for many years. In April 1965, white supremacists had burned crosses in front of twenty-five black residences in integrated neighborhoods of the city.[49] In the weeks leading up to the Detroit rebellion, three incidents exacerbated racial tensions. On June 12, a mob of more than eighty whites waged a miniriot and smoke-bombed the house of an interracial married couple—a black man and a white woman—who had moved into a suburban white neighborhood. On June 23, a black couple—Mr. Thomas, who worked at a local Ford plant, and Ms. Thomas, his pregnant wife—went to Rouge Park in a white neighborhood. A mob of more than fifteen whites harassed them, threatened to rape Mrs. Thomas, cut the wires on their car so they could not leave, and then shot Mr. Thomas three times, killing him and causing Ms. Thomas to miscarry. Six of the whites were arrested, but only one was charged, and he was eventually let off by a jury. In fact, at that time, no white had ever been found guilty of murdering a black person in Detroit. On July 1, Vivian Williams, a young black prostitute, was killed, and rumors circulated that she had been killed by a policeman.

A police raid of a "blind pig" bar on Twelfth Street had sparked the outbreak. Blind pigs were important social institutions in Detroit's black communities dating back to the early twentieth century. When white establishment bars started admitting blacks after 1948, the blind pigs were "underground" bars that mostly served blacks after 2:00

A.M., when state laws forbade the sale of liquor. Police customarily took protection bribes from the operators and raided those that refused to pay, creating resentment among many in the black community. In the early hours of July 23, the blind pig in the dingy second-floor apartment at 9125 Twelfth Street hosted a raging party for two black veterans returning from Vietnam and another soldier departing for the war.

As the eighty or so patrons, almost all of them black, were arrested and brought down to the street to be loaded into paddy wagons, a crowd began to gather. Word spread, and soon onlookers greatly outnumbered the police. Several people saw the police dragging the men down the stairs. Many in the gathering crowd believed that the police were using excessive force, and tensions rose. A young black nationalist began to shout "Black Power, don't let them take our people away; look what they are doing to our people. . . . Let's kill them whitey motherfuckers . . . let's get the bricks and bottles going. . . . Why do they come down here and do this to our neighborhood? If this happened in Grosse Pointe [an affluent white neighborhood], they wouldn't be acting this way."[50] Someone threw a beer bottle, and the crowd went wild.

Even before this episode, there had been a strong black nationalist presence in Detroit that provided an anticolonial assessment of conditions in the black community and called for rebellion. In addition to RAM and the Student Nonviolent Coordinating Committee, these activists included Uhuru, Reverend Albert Cleage and the Black Christian Nationalist Movement, the Afro-American Unity Movement, radical activists and authors Grace Lee and James Boggs, and the Malcolm X Society. A SNCC delegate from Cincinnati at the Second Black Arts Conference in late June said, "We already had our riot and we're here to show you how it's done."[51] The Afro-American Unity Movement was already preparing for urban rebellion and had already had several confrontations with police before the Detroit uprising. RAM had developed plans for seizing control of the city's industries should a rebellion take place.

During the rebellion, representatives from the Malcolm X Society contacted the mayor of Detroit and the governor of Michigan, claiming they would bring a cessation of "all hostilities" if the officials would meet a number of key demands, including those for community control over the police, the school board, and urban renewal. After the uprising, several newspapers published allegations that RAM was responsible for systematic burning and sniping, but these allegations were never proven.

Unlike the young black nationalists whose politics coincided with those of the rebels on the streets, black political leaders who attempted to quell the rebellion were booed and chased out of the neighborhood. This division between established leadership and young militants became clear in one community meeting during the uprisings. A young black steelworker from the Twelfth Street neighborhood told the politicians, "You leaders have failed the black community . . . . The black leadership brought it [the rebellion] on the black people."[52]

While liberal politicians' rhetoric about the Detroit rebellion emphasized the poor conditions blacks faced and the need for an ameliorative response, on the ground the state response was repressive. When the local police was unable to contain the rebellion, the mayor and the governor called in the National Guard and Michigan State Police and asked President Johnson to send in the army, which he eventually did. Soon, the police not only had bayonets and armored personnel carriers but were also backed up by tanks, army choppers, and machine guns. When the National Guard arrived on July 23, the troops were instructed "to shoot any person seen looting." By that evening, the police, the guardsmen, and the state police were all firing at fleeing looters. The next day, with backup from the National Guard, the police unleashed their full repressive force against the rebels, attempting to reestablish their "dominance and control" and to "teach the bastards a lesson." Many law enforcement officers believed their job was to put blacks back in their place. "I'm gonna shoot anything that moves and that is black" said a guardsman. White firemen shouted to guardsmen while they frisked two blacks on July 25, "Kill the black bastards! Control those coons. Shoot 'em in the nuts!"[53]

The rebels had no illusions that the government would act in their favor. Many explicitly saw their rebellion as an assertion of Black Power. One rebel confronted a cop with the words "You can't do anything to me White man. Black Power!"[54] As the government brought down increasingly repressive force, the rebels responded in kind.

At its height, the rebellion can best be described as an insurrection. Large crowds of looters in the early part of July 23 gave way to roving bands of looters and fire bombers, who were much harder to control. Some coordinated their tactics by shortwave radio. Apparently, the rebels saw all government officials as the enemy, and they attacked firemen as well as policemen.

By 4:40 P.M. on July 24, rebels had stolen hundreds of guns from gun shops. As police began to shoot at the looters, black snipers started shooting back. Hubert Locke, executive secretary of the establishment Committee for Equal Opportunity, called it a "total state of war." Police officers and firemen reported being attacked by snipers on both the east and west sides of the city. Snipers made sporadic attacks on the Detroit Street Railways buses and on crews of the Public Lighting Commission and the Detroit Edison Company. Police records indicate that as many as ten people were shot by snipers on July 25 alone. A span of 140 blocks on the west side became a "bloody battlefield," according to the *Detroit News*. Government tanks and armored personnel carriers "thundered through the streets and heavy machine guns chattered. . . . It was as though the Viet Cong had infiltrated the riot blackened streets." The mayor said, "It looks like Berlin in 1945."[55]

The black uprisings in Detroit and Newark were the largest of 1967 but by no means the only ones. Urban rebellions rocked cities large and small all across America. According to the Kerner Commission, 164 such rebellions erupted in the first nine months of the year.[56]

The urban uprisings marked a significant shift in Black America's relationship both to the Civil Rights Movement and to white-controlled law enforcement. Since the urban conflicts during World War II, the United States had seen few such disturbances until the Harlem rebellion in 1964. But by the summer of 1967, Black America was approaching full-scale violent revolt. The promise of full rights and upward mobility had helped contain the aspirations of Black America since the war. However, in the ghettos of the North and West, despite the achievement of citizenship rights, black subordination not only persisted but all too often expanded. With white flight and the desertion of the inner cities to blacks, urban governments sought to address the problems of their swelling ghettos through containment, relying increasingly on police force.

According to the Kerner Commission, the urban rebellions of 1967 responded to the "accumulation of unresolved grievances and . . . widespread dissatisfaction among Negroes with the unwillingness or inability of local government to respond."[57] Among the factors contributing to this dissatisfaction, according to the commission, were pervasive discrimination and segregation, black in-migration and white exodus, the convergence of segregation and poverty in the ghettos, disappointment with the Civil Rights Movement, violence by white vigilante groups reacting against black civil disobedience, frustration and powerlessness, a new mood of enhanced racial pride, and emerging views of the police as a symbol of white power—offering protection for white citizens while oppressing blacks with impunity.[58] The commission assigned special importance to police actions, believing that law enforcement's overstepping of power had not only triggered the rebellions but also generated the tensions that preceded them.[59]

As the censured analysis by the commission's research director Robert Shellow suggests, these conditions are best understood not as psychological factors prompting individual "rioters" to act but rather as the impetus for political acts of black rebellion. Rebellion reemerged as a political avenue precisely because of the limitations of the civil rights victories. These victories left untouched the economic and material dimensions of black subordination. With persistent racial subordination in the face of rhetorical freedom, pressures mounted. In the summer of 1967, the floodgates lifted, and the dream of black nationhood poured through the channels of urban rebellion.

VANGUARD OF THE BLACK REVOLUTION

Despite its early influence, the Black Panther Party started as just one of many small Black Power organizations. But coupled with the attention garnered from Sacramento, the wave of urban rebellions in the summer of 1967 confirmed the Party leaders' confidence in their political program. When Black America rebelled, Huey P. Newton and the Black Panther Party were prepared to seize the time. They were no mere ideologues giving lip service to the sentiments of the rebels. They had seen the wave of black revolt approaching. They had recognized its power and analyzed its character, and they had prepared the Party to organize it—to become its leading force. They had begun to position themselves as the vanguard of the black revolution.

Tentative No More

The Party's first assertions of its vanguard status were tentative. When the Black Panthers first published their ten-point platform and program at the beginning of the summer, they included this disclaimer above it: "To those poor souls who don't know black history, the beliefs and desires of the Black Panther Party for Self Defense may seem unreasonable. To black people, the ten points covered are absolutely essential to survival. We have listened to the riot producing words 'these things take time' for 400 years. The Black Panther Party knows what black people want and need. Black unity and self defense will make these demands a reality."[60] In the statement, the Party appeared to be trying to explain itself and did not yet seem confident of its growing influence. This disclaimer also appeared in several subsequent issues of the newspaper. Yet as urban rebellions spread, the confidence of the Party's leadership grew.

At 1:00 P.M. on June 29, 1967, Bobby Seale called a press conference on the steps of the San Francisco Hall of Justice. With television cameras rolling, Seale unfurled and read Minister of Defense Huey Newton's "Executive Mandate No. 2" drafting Stokely Carmichael into the Black Panther Party for Self-Defense and investing him with "the rank of Field Marshall, delegated the following authority, power and responsibility. . . . To establish revolutionary law, order and justice in the territory lying between the Continental Divide East to the Atlantic Ocean; North of the Mason-Dixon Line to the Canadian Border; South of the Mason-Dixon Line to the Gulf of Mexico." At the press conference, Seale presented a challenge to Carmichael: "I know you have questions you want answered, but there is only one question that is pertinent at this time, and that is this: Whose Authority and Program is Stokely Carmichael going to acknowledge, that of the warmonger Lyndon Baines Johnson or Minister of Self Defense, Huey P. Newton." The front page of the *Black Panther* pointed out that Carmichael was the first well-known "Afro-American leader" to take a stand against the draft and that many others had followed in his path, including Muhammad Ali and Martin Luther King.[61]

Although the press conference drew little coverage, it dramatically illustrated the Black Panther Party's evolving self-perception. The Party not only presented the United States as an imperialist power but also positioned itself as the sole legitimate alternative. By presenting Carmichael with a choice between two authorities—President Lyndon B. Johnson or Huey P. Newton, minister of defense of the Black Panther Party—the Panthers implied that if Carmichael did not accept Newton's authority, then he accepted Johnson's. Further, in delegating Carmichael to "establish revolutionary law" for the entire United States east of the Mississippi, Newton did not simply claim authority over Black America but posed a revolutionary challenge to America as a whole.[62]

In the same issue in which the Panthers enlisted Carmichael for revolutionary leadership, they removed the disclaimer from their Ten Point Program. They now proclaimed rather than argued the viability of the program. Carmichael would eventually join the Black Panther Party, but not until the following year. While the Party was not yet very large or influential, by the end of the summer, it had reinvented the politics of self-defense. The intense wave of summer rebellions demonstrated the Party to be highly attuned and bolstered the leadership's confidence in its revolutionary vision. This new confidence expressed itself in Party relations with other political organizations.[63]

Bootlickers

As the Party began to take more seriously its goal of becoming the vanguard of the black revolution, it came into increasing conflict with more moderate black political organizations. In July 1967, CORE held a conference in Oakland, bringing together representatives from a range of black political organizations: representatives of the local CORE chapter led by Wilfred Ussery, Floyd McKissick and James Farmer from the national CORE, Afro-American Association leader Donald Warden, Elijah Turner, California Assemblyman Willie Brown, SNCC Chairman H. Rap Brown, and Muhammad Ali. CORE asked the Black Panthers to serve as bodyguards for the event but refused to allow Newton to speak or to list the Black Panther Party in the program as a conference participant. The organization took the further step of asking the sheriff of San Mateo County to telephone Newton and Seale to inform them that they could carry guns for that day only as body guards at the event.

The Panthers were insulted and offended. Refusing to participate on these terms, they published a response in their newspaper that articulated their developing view of their political role and distinguished this role from that of CORE and its allies. The Panthers argued that black people "must develop the concept of a Foreign and Domestic Policy for Afro-America. . . . We have to start viewing reactionary black leaders as BLACK AGENTS OF THE WHITE MOTHER COUNTRY. And reactionary black organizations can be viewed as BLACK FRONTS FOR THE WHITE MOTHER COUNTRY."[64]

Following the conference, the *Black Panther* began to critique not only the police and white political leaders but also black political leaders and organizations that it viewed as counterrevolutionary. On July 20, the Black Panthers introduced their "Bootlicker" column. The idea was to identify "bootlicking," or counterrevolutionary, black leaders who were subservient to the "White power structure." The column was replete with photos, derogatory graphics, and articles critical of black leaders and organizations they saw as accommodationist—not only Ussery and CORE, but also California Assemblyman Willie Brown and the National Association for the Advancement of Colored People.[65]

Paper Panthers

The Black Panther Party did not confine itself to criticizing mainstream black political organizations. Increasingly confident in positioning the organization as a vanguard party, the Panthers also criticized other black nationalist organizations that did not live up to their revolutionary rhetoric. A particularly bitter rift had occurred between the Black Panther Party for Self-Defense and the Black Panther Party of Northern California, led by Huey and Bobby's former comrades from the West Coast RAM. A disagreement about tactics had been brewing for years, even when Huey and Bobby had worked with the Soul Students Advisory Council at Merritt College. The split widened as Huey and Bobby's Black Panther Party for Self-Defense gained in stature. Jockeying for media attention, RAM twice accepted credit for Panther activities, including the Black Panther escort of Betty Shabazz and the action in Sacramento. The fact that RAM carried unloaded weapons, a tactic that Huey adamantly opposed, did not help matters.

David Hilliard, one of Huey Newton's childhood friends who became active in the Party, coined the phrase "Paper Panthers" to describe the RAM group. RAM members were armchair revolutionaries who did not know the first thing about fighting an actual revolution, argued Hilliard, who would soon rise to the rank of chief of staff, assuming primary leadership of the Party's operation. The phrase stuck, and after the Newark rebellion in July 1967, the Black Panthers published a graphic of a "Paper Panther" in their newspaper replete with bullet holes and labels identifying the group as "conservative," "misguided," "reactionary," and "counterrevolutionary." The message was clear: The Black Panther Party for Self-Defense was the truly revolutionary Party, the vanguard of the black revolution, and no substitutes would be accepted.[66]

Mockery was not enough to resolve the conflict. According to Newton's memoirs, he confronted Roy Ballard of the Black Panther Party of Northern California about the rumor that Ballard's group carried unloaded guns. Ballard reportedly admitted that he did not even own any bullets. Huey reported that a few weeks later, he and his Panthers "went to San Francisco where the 'Paper Panthers' were having a fish fry, and issued an ultimatum: They could merge with us or change their name or be annihilated. When they said they would do none of these things, we waded in. I took on one and hooked him in the jaw. It was a short battle, ending a few moments later when somebody fired a shot in the air and people scattered. After that, the Paper Panthers changed their name."[67]

GENDER IN THE VANGUARD PARTY

As the Black Panthers garnered influence and self-confidence and sought to redefine their political strategy, the gender politics of the Party shifted as well. All the original Party members were men. They sought to educate and politicize the male "brothers on the block." And part of their project was to assert a strong black masculinity. In Newton's early essay "Fear and Doubt," he described the crisis of manhood he saw facing black men: "As a man, he finds himself void of those things that bring respect and a feeling of worthiness. . . . He ultimately blames himself. . . . He may father several illegitimate children by several different women in order to display his masculinity. But in the end, he realizes that he is ineffectual in his efforts. . . . He is asked to respect laws that do not respect him."[68]

Contrary to some critics, Newton laid out a position that was distinct from the Moynihan Report—a policy study for the War on Poverty issued in 1965 by the U.S. Department of Labor—which blamed the social castration of black men on the pathology of black matriarchal culture. Newton saw the problem not as a cultural difficulty endemic to black people but as a form of oppression imposed on black men by the racist social structure. In the Black Panthers' program to assert a revolutionary masculinity, black men were to become men by standing up against and seeking to destroy the oppressive system that was denying them their humanity. This politics challenged both the Uncle Tom role of black male deference to white power and the civil rights politics of turning the other cheek in pursuit of integration.[69]

Within months of its founding, the Black Panther Party attracted the participation of women, who soon became trusted and invaluable members. From the start, women participated in all Party activities, including the more militant ones. The Party's initial tactic of challenging the police principally attracted men but also attracted some women. The Panther entourage that confronted the police while escorting Betty Shabazz at the San Francisco Airport included women. And women Panthers participated in the "invasion" of the capitol building in Sacramento. Pictures of Panther women carrying guns appeared in the earliest issues of the *Black Panther*. Early issues of the newspaper represented women as valued Party members: as soldiers, poets, and writers.

In the summer of 1967, as Party influence grew, more women joined the Party. With the Party's growing confidence in its role as a revolutionary vanguard, Panther women increasingly wrote, and were written about, in the *Black Panther*. Not surprisingly, these pioneer Panther women applauded the idea of revolutionary nationhood and the bold masculinity of the Black Panther Party. In a recruitment pitch aimed at women, Barbara Arthur emphasized the appeal of a black political organization led by and consisting of revolutionary black men: "The Black Panther Party is where the BLACK MEN are. I know every black woman has to feel proud of black men who finally decided to announce to the world that they were putting an end to police brutality and black genocide. . . . Become members of the Black Panther Party for Self Defense, Sisters, 'we got a good thing going.'"[70]

Sister Williams not only embraced the pride and power these men exuded, but she also noted the deep appeal of the revolutionary love that Panther men held for "their brother": "Respect and dignity have long been abstractions to the majority of Black Men. This is no longer the case. The Black Panther Party for Self-Defense are Black Men with pride, self-respect and most of all love for their brother. These Black Men who express fervor, spirit and boldness of heart kindle in me, a Black Woman, the feeling of wanting to help plan, work, experience, and most of all share not only these feelings with him but the togetherness of wanting and now going about getting our freedom together."[71] Williams endorsed the Party as essential to black liberation. She validated the Party's claim to be the vanguard of the black revolution.

Powerful images of handsome black men and beautiful black women in the *Black Panther* projected the Party's appeal to allies, supporters, and recruits. On occasion, the early Party imitated Madison Avenue tactics, blatantly exploiting black female beauty to sell the Party. Underneath an attractive photo of Panther secretary and newspaper editorial staff person Audry Hudson, was a caption that read in part, "Besides being very beautiful to look at, (as you can see for yourself) the sister is a very beautiful person. She has gotten herself together and enlisted in the struggle for the total liberation of her people. She is a welcomed addition to the swelling ranks of the Vanguard Party of the black liberation struggle."[72]

Early articles by women in the *Black Panther* about issues of gender and sexuality ranged widely in tone, subject matter, and consciousness. In a complex analysis of the distinction between revolutionary and bourgeois black romantic relationships, Judy Hart contended, "At this stage in the black revolution the relationships between black men and black women are taking on new and crucial meanings. . . . With the black revolution being no more than the fusing of separate frustrations, desires, convictions, and strengths toward a common liberation, the black man and his woman cease to be simply a couple . . . but a fusing, a deepening of two black minds, souls, and bodies passionately involved not only in each other but in 'the movement.'"[73]

Hart argued that within the constraints of bourgeois society, it is impossible for black women and men to work together. She appealed to black women to commit to the revolution and relate differently to black men. She wrote that bourgeois black women necessarily relate to black men as tools to use for their own gain, and in seeking to succeed according to the dominant society's standards, they despise black men just as the racist society despises them. Hart decried the dysfunctional black household "in which the male can't function unless he's drunk, it's the first of the month, or he's physically asserting himself by yelling, beating, or fucking." By embracing revolutionary struggle, a different kind of relationship becomes possible. "Socially, the Negro man becomes extinct, outmoded. Social barriers and distinctions disappear, replaced by a communal unity." The revolutionary black man's "total commitment . . . is an invitation to the black woman to join with him in the pursuit of a life together, removing the shackles of White Racist America and establishing a solid foundation of blackness from which to build."[74]

Even in her nuanced treatment of gender and sexuality, Hart presented the man's revolutionary role as central and the woman's revolutionary role as supportive. This patriarchal orientation of Black Panther politics, common to most black nationalist and other movement organizations at the time, is evident throughout the Party's early actions and communications. Telling contrasts, such as the iconic representation of Huey as "Black Warrior Prince" set against the relatively obscure representation of the Panther woman as "Woman Warrior," speak to the initial masculine identity of the Party.

The Party's founding, early history, and ongoing struggles as a male-oriented organization affected all men and women who subsequently joined the Party. Not surprisingly, therefore, making the Black Panther

Party into a mixed-gender organization that modeled gender and sexual equality remained a hard-fought battle and an elusive goal. Difficult struggles to master these issues hounded the organization throughout its existence. Rhetorical commitments to gender and sexual equality at all levels of the Party could not on their own overcome real and fractious gender and sexual contradictions. However, over time, as more and more black women joined the Party, their work and leadership helped shape the entirety of the Party's politics. Their influence was particularly critical in giving a more positive cast to the Party's evolving gender and sexual politics and dynamics.

Women and some men in the Party demanded and led the Party's often frank and difficult engagement with the increasingly wide range of gender equality issues, particularly the question of how to define black women's role in a revolutionary nationalist movement. Thus, the rank-and-file members of the Party were the primary shapers of the organization's internal gender politics. The talented and audacious black women who increasingly joined the Party were far more active than the men in forcing the Party to focus on critical gender and sexuality concerns. In the summer of 1967, these intra-Party debates on gender and sexuality were just warming up. During the next several years, these debates would become increasingly intense, shaped by the parallel conversations about gender and sexual issues within the Black Liberation Struggle and black communities, as well as in the growing Women's Liberation Movement, Gay and Lesbian Liberation Movement, and sexual revolution.[75]

In the summer of 1967, with the core Panther practice of armed patrols of the police outlawed, yet with the Party's stature enhanced by its Sacramento actions, Newton had sought to build upon the success of the police patrols and articulate a revised politics of armed self-defense against the police. Attracted to Newton's courage, and building upon the Panther's newfound fame, new Panther recruit Eldridge Cleaver used his networks and eloquence to forge powerful alliances with other leftists and black nationalists. The Newark and Detroit rebellions, the largest and most violent of the period coming just weeks after publication of some of Newton's key theoretical writings, revealed the Panthers to be highly attuned to ghetto sentiment—and deepened the Panthers' confidence in their vanguard politics. And as the Party developed, it attracted more women members, who began to transform the gender politics of the Party. As the summer of 1967 gave way to the fall, the Panthers' new politics were put to the test.

4

Free Huey!

After dinner with his family on October 27, 1967, Huey Newton walked to his girlfriend LaVerne Williams's house at 5959 Telegraph Avenue in Oakland. It was Friday night, and the two had plans to go out. On the way over he thought about where they might go that evening. When he arrived, LaVerne was not feeling well. He offered to stay in with her, but she insisted that he go out and enjoy himself and lent him her car.[1]

Newton started up LaVerne's tan 1958 Volkswagen Beetle and drove to Bosn's Locker, his favorite bar. After casual conversation with friends over a rum and coke, he left the bar and went to the nearby Congregational church on Forty-Second and Grove. The church held Afro-American history classes on Wednesday nights, and Newton knew that there would be a church social on Friday. When he arrived, the social was in full swing, replete with dancing and cards. There he met up with Gene McKinney. They stayed until the social ended at 2:00 A.M. and then drove to a party at the home of Mrs. Verde Johnson on San Pablo Avenue near Thirty-Seventh. The pair of friends stayed until sometime after 4:00 A.M., at which point they decided to drive to a restaurant on Seventh Street that served soul food all night long.

The early morning of October 28 was cool, dark, and slightly misty. Officer John Frey of the Oakland police force sat alone in his patrol car on Willow Avenue at the corner of Seventh Street. Officer Frey (pronounced "fry") had just turned twenty-three. Married, though separated, Frey was a large man, over six feet tall and more than two hundred pounds. In his year and a half on the force, Frey had already developed quite a reputation. A ten-year veteran of the Oakland Police Department told a reporter from *Ramparts,* "Frey is not what I would categorize as a good cop." Frey had been implicated in numerous incidents of racism. H. Bruce Byson, an English teacher who invited Frey to speak about police work to his class at Clayton Valley High School, reported that Frey told the class that "niggers" in the neighborhood he patrolled were "a lot of bad types." In the trial eventually held to adjudicate the events of that early morning, Elford Dunning, an accountant for Prudential Life Insurance, testified that Frey had racially harassed him during a traffic accident, and when Dunning complained that Frey was acting like the Gestapo, Frey loosened his holster, put his hand on his gun, and said "I *am* the Gestapo" and ordered Dunning into the police car. Earlier on the evening that Huey Newton and Gene McKinney drove to get soul food on Seventh Street, Frey had intervened in a dispute between a black grocery clerk named Daniel King and a white man without pants on who claimed King had stolen his pants. According to King, Frey called him a nigger and held his arms so the white man could beat him.[2]

Several hours after Frey had released King, Newton and McKinney drove by his parked patrol car. Sitting on the dashboard in front of Frey was a list of twenty cars that the Oakland police had identified as Black Panther vehicles. Second to last on the list was "Volkswagen, 1958, sedan, tan, AZM489." Frey called for backup and pulled out after the Volkswagen. When Newton saw the red beacon lights in his rear-view mirror, he pulled over near the corner of Seventh and Campbell.

HUEY MUST BE SET FREE!

When physician Mary Jane Aguilar saw an *Oakland Tribune* photograph of Huey Newton taken hours after he was pulled over by Frey, she wrote a letter to the Black Panther Party:

> I can remember nothing in my medical training which suggested that, in the care of an acute abdominal injury, severe pain and hemorrhage are best treated by manacling the patient to the examining table in such a way that the back is arched and belly tensed. Yet this is precisely the picture of current emergency room procedure which appeared on the front page of a local newspaper last week-end. Looming large in the foreground of the same picture, so large as to suggest a caricature, was a police officer. Could it have been he who distracted the doctor in charge of the case to position the patient in this curious way?[3]

There are conflicting accounts of what happened near the corner of Seventh and Campbell Streets in Oakland that morning. In the murder trial that followed the incident, the jury was not able to put together a clear and compelling account from the evidence and testimony presented in the courtroom. But at some point during the early hours of the day, Newton and Gene McKinney arrived at David Hilliard's house. Newton had a gunshot wound in his abdomen, so David and his brother June Hilliard rushed Newton to the Kaiser Hospital emergency room. Soon the story was all over the news: Officer Frey was dead, and Huey P. Newton, minister of defense for the Black Panther Party, had been arrested as the prime suspect in his murder.[4]

Well before the news stories hit the press, the Black Panther Party sprang into action. Over the preceding months, a small but growing number of people had come to view Newton as the leader of the vanguard of black revolution. In the months following the Panthers' action in Sacramento, the Party had increased its capacity, not only by growing its membership and improving its ability to organize people but also by strengthening its political analysis, its newspaper, and its relationships with other political organizations. Now that Newton would face capital charges for a confrontation with the Oakland police and could be sent to the gas chamber, his release became the central cause of the Party.

Beverly Axelrod introduced Newton to her mentor Charles Garry, who she felt would be the ideal lawyer for such a high-profile, politically charged case. Garry, the son of Armenian immigrants, was known as a passionate trial lawyer. His raw eloquence and brilliant maneuvers elicited revealing responses from witnesses under cross-examination. A former president of the San Francisco chapter of the National Lawyers Guild and an avowed Marxist with a strong commitment to social justice, Garry had defended more than thirty capital cases, and not one of his clients had been executed. Garry offered to represent Newton, and Newton accepted.[5]

From the start, Newton and the Black Panther Party viewed the trial as a political contest rather than merely a legal proceeding. The Party put out the sixth issue of its newspaper with the picture of Huey in his wicker throne on the front page and the bold headline, "Huey Must Be Set Free!" After explaining that Huey had been shot and arrested and that Officer Frey had been shot and killed, the editorial discussed the case in terms of racial politics:

The shooting occurred in the heart of Oakland's black ghetto. Huey is a black man, a resident of Oakland's black ghetto, and the two cops were white and lived in the white suburbs. On the night that the shooting occurred, there were 400 years of oppression of black people by white people manifested in the incident. We are at that crossroads in history where black people are determined to bring down the final curtain on the drama of their struggle to free themselves from the boot of the white man that is on their collective neck. . . . Through murder, brutality, and the terror of their image, the police of America have kept black people intimidated, locked in a mortal fear, and paralyzed in their bid for freedom. . . . They are brutal beasts who have been gunning down black people and getting away with it. . . . Huey Newton's case is the showdown case. . . . We say that we have had enough of black men and women being shot down like dogs in the street. We say that black people in America have the right to self defense. Huey Newton has laid his life on the line so that 20,000,000 black people can find out just where they are at and so that we can find out just where America is at.[6]

The Panthers argued that Newton was resisting the long-perpetrated oppression of blacks by police when he was shot and imprisoned. The Party turned the state's accusations against Newton around, using the case to mobilize support and put America on trial.

STOP THE DRAFT WEEK

In the weeks leading up to Newton's arrest, the Bay Area antiwar movement had experienced its own conflict with the Oakland police. As resistance to the Vietnam War intensified, white antiwar activists began getting a taste of police repression—and this experience was to deepen their alliances with the Panthers. By October, the draft resistance movement was gathering steam.[7] No longer were the students and the antiwar activists simply Americans expressing their view within established channels. Inspired by Black Power, emboldened by the ghetto rebellions, many draft resisters saw themselves as subjects of empire who sought self-determination, much like the Vietnamese. They rejected the legitimacy of the war, the draft, and the government more generally, seeking to resist by any means.

"This week," a demonstrator wrote from Oakland at the end of Stop the Draft Week in mid-October, "the first crack appeared in the egg that will hatch white revolution in America." Demonstrators sought to emulate the radical tactics of the ghetto rebellions of July. According to Frank Bardacke, an antiwar activist who would face the heaviest charges from the Stop the Draft Week protests in Oakland, the draft card burning was the defining act that set the tone for active resistance to authority: "Young men burning their draft cards on Sproul Hall steps changed the political mood of the campus. This example and that of hundreds who turned in their draft cards gave the rest of us courage."[8] "We too are the Vietcong," Hal Jacobs of the Students for a Democratic Society told a Resistance rally in preparation for Stop the Draft Week at UC Berkeley.[9]

Day one, Monday October 16, was relatively calm. Some 300 resisters turned in their draft cards at the Federal Building in San Francisco, and another 120 were arrested for a nonviolent sit-in at the Oakland Induction Center. But the next day, confrontations with police intensified. While Monday had been reserved for the more pacifist groups, Tuesday's event was organized by those ready to take the resistance to a new level, including SDS, the Student Nonviolent Coordinating Committee, and the Independent Socialist Club, which instructed "those in the militant action" to "wear a hat and thick clothes, carry a handkerchief and change, and arrange for someone to have bail ready." One of the speakers was George Ware, the SNCC field secretary who had recently traveled to Cuba with Stokely Carmichael.

Emboldened by the Black Power movement and what one organizer called "vicarious intoxication by the summer riots," resisters attempted to shut down the induction center in Oakland and met brutal repression. Under the front page headline "Cops Beat Pickets," the *San Francisco Chronicle* described the police action: "Police swinging clubs like scythes cut a bloody path through 2500 antiwar demonstrators who had closed down the Oakland Armed Forces Examining Station yesterday . . . their hard wooden sticks mechanically flailing up and down, like peasants mowing down wheat." More than twenty people were injured, and twenty-five were arrested. In the next two days, ninety-seven more were arrested during peaceful pickets.

At 6:00 A.M. on Friday, ten thousand demonstrators surrounded the Oakland induction center. Many were dressed for conflict with the police, wearing helmets and shields. They painted the streets and built barricades using benches, large potted trees, parking meters, garbage cans, cars, and trucks. Some of these vehicles had been stolen and then positioned in the intersections with the air let out of the tires. In this way, the resisters shut down many of the intersections surrounding the induction center and prevented buses from reaching it. The confrontation grew into a violent melee that soon spread over a twenty-block area of downtown Oakland.[10]

The Panthers had claimed to be fighting an anticolonial war all along. Now antiwar activists increasingly saw their struggle too as a fight against imperialism, and the "Free Huey!" campaign became a lightning rod for the anti-imperial Left. "Free Huey!" bumper stickers appeared all over the Bay Area. White as well as black support for Huey's immediate release from prison boomed. As *Ramparts* writer Gene Marine explained, this outpouring of support had little to do with whether Newton's shooting and jailing were unjust. Instead, the groundswell of support reflected the increasingly widespread belief that "justice was impossible." "Once the white radical could accept the idea that white America is the mother country and black America the colony," wrote Marine, "his problem with the cry of 'Free Huey!' disappeared; he was in the position of a Frenchman opposed to his nation's colonial adventure in Algeria."[11]

Both Black Power organizations and New Left groups rallied in support of Huey. The day of the shooting, SNCC headquarters sent a telegram to Huey at Kaiser Hospital:

> Violent cop attack against you is part of White America's plan to destroy all revolutionary Black men. Brothers and sisters in SNCC support you all the way. We praise and welcome your fine example of armed self-defense. Your action is inspiration for black men everywhere. SNCC stands united with you and ready to help in any way possible.[12]

Telegrams and articles supporting Huey and demanding his release poured in from New Left allies such as the Progressive Labor Party and Bob Avakian of the Community for New Politics.[13]

At one "Free Huey!" rally outside the trial at the Alameda County courthouse, Bobby Seale climbed on top of a car to speak to the crowd. The police ordered him down, and he complied. When a young protestor challenged him for following police orders, he explained his actions: "What do you want me to do, just jump up and off some cop? That [would] do Huey a lot of good, wouldn't it—a big shootout in front of the trial?"[14]

Building on the political strategy they had developed in facing legal challenges after the Sacramento action, Newton and the Panthers insisted on a political approach to the trial. They would follow the law to the letter and strive to exonerate Huey through legal channels, to "exhaust all legal means," but the principle behind the case would be political.[15] They would use Huey's trial as a forum to put America on trial, to expose its inherent racism and injustice. If confronted with a strategic choice about whether to advance the political project or Newton's personal interests, the Panthers would give priority to the political path. This decision reflected their belief that the political system was inherently unjust and that Huey would be put to death. They designed their legal approach to call attention to state repression and to advance the Panthers' cause. Further, the Panthers believed that only a powerful mass political campaign could save Huey's life.

KATHLEEN

One of the first recruits to join the "Free Huey!" campaign was Kathleen Neal, who would go on to become a key player in the Panther leadership.[16] Neal had grown up in Tuskegee, Alabama, and other college towns where her father Ernest Neal worked as a professor. When Dr. Neal joined the U.S. Foreign Service, Kathleen lived for stints in New Delhi, the Philippines, Liberia, and Sierra Leone. Always an honor student in American schools abroad, she later attended boarding school in the United States, went to Oberlin College, and completed a government internship in Washington, D.C.[17]

Neal's experiences as a young black woman growing up in the South in the 1950s made her want to challenge injustice. Seeing powerful women leaders of SNCC in action made her wonder how she too might advance a revolution for black liberation. This search led her first to SNCC and then to the Black Panther Party. "I saw Gloria Richardson standing face to face with National Guard soldiers, bayonets sticking from the guns they pointed at the demonstrators she led in Cambridge, Maryland," Neal later wrote. "I saw Diane Nash speaking at Fisk University, leading black and white Freedom Riders onto Greyhound buses that got set on fire when they reached Alabama. I saw Ruby Doris Robinson holding a walkie-talkie, dispatching the fleet of cars that transported civil rights workers across the state of Mississippi during the 1964 Freedom Summer. These women were unfurling a social revolution in the Deep South. Gloria Richardson, Diane Nash, and Ruby Doris Robinson all worked with the Student Nonviolent Coordinating Committee. . . . That's where I was determined to go."[18]

In 1966, Neal went to work in SNCC's New York office, then to Atlanta as the secretary of SNCC's Campus Program.[19] There, she helped organize a black student conference in March 1967 at Fisk University in Nashville, Tennessee, where she first met Eldridge Cleaver.[20] She later recalled their first encounter:

What startled me most about him—a brilliant writer, and eloquently lucid speaker, as well as a tremendously handsome and magnetic person—was that he referred to himself as a "convict." Seeing him at the conference as he moved about with supreme confidence, an ease that approached elegance and a dignified reserve that all combined to give him an air that could best be described as stately, it seemed hard to conceive of this powerful man as a "convict." He exuded strength, power, force in his very physical being. To think of such a man caged up and designated for the dungheap of history was impossible.[21]

On the plane back to Washington from the conference, Kathleen wrote a passionate love poem to Eldridge, titling it "My King, I Greet You," in answer to "My Queen, I Greet You," the open love poem he had written to all black women (from all black men).[22] Three weeks after Huey Newton's arrest, Kathleen moved to San Francisco to join the Black Panther Party. Another month and a half later, just after Christmas 1967, Kathleen and Eldridge were married. Alprentice "Bunchy" Carter, who had served time with Eldridge in Soledad Prison, was the witness.[23]

Kathleen—now Kathleen Cleaver—threw herself fully into the campaign to free Huey. She helped organize demonstrations, wrote leaflets, held press conferences, attended court hearings, designed posters, spoke at rallies, and appeared on television programs.[24] She had more formal education than most Panthers and soon was appointed to sit on the Central Committee as communications secretary of the Black Panther Party.

The work of Kathleen Cleaver in the Party was important in the ongoing and at times challenging process of integrating black women into an organization that had begun as a male formation. The male chauvinism that women like Cleaver all too often confronted within and outside the Party made women's participation all the more challenging. Over time, as issues of gender and sexuality became increasingly important to the Party's development, women like Cleaver modeled strikingly influential and vital roles for black women in the Black Panther Party in particular and in black nationalist organizations in general. The tradition of radical black women activists such as the strong black women leaders in SNCC shaped the activism of Panther women like Cleaver. However, most Panther women ultimately improvised their revolutionary roles precisely because there was no guidebook, no single model. As Cleaver acknowledged in a 1970 interview, "Of all the things I had wanted to be when I was a little girl, a revolutionary certainly wasn't one of them. And now it was the only thing I wanted to do. Everything else was secondary. It occurred to me that even though I wanted to become a revolutionary more than anything else in the world, I still didn't have the slightest idea what I would have to do to become one."[25]

On January 16, 1968, at 3:30 A.M., police knocked down the door to Kathleen and Eldridge's apartment without a warrant. Armed with shotguns and pistols, cursing and yelling at the Cleavers, they threw around papers and furniture as they searched the apartment; when nothing of interest turned up, they left.[26] In response, from prison Huey Newton issued Executive Mandate No. 3, ordering all members of the Black Panther Party to keep guns in their homes and to defend themselves against any police officers or others who attempted to invade their homes without a warrant.[27] Accompanying the mandate was a bold photo of Kathleen, dressed in a long black leather jacket standing in the doorway to her apartment. In her arms she bore a large shotgun, pointed toward the camera, and the heading read "Shoot Your Shot!" With such actions, the Party sought to solidify the ethic it had established at the outset: both women and men bore responsibility for armed self-defense.[28]

PEACE AND FREEDOM PARTY

After Huey's arrest and imprisonment, Eldridge's role became "increasingly important, especially in the Party's collaboration with the white radicals in the Free Huey movement," Kathleen later recalled.[29] The most important early alliance was with the Peace and Freedom Party (PFP), founded by *Ramparts* editor Robert Scheer and other leaders of the Community for New Politics on June 23, 1967. The initial idea for the party, part of a national network of antiwar political organizations, picked up momentum as the black rebellions spread across the country that summer. After Martin Luther King Jr. gave the keynote address to 125,000 people at an antiwar rally in New York that April, many urged King to run for president of the United States. The Peace and Freedom Party sought to promote a strong antiwar and antiracist politics in opposition to the establishment Democratic Party, which was resolutely prowar and had distanced itself from the insurgent Black Liberation Struggle. The party garnered support from a range of progressive and left-wing organizations in the Bay Area and Los Angeles, including the Independent Socialist Club and the Communist Party. Yet from the start, party members had conflicting ideas about how to advance the party's "ideological support for racial equality."[30]

On July 12, 1967, the membership of the Peace and Freedom Party voted to seek official registration of a candidate on the November 1968 ballot. To do so in California, the party needed to obtain sixty-seven thousand signatures. But a lack of consensus on the politics of race made achievement of this goal a major challenge. About twenty-five hundred activists, predominantly white and affiliated with a range of leftist organizations, gathered for the National Conference for New Politics in Chicago in early September. King spoke at the convention but declined to run as a peace candidate for president. Serious conflict arose when the three hundred black delegates formed a Black Caucus and proposed that half the posts on all conference committees be filled by members of their caucus. The conference leadership, needing black participation to legitimate their politics, voted in favor of the proposal—but important organizations opposed, notably members of the California Peace and Freedom Party such as Bob Avakian.[31] Two weeks later, the California Peace and Freedom Party held its statewide conference to rally support for the California registration drive. Of the hundred fifty delegates who attended, about 10 percent were black. Again the black delegates formed a caucus and proposed that they be given 50 percent of voting rights. This time the proposal was defeated, and the entire Black Caucus walked out. The Communist Party representatives and others followed them.[32]

Now almost exclusively white and desperate to salvage its antiracist and antiwar alliance in time for the registration deadline on January 3, leaders of the Peace and Freedom Party approached black organizations for support. SNCC and other black groups, however, rebuffed them.[33] The results were disastrous. As December arrived, with less than a month to go before the registration deadline, the PFP had collected only about twenty-five thousand of the required sixty-seven thousand signatures. On December 18, with less than two weeks remaining, the California Supreme Court rejected the Peace and Freedom Party's suit to extend the registration deadline and reduce the number of signatures required.[34]

By this time, the October 28 shooting and the "Free Huey!" campaign had thrown the Black Panther Party into the national spotlight. Through Avakian, Scheer, and others, the Peace and Freedom Party approached the Panthers to propose a coalition. As Peace and Freedom organizing committee member Mike Parker recalled,

> We started out as a predominantly White group based on the anti-war movement, and from the very beginning we had the position that there could be no peace unless it was a peace among free men—that you did not

have a true peace just because there was no war if people were oppressed. And so we made our slogan "Peace and Freedom" just to make it clear that we stood not only for ending the war in Vietnam and other wars but also for ending oppression. We were looking for groups in the Black community to work with and we found that the only group in the Black community that was even willing to talk with us about these kinds of questions in a serious way . . . was the Black Panther Party for Self Defense.[35]

The coalition was announced on December 22, 1967. The white Left in Northern California, so troubled by the question of how to relate to Black Power, was surprised and enthralled. The *Berkeley Barb*, a weekly underground newspaper, called the coalition an "unprecedented combination of Black and white activists . . . the first such militant alliance since the 'Black Power' concept was outlined by Stokely Carmichael last year."[36] The coalition initially sought to ensure that Huey Newton received a fair trial but later demanded that Huey be set free unconditionally. The Peace and Freedom Party contributed $3,000 and use of its sound equipment to the "Free Huey!" campaign.[37]

The Black Panther Party offered much needed legitimacy to the Peace and Freedom Party's racial politics. With the Black Panthers at the table, many of the high-profile supporters who had walked out over the Peace and Freedom Party's racial politics in September returned to endorse the registration drive, including James Vann of the Oakland Congress of Racial Equality, Si Casady of the California Democratic Council, and representatives of the Communist Party. The day after the announcement of the coalition, new registrations in Berkeley alone jumped to more than 500—reaching 1,200 per day by the end of the week. By the deadline on January 3, over 105,000 signatures had been gathered: the Peace and Freedom Party would be on the November ballot in California.[38]

The coalition proved to be mutually beneficial. As a *Black Panther* editorial explained, "What we wanted and needed were people who were willing to work. . . . The Peace and Freedom Party was willing to work. In return, we were willing to hold rallies with them, to share platforms with them, and to recommend them to Black people who had their minds set on participating in electoral politics. . . . The Peace and Freedom Party acknowledges that we were helpful to them in gaining enough signatures to get on the ballot. We are glad that they made it and that we were instrumental in the success."[39]

The Party also keenly understood that the Black Liberation Struggle needed nonblack allies, particularly progressive white allies. An editorial in the *Black Panther* explained why this alliance was important: "The increasing isolation of the black radical movement from the white radical movement was a dangerous thing, playing into the power structure's game of divide and conquer. We feel that in taking the step of making the coalition with the Peace and Freedom Party, we have altered the course of history on a minor, but important level."[40]

From its inception, the Black Panther Party had embraced both an uncompromising commitment to black liberation and a principled rejection of a separatist black politics. The coalition with the Peace and Freedom Party, which a number of black nationalists criticized, illustrated both. Explaining the Party's position to its expanding black base was critical. "Because our Party has the image of an uncompromising stand against the oppression of the white power structure on Black people, we could take this step without getting shot down with the charge of selling out."[41]

As the Black Panther Party promoted the "Free Huey!" campaign, it built on emerging alliances with students and white antiwar activists, advancing an anti-imperialist political ideology that linked the oppression of antiwar protestors to the oppression of blacks and Vietnamese. Bobby Seale elaborated this position at a January 28, 1968, rally at UC Berkeley supporting students who had been arrested during Stop the Draft Week. Citing Newton's article "On the Functional Definition of Politics," Seale spoke to the crowd about self-defense power and the parallels between the Vietnamese and the black American liberation struggles. He pointed out that the antidraft students were locked up right alongside Huey Newton in the Alameda County jail. He made common cause with the students, arguing that the antiwar demonstrators faced a plight like that of the black community:

> Black people have protested police brutality. And many of you thought we were jiving, thought we didn't know what we were talking about, because many Black people in the community probably couldn't answer your questions articulately. But now you are experiencing this same thing. When you go down in front of the draft [board], when you go over and you demonstrate in front of Dean Rusk, those pig cops will come down and brutalize your heads just like they brutalized the heads of black people in the black community. We are saying now that you can draw a direct relationship that is for real and that is not abstract anymore: you don't have to abstract what police brutality is like when a club is there to crush your skull; you don't have to abstract what police brutality is like when there is a vicious service revolver there to tear your flesh; you can see in fact that the real power of the power structure maintaining its racist regime is manifested in its occupying troops, and is manifested in its police department—with guns and force.[42]

Antiwar activists eagerly took up the analogy. Free Speech Movement veteran and Communist Party member Bettina Aptheker spoke after Seale and emphasized the escalating repression of the antiwar movement and its common cause with both the Black Liberation Struggle and the "Free Huey!" campaign. "The ghettos have become occupied territories in the United States. This peace movement should have called for the immediate withdrawal of troops in July from Newark and Detroit. It failed to do that and it should have done that just as it calls for the immediate withdrawal of troops from Vietnam," she exhorted. "For a long time the ghetto communities in this country have borne the brunt of the assault on the democratic rights of all of us, and it is now perhaps first coming home to us that to defend the rights in the ghetto is to defend our own rights."[43] Bob Avakian also spoke, noting that Huey's case and that of the draft resisters were "interrelated" and together posed a fundamental challenge to "power in this society." He explained, "The Black Liberation Movement poses that challenge. The Antiwar Movement and the Antidraft Movement as it moves towards resistance is beginning to pose that challenge. And they are responding the way all blind tyrants respond when their power is challenged. By brute force and by attempting to mitigate that brute force through the veneer of a court apparatus which we all know is rigged."[44]

A few weeks later, the *Black Panther* carried a cartoon by Emory Douglas titled "It's All the Same" that graphically illustrated the three-part anti-imperialist analogy. The cartoon featured three identical drawings of a filthy pig in uniform surrounded by flies and carrying a machine gun, napalm, mace, and a pistol. The first panel identified the pig as the local police. The second panel identified the pig as the National Guard. The third panel identified the pig as the Marines. The Peace and Freedom Party picked up and distributed the graphic, citing the Black Panthers, to bolster its argument that the oppression that antiwar activists faced for opposing the war was part and parcel not only of the struggle for black liberation but also of the international struggle against imperialism.[45]

COMING OF AGE

On February 17, 1968, Huey Newton's twenty-sixth birthday, the Black Panther Party came of age. In a massive, predominantly black rally in the Oakland Auditorium, while Newton sat in jail, the Black Panthers announced a merger with SNCC. The terms of the merger were ambiguous; SNCC itself was in crisis, and the merger did not last long. But for the Black Panther Party, an organization that only a year earlier had barely been known outside of Oakland, the event marked an important step in the maturation of its politics and its emergence on the national political stage.

In the center of the auditorium stage sat Huey's wicker throne from the famous photograph, empty of course. In addition to Eldridge Cleaver, who served as master of ceremonies, and Bobby Seale, the day's speakers included three of the most famous leaders of SNCC: James Forman, H. Rap Brown, and Stokely Carmichael. Bob Avakian from the Peace and Freedom Party and Berkeley Councilman Ron Dellums were also on stage, as was Armelia Newton, Huey Newton's mother.

Seale focused most of his speech on the need to stand up to police brutality and organize to free Huey. He also spelled out a fuller view of the Panthers' politics. Summarizing the Panthers' Ten Point Program, he emphasized the need to serve the community, describing a Panther campaign to erect a stoplight at 55th and Market Streets in Oakland, where speeding cars had killed several children. He then delved into the Party's position on whites:

> When the Man walks up and says we are anti-white, I scratch my head, I say, " . . . what does he mean by that?" He says, "Well, I mean, you hate white people." I say, "Me? Hate a white person?" I say, "Wait a minute, man, let's back up a little bit. That's *your* game. That's the Ku Klux Klan's game." I say, "That is the Ku Klux Klan's game to hate me and murder me because of the color of my skin." I say, "I wouldn't murder a person or brutalize him because of the color of his skin." I say, "Yeah, we hate something, alright! We hate the oppression that we live in! We hate cops beating black people over the heads and murdering them. That's what we hate!" If you've got enough energy to sit down and hate a white person just because of the color of his skin, you're wasting a lot of energy. You'd better take that same energy and put it in some motion out there, and start dealing with those oppressive conditions, and you're going to find out just what you hate, and what you're going to stop.[46]

H. Rap Brown then spoke eloquently about the importance of freeing Huey. But in contrast to Bobby, he framed this question in terms of generic opposition to whites:

> Huey Newton is the only living revolutionary in this country today. He has paid his dues! He paid his dues! How many white folks you kill today? . . . Yes, politics IS war without bloodshed; and war is an extension of those politics. But there is no politics in this country that is relevant to us . . . to black people.[47]

Stokely Carmichael extended the point:

The major enemy is the honky . . . THAT's the major enemy! THAT is the major enemy! And whenever anybody prepares for revolutionary warfare, you concentrate on the major enemy. We're not strong enough to fight each other and also fight him. We WILL not fight each other today! We WILL not fight each other. There will BE no fights in the black community among black people. There will just be people who will be offed. There will be no fights, there will be no disruptions. We are going to be united! . . . Now then, some people may not understand brother Rap when he talked about whom we ally with. He said we have to ally with Mexican Americans, Puerto Ricans, and the dispossessed people of the earth; he did not mention poor whites. . . . Who do you think has more hatred pent up in them, white people for black people, or black people for white people? White people for black people, obviously. The hatred has been more. What have we done to them for them to build up this hatred? Absolutely nothing. Yet . . . we don't even want to have the chance to hate them for what they've done to us, and if hate should be justified *we have the best justification in the world for hating the honkys*! We have it! We have it! We have it![48]

SNCC, as much as any organization, had given birth to the idea of forming a Black Panther Party. SNCC was born in the South out of the early 1960s fight against Jim Crow. Perhaps more than any other organization, it was responsible for mobilizing the nonviolent civil disobedience that brought de jure racial segregation to its knees. From 1965 through 1967, SNCC had nurtured the shift of a militant younger generation toward black nationalism and the call for Black Power. As SNCC chairman, Stokely Carmichael had initiated several Black Panther organizations in various cities in 1967. Yet even as SNCC spread the powerful message of Black Power, the organization had never developed a practical strategy to sustain these Black Panther organizations or the broader movement politically. SNCC had no real constituency, no effective tactics, no institutional framework for advancing Black Power politics. By Huey's birthday on February 17, 1968, SNCC was starting to collapse.

The Black Panther Party for Self-Defense filled the vacuum left by SNCC. Among black nationalists and the Left, Newton was now widely viewed as a political prisoner: a radical activist being railroaded to prison for his politics. Using the political framework it had developed following Sacramento, the Black Panther Party could now turn all its energies toward freeing him. If SNCC was the mother and the Black Panther Party the child, then on the very stage that SNCC and the Black Panther Party had announced their merger to the world, the

Panthers, as every child must, now left its mother behind to strike out on its own.

The SNCC leaders criticized the Panthers' politics of aligning with white leftists, including their decisions to hire a white lawyer and raise money from whites to defend Huey. More broadly, SNCC leaders suggested that the Black Panther Party was good at particular tactics but not a fully effective political entity. SNCC, its leadership suggested, was the senior partner in the SNNC–Black Panther Party alliance, the partner with the stronger overarching political view. In his February 17 speech, Carmichael implied that the Black Panther Party for Self-Defense was principally concerned with self-defense activities, or at least ought to be.

In the next issue of the *Black Panther,* the Party dropped "for Self-Defense" from its name and became simply the Black Panther Party.[49] While the rhetoric of the SNCC leaders roused as much enthusiasm from the crowd at Huey's birthday celebration rally as did the speeches by Panther leaders, the Panthers were the ones with a practical program. Several thousand people left the Oakland Auditorium that night with a shared commitment to help "Free Huey!"[50]

The Black Panther Party was now a key model for the new Black Power politics. According to the Panthers, black communities were colonies within the mother country. The oppressive imperial American state denied black people political and economic power, so blacks had no moral obligation to obey its laws. They had a moral obligation to resist. In particular, the Party politicized black people's conflicts with the police. The police were not officers of justice—they were pigs, foul traducers, and foreign troops oppressing black people. Those who challenged the police were not criminals—they were anti-imperialists. The "Free Huey!" campaign rejected the legitimacy of the police and demanded Huey's freedom irrespective of the details of the case. The Panthers turned the charges around and put America on trial.

Building upon foundations laid after Sacramento, the "Free Huey!" campaign drew strong support from SNCC and leading Black Power activists, on the one hand, and the Peace and Freedom Party and the broader Left, on the other. Then, in April, the living symbol of the insurgent Civil Rights Movement, who for many embodied that movement's continuing promise, was extinguished.

5

Martyrs

On Thursday, April 4, 1968, at 6:01 P.M., Martin Luther King Jr. stepped onto the balcony outside his second-floor room at the Lorraine Hotel in Memphis, Tennessee. King and his aides were in Memphis organizing support for a strike by thirteen hundred black sanitation workers. The effort was part of King's new emphasis on the alleviation of poverty and opposition to the Vietnam War. King's fame brought widespread attention to the sanitation workers' strike, and over the previous week, conflicts between police and black strike supporters had become violent.

King had returned to the hotel after a long day of organizing and was headed to dinner. He wore a black silk suit and white shirt. Jesse Jackson, one of King's associates standing in the courtyard below, introduced Ben Branch, a musician from Chicago who was scheduled to play at the rally that evening. King took hold of the green iron balcony railing and leaned over it to chat. "Do you know Ben?" Jackson asked. "Yes, that's my man!" King beamed. King asked Branch to play the gospel favorite "Precious Lord, Take My Hand," at the rally. A shot rang out, and the bullet tore through the base of the right side of King's neck. An hour later, at 7:05, doctors at St. Joseph's Hospital pronounced King dead.[1]

That evening, Black Memphis erupted with fires, broken windows, and sporadic attacks on police with bricks, bottles, and some gunfire. Over the next three weeks, violent rebellions swept the nation, igniting communities in more than 120 cities. Black neighborhoods in Washington, D.C., Baltimore, and Chicago were devastated. President Johnson deployed forty-four thousand soldiers and National Guardsmen to restore order. Police arrested twenty-one thousand, and forty-six people were killed.[2]

By the time of King's assassination, a wide rift had opened in the Black Liberation Struggle. On one side were moderate organizations such as the Urban League and the National Association for the Advancement of Colored People. As the movement successfully challenged legal segregation, these venerable groups offered vital legal and institutional support.[3] But in the civil rights insurgency that peaked in the early 1960s, these organizations played a supportive role, rather than leading the sit-ins, marches, and frontline civil disobedience. With formal segregation defeated by the late 1960s, leaders like Urban League director Whitney Young and NAACP director Roy Wilkins joined the establishment, seeking to consolidate the gains of formal racial equality. On the other side, young activists—frustrated by the lack of material progress, particularly in the urban areas outside the South—sought new, often more confrontational ways of advancing Black Power.

In the months before his death, King endeavored to bridge these divergent paths. More than any other individual, King was widely revered for his role in helping to destroy Jim Crow. With this stature, he could not easily be ignored nor repressed. Further, King and his organization—the Southern Christian Leadership Conference (SCLC)—had a strong base rooted in the black churches of the South and had worked closely with other organizations both in supporting and leading frontline civil disobedience. As the movement defeated Jim Crow and the challenge to legal segregation became moot, King increasingly championed the struggle against poverty and publicly opposed the war in Vietnam—gaining the cautious respect of the radical young activists. His leftward turn toward anti-imperialism increasingly incurred the wrath of the establishment.

Shortly before his death, King told reporters, "Our program calls for a redistribution of economic power." Blacks, he explained, must help lead the struggle "to reform the structure of racist imperialism from within."[4] An article in the *New York Times Magazine* right before his death explained that King had "come to believe that war and poverty are inseparable issues." King's "plans are calculated to disturb whatever peace of mind the President enjoys these days."[5] King was leading plans for an interracial march in the nation's capital that would mobilize thousands of poor people and their supporters to "re-establish that the real issue is not violence or nonviolence, but poverty and neglect."[6] King's persistent insurgency angered the Johnson administration, which trumpeted recent civil rights victories. Despite their history of working together, Dr. King and President Johnson had been "virtually out of touch since Dr. King began to condemn the Administration's policy in Vietnam two years ago," the *New York Times* explained in a front-page article published just days before King's assassination.[7]

An establishment chorus denounced King's Poor People's March as well as his increasingly vigorous opposition to the Vietnam War. Robert Byrd, the Democratic senator of West Virginia, called King a "self-seeking rabble rouser" and called for a restraining order to block the planned April demonstrations against poverty.[8] The day before King was killed, a federal court had issued a restraining order prohibiting him from holding a demonstration in Memphis. Angry and defiant, King called the order "illegal and unconstitutional," and refused to obey it.[9]

But when King died, the establishment quickly put aside its wrath and sought to claim him as a martyr for America. On the evening after King's assassination, President Johnson addressed the nation, asking "every citizen to reject the blind violence that has struck Dr. King, who lived by non-violence." The president emphasized King's nonviolent tactics and ignored the insurgent character of his leadership, appropriating the symbolism of King's death for America: "Martin Luther King stands with our other American martyrs in the cause of freedom and justice."[10]

The following day, on April 5, President Johnson attended a memorial for King at the Washington Cathedral. He entered the cathedral with an entourage that included Roy Wilkins; Whitney M. Young Jr.; Thurgood Marshall, the civil rights lawyer appointed by Johnson as the first black Supreme Court justice; Chief Justice Earl Warren, who crafted the landmark *Brown v. Board* civil rights decision; Robert Weaver, Johnson's secretary of housing and urban development and the first black member of a presidential cabinet; Vice President Hubert Humphrey; and Secretary of Defense Clark Clifford.[11] The message was clear: Johnson was signaling his administration's commitment to racial equality and its support of the civil rights establishment.

Johnson presented King as an "American martyr" sacrificed to the cause of formal racial equality embraced by the establishment and embodied in the Civil Rights Act of 1964 and the Voting Rights Act of 1965. Every avowed presidential candidate at the time, including former Republican Vice President Richard Nixon, Senators Robert Kennedy and Eugene McCarthy, and Vice President Humphrey, flew to Atlanta to attend Dr. King's funeral on April 9, as did fifty congressmen, thirty senators, and several state governors.[12] Young black activists at the funeral complained that the politicians were "vote-seeking" and crying "crocodile tears."[13]

With King gone, the SCLC no longer offered an effective conduit for the realization of black political aspirations. Without King's celebrity and credibility, SCLC had difficulty attracting participation in the Poor People's Campaign, and its protests drew less public attention and support from allies. SCLC initiated fewer and fewer insurgent protests and saw its membership and funding wither.[14] "People had confidence in him," explained SCLC leader Andrew Young in July 1968, but they "have not demonstrated a willingness to take us [the post-King leadership] seriously."[15]

The rift between the civil rights establishment and young urban blacks became harder to bridge. Stokely Carmichael, the preeminent voice of the young guard, held a press conference the day after King's assassination and declared, "I think white America made its biggest mistake when she killed Dr. King last night because when she killed Dr. King last night, she killed all reasonable hope. When she killed Dr. King last night she killed the one man of our race that this country's older generations, the militants and the revolutionaries, and the masses of black people would still listen to. Even though sometimes he did not agree with them, they would still listen to him."[16]

LIL' BOBBY HUTTON

On the evening of April 6, two days after King's death, at a little after 9:00 P.M., three carloads of armed Black Panthers pulled over to the curb on Union and 28th Streets in largely black west Oakland. Eldridge Cleaver was driving the lead car, an old white Ford with a Florida license plate that a member of the Peace and Freedom Party had donated to the Panthers. The entourage included David Hilliard, seventeen-year-old Lil' Bobby Hutton, and six other rank-and-file Panthers.[17] Cleaver opened the door and walked around to the passenger side of the Ford, reportedly to urinate. A moment later, several police cars pulled up and shined a spotlight on Cleaver. Words were exchanged, then gunfire. The Panthers ran for cover, the police quickly cordoned off a two-block area, and neighbors gathered in the streets. An hour and a half later,

Cleaver, having been shot in the foot and rear, his lungs burning from tear gas and firebomb smoke, emerged stark naked from a burning basement, surrendered, and was taken into custody. Lil' Bobby Hutton emerged from the basement unarmed. Police shot him dead.[18]

The following day, Bobby Seale held a press conference. Speaking quietly and carefully, he charged the police with racism, repression, and murder: "Bobby Hutton had his hands in the air, and was shot and murdered" by the Oakland police. Seale and Charles R. Garry, the Panthers' lawyer, called for the indictment of the policemen who had killed Bobby Hutton. Seale described the shoot-out as an ambush by police, and explained that the Panthers bore arms in self-defense. He noted, "A panther never attacks anyone, but when he is pushed into a corner . . . like the brothers were last night, he has one thing to do: to defend himself." The Black Panthers wanted peace, he explained, but peace could be obtained only through armed self-defense. "Our brother Martin Luther King exhausted all means of nonviolence."[19]

At the April 12 funeral for Hutton, two thousand people packed into the Ephesian Church of God in Christ in Berkeley, with a hundred uniformed Black Panthers forming the honor guard. The Reverend E. E. Cleveland called down "shame" on the powerful for failing to improve the lot of blacks. After the service, the Panthers held an outdoor rally and proclaimed that Bobby Hutton had been assassinated because of his Panther politics. Now Seale was angry. "There are pigs on tops of the library behind you. They are up there on other buildings. . . . They must know that every time these racist pigs attack us we are going to defend ourselves." Seale cried out, "Free Huey!" and the crowd answered: "Free Huey!"[20]

The Black Panther leadership charged that Hutton had posed a challenge to racism and that the police had killed him to repress this challenge. From prison, Cleaver wrote his account of the shoot-out, published in *Ramparts:*

> The Oakland Police Department MURDERED Little Bobby, and they cannot have that as a victory. . . . We must all swear by Little Bobby's blood that we will not rest until Chief Gains is brought to justice, either in the courts or in the streets; and until the bloodthirsty troops of the Oakland Police Department no longer exist in the role of an occupying army with its boots on the neck of the black community, with its guns aimed at the black community's head, an evil force with its sword of terror thrust into the heart of the black community. That's what Little Bobby would ask you to do, Brothers and Sisters, put an end to the terror—by any means necessary.[21]

Many notables joined the Panthers in praising Hutton's courage and contribution to the Black Liberation Struggle. Stokely Carmichael said, "Hutton understood that power comes out of the barrel of a gun." Betty Shabazz, the widow of Malcolm X, sent a telegram: "Shot down like a common animal, he died a warrior for black liberation." A group of professors from the University of California, the University of San Francisco, San Francisco State College, and San Jose State College called for an investigation of the Oakland Police Department by the U.S. Civil Service Commission.[22] Harry Edwards, professor of sociology at San Jose State and a prime mover behind the successful movement for black athletes to boycott the 1968 Olympics, said, "You can no longer ignore the Black Panthers" and announced his intention to join.[23] Marlon Brando attended Hutton's funeral and said, "That could have been my son lying there."[24] A letter to the editor of the *San Francisco Chronicle,* signed by a list of notables that included James Baldwin, Ossie Davis, Elizabeth Hardwick, LeRoi Jones, Oscar Lewis, Norman Mailer, Floyd McKissick, and Susan Sontag, compared the murder of Hutton to the murder of King: "Both were acts of racism against persons who had taken a militant stand on the right of black people to determine the conditions of their own lives. Both were attacks aimed at destroying this nation's black leadership."[25]

NEW DAY IN BABYLON

By 1968, the Civil Rights Movement had unraveled as the defeat of formal racial subordination eliminated targets for effective civil rights mobilization. But more than any other figure, King had embodied the promise of liberation through nonviolence and appeals to American morality. His persistence as he sought to broaden the civil rights struggle to address war and poverty kept hope alive. For many young activists, when King died, the promise of the civil rights struggle died with him.

De facto racial subordination of black people persisted. Many schools, neighborhoods, and professions remained segregated in practice. Many police departments, fire departments, and local governments in areas with large black populations remained exclusively or predominantly white. Many black people remained locked in poverty and in squalor. And in some holdout areas, such as "Bloody Lowndes" County, Alabama, protection of black residents' civil rights was seriously lacking well past the passage of the federal 1964 Civil Rights Act and the 1965 Voting Rights Act.

But by 1968, even in "Bloody Lowndes," the political dynamic had changed.[26] As the Civil Rights Movement dismantled Jim Crow through the mid-1960s, it ironically undercut its own viability as an insurgent movement. Whereas activists could sit in at lunch counters or sit black and white together on a bus or insist on registering to vote where they had traditionally been excluded, they were often uncertain how to nonviolently disrupt black unemployment, substandard housing, poor medical care, or police brutality. And when activists did succeed in disrupting these social processes nonviolently, they often found themselves facing very different enemies and lacking the broad allied support that civil rights activists had attained when challenging formal segregation. By 1968, the civil rights practice of nonviolent civil disobedience against racial exclusion had few obvious targets and could no longer generate massive and widespread participation.[27]

Civil rights as an ideal remained more important than ever. Black activists continued to emulate the nonviolent direct action of the Civil Rights Movement's heyday in their struggles for school busing, economic opportunity, and affirmative action. For decades to come, countless black activists would work tirelessly in the legal and political arenas to bring to fruition the seeds of racial equality planted by the Civil Rights Movement. And many others would emulate the Civil Rights Movement in pursuing their own environmental, identity, and social causes.

But black liberation activists who were committed to continued nonviolent insurgency had no coherent alternative politics for which to claim King. Because of his fame and stature, King had remained a threat to the establishment. Actions he participated in garnered wide attention and support that they could not have attracted without him. But King had yet to convert that fame and stature into a viable practical basis of a new insurgency. Thus, there was no viable new insurgent movement that could claim King as its martyr.

President Johnson and the American establishment sought to appropriate King as an American martyr: a powerful symbol for American democracy. Members of the establishment quickly forgot King's continued insurgency and his efforts to broaden the struggle. Instead, they sought to make King their own, trumpeting racial progress to burnish American democratic credentials. Lacking the practical means to sustain civil rights insurgency and eager to join the establishment, the moderate civil rights leadership quickly embraced this symbolism.

In this environment, Lil' Bobby Hutton became a very different kind of martyr from King. He was virtually unknown and ignored by the establishment. Hutton had died standing up to the brutal Oakland police; he died for black self-determination; he died defying American empire like Lumumba and Che and hundreds of thousands of Vietnamese had before him. Unlike King in 1968, Lil' Bobby Hutton represented a coherent insurgent alternative to political participation in the United States—armed self-defense against the police and commitment to the revolutionary politics of the Black Panther Party.

Eldridge Cleaver wrote, "If we understand ourselves to be revolutionaries, and if we accept our historic task, then we can move beyond the halting steps that we've been taking. . . . Then there will be a new day in Babylon."[28] So long as King persisted in his efforts to broaden civil rights insurgency, many young activists held on to the hope that he would succeed. But when King and Hutton were killed, a new day arrived. As the federal government inched toward establishing a national holiday in honor of Martin Luther King Jr., Hutton became the first martyr of the Panther revolution.

ECLIPSING SNCC

In the spring of 1968, the Black Panthers joined forces with the Student Nonviolent Coordinating Committee to begin discussions with Third World representatives in the United Nations in an effort to advance their program. The Panthers sought support for the "Free Huey!" campaign and for a proposed black plebiscite. The goal of the plebiscite, according to Eldridge Cleaver, was to give blacks in America the opportunity to vote "whether they want to be separated into a sovereign nation of their own, with full status and rights with the other nations of the world, including UN membership and diplomatic recognition by the other nations of the world." Malcolm X had earlier publicized this notion. James Forman, then jointly appointed the chairman of international affairs of SNCC and the minister of foreign affairs of the Black Panthers, conducted an informal poll of key U.N. representatives and found some support for the proposed plebiscite.[29]

Underlining the importance of the proposal, on May 4, the Black Panther Party expanded point ten of its Ten Point Program to read, "We want land, bread, housing, education, clothing, justice and peace, and as our major political objective, a united nations supervised plebiscite to be held throughout the black colony in which only black colonial subjects will be allowed to participate, for the purpose of determining the will of black people as to their national destiny."[30]

The Panthers and SNCC developed plans for a high-profile joint delegation to the United Nations in July. But by the time of the trip, tensions were building within SNCC, and the organization was struggling to redefine itself in the post–civil rights era. Stokely Carmichael and James Forman wrestled for control, advancing different visions of SNCC's role within the Black Power movement and of its relationship with the Panthers.[31]

Forman and Carmichael both traveled to Oakland for the "Free Huey!" rally at the start of Newton's trial on July 15.[32] Then, on July 19, both Forman and Carmichael traveled to New York for a Panther press conference at the United Nations and a series of community rallies in Harlem, Brooklyn, and Newark to support the plebiscite. There, they met up with a Panther contingent that included Chairman Bobby Seale, Minister of Information Eldridge Cleaver, Chief of Staff David Hilliard, Father Earl Neil, Minister of Education George Murray, and Field Marshall Donald Cox. Fliers were printed, and a flurry of meetings were called to advance the U.N. campaign. A Panther press statement said that in addition to support for the "Free Huey!" campaign and the black plebiscite, the Panthers were calling upon "the member nations of the United Nations to authorize the stationing of UN Observer Teams throughout the cities of America wherein black people are cooped up and concentrated in wretched ghettos." After meeting with several U.N. delegations and talking with the press, the Black Panthers filed for status as an official "nongoverning organization" of the United Nations.[33] While the notion of the black plebiscite was intriguing to many, it failed to gain traction.

Underneath the united activity, SNCC was fragmenting. The evidence suggests that the Black Panthers sided with Carmichael against Forman. On Wednesday July 24, a delegation of Carmichael supporters and Panthers confronted Forman at his office on Fifth Avenue in New York City. The press reported allegations that a Black Panther stuck an unloaded pistol into Forman's mouth and squeezed the trigger three times, but Forman denied the story.[34] Nonetheless, shortly after the July trip to New York, SNCC sided with Forman, passing a resolution terminating Stokely Carmichael's position, and officially cutting off their relationship with the Panthers. The SNCC resolution claimed that Carmichael had engaged "in a power struggle both within and outside of S.N.C.C. with another organization member (Forman) which . . . threatened the existence" of SNCC.[35]

With Jim Crow vanquished and SNCC struggling to transition out of the South and remain politically relevant, the Black Panther Party captured the imagination of the younger generation of black activists. Legendary SNCC founder Ella Baker, speaking in 1968, explained SNCC's predicament: "S.N.C.C. came North when the North was in a ferment that led to various interpretations of what needed to be done. With its own frustrations, it could not take the pacesetter role it took in the South. They were unable to sense that the milieu and factors of change were more than they had dealt with before. And the frustration that came to individuals that had gone through the Southern experience rendered them unable to make a historical decision that perhaps their days were over."[36] The *New York Times* noted the Panthers' eclipse of SNCC: "The Student Nonviolent Coordinating Committee, which emerged from the rural South eight years ago to become a pacesetter in the national Civil Rights movement, is in serious decline. It has lost much of its power and influence to the northern slum-born Black Panthers."[37]

ALLIES

On May 14, Kathleen Cleaver announced Eldridge's candidacy for the Peace and Freedom Party nomination for president. Eldridge was temporarily in Vacaville Prison on a parole violation stemming from the confrontation with police in which Bobby Hutton had been killed. The conflict increased Cleaver's notoriety, and the *Black Panther* carried a full-page promotion of his candidacy for president, along with a full-page spread on Kathleen Cleaver's campaign for the California State Assembly. The Panthers saw both campaigns as opportunities to build influence and broaden their support within the Left. Kathleen's candidacy directly challenged Willie Brown, the popular incumbent black California state assemblyman who had refused to support the Panthers. Eldridge Cleaver's run for president represented disaffection with both the Democratic and Republican Parties and was, in the words of the *New York Times,* an effort "to use the traditional election process to win an audience and to organize for the radical movement." As Eldridge explained in a "black paper" presented at a Peace and Freedom Party convention, the Panthers sought to "focus attention . . . on a revolutionary leader with a revolutionary program within the conventional political context. . . . In practical terms, this kind of campaign becomes another tool for political organization for black power. . . . We want to pull people out of the Democratic Party, out of the Republican Party, and swell the ranks of the Black Panther Party and the Peace and Freedom Party."[38]

After building an alliance with Latinos within the Peace and Freedom Party and after a series of state primaries and much wrangling, Eldridge Cleaver emerged as the clear favorite. On August 18, he formally secured the nomination of the national Peace and Freedom Party convention as its candidate for president of the United States with 161.5 delegate votes, outshining the 54 votes for the runner-up, civil rights activist and comedian Dick Gregory.[39]

On August 25, the Panthers held a rally at De Fremery Park in west Oakland that they ceremoniously renamed Bobby Hutton Memorial Park in honor of the martyred Panther youth. The rally attracted a cross-section of Panther supporters, bringing them together to strengthen their anti-imperialist identity, binding them across race and social position to forge a revolutionary rejection of American empire.[40]

The crowd gathered in the hot sun and under the cool shade of the park's oaks to listen to the speakers and show their support for Huey Newton. Although Hutton Park lies in the heart of Black west Oakland, more than half the people who turned out that day were whites, Latinos, and Asian Americans. The crowd was a rich tapestry of the times and vividly represented the diverse allies that increasingly supported the Black Panther Party. Hundreds sat on the grass, mostly young nonblack activists. Some were older and more professional looking, such as the woman in her fifties with a striped blouse and permed blonde hair sitting behind two young activists, one wearing a leather vest and the other without a shirt. Hundreds more, mostly black, stood stretched out across the park, under the trees, near the neighboring houses, squeezing into view of the stage. There were well over a thousand people in all. A heavyset man in his thirties—almost twice the age of many Panthers—with short cropped hair and wearing a checkered button-down shirt leaned back with arms crossed and chewed on a cigarette butt as he listened to the speakers. Another black man, tall and muscular with a goatee and Italian felt hat, stood nearby, crossed his arms, and listened. A woman in her early twenties wearing a paisley print dress and head wrap and sandals and adorned with gold bracelets and hoop earrings held her fingers to her lips and tilted her head pensively. A heavyset grandmother with a print dress and Malcolm X glasses held up her homemade "Free Huey" banner with both hands, and her grandchildren stood nearby with homemade "Free Huey" headbands, complete with flower ornaments. Dozens of photographers weaved through the crowd snapping photos. Uniformed Panthers stood at attention along the periphery for the crowd to see. Another Panther strode pointedly through the crowd, talking logistics into a boxy walkie-talkie with an antenna the size of a fishing rod. Police were scattered along the park's edges, with helicopters circling above them for backup.

At the front of the park sat the Peace and Freedom Party bus, its roof sporting a stage platform and sound system. The bus featured a large "Free Huey!" sign with dozens of bumper stickers supporting Cleaver's presidential campaign as the Peace and Freedom candidate. A Black Panther security squad of two dozen young men lined up in front of the bus facing the crowd. They wore white T-shirts emblazoned with the Panther logo and "Black Panther Party" in bold print, each wearing black pants and a black beret cocked to the right. Bobby Seale spoke, then Stokely Carmichael, and next Kathleen Cleaver. Allies Reies Tijerina—the Chicano insurgent leader—Richard Aoki, and Bob Avakian took turns speaking.

Someone cleared the mike and all eyes turned for the main event, the speech by Eldridge, the newly anointed national candidate for president on the Peace and Freedom Party ticket. Cleaver exhorted the multiracial audience to "Free Huey!" He reminded his listeners of their collective identity—their shared rejection of American power—and of the importance of their struggle: "I would love to sit around on my ass drinking wine, smoking pot and making love to my wife, but I can't afford to be doing that while all these pigs are loose. . . . Here I am, a convict. A whole lot of respectable people have nominated me for President. I'm not going to get elected . . . I'm a symbol of dissent, of rejection. Every page of American history is written in human blood, and we can't endorse it. We cannot endorse it. Close it! Close the motherfucker and put it on the shelf."[41]

Origins of the New Left

The multiracial New Left would prove a crucial ally of the Black Panther Party. Even before the founding of the Black Panther Party, Black Power helped to spark draft resistance and the development of the New Left. The New Left's own self-understanding evolved in relation to Black Liberation Struggle. In the wake of the Civil Rights Movement, the New Left imagined itself a revolutionary partner in Black Liberation. Stepping back and tracing the development of the New Left is key to understanding why it would so ardently embrace the Black Panther Party.

Students for a Democratic Society, the main New Left organization, grew in part out of student involvement in the Civil Rights Movement of the early 1960s. It had a young, privileged, and predominantly white constituency. It was not anti-imperialist in the beginning. In the early 1960s, SDS spurned active draft resistance. As late as mid-1965, it had only three thousand nominal members nationally and little influence. The major growth of the New Left came with draft resistance between 1966 and 1968.[42] This draft resistance built upon SDS's embrace of revolutionary anti-imperialism and the Black Liberation Struggle.

Contrary to popular thought, draft resistance was not simply a response to high rates of military induction. The U.S. government conducted a military draft continuously from the time before the nation's entrance into World War II until the draft ended in 1973. Throughout this period, there was little opposition to the draft until widespread resistance began in 1967. In fact, almost ten times as many young men were drafted annually during the height of World War II—with a peak of more than 3.3 million draftees in 1943—than during the Vietnam War. Yet there was relatively little resistance to the draft. Similarly, draft resistance was negligible during the Korean War despite the fact that almost twice as many young men were drafted per year as during the Vietnam War—peaking at 551,806 in 1951. When wide draft resistance first erupted in 1967, annual inductions were only 228,263.[43]

Through the first half of the twentieth century, open draft resistance was not a viable political option. When a war effort was widely considered legitimate, heavy repression could be leveraged against those who refused to fight for their country. During World War I, conscientious objectors were beaten, tortured, locked in solitary confinement, and some were sentenced to death, though never executed. During World War II, some conscientious objectors were used for live human medical testing, such as experiments subjecting them to repeated lice bites.[44]

As the Johnson administration began to escalate the Vietnam War in 1965, most Americans still saw draft resistance as cowardly or even traitorous. A national poll that year found that 63 percent of Americans favored the draft and only 13 percent opposed it. Early acts of resistance were sometimes met with public violence. On March 31,

1966, 11 clean-cut white pacifists protested the draft in front of the district courthouse in South Boston. As the protest was announced on the radio, antagonistic counterdemonstrators began to arrive. This shouting crowd of around 250 soon surrounded the pacifists, calling them "cowards." When four pacifists took out their draft cards and lit them on fire, the hostility exploded, with members of the mob shouting "Shoot them!" and "Kill them!" and then knocking the demonstrators to the ground and beating them.[45]

Although popular imagery portrays draft resisters as mostly white, black SNCC activists were among the first to mobilize resistance to the draft during the Vietnam War. SNCC activists almost universally opposed the war, and they had good reason.[46] In 1966, the Pentagon admitted that "proportionately more Negroes have been killed in Vietnam ground combat than other Americans."[47] SNCC activists asked why black Americans should serve a country and a government that disrespected and mistreated them because they were black. A sense of betrayal by the federal government also fostered black anti-imperialism and draft resistance, especially among black movement leaders.[48]

With the emergence of "Black Power," SNCC activists had intensified their opposition to the war, inventing the slogan "Hell no, we won't go!" SNCC launched daily demonstrations at the Atlanta induction center. Twelve blacks were arrested. By the fall of 1966, as white students began cautiously signing symbolic "We Won't Go" statements, induction refusals by blacks were already widespread.[49]

Feeling politically isolated for his embrace of draft resistance, Stokely Carmichael, SNCC's chairman, approached SDS for support.[50] In July 1966, at Carmichael's behest, SDS and SNCC published a joint statement to the House Committee on the Armed Services cosigned by Carmichael and Carl Oglesby, president of SDS. The statement marked a crucial step in the antiwar movement. It asserted the three part anti-imperialist analogy that would later be adopted and spread by the Black Panther Party. Carmichael and Oglesby argued that blacks, Vietnamese, and draftees shared a common oppressor, and asserted a powerful moral justification for resisting the draft: "In a supposedly 'free society' conscription is a form of legalized enslavement of the worst kind: a slave had to serve his master's economic interest with labor and sweat; but a draftee must serve the 'national interest' with murder and his own blood. Black men in the United States are forced to kill their colored brothers in Vietnam for $95 a month and the risk of death, injury and disease; this is why we oppose the draft."[51]

Despite signing on to the joint statement, SDS had not yet fully embraced its implications and was still reluctant to organize draft resistance. Some smaller antiwar organizations such as End the Draft were trying to enlist SDS in draft resistance, but many SDSers were afraid of the repression likely to come with a serious challenge to the draft.[52]

This changed in October 1966 when SDS organized the Black Power conference in Berkeley—the same conference that encouraged Newton and Seale to found their party—and invited Stokely Carmichael as the keynote speaker. Carmichael focused most of his speech on the question of Vietnam. "The war in Vietnam is an illegal and immoral war," he said. He compared the plight of black people in America to the plight of the Vietnamese. He argued that in order to be relevant to most people, SDS needed to start organizing draft resistance: "The peace movement has been a failure because it hasn't gotten off the college campuses where everybody has a 2S and is not afraid of being drafted anyway."[53]

In the months preceding the conference, while antiwar organizing was prevalent, there was little discussion of the draft on the UC Berkeley campus.[54] The Black Power conference, however, dramatically changed the focus of the campus antiwar movement. The day after Carmichael's speech, the campus chapter of SDS, the organizers of the conference, formed an antidraft committee and distributed a flier inviting the public to a workshop that evening: "One of the purposes of the Black Power Conference has been to stimulate new ideas and discussions as to where the Movement at Berkeley will go from here. Black Power offers a challenge to white radicals to organize themselves . . . STOP THE WAR! STOP THE DRAFT! . . . If you want to discuss possibilities of Direct Action to help stop the war and benefit yourself, come to the workshops."[55] Other antidraft activities on campus followed. A week later, the campus Community for a New Politics organized a workshop called You and the Draft. An organization called Resistance launched on campus and explained its position: "Today Vietnamese men, women and children will die. They will die at the end of an American soldier's bayonet, they will burn to death from the napalm dropped from American planes. These executions are performed daily by ordinary American guys, most of whom are not in Vietnam by choice. They were drafted. Our government ordered them there." Within months, there was a deluge of meetings, organizations, conferences, and protests on campuses across the country, all focused on the draft.[56]

Less than two months after the Black Power conference, as the Panthers organized their first patrols in Oakland, SDS formally embraced draft resistance at its National Council meeting at Berkeley.[57] An accompanying report published by SDS in January 1967 compared anti-draft resistance to "the revolt of slaves against their masters" and said that SDS was moving into a new phase, from "protest to resistance."[58]

The new approach to draft resistance was compelling because of its universality. The black anti-imperialism championed by SNCC compared the plight of blacks in the United States with the plight of the Vietnamese and others throughout the world who were waging struggles against colonialism and imperialism. At SNCC's invitation, student antiwar activists came to see themselves as fighting for their own liberation from the American empire. The imperial machinery of war that was inflicting havoc abroad was forcing America's young to kill and die for a cause many did not believe in. Young activists came to see the draft as an imposition of empire on themselves just as the war was an imposition of empire on the Vietnamese.[59]

SDS leader Greg Calvert encapsulated this emerging view in the idea of "revolutionary consciousness" in a widely influential speech at Princeton University that February. Arguing that students themselves were revolutionary subjects, Calvert sought to distinguish radicals from liberals, and he advanced "revolutionary consciousness" as the basis for a distinct and superior morality: "Radical or revolutionary consciousness . . . is the perception of *oneself* as unfree, as oppressed— and finally it is the discovery of oneself as *one of the oppressed* who must unite to transform the objective conditions of their existence in order to resolve the contradiction between potentiality and actuality. Revolutionary consciousness leads to *the struggle for one's own freedom in unity with others who share the burden of oppression.*"[60]

The speech marked a watershed in the New Left's self-conception.[61] Coming to see itself as part of the global struggle of the Vietnamese against American imperialism and the black struggle against racist oppression, the New Left rejected the status quo as fundamentally immoral and embraced the morality of revolutionary challenge. From this vantage point, the Vietnam War was illegitimate, and draft resistance was an act of revolutionary heroism.

As this radicalized draft resistance came to life, it had an explosive impact on an antiwar movement that had been weak and disoriented. In the first few months of 1967, a flurry of "We Won't Go" statements, antidraft unions, and pickets at induction centers took place throughout the country, many instigated by SDS, but some arising independently.[62]

A quarter million people turned out on April 15, 1967, for the Spring Mobilizations against the War in New York and San Francisco—the largest antiwar protest to date in American history. Speakers in New York included Martin Luther King Jr., James Bevel of the SCLC, Floyd McKissick of the Congress of Racial Equality, singer and civil rights activist Harry Belafonte, and Stokely Carmichael. As Carmichael spoke, members of the crowd shouted out "Black Power!" He called the war "brutal and racist" and demanded an end to the draft. Many marchers took up the chant started by SNCC: "Hell No, We Won't Go!" Some protestors displayed flags of the National Liberation Front of Vietnam, asserting that they were not only appealing for America to have a better policy but also allying themselves with the Vietnamese revolution.[63] In San Francisco, a contingent of black nationalists led the march carrying a streamer that read "The Vietnam N.L.F. Never Called Us Niggers." Keynote speaker Coretta Scott King, Martin Luther King's wife, told the audience that "freedom and justice in America are bound together with freedom and justice in Vietnam." Future Panther minister of information Eldridge Cleaver, at that time a representative of the Organization of African Unity, added, "We are against this racist, vicious power structure."[64]

Because of the high stakes—potentially five years in prison—and the lack of wider support, very few had seriously considered public burning of draft cards as a viable tactic. But in unprecedented defiance of U.S. legitimacy, over 150 people burned their draft cards during the rally in Central Park that day.[65]

Two weeks later, Muhammad Ali, the heavyweight boxing champion of the world, refused induction, arousing further acts of draft resistance. Due in no small part to the influence of Malcolm X, early black resistance to the draft was widespread, not limited to SNCC. Muhammad Ali was a member of the Nation of Islam, recruited by Malcolm X in 1963. As heavyweight champion, he soon became a symbol of Black Power. Every time he stepped into the ring, much more than the title was at stake.[66] In early 1966, as the demand for troops in Vietnam increased, the Selective Service System expanded its pool for draft eligibility, and Ali was reclassified as I-A—ready and eligible.[67] In February 1966—months before SDS's first tentative support of SNCC's antidraft stance—Ali told the press, "I'm a member of the Black Muslims and we don't go to wars unless they are declared by Allah himself. I don't have no personal quarrel with those Vietcong."[68]

Ali's statement posed a clear challenge to the legitimacy of the war effort, and many politicians were quick to condemn him. Pennsylvania congressman Frank Clark called Ali "a complete and total disgrace to the land."[69] When Ali, then still using his original name, Cassius Clay, refused to apologize for his remarks, Governor Kerner of Illinois, Mayor Daley of Chicago, and other political figures sought to cancel his scheduled championship fight in Chicago.[70] Closed-circuit telecasts of his fights were banned in Boston, Miami Beach, and elsewhere.[71] The government confiscated his passport.[72]

On April 28, 1967, the day Ali was to be inducted into the army and two weeks after the card burning in Central Park, young black protestors including H. Rap Brown flocked to the induction center in Houston. When Ali's name was called, he refused to step forward. "Why should they ask me and other so-called Negroes to put on a uniform and go 10,000 miles from home," Ali explained to the press, "and drop bombs on brown people in Viet Nam while so-called Negro people in Louisville are treated like dogs and denied simple human rights?"[73] Ali was sentenced to a maximum penalty of five years in jail and a $10,000 fine for refusing induction.[74]

Ali's actions, on the heels of the Central Park card burning, suggested that widespread draft resistance was possible. Many in government and the press worried that if the resistance grew large enough, the war effort might be compromised. The influential *New York Times* columnist Tom Wicker explained,

> The issue raised by the remarkable Ali remains, because he has made it quite clear that whether or not the courts finally rule in his favor, whether or not the Government, in both its administrative and judicial processes, has given his claims due and fair hearing—whether or not, in short, his position is *legally* justified, he will simply refuse to serve in the armed forces. . . . What would happen if all young men of draft age took the same position? . . . If the Johnson Administration had to prosecute 100,000 Americans in order to maintain its authority, its real power to pursue the Vietnamese war or any other policy would be crippled if not destroyed. It would then be faced not with dissent, but with civil disobedience on a scale amounting to revolt.[75]

Preparations were under way for massive antiwar protests in Washington, D.C., and Oakland in October 1967. Smaller actions were planned for the same time in Los Angeles, Portland, Denver, Kansas City, St. Louis, Chicago, Des Moines, Cedar Rapids, St. Paul, Boston, New York, Philadelphia, Ann Arbor, Yellow Springs, Champaign-Urbana, Bloomington, Puerto Rico, and London.[76] Following the ghetto rebellions in July, the National Mobilization Committee to End the War in Vietnam (MOBE), a national coalition of peace organizations, announced at a press conference that it supported the urban uprisings and said that the actions planned for October would "obstruct the war machine." MOBE proclaimed there was "only one struggle—for self-determination—and we support it in Vietnam and in black America."[77]

A new spirit had swept the antiwar movement. That October, draft card burnings increased almost tenfold.[78] Activist scholars Paul Lauter and Florence Howe described the spontaneous outbreak of a draft card burning at the Pentagon:

> Suddenly as the daylight died two or three tiny flames burst from different places in the crowd. There was only red in the west, and the earth was black, when dozens of draft cards began to burn, held aloft, amid increasing cheers and applause. One by one, the lights flickered, burned, then went out. The burnings traveled to the other side of the Mall, beyond the soldiers that split our large group from a small one on the right, and eventually down to the grassy plains below. The sight silenced even the cheering.[79]

Thousands of draft resisters stormed the Pentagon. Military police and U.S. marshals beat the demonstrators and released tear gas, reoccupying the grounds yard by yard. Among the protestors, 647 were arrested and 47 hospitalized.[80] A line had been crossed. No longer were the students and antiwar activists simply Americans expressing their view within established channels. Now, inspired by Black Power and emboldened by the ghetto rebellions, many antiwar activists declared themselves revolutionaries, seeking self-determination through resistance.

New Left: Free Huey

While Black Power was a key influence on the emerging draft resistance movement, the Black Panther Party remained relatively insignificant politically until April 1968. Few in the New Left outside the Bay Area had done anything to support the Panthers. SDS, by far the largest and most influential New Left organization—with thirty-five thousand members at three hundred colleges and universities—had no relationship to or position on the Panthers.[81] The organization's *New Left Notes,* the largest New Left newsletter, had not carried a single story on the Black Panther Party.[82]

This situation changed with the assassinations of King and Hutton. For many young activists opposed to the Vietnam War, King had embodied the hope that America had a moral conscience and that justice would prevail through peaceful means. His assassination dashed their hopes. Following the slayings of King and Hutton, hundreds of thousands of students joined SDS-led actions on campuses from coast to coast, often in coalition with black student organizations. In Boston, twenty thousand students marched on city hall demanding that the police and National Guard "be kept out of the ghetto." At Michigan State University in East Lansing, students took over the administration building and held a sit-in, demanding the addition of black history courses, equal hiring practices, and sanctions against companies that discriminated against blacks. The response to King's death fueled SDS's planned "Ten Days of Resistance" to protest the war, and at least fifty colleges and almost a million students participated in a nationwide "student strike" on April 26.[83]

After the April killings, the New Left increasingly looked to the Black Panthers for leadership. Already embracing anti-imperialism by the time of King's assassination, SDS now made support for the Black Panther Party one of its key causes. On April 12, 1968, SDS affirmed its support for the Black Panther Party:

> Students for a Democratic Society . . . demands the immediate release of Eldridge Cleaver, Huey P. Newton, and all other political prisoners being detained by the state of California. The racist cops of Oakland, who have long oppressed and denied basic human rights to black people, are the real criminals loose on the streets of our country. They are the ones, along with the slumlords and politicians in the white power structure, who should be imprisoned, not Eldridge Cleaver, Huey Newton, or any other black man fighting for self-determination and freedom.[84]

On April 15, the cover of *New Left Notes* featured a photo of Bobby Hutton and a long article on the Panthers under the headline "Oakland Police Attack Panthers." The article detailed the police slaying of Hutton and examined the repressive actions against the Panthers over the preceding months.[85] The issue also ran a full reproduction of the Panther Ten Point Program and implored SDS members to combat repression of the Black Panthers. The "systematic political persecution of the Black Panther Party MUST BE RESISTED. Distribute information about the Panthers and raise money for their work and defense. Funds should be sent to our brothers."[86] In July, the SDS convention passed a major resolution in support of the Black Panthers asserting that "Huey must be set free!" They pledged to "give full support, in whatever manner is needed," both to free Huey and to support the Panthers generally.[87]

Monday July 15 marked the opening day of Huey Newton's trial on charges of murdering a police officer. The Panthers argued that Newton, not Officer Frey, was the one who had been attacked and that the trial was yet another act of political repression. They brought their case to the court of public opinion, organizing a rally in front of the imposing granite Alameda County courthouse in Oakland that morning.[88]

Numerous New Left organizations participated in the mobilization, including the Western Mobilization against the War, the Brown Berets, the Peace and Freedom Party, and the Iranian Students Association. By 10:00 A.M., over twenty-five hundred supporters had gathered, surrounding the courthouse, filling the courthouse plaza, and spilling into the street. Members of the Oakland Sheriff's Department, wearing helmets covering their faces and armed with billy clubs and guns, guarded every doorway to the courthouse. Reporters came from across the country and as far away as London to cover the event.[89]

At the top of the courthouse steps, 250 members of the Black Panther Party lined up, the women standing on the top tier. The women wore simple dark-colored knee-length dresses with belts, their hair in naturals. The men, standing in three files below, wore the Panther uniform of black leather jackets, light turtleneck sweaters, and black berets cocked to the right. An assigned section leader began a chant, and soon the Panthers were rocking, clapping, and singing in unison:

(Women) No more brothers in ja-il,
(Men)   Off the pigs!
(Women) The pigs are going to catch he-ll,
(Men)   Off the pigs!
(Women) No more brothers in ja-il,
(Men)   Off the pigs!
(Women) The pigs are going to catch he-ll,
(Men)   Off the pigs!

Members of the Asian American Political Alliance carried signs with Chinese lettering reading "Chairman MAO says: FREE HUEY" and "Yellow Peril supports Black Power."[90] A large flagpole stood in the middle of the courthouse plaza, and someone in the crowd shouted, "Cut the rope! Take the fuckin' flag down!" After a brief debate among the Panther supporters, Bob Avakian cut the rope on the flagpole, sending the American flag to the ground. Several demonstrators grabbed the flag and lit it on fire. A phalanx of police wearing riot helmets and thrusting nightsticks quickly beat a path through the crowd to the flagpole. The pitch of the chant intensified as uniformed Panthers pushed toward the police:

(Women) No more pigs in our community,
(Men)   Off the pigs!

Bobby Seale told the crowd that if Huey "is going to be tried at all, he's got to be tried by his peers—not the Negro maids working up on the hill but his peers, people on probation, people they've been running through their jails. . . . Huey ain't on trial, the black people are on trial here." Seale argued that this was not the time or place to fight the police. But, he warned, "If anything happens to Huey P. Newton, the sky's the limit." The Panthers then began a circular march around the courthouse, fists pumping a Black Power salute in time with the chant:

Black is beautiful,
Free Huey!
Set our leader free,
Free Huey!

SDS fully embraced the "Free Huey!" campaign, emphasizing the centrality of the Panthers to the New Left and suggesting that mobilization to resist repression of the Panthers was necessary to achieve its own political goals. In coverage of the Free Huey rally in Oakland, SDS declared, "The real question for the Panthers and the whole radical movement in this country remains: Can Huey be set free?"[91]

Cleaver at Berkeley

By the fall of 1968, the Panthers became such a potent symbol of revolution that simply asking them to speak was often considered a highly disruptive act. Such was the reaction when several undergraduate students at the University of California, Berkeley, organized an experimental course on racism in America called Social Analysis 139X, Dehumanization and Regeneration of the American Social Order. At the time, few black studies courses were available on campus, and the students sought to challenge dominant perspectives on race. They convinced several professors to facilitate the course, including sociologist Troy Duster and psychologist Edward Sampson, and they invited Eldridge Cleaver to deliver ten guest lectures.[92]

The reaction of establishment political leaders was immediate and extreme. Within twenty-four hours of the public announcement of the class, California governor Ronald Reagan demanded that the University of California Board of Regents promptly uninvite Cleaver and blasted the university administration, declaring, "In one single act, the Berkeley administrators would undo years of academic commitment and dedication to the highest values of the teaching profession." Max Rafferty, the conservative state superintendent of public instruction, and Jesse Unruh, Democratic leader of the State Assembly, also jumped on board to condemn the university administration. The State Senate and Assembly both voted to censure the university.[93]

While Cleaver could not be easily ignored, neither could he be easily repressed. Only a small percentage of Californians actively ascribed to the Black Panthers' revolutionary anti-imperialist politics, but elements of the Party's position had broad appeal. Most blacks wanted a serious treatment of black history and greater black student enrollment. The university seemed unlikely to provide either without a struggle. For those opposed to the war, in late 1968, neither the Democratic nor Republican Party appeared to be listening to them. For faculty across the state and the country, the issue of intellectual freedom loomed large: would politicians be allowed to silence controversial and provocative viewpoints and interfere in university curricula? For these reasons, suppressing Cleaver proved to be widely unacceptable, even to many who believed the Panthers' revolutionary program was extreme. The op-ed pages in California newspapers were filled with conflicting opinions on the "necessary" or "disturbing" character of Cleaver's planned lectures.[94]

As Cleaver traveled from campus to campus in late September and early October, he stirred up the controversy, assailing "Mickey Mouse Ronald Reagan" and the others in front of packed meetings overflowing with cheering student activists. Burnishing his hypermasculine image, a jocular Cleaver contended, "It is my belief that Ronald Reagan is a punk, a sissy, and a coward, and I challenge him to a duel. I challenge the punk to a duel to the death and he can choose his own weapon: it could be a baseball bat, a gun, a knife, or a marshmallow. I'll beat him to death with a marshmallow."[95]

When the UC Board of Regents passed a resolution in late September to restrict Cleaver to one lecture, opposition exploded. Important segments of the black political establishment, believing that the edict undermined black educational interests, challenged the regents. The California Negro Leadership Conference described the censorship of Cleaver as racist and warned that if Cleaver was not allowed to lecture, it would ask black legislators to deny support to the university and seek to have federal funding withheld under the Civil Rights Act. Dr. Carleton Goodlett, publisher of the San Francisco based black newspaper the *Sun Reporter,* said he would launch a campaign "in which the black middle class will disassociate themselves from all UC programs."[96]

More than two thousand students turned out for an organizing meeting at UC Berkeley and voted unanimously to demand that Cleaver be allowed to give all ten lectures. The Student Senate voted overwhelmingly to demand that the regents rescind their decision and to ask the faculty Academic Senate to reject it. The student senates at three other University of California campuses, the National Student Association, and seven university student body presidents all announced their support for the lecture series. Student demonstrators at UC Santa Cruz heckled Reagan and disrupted a Board of Regents meeting there, protesting the Cleaver policy and demanding creation of "a college dedicated to the black experience." Students at Berkeley occupied the College of Letters and Science headquarters and the chancellor's office and lit a protest bonfire on the campus's Sproul Plaza.[97]

Faculty members were also agitated. Responding to faculty outcry about political interference in the curriculum, the president of the University of California announced, "The faculty still has authority over courses. It has not been affected in any way." The UC Berkeley faculty Academic Senate in turn voted to repudiate the Board of Regents' censure by 668 to 114. Faculty senates at both the Los Angeles and San Diego campuses of the University of California voted similarly in support of UC Berkeley's faculty. Cleaver would be allowed to hold all ten lectures, although students would not receive credit for attending. One thousand students signed up for the hundred-seat class. When the victorious Cleaver finally lectured, he adopted a serious tone, avoiding obscenities, not once alluding to the controversy, and confining his comments to an analysis of his topic, "The Roots of Racism."[98]

Even as the political establishment appropriated Martin Luther King Jr. as a martyr for America, Black Panther Lil' Bobby Hutton confronted the police and became a martyr for revolution. Tens of thousands of allies mobilized in support of Newton, Hutton, Cleaver, and their Party. But the true litmus of the Panthers' politics would be the response of young blacks throughout the country.

6

National Uprising

The turning point in Ericka Huggins's life came a week after King's death, at the funeral of Lil' Bobby Hutton in Oakland on April 12, 1968. This was the moment when she committed her life to the revolution and the Black Panther Party. Huggins later recalled,

> What awakened me, what changed my life and my mind . . . was Bobby Hutton's face at his funeral. . . . My entire life and mind was changed from that point on. . . . I had read about the Party and I had read about all the things in history that had been done to black people—lynching, murder, tortures, etc.—but I was convinced when I had direct confrontation with the brutality, the cruelty, and the doggishness of the police. His face had been entirely shot out. The entire portion of his face was gone and had been puttied into place and made up. He was no longer the seventeen year old person he had been, not physically or anything else. He wasn't. And the police were in the balconies of that church. They were everywhere. I had never seen anything like that in my life. I mean I had never been directly involved.[1]

Born in 1948 to a working-class family in Washington, D.C., Huggins had one younger sister and a younger brother. Among the children, she was the pensive, reclusive, existential one. After high school, she went to historically black Cheyney State College in Pennsylvania with dreams of becoming a teacher and working with disabled children. But Cheyney offered no challenges, educational, political, or otherwise. Huggins found both the curriculum and the student life lacking, and in 1966, she transferred to Lincoln University, another historically black institution in Pennsylvania. At Lincoln, her world began to open up. Here she was turned on to the ideas of Malcolm X and joined the black student organization, where she met John Huggins in early 1967. John had been raised in a well-heeled black family in New Haven, Connecticut. He had served in the navy and was a Vietnam veteran. John was sensitive and had shaggy hair. The two quickly fell in love and soon married.

Ericka and John immersed themselves in black student activities, but something was missing. More and more, they felt removed from the real problems faced by most black people. As the black urban rebellions spread, they felt like "armchair revolutionaries"—committed to the idea of Black Liberation Struggle yet distant from it. Consequently, they dropped out of school and in November 1967 moved to Los Angeles, a hotbed of black politics, looking to get involved. In April 1968, at the funeral of Lil' Bobby Hutton, Ericka and John committed their lives to the revolution.

LOS ANGELES

One of the first people Ericka Huggins recruited to join the Black Panther Party was an articulate and striking young woman named Elaine Brown.[2] Raised poor in a Philadelphia row house in a Jewish neighborhood, Brown was the only child in a household of adults—her single mother, her aunt, and her grandmother and grandfather. After high school, she enrolled in Temple University but soon dropped out, joined the working world, and moved to Los Angeles. Through intelligence, hard work, wit, and a series of affluent white lovers, Brown made her way into a world of glamour and wealth, but she could never escape racism. She reached a personal turning point in 1967, when, as the guest of the owner of a luxurious hotel in Las Vegas, she was denied service at a nearby beauty shop because of her race. The hotel owner disciplined the beauty shop manager, but the incident showed that she could not escape her blackness. She soon started making friends with Los Angeles black nationalists.[3]

At the time, the Black Power ferment in Los Angeles centered on the Black Congress. After the Watts rebellion in 1965, Black Power organizations had proliferated and developed the Black Congress as a united front. One member organization was the Community Alert Patrol led by Ron "Brother Crook" Wilkins. After Watts, Brother Crook became widely known for pioneering patrols of police, a tactic taken up and modified by Huey Newton. Members of CAP would follow the police with cameras and tape recorders to ensure that they did not commit acts of brutality against members of the black community.[4]

Harry Truly's Black Student Alliance was another member of the Black Congress. Truly taught sociology at California State University, Los Angeles, during the day and led the alliance by night. He had a vision of bringing all black student organizations across the country into the alliance and creating a revolutionary force. Truly was well read and deeply committed. His compelling vision for Black Power was just one of many in the Black Congress of Los Angeles at the time. The congress also included representatives from the Congress of Racial Equality, the Freedom Draft Movement, SLANT (Self Leadership for All Nationalities Today), the Afro-American Association, the Afro American Cultural Association, Black Resistance against Wars for Oppression, Black Unitarians for Radical Reform, Black Youth Conference, Citizens for Creative Welfare, Immanuel Church, L.A. County Welfare Rights, the National Association for the Advancement of Colored People, Operation Bootstrap, Parent Action Council, Underground Musicians Association, and the Watts Happening Coffee House.[5]

The most influential organization in the Black Congress in late 1967 and early 1968 was Ron Karenga's US, pronounced "us," as in "not them." Karenga's group sought to transform society through a cultural, rather than a political, revolution. According to historian Scot Brown, "As a cultural nationalist vanguard, the US Organization saw itself as a mirror of African Americans' progressive future." Through the creation of an alternative and progressive culture, US held that black people would transform their own world and the larger society. Karenga and US were not adverse to political action, but they saw culture as the principal vehicle for change. For them, heightened cultural awareness was the key to social transformation. Members dressed in dashikis and ceremonial African garb. Male members shaved their heads. Karenga spoke several languages, including Swahili, which he taught widely. Within US, Karenga was the central authority and was called Maulana, or "master teacher," by his followers. US is best known today for starting the holiday Kwanza.[6]

Another Black Congress member was the Black Panther Political Party, led by John Floyd, a schoolteacher. The L.A. Black Panther Political Party, which grew out of Stokely Carmichael's efforts to proliferate the Black Panther Party originated in Lowndes County, Alabama, started independently of the Oakland Black Panther Party. The fifth issue of *Harambee* (Swahili for "Let's pull together"), the Los Angeles Black Congress newsletter edited by Ron Karenga, popularized the Black Panther idea and symbol in Los Angeles. The issue, published on November 3, 1966, reproduced a Lowndes County flier, a speech by chair John Hulett, and a front-page spread dedicated to the Lowndes County Black Panther Party. Soon thereafter, John Floyd started the L.A. Black Panther Political Party. When the Oakland Black Panther Party for Self-Defense forged an alliance with the Peace and Freedom Party in June 1967, John Floyd supported the effort, filing documents to verify the Black Panther Party's existence as a statewide organization and explaining to the press, "For all intents and purposes, we are a statewide party." But in practice, the two organizations hardly communicated. In late 1967 or early 1968, Angela Davis—at that time working on her PhD in philosophy with Herbert Marcuse at the University of California, San Diego, joined Floyd's organization.[7] Around this time, Elaine Brown was becoming active in the Black Congress. She began working with John Floyd to put out *Harambee* and became particularly close to Sandra Scott and Harry Truly of the Black Student Alliance.[8]

Beneath the surface of Black Power unity at the Los Angeles Black Congress lay deep conflict. Black Power had posed a question, but there was no single answer. The term meant different things to different people and organizations in the Black Congress. Everyone in the Black Congress sought dignity and empowerment. Most rejected the integrationism and nonviolence of the Civil Rights Movement. Many organizations in the congress viewed the black community as a colony and agreed on the need for self-determination. Black people, they agreed, needed to develop their own sources of political, economic, and cultural strength. But how to achieve this and how best to appeal to the people proved to be points of contention.

In every insurgent movement, conflicting visions compete. As movement groups challenge the legitimacy of the state and the established social order, each asserts its own vision as an alternative. The stakes appear high, especially the ability to claim leadership of the revolution and the potential to set the direction for the future. Certainly, the conflict in Los Angeles was intense. Organizations constantly jockeyed for control within the Black Congress, and at times, these conflicts became violent.[9] Recalling a gun battle that broke out between the United Front and members of Ron Karenga's US at the November 1967 Black Youth Conference, Angela Davis explained, "Beneath the façade of unity, under the wonderful colors of the bubas, lay strong ideological differences and explosive political conflicts, and perhaps even agents provocateurs."[10] The incident at the conference was not unique. In another incident, fifteen members of US were arrested, for allegedly beating three men who interrupted a "soul session."[11]

In early 1968, the Oakland-based Black Panther Party began organizing a chapter in Los Angeles—the first outside the Oakland Bay Area—and the dynamics in the Black Congress quickly changed. The politics developed by Huey Newton, Bobby Seale, and Eldridge Cleaver resonated with young blacks in Los Angeles, providing new conduits for action. Like Ron Karenga and US, the Black Panthers had a compelling theory about the source of black people's suffering, a vision for advancing black dignity and power, and they had created a disciplined organization to advance that vision in tangible ways. US, however, never sought to become a mass organization, emphasizing educational and cultural activities accessible to only a few. As Scot Brown has observed, "US leaders saw no need for a large membership. Their goal was to ideologically influence other organizations with its united-front approach, and thus direct the course of the coming 'cultural revolution.'"[12]

Unlike US, the Black Panther Party recognized the explosive potential of the Watts rebellion as a political force and developed a program and activities to organize black folks on the street. Like Brother Crook's community alert patrols, the Black Panther Party asserted black dignity and self-determination by holding the police accountable. But unlike Brother Crook, the Black Panthers created a track record of winning such confrontations, legally backing off police with loaded weapons and storming the state capitol in Sacramento. When the law was changed to prevent the Panthers from engaging in these confrontations, Huey Newton had allegedly killed a policeman in self-defense. Many in the Black Congress considered Newton's resistance heroic and embraced the "Free Huey!" campaign.

In January 1968, Eldridge Cleaver recruited Alprentice "Bunchy" Carter to organize a chapter of the Black Panther Party in Los Angeles. Elaine Brown recalled the first time she met Carter:

> "My name is Bunchy," he said coolly. "Bunchy," he reiterated "like a bunch of greens," answering a question someone a long time ago had found the courage to ask. His face was black alabaster; his eyes, black diamonds, set off by carved eyebrows and distinct black eyelashes. His skin was as smooth as melted chocolate, unflawed, with a reddish gloss. He was the

vision of Revelations, a head of soft black wool refined to an African crown. He stroked his rich mustache as he spoke, head back, feet apart, an olive-green leather coat tossed over his strong shoulders. Everybody had heard of Bunchy.[13]

Cleaver and Bunchy had become friends at Soledad State Prison, where they had joined the Nation of Islam and become politicized by Malcolm X. Before Soledad, Bunchy had a brief career as a middle-weight boxer and then joined the five thousand–member Slauson gang and founded its most feared branch, the Slauson Renegades. Widely known as the "Mayor of the Ghetto," he was considered by many to be the most dangerous man in Los Angeles. Bunchy was not only tough, he was charismatic. His authority came from his intelligence and creativity as well as his street credentials. He wrote poetry and having studied revolutionary theory during his years in prison, could fiercely debate the theories of Fanon, Che, Lenin, and Mao.[14]

The strong respect Bunchy garnered on the streets separated him from the regular participants in the Black Congress. Because of Huey Newton and the Panthers' courageous stance against the police, Bunchy could relate to the Oakland-based Black Panther Party, as could his street protégés.[15] When Bunchy formed a branch of the Oakland-based Black Panther Party in Los Angeles, he brought many former members of the Slauson gang into the Party with him.[16]

In January 1968, Bunchy attended a poetry reading organized by the Black Congress to announce the launch of the Los Angeles chapter of the Black Panther Party, the first outside the Oakland Bay Area. He brought twenty street-hardened soldiers dressed in black leather jackets and gloves and carrying armed pistols and sawed-off shotguns. Uninvited, Bunchy and his "wolves" stormed the hall midreading and surrounded the Black Congress members who were there. Conversation stopped, and someone called for Bunchy to "blow," to recite a poem. After reciting the fierce "Niggertown" and tender "Black Mother," both of which he had written, Bunchy thanked the audience for letting him "blow." Next he gestured to one of the wolves, who unfurled a poster of Huey Newton on his wicker throne. Bunchy declared that Huey Newton was the leader of the Black Liberation Struggle and announced that he was forming the Southern California chapter of the Black Panther Party:

> [Huey] set the example and showed us that we, too, must deal with the pig if we are to call ourselves men. We can no longer allow the pig's armed forces

to come into our communities and kill our young men and disrespect our Sisters and rob us of our lives. The pig can no longer attack and suppress our people, or send his occupying army to maraud and maim our communities, without suffering grave consequences. . . . From this point forward, Brothers and Sisters, if the pig moves on this community, the Black Panther Party will deal with him.[17]

Bunchy then commanded that no one else, including John Floyd, was to use the Black Panther name or logo without authorization from the Central Committee of the Party in Oakland. At the suggestion of James Forman of the Student Nonviolent Coordinating Committee, Floyd changed the name of his group to the West Coast chapter of SNCC and helped to mobilize the "Free Huey!" rally in February.[18]

A wide array of organizations in the Black Congress, including Karenga's US, supported the Black Panther argument that Huey was a political prisoner. They demanded he be set free, and many pitched in to organize the "Free Huey!" rally planned in Los Angeles on February 18, 1968 (the day after the "Free Huey!" rally at the Oakland Coliseum).[19] Amid the show of unity, though, tensions and disputes emerged as representatives of the participating organizations jockeyed for authority and sought to assert competing visions. In a meeting just before the rally on February 18, an angry dispute erupted among US, the Black Panther Party, and two factions of SNCC over whether police should be allowed to provide security at the rally. The Panthers and Carmichael asserted that the police should be removed, but Karenga—still the most influential voice in the Black Congress—prevailed, asserting that confrontation with the police should be avoided at that point.[20] The February 18 rally drew at least five thousand people. Speakers included Bobby Seale, Stokely Carmichael, H. Rap Brown, James Forman, Ron Karenga, and radical Chicano activist Reis Tijerina.[21] In late February, the Party moved its office in the Black Congress building to a new space at 4115 South Central in Los Angeles.[22]

When Martin Luther King Jr. was killed in April, the Black Panther Party quickly became the dominant presence in the Los Angeles Black Power scene. Hundreds of young black Angelenos flocked to join the Panthers. People such as Elaine Brown and Ericka and John Huggins, who had been seeking a way to advance Black Power, found what they were looking for in the Party of Bunchy Carter and Huey Newton. Many of the smaller organizations, such as Harry Truly's Black Student Alliance, dissipated. By early 1969, the Black Congress would be defunct.[23]

The Black Panther Party offered black people more than an alternative; it promised dignity. By standing up to the police, Huey Newton showed that black people could break patterns of racial submissiveness and deference. Eldridge Cleaver claimed that Newton was the true heir to Malcolm X: "Malcolm prophesied the coming of the gun to the black liberation struggle. Huey P. Newton picked up the gun and pulled the trigger."[24] Newton had created a black anti-imperialist politics of armed self-defense that, unlike other versions of Black Power, held strong appeal for alienated and marginalized blacks. The Panthers recognized that many black people already lived in a state of war. The violence of the ghetto rebellions reflected the raw desperation of everyday life. The Panthers believed these forces could be organized and strove to channel the desperation and violence of everyday black life into powerful political resistance.

Newton's example of armed self-defense against the police inspired many young activists in L.A., and they sought to emulate it. In the second week of August 1968, more than seventy thousand people and seventy organizations participated in the Watts Festival in South Central Los Angeles commemorating the third anniversary of the Watts rebellion.[25] Tensions between police and the community were running high, and on Monday August 5, a gunfight broke out during the festival at Will Rogers Park in Watts, and six people were wounded.[26] Later that day, police pulled over four Black Panthers driving a black 1955 Ford sedan at a service station at the corner of Adams and Crenshaw. Anthony Bartholomew later reported, "The police knew we were Panthers and were following us."[27] The Panthers were armed and refused to submit to police. A gun battle erupted. Police killed Stephen Kenna Bartholomew, twenty-one years old, with multiple gunshots to the head and lower body; Robert Lawrence, twenty-two years old, with multiple gunshots to the head and left shoulder; and Thomas Melvin Lewis, just eighteen years old, with shots to the abdomen and left leg. In the battle, the Panthers wounded two police officers; one Panther, Anthony Bartholomew, escaped.[28]

SEATTLE

The funeral of Bobby Hutton transformed the life of Aaron Dixon, a student from Seattle, much as it did Ericka Huggins's life. A member of SNCC, Dixon and his brother Elmer were in San Francisco for the West Coast Black Student Union conference, and they crossed the Bay

Bridge to attend Bobby Hutton's funeral on April 12, 1968. Aaron later recalled the overwhelming cries of Hutton's mother. Looking into the casket "was almost like looking into a vision of the movement, and it was not what we had expected. It was not the glory and the victory we had romanticized about." After the funeral, Dixon met Warren Wells, Kathleen Cleaver, and Bobby Seale. Seale's speech was mesmerizing. Decades later, Dixon remembered sharing a drink with Seale and could still visualize Seale's dramatic portrayal of a black man chained up and struggling to be free.[29]

When the Dixon brothers returned to Seattle, they rented an office and opened the first chapter of the Black Panther Party outside of California. Within two months, more than three hundred people joined the chapter, women as well as men. Some, such as Kathy Jones, were high school students; others were in their twenties. A few, such as Ron Carson, who ran a local poverty program and carried a pistol, were over thirty. Most were black but some were Asian, such as Guy Kurose, and had grown up in the neighborhood. A few came from college, including Kathy Halley, who later changed her name to Nafasi and became one of Aaron's closest confidants. Others, such as Bobby White, Bobby Harding, and Mike Tagowa, were Vietnam veterans. White was a dynamic poet and writer who became the chapter's lieutenant of information. Some Seattle Panthers, such as Chester Northington, John Eichelburger, and Bruce Hayes, came with experience from other black nationalist organizations. Others, such as Warren Myers and Steve Phillips, had been involved in street life and saw the Party as a way of getting back at the police while redeeming themselves in the community. Lewis Jackson was a hardened fighter from New Orleans with a thick Creole accent, who sported a tattoo of a football between his eyebrows. He carried a .45 when he joined the Party and soon became Aaron's bodyguard. Joyce Redman had a reputation as the fiercest sister in the neighborhood. Maud Allen was a stickler for rules.

"Since the death of Martin Luther King," Aaron Dixon later recalled, "my life and the life of many other black youth throughout America had taken on an overwhelming sense of urgency. Suddenly it seemed that the movement had accelerated. We were now almost totally consumed with the fight for justice and the right to determine our own destiny. For me school had now taken a back seat to the emerging struggle."[30]

The Seattle Black Panther office became a community headquarters, and the phone was constantly ringing with people asking for help.

The Panthers frequently helped people with problems with landlords, spousal abuse, or the police. In one incident, a landlord had removed the front door when a family was late in paying the rent. The Panthers went to the landlord's house, took back the tenants' door, and hung it back on the hinges. In another case, parents reported frequent beatings of black children at the predominantly white Rainier Beach High School. Three cars of armed Panthers drove to the school, patrolled the hallways, and told the principal that if he did not provide security for the black students, they would. The principal quickly complied.[31]

Like their comrades in California, the Seattle Panthers increasingly came into conflict with police. In May 1968, Buddy Yates was arrested for interference with an arrest. In June, Aaron Dixon was arrested for the same, and Gary Owens was charged with addressing a cop as "pig." In July, Seattle police accosted and beat Panthers Bobby Harding, Bobby White, and Joe Atkins.[32]

At seventeen years old, Seattle Black Panther Welton Armstead was tall yet slight of frame. A new father, he walked in exuberant strides, his energy infectious. He was highly intelligent, perceptive, and reasonable, and many older men looked to him for answers. He quickly climbed the Party ranks and earned authority in the Seattle chapter. On a dreary Tuesday afternoon in Seattle, October 15, 1968, Armstead decided to tint the windows on his car. The car was parked in front of his house, and Armstead worked in the street. At about 4:20 P.M., a police car pulled up. Officer Erling J. Buttedahl got out, asked Armstead what he was doing, and accused him of stealing the car. Armstead denied the charges. Armstead's mother came out of the house and later would claim that the police were harassing her son. Armstead decided that he would defend himself and his family from harassment. He got his rifle and asked the police to leave him alone. Officer Buttedahl shot Armstead dead and arrested his mother and sister for interfering with an arrest.[33]

NEW YORK

In the weeks following King's assassination, the Black Panther Party also opened a chapter in New York City's Harlem. The black nationalist ferment of late 1960s New York had deep roots in Harlem that went back at least as far as Marcus Garvey's Universal Negro Improvement Association in the late 1910s and 1920s. Malcolm X achieved his greatest impact and notoriety in Harlem in the 1950s and 1960s. SNCC had a New York City office and had even flirted with the idea of creating a New York–based Black Panther Party in early 1966.[34] The effort collapsed long before SNCC's partial merger with the Panthers in February 1968. When King was killed in April, SNCC helped jump-start the New York Panther chapter, this time under Oakland's leadership. With the "Free Huey!" campaign picking up momentum as the case headed to trial, tales of the Panthers storming the legislature in Sacramento, news of Cleaver's presidential bid, and the martyrdom of Lil' Bobby Hutton, the Oakland-based Black Panther Party exemplified the direct enactment of Black Power that so many black New Yorkers craved.

In April, just weeks after King's death, Joudon Ford took the reins as the new captain for the New York Black Panther Party, setting up a temporary office in the SNCC headquarters in downtown Manhattan.[35] In addition to his civil rights experience with SNCC, eighteen-year-old Ford had served in the Civil Air Patrol before joining the Panthers. He was looking for a practical way to build Black Power and was drawn to the Panthers because of their track record of militancy. "The Panther Party," Joudon later recalled, "seemed to be the most serious black organization, but there was also the military aspect."[36]

Joudon Ford was an organization man and diligently set about building the first East Coast chapter of the Party. Assisted by David Brothers—the newly assigned forty-year-old chairman of the New York chapter—Ford organized and taught political education classes and self-defense training.[37] He led his members into open verbal confrontations with the police. He convinced the Brooklyn campus of Long Island University to let the Panthers use an auditorium for monthly citywide meetings and diligently hashed out internal conflicts to create order in the New York chapter.[38] His job was not easy, especially with the challenges posed by the chapter's rapid growth. At one point, Joudon called David Hilliard, Panther chief of staff in Oakland, to ask how to keep shady people out of the party. "When I find out," Hilliard told Ford, "I'll let you know."[39]

On May 20, the Black Panther Party held a benefit performance at the Fillmore East in the East Village to help raise $200,000 bail for Eldridge Cleaver and six other Panthers arrested in the April 6 shootout in Oakland. The benefit, which featured several plays and performances by Amiri Baraka (LeRoi Jones) and Ed Bullins, drew twenty-six hundred people. James Forman of SNCC was the event's emcee, and Kathleen Cleaver spoke about Lil' Bobby Hutton's martyrdom and her husband's case. The Party tapped into the emerging consensus that the Panthers epitomized Black Power, drawing upon its national networks and its new relationship with SNCC to raise funds and build a strong presence in New York.[40]

Two of the first New Yorkers to join the Black Panther Party were Lumumba Shakur, appointed section leader for Harlem, and Sekou Odinga, named section leader for the Bronx. After attending Andrew Jackson High School in Queens together, the two men had been politicized in prison, joined Malcolm X's Organization of Afro-American Unity (OAAU) in 1964, and—dissatisfied with other black nationalist organizations—turned to the Black Panther Party after Martin Luther King's death.[41]

Lumumba's racial politics had deep roots. His father was a Black Muslim, and his grandfather "was arch anti-white repression," Lumumba recalled. "He would sit down and talk about white repression for days. My grandfather was a cop for three days until a white man told him no nigger was going to arrest *him,* and Grandpa whipped that cracker half to death."[42]

Perhaps the turning point in Lumumba's life was an event that took place in December 1959. Lumumba—sixteen years old at the time— boarded a bus in Jamaica, New York, with about fifteen friends after a party. He sat next to a large white man in a U.S. Navy uniform. The man said that where he came from "niggers" did not sit next to white people. Lumumba told the man that this was not the South, and the man punched Lumumba in the face. "All pandemonium broke out in the bus, and that cracker was whipped mercilessly. Later I found out that cracker was cut every place except the soles of his feet."[43] Lumumba got off the bus but was soon picked up by the police. The police took him to the hospital, and the white man identified Lumumba as the one who had beaten him. The police beat Lumumba badly in front of the doctors and nurses, right in the middle of Jamaica Hospital. Later in court, the white man admitted that he had punched and attacked Lumumba first, "because niggers aren't supposed to sit next to white people on buses." The judge ordered the statement stricken from the record, saying it was not relevant to the issue being decided. The judge set bail at $10,000 for Lumumba and dispatched him to jail for seven months pending trial. Lumumba's state-appointed lawyer told him to plead guilty to "attempted assault two" and said that he would receive a sentence of time served. Lumumba pled guilty as instructed, but his lawyer never made a deal, and he was sent to jail for five years.[44]

In jail, prisoners had to fight continually to protect themselves or suffer the consequences—often rape. Guards cultivated racial and gang conflicts among the prisoners and often sat as spectators at their fights, "like they were in Madison Square Garden."[45] Lumumba resented being used in this way and became increasingly politicized in prison, organizing black inmates into a united block.[46]

In New York state's Comstock Prison, Lumumba again met up with Sekou Odinga. There in 1963, Lumumba tried to get assigned to work in the bakery. Of 1,800 prisoners in Comstock, 1,300 were black. But black prisoners were confined to working as dishwashers, in labor gangs, in the laundry, or in other low-skill jobs; no black prisoners were allowed to work in any of the shops or prison jobs where they could learn a trade, such as the bakery or the auto shop. Lumumba asked the deputy warden for reassignment to the bakery, but the official told him that the bakery jobs were only for white prisoners. Sekou and every other black prisoner who requested assignment to a skilled shop or job received the same response. Consequently, Lumumba, Sekou, and a number of the black prisoners decided that the only way to change the situation was through violent confrontation. They secretly organized and in late September 1963, they rioted. Some 450 prisoners fought guards with fists, stones, and wooden planks; 23 of them were injured. New York Prison Commissioner McGinnis visited Comstock to investigate. Lumumba met with him and told him why they had rioted. Lumumba and 13 other prisoners who had organized the riot were transferred to Attica. Yet the policies in Comstock were changed, with black inmates "assigned to every professional school, shop, trade, and job in Comstock" from then on.[47]

When Lumumba got out of prison in December 1964, he joined Malcolm X's Organization of Afro-American Unity. A couple months later, Malcolm X was dead. In April, he got in touch with Sekou, his childhood friend, who also joined OAAU. Lumumba, however, was put off by the male chauvinism in OAAU and its lack of impact, so the two quit and looked for another organization that exemplified the vision and direction of Malcolm X. They could not find anything satisfactory in New York. In 1967, they joined with other black nationalists in Jamaica Queens and organized the Grass Root Front. "Our aim was to take the anti-poverty programs from the hands of the religious pimps and preachers and guarantee the grass-root people control of the anti-poverty programs," Lumumba explained years later. "When the community people began to get more control of the anti-poverty programs, the religious pimp-preachers called OEO [Office of Economic Opportunity] and the pigs. It was a split within the Grass Root Front because Sekou, Larry Mack, and I wanted to inflict a political consequence. The other brothers did not agree with us. So we quit and told them that they were jiving."[48] Sekou recalled, "We were all very young and inexperienced and got caught up in a local anti-poverty program. By 1967 I was thoroughly disillusioned with that, when I heard about the Black Panther Party in Oakland, California. . . . By the spring of 1968, we heard that representatives from the [Black Panther Party] were coming to New York and there was a possibility of organizing a chapter. I attended the meeting and decided to join and help build the [Party] in New York."[49]

In the spring of 1968, the Black Panther Party attracted many of New York's most politically active young blacks. An experienced tenants' rights activist, Kuwasi Balagoon had traveled to D.C. to protest opposition to rat-control legislation in Congress, a key issue for renters in New York City. He and his fellow protesters brought live rats to the demonstration in the House of Representatives and were beaten by police. Next he joined the central Harlem Committee for Self-Defense.[50] Yet none of these efforts satisfied Balagoon's feeling that he had to do something more serious for black people's liberation—a feeling that only intensified with King's assassination. Then he heard about the Black Panther Party:

> When I heard that Huey Newton had been involved in a shootout with two pigs and one had died, I thought I'd check this brother out, as he seemed to be a sure enough leader. And when the Panthers came to New York, I checked them out, and found the ten-point program unquestionable, and the fact that it was community-based a good thing. Digging that the cadre believed that political power stems from the barrel of a gun made me feel instant kinship. So I joined, and extended my energies and skills to the black community and mankind through the Party.[51]

Drawn to the Black Panthers' militancy, Afeni Shakur joined the Party as soon as it came to New York in the spring of 1968 and married Lumumba.[52] She was sick of turning the other cheek and believed that the Panthers offered a real alternative. Shakur had been impressed by the way in which the Panthers responded when a policeman tried to take one of their guns in Sacramento. The Panther holding the gun had asked the policeman, "Am I under arrest?" When the policeman responded that he was not, the Panther told the policeman, "Then take your hands off my motherfucking gun. I have a constitutional right to have this gun." "In 1967 that in itself was enough to blow anybody's mind," Shakur later recalled.[53]

From that time on, Shakur waited eagerly for the Party to spread to New York so that she could join: "All I did then was wait for the Black Panther Party to come to New York. Somebody told me they were coming; you know, I knew they just *had* to come, they just couldn't stay on the Coast. . . . Nothing that strong could stay in one area. I just knew from the beginning that it would branch out into something beautiful—it had to. I just knew there were niggers all over the place that felt like I did. The Party got here around April."[54]

Others joined the Party for similar reasons. David Parker, a seventeen-year-old rank-and-file New York Panther explained the appeal to the *New York Times* in 1968: "Why am I a Black Panther? Well, I've been listening to Brother Malcolm's records for a long time. I know what he said and I've just been waiting for the Panthers to come here." Paraphrasing Malcolm X, he argued that the Panthers offered change: "Change, change by any means necessary." Bill Hampton, a twenty-seven-year-old New York Panther, married father of three, and former executive in training with the Olin Mathieson chemical company, told the *Times*, "We're revolutionaries and we're fighting a war" for the survival of black people. "People have to realize that 'the man' is not just moving on us Panthers, but he is moving on all black people. . . . They see us as a threat and realizing this the man has to put it down. That's why the police run around here now trying to get something started." Hampton described police as "Gestapo forces that occupy the black community" and asserted, "They have got to be forced out of our community . . . their power is on their hips. Take those guns away from those pigs and they are nobodies. The only way to counteract this power is with a gun in your hand."[55]

Abayama Katara, still a student at Franklin High School when he joined the Panthers, recalled one of the experiences that convinced him the police were an occupying force:

> One night my family was sitting in the living room and I heard what sounded like firecrackers. I looked out the window and saw a black man running down the street with what looked to be an army of cops running after him. (I found out later he had tried to hold up a store and a rookie cop had fired on him.) There were people all over the street, but the cops didn't even tell them to get down, they just kept on firing. When the brother got to 135th Street he stopped on the corner and held his hands up, but the cops just kept coming and shooting. People were shouting out of the windows at the cops telling them to stop, couldn't they see the brother was trying to give up, and so the cops started pointing their guns at the windows, telling everybody to keep inside and mind their own business. And about

then a bullet chipped a piece of brick between the window I was hanging out of and the apartment next to ours. We never did figure out whether that bullet ricocheted or whether one of those cops just wanted to see a lot of black blood, but it was sure hard to see where it could have ricocheted *from*. They finally caught up with the brother in the schoolyard, and you could hear him screaming all the way down the street as they dragged him to a patrol car.[56]

When Katara heard that the Panthers were taking on the issue of police abuse, he went to a Party meeting. There, he found a way of thinking about the police that transformed his perspective and in turn changed his life. Panthers kept talking about "pigs," and Katara did not know what they meant. After the meeting, he asked one of the Panthers if he knew what a pig was. "Man, he looked at me as if I asked him what earth was. After he finished running it down, I was souped up for a motherfucker. I left the house saying 'pig' over and over again. I got on a bus and everybody must have thought I was bugged out, because all the way home I just kept on saying 'pig,' because the way the brother ran it down, it fit perfectly."[57] More than an insult, calling the police (and other authorities) pigs rejected their legitimacy, denounced their Gestapo-like behavior as inhuman, and asserted the moral superiority of the oppressed. Katara felt liberated.

As a Black Panther, Katara soon became president of the Afro-American history club at Franklin High School. His club tried to educate classmates, displaying posters in the hallway of three phases of the Black Liberation Struggle. The first phase was illustrated by the image of a black woman being beaten by Bull Connor's police and dogs; the second, by pictures of members of the Student Nonviolent Coordinating Committee taking nonviolent action; and the third, by pictures of the Black Panther Party in action, including a photo of Kathleen Cleaver with a shotgun. The principal ordered them to remove the violent photos, but the students argued that there were far more violent scenes in their history books. Soon the posters became a point of contention in the ongoing struggle between black community activists and school officials for control of the school district, a struggle in which the New York Black Panther Party played an active part in late 1968.[58]

While the New York Panthers became heavily involved in issues of housing, schools, and welfare, as well as their program of political education, their conflicts with police were the activities that garnered the most media attention and mobilized allied support. On August 1, twenty-year-old Gordon Cooke and seventeen-year-old Darrell Baines, both Party members, were working in the Panther office at 780 Nostrand Avenue in the Bedford-Stuyvesant section of Brooklyn. A little before 2:30 P.M., they went out onto the sidewalk in front of the office and sought to rally neighbors to protest police abuse. Cooke shouted into the bullhorn, calling the police "racist," "pigs," and "crackers." He soon attracted a crowd of about fifty people. Someone called the police. Two officers arrived on the scene, waited nearby, and then walked into the store next to the Panther office and called for backup. One officer asked Cooke if he had a permit to use the bullhorn. Another asked Baines who was in charge, and Baines said he was. The officer called Baines over to the patrol car, but Baines refused, and the officer tried to grab him. Police later claimed that Baines kicked an officer in the groin. According to Cooke, he saw the police roughing up Baines and tried to intervene. The policeman started to beat Cooke over the head with his nightstick. Soon other police cars arrived, and several policemen blocked off the other Panthers while six of their fellow officers beat Cooke with nightsticks. Even after Cooke was handcuffed and on the ground, they continued to beat him on the pretense that he was resisting arrest. Cooke was taken to Brooklyn Jewish Hospital, where he was treated for head lacerations, and then arrested for resisting arrest and interfering with an officer. Baines was arrested for assault, harassment, and resisting arrest.[59]

Later that afternoon, 350 Panthers turned out for the arraignment of Darrell Baines and Gordon Cooke at the Brooklyn Criminal Court. Judge John Furey, who had served for ten years in the New York Criminal Court, placed the two defendants on parole. The judge explained later that Baines and Cooke had no previous records, and "under the circumstances, with the group that was there and the charges that were brought, it seemed foolish to needlessly put them on bail."[60]

Early the next morning, two policemen came to the Crown Heights neighborhood in Brooklyn on a domestic dispute call. As they got out of the police car, they were hit and wounded by birdshot fired from a shotgun by one or two people hiding in the bushes thirty feet away. The shooters ran and escaped. The *New York Times* reported a rumor, which the police denied, that a Black Panther button was found at the scene near two shotgun shells.[61] Panther captain Joudon Ford denied any Panther involvement in the shooting.[62]

Outraged that Judge Furey had treated the Panthers "lightly," ten patrolmen from Brooklyn's Grand Avenue station organized a petition charging Furey with allowing Panthers to wear hats and curse in his courtroom and calling for his resignation. The petition demanded that the police union—the Patrolmen's Benevolent Association (PBA)—call for Furey's resignation and threatened that the signatories would resign and withhold dues from the PBA if the group did not take this action.[63] A Brooklyn Bar Association subcommittee responded by asking the police commissioner to investigate the charges that Furey had allowed Panthers to act disrespectfully in his courtroom. The PBA launched its own investigation.[64] Spurred by the petition, a group of officers began a new organization called the Law Enforcement Group (LEG). The group claimed that officers were not receiving the support they needed generally and called for widespread changes, beginning with a grand jury investigation of alleged "coddling of accused criminals by the Criminal Courts" and including the "abolition of the Police Department's Civilian Complaint Review Board," prevention of "another Warren Court," and "removal of civilians from clerical duties in police stations."[65] Sensing a challenge to their customary policing practices, these officers sought to beat back what they saw as a serious move to undermine their authority.

Civil liberties groups responded, calling the coddling charge "an absurdity." These groups identified LEG as a "frightening power play to take over the judiciary" and an "undisguised declaration of war against the black militant communities." Ira Glasser, the spokesman for the New York Civil Liberties Union said, "If the program they wanted was instituted we would wind up with an open police state."[66]

Several weeks later, on August 21, as public attention faded, a group of young blacks that included several Brooklyn Panthers ignited a pile of trash heaped in the street on Nostrand Avenue near the Panther office. When firemen and police responded to the rubbish fire, rebels attacked them with bottles, bricks, cans, and stones and then began smashing storefront windows and looting stores along a twelve-block commercial stretch of Nostrand Avenue. Police quickly quashed the rebellion and arrested seven participants: George Correa, Darrell Baines, John Martinez, Morris Holman, Ricky Fletcher, Patricia Riley, and Fremont Dunn. Some one hundred police officers packed into the Brooklyn Criminal Court for a hearing on the rebels' case later that day, and the district attorney asked the court to set an extrahigh bail: "We have reason to believe that these defendants are members of the ultramilitant Black Panther Party. We feel there is a danger that they may not reappear in court unless high bail is set. Their actions show clearly a lack of respect for authority." The judge proceeded to set an unusually high bail of $50,000 each for twenty-two-year-old Correa and seventeen-year-old Baines and $11,500 for seventeen-year-old Martinez, each charged with resisting arrest and possessing stolen property. More standard bail of $1,500 each was set for the remaining four defendants.[67] Rather than stifle protest, the punitive bails ignited further resistance.

While street rebellions were common among urban black youths in the late 1960s, these rebels were different, claiming common cause with the anti-imperialist struggles in Vietnam and the domestic draft resisters. In addition to twenty Panthers who rallied for the rebels and turned out for further court hearings the following week, the white Left saw the Panthers as allies in their own anti-imperialist struggle and responded to the police repression with resistance. William Kunstler, a renowned left-wing lawyer took the Brooklyn Panthers' case and argued that the bail was "unconstitutionally excessive," part of the "police vendetta against the Black Panthers in New York." Members of the predominantly white Peace and Freedom Party and also the Columbia Strike Committee organized demonstrations outside the courthouse protesting the unusually high bail. The protestors carried signs saying "Hands Off Black Panthers," "White Radicals Defend Black Panthers," and "Stop Cop Harassment of the Black Panther Party." The court reduced bail to $20,000 for Correa, $10,000 for Baines, and $2,500 for Martinez.[68]

At a September 4 preliminary hearing for Correa, Baines, and Martinez, 150 whites, many of them off-duty policemen associated with LEG, packed the courtroom. The cops positioned themselves behind the Panthers in the courtroom, poking them in the back with their nightsticks, cursing, and saying, "White tigers eat black panthers." When the small group of Panthers left the courtroom and made their way to the elevator, the police beat them up and attacked a few white members of Columbia University's Students for a Democratic Society who had come to support the Panthers. The *New York Times* reported, "About 150 white men, many of whom were off-duty and out-of-uniform policemen, attacked a small number of Black Panther party members and white sympathizers yesterday on the sixth floor of the Brooklyn Criminal Court." Many of the off-duty police wore "Wallace for President" buttons, referring to George Wallace, the white supremacist former governor of Alabama who was running for president of the United States. The off-duty policemen beat the Panthers and their white supporters with blackjacks. LEG officers called the Panthers "niggers" and "motherfuckers" while beating them. Uniformed police pretended to try to stop the beating but actually dropped their billy clubs so the off-duty officers could use them to beat the Panthers. According to the *Times*, two of the Panthers had blood gushing from their heads after the beating. New York Panther chairman David Brothers, the Peace and Freedom Party nominee for the 12th Congressional District at the time, was kicked and stomped in the back more than twenty times. Panther section leader Tom McCreary suffered a fractured skull.[69]

Katara, one of the Panthers in the delegation that day, recalled fleeing from the off-duty police who were beating them, with nowhere to turn. The Panthers finally got into an elevator and tried to go down, but the elevator went up. Everywhere they went, the off-duty police were waiting for them. They exited the elevator, and Joudon Ford called the mayor's office but could not get through. They went to the offices of the Human Rights Commission and City Council but found no one there. They fled into another courtroom and asked the judge there for help. He finally called a court guard to escort the Panthers downstairs. When they went outside, the police were waiting for them, and the Panthers split up and ran. The police chased them. Katara made it into the subway and took off his beret and black shirt so that the off-duty police would not recognize him and was able to ride home safely.[70]

The next day, Mayor John Lindsay and Police Commissioner Leary verified that off-duty policemen had participated in the attack, and they promised swift action, "including criminal prosecution if that is warranted by the facts."[71] The day after the courtroom beating, a group of Panthers and their attorneys Kunstler and Gerald Lefcourt met with representatives of Mayor Lindsay's office and answered questions about the attack.[72]

In the following days, the Panthers and their allies turned up the political and legal pressure. On September 7, the New York state NAACP called upon the district attorney to conduct a grand jury investigation into the beating.[73] Two weeks later, Acting District Attorney Elliott Golden ordered a "thorough grand jury investigation" into the September 4 attack on Black Panthers in the Brooklyn Criminal Court.[74] On September 10, the Black Panther Party filed a suit in the U.S. District Court for the Southern District of New York, charging the New York City Police Department with systematic "violence, intimidation and humiliation," asking for community control of the police, and seeking injunctions forbidding the police from harassing Black Panthers. The National Lawyers Guild, the National Emergency Civil Liberties Committee, and the Law Center for Constitutional Rights all sponsored the suit.[75] The Panthers' web of support was widening.

A couple days later, at 2:05 on the morning of September 12, another ambush of police occurred in Brooklyn. Two officers were patrolling on Schenectady Avenue only a few feet from where the other two officers had been ambushed on August 2. Signs nearby announced a $10,000 reward for information leading to the arrest and conviction of the gunman who had shot the other officers. Two blasts from a .308 rifle burst through the front windshield of the patrol car, injuring both officers and shattering the windows on the right side of the car. The officers were admitted to Kings County Hospital.[76]

FROM COAST TO COAST

At the time of the killings of Martin Luther King Jr. and Bobby Hutton in early April of 1968, the Black Panther Party was essentially a local organization based in Oakland, with a satellite chapter beginning to organize in Los Angeles. Although the Black Power ferment was brewing in most major U.S. cities, the Party had not yet achieved national influence. This quickly changed in 1968. As Kathleen Cleaver later recalled, "The murder of King changed the whole dynamic of the country. That is probably the single most significant event in terms of how the Panthers were perceived by the black community."[77] Seeking effective ways to advance their communities' interests, young blacks flocked to the Black Panther Party and its politics of armed self-defense. The Party did little recruiting. Instead, young activists from around the country contacted the Party asking how they could join, and the Party responded by opening new Black Panther offices in Los Angeles, New York, Seattle, and at least seventeen other cities by the end of the year, including Albany, Bakersfield, Boston, Chicago, Denver, Des Moines, Detroit, Fresno, Indianapolis, Long Beach, Newark, Omaha, Peekskill, Philadelphia, Richmond, Sacramento, and San Diego.[78]

Young blacks were drawn by the Panthers' strategy of armed self-defense against the police because it simultaneously gave them a powerful means to resist and was difficult to repress. Facing the resistance of organized and armed young blacks, police departments could no longer maintain brutal containment policing practices with impunity. By arming and organizing, and advocating revolution, Black Panthers challenged the legitimacy of the state. Yet the Party remained aboveground, refraining from overt direction of armed struggle. For example, Newton's Executive Mandate No. 3, issued from prison in March 1968, ordered all Panther members to obtain firearms, and to fire on anyone—including police—who attempted to enter their homes without peaceably producing a legal warrant. Without any offensive direction, the Party thus created the conditions under which an increasing number of armed confrontations between Panthers and the police occurred. The Party effectively argued to potential allies that these confrontations reflected the widespread pattern of oppression of blacks and that the only change was the Black Panthers' decision to claim their right to defend themselves.

By framing this practice of armed self-defense as part of a global anti-imperialist struggle, the Panthers were able to draw broad support both from other black political organizations and from many nonblacks. These allies provided crucial financial, political, and legal support that enabled the Panthers to mount top-notch, unprecedented legal defenses against the many charges they faced, and they often won their cases in court. The allied support the Panthers received not only enabled the Party to grow but also demonstrated the efficacy of its politics. If the Panthers had simply been jailed and killed, with little allied support, the Party would have quickly dissolved. Instead, the Black Panther Party rapidly expanded to become the most influential black movement organization in the United States by December 1968. The insurgency was escalating.

FIGURE 1. The original Black Panther logo is displayed by Jesse W. Favor, a candidate for sheriff of Lowndes County, Alabama, in preparation for the nominating convention on May 3, 1966. (AP Photo)

SATURDAY

GREEK THEATER

BERKELEY CONFERENCE ON

BLACK POWER
and ITS CHALLENGES

9:45 - MIKE MILLER - " HISTORY OF BLACK POWER IN SNCC"

10:00- IVANHOE DONALDSON

10:40- A STATEMENT FROM I

11:00- TERRY CANNON (Editor

11:30- RON KARENGA (from W

11:50- CLAY CARSON (from W

12:00- ELIJAH TURNER (Oakla

12:20- "TWO VIEWS ON BLAC

   -- JAMES BEVEL (Sou

   -- IVANHOE DONALD

1:40- RENNIE DAVIS (Chicago

2:10- PANEL _ "BLACK POW

  -Watts: DANNY GREY

      BROTHER LE

  - Richmond: KATHERI

  - Oakland: ELIJAH TUI

  - Moderator: MIKE MII

3:10- "ORGANIZING STUDEN

  --MIKE SMITH (SDS)

  --MIKE PARKER (SDS

3:50- JAMES BEVEL (Southe

4:30- STOKELY CARMICHAE

The **BLACK PANTHER**

VOLUME 1   APRIL 25, 1967

P.O. BOX 8641 OAK. CALIF. EMERYVILLE BRANCH

INSTITUTION *BLACK COMMUNITY NEWS SERVICE*

NUMBER 1

PUBLISHED BY THE BLACK PANTHER PARTY FOR SELF DEFENSE

FEB 1 9 1993

WHY WAS DENZIL DOWELL KILLED

APRIL FIRST
3:50 a.m.

"I BELIEVE THE POLICE MURDERED MY SON" SAYS THE MOTHER OF DENZIL DOWELL.

Brothers and Sisters of the Richmond community, here is the view of the family's side of the death of Denzil Dowell as compiled by the Black Panther Party for Self Defense, concerned citizens, and the Dowell family. As you know, April 1st, 1967, Denzel Dowell (age 22), was shot and killed by an "officer of the Martinez Sheriff's Department", so read the newspaper.

But there are too many unanswered questions that have been raised by the Dowell family and other neighbors in the North Richmond community. Questions that don't meet the satisfaction of the killing of Denzil. The Richmond Police, the Martinez Sheriff's Department, and the Richmond Independent would have us black people believe something contrary to Mrs. Dowell's accusation. That is, her son was "unjustifiably" murdered by a racist cop.

There are too many questionable facts supporting the Dowell family's point of view.

These questionable facts are as follows:

1. Denzil Dowell was unarmed so how can six bullet holes and shot gun blasts be considered "justifiable homocide"? (Con't Page 2)

WE BLACK PEOPLE ARE MEETING SATURDAY 1:30 AT 1717 SECOND STREET LET US SUPPORT THE DOWELL FAIMLY EVERY BLACK BROTHER AND SISTER MUST UNITE FOR REAL POLITICAL ACTION

FIGURE 2. *(above)* Disseminated nationally by Stokely Carmichael, the Black Panther Party name and logo first appeared in the Oakland Bay Area on this flier for a Black Power conference on October 29, 1966, featuring Carmichael and organized by the Students for a Democratic Society. (H. K. Yuen Collection)

FIGURE 3. *(below)* Huey Newton and Bobby Seale soon adopted the Black Panther logo, displayed here in the first issue of their newspaper, published April 25, 1967. (© Dr. Huey P. Newton Foundation)

FIGURE 4. Black Panther founders Bobby Seale *(left)* and Huey Newton *(right)* pose with their weapons outside their first office on 56th and Grove Streets in Oakland, February 1967. (AP Photo/San Francisco Examiner)

FIGURE 5. An armed Black Panther contingent at the California Assembly building in Sacramento protests the proposed Mulford Act, which would prohibit their armed patrols of police, May 2, 1967. (Walt Zeboski/AP Photo)

FIGURE 6. Huey P. Newton, leader of the Black Panther Party, seated in a wicker throne. The Party began distributing this now-iconic image as part of its reconception as a revolutionary vanguard following cessation of armed patrols of the police during the summer of 1967. (© Dr. Huey P. Newton Foundation)

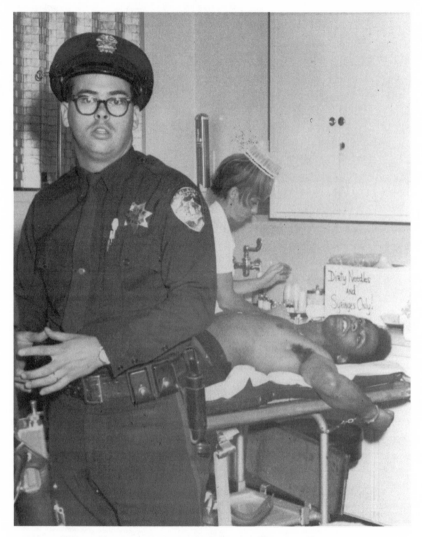

FIGURE 7. Newton lies manacled to a hospital gurney after an early-morning confrontation on October 28, 1967, in which he was shot in the abdomen and Oakland police officer John Frey was killed. (AP Photo)

FIGURE 8. *(above)* Speakers at the Huey Newton birthday celebration at the Oakland Auditorium, February 17, 1968, include, *from right to left*, Alprentice "Bunchy" Carter, leader of the newly founded Los Angeles Black Panther Party chapter, who was later killed in a conflict fostered by the FBI COINTELPRO; Student Nonviolent Coordinating Committee leaders James Forman, H. Rap Brown, and Stokely Carmichael; Bobby Seale; Carver Chico Nesbitt; unknown boy; and Ron Dellums. The renowned SNCC leaders were exploring a merger with the Black Panther Party at the time. The empty wicker throne highlights Newton's absence, as he sat in prison awaiting his trial on capital charges. (© Dr. Huey P. Newton Foundation)

FIGURE 9. *(below)* The Black Panther Party's first member, Lil' Bobby Hutton, poses armed in front of the Oakland jail, 1967. On April 8, 1968, four days after the assassination of Martin Luther King Jr., Oakland police killed Hutton. (© Ron Riesterer)

FIGURE 10. *(above)* Actor Marlon Brando and Black Panther members in uniform were among those attending Lil' Bobby Hutton's funeral on May 12, 1968. (Dan Cronin/New York Daily News Archive/Getty Images)

FIGURE 11. *(below)* Black Panthers hold a rally in New York City. Following the killings of Lil' Bobby Hutton and Martin Luther King, the Black Panther Party quickly expanded, opening chapters in cities throughout the country, including an important branch in New York City. (© Roz Payne)

FIGURE 12. *(above left)* Alprentice "Bunchy" Carter, leader of the Los Angeles chapter of the Black Panther Party, was killed on the University of California campus in Los Angeles on January 17, 1969, by members of the US organization, in a confrontation actively instigated, if not directly planned, by the federal government's COINTELPRO. (© Dr. Huey P. Newton Foundation)

FIGURE 13. *(above right)* John Huggins, born to a well-heeled family in New Haven, dropped out of college to join the Black Panther Party and played a key role in organizing the Los Angeles chapter, the first chapter to open outside the Oakland Bay Area. Three weeks after his wife, Ericka Huggins, gave birth to their daughter, Mai, on January 17, 1969, Huggins was killed alongside Carter in the UCLA campus confrontation instigated by COINTELPRO. (© Dr. Huey P. Newton Foundation)

FIGURE 14. *(below)* Ericka Huggins left college in Pennsylvania and traveled to California to join the Black Power movement. At the funeral for Lil' Bobby Hutton, she and her husband, John, committed their lives to revolutionary struggle and to the Black Panther Party. When John was killed less than nine months later, Ericka moved to New Haven and became an important Party leader there. Her trial on conspiracy charges, eventually dismissed, was one of the most celebrated political trials of the decade. She went on to direct the award-winning Oakland Community School and now lectures and consults widely. (Dave Pickoff/AP Photo)

FIGURE 15. Bobby Seale speaks at a "Free Huey!" rally in "Lil' Bobby Hutton Park" on July 14, 1968. The bus and sound system were on loan from the Peace and Freedom Party. James Forman *(seated middle)* and Chief of Staff David Hilliard *(seated right)* share the stage with Seale. (© 2011 Pirkle Jones Foundation/Ruth-Marion Baruch)

FIGURE 16. *(above) Left to right,* Black Panthers Mary Ann Carlton, Delores Henderson, Joyce Lee, Joyce Means, and Paula Hill rally in "Lil' Bobby Hutton Park," August 25, 1968. (© 2010 Pirkle Jones Foundation/Pirkle Jones)

FIGURE 17. *(below)* Allies attend a "Free Huey!" rally in "Lil' Bobby Hutton Park," the summer of 1968. As in most large Black Panther rallies, the audience was mixed racially, featuring many nonblack as well as black supporters. (Stephen Shames/Polaris Images)

FIGURE 18. Kathleen Cleaver, Black Panther communications secretary, poses armed to illustrate the Party's Executive Mandate No. 3, which ordered all members to keep guns in their homes and to defend themselves against any police officers or others who attempted to invade without a warrant. (© Alan Copeland)

FIGURE 19. *(above)* "It's All the Same," a graphic by Emory Douglas published in the *Black Panther* and subsequently disseminated by New Left activists, makes the point that all state violence is similar, whether meted out by local police (against blacks), the National Guard (against protestors), or the U.S. Marines (against the Vietnamese). (© 2012 Emory Douglas/Artists Rights Society, New York)

FIGURE 20. *(below)* Students and Black Panther supporters listen to Eldridge Cleaver, Black Panther minister of information, speaking on Sproul Plaza at the University of California, Berkeley, on October 3, 1968. (© 2010 Pirkle Jones Foundation/Pirkle Jones)

FIGURE 21. Black Panther Charles Bursey serves breakfast to children, June 20, 1969. In 1969, the Black Panther Party made community programs its core activity. (© 2011 Pirkle Jones Foundation/Ruth-Marion Baruch)

FIGURE 22. *(above left)* Black Panther Bill Whitfield serves breakfast to children in Kansas City, Missouri, April 16, 1969. (William Straeter/AP Photo)

FIGURE 23. *(above right)* The Panthers launched the first Free Breakfast for Children Program at St. Augustine's Episcopal Church in Oakland. (Stephen Shames/Polaris Images)

FIGURE 24. *(below)* Students attend class at the Black Panther Party Children's Institute, a precursor to the Oakland Community School. (Stephen Shames/Polaris Images)

FIGURE 25. *(above)* Members of the Black Panther Party distribute free clothing to the public in New Haven, September 28, 1969. (David Fenton/Getty Images)

FIGURE 26. *(below)* Panther Cubs and members of the San Francisco chapter of the Party give the Panther salute. (© Bettmann/Corbis/AP Images)

PART THREE

Resilience

First you have free breakfasts, then you have free medical care, then you have free bus rides, and soon you have FREEDOM!

—Fred Hampton, Deputy Chairman, Black Panther Party, Illinois

One of our primary aims in counterintelligence as it concerns the [Black Panther Party] is to keep this group isolated from the moderate black and white community which may support it. This is most emphatically pointed out in their Breakfast for Children Program, where they are actively soliciting and receiving support from uninformed whites and moderate blacks. . . . You state that the Bureau under the [Counterintelligence Program] should not attack programs of community interest such as the [Black Panther Party] "Breakfast for Children." You state that this is because many prominent "humanitarians," both white and black, are interested in the program as well as churches which are actively supporting it. You have obviously missed the point.

—J. Edgar Hoover to FBI Special Agent in Charge, San Francisco, May 27, 1969

You can kill a revolutionary, but you can't kill a revolution!

—Fred Hampton

7

Breakfast

Polly Graham knew about hardship and struggle. In the 1940s, she had been part of a failed attempt to organize low-wage black workers in the R. J. Reynolds Tobacco Factory in Winston-Salem, North Carolina. But virulent anti-unionism, magnified by racism and anti-Communist hysteria, had beaten that noble and long-forgotten effort. Almost thirty years later, on March 4, 1970, she opened the door of her rented home to find police handing her an eviction notice. Because the property had already been condemned in a legal hearing, she understood that she owed no rent until the landlord made the necessary repairs. The landlord believed and acted differently. Confronted with the seemingly impregnable power of the police, Polly Graham went to the local office of the Black Panther Party for help.

The local Panthers immediately sprang into action, sending a contingent to Ms. Graham's home, where, with two armed Panthers standing guard, they replaced belongings that had been removed from the home by eviction police. In addition to resecuring Ms. Graham in her home, armed Panthers stood guard over the nearby homes of Pauline Greer and Minnie Bellamy to prevent similar evictions of these two elderly women.

The neighborhood temperature reached a boil. A standoff ensued between the police, trying to carry out evictions, and the Panthers, trying to keep these elderly black women from being tossed from their homes. Other community activists joined the fray. Lee Faye Mack, emboldened by the Panther presence, encouraged the crowd to "Go get your pieces." A cofounder of Mothers for Black Liberation and a Party adviser, Ms. Mack personified the increasingly tight bond between the poor and working-class black community of East Winston-Salem and the Panther Party. As Larry Little, the irrepressible leader of the local Panthers, recalled, after Ms. Mack spoke, even little "old ladies" went home and returned with "their double-barrel shotguns" to face down the eviction cops. Only after a third party paid Ms. Graham's rent did the standoff cool down.[1]

Still, Winston-Salem's black community remained on edge. Three months later, in June 1970, Sara Alford seriously cut herself on a glass jar in the A&P Supermarket in the black Carver neighborhood. When Ms. Alford asked store management to pay for her anticipated medical bills they refused. As word of the store's refusal spread, black outrage about the store's position sparked a community-wide boycott and picket of the local A&P. Larry Little told store officials, "Either you make the A&P relevant to the needs of the black community or get out." A protest against the store's disregard for Ms. Alford's injury escalated into a broader protest against discriminatory and disrespectful treatment endured by many black patrons of A&P. Protestors demanded that the store end its discriminatory hiring practices and employ blacks in substantial positions. The Party and its supporters demanded that the store contribute to its free breakfast program (formally known as the Free Breakfast for Children Program). Eventually, the store relented and agreed to the demands, including payment of Ms. Alford's medical bills.[2]

Reenacted countless times in black communities across the country, similar confrontations between the Panthers and authorities helped build strong local Party chapters. Local Party chapters frequently served as community sounding boards and social service agencies—as black people's stewards—deeply committed to social justice and community betterment. The Party essentially said to the community, Bring your concerns to us. And they did. Jamal, a Philadelphia Panther recalled,

> The offices were like buzzing beehives of Black resistance. It was always busy, as people piled in starting at its 7:30 A.M. opening time and continuing 'till after nightfall. People came with every problem imaginable, and because our sworn duty was to serve the people, we took our commitment seriously. . . . When people had been badly treated by the cops or if parents were demanding a traffic light in North Philly streets where their children played, they came to our offices. In short, whatever our people's problems were, they became our problems. We didn't preach to the people; we worked with them.[3]

Community members brought all kinds of disputes to the local Party: job-related conflicts, evictions, rent struggles, gang violence, safety concerns, legal and criminal justice problems, consumer complaints, and issues with government social services, public and private utilities, and the underworld economy (numbers runners, pimps, prostitutes, drug dealers). If the local Party judged that redress was necessary, it took action. In doing so, it provided community members with a vital source of remediation that was often unavailable from the state. Its actions, in turn, attracted more members and supporters.

The Party saw itself as inextricably tied to the local black community. The most critical aspect of the Black Panther message proved deceptively simple: We are you; your problems are our problems. As one Party comrade explained, "The exploited . . . people's needs are land, bread, housing, education, . . . , clothing, justice, and peace, and the Black Panther Party shall not, for a day, alienate ourselves from the masses and forget their needs for survival."[4]

FROM GUNS TO BUTTER

By the fall of 1968, membership in the Black Panther Party was mushrooming. Local activists in cities throughout the country had heard of the Black Panther Party and contacted national headquarters wanting to join and start their own local chapters. Chief of Staff David Hilliard later recalled the deluge of calls from people "asking to start a chapter. We get calls all day long. Des Moines, Virginia Beach, Atlanta. Since we're three hours behind the East Coast, the requests often start as early as eight A.M."[5] As Party membership and influence grew, so did repressive action by the state. The Party sought meaningful activities for members that would serve the community, strengthen the Party, and improve its image in the public relations battle with the state. In this context, community programs quickly became a cornerstone of Party activity nationwide.

The Black Panther community programs began in early 1969 under Bobby Seale's leadership, marking an important transformation in the Party's political practice. In the fall of 1968, Eldridge Cleaver went into exile to avoid returning to prison when his parole was revoked.[6] With Huey Newton in prison, Seale, a staunch advocate of community programs since his days working in the government poverty program in Oakland, became primarily responsible for setting Party policy.[7]

The Black Panther Party announced its intention to launch the Free

Breakfast for Children Program in Oakland in September 1968. The call for volunteers and donations went out before Christmas.[8] The Party launched its first free breakfast program at Father Earl A. Neil's St. Augustine's Episcopal Church in west Oakland in late January 1969. Parishioner Ruth Beckford-Smith coordinated the program. Beckford-Smith first became interested in the Black Panthers while teaching Afro-Haitian dance to young women at the church, including LaVerne Williams, Huey Newton's girlfriend. When the Party decided to organize a breakfast for children at St. Augustine's, Beckford-Smith volunteered to coordinate the program and helped organize it. The first day the program opened it served 11 children. By the end of the week, the program was serving 135 children daily at St. Augustine's. The *San Francisco Chronicle* covered the program and reported the "unspoken lesson" children would learn: "power in a community begins with people who care."[9]

By March 1969, the Black Panthers opened another Free Breakfast for Children Program at the Sacred Heart Church in San Francisco's Fillmore district.[10] By April, the Party reported feeding more than twelve hundred children per day at nine facilities in Oakland, San Francisco, and Vallejo in California; in Chicago; and in Des Moines, Iowa.[11]

Seale went to prison that August, and David Hilliard, chief of staff of the Party, took the reins of the national Party organization. Hilliard continued to give priority to development of the Free Breakfast for Children Program, and during his tenure, the program spread like wildfire, becoming the most important Panther activity.[12] By November, the Party reported feeding children free breakfast daily in twenty-three cities across the country, from Seattle to Kansas City and New York.[13] At the height of the effort, between 1969 and 1971, at least thirty-six breakfast programs were operating nationwide with larger chapters running multiple sites.[14]

David Hilliard was born May 15, 1942, in rural Rockville, Alabama, the youngest of Lee and Lela Hilliard's twelve children. David's father always worked—often as a logger or tapping turpentine. His mother always worked when she was not nursing one of her babies. With such a large family, the Hilliards were poor, living in a four-room shack without flush toilets and scraping together meals. As the baby of the family, David was protected. He became an independent thinker, quite stylish and averse to drudgery. Extremely willful in his dealings with the world, he remained exceptionally loyal and deferential to family elders.[15]

Under Jim Crow, blacks were expected to kowtow to whites. The Hilliards, though, did not always comply. After a fight with a white man in the early 1950s, David's eldest brother, Bud, fled to Oakland, California. David later recalled being impressed by Martin Luther King and nonviolent civil rights activists but disagreeing with their approach: "The passivity of the civil rights demonstrators contradicts my family's most fundamental belief: you don't stand idly by and be kicked, you fight for yourself."[16] When David was eleven, his mother moved to Oakland to join Bud, bringing David and eventually other family members along. In Oakland, David became close friends with fellow elementary school student Huey Newton. This friendship eventually shaped the course of his life. At seventeen, he married his sweetheart, Patricia, dropped out of high school, and entered the workforce. Within three years, he and Patricia had three children: Patrice, Darryl, and Dorion.

David Hilliard's ascent to Party leadership was gradual. He was first and foremost loyal to Huey, his childhood friend. As he became increasingly involved in the Party, the Panthers became his family. Until the summer of 1969, when he was thrust into primary Party leadership, Hilliard was always deferential, following the lead of Huey, then Eldridge, then Bobby. He was not eager to participate in big, head-on confrontations with the state and did not participate much in the early patrols of police, the armed rallies in Richmond, the armed action in Sacramento, or later confrontations; he went along with Eldridge on the April 6, 1968, armed action only under duress.

Rather than gravitating toward the military side of the Party, Hilliard saw the Party as one big extended family, building on the communal traditions he had experienced in the black rural South. He later recalled, "When I think about the influences that inspired the spirit and work of the Black Panther Party . . . the most important members of the Party . . . were imbued with the moral and spiritual values of their parents; and the work that went into the Party, our dignity as an independent people, the communal ideal and practice that informed our programs, all stem in part from the civilization of which my mother and father were so representative a part."[17]

In addition to his communal ethic, his working man's sense of organization, discipline, and efficiency—gained during a work life that included laboring on the docks—became an important characteristic of his leadership. He proved to be a good administrator, in constant communication with the diverse and rapidly growing local leadership of the Party in cities across the country. He worked hard to keep the local chapters around the country united under a singular program. Under his leadership, the Panthers' community service programs flourished. And through the period of the greatest repression, the Party continued to grow. Hilliard's leadership and especially the community programs he championed contributed significantly to that growth.

During the year Hilliard served as the senior ranking Panther not in prison or exile, from August 1969 through August 1970, the Black Panther Party developed an impressive array of community programs in Panther chapters throughout the country. These programs eventually included the Free Breakfast for Children Program, liberation schools, free health clinics, the Free Food Distribution Program, the Free Clothing Program, child development centers, the Free Shoe Program, the Free Busing to Prison Program, the Sickle Cell Anemia Research Foundation, free housing cooperatives, the Free Pest Control Program, the Free Plumbing and Maintenance Program, renter's assistance, legal aid, the Seniors Escorts Program, and the Free Ambulance Program.[18] Larger and more established chapters tended to run the most diverse range of programs. The histories of specific programs in local chapters were often episodic, at times short-lived, depending upon the strength and viability of a given chapter at a particular moment. Virtually all chapters ran at least a Free Breakfast for Children Program at some point.

The breakfast program quickly became an important public face of the Party as well as its cornerstone activity. In 1969, it moved front and center for the Party programmatically, politically, ideologically, and publicly. The Party claimed to have fed twenty thousand children in the 1968–69 school year and said it hoped to feed one hundred thousand in 1969–70.[19] As "the most respected and popular" of the Party's programs, former Detroit Panther JoNina Abron has observed, these breakfast services enjoyed widespread support within black neighborhoods.[20]

The Free Breakfast for Children Programs adopted a rigorous common routine. Members had to be at the sites early in the morning, in time to prepare the food and be ready for the arriving children before they ate and then headed off to school. Transporting some of the children from home to the site and then to school was another vital yet often trying logistical job. While the children ate their meal, members taught them liberation lessons consisting of Party messages and black history. Miriam Ma'at-Ka-Re Monges recalled that in the breakfast program at the Ralph Avenue Community Center in the Brownsville section of Brooklyn, "Party Members and students cooked and served large pots of grits and eggs. We cajoled supermarkets for donations and we fed hundreds of children. Most importantly, we also nourished their minds with Black History lessons as they ate their meals. Sometimes we fed parents of the children."[21] The Brownsville breakfast program was not unique in its willingness to feed not just the hungry children but also other hungry community members.

Feeding "hundreds of kids a day and approximately 1,200 per week" as the Los Angeles chapter did at one time demanded strong publicity, marketing, organizational, and executive skills. In Los Angeles, Flores Forbes notes,

> The organizing effort began with us going door-to-door in the projects, passing out free papers with leaflets advertising the program. We talked to parents, kids, and storeowners near the projects. We explained why we had started the program: to help the kids grow and intellectually develop because children can't learn on an empty stomach. The breakfast program was an excellent organizing tool, helping us make friends and comrades in the projects. . . . The response was overwhelming. All types of parents agreed to host and serve our efforts. We held the program in the homes of junkies, drug dealers, regular public assistance recipients, gamblers, and gang bangers. Store owners donated bread, eggs, bacon, sausage, milk, and paper products. In addition to our organizing activities, we cooked, served the food, knocked on doors to let the kids know which apartment the food was being served in, and on many an occasion made last-minute pick-ups of donations from stores.[22]

Businesses donated food and supplies to the local breakfast programs for a mix of reasons, including altruism and the promotion of positive community relations. Businesses that chose not to help out faced the Party's wrath. At times the Panthers' cajoling blended into harassment and strong-arming. Far more common were boycotts and pickets of businesses that refused to assist the programs. Equally common was the tactic of calling out, or publicly shaming, those who refused to help. Churches and other community-based organizations that refused to help, notably those who refused to sponsor or allow breakfast programs on their premises, faced similar treatment. For starters, the Panther newspaper and Panther representatives railed against the non-supportive businessperson or community leader as a "capitalist pig." Other epithets included "religious hypocrites," "lying preachers and merchants," and "avaricious businessmen."[23]

Multiple ideological goals linked these programs, which, broadly speaking, helped to "raise public consciousness about hunger and poverty in America."[24] More specifically, the free breakfast programs highlighted the fact that hunger impeded a child's ability to learn. Politically, the breakfasts shed light on the government's failure to address childhood poverty and hunger—pointing to the limits of the nation's War on Poverty. The U.S. government spent only $600,000 on breakfast programs in all of 1967. Government-sponsored breakfast programs grew rapidly as the Panthers pioneered their free breakfast program. By 1972, government-sponsored breakfast programs were feeding 1.18 million children out of the approximately 5 million who qualified for such help.[25]

Attacking the serious problem of childhood hunger was a way to win people's hearts and minds. "While we might not need their direct assistance in waging armed revolution," acknowledged Forbes, "we were hedging our bets that if we did, they would respond more favorably to a group of people looking out for their children's welfare."[26] The FBI and police agreed. In Baltimore, as in other places, they castigated these programs "as a front for indoctrinating children with Panther propaganda." As a result, the national repression apparatus went into overdrive to destroy the free breakfast programs. Police and federal agents regularly harassed and intimidated program participants, supporters, and Party workers and sought to scare away donors and organizations that housed the programs, like churches and community centers. Safiya A. Bukhari discovered that participation in one of the Harlem free breakfast programs fell off after the police spread a false rumor among black parents that the children were being fed "poisoned food." A police disinformation campaign in Richmond, California, suggested that the Party used the Free Breakfast for Children Program to spread racism and to foment school riots. Student participation began to decline, forcing local Panther leaders to combat the official disinformation.[27]

The police were not above raiding breakfast program locations, even while the children were eating. The Baltimore Panther branch was comparatively small, but as Judson L. Jeffries demonstrates, the branch endured "an excessive amount of violent repression, and not even children were spared harassment by the police." One morning, the Baltimore police disrupted the children's breakfast, barging menacingly onto the premises. A witness recalled, "They walked around with their guns drawn and looked real mean. The children felt terrorized by the police. [The police] were like gangsters and thugs." The *Black Panther* explained that in Baltimore, "the hired mercenary pig forces" terrorized the community, the Party, and especially the Free

Breakfast for Children Program. Ronald Davis, co-coordinator of the Baltimore program, reported that "the foul minions of legal brutality and murder" had encircled the church sponsoring the program. The police were, he wrote, "armed to the teeth with the weaponry of the fascist war machine. After holding the people in check, with guns, the pigs proceeded to force their way into the Children's Breakfast Program under the false excuse of looking for . . . suspects. Once the Gestapo shock troopers left the Breakfast Hall, they kicked in the door of Sister Angeline Edison, a former member of the Party, and kidnapped her and her son from her home with guns pointed at her and surrounding her, all under the pretentious lies of justice."[28]

HEALTH CARE AND BEYOND

The success of the Panthers' Free Breakfast for Children Program led the Party to initiate free health clinics and a range of other community programs. Many blacks were poorly served by the health care system, and some had never seen a doctor. Despite the health care initiatives within the federal government's War on Poverty—particularly the newly created neighborhood health centers targeting the needs of inner-city communities—many residents in these communities received only limited, if any, health care attention.[29]

In response, the Party created a series of free medical clinics across the country. These clinics relied on the volunteer services of local doctors, medical students, interns, residents, nurses, and community folk as well as donated or low-rent clinic space. These public Panther-run clinics, such as those in Berkeley and Cleveland, offered services to all who came, black and nonblack alike. In some cities, like Baltimore, the Party formed coalitions with like-minded individuals and groups to run free clinics in the community.[30]

For the Party, the focus was plain and urgent: to address within its limited resources the pressing health care concerns of poor black communities that sorely lacked adequate medical facilities and professionals. Clinic services "included first aid care, physical examinations, prenatal care, and testing for lead poisoning, high blood pressure, and sickle cell anemia." If necessary, clinicians referred patients to specialists for follow-up care. There were at least eleven such clinics, including those in Kansas City, Seattle, and New Haven. Chicago's Spurgeon "Jake" Winters Free Medical Care Center was one of the best-run and most-respected Panther health clinics, serving over two thousand people in its initial two months. "Medical teams from the Winters clinic went door-to-door assisting people with their health problems," according to Abron. "The clinic's staff included obstetricians, gynecologists, pediatricians, and general practitioners." Milwaukee's People's Free Health Center emphasized preventive medicine and health care education on "sickle cell anemia, drug abuse, children's health and birth control" as well as free health care screenings. The clinic also sponsored discussions on black social relations, including relations between black women and men, and concerns of black youth.[31]

The Party's sickle-cell-anemia testing program and its Sickle Cell Anemia Research Foundation made a serious contribution to black health care in America. The Party worked hard to publicize the seriousness of the disease, which afflicts about one in five hundred African Americans.[32] Before the Panthers launched a public awareness campaign in 1971, black and mainstream awareness of the disease was limited. After the Panther's publicity offensive on behalf of battling the disease, more and more blacks learned of the disease and got tested for it. In the Panther clinics, health care professionals referred those with the disease or with the sickle-cell trait for further counseling and, if necessary, treatment. The Panthers' Sickle Cell Anemia Research Foundation provided a public face to the disease, promoting pioneering work that led to advances in scientific understanding and medical treatment of the disease.[33]

The Party's health care programs included efforts to combat drug addiction. Often led by ex–drug addicts who worked with the Party, these initiatives focused on treatment and rehabilitation. In Boston's South End neighborhood, "Project Concern" was "run by ex-addicts who have acquired a political consciousness and therefore realize the necessity of quitting drugs in order to survive." The Party lauded the project's ideological thrust as well as its health advocacy and gave special praise to the brothers who ran and participated in the program. These brothers built their program "on the revolutionary ideology of capitalism plus dope equals genocide." Dope, they argued, was part of the oppressor's plan "to ensure our enslavement." A similar initiative, People for the People, offered "drug control and education" in "the heavily drug-infested" community of Corona-East Elmhurst in Queens, New York.[34]

Despite these successes, state repression continued. Local police and the FBI worked to undermine the Party's health clinics and the Panthers' health care activism. In 1971, Cleveland Panthers worked hard to transform their health clinic into a larger People's Free Health Clinic. On August 18 that year, a dynamite explosion severely damaged the clinic. The blast was widely believed to be the handiwork of the state, and Panther Jimmy Slater suggested that the police and FBI counterintelligence were responsible for blowing up the clinic, though definitive proof is lacking. "Any positive program that served and mobilized the community was attacked. It was one of the things we had going on that served a lot of people who needed free medical aid, and it was attacked to undermine the party's efforts."[35]

That same summer, early Sunday morning on July 5, the Party's Franklin Lynch People's Free Health Center in Boston was hit by thirteen shots, causing limited damage. Due to the loud noise of the July 4 fireworks and firecrackers, the attack went undetected until early Sunday morning. The shots were allegedly fired by local police, and clinic patrons and workers, community folk, and party members were outraged. The Boston Party chapter resolved that "the strength, the love and determination of the people has built the Free Health Center up to what it is today, and the same strength, love, and devotion of the people will make the Free Health Center stand up to future attacks by Mayor White's Gestapo pig force."[36]

The Party's advocacy of public health care for blacks revealed the group's deep commitment to a holistic view of health that was both environmental and physical. For the Party, the well-being of individual black bodies and the collective black community reflected the overall welfare of the larger black body politic. Improving the health status of blacks thus went hand in hand with improving their political, economic, and social status. In the Party's view, black political activism and black public health activism were interwoven.

Complementing the Party's health care activism were several programs that addressed the most basic material needs of poor black communities. The Free Food Distribution Program, the Free Clothing Program, and the Free Shoe Program were extremely well received. Also popular were targeted give-away initiatives featuring free food, clothing, and shoes, sometimes in conjunction with a Party rally. Free-food rallies organized by the Winston-Salem Black Panther Party chapter inaugurated the Joseph Waddell Free Food Program to honor a beloved comrade who had died in state prison under suspicious circumstances. One rally drew over two thousand people to the Kimberly Park Housing Project, where Party members gave out free food and shoes for children.[37]

A lack of adequate ambulance services was an especially galling problem in Black Winston-Salem. On October 17, 1970, fifteen-year-old Alan "Snake" Dendy was shot and then died when the drivers of the county ambulance that arrived on the scene refused to move his body, claiming they lacked authorization to do so. Responding to community outrage at the injustice, the local Panther chapter swung into action. By June 1971, the group had acquired an old hearse that it retrofitted as an ambulance. Party members had already been taking emergency medical technician (EMT) and first-aid classes at Surry Community College, and by summer's end, they were certified as EMTs. The chapter was thus able to begin operating its own ambulance before the year was out.[38]

The free emergency ambulance service was a big success and was named the Joseph Waddell People's Free Ambulance Service to commemorate the Panthers' recently deceased comrade. Waddell's $7,000 life insurance death benefit went to the local chapter, which used the money to subsidize the free ambulance program. Operating for over two years, the service at its height featured twenty-four-hour service and twenty certified EMTs who were Party members. The Forsyth County commissioners granted the chapter a franchise to operate.[39]

Another popular Panther effort, the Free Busing to Prison Program, helped incarcerated blacks stay connected to their families and communities. Because so many inner-city blacks could not afford transportation to and from prisons (which were often located in out-of-the-way rural sites) to visit relatives and friends, the busing program proved very popular, though it was expensive to maintain and suffered from chronic underfunding and persistent state efforts to destroy it.[40] The busing program had multiple political aims. First, it helped sustain connections between imprisoned blacks and their home communities. "Just because a Brother or Sister commits a crime, is it correct for them to be cut off from their loved ones, friends and community with no communication?" asked Milwaukee's Ronald Stark.[41]

Another aim of the Free Busing to Prison Program was to highlight the unjust incarceration of a disproportionate number of blacks and bring attention to the wrongful imprisonment of Panthers and other black political prisoners through bogus charges. The Panthers also sought to expose the alarming racism underlying these wrongs—an entire criminal injustice system for blacks and poor people. The extreme state repression of the Party, the unjust imprisonment of so many Party members, and the devastating consequences of both only heightened the ideological and practical significance of the Party's Free Busing to Prison Program.[42]

After becoming a member of the Detroit branch, JoNina Abron's involvement in the busing program introduced her to the Party's other community service programs:

> I drove one of the vans that transported families to visit their incarcerated relatives at Jackson State Prison. Having grown up as the sheltered daughter of a minister and a music teacher, I was overwhelmed by my experience at Jackson State Prison, which was my first visit to a penitentiary. Another service that the [Black Panther Party] provided for prison inmates was the free commissary program. [Party] members secured donations of personal hygiene items and non-perishable foods and sent care packages to prisoners. The party also offered attorney referral services for prison inmates.[43]

Just as the Party's free medical clinics at times led to cooperation with local allies and outlasted the Party's active involvement, several of the Free Busing to Prison programs lived beyond the Party. In Cleveland, for instance, Panther JoAnn Bray's work with the Party's Free Busing to Prison Program continued after the local Party itself collapsed. With ongoing community support and a $16,000 grant, Bray was able to keep the buses running for several years in the 1970s, changing the program's name to the People's Busing Program and charging a small fee.[44]

Panthers at all levels and from all class backgrounds had endured the racism of public schools and knew firsthand the crying need to remake fundamentally black public school education. The Black Panther Party thus committed itself to a relevant and empowering education for black children. Point 5 of the Party's platform demanded an education "that exposes the true nature of this decadent American society" and "teaches us our true history and our role in the present-day society." Such an education had to be probing and affirmative. It had to create highly skilled citizens dedicated to advancing the best interests of the black nation within the American nation.

Building upon the tradition of black self-empowerment, alternative black schools dotted the progressive landscape before the Panthers came on the scene. The citizenship schools of the Civil Rights Movement, led by Septima Clark, helped many blacks master the knowledge and mechanics necessary to register to vote in the South before the Voting Rights Act. Freedom Summer 1964 in Mississippi featured a series of freedom schools that taught the fundamentals alongside black history and culture as well as the Civil Rights Movement's ideology and goals.

These efforts contributed to the larger social changes transforming Mississippi and the rest of the former Confederacy.[45]

The Panthers' liberation schools extended this tradition by insisting on a Black Power revolution: the inclusion of black perspectives, experiences, and knowledge in the formal and informal school curricula. The liberation schools typically served children in kindergarten through the eighth grade and included meals, social welfare help for needy students and families, and extended hours. These schools also featured black history and culture, a diverse and rich academic and political curriculum, and lessons in the Party's ideology, goals, and activities. Whereas the Party saw these schools as training grounds for well-equipped citizens, sensitive to issues of class, race, and socialism, the Black Panther Party's enemies—principally state and federal governments—saw them as purveyors of anti-American and antiwhite propaganda.

The Panthers launched at least nine liberation schools across the nation, from Seattle to the Bronx, with the first established in Berkeley in June 1969. These institutions varied in longevity, structure, substance, and effectiveness. Because of the Party's emphasis on education and the Panthers' own often negative experiences with the mainstream education system, Party members labored hard and long to make these schools effective. Still, government misinformation and bad publicity led to the demise of several efforts, such as Black Panther Party–sponsored liberation schools in Des Moines and Omaha.[46]

Variations on the Panthers' central educational model sprouted up throughout the United States. Building upon the Party's broader community-based educational work, the Philadelphia chapter sponsored a People's Free Library that featured texts by black authors. In the summer of 1970, the Cleveland chapter ran a summer liberation school with meals and ten hours of instruction for twenty-five children. In Brooklyn, the local Party ran a liberation school that supplemented the basics with an Afrocentric focus. According to Miriam Monges, the schools emphasized "rudimentary aspects of the Afrocentric paradigm. . . . We taught African history lessons and sponsored African dance classes."[47]

The most substantial and successful Party liberation school was the flagship Intercommunal Youth Institute (IYI) in Oakland. Founded in January 1971, the school graduated its first class in 1974 and lasted through 1982, well after the rest of the Black Panther Party organization had disintegrated. The IYI's first class had twenty-eight students, most of whom were children of Party members. At its height, the school had a waiting list of four hundred. Working with students from ages two and a half to eleven, the faculty, led from 1973 to 1981 by Ericka Huggins and a strong group of mostly women teachers, taught a demanding program to a student body with wide-ranging abilities and often challenging backgrounds.[48]

Adopting a pedagogy that grouped students by ability and achievement rather than by age, the IYI sought to do its best by each student. The Party provided meals to students, and when the school expanded to encompass a middle school, it provided housing for some of the older children. The school also at times hosted other programs, including a GED (high school equivalency) program and instruction in martial arts. At its height, the school was commended by Governor Jerry Brown and the California State Assembly for "having set the standard for the highest level of elementary education."[49]

SHIFTING GENDER DYNAMICS

Women were a pivotal force in the Panthers, at times constituting a majority of the Party's membership. Panther women energized the local branches and played a central role in creating the indigenous culture of struggle that gave the local chapters their resonance and distinctiveness. They kept the community programs alive and did most of the painstaking day-to-day social labor necessary to sustain the chapters. Providing informal child-care networks and day-care centers, assisting elderly and infirm community members with their housing, food, medical, and even more personal concerns were generally the province of Panther women. The Party heavily recruited women to staff programs like the Free Breakfast for Children Program, where women, notably mothers, garnered special praise for their work. Reflecting traditional gender norms, the Party newspaper enthusiastically endorsed these kinds of programs as fundamentally maternalist: particularly well suited to mothers', and by extension to women's, sensibilities and commitments.[50]

In its early years, especially before 1968 and the explosive subsequent growth in Party membership, the organization was largely male. The Black Panther Party got its start as "a male-centered, male-dominated organization."[51] The group's initial rhetorical and programmatic emphasis on arming members for self-defense, organizing the "brothers on the block," and revitalizing black manhood highlighted the Party's masculinism.

Even after women began to join the Party en masse in 1968 and the struggle to achieve gender equity intensified, the Party never overcame what Tracye Matthews has aptly called its "masculine public identity." Nevertheless, Frankye Malika Adams, speaking from her experiences at the grassroots level and reflecting a widely held view among Party members, noted, "Women ran the [Black Panther Party] pretty much. I don't know how it came to be a male's party or thought of as being a male's party. Because these things, when you really look at it in terms of society, these things are looked on as being women's things, . . . feeding children, taking care of the sick. . . . We actually ran the [Party's] programs."[52]

The gendering of the Party's community programs as female and the public face of the Party as male became entrenched for two major reasons. First, the Party's continuing masculinism and the society's deeply ingrained gender norms undercut the women's serious battles against sexism within the Party. Second, even as women's participation became increasingly central to the operation of the Party and questions of gender equity loomed large, the Party had no formal and effective mechanisms to root out sexism and misogyny. Consequently, despite the Panthers' antisexist rhetoric and efforts and the efforts of many Panther men and women to confront these ongoing problems, the problems persisted. Ericka Huggins recalls visiting a local chapter where women prepared the food and then waited in the kitchen until Panther men had eaten before serving themselves—a dynamic she quickly ended.[53]

Just as the lure of guns proved compelling for many recruits, both women and men, community service programs brought innumerable men and women into the Party and actively engaged large numbers of Panthers of both genders. Indeed, while women often ran many of the Free Breakfast for Children Programs, male participation in the programs was widespread, sensitizing innumerable Panther men to the importance of family, children, and gender issues for the Party as well as for black communities and the larger society. The Free Breakfast for Children Program specifically and the community service programs generally provided a powerful counter to the misleading stereotype of the Party as a bunch of gun-toting men.

Many of the Party members who served black communities in the free breakfast and other community programs lived in low-cost, no-frills communal arrangements within black communities known as Panther pads or Panther cribs. To the extent that these homes operated along egalitarian and democratic lines, they worked for all involved. In part, Panther pads reflected the Party's critique of conventional familial norms. As Huey Newton once noted, the traditional nuclear family in particular and conventional familial norms in general were "imprisoning, enslaving, and suffocating."[54] The Party's open and nonmonogamous communal living arrangements aimed to offer freer and more fulfilling lives.

In fact, these Panther pads often perpetuated the very practices they were supposed to alleviate, reinscribing male privilege and sexist attitudes. Thus, women were primarily responsible for housework and bore the brunt of the responsibility for open relationships with men, taking on family planning and reproductive concerns—notably birth control and abortions. Similarly, pregnancy and child care were primarily women's responsibility, so single mothers with children were often expected to pull the same load as their single and childless comrades. Rather than ushering in greater gender and sexual equality, these Panther pads all too often replicated gender and sexual inequality.[55]

THE POLITICS OF COMMUNITY SERVICE

The Party's community service programs were fundamentally political programs as well as socioeconomic ones and were thus vital to the Party's developing political ideology and practices. Writing in 1969, Bobby Seale maintained that the programs were not "reform programs" but "revolutionary, community, socialistic programs." This distinction—by casting the programs as part of a broader insurgency to change the American capitalist system to a more equitable socialist one—was crucial to the Party's political and ideological integrity. In the Panthers' view, the programs were revolutionary, not reformist. As Seale explained, "A revolutionary program is one set forth by revolutionaries, by those who want to change the existing system to a better one," whereas "a reform program is set up by the existing exploitative system as an appeasing handout, to fool the people and to keep them quiet. Examples of these programs are poverty programs, youth work programs, and things like that."[56]

The Party's community-based revolutionary ethos epitomized the pervasive desire within Black Power movements to empower black communities. The Party attracted large numbers of members and supporters, from various classes and races, who wanted to be part of a dynamic liberation movement rooted in the day-to-day struggles of ordinary black people, most of whom were poor and working class.

"Unlike the Niagara Movement, the National Association for the Advancement of Colored People, or the Urban League," Miriam Monges reminds us, "the Party's origins lie enmeshed among the black downtrodden. [Black Panther Party] offices were always located in the center of low-income areas of African American communities."[57] The short-lived and all-black Niagara Movement (1905–9), the interracial NAACP (1909-present), and the interracial Urban League (1911-present) all began as middle-class-led movements. The Black Panther Party, as a movement primarily identified with the black working class and underclass, linked itself to movements like the Nation of Islam, Garveyism, and varieties of black worker- and union-based activism dating back to the nineteenth century.[58]

Through direct service to the community, the Panthers accomplished several pressing functions. First, the services provided concrete aid to an impressive number and cross-section of folk—whites, blacks, and other people of color—materializing the notion of service to the community. In addition to providing their own labor, the Panthers generated alternative bases of funding and resources to serve impoverished communities, collecting individual and local business donations.

Second, these programs accomplished crucial educational and political work within communities, conveying the insufficiency of the capitalist welfare state to meet even the most basic needs of its citizens, especially its black citizens. As Ryan Nissim-Sabat has pointed out, the piecemeal yet serious efforts of these community programs represented a broader offensive "to compensate for the inadequate institutions of the state and to raise the consciousness of people in their local communities."[59] As Yvonne King, deputy of labor in the Party's Chicago chapter, observed in the spring of 1969, "Hunger among schoolchildren illustrates one of the basic contradictions in American society. America is one of the richest nations in the world, able to send countless numbers of rockets into space at the drop of a dollar, yet people are starving."[60] The Free Breakfast for Children Program in particular enabled the Party to crystallize these stark contradictions and heighten black awareness of such structural inequities. This deepening awareness then pushed black communities to create other programs to ameliorate the crushing problems stemming from systemic inequalities.

Third, the Panthers' programs expanded communities' understanding of the process of grassroots institutional development—how to create and sustain their own much-needed institutions from the ground up. Building upon these communities' tradition of active self-help, the

Party revitalized and modeled grassroots black community development and institution building. Its programs offered concrete examples of Black Power's vision of community empowerment. The ultimate goal of these institutions was clear: self-determination. Empowering black communities to take control of their own affairs and manage them in their best interests was central to the Party's social service programs.

Fourth, these programs not only kept the Party alive in the face of awesome state repression, they also initially enabled it to grow during these trying times. Party members' arduous work with very little formal remuneration—particularly in the breakfast programs and free medical clinics—won the Panthers' strong support in black communities and contributed substantially to the Party's "street credibility." This vital work likewise had strong support from liberal and progressive blacks and whites.

The Party's emphasis on direct community service as a means of advancing black community self-determination and ameliorating the ills besetting them linked it to the historic organizing tradition of the Black Liberation Struggle. Just as the Student Nonviolent Coordinating Committee's extraordinary organizing work helped galvanize the Southern Civil Rights Movement, the Panthers' organizing efforts were vital to galvanizing the national Black Liberation Struggle.[61] The social service programs linked the Party's organizing work to a long tradition, including the work of organizations like the postwar Nation of Islam, with its successful rehabilitation programs for black male prisoners, exemplified by the rehabilitation of Malcolm X.[62] These kinds of formal programs constituted concrete steps to advance the best interests of the black nation within the American nation. Black Panthers saw their own community-based programs as part of their commitment to a black nation-building project, an expression of the Party's revolutionary nationalism.

Even as the state wrenched into overdrive to decimate the Party in 1969 and 1970, the community service programs attracted innumerable new Party members and supporters and enabled the Party to keep growing. Jimmy Slater explained that he joined the Cleveland chapter because of "the many different positive programs sponsored by the party."[63] Flores A. Forbes noted that "the work I most enjoyed" was the community service programs, particularly the free breakfast programs for children in the four main Watts housing projects.[64]

The state marshaled its vast and enormous powers and labored overtime to destroy the Party. In late August 1970, a series of Gestapo-like raids of several Panther headquarters by the notorious Philadelphia police proved disastrous for the Party, causing extensive property loss and damage and subjecting arrested Party members to humiliating public strip searches in front of the media and the community. Still, the community did not abandon the Party. Instead, in early September, ignoring police orders, community members labored to return the North Philadelphia office to a habitable state. Clarence Peterson remembered, "It was the most beautiful experience I've ever had in my whole life. I really cried because the people opened up our offices again. . . . We did not think our office would open again. The people in the community put everything back in the office. They put furniture back . . . they fed us for about a week . . . they kept our kids. It was something that I have never seen or heard of before. It was really something . . . it was out of sight . . . they told the cops that these are our Panthers, so leave them alone."[65] Precisely because the Panthers responded as best they could to the pressing concerns of their home communities, these communities embraced their Panthers, and the ties between local Panthers and local communities deepened. This deepening support came just in time.

8

Law and Order

On Sunday night September 8, 1968, Newton was convicted of manslaughter in the killing of Officer Frey and sentenced to two to fifteen years in prison. He was acquitted of wounding the other officer. Many Panthers and their supporters were disappointed that their efforts had not saved Huey. Newton's lawyer, Charles Garry, promised to appeal the decision. According to the *New York Times,* many police saw the sentence differently and wanted Newton executed for the killing of Frey. About thirty hours after Newton's conviction, at 1:30 in the morning on September 10, two white on-duty uniformed police officers shot up the windows and office of the Black Panther headquarters at 4421 Grove Street in Oakland.

Residents of the area awoke to the sound of gunfire. Witnesses who saw the shooting said that the police shot at the office from inside their parked car, across four lanes of Grove Street. According to police sources, the officers fired more than a dozen bullets. The pattern of the bullet holes left by the shooting suggested that the officers were aiming at a poster of Newton in the wicker throne in the office front window.[1]

Insurgency destabilizes traditional political arrangements, forcing various constituencies to take sides on contentious issues and leading to realignments. Such realignments are often accompanied by brutal attempts by traditional authorities to repress insurgents. In the United States in 1968, just such a political realignment took place. By 1968, the broad insurgency of which the Panthers were part—encompassing the ghetto rebellions and draft resistance—made status quo political arrangements ungovernable.

The governing Democratic coalition split along two axes—race and the Vietnam War. In the 1968 presidential election, Republican Richard Nixon seized the day with a "Law and Order" platform that attacked the Democrats by attacking the insurgents. Nixon's victory that year brought increasingly virulent state repression of the Black Panthers alongside broad alienation of blacks and liberals.

COINTELPRO

Even before Nixon's election, as the Black Panther Party mobilized young blacks in cities across the country, the federal government had targeted the Party for concerted repressive action. From the inception of the Federal Bureau of Investigation in 1908, the agency had targeted both leftists and black political organizations for covert investigation and at times disruption. Prime targets included Marcus Garvey's Universal Negro Improvement Association, the Communist Party, the Wobblies (Industrial Workers of the World), and the National Association for the Advancement of Colored People.[2] In 1956, the FBI formalized and consolidated its disruptive (rather than intelligence-gathering) activities into the first counterintelligence program, or COINTELPRO, specifically targeting the Communist Party USA.[3]

During the early days of the Civil Rights Movement, the FBI assiduously monitored the activities of civil rights activists but did little to protect them from illegal violence and sometimes zealously prosecuted movement leaders. Yet through 1963, the FBI did little to actively and directly repress the Civil Rights Movement.[4] However, by the end of 1963, as the movement attained international coverage and support, the FBI had undertaken extensive efforts to hound and discredit Martin Luther King Jr., and it continued this activity until his death five years later. The agency disseminated damning information—some obtained through spying and some fabricated—to political leaders, funders, allies, churches, and journalists, alleging, for example, that King was under Communist influence or that he was having extramarital affairs. Sometimes the FBI alleged misappropriation of funds or various forms of hypocrisy. Though the FBI persisted in its efforts to discredit King, the campaign against him waned from December 1964 until 1967, when he came out against the Vietnam War.[5]

In the summer of 1967, the FBI dramatically shifted the direction and intensity of its repression of black political organizations. In the summer of 1966, Stokely Carmichael first called for Black Power, and the Black Liberation Struggle entered a new phase. Organizations like the Student Nonviolent Coordinating Committee and the Revolutionary Action Movement declared common cause with the Vietnamese in opposing the American empire. By the following year, the tenor of the movement had become more nationalist and more confrontational. Urban rebellions raged in ghettos throughout the country. In Newark and Detroit, participants in the rebellions proclaimed black nationalist goals and called for armed resistance against the state. Thousands of young blacks rebelled. On April 4, 1967, Martin Luther King Jr. joined the younger generation of black movement leaders in publicly denouncing U.S. involvement in the war in Vietnam.[6]

Many in the federal government believed the growing black rebellion constituted a threat to the internal security of the country. On August 25, 1967, FBI director J. Edgar Hoover sent a memo to twenty-three FBI field offices around the country instructing agents to initiate counterintelligence activities against black nationalist organizations:

> Offices receiving copies of this letter are instructed to immediately establish a control file . . . and to assign responsibility for following and coordinating this new counterintelligence program to an experienced and imaginative Special Agent well versed in investigations relating to black nationalist, hate-type organizations. . . . The purpose of this new counterintelligence endeavor is to expose, disrupt, misdirect, discredit, or otherwise neutralize the activities of black nationalist, hate-type organizations and groupings, their leadership, spokesmen, membership, and supporters. . . . Efforts of various groups to consolidate their forces or to recruit new or youthful adherents must be frustrated.[7]

The memo targeted six "black nationalist hate-type" organizations. Most revealing was the inclusion of King's Southern Christian Leadership Conference on the list. This was noteworthy because King and the other Christian ministers in the SCLC continued to call for nonviolence and rejected black nationalism outright, advocating instead for reforms within the political framework of the United States that would address the plight of blacks and other poor and dispossessed Americans. After the defeat of Jim Crow in the mid-1960s, King and the SCLC redirected their efforts and sought to heed the concerns of young blacks, calling for redress of the problems of poverty and for an end to the Vietnam War. In Hoover's view, these political positions qualified the SCLC as a leading "black nationalist, hate-type" organization and a dire threat to national security.[8] The Black Panther Party, at the time still a local organization in the Oakland Bay Area, was not mentioned.

On March 4, 1968, J. Edgar Hoover expanded the COINTELPRO against black nationalists to forty-one field offices, and in a new memo established the following five long-term goals for the program:

1. Prevent the coalition of militant black nationalist groups. In unity there is strength; a truism that is no less valid for all its triteness. An effective coalition of black nationalist groups might be the first step toward a real "Mau Mau" in America, the beginning of a true black revolution.

2. Prevent the rise of a "messiah" who could unify, and electrify, the militant black nationalist movement. Malcolm X might have been such a "messiah;" he is the martyr of the movement today. Martin Luther King, Stokely Carmichael and Elijah Muhammad all aspire to this position. Elijah Muhammad is less of a threat because of his age. King could be a very real contender for this position should he abandon his supposed "obedience" to "white, liberal doctrines" (nonviolence) and embrace black nationalism. Carmichael has the necessary charisma to be a real threat in this way.

3. Prevent violence on the part of black nationalist groups. This is of primary importance, and is, of course, a goal of our investigative activity; it should also be a goal of the Counterintelligence Program. Through counterintelligence it should be possible to pinpoint potential troublemakers and neutralize them before they exercise their potential for violence.

4. Prevent militant black nationalist groups and leaders from gaining respectability, by discrediting them to three separate segments of the community. The goal of discrediting black nationalists must be handled tactically in three ways. You must discredit these groups and individuals to, first, the responsible Negro community. Second, they must be discredited to the white community, both the responsible community and to "liberals" who have vestiges of sympathy for militant black nationalists simply because they are Negroes. Third, these groups must be discredited in the eyes of Negro radicals, the followers of the movement. This last area requires entirely different tactics from the first two. Publicity about violent tendencies and radical statements merely enhances black nationalists to the last group; it adds "respectability" in a different way.

5. A final goal should be to prevent the long-range growth of militant black nationalist organizations, especially among youth. Specific tactics to prevent these groups from converting young people must be developed.[9]

One month later to the day, Martin Luther King Jr. was assassinated.

Following the assassinations of King and Bobby Hutton, the Black Panther Party quickly spread across the country and attained tremendous influence. By the fall of 1968, the Party had clearly emerged as the nation's leading black movement organization. The party's rhetoric and ideology did not change significantly in this period, nor did its tactics. The Party was no more militant in action or rhetoric in September 1968 than it had been in March. What changed was the party's influence, its growing national scope, and the political challenge it now posed to the status quo. While the FBI did not mention the Black Panther Party in earlier COINTELPRO memos targeting black nationalist organizations, the agency now began to focus its attention on the Panthers. According to an FBI internal memo in September 1968:

> The extremist [Black Panther Party] of Oakland, California, is rapidly expanding . . . [It] is essential that we not only accelerate our investigations of this organization, and increase our informants in the organization but that we take action under the counterintelligence program to disrupt the group. . . . The attached letter will instruct the field to submit positive suggestions as to actions to be taken to thwart and disrupt the [Party]. . . . These suggestions are to create factionalism between not only the national leaders but also local leaders, steps to neutralize all organizational efforts of the [Black Panther Party], as well as create suspicion amongst the leaders as to each other's sources of finances, suspicion concerning their respective spouses and suspicion as to who may be cooperating with law enforcement. In addition, suspicion should be developed as to who may be attempting to gain control of the organization for their own private betterment, as well as suggestions as to the best method of exploiting the foreign visits made by [Party] members. We are also soliciting recommendations as to the best method of creating opposition to the [Black Panther Party] on the part of the majority of the residents of the ghetto areas.[10]

THE HAWK IS DEAD

Even as the federal government targeted the Black Panther Party for intensive repression in 1968, deepening cleavages in the ruling Democratic Party coalition increased the salience of the Panthers' politics. The divide in the Democratic coalition over the politics of race was not new. In the early 1960s, the Civil Rights Movement had forced the national Democratic Party's hand on the question of civil rights for blacks. President Lyndon Johnson's support of civil rights won broad support but alienated many southern Democrats. Johnson had won the presidency in a landslide in 1964, winning every state but five in the Deep South and Arizona. The ongoing Black Liberation Struggle in the mid-1960s deepened the divisions over race in the Democratic coalition. Liberals in the Democratic Party supported full equal civil rights for blacks but could not support calls for black self-determination by the younger generation of Black Power activists. Conversely, many traditional southern Democrats assailed liberals for "encouraging rebellion" and called for uncompromising repression of black activists.

The mid-1960s also brought a new divide over the Vietnam War. The public came to oppose the war, with one Gallup poll showing that 58 percent believed the war was a mistake by October 1968.[11] President Johnson's difficulty appeasing opponents of the war had first become serious in 1967 with the spread of draft resistance. Johnson could not simply ignore the draft resistance as he had earlier shrugged off more passive protests against the war; the card burning and induction refusals challenged his leadership. Consequently, the president sought to discredit the antiwar movement. He repeatedly pressed the FBI and Central Intelligence Agency to investigate links between the antiwar movement and foreign governments. His administration leaked allegations to the press about Martin Luther King Jr.'s "communist" aides and the Communist affiliations of other leading antiwar organizers in order to discredit the protest among liberals. But these efforts failed. While many Americans said they opposed the militancy of the draft resisters, the draft resistance movement ate away at Johnson's credibility.[12]

The draft resistance movement challenged the legitimacy of the war. The anti-imperialist idea that the Vietnamese were fighting for their liberation contradicted the administration's assertion that the North Vietnamese National Liberation Front (NLF), or Vietcong, was unpopular and would be rapidly defeated. Like the Civil Rights Movement, the militancy of the draft resistance forced the federal government to intervene to maintain social order. Also like the Civil Rights Movement, the protests increasingly resonated with popular sympathies. By December 1967, support for the war was declining; some 45 percent of people polled thought the Vietnam War was a mistake.[13] But unlike the Civil Rights Movement, draft resistance specifically violated federal rather than local policies.

After the Pentagon protests, with graphic challenges to Johnson's leadership and no end of the war in sight, support for Johnson's handling of the war fell to a low of 28 percent. A week later, Secretary of Defense Robert McNamara told Johnson that he strongly disapproved of the president's Vietnam policy and resigned. Criticism in the press ballooned, and challenges in Congress became bolder. In November 1967, Minnesota senator Eugene McCarthy defied political convention and announced that he would seek the Democratic Party nomination for the 1968 presidential election, thereby challenging the incumbent president from his own party. McCarthy framed his campaign almost entirely as a crusade against the war in Vietnam.[14]

Increasingly worried that the antiwar movement was eroding confidence in both his leadership and the war effort, Johnson launched a public relations campaign to allay public fears about the war's progress. The handsome young general William Westmoreland was particularly effective, assuring TV audiences he was "very, very encouraged" that the United States was "making real progress."[15]

Then came the Tet offensive. Without warning, on the eve of "Tet," the Vietnamese New Year, January 30, 1968, the National Liberation Front simultaneously attacked the U.S.-supported Vietnamese government in thirty-six of the forty-four provincial capitals of South Vietnam, causing a widespread breakdown in government authority and suspension of the constitutional process by South Vietnamese president Nguyen Van Thieu. In the South Vietnamese capital of Saigon, NLF forces penetrated the supposedly invulnerable U.S. embassy, and the press carried pictures of American soldiers lying dead inside the compound. In four days of fighting, 281 American troops were killed and 1,195 were wounded. Fighting persisted in Saigon for a week. In Hue, the former imperial capital in central Vietnam, the NLF seized power. It took three weeks of aerial bombing and the destruction of eighteen thousand of the twenty thousand houses in Hue for U.S. allies to reclaim the city. All told, at least twelve thousand Vietnamese civilians were killed and countless refugees had to be evacuated to restore order in South Vietnam.[16]

In the United States, the reports of the Tet offensive intensified public concern that the war was wrong and that it would be long and bloody and cost many more American lives. The bloody battle belied Johnson's assertion that American victory was near and strengthened the claim of many in the antiwar movement that the NLF had popular support and that people were fighting for self-determination and would to go to any length to resist U.S. imperialism. The "Vietcong remain adamant in their struggle to overthrow the South Vietnamese Government and force the United States out of the country," the *New York Times* reported, quoting a captured NLF soldier: "An easy victory costs little blood, a difficult victory costs much blood. . . . Regardless, the result will be victory."[17]

Public approval of Johnson's handling of the war plummeted after Tet.[18] A February poll showed that for the first time, a majority of

Americans believed that it was a "mistake" to keep U.S. troops in Vietnam.[19] The press also turned against the war. Even Walter Cronkite, the nation's most respected anchorperson, renowned for his journalistic objectivity, came out against the war. In February, upon returning from an investigative tour of Vietnam, he reported that the president's policies were failing there.[20]

On March 12, Eugene McCarthy, critical of Johnson's handling of the war, almost beat him in the New Hampshire primary, garnering 42 percent of the vote to Johnson's 49 percent. Four days later, with Johnson's vulnerability clear, Robert Kennedy—the former attorney general, younger brother of slain President John F. Kennedy, and now a senator with powerful political and financial backing and widespread appeal—entered the race.[21]

Johnson circulated a draft speech to several close advisers on March 28 taking a hard-line, hawkish stance advancing the war. Clark Clifford, Johnson's newly appointed secretary of defense and one of his closest advisers, told the president he could not give the speech. "What seems not to be understood," he said, "is that major elements of the national constituency—the business community, the press, the churches, professional groups, college presidents, students, and most of the intellectual community—have turned against this war."[22] In the last days of March, Johnson reassigned General Westmoreland and denied the military's request for 209,000 new troops, setting a ceiling of 549,500 troops for Vietnam. Johnson's advisers drafted a new speech. On March 31, the president gave this revised speech to the nation largely as drafted. He said he was moving toward de-escalation in Vietnam, halting bombing north of the 20th parallel, and hoping to open peace talks with the communists.[23]

Then Johnson made an announcement that surprised many of his advisers as well as much of the nation. Lyndon B. Johnson, who had won the 1964 presidential election with more than 90 percent of the electoral college and the largest percentage of the popular vote ever recorded in U.S. history, announced he would not seek re-election in 1968.[24] Exuberant college students poured out of dormitories across the country cheering, "The hawk is dead!"[25]

DEMOCRATS BETRAY THE BASE

Despite widespread opposition to the war, Vice President Hubert Humphrey soon entered the presidential race with the support of the Democratic Party establishment, pledging to pursue the war. On June 5, on a platform critical of the Vietnam War, Robert Kennedy won the California Democratic primary. Many antiwar liberals celebrated the victory, rallying around Kennedy as the likely Democratic nominee. But at his victory celebration that evening at the Ambassador Hotel in Los Angeles, Kennedy was assassinated.

The Democratic nomination and the party's position on Vietnam would be decided at the Democratic National Convention that August in Chicago. The National Mobilization Committee to End the War in Vietnam ("the MOBE"), a coalition of ideologically diverse antiwar organizations that had organized the Pentagon protests, planned demonstrations to take place outside the convention.[26] Organizers also invited the Black Panthers to speak. In late August, Bobby Seale and David Hilliard flew to Chicago.[27]

Only when challenged do authorities reveal where they are willing to compromise and what they will do to hold onto power. Despite widespread opposition to the war among registered Democrats, the party leadership was not willing to cede ground on its Vietnam policy. Yet the vociferous resistance within the party challenged the legitimacy of the Democratic leadership, which attempted to repress the resistance. In preparation for the convention, Chicago mayor Richard Daley sealed off the convention site with barbed wire, refused to grant permits to many protestors and stalled on other requests, placed all twelve thousand Chicago police officers on twelve-hour shifts, mobilized more than five thousand National Guardsmen and provided them with riot training, and called in six thousand U.S. Army troops equipped with flamethrowers, bayonets, bazookas, and machine guns mounted on Jeeps.[28]

Small but disruptive protests through the weekend of August 24 and the early part of the week encountered aggressive police. A troop of 150 police broke up a protestor encampment at Lincoln Park with tear gas and nightsticks.[29] Many in the black community watched the conflict with interest, remembering Daley's "shoot to kill" orders during the black rebellion in Chicago following King's assassination in April. Hundreds of young black people from the Chicago area joined the confrontations.[30] Police removed badges and beat both protestors and news reporters with abandon.[31]

Inside the convention hall, the Democratic Party leadership was busy repressing another kind of challenge. During the primary election, registered Democrats had displayed overwhelming opposition to the administration's policy in Vietnam, and 80 percent had voted for candidates critical of the Vietnam War. True to the voters, a group of anti-war delegates proposed a plank to the platform committee calling for de-escalation in Vietnam along the lines proposed by McCarthy and Kennedy. But the platform committee endorsed a prowar plank and pushed this through on the floor a few days later. Then, on Wednesday August 29, although antiwar candidates McCarthy and Kennedy had received the vast majority of the primary votes cast, convention delegates handpicked by party machine leaders nominated prowar Hubert Humphrey for president. Downtown Chicago exploded that night.[32]

More than ten thousand people gathered for a legally sanctioned nonviolent protest at Grant Park across the street from the Hilton Hotel where many delegates were staying. When someone lowered the American flag, the police swooped in, bloodying a number of protestors. Black Panther chairman Bobby Seale told the protestors: "If you dissent, your heads will be whipped and your skulls will be cracked. . . . Every time the people disagree with the basic decisions of the power structure it sends in its arms, guns, and force to make them agree."[33]

Tom Hayden, a founder and former president of the Students for a Democratic Society, took the microphone and called for the protestors to shake up the city: "The city and the military machinery it has aimed at us won't permit us to protest in an organized fashion. Therefore, we must move out of this park in groups throughout the city, and turn this overheated military machine against itself. Let us make sure that if blood flows, it flows all over the city. If they use gas against us, let us make sure they use gas against their own citizens."[34] The action on the street was electric as young people of various races and social classes confronted the police head-on. SDS developed "affinity groups" to act in a "guerilla" fashion, avoiding police attack and moving the melee into the busy streets of Chicago.

Now disillusioned, many of the antiwar liberal kids who had poured their hearts into McCarthy's campaign joined the radicals confronting the police in the streets. Even those who had tried to quiet the protests earlier because they believed they would dampen McCarthy's chances joined in. Some threw rocks at the police, who in turn stormed McCarthy's headquarters on the fifteenth floor of the Hilton, tossing several staff members out of bed and breaking a club over one's head. The McCarthyites' anger grew: "Well, from now on it's the Battle of Algiers," one declared. Soldiers chased protestors through the streets of downtown Chicago, spraying them with tear gas through converted flamethrowers. The gas was so thick that even Democratic nominee

Hubert Humphrey had trouble breathing in his suite in the Hilton many stories above the street. The carpet in the hotel lobby was covered with vomit from those made sick by the gas. Out on the streets, small groups of protestors, confronted by police, dispersed, circled, and regrouped. The police lined up platoon style, shouting "Kill, Kill, Kill" with clubs raised. Any protestor the police caught, along with many news reporters and other bystanders, were knocked to the ground and beaten. One group was pushed through the plate-glass window of the Hilton's Haymarket Lounge by police.[35]

Senator Abraham Ribicoff of Connecticut condemned Daley for "Gestapo" tactics. Other official delegates held up signs comparing Chicago to Prague, where Soviet troops and tanks were crushing a liberal Czech movement.[36] All told, more than 1,000 people, including 192 police, were injured and 662 were arrested. One young man was shot to death by the police.

Panther minister of information Eldridge Cleaver held a press conference, announcing, "We have been driven out of the political arena. . . . We will not dissent from the American Government. We will overthrow it."[37] Renowned journalist I. F. Stone declared, "The war is destroying our country as we are destroying Vietnam." Kennedy aide Richard Goodwin said, "This is just the beginning."[38] In the revolutionary mood following Chicago, tens of thousands of young people joined the New Left. The greatest growth was in the months following Chicago. By the time of the presidential elections in November, SDS alone had at least eighty thousand members—up from thirty-five thousand in April.[39]

THE GREATEST THREAT

The insurgents had split the governing Democratic coalition. The Democratic Party leadership was unwilling to yield to the antiwar position of the party base. The Democrats had embraced civil rights, losing traditional support from the Dixiecrats. But they had failed to address the persistent poverty, lack of political representation, ghettoization, and police brutality that were the core concerns of Black Power activists.

Richard Nixon took advantage of the fractures in the Democratic coalition by seeking to unify the Republican Party behind a "Law and Order" platform. He attacked the Democrats by attacking the rebels. He blamed the flagging war effort in Vietnam and the growing black and antiwar rebellions on the Democrats' weakness. "The long dark night for America is about to end," Nixon pledged.[40] Nixon called for tough government action to repress the rebels: "It is too late for more commissions to study violence. It is time for the government to stop it. The people of this country want an end to government that acts out of a spirit of neutrality or beneficence or indulgence towards criminals. We must cease as well the granting of special immunities and moral sanctions to those who deliberately violate public laws—even when those violations are done in the name of peace or civil rights or anti-poverty or academic reform."[41]

Positioning himself to capture the conservatives in the Democratic Party who were deeply troubled by social unrest and wanting to attract as much of the white supremacist vote as he could, Nixon conflated crime, ghetto rebellion, civil rights, and student protest. The gambit worked. On November 5, by the thinnest of margins, Nixon was elected the thirty-seventh president of the United States.[42]

From the first days of his presidency, Nixon took a personal interest in repressing the Black Panther Party. In early 1969, he asked FBI director Hoover how extensively the Justice Department was targeting the Party. Nixon was displeased when Hoover reported little action and said he would inform Attorney General John Mitchell of the importance of moving against the Panthers.[43] In response, Mitchell's Justice Department identified the Panthers as a "menace to national security" and set up a task force on extremism—independent of FBI activities— whose main charter was to repress the Panthers. One plan of action the department considered was wide legal prosecution of Black Panthers for "conspiring to advocate the violent overthrow of the government" under the Smith Act that had been used to jail Communists in the 1950s.[44]

On July 15, 1969, Hoover publicly announced that of all the black nationalist groups, "the Black Panther Party, without question, represents the greatest threat to the internal security of the country."[45] This statement stood in stark contrast to earlier public statements by the FBI about the Panthers. The FBI report for fiscal year 1968, which was released on October 1, 1968, barely mentioned the Panthers, and its report for 1967 had not mentioned them at all.[46] But by the fall of 1968, the FBI was secretly developing what would become its most intensive program to repress any black political organization. Of 295 actions initiated by the FBI's Counterintelligence Program to destabilize black nationalist organizations, 233 of them—or 79 percent—targeted the Black Panther Party.[47] Federal actions against the Panthers ranged from spreading false information about misappropriation of party money to fomenting marital strife, and in some cases, participating in planned killings of Panther leaders.

COINTELPRO aimed to undermine the Black Panthers' ability to threaten the political status quo. Toward that end, its agents tried to foster divisions between the Panthers and potential recruits and between the Party and other organizations, as well as among the Black Panthers themselves.

No aspect of the Black Panther program was of greater concern to the FBI than the Free Breakfast for Children Program, which fostered widespread support for the Panthers' revolutionary politics. Hoover drove home this point in an airtel to the special agent in charge in San Francisco on May 27, 1969:

> You state that the Bureau under the CIP [COINTELPRO] should not attack programs of community interest such as the [Black Panther Party] "Breakfast for Children." You state that this is because many prominent "humanitarians," both white and black, are interested in the program as well as churches which are actively supporting it. You have obviously missed the point. . . . You must recognize that one of our primary aims in counterintelligence as it concerns the [Party] is to keep this group isolated from the moderate black and white community which may support it. This is most emphatically pointed out in their Breakfast for Children Program, where they are actively soliciting and receiving support from uninformed whites and moderate blacks.[48]

The FBI took extensive measures to undermine support for the Panthers' breakfast program. For example, agents sent forged letters and incendiary propaganda to supermarkets to dissuade them from providing food and impersonated concerned parishioners to dissuade churches from providing space for the program.[49]

Various branches of the federal government mobilized to address the political threat posed by the Panthers. In response to White House interest in Internal Revenue Service (IRS) support of efforts to repress "ideological organizations," the IRS established the Activist Organizations Committee in July 1969 to "collect basic intelligence data" on members of the Black Panther Party, organizations that did business with the Black Panther Party, and other "radical" political organizations. The FBI supplied the IRS with the names of individuals and organizations. The IRS, in return, supplied detailed personal financial information and also targeted these individuals for special enforcement of tax regulations.[50]

In June 1970, a joint report by the FBI, the CIA, the Defense Intelligence Committee, and the National Security Agency identified the Black Panther Party as the most "active and dangerous" black nationalist threat to internal security. The report expressed particular concern about widespread grassroots support for the Party, noting, "A recent poll indicates that approximately 25 percent of the black population has a great respect for the [Black Panther Party], including 43 percent of blacks under 21 years of age." The report also emphasized the large, 150,000 weekly circulation of the Panther newspaper, 189 speaking engagements on college campuses in 1969, strong support from the Students for a Democratic Society and other New Left groups, the appeal of the Black Panthers to blacks in the military, and the Party's international support from students in Europe, guerilla movements in the Middle East, and the governments of Cuba, North Korea, and Algeria.[51]

Before Nixon's election as president, there had not been a single police raid of a Black Panther office. Police had stopped and arrested small groups of Panthers selling the *Black Panther* newspaper. They had also confronted Panthers in spontaneous conflicts outside Panther offices in New York and Denver, and in the Bay Area, they had raided the homes of Bobby Seale and the Cleavers, encountering minimal resistance.[52]

But state repression of the Panthers intensified after Nixon's election. Even before Nixon took office in January 1969, police and federal agents began staging raids on Panther offices. It is not clear whether the wave of raids of Panther offices that followed was the independent response of local police to the victory of Nixon's Law and Order campaign in the polls or whether the FBI systematically encouraged the change in policy nationwide. In either case, no form of repression was more direct, more provocative, or more violent. In January 1968, Newton had issued Executive Mandate No. 3, commanding Panthers to defend their homes and offices with guns against trespass by police who could not produce legal warrants. Panthers around the country took this mandate seriously, preparing for unwarranted raids by police and in some cities fortifying their offices for attack. In this context, raids on Panther offices were essentially acts of war—usually planned confrontations in which authorities expected armed resistance.

At 8:00 A.M. on December 18, 1968, police and federal agents stormed the Panther office in Indianapolis, shooting tear gas canisters through the window and arresting three Panthers. They then ransacked the office. Photos show everything in the office tossed about and destroyed.

Federal marshals claimed they were searching for unregistered weapons, but they found none.[53]

After a wedding reception for Lauren Watson, chair of the Denver Black Panthers, at a Panther office and cultural center in December 1968, police raided and ransacked the center. They ripped and damaged books and cultural objects. Photos taken after the raid show the center in disarray, with strewn papers and broken furniture. The wedding had been attended by some of Denver's most prominent black leaders, and the black press covered the raid. No Panthers were in the office at the time of the raid.[54]

On December 27, 1968, one hundred police and FBI agents—weapons drawn—knocked down the door of the Des Moines Panther headquarters. They ransacked the office, confiscated some papers, and arrested two Panthers on charges of arson at a local lumber company.[55]

That same month, at 4:15 on a Sunday morning, two white men dressed in police uniforms pulled up in front of the Newark Black Panther office in an unmarked vehicle and threw two small bombs at the office. The bombs shattered parts of the front wall and window and started a fire in the office; four Panthers were injured, including Carl Nichols, who suffered a broken arm and burns on his legs. Police spokesmen alleged that the Panthers were the ones who had earlier shot up the front of the Newark police station with a machine gun but denied Panther charges that the bombing of the Panther office was retaliation for that shooting.[56]

The New York chapter of the Black Panther Party was one of the largest, most active, and most effective. At 1:00 A.M. on April 2, 1969, based on the allegations of three paid informants, a New York grand jury indicted twenty-one Black Panthers for plotting to bomb department stores, police stations, and the Brooklyn Botanical Garden. At 5:00 in the morning, New York police simultaneously raided five Black Panther houses, arresting twelve Panthers. Other members of the chapter were already in police custody; a few escaped capture and went into exile. Those indicted were Afeni Shakur (the mother of future rap star Tupac Shakur), Lumumba Shakur, Dhoruba (Richard Moore), Sekou Odinga (Nathanial Burns), Jamal (Eddie Joseph), Joan Bird, Cetawayo (Michael Tabor), Kuwasi Balagoon (Donald Weems), Robert Collier, Richard Harris, Ali Bey Hassan (John J. Casson), Abayama Katara (Alex McKiever), Kwando Kinshasa (William King), Baba Odinga (Walter Johnson), Shaba Ogun Om (Lee Roper), Curtis Powell, Clark Squire, Larry Mack, Mshina (Thomas Berry), Lonnie Epps, and Mkuba

(Lee Berry). While the evidence against them was flimsy, the judge set bail prohibitively high: $100,000 each for most of the "Panther 21." Although all twenty-one defendants were eventually acquitted, most of them remained in jail for two years while the trial proceeded, incapacitating most of the New York Panther leadership. The case became a major cause for further mobilization of Panthers and their allies across the United States.[57]

Just after midnight on April 27, 1969, a bomb exploded in the Des Moines Black Panther headquarters, demolishing one side of the building, including the bathroom, kitchen, conference room, and distribution room. Photos show half the building obliterated, with large sections of the walls and roof destroyed. Six Panthers were in the other half of the building at the time; miraculously, no one was seriously hurt. Police arrived less than thirty seconds later, cordoned off the building, and began seizing documents from inside the house. When some of the Panthers objected, police used mace against them and arrested three of them for disturbing the peace and resisting arrest. The Panthers charged the police with bombing the office and argued that the unnatural quickness of their arrival after the explosion showed that they knew of the bombing in advance.[58]

On April 28, 1969, after a Panther rally to mobilize support for the "Free Huey!" campaign, police raided the San Francisco office of the Black Panther Party. Carrying Thompson submachine guns and M16 rifles, police kicked in the front door, shooting bullets into the office and filling it with tear gas. Eleven Panthers fled through the back door, and police arrested all of them. Nine of the eleven were later released without charge; Cleveland Brooks was booked for disturbing the peace, and Panther Field Marshal Donald Cox was arrested for suspicion of assault on a police officer.[59]

At 1:00 A.M. on June 5, 1969, police surrounded Panther headquarters in Milwaukee and arrested five Panthers standing outside on charges of carrying concealed weapons and loitering.[60]

At 9:15 P.M. on June 15, 1969, police sought to disperse a gathering of blacks in a local park across the street from the Black Panther Party office in Sacramento. The crowd, including many women, resisted, and the confrontation became violent, with police spraying mace and beating people, who in turn threw rocks and bottles at the police. Police tried to cordon off the crowd, and many of the participants retreated to the Black Panther office. Police fired dozens of shots into the office, and Panthers escaped out the back doors. Police then ransacked the office, smashing windows, strewing papers on the floor, and breaking office equipment. Shooting between police and local residents continued for six hours. Fifteen people, many of them police, suffered gunshot wounds. By the end of the episode, police had arrested thirty-seven people, including several Panthers, whom they beat in jail.[61]

On July 14, 1969, police raided the Black Panther office in San Diego, confiscating the weapons stash—which the Panthers claimed were all legal—overturning the desks, and strewing papers on the floor.[62]

On August 9, 1969, at 9:00 P.M., dozens of police surrounded the Black Panther Party office in Richmond, California. The Panthers called their radio contacts, who promptly made an announcement on air, and dozens of people from the neighborhood quickly turned out to observe the police. After a short while, the police got in their cars and left.[63]

In the early morning of September 2, 1969, police surrounded a Panther house in San Diego and ordered the occupants—two women and a baby—to leave their home. When the police could not produce a warrant, the women refused to leave or to let the police in. The police fired tear gas canisters into the house through a window. Neighbors turned out and began throwing rocks and bricks at the police, who proceeded to arrest most members of the crowd. Eventually, the two women came out of the house with the baby, and the police arrested them too. Next the police ransacked the house, seizing Panther arms and ammunition. They claimed they were looking for Ronald Freeman, a Panther captain, who was wanted on suspicion of murder.[64]

On September 23, 1969, FBI agents and Philadelphia police surrounded the Philadelphia Black Panther headquarters. They arrested everyone inside and confiscated the Panthers' files and an M14 rifle.[65] These and other actions only served to incite people's anger.

The political realignment of 1968 held far-reaching consequences for the Black Panthers that would set the context for the next phase of the Party's development through 1969 and much of 1970. Nixon's "Law and Order" victory intensified state repression of the Panthers. Simultaneously, large portions of society, including many black people and opponents of the war, felt betrayed by the political establishment. For many, harsh repression confirmed the anti-imperialist view that the government did not serve the interests of the people. Even as right-wing Nixon seized the presidency, the Left expanded and deepened its commitment to fight imperialism. The more the state attempted to repress the Panthers, the more influential the Party would become.

9

41st and Central

By January 1969, the Los Angeles chapter of the Black Panther Party had consolidated its status as a leading black nationalist organization in the city, rivaled only by Ron Karenga's US organization. The Los Angeles Panther chapter was not yet a large organization, but the killings of Panthers Bartholomew, Lawrence, and Lewis by police in the shoot-out at the gas station during the Watts festival in August 1968 had not scared everyone away either. If anything, the fact that these Panthers stood their ground and fought the police to the death strengthened the Party's revolutionary credentials and drew new recruits, including alienated Vietnam War hero Geronimo Pratt.

In addition to earning a Purple Heart, Sergeant Elmer "Geronimo" Pratt—a former high school quarterback from Morgan City, Louisiana—had earned many honors in his first tour of duty in Vietnam, including the Soldier's Medal and the Air Medal. He lost many friends in combat and had been wounded in action several times, including once by shrapnel from a land mine. Medics reported that only the extra sandbags with which Pratt had lined the bottom of his jeep had saved his life. In the incident that earned him the Soldier's Medal, Pratt saved the lives of fellow soldiers when their helicopter crashed. Pratt's citation read, "Pfc. Pratt, disregarding his own safety, entered the burning aircraft. Aware of the possibility of enemy activity in the area and the likelihood of an explosion in the helicopter, Pfc. Pratt made repeated trips into the aircraft until all five occupants had been removed and taken a safe distance from the flaming wreckage. His heroic and selfless action, at the risk of his own life, is in keeping with the highest traditions of the military service and reflects great credit upon himself, his unit and the United States of America."[1]

Pratt was a committed soldier, and he later recalled that he simply saw his ordeals in Vietnam as part of the job. He was ready, even eager, to return to Vietnam. But in the summer of 1967, Pratt was sent to Detroit to put down the black uprising there. He later recalled, "They took away our dignity as soldiers. One month we're risking our lives for our country, and the next we're getting ready to fire on our own people. I knew if the order came I couldn't obey it."[2]

When Pratt was sent back to Vietnam for a second tour of duty, he saw things in a new light. He began having nightmares and became critical of the war. "After a while," recalled Pratt, "I began to see the war as another kind of racism. . . . All we ever heard was 'gooks,' 'Buddha-heads,' 'slopes,' same way our daddies heard 'Krauts' and 'Japs.' You got to make people subhuman before you kill 'em. I saw things I don't want to remember. I *did* things I don't want to remember. That second tour was a bad time."[3] Martin Luther King Jr.'s assassination in April 1968 was a wakeup call for Pratt. People back home had been telling him that a race war was approaching, and that they needed him. By June, he was back in Morgan City with an honorable discharge.

In September 1968, Pratt traveled to Los Angeles, where he met Bunchy Carter through a family friend. He arrived only a few weeks after police killed three Panthers at the Watts Summer Festival. Pratt agreed to share his military knowledge to help Bunchy train the Black Panthers in more effective self-defense measures. According to Pratt, Bunchy gave him the honorary name "Geronimo ji Jaga," after the fierce warriors of the Jaga people of the Congo. Geronimo became Bunchy's right-hand man and stayed in Los Angeles to train the Panthers.[4]

John and Ericka Huggins and Elaine Brown shared a communal apartment that served as an informal headquarters for the Party leadership, and the Panthers rented a two-story office where they conducted political education classes, meetings, and other official Party activities. In December 1968, Ericka gave birth to baby girl Mai Huggins. While Ericka cared for the baby, John and Elaine, along with Bunchy Carter and Geronimo Pratt, participated in the High Potential Program at the University of California, Los Angeles. Funded partly by the federal government, the special program admitted black students deemed to have high potential despite a lack of formal academic credentials.

The Panthers took college classes and worked to organize other black UCLA students. In line with instructions from the national office, they sought to organize L.A.'s first Free Breakfast for Children Program and set up a meeting with the head of food services at a UCLA dormitory to discuss whether the dorm would donate leftover food to the program.[5] But before the Panthers could open the first community program, crisis struck.

In the fall of 1968, the FBI had accelerated a program to undermine the growing political influence of the Black Panthers. Taking note of the growing tension between the Black Panther Party and the US organization in Southern California, the FBI sought to escalate the conflict. FBI Director J. Edgar Hoover sent a memo to field officers on November 25, 1968, with the following instructions: "For the information of recipient offices a serious struggle is taking place between the Black Panther Party and the US organization. The struggle has reached such proportion that it is taking on the aura of gang warfare with attendant threats of murder and reprisals. In order to fully capitalize upon [Black Panther Party] and US differences as well as to exploit all avenues of creating further dissension in the ranks of the [Party], recipient offices are instructed to submit imaginative and hard-hitting counterintelligence measures aimed at crippling the [Black Panther Party]."[6]

Field offices quickly responded to Hoover with plans for escalating the conflict, and the Los Angeles office reported back to Hoover, "The Los Angeles Office is currently preparing an anonymous letter for Bureau approval which will be sent to the Los Angeles Black Panther Party supposedly from a member of the 'US' organization in which it will be stated that the youth group of the 'US' organization is aware of the [Black Panther Party] 'contract' to kill RON KARENGA, leader of 'US,' and they, 'US' members, in retaliation, have made plans to ambush leaders of the [Party] in Los Angeles. It is hoped this counterintelligence measure will result in an 'US' and [Black Panther Party] vendetta."[7]

Tensions between Ron Karenga's US organization and the Panthers came to a head over the leadership of the Black Student Union on the UCLA campus and the direction of the new Black Studies Program there. Karenga, as a formal community adviser appointed by the university administration, supported one candidate for director of the new program; the Black Panthers wanted a role in the decision-making process and opposed Karenga's candidate. The university administration planned to announce the new director of the Black Studies

Program on January 21. At two large and confrontational meetings of the Black Student Union on January 15 and January 17, no resolution was achieved. Most of the black students appeared to support the Black Panther position. Elaine Brown and John Huggins were elected to an ad hoc committee to represent Black Student Union concerns, and John Huggins and Bunchy Carter emerged as leading contenders in the upcoming election for the Black Student Union presidency.

At about 2:40 P.M. on January 17, as the Black Student Union adjourned and about 150 students poured out of the meeting at Campbell Hall, the conflict became violent. Ranking members of the US organization fired guns at Los Angeles Black Panther leaders; they shot John Huggins in the back and Bunchy Carter in the chest, killing them both.[8]

Fleeing campus, Panthers gathered at the Century Boulevard home shared by John and Ericka Huggins, their three-week-old daughter, Mai, and Elaine Brown. When Elaine Brown told Ericka that John had been killed, Ericka's eyes glazed over; she started making coffee for the guests. About 150 police officers surrounded the house. Brown and two other Panther women hid under the bed with Ericka Huggins and Mai wrapped in a coat as police kicked down the door. Police arrested all seventeen Panthers in the house.[9]

Initially, no members of US were arrested. Playwright Donald Freed, the National Lawyers Guild, and other Panther allies quickly mobilized to raise bail and activate a legal defense. Within a few days, all charges against the Panthers were dropped, and the Panthers were released. Funeral services for Bunchy Carter took place at the Trinity Baptist Church in Los Angeles on Friday, January 24. Hundreds of people, including Kathleen Cleaver and James Baldwin, attended. Bobby Seale flew down to lead the services. While documentation of the FBI's involvement in escalating the conflict with US would not be revealed for years to come, the Panther leadership believed from the start that the attack was part of a government plot. At Bunchy Carter's funeral, Bobby Seale denounced Ron Karenga as a "reactionary" and a "tool of the power structure."[10]

The Panthers rallied around their dead as martyrs in a revolutionary war against the U.S. government. On January 25, 1969, the front-page headlines of the *Black Panther* declared, "A Political Assassination." Several articles in that issue argued that Ron Karenga and US were government pawns and that government forces had put them up to murder the Panthers to serve the ends of the state. The evidence the *Black Panther* presented to support this argument was circumstantial but powerful. The Panthers posited that their members had been attacked and killed by both police and the US organization, while US had never been attacked by police or by the Panthers. They pointed out that US received government funding; the Panthers did not. Panthers organized programs serving masses of poor black folks; US did not. The government conducted violent raids on Panther offices and activities nationally but had a peaceable relationship with US. US cooperated with the police to repress disturbances at high schools; the Panthers did not. Moreover, the Panthers argued that they were not especially invested in the outcome of the conflict at UCLA and would never have come to blows over it. The *Black Panther* explained, "[The] issue of the control of UCLA's Black Studies Program is not an objective of the Black Panther Party. The Black Panther Party would not trade one block of Central Avenue [a low-income black neighborhood] for the whole city of Westwood [where UCLA is located] because the Black Panther Party is based on the masses of Black people, and gets its strength from the same."[11]

At the time, Panther leaders had no direct knowledge of the FBI's role in fomenting the killing, but they had a strong grasp of the political dynamic at hand. The Panthers were correct in surmising that the killings were not part of the normal course of conflict between the Party and a rival black nationalist organization. Evidence would emerge later showing that the state had a hand in stirring up the conflict that contributed to the killings of John Huggins and Bunchy Carter. Yet the Panthers did not know at that time, and we still do not know today, to what extent US members were working directly with the FBI or police and whether the killings were planned and implemented under direction of the government. Police issued warrants for the arrest of the Stiner brothers, George and Larry, rank-and-file members of US, who had been present at the time of the killing. The Stiner brothers turned themselves in to police and received life sentences for conspiracy to commit murder. But US members Claude Hubert-Gaidi, whom witnesses said was the actual shooter, and Harold Jones-Tawala, who played a central role in the violent conflict that day, both disappeared and never stood trial.[12]

In the months that followed, the Panthers rallied around their martyrs, drawing on the outpouring of allied support to advance their revolutionary program. L.A. Panther Gwen Goodloe attended the Los Angeles Conference of Baptist Ministers and received an endorsement for the free breakfast program, which the Panthers hoped would help them obtain use of church space to prepare and serve breakfast. The Seventh-Day Adventist Church on Santa Barbara Avenue (now Martin Luther King Jr. Boulevard) near South Budlong Avenue in South Central Los Angeles provided free facilities for the program. Donald Freed helped form Friends of the Panthers, which started holding public meetings on March 8, to help organize an L.A. breakfast program and to raise funds. UCLA agreed to provide leftover cafeteria food for the program. The Panthers named the first Free Breakfast for Children Program in L.A. after John Huggins and began serving daily breakfasts on April 29.[13]

Hollywood stars like Jean Seberg donated thousands of dollars to support Panther operations in L.A.[14] At the end of October, the L.A. Panthers opened the Walter "Toure" Pope Community Center, named after a young Panther killed in a shoot-out with L.A. police earlier that month. The Panthers started another free breakfast program at the community center, where they also organized political education classes and held larger community events. One Saturday in November, about 150 adults, including 45 soldiers from Camp Pendleton, visited to express solidarity, eat breakfast with the children, and denounce the actions of the U.S. military—comparing the injustice of the war in Vietnam to the war the Panthers were fighting at home.[15] With help from the Panthers, their Chicano allies Los Siete de la Raza also opened a free breakfast program in Los Angeles at the Ramona Gardens housing project in October.[16] By November, plans were in the works to open a Bunchy Carter Free Health Clinic, and several doctors and nurses had volunteered their time to organize the launch and operation of the facility.[17]

As the Southern California Panther chapter grew and became more involved in the black community, repression increased. Police regularly pulled over known Panthers, often arresting them only to drop the charges later. On May 1, police raided the Adams Boulevard office of the Black Panther Party, arresting eleven Panthers and seizing three guns. Police booked two of the Panthers on charges that included "suspicion of assault with a deadly weapon" and released the rest. The *Black Panther* reported that in a single month that spring, L.A. police performed fifty-six arrests involving forty-two Panthers. The bail for these fifty-six arrests totaled more than $100,000, but with legal support from Panther allies, bails were reduced, and most of the charges were dropped.[18]

Despite growing community support for the Panthers, the FBI was apparently pleased with the effects of the US-Panther conflict they had helped create and continued to foment tensions between the two organizations through covert counterintelligence actions, such as distributing incendiary cartoons ridiculing the Panthers and attributing them to US.[19] On Friday, August 15, 1969, San Diego Black Panther leader Sylvester Bell was shot and killed by members of US as he sold copies of the *Black Panther* in the parking lot of a shopping center in southeast San Diego.[20] The FBI special agent in charge in San Diego wrote to FBI Director Hoover to celebrate the development and propose further FBI activities to escalate the US-Panther conflict:

> Shootings, beatings, and a high degree of unrest continues [sic] to prevail in the ghetto area of southeast San Diego. Although no specific counterintelligence action can be credited with contributing to this over-all situation, it is felt that a substantial amount of the unrest is directly attributable to this program. . . . In view of the recent killing of [Black Panther Party] member SYLVESTER BELL, a new cartoon is being considered in the hopes that it will assist in the continuance of the rift between [the Panthers] and US. This cartoon, or series of cartoons, will be similar in nature to those formerly approved by the Bureau and will be forwarded to the Bureau for evaluation and approval immediately upon their completion.[21]

The Panthers were at war, and the Panther National Central Committee placed Geronimo Pratt in charge of the Southern California chapter. Pratt proceeded to fortify the L.A. offices. He assigned Panthers to dig tunnels in the basement and use the dirt to fill sandbags. Pratt recalled, "We stuffed sandbags in the panels behind our walls, below our ceilings, up under our roof. We put up *tons* of dirt. It was all defensive structure. No bullet was gonna penetrate three-foot walls."[22]

At 5:30 P.M. on Wednesday November 12, seventy-five police officers surrounded the L.A. Panther headquarters on Central Avenue near 41st Street, where a meeting was under way. They positioned sharpshooters on roofs and paddy wagons at the corners. The Panthers called the media, and soon reporters and many local residents gathered outside. The police left.[23]

Almost four weeks later, at 5:00 A.M. on December 8, police simultaneously raided three Panther buildings in Los Angeles—the home of Geronimo Pratt, the Toure Community Center, and the chapter headquarters on Central Avenue. At Pratt's home, the police knocked down the door, shot up the house, and arrested everyone inside, including Pratt; his wife, Saundra; Long John and Kathy Kimbro; and Evon Carter—Bunchy Carter's widow—and the two Carter children, Michelle, eight, and Osceola, eight months. At the same time, another police party raided the community center, shooting up the building and arresting Panthers Al Armour, Sharon Williams, Craig Williams, and Ike Houston.

At 41st and Central, it was war. The initial raid by seventy-five police officers on L.A. Panther headquarters met fortified resistance. Police and Panthers exchanged fire. Hundreds of police reinforcements arrived, as did hundreds of observers and the news media. The Panther sandbags absorbed most of the police rounds. Metal grilles the Panthers had installed over the windows prevented police from launching tear gas and smoke canisters into the building. Panthers tore filters from cigarettes and stuck them in their noses as makeshift gas masks against the tear gas that did seep in.

Pioneering the first-ever Special Weapons Assault Team (SWAT), the raiding officers came dressed for war. The SWAT officers wore black jumpsuits with black boots, head coverings, and flak jackets. They wore gas masks, carried M16 rifles, and carried bandoliers of ammunition over their shoulders. From behind the relative safety of armored cars and vehicles borrowed from the National Guard, police fired five thousand rounds of ammunition into the Panther headquarters. Panthers returned fire with rifles and submachine guns and lobbed homemade Molotov cocktails at the police. Police attempted to penetrate the roof with a dynamite charge dropped from a helicopter, but the roof held.

The fighting went in waves. Police tried to gain position but could not penetrate the Panther fortress. With intensive exchanges, the sky would fill with thick smog. Then, with a pause in the shooting, a breeze would clear the air. The battle raged almost five hours. Police requested use of a grenade launcher from the army and were granted permission from the Pentagon. Then, at 9:45 A.M., Panthers waved a white flag from a window and the shooting stopped.

Renee "Peaches" Moore, nineteen, wearing a torn and bloodied yellow dress, emerged carrying the flag. She told reporters, "We gave up because it's not the right time. We'll fight again when the odds are more in our favor." Panthers Bernard Smith, Gil Parker, Wayne Pharr, Will Safford, Tommie Williams, Paul Redd, Jackie Johnson, Robert Bryan, Melvin "Cotton" Smith, Roland Freeman, and Lloyd Mims followed, and all were arrested. All but four of the Panthers were teenagers; three were in their early twenties, and Melvin "Cotton" Smith was forty-one. Three Panthers and three police were injured in the confrontation.[24] Robert Bryan later recalled that what had kept the Panthers fighting were the lines from Bunchy Carter's poem "Black Mother":

A slave of natural death who dies,
Can't balance out two dead flies.
I'd rather be without shame,
A bullet lodged within my brain.
If I were not to reach our goal,
Let bleeding cancer torment my soul.[25]

Mainstream allies rallied in support of the Black Panthers in the days following the December 8 police raid. Black state senator Mervin Dymally, in whose district the shoot-out took place, told reporters, "We need to raise some national voice against what is happening to the Panthers. I think it's a national plan for police repression. One must conclude that this is not an isolated incident."[26] Moderate black leaders feared that if the Panthers could be so violently repressed, other blacks could as well.[27] John W. Mack, executive director of the L.A. Urban League, said that police action against the Panthers had "the potential for spreading to other blacks." Earl E. Raines, executive secretary of the Los Angeles chapter of the NAACP told the press, "The black community is affected. . . . Next time it may be you." A coalition of major black organizations in Los Angeles, including the National Association for the Advancement of Colored People, the Urban League, the Congress of Racial Equality, the Southern Christian Leadership Conference, Operation Breadbasket, and the Conference of Black Elected Officials called for a massive rally at city hall on December 11 to protest the police raid of the Panther offices. Other allies mobilized as well. The Socialist Workers Party held a press conference in support of the Panthers. High school students organized a picket of the Hollywood police station. The American Civil Liberties Union (ACLU) volunteered to help with the Panthers' case. ACLU attorney Fred Okrand protested the high bail set for the Panthers arrested in the raids.[28]

On Thursday December 11, at the rally endorsed by mainstream black leadership, about four thousand protestors rallied at Los Angeles City Hall to protest the police raid of Panther headquarters on Central Avenue. Most of the protestors were young and black. Participants held signs with slogans such as "Stop Mass Murder," "Stop Panther Killing," "Pigs Will Be Pigs," "End Political Repression," and "Free All Political Prisoners." Sharing a stage with NAACP and other mainstream black supporters, Elaine Brown told the crowd, "These young warriors . . . established a lesson that should never be forgotten—the power really does belong to the people." Angela Davis said, "This is fascism; there's no doubt about it." The crowd moved from city hall and took over the Hall of Justice, where one young protestor addressed the crowd from the steps: "We have done what we have done today to show that the City Hall, this building, or any other building belongs to the people. The glorious warriors arrested Monday are on the top three floors of this building . . . We are here to show them we will get them out . . . to show them that eventually we will take power and we will destroy this goddamn place."[29]

In 1969, the state's repressive actions did not crush the Los Angeles Panthers. We need only compare the nascent Los Angeles chapter in January 1969 to the larger, better resourced, and highly militarized organization that police encountered when they tried to raid the Panthers' offices and were held at bay in the miniature one-day urban war of December 1969. Rather than weakening the Panthers, the intensive campaign of state repression during the year drove more members, funding, and allied support to the Party. In cities across the country, the pattern was similar. Repressive state actions in 1969 fueled growth of the Party.

10

Hampton and Clark

Fred Hampton was a natural leader. He dressed casually and was not flashy, but he had a strong, bold presence. People trusted him. He had been raised in a loving and close-knit family and attended church and Bible study throughout his childhood. He was a top athlete in high school, and an A student. He never used drugs or drank. Even as a young man, when he spoke, the words flowed sharp and lyrical in the best of the black church tradition. People opened their eyes and listened. And he was fearless.[1] Born August 30, 1948, the youngest of three children in a strong family from Louisiana, Hampton grew up in Maywood, Illinois, a working-class suburb of Chicago. In September 1967, he became the president of the youth council for the National Association for the Advancement of Colored People branch there. In that capacity, he helped organize a student boycott of his high school, Proviso East High, when black girls were excluded from the homecoming queen's retinue. When black students protested, white students responded with violence, beating black students with bats and blackjacks. Hampton organized groups of black students to fight back. In response to the interracial violence, Maywood police imposed martial law and set up checkpoints in the city's black neighborhoods. Hampton brought in representatives from the national NAACP and led the boycott of Proviso East High, demanding retraction of the martial law.[2]

Bobby Rush was a more scholarly type activist—a sharp thinker and a good administrator but not much of a public speaker. He had grown up in the Chicago Student Nonviolent Coordinating Committee; by 1968, he was codirecting the small SNCC chapter there, and he had an ongoing relationship with Stokely Carmichael. As tensions heightened between Stokely and other SNCC leaders in the spring of 1968, and following King's assassination, Stokely encouraged Rush to start a Black Panther chapter in Chicago. According to Rush, "The problem with SNCC was that it didn't have any specific activities."[3] Stokely arranged for Rush to travel to California to meet Donald Cox, and through Cox, to meet David Hilliard and Bobby Seale. The Panthers' approach impressed Rush, and he began seeking partners to build a Panther chapter in Chicago. When Rush heard Hampton speak at a black leadership conference at the headquarters of the Chicago gang Black P. Stone Nation, he knew Hampton was his key to success; Rush recruited him to join the Panthers. Rush and Hampton, along with Bob Brown—Rush's SNCC codirector—organized what would soon become the Party's major hub in the Midwest.[4]

ATTEMPTED PROVOCATION

In Chicago in the late 1960s, gangs were an important political force in black neighborhoods—none more so than the Blackstone Rangers. From their start in the early 1960s, the Rangers had focused on community building as an adjunct to their illegal activities, which included drug trafficking and extortion. As a result, they constituted a sort of parallel government on the South Side, protecting members of their neighborhood from other gangs and the police and providing some community services. By the late 1960s, they had swallowed up most of the smaller gangs in the area as part of the "P. Stone Nation" and had more than thirty-five hundred dedicated members, possibly as many as eight thousand. The gang organized cultural activities, such as a play coordinated by singer/songwriter/jazz pianist Oscar Brown Jr., and developed a loose affiliation with Black Power politics. Just before the big Chicago rebellions in the summer of 1967, a large block of federal money was channeled to Chicago, including a $957,000 grant from the Office of Economic Opportunity earmarked for at-risk youth. The Rangers and their main gang rivals, the Disciples, received the grant to help run a job-training program for unemployed black youth on Chicago's South Side. The Rangers also developed a wide range of other community and entrepreneurial activities, including a youth center and a restaurant.[5]

In December 1968, having quickly built a powerful Panther base in

Chicago, Fred Hampton entered discussions with Jeff Fort, leader of the Rangers, about merging the Panthers and the Rangers. The merger promised to boost the Panthers' membership and street presence. The FBI saw the potential merger as a political threat and sought to foster conflict between the two groups. The Chicago FBI field office suggested, in a memo to FBI headquarters on December 16, that spreading false rumors that the Black Panther Party leadership was disparaging Fort "might result in Fort having active steps taken to exact some form of retribution towards the leadership of the [Black Panther Party]." Hampton and a small entourage of Panthers went to the Rangers' headquarters on December 18 around 10:30 P.M. to discuss the potential merger. Hampton suggested to Fort that by joining forces, they could take over all the other Chicago street gangs. According to an FBI informant, Hampton told Fort that "they couldn't let the man keep the two groups apart." Fort was interested in a merger, the informant reported in an FBI memo, but he wanted the Panthers to join the Rangers, not the other way around, and he put on a show of strength: Fort "gave orders, via walkie-talkie, whereupon two men marched through the door carrying pump shotguns. Another order and two men appeared carrying sawed off carbines then eight more, each carrying a .45 caliber machine gun, clip type, operated from the shoulder or hip, then others came with over and under type weapons. . . . After this procession Fort had all Rangers present, approximately 100, display their side arms and about one half had .45 caliber revolvers . . . all the above weapons appeared to be new."[6] Fort told Hampton that he supported the Panthers but that the Rangers were not to be considered members of the Party, and he gave Hampton a new .45 caliber machine gun to "try out."

Over the next two weeks, discussions deteriorated, and the Chicago office of the FBI suggested to headquarters that the time was right to provoke the Rangers to take violent action by sending a forged letter to Fort:

Brother Jeff:
I've spent some time with some Panther friends on the west side lately and I know what's been going on. The brothers that run the Panthers blame you for blocking their thing and *there's supposed to be a hit out for you.* I'm not a Panther, or a Ranger, just black. From what I see these Panthers are out for themselves not black people. I think you ought to know what they're up to, I know what I'd do if I was you. You might hear from me again.

[signed:] *A black brother you don't know.*[7]

The FBI field office suggested sending the letter to Fort rather than Hampton because Fort was more likely to respond with violence: "It is believed the above may intensify the degree of animosity between the two groups and occasion Fort to take retaliatory action which could disrupt the [Black Panther Party] or lead to reprisals against its leadership. Consideration has been given to a similar letter to the [Party] alleging a Ranger plot against the [Black Panther Party] leadership; however, it is not felt this would be productive principally because the [Party] at present is not believed as violence prone as the Rangers to whom violent type activity—shooting and the like—is second nature."[8] J. Edgar Hoover approved the proposal, and the field office sent the letter to Fort.[9]

The FBI's effort may have helped prevent a merger between the Panthers and the Rangers, but it did not precipitate widespread violence between the groups. Hampton and Fort figured out that the government was attempting to create a deadly conflict between them and decided not to take the bait.[10]

ICE CREAM

In early 1969, Fred Hampton initiated the Chicago Panthers' first free food distribution. Hampton imagined himself a modern-day Robin Hood and "appropriated" an ice cream truck in Maywood, passing out more than four hundred ice cream bars—worth a total of seventy-one dollars—to neighborhood children. The Maywood police apparently did not appreciate his sense of justice and arrested him on charges of robbery and assault.[11]

In the weeks that followed, Hampton and the Chicago Panthers organized their first official program, a Free Breakfast for Children Program, which opened on April 1, 1969. Within two weeks, the Panthers had fed more than eleven hundred grade-school children, drawing new community support and also making it hard to ignore the political dimensions of Hampton's case.[12] During his trial that April, Hampton appeared on a local television show publicizing the free breakfast program, and appealing for public support for the Panthers.[13]

On April 9, 1969, Hampton was convicted of robbery and assault. Maywood Police Chief Kellough attempted to prevent the court from releasing Hampton on bail pending sentencing. But in part due to the efforts of Hampton's civil rights attorney, Jean Williams, Hampton was released on $2,000 bail.[14] Williams planned to appeal Hampton's conviction on the grounds that newspaper articles about the Panthers during the trial had prejudiced the jury.[15]

Following the ice cream trial and the attention it brought, Hampton called the Chicago Panthers' first press conference, in which he challenged the legitimacy of the state, asserting a higher morality underlying the Panthers' revolutionary program and calling on people to mobilize to support the Panthers against state repression. Hampton argued that the Black Panther Party, not the government, acted in the interests of the people: "Our case should be taken to the people and the people will not tolerate any oppressive system or force that attempts to jail the very people who feed their hungry children." Hampton announced that the Chicago Panthers intended to establish a community patrol of police, open liberation schools throughout the city, and set up free health clinics. "We're being harassed constantly by the pigs, and they're arresting us as fast as they can on any kind of charge, such as traffic violations, smoking on buses, carrying concealed weapons, just anything," Hampton explained. "But no matter how many of us they try to lock up, force underground or even kill, the vanguard of the people's revolution, the Black Panther Party will still go on. We are servants of the people, and any people who launch attacks against the servants of the people are enemies of the people."[16]

The Chicago Panthers sought to mobilize a broad New Left alliance in support of Hampton. While Hampton was out on bail, they held a mock court with nonblack allies enacting the trial of Fred Hampton as an educational exercise. Hampton told the New Leftists, "We gonna fight racism not with racism, but with solidarity. We not gonna fight capitalism with Black capitalism, but we gonna fight it with socialism. We not gonna fight reactionary pigs . . . with any reaction on our part. We gonna fight their reaction when all of us get together and have an international proletarian revolution."[17]

The fledgling Chicago Panthers seized the attention of the Party's national leaders. When Panther chairman Bobby Seale visited Chicago, he joined Hampton and Rush in a church mobilization and spoke to an audience of blacks of various classes and New Leftists of various hues, explaining the revolutionary cross-race logic of Hampton's action: "I'm so thirsty for revolution. I'm so crazy about the people. We're going to stand together. We're going to have a Black Army, a Mexican American Army, an alliance in solidarity with progressive Whites, All of us. And we're going to march on this pig power structure. And we're going to say: 'Stick 'em up motherfucker. We come for what's ours.'"[18]

On Monday May 26, with Illinois state attorney Edward V. Hanrahan publicly pressuring the judge, Fred Hampton was sentenced to two to five years in prison for robbery and assault. In a joint press conference at the Chicago Panther headquarters, Robert L. Lucas, national director of the Black Liberation Alliance and a former leader of the Congress of Racial Equality, condemned the sentence, noting that Hampton's breakfast for children program fed three thousand children throughout Chicago, making Hampton a threat to Mayor Daley and the political establishment. "This type of program poses a devastating threat to the Daley political machine and the black lackeys who front for him in the city's wards."[19]

As late as March 1969, the Chicago Panther chapter was still small and garnered little local influence or national attention. While Rush and Hampton teamed up in June 1968, the Black Panther national office did not officially recognize the chapter until October, and the first Chicago office was not opened until November 1, 1968.[20] There was no coverage of the Chicago Panthers in the Black Panthers' own newspaper until May 1969.[21] But as the state attempted to repress the Chicago Panthers in the spring of 1969, their membership grew, and they gathered increasing attention from the national office, local blacks, and New Left allies.

On April 9, the same day that Fred Hampton was convicted of robbing an ice cream truck, as Bobby Seale and the rest of the Chicago Eight were arraigned in Chicago on conspiracy charges for their part in the rebellion at the Democratic Convention, the Black Panthers joined with the Students for a Democratic Society to organize a rally in downtown Chicago. Speaking to the more than five hundred people gathered at the rally, the Panthers proclaimed their position as the "vanguard of the revolutionary struggle today." Seale and Hampton jointly spoke of plans for a massive organizing drive in Chicago that summer in preparation for Seale's trial in September.[22]

Federal efforts to repress the Chicago Panthers continued. In early April, undercover Chicago police approached Panthers and offered to sell them illegal submachine guns. On April 11, in what the New Left *Guardian* called a clear case of "provocation and entrapment," seventy-nine federal agents and Chicago police, in a raid using hidden floodlights for their public relations effect, arrested three Panthers—Merrill Harvey, Michael White, and Field Secretary Nathaniel Junior—for the attempted purchase of automatic weapons. The court set bails ranging from $65,000 to $75,000 for each of the three Panthers. The same court had released two white men in January on only $4,000 bail for selling similar weapons, presumably a greater offense.[23]

By the end of May, advancing their community programs and alliance politics in the face of overt repression, the Panthers were building a strong organization in Chicago. Energetic activists in their late teens and early twenties led many of the initiatives. Twenty-year-old Panther Barbara Sankey, who grew up on the West Side of Chicago and had been drawn to the Panthers by the activities surrounding Huey's trial, directed the Free Breakfast for Children Program. The program served about five hundred breakfasts to children every week at three Chicago sites. One meat company gave the Panthers fifty pounds of sausage every week, and the Joe Lewis Milk Co. donated five hundred cartons of milk to the program every week.

Twenty-year-old Billy Brooks, who also grew up on Chicago's West Side, directed the "internal education cadre" of fifteen Panthers. Each member was required to closely read a dozen books—six by or about Mao Zedong, three by or about Malcolm X, and one each by Huey Newton, Frantz Fanon, and Karl Marx. In turn, each member had to help other Panther members understand these texts. The reading list reflected the Panthers' increasingly explicit embrace of Marxist, and especially Maoist, theory and ideology.

Deputy Minister of Information Rufus "Chaka" Walls, with a staff of twenty Panthers, was in charge of distributing the *Black Panther*. Walls, at twenty-eight, was older than most Panthers and was president of the Black Student Association at a local community college. By late May, the Chicago chapter was selling about eight thousand copies of the newspaper per week and was planning to increase sales to fifteen thousand copies a week. Chicago Deputy Minister of Health Ronald Satchel, who grew up in a middle-class family and had recently dropped out of the University of Illinois, was only eighteen. He and a group of about ten Panthers were trying to organize a medical clinic, but they were having a hard time getting doctors to donate their time. Communications Secretary Ann Campbell—with a staff of three—served as the office manager, oversaw communications within the chapter and reports to the national office, and handled the mail. Yvonne King, in her early twenties and new to Chicago, initially organized black workers in her position as deputy minister of labor and then took on the role of field secretary, overseeing community programs.[24]

The two-story Chicago Black Panther office at 2350 West Madison Street was a formidable presence in the community. Under three large bay windows on the second floor, a sign with large hand-painted black lettering on a white background read "ILL. CHAPTER BLACK PANTHER PARTY." The sign was bookended on the left and right by life-size mirror images of a black panther springing into action in defense of the office and against any attackers. Beneath the sign hung seven posters of the Panthers' most famous and powerful images: Huey Newton and Bobby Seale armed in defense of the original Panther office, Eldridge Cleaver speaking, Malcolm X, an Emory Douglas painting of Bobby Hutton, and Huey on the wicker throne.[25]

RAIDS

As the Chicago Panthers grew in number and political strength, state efforts to repress them escalated. At about 5:30 in the morning on Wednesday June 4, the FBI raided the Chicago Black Panther headquarters on Madison Street. Agents, armed with machine guns, rifles, and handguns, used sledgehammers to break down the two steel doors to the second-floor office. Without presenting search warrants, they proceeded to sack the office and arrest the eight Panthers present. The FBI agents told the press they had found several guns and ammunition in the office, but the weapons were not automatic and did not violate any federal regulation. Bobby Rush held a press conference later in the day decrying "illegal" FBI tactics; the Panthers, he said, planned to press charges. Rush said the FBI agents left the office in complete disarray, creating more than $20,000 in property damage, including destroying two desks and assorted office equipment and confiscating a safe containing $3,000, which the Panthers planned to use to equip a health clinic they hoped to open in July. The agents also took cereal meant for the free breakfast program. Rush described the raid as part of a concerted national effort by the FBI to crush the Panthers, citing similar raids in Detroit, New York, Connecticut, San Francisco, Indianapolis, Des Moines, and Denver. Michael Klonsky, area leader of the Students for a Democratic Society, joined Rush in the press conference and said that SDS supported the Black Panthers 100 percent in resisting illegal state repression.[26]

On Tuesday June 10, 1969, a Cook County grand jury indicted Fred Hampton, his bodyguard William O'Neal, and fourteen other leading members of the Illinois Black Panther Party on charges that included kidnapping and unlawful use of a weapon. The state's attorney, Edward V. Hanrahan, said that the charges stemmed from the kidnapping and torture of a woman who had stored guns for the Panthers and then hidden them. Bail was originally set at $100,000 for most of the accused but $10,000 for O'Neal. Hampton was never convicted on the charges, but William O'Neal was later exposed as a provocateur working secretly for the FBI.[27]

On the morning of July 14, 1969, Larry Roberson and fellow Panther Grady Moore were selling the *Black Panther* newspaper when they saw two police officers questioning black patrons about a suspected theft of two baskets of produce from a nearby market. According to the Panthers, the police had lined up more than a dozen people—mostly older black men—against the wall and were harassing them. The police maintained that they were simply investigating a report of stolen produce when Roberson and Moore approached and asked them what they were doing. The officers said that when they told Roberson and Moore to leave, they became belligerent, calling themselves "protectors of the community." The Panther newspaper reported that Moore and Roberson were not armed, but police told the press that Roberson drew a gun and started shooting at them. Roberson was shot three times by police and taken by ambulance to the county hospital, where he was admitted in good condition. Both Moore and Roberson were arrested on charges of attempted murder. No police officers were wounded.[28]

Two weeks later, Chicago police raided the Black Panther office a second time. They arrived at 1:15 A.M. on Thursday July 31, following a community rally outside the Black Panther office Wednesday afternoon. Twenty-four police cars shut down Madison Street in front of the Panther office, and the officers attempted to storm the building. Hampton was in jail on the ice cream charges, and no Panther leaders were in the office at the time, but three rank-and-file Panthers—Joseph "Pete" Hynam, Larry White, and Alvin Jeffers, each armed with a hand gun—held off police for thirty-five minutes until they ran out of ammunition. Eventually, police shot through the steel door and made their way upstairs, beating the Panthers with rifle butts, knocking Larry White unconscious and breaking his jaw, badly injuring the others, and arresting them on charges of attempted murder. Then, according to the Panthers, the police used gasoline to burn down the upper half of the Panther office. Video footage documents the charred office and the hundreds of bullet holes riddling the building façade and front door. Police claimed that the Panthers fired first, sniping at passing police cars, and that the fire was caused by tear gas canisters. Panthers reported that people on the street threw bottles and rocks at the police during the incident and later helped with repairs.[29]

By this point, the Panthers and their allies understood they were under siege and prepared for further raids. Video footage by concerned Panther allies shows more than a dozen rank-and-file members cleaning and readying guns in the Chicago office. In the video, one Panther, a woman, asks various members for their blood types, marking their answers on a clipboard. Another passes out cloth for people to use to cover their mouths and faces in the event of a tear gas attack.[30]

In the early morning hours of Saturday October 4, police again raided the Chicago Panther headquarters. The raid was in many respects a repeat of the July 31 police raid. Officers' bullets riddled the front door and walls of the office. The police set the office on fire, smashed equipment, and destroyed stores of food designated for the free breakfast programs. After Panther resistance abated, police arrested six Party members on charges of attempted murder, alleging that they had tried to snipe at police from the headquarters rooftop. Again, Panthers alleged that the police intentionally set the fire. Neighbors carried water up to the office in buckets to help extinguish the flames. Hampton, from jail, maintained that again police took money intended for the breakfast program.[31] National Chief of Staff David Hilliard sought to build support for the Panthers' community policing initiative, declaring that the raid provided further proof of the need for community control of the police. He said that raids like the one on October 4 in Chicago "will continue and be escalated unless we move to circulate, as soon as possible, the petition for Community Control (decentralization) of police."[32]

With the repeated raids and arrests of local Panthers that fall, many black organizations lined up in support of the Panthers. Many believed that such repression posed a threat to all black people: what could be done to the Panthers could be done to them as well. On November 3, a large coalition of black groups united to protest the government treatment of the Black Panther Party. The participating groups included a number of black gangs, including the P. Stone Nation and the Conservative Vice Lords, as well as representatives from other radical black groups, such as the Black Liberation Alliance. The coalition also included black political leaders such as Jesse Jackson, who had closely worked with Martin Luther King Jr. and was the director of the Southern Christian Leadership Conference's Operation Breadbasket. The coordinator of the rally, Reverend C. T. Vivian, another important

King ally, told the press, "This is a picture of illegal court systems operating against black men."[33]

Some in the coalition believed that resisting the repression of the Panthers was a matter of life and death. And for good reason. In July, the ambulance had delivered Larry Roberson to the county hospital in good condition after being shot by police. Yet he died in the hospital on September 4 from some combination of injuries sustained in the shooting and improper medical care.[34]

What made the stories of Panther repression so compelling to many young blacks in Chicago was not how unusual they were but how common. The summer had been filled with violence, and many young black people had died in conflicts with the Chicago police. On October 5, police shot sixteen-year-old John Soto in the back of the head, killing him. Eyewitnesses said police, unprovoked, had fired as Soto walked away. Soto's older brother, Michael Soto, a black community activist and a decorated army sergeant on leave from Vietnam, helped organize rallies to protest John's killing by police. On October 10, police fatally shot Michael Soto as well, claiming they had caught him in a robbery attempt.[35] In August, police killed nineteen-year-old Linda Anderson by firing a shotgun through her apartment door. They claimed they had been trying to protect her from rape by an acquaintance.[36] In 1969 and 1970, Chicago police killed fifty-nine blacks versus nineteen whites in a city where whites outnumbered blacks by more than two to one. A black person in Chicago was six times more likely to be killed by the police than a white person.[37]

Panther Spurgeon Jake Winters, nineteen, knew Roberson and took the police actions harder than most. A scrawny and studious kid, he had received a scholarship to the Catholic Xavier University. But on Thursday November 13, 1969, he was not thinking about school. The city was cold. Snow fell lightly on the streets. Winters' heart was full of rage. He went with his friend and fellow Panther Lance Bell to their hideout at the abandoned Washington Park Hotel on 58th Street at Calumet Avenue. At some point someone called the police and Bell fled, leaving Winters to stand alone. As the first police officer approached the abandoned building, Winters picked up one of two rifles, took aim, and pulled the trigger. The officer fell dead. In the ensuing rush of police cars and sirens and volley after volley of police fire, Winters ran from room to room shooting at the police through the windows of the empty hotel. Over the next twenty minutes, in the storm of his rage, Winters wounded nine officers and totaled five police cars. One police officer and military veteran later recalled that the firefight was hotter than any he had experienced in Vietnam.

Bleeding badly, Winters escaped out of the east side of the building and through a dark tunnel leading to King Drive and Washington Park. Instead of fleeing into the safety of his neighborhood, he climbed the nearby stairs. This was his last stand, and he waited, gun in hand. When the first officer came through the tunnel, Winters shot him, knocking him to the ground. Then, as other officers rushed forward, Winters walked to the fallen officer, purposefully raised his gun, and shot the officer in the face, killing him, as the remaining officers gunned Winters down.[38]

DECEMBER 4, 1969

As directed by national headquarters, the Chicago FBI office had first established a counterintelligence program against the Chicago Black Panther Party in the fall of 1968, at which point agents began closely monitoring the Panthers via a warrantless wiretap of their office and other means. A special FBI Racial Matters Squad was organized to spearhead actions against the Panthers. Roy M. Mitchell, a special agent in the squad, was the person who had approached William O'Neal while he was a prisoner in the Cook County jail and recruited him to infiltrate the Panthers and provide information to the FBI. On November 1, the day the Chicago Black Panther office opened, O'Neal, already on the FBI payroll, went to the office and joined the Black Panther Party. As a seemingly eager early recruit, O'Neal soon was appointed chief of security for the Chicago Panthers.[39]

The Chicago FBI worked closely with local law enforcement, mostly through the offices of Edward V. Hanrahan, who was elected Cook County state's attorney in November 1968. Hanrahan created a Special Prosecutions Unit (SPU), putting Assistant State's Attorney Richard Jalovec in charge. Starting in April 1969, FBI Special Agent Mitchell worked closely with Jalovec to target the Panthers. That June, as the FBI began coordinating raids on the Chicago Panther offices, a special squad of nine Chicago police officers was assigned to report directly to the Special Prosecutions Unit, which in turn was working closely with the FBI Racial Matters Squad.[40]

On the night of November 13, FBI Special Agent Mitchell met with informant William O'Neal and showed him photos of the two dead police officers killed earlier that day by Spurgeon Winters. In a series of meetings in the following days, Mitchell had O'Neal help map out the exact layout of Fred Hampton's apartment, including the specific location of his bed and nightstand. He also asked O'Neal to keep tabs on who was coming and going from the apartment and to determine what weapons were kept there.[41]

Armed with this information, a raiding party of fourteen SPU officers arrived outside Hampton's apartment at 4:30 A.M. on December 4. They did not bring the standard raiding equipment they had used in previous Chicago Panther raids, such as tear gas or sound equipment; instead, they carried a Thompson submachine gun, five shotguns, a carbine, nineteen .38 caliber pistols, and one .357 caliber pistol. The assault was quick and decisive. Within fifteen minutes, Fred Hampton was dead, shot twice through the head while he lay in bed. Peoria, Illinois, Panther leader Mark Clark, in Chicago attending a statewide meeting of Party leaders, was also dead. The seven other Panthers in the apartment—four with bullet wounds—were arrested on charges of attempted murder, aggravated battery, and unlawful use of weapons. One SPU officer was shot in the leg.[42]

Hanrahan told the press that the Panthers fired first and continued to shoot repeatedly despite warnings from police that they were at the door: "The immediate, violent, criminal reaction of the occupants in shooting at announced police officers emphasizes the extreme viciousness of the Black Panther Party. So does their refusal to cease firing at the police officers when urged to do so several times." Panther survivors claimed the SPU never knocked and came in shooting.[43]

The Chicago FBI viewed the raid as a success, attributable in part to the information provided by William O'Neal. Following the raid, the Chicago field office wrote to the FBI headquarters requesting a $300 bonus for O'Neal: "[Prior to the raid], a detailed inventory of the weapons and also a detailed floor plan of the apartment were furnished to local authorities. In addition, the identities of [Black Panther Party] members utilizing the apartment at the above address were furnished. This information was not available from any other source and subsequently proved to be of tremendous value . . . to police officers participating in a raid . . . on the morning of 12/4/69. The raid was based on the information furnished by the informant." The bonus was approved.[44]

Before sunrise on Friday December 5, the morning after Hampton and Clark were killed, police raided Bobby Rush's South Side apartment, but Rush was not there.[45] Later that same day, still alive and free, Rush began conducting tours of the blood-stained and bullet-ridden apartment where Hampton and Clark had been killed. He told the reporters and community residents who lined up to see the apartment, "This was no shootout. Nobody in the apartment had a chance to fire a gun and we can prove it by the fact that there are no bullet holes outside in the hallways or outside, just big gaping holes in Fred's bedroom where they fired on him." The *New York Times* reported, "Most of the rooms and walls appeared to be free of scars, pockmarks and bullet holes. There were clusters of bullet holes and the gouges of shotgun blasts in the places where the Panthers said the two men had been killed and four others had been wounded. . . . There were no bullet marks in the area of the two doors through which the police said they entered."[46]

WE ARE ALL BLACK PEOPLE

There was an immediate outpouring of support for Hampton, Clark, and the Panthers. By early evening, three Chicago aldermen, the Afro-American Patrolmen's League, the Illinois division of the American Civil Liberties Union, and a variety of black community groups had called for an independent investigation of the incident.[47] New Left attorneys Francis Andrew, Kermit Coleman, and James Montgomery stepped forward to represent the Panthers and the families of Hampton and Clark.[48] Black Chicago alderman and funeral home director A. A. Rayner, who viewed the Panthers as a much-needed "youth group" and had previously supported them by cosigning their office lease, offered to hold Fred Hampton's body at his funeral home for public viewing.[49]

Rush, working with Rayner, and Hampton's mother and father, arranged for an independent autopsy of Hampton at Rayner's funeral home that evening.[50] Dr. Victor Levine, who had served as chief pathologist for the Cook County coroner in the 1950s, conducted the autopsy, assisted by Dr. Carl Caldwell and Dr. Quentin Young. The three doctors found that Hampton had been killed by bullets shot from an angle slightly above and behind his head as he was lying down. They found no powder burns on his hands, contradicting police claims that Hampton had fired at them.[51]

On that same Friday, Rush learned that a warrant had been issued for his arrest on charges of failing to register a gun. He arranged to surrender publicly to police on Saturday at a meeting organized by Operation Breadbasket. An overflow crowd of five thousand people, mostly black and many middle class and middle-aged, crammed into the Capitol Theater to witness the surrender. Rev. Jesse Jackson spoke to the crowd, contending that the problem was the exclusion of black people from leadership in the police department. He maintained that white police should be withdrawn from the black community, or black people should be appointed to leadership in the police department: "If we're 42 percent of the population, then we should have 42 percent of decision-making jobs in the department."[52]

Fred Hampton's brother Bill also spoke, delivering a message from his parents asking people to maintain the peace—not to riot but to unite. He reported that the independent autopsy conducted Friday at Rayner's Funeral Home confirmed that Hampton had been murdered while he slept. When Rush walked on stage and embraced Jackson, the crowd cheered wildly. Rush told the audience, "I am turning myself in to black people, who will dictate my future actions." Police then took Rush into custody. A black ACLU lawyer and the head of the Afro-American Patrolmen's League accompanied Rush to prevent police wrongdoing.[53]

Later that day, released on $1,500 bond, Rush appeared at a Panther rally at the Church of Epiphany. More than three thousand people crammed into the church, and more than one thousand others were turned away. The audience was again predominantly black, but this group was younger, less affluent, and more radical; some three hundred whites and a number of Puerto Rican New Leftists were in the crowd as well. Speakers, including city officials, a college president, a representative of the Puerto Rican Young Lords Organization, a representative of the Communist Party, and various Black Panthers, paid homage to Hampton and Clark. When Rush spoke, he told the audience that the killing of Hampton and Clark threatened them all: "Wake up and see the handwriting on the wall with your lives being threatened and murderers at your doorstep." Someone passed him a note, which he paused to read. He looked up at the audience and reported that Ronald Satchel, the Chicago Panther deputy minister of health, who had been shot five times by police in the December 4 raid, was in critical condition: "We just got word from the hospital that brother Ronald is fighting for his life." The audience gasped. "If he dies, this beautiful brother . . ."—Rush's voice broke off, and two uniformed Panthers leapt to his side. Rush composed himself and continued: "Brother Ron was a former medical student, nineteen years old. He was getting ready to open the Panther's free medical center before he was gunned down. And now he's fighting for his life."[54]

Another Panther speaker angrily denounced the "pig power structure that has murdered our dear brothers." When the speaker urged the audience to "get you some guns and defend yourselves against the pigs," the crowd broke into a foot stomping, handclapping chant:

All Power to the People!
Right On!
All Power to the People!
Right On![55]

The Panthers used the public attention to organize support through popular education, offering more tours of the apartment where Fred Hampton and Mark Clark had been murdered. In the following weeks, thousands of people—and many journalists—flocked to the apartment to mourn the deaths and to consider the evidence for themselves. Most who came were black, representing a wide swath of society, from high school students to professionals in suit and tie, "workmen in paint-stained clothes, middle-aged women in flowered hats, neatly dressed office workers, elderly people and postal workers in gray uniform," according to the *New York Times*. "Many [gave] a clenched fist salute" as they left. Young New Leftists from across the city put on their political buttons espousing radical causes and made the trip to learn about Fred Hampton. Tours of the apartment ran all day and continued until 8:00 each evening. Panther tour guides showed visitors unscathed walls where police had entered and where they reportedly had stood during the raid, and then the clusters of bullet holes and large pools of blood where the Panthers had been shot. Tours continued until December 17, when Cook County authorities halted them by sealing off the apartment.[56]

The National Black Panther Party understood and sought to portray the killing of Hampton and Clark as political assassination and as part of a national government conspiracy to repress the Party. Chief attorney for the Panthers Charles Garry made a claim, widely publicized in the mainstream press, that Hampton and Clark were the twenty-seventh and twenty-eighth Panthers killed by police since January 1968.[57] Panther Chief of Staff David Hilliard declared, "The organized attempt to destroy the B.P.P. [has] brought to the attention of the American people the atrociousness of the American Government, in terms of its subjects. People are moving for their freedom. The very fact that they attacked us so openly shows that they're a very brutal people—that they are barbarous, criminal elements against society."[58]

While the number of people who agreed with the Black Panthers' revolutionary politics was relatively small, many were concerned that the killing of Hampton and Clark was part of a pattern of government repression that posed a broader threat to life and freedom. Many mainstream political organizations—including the NAACP, CORE, the American Jewish Committee, the mayor's office of Maywood, the Chicago ACLU, and the United Auto Workers—joined the call for an independent investigation of the killings.[59]

The director of the Chicago Urban League contended, "Whatever the Panthers believe in, they shouldn't be shot down like dogs in the street."[60] On December 8, the *Chicago Daily Defender,* the nation's largest black newspaper, decried the apparent government conspiracy to repress the Panthers: "Are blacks to be murdered for what they believe or what they say? Is the slaying of leaders of the Black Panthers across the nation a part of a national conspiracy to destroy their organization? These and similar questions are being asked in the black community of Chicago even by those who have little or no sympathy for the Panther Party."[61]

Simultaneously, the New Left took to the streets. Sixty-five young New Leftists were arrested on Park Avenue in New York on December 9 for protesting Hampton's killing outside an award dinner attended by President Nixon. Many of the protestors were charged with breaking windows at Saks Fifth Avenue and five other upscale stores, and with assaulting police officers.[62] And at Panther offices nationwide, young white allies—some of them lawyers—held around-the-clock vigils to prevent further raids, some bringing their bedrolls and sleeping in the Panther offices each night. Allan Brotsky, a lawyer, explained, "We feel this will be a deterrent to lawless raids by the police on Panther headquarters."[63]

On Tuesday December 9, Fred Hampton's parents, working with the Panthers and SCLC, held memorial services for their slain son. About five thousand people jammed into a church in Maywood and crowded around loudspeakers outside. The Rev. Ralph Abernathy, a close associate of Martin Luther King Jr. and head of the SCLC, delivered the main eulogy, declaring, "If the United States is successful in crushing the Black Panthers, it won't be too long before they will crush SCLC, the Urban League and any other organization trying to make things better."[64] Bobby Rush asked the mourners to channel their sorrow into active support for the struggle: "We can mourn today. But if we understood Fred . . . that his life wasn't given in vain, then there won't be no more mourning tomorrow. Then all our sorrow will be turned into action."[65] Following the memorial for Fred Hampton, who had been born in the suburbs of Chicago, Hampton's parents sent their son's body "home" to be buried in Haynesville, Louisiana, where they had both been born.[66]

Wide black support for an independent investigation continued to grow. On the day of the memorial, six black Chicago aldermen—Wilson Frost, George Collins, Fred Hubbard, Robert Biggs, William Shannon, Kenneth Campbell, and Ralph Metcalf—submitted a resolution to the city council calling for an independent investigation: "All of Chicago is entitled to complete clarification of every obtainable fact and circumstance surrounding the deaths of Fred Hampton and Mark Clark."[67] The same day, the Afro-American Patrolmen's League issued a statement denouncing Hanrahan's Special Prosecutions Unit. The league announced that it would begin its own investigation into the shooting. A spokesman pointedly questioned Hanrahan's motives and told the press that the shootings were "obviously political assassination."[68] Also that day, the Chicago Conference on Religion and Race, an alliance of Chicago's black churches, issued its own call for an inquiry.[69] The Northern Area Conference of the NAACP issued a statement condemning the police murder of Fred Hampton and the repression of the Black Panther Party: "Although we may differ with the Black Panthers in political philosophies . . . WE ARE ALL BLACK PEOPLE and when these kinds of actions are held by our police departments, we feel that all Black people are being threatened with the loss of their very lives." The statement called on U.S. Attorney General Mitchell and President Nixon to investigate the killings.[70]

On December 11, Hanrahan delivered to the *Chicago Tribune* exclusive police photographs of Hampton's apartment, claiming they proved that the Panthers had initiated the gun battle and that they showed bullet holes where the Panthers had fired at police. But after further investigation, the *New York Times* reported that many of the photos did not represent what their subtitles claimed. One depicted nail heads in the apartment kitchen doorjamb rather than bullet holes. Another photo that police claimed showed bullet marks on the outside of a bathroom door actually depicted the inside of a bedroom door.[71]

Hanrahan's deceit further fueled community outrage. On December 15, a coalition of more than one hundred black community groups calling itself the United Front for Black Community Organizations (but with no apparent involvement of the Black Panthers, who opposed separatist measures), announced a curfew barring whites from black neighborhoods. The curfew announcement read, "Effective immediately, a 6 P.M.-6 A.M. curfew is established for all whites in the black community. No whites will be permitted to enter the black community—for any reason—during those hours and all whites inside the black community must leave by the 6 P.M. deadline." Reverend C.T. Vivian, leader of the coalition, noted, "In recent days, the forces of power in Chicago have stepped up their campaign to oppress and repress black people. . . . We see these atrocities not as individual or isolated incidents but as a calculated pattern, a conspiracy by the forces of power in this city to crush the black drive toward liberation."[72] Prominent members of the coalition quickly denounced the curfew, saying that they had not been consulted, and the curfew was withdrawn.[73]

National black political figures condemned the government and praised the Panthers. Harlem congressman Adam Clayton Powell charged federal officials with conspiring to "exterminate" the Black Panthers.[74] Jesse Jackson published a column in the *Chicago Daily Defender* endorsing the Black Panther explanation that Fred Hampton had been murdered by police while he slept, calling his murder a "crucifixion" and calling on black people to "resurrect" his spirit for liberation.[75] Having returned to the United States from exile, radical Robert Williams spoke publicly about the repression of the Black Panthers: "It is not just a campaign against Panthers. It is not a campaign just against the Blacks. It is a campaign against all of those who oppose what is taking place in America today. It is against the resisters, those who resist imperialism, those who resist fascism, those who are nonconformists. . . . What is happening to the Panthers is happening to all of us. . . . I'm proud to return to this country and to find the new spirit that now exists among the Panthers. . . . And I'm happy to join my support."[76]

Even moderate national black and political leaders supported the idea of a public investigation. Whitney Young, national executive director of the Urban League, sent a telegram to Attorney General John Mitchell calling for a special investigation of the killing of Hampton and Clark and of the repression of the Black Panther Party nationally.[77] Roy Wilkins, executive director of the NAACP, made a similar statement.[78] Congressman Edward Koch of New York said at an antiwar rally, "I don't agree with the goals or methods of the Black Panthers, but civil liberties transcend the issue of the Panthers' goals."[79]

Five black U.S. congressmen—Louis Stokes from Ohio, Charles

Diggs from Michigan, Adam Clayton Powell from New York, John Conyers from Michigan, and William Clay from Missouri—toured the apartment with Bobby Rush and held a five-and-a-half-hour public hearing on Chicago's West Side to hear community concerns about the shootings. Representatives Shirley Chisholm of New York and Augustus Hawkins of California also declared their support. David Hilliard and Charles Garry flew to Chicago to participate. Louis Stokes told reporters that he agreed with the Panthers' interpretation of the evidence in the apartment: "All the physical evidence appears to be that there was shooting into the apartment but not shooting out. The wall appears to tell the story of what happened here."[80]

In explaining the outpouring of black support for the Panthers in the wake of the Hampton and Clark killings, the *New York Times* quoted one protestor: "A well-dressed Negro mother summed up the feeling of the black community here as she walked with her family to a packed rally in a church a few days after the shootings. 'They came in and killed Fred Hampton,' she said in a soft, very even tone. 'And if they can do it to him, they can do it to any of us.'"[81]

On December 19, the internal Chicago police investigation found no fault on the part of Hanrahan's SPU, a finding echoed in a report by the Cook County coroner.[82] In response to public pressure, the Justice Department appointed a federal grand jury to investigate the killings of Hampton and Clark.[83]

On January 6, Bobby Rush informed the press that results of a blood test of Fred Hampton in the independent autopsy revealed a heavy dose of Seconal, a drug that induces sleep. Rush charged that the killing of Hampton was a government conspiracy and that Hampton had been drugged by an FBI infiltrator to facilitate his murder.[84] Hampton's fiancée, Deborah Johnson (Akua Njeri), who was eight months pregnant at the time of his killing and was arrested in the raid, later recounted Hampton's strange behavior the night of the raid. She said that Hampton never got up from bed during the raid and remained silent. He woke up and slightly lifted his head as guns were being fired but barely moved and never said anything. After the first wave of shooting, police arrested Johnson and pulled her out of the bedroom and into the kitchen. She said she heard a police officer say, "He's barely alive, he will barely make it." Then the police started shooting again. She says she heard "a sister" scream. Then a police officer said, "He is good and dead now."[85]

Meanwhile, throughout 1970, national mobilizations in support of the Chicago Panthers continued. A number of New Leftists in New York City formed a group called the December 4 Movement to show "solidarity with the Black Panthers." On March 14, 1970, the group held a rally at Columbia University featuring Abbie Hoffman, French writer Jean Genet, Panthers Afeni Shakur and Zayd Shakur, and Juan Ortiz of the Young Lords. Following the rally, several hundred students marched around campus breaking windows and then took over the university's business school building. They promised to occupy the building until the university administration agreed to pay reparations to the Black Panther Party.[86]

On May 8, 1970, the state's attorney Edward V. Hanrahan dropped all charges against the seven surviving Panthers arrested in the December 4 raid, saying that there was no proof that any of the defendants had fired at police.[87] One week later, a federal grand jury issued a 250-page report finding that at least eighty-two bullets had been fired by the SPU officers, and only one shot appeared to have been fired by a Panther.[88]

After more than a decade of legal wrangling during which the case went all the way to the Supreme Court, the government eventually settled in 1982, agreeing to pay $1.85 million to the estates of Hampton, Clark, and the Panther survivors of the incident, with the federal, county, and city governments agreeing to split the bill.[89]

Fred Hampton was a revolutionary. The unusual aspect of his case was not that the state killed him—states often kill their enemies with impunity—but rather the broad mobilization in response to his assassination. If not for this support, the Chicago Panthers initially accused of starting the shoot-out and thus being responsible for Hampton's death would likely have been convicted. The outrageous details of the killing would never have been exposed. But the Chicago Panthers were building support by addressing the needs of many poor Chicago blacks and organizing them politically. While mainstream black political organizations such as the Urban League and SCLC did not support the Black Panther Party's political practices or its call for revolution, in 1969, they viewed the activities of the Chicago Panthers as an influential effort by young blacks to redress their plight. Despite their differences with the Panthers, the moderate black leaders of these organizations allied with the Party to expose and challenge state repression because they felt threatened by the killing of Fred Hampton and Mark Clark. In other cities, nonblacks provided the Panthers' vital base of allied support.

11

Bobby and Ericka

On January 23, 1969, Ericka Huggins—carrying her three-week-old daughter, Mai—brought the body of her husband, John, to his hometown of New Haven, Connecticut, for burial. John's parents still lived and worked in New Haven, which was the location of Yale University and a declining industrial city with extreme poverty and a sizable black ghetto. Ericka and Mai moved in with John's parents.[1] In the preceding months, the Panthers had begun organizing a chapter of the Party in Bridgeport, Connecticut, but their plans changed after John Huggins's funeral. The *Black Panther* carried Ericka Huggins's image on the front page, and she became an important national figure. Soon, the Panther focus in Connecticut shifted to New Haven, and the state's few Panthers gathered around Ericka.

When Warren Kimbro attended John Huggins's funeral in New Haven on January 24, 1969, he was thirty-five years old and going through a midlife crisis. Frustrated at work and in his marriage, he was greatly impressed with the newly widowed twenty-one-year-old Ericka Huggins. He joined the Black Panther Party and soon became infatuated with her. Kimbro quit his well-paying city job, offered his home for Panther activities, and separated from his wife and children. Ericka Huggins, while wise and exceptionally strong by most accounts, was not only a young widow but also a brand-new mother in need of emotional support. She soon succumbed to Kimbro's advances.[2]

Huggins and Kimbro quickly drew about a dozen committed members to the Party and began running the Connecticut Panther chapter out of Kimbro's house on Orchard Street in New Haven. They offered political education classes, tried to start a breakfast program, regularly made public speeches, and started attracting attention. In one provocative flier, they charged the city with murder for its housing policy: "Wanted for Murder by the people of New Haven for the use of lead paint in already inadequate Housing. We Charge these people: Murderer No #1 Mayor Richard C. Lee, Police Chief James Ahern . . . with these crimes: conspiracy with the intent to commit murder, premeditated murder. We charge all slum land lords with the same crimes."[3]

The FBI paid close attention to the New Haven Panthers, tapping their phones and infiltrating their ranks with several undercover informants. In March, FBI Director Hoover fiercely reprimanded the New Haven field office for not producing hard-hitting counterintelligence measures for dealing with the Panthers there: "To date you have submitted no concrete recommendations under this program concerning the Black Panther Party, despite the fact this extremely dangerous organization is active in four cities in your Division."[4] In early May, New Haven Police Department wiretaps revealed that Bobby Seale would be speaking at Yale University later that month to raise funds for legal fees. The police passed on this information to the FBI.[5]

On Saturday May 17, New York Panther George Sams showed up at the New Haven Panther office with Alex Rackley in tow. Rackley was nineteen years old, homeless, desperate, and eager to please. He had joined the Panthers in New York looking for a place to fit in. Sams was a bully. He was short, stocky, unkempt, and usually carried at least two pistols in his brown trench coat. Earlier expelled from the Party for stabbing another Panther in Oakland, Sams was reinstated at the request of Stokely Carmichael, whom he had once served as a bodyguard.[6]

Sams had shown up in New York earlier that spring as police began arresting most of the Party leadership there in multiple raids. He called himself "Crazy George" and claimed that he was sent "to straighten out" unreliable Party chapters.[7] In New York, Sams openly drank and used drugs in violation of Party rules and showed off his .45 caliber pistol. One Party member reported that he had beaten and raped a female Panther when she refused to have sex with him.[8]

Sams met Alex Rackley in Harlem and "disciplined" him for looking like a "pickaninny," beating him and ordering him to run around the block. Shortly thereafter, Sams drove Rackley to New Haven. According to New Haven Panther Francis Carter, Sams was the "kiss of death." When he arrived, Carter observed, "the whole family cohesiveness-camaraderie we were experiencing stopped."[9]

When Sams arrived in New Haven, he claimed that he had been sent by the national headquarters to weed out spies. Violent, heavily armed, and scary, he immediately took control of the fledgling New Haven chapter. He charged Rackley with being a spy and set up a kangaroo court to interrogate him. With the help of Warren Kimbro and young new Panther recruit Lonnie McLucas, Sams tied Rackley to a chair and tortured him. The two beat Rackley with a club, twisted coat hangers around his neck, and poured boiling water over him. Sams ordered Ericka Huggins to record the "proceedings" on audiocassette, and the recording captures Rackley desperately screeching for mercy.[10]

On the evening of May 20, three days after Sams had brought Rackley to New Haven, Sams announced that he would drive Rackley to the bus station and let him go. With Kimbro and McLucas, Sams took Rackley to a wooded swamp in the suburbs. Sams handed Kimbro his .45 and said "Ice him. Orders from National." Kimbro shot Rackley in the back of the head, killing him. Sams then took the gun back and handed it to McLucas, telling him to finish Rackley off. McLucas shot Rackley in the chest.[11]

The police and FBI had gathered extensive information on the New Haven Panther headquarters through paid informants and wiretapping. The night of May 20, Kelly Moye, a police informant, called Nick Pastore, the head of the information division of the New Haven police, and warned him that Sams and others were about to transport something important in Sams's green Buick Riviera. New Haven police chief James Ahern later said that he and his colleagues suspected that the Panthers had kidnapped someone and that the hostage was in transit. Police, however, did nothing to stop Rackley's torture or murder, later claiming that they did not know he was being tortured and that they had tried to follow the car that carried Rackley to his death, but it had eluded them.[12]

The next day, police recovered Rackley's body, and late that night, they conducted raids to arrest Ericka Huggins, Warren Kimbro, Lonnie McLucas, Francis Carter, and four other young female Panthers on murder charges.[13] In early August, Sams was arrested in a gun incident that embarrassed the fledgling Panther chapter in Halifax, Nova Scotia, and he was soon extradited to the United States for trial, where he turned state's evidence.[14] Within days, the Justice Department created a special unit with the "purpose of instituting federal prosecution against the [Black Panther Party]."[15] On August 19, on the basis of Sams's testimony, Bobby Seale, chairman of the Black Panther Party, was arrested in Berkeley, California, on capital charges of conspiracy to commit murder for allegedly ordering the killing of Alex Rackley.[16] The state made a deal with Kimbro, offering him a light sentence and a return to his middle-class life in exchange for turning state's evidence and pinning the murder on Panther higher-ups. Kimbro and Sams each served four years and were released.[17] Lonnie McLucas maintained the innocence of the Party leaders and was slated to face trial.

Panther field marshal Landon Williams was also in New Haven during Alex Rackley's torture and murder, and Sams testified that he had been taking orders from Williams and that Williams in turn was taking orders from Black Panther national headquarters. It is clear that Sams directed the gruesome events, and in the end, the state found insufficient evidence to support Sams's claim that he was following orders from Williams. Williams pled guilty on lesser charges of conspiracy to murder and received a suspended sentence in November 1971.[18]

Hoping to pin the murder on national Panther leaders Bobby Seale and Ericka Huggins, the state prosecuted a long and costly trial in an attempt to convict them. But its efforts failed, and all charges against Seale and Huggins were dismissed.[19]

The extent of the state's involvement in setting up Seale and Huggins remains unclear. The FBI has resisted legal requests to release records of wiretaps of the New Haven Panther headquarters, which might reveal that the agency knew about Rackley's kidnap and torture but did not act to prevent it.[20] Even more grave are suggestions that Sams directed the torture and murder of Rackley while on the FBI's payroll. Sams was the only first-hand witness to name Seale or other national Panther officials in the Rackley case, and authors Churchill and Vander Wall argue that the state based its charges on "material provided by 'a *trusted ten year informant*,'" and that this FBI informant was likely Sams.[21] Was it a coincidence that Sams showed up in New York as the New York 21 conspiracy broke, just in time to step into the power vacuum left by their arrest? Was it a further coincidence that he drove Rackley to the fledgling New Haven chapter two days before Seale was scheduled to arrive?[22]

On February 17, 1969, three months before Sams arrived in New Haven with Alex Rackley in tow, William O'Neal—the FBI infiltrator who provided the information used by the Chicago Special Prosecutions

Unit in the killing of Hampton and Clark—wrote in the *Black Panther* that he used "intensive" torture methods to obtain a confession from a rank-and-file Panther, Derek Phemster, and that Phemster was an FBI informant.[23] William O'Neal was one of the most valued and highly placed FBI infiltrators in the Black Panther Party, and it is not credible that the FBI would have paid him to torture and expose its other informants. More likely, the FBI directed O'Neal to publish the article to normalize the idea of torturing suspected informants and suggest its efficacy.

When police arrested the Black Panther suspects in New Haven the day after Rackley was murdered, Sams had already left town. But he left behind the tape recording he had made of Rackley's torture, and police had no trouble locating and confiscating the tape when they arrested the New Haven Panthers.[24] After those arrests, Sams traipsed in and out of various Panther offices nationally, with police and FBI raids following close behind. But, as Donald Freed has noted, "As George Sams traveled around the country, spending large sums of money, certain things began to happen to the Panthers. Each city he visited was thereafter subjected to predawn raids by combinations of city, state and federal police. But Sams was never caught; he always managed to leave before the raids were made."[25] The *New York Times* reported Sams's unlikely narrow escape from an FBI raid of the Chicago Panther headquarters in June.[26] Sams was not arrested until August, when police raided Black Panthers to derail an organizing effort in Halifax, Nova Scotia. In her book on the Black Panther effort in Halifax, Jennifer Smith argues that Sam's actions in Halifax are hard to explain unless he was seeking to undermine the Party.[27]

FREE BOBBY AND ERICKA!

Whoever was ultimately responsible for deciding to murder Alex Rackley, there was no credible evidence of Bobby Seale's involvement. The government's strained efforts to pin the murder on him became a rallying point for potential allies. Many progressives already saw Seale as a target of government repression. Despite his minimal involvement in the protests at the Democratic National Convention in Chicago, a federal grand jury indicted him on March 20, 1969, for conspiracy to incite riots along with the other "Chicago Eight": Rennie Davis, David Dellinger, John Froines, Tom Hayden, Abbie Hoffman, Jerry Rubin, and Lee Weiner.

At the time, Seale's attorney Charles Garry was undergoing surgery.

When the judge refused to delay the trial, Seale insisted on representing himself. The judge denied him that right, and Seale insisted he was being railroaded. Seale refused to be silenced and continued to press his constitutional right to defend himself, arguing, "You have George Washington and Benjamin Franklin sitting in a picture behind you, and they were slave owners. That's what they were. They owned slaves. You are acting in the same manner, denying me my constitutional rights."[28]

On October 29, the judge—unwilling to let Seale defend himself and unable to silence him—ordered Seale shackled to a chair and gagged. Seale continued to bang his chair and shout through his gag, demanding the right to defend himself. On November 5, the judge sentenced him to four years in prison on sixteen counts of criminal contempt of court and severed his case from that of the remaining seven defendants.[29] Every newspaper and TV news program featured depictions of Seale bound but undeterred.

Many potential allies saw the conspiracy charges against Bobby Seale as a state effort to stifle political dissent. On September 16, following Seale's arrest in San Francisco, an interdenominational group of ministers and priests held a sit-in at the U.S. marshal's office in San Francisco, nonviolently taking over the office. They argued that the conspiracy charges against Seale were "designed and enforced for the purpose of suppression of political dissent" and that "the Department of Justice is relating to the Panthers like the Department of Defense is relating to the Vietnamese." Eight of them were arrested.[30] The month after Seale was gagged and shackled in the Chicago court, the New Mobilization Committee to End the War in Vietnam (New MOBE)—the largest antiwar coalition in the United States at the time—sent a telegram to the Black Panther Party decrying the violation of Seale's rights and his mistreatment in court. New MOBE called for the immediate dismissal of charges against Seale and impeachment of the judge.[31]

Solidarity committees in Scandinavia launched a wave of rallies, displaying signs with pictures of Seale under the headline "Kidnapped" and others reading "Kapitalism + Racism = Fascism." Allies flew *Black Panther* editor "Big Man" Howard to Stockholm to speak on Seale's persecution at a joint anti-imperialist rally with the National Liberation Front of Vietnam.[32] In November South Africa's leading anti-apartheid organization, the African National Congress (ANC), sent a letter to the Black Panther Party expressing concern for political prisoners Bobby Seale and Huey Newton. The ANC also offered a shared vision of liberation: "Our struggle like yours is part of the larger struggle against international imperialism now being conducted in Vietnam, in the Middle East and most of the Third World. We, therefore, unhesitantly express our solidarity with you in your efforts to free Comrade Bobby and Huey. More than this we wish to express our solidarity with the Black Panther Party in its life and death struggle against our common enemy: fascist racism. It is not without significance that our demand is identical to yours . . . Power to the People!"[33]

After Seale's indictment in August for his alleged involvement in the Connecticut conspiracy, the Black Panther Party national office sent Doug Miranda to New Haven to develop and lead the Panther chapter there. Miranda, nineteen, had developed a reputation as one of the most effective young organizers in the Party. National headquarters chose him for the crucial role of organizing support for Seale and Huggins.

Miranda had joined the Black Panther Party through his involvement in the Third World Strike for Ethnic Studies at San Francisco State College (see chapter 12), and he had demonstrated his organizing skills during the launch of a Panther chapter in Boston. Party leaders recognized Miranda as one of their best organizers. He built trust and won loyalty. When needed, Miranda could also mete out discipline. At one Panther meeting in Boston, Miranda ordered latecomers to stand with their arms outstretched. "Repeat after me," he commanded. "Tardiness is a hardy corrosive that would destroy the party. I would rather destroy my arms than destroy the party!" His success with Harvard students also proved he knew how to deal with privileged allies. Once in New Haven, Miranda demonstrated his intellectual acuity to Yale students, trouncing a representative of Students for a Democratic Society in a public debate on Marxism. Miranda ably raised funds to support the New Haven chapter by securing regular donations from wealthy students, an activity that the FBI closely monitored through wiretaps.[34]

Under Miranda's leadership, the New Haven Panther chapter quickly developed. He set up an office on Sylvan Avenue in the predominantly black neighborhood called "the Hill." At a news conference on October 1, Miranda announced the formation of the Coalition to Defend the Panthers as a central part of their effort to mount a defense outside the courtroom. The coalition would focus on fund-raising for the legal defense and would challenge the vilification of the Panthers in the mainstream press, seeking to create a political climate conducive to the Black Panthers' case. The Panthers wanted the coalition to be a source of broad support, encompassing progressives and liberals and not just radicals: "The Coalition will be broad enough to include people who do not necessarily agree with the whole Panther program, but who do believe in any case that the Panthers are being persecuted for their political beliefs. The main line of the Coalition in its educational work will be that the Panther case has received such prejudicial coverage in the press that a 'fair trial' is impossible, and that therefore the Panthers should be freed immediately."[35]

At the time of its launch, the coalition comprised fifteen organizations, including national left and progressive organizations such as SDS and the Women's International League for Peace and Freedom; black community organizations from New Haven such as the Hill Parents Association; Yale organizations such as the Yale Divinity School Association and the Yale Black Law Students organization; and New Haven's leading leftist organization, the American Independent Movement.[36]

On October 8, the New Haven Black Panthers launched the John Huggins Free Breakfast for Children Program at the Newhallville Teen Lounge on Shelton Avenue. They teamed up with a welfare rights organization called Welfare Moms of New Haven to promote the breakfast program and build support for the Black Panther Party. Soon, they were feeding seventy to eighty kids each morning. On Wednesday nights, the Panthers held a popular ideology class on Columbus Avenue. They intermittently distributed free clothing and worked with existing black community groups on lead-abatement projects in black neighborhoods. Several months later, an open house at the Panther Community Information Center on Sylvan Avenue attracted hundreds of people, mostly working-class and low-income black residents of the neighborhood.[37]

Women's Liberation, a predominantly white feminist group in New Haven, planned a rally for November 22, 1969, to protest the plight of the five women Panthers incarcerated there. The group argued that, with the women being held without bail and not allowed visitors, their "right to interview lawyers crucial to the preparation of their defense has been denied in direct violation of their constitutional rights." Three of the five incarcerated Panther women were pregnant. Women's Liberation argued that the women were being denied adequate diet, exercise, and health care. "To hold these women under these conditions while they're still in pre-trial status makes a mockery of the 'presumption of innocence' which is their constitutional guarantee." On the day of the rally, about five thousand women and their male allies gathered at Beaver Pond Park and marched to the courthouse chanting,

"Off Our Backs!" "Power to the People!" and "Free Our Sisters, Free Ourselves!" A group of New Haven mothers on welfare led the procession, followed by women members of the Black Panther Party and representatives of predominantly white feminist organizations from several states, with men marching in solidarity behind them.

At the courthouse, Beth Mitchell, the communications secretary of the Harlem Black Panther Party, addressed the crowd: "We demand immediate freedom for the Connecticut Panthers and for all political prisoners. We demand an end to their isolation and sleepless nights. We demand adequate diet, exercise, and clothing. We demand their right to choose counsel. We demand their right to prenatal and maternity care by doctors of their choice. We demand the right for these mothers to make their own arrangements for the custody of the children in accordance with their wishes and the wishes of the Black Panther Party."[38]

To build support for their case, the Panther national leaders also sent Charles "Cappy" Pinderhughes, a former journalist, to accompany Miranda and develop a local newsletter. The *People's News Service* captivated and informed, advancing the Panther perspective and helping to mobilize support for Seale, Huggins, and the other Panthers in New Haven. In March, J. Edgar Hoover ordered the New Haven FBI to "furnish six copies of this bulletin on a regular basis," noting that the "paper is chock full of reports—from jail, from New Haven black neighborhoods, about police confrontations, conditions at Elm Haven [housing projects], diatribes against the system, news on national Panther cases. . . . [It retains] real local flavor."[39] By April 1970, the FBI noted that thirty "hard core" committed Black Panther members, supported by many more peripheral members and allies, were working around the clock to forge a strong and organized Panther presence in New Haven.[40]

As the New Haven Panthers mobilized, allied support grew, albeit slowly at first. On December 18, five Yale students interrupted a large class in Harkness Hall and recited a list of names of Black Panther Party members who had been killed. The students told the press they were "protesting the persecution of the Black Panther Party." The Yale administration did not take kindly to the intrusion and expelled all five students, informing them that they could reapply for admission the following term if they wanted to return.[41]

The Women's International League for Peace and Freedom, at their meeting in Philadelphia on February 14, 1970, passed a resolution expressing solidarity with Bobby Seale and the Black Panthers:

We call upon our lawmakers and all agencies of the government to respect the human and constitutional rights of all members of society. An orderly society with freedom and justice for all will not be attained until and unless the right of each individual to live in human dignity, to be free from racial discrimination, and to express his political views without persecution is recognized and enforced. We reaffirm our support of those, like ... the Black Panther Party, who courageously assert their constitutional rights in the face of lawful and oppressive governmental interference.[42]

On March 2, six hundred people—many of them black—rallied in front of the American embassy in London calling for the release of Bobby Seale and expressing solidarity with the Black Panther Party. A number of the protestors fought with police, and sixteen were arrested. On March 14, the National Student Union in Kamerun (now Cameroon) wrote to the Black Panthers to express its solidarity and to assert that the Panthers' struggle in the United States was an extension of the international fight against colonialism, analogous to the victorious Kamerun armed struggle against French imperialism. The Black Nationalist Malcolmites and the British Tricontinental Organization also extended their solidarity and support.[43]

That month, as the Connecticut trial approached, the famous French author Jean Genet traveled to New Haven to support the Panthers. He took up the core Panther notion that black communities in the United States were treated as "the Black Colony" and argued that Bobby Seale was being persecuted for refusing to follow the docile script laid out for blacks by their oppressors: "Bobby Seale and his comrades have over-stepped our [white] boundaries, they speak and act as responsible political people. . . . Because of his exceptional political stature, Chairman Bobby Seale's trial which just started is, in fact, a political trial of the Black Panther Party, and on a more general basis, a race trial held against all of America's Blacks." French filmmaker Jean-Luc Godard also traveled to New Haven to support the mobilization effort for Bobby Seale and the Black Panther Party. He told a packed crowd of six hundred gathered at the Yale Law School, "The outcome of this trial will very much affect the Panthers' effort to make a class struggle instead of a race war in this country. United States political leaders are trying to destroy the liberation struggle of the people. . . . You must all participate in the political actions in this city, not just as individuals, but as members of a society struggling against the rise of fascism."[44]

THE PANTHER AND THE BULLDOG

In mid-March, with the pretrial hearings for the New Haven Panthers approaching, the Black Panther Defense Committee opened its own office on Chapel Street in New Haven and began organizing a massive nonviolent protest for May 1—May Day—in support of the Panthers. The lead organizer for the committee was Ann Froines, whose husband, John Froines, was one of the Chicago Seven (known as the Chicago Eight before the judge severed Bobby Seal's case). The committee sought to tap into Panther alliances with national antiwar and countercultural leaders.[45]

As pretrial hearings for Panther Lonnie McLucas began in mid-April, Panthers and their allies in New Haven mobilized. They first targeted Yale, seeking to force the university to take a stand on the Panther trials. About seventeen hundred people, mostly Yale students, gathered in the campus's Woolsey Hall for a Panther presentation. Artie Seale, Bobby's wife, told the crowd, "Either you're with us or against us." A group entered the courthouse chanting pro-Panther slogans; police arrested two people from the group and expelled the rest from the building. The protesters rallied with Panther speakers Doug Miranda and Artie Seale across the street from the courthouse on the New Haven Green. Some students smashed windows at the nearby Chapel Square Mall and fought with police. Police arrested five people, including a Yale graduate student charged with photographing the police on the courthouse steps in violation of a local "emergency directive."[46]

The trial was a central concern of the Panther organization nationally, and that afternoon, David Hilliard attended the pretrial hearings accompanied by Panther minister of culture Emory Douglas and French author Jean Genet. At this point, Hilliard was the highest-ranking Panther leader not in jail or exile, and he had been in charge of the Party's daily operation since Seale had been arrested in late August. When Seale's lawyer Charles Garry handed Hilliard a note, police grabbed Hilliard and tried to seize the paper. Douglas and Genet defended Hilliard. Police confiscated the note, arrested Hilliard and Douglas (but not Genet), and the judge sentenced each to six months in jail—the maximum sentence for one count of criminal contempt of court. In the eyes of many potential supporters, the arrests and sentencing were further evidence that the government and legal system were targeting Panthers.[47]

The incident was a turning point for Panther support in New Haven, especially among Yale students. The Panthers had argued that police in Chicago and New Haven had targeted Seale because of his political views and influence. That Hilliard—the top Panther leader who was still free—was incarcerated so swiftly for a questionable infraction supported this argument. The next day, April 15, 1970, a group of four hundred Yale students passed two resolutions supporting the fourteen Black Panthers awaiting trial in New Haven. One resolution called for a three-day moratorium on classes. The other called for Yale to donate $500,000 to the Black Panther legal defense fund.[48]

Doug Miranda met with various Yale groups to build student support. At one meeting, he told Yale students, "You ought to get some guns, and go and get Chairman Bobby out of jail." After the meeting, a group of black Yale undergraduates confronted Miranda about his incendiary tactics. Miranda said he did not actually expect the Yalies to use violence, "But they ain't done shit yet except talk. We're trying to get a strike going here, man! Now you can't just tell them, 'Strike!' You've got to give them something more extreme, and then you let them fall back on a strike."[49]

The next day in Cambridge, Massachusetts, an offshoot of the Students for Democratic Society and Abbie Hoffman of the Chicago Seven organized a rally at Harvard University in support of the New Haven Panthers. About 3,000 people showed up, and Harvard locked the gates along the protestors' route, shutting them out of the campus. The crowd threw rocks and bricks through windows, lit trash fires, and fought with police. Police beat marchers—including female students from Radcliffe—with nightsticks; 214 people were hospitalized.[50]

The potential for violence in New Haven was much greater. On April 19, about fifteen hundred people crammed into Yale's Battell Chapel for a Panther teach-in. Doug Miranda called for a student strike: "Take your power and use it to save the institution. Take it away from people who are using it in a way it shouldn't be used. You can close down Yale and make Yale demand release. You have the power to prevent a bloodbath in New Haven. . . . There's no reason why the Panther and the Bulldog [Yale's mascot] can't get together! . . . That Panther and that Bulldog gonna move together!" Audience members jumped to their feet to deliver a standing ovation. Students rushed to join the preparations, and Miranda's imagery became a central organizing motif. Students printed graphic images of the panther and bulldog logos on T-shirts and pamphlets to aid in organizing the strike for May Day.[51]

The next day, the Yale College Student Senate, the school's formal student government, approved a resolution calling for a student strike and asking classmates to endorse it. The same day, the Chicago Seven held a press conference in New York in which the Reverend Ralph Abernathy, head of the Southern Christian Leadership Conference, was the featured speaker. He urged liberals and progressives to join the May 1 rally in New Haven to support Bobby Seale and the Black Panthers. Abernathy said that the "racist justice" that drove Martin Luther King Jr. to the streets in the South "is now driving us to the streets of the North—New York, New Haven, Chicago, signaling the beginning of the end of the Mitchell-Nixon-Agnew-Thurmond era." Denouncing the jailing of Hilliard and Douglas, he declared, "Southern-style justice has come to New Haven. . . . This is nothing more than legal lynching."[52]

Despite parallels to the recent Chicago trials, the Panthers understood that the political dynamics in New Haven were quite different. In Chicago, Seale had been tried on charges that were, on their face, absurd. He had not participated in organizing the Chicago mobilizations. He had been in Chicago for only a few hours, where he spoke once briefly, with little in his speech offering ammunition for his arrest. He had had almost no discernible role in instigating the rebellion outside the Democratic National Convention. The court's decision to deny him his right to defend himself rested on shaky legal ground. Seale's refusal to participate politely in a trial that appeared designed to railroad him had garnered broad political support. But New Haven was a different story. Alex Rackley had been brutally murdered. And while the Panthers argued that the FBI had gone to great lengths to frame Seale, murder was a serious matter. The allegations had to be addressed carefully. Open defiance of the court proceedings would be impolitic.

In a private meeting on April 21, the Panthers met with Judge Harold Mulvey. The Panthers wanted to establish a cordial relationship, and so did the judge. Public outcry about the jailing of Hilliard and Douglas bode poorly for the judge should the relationship with the Panthers become polarized. So he and the Panthers agreed that Seale would apologize publicly in exchange for Hilliard's and Douglas's release. That day, Seale said in court, "I respect your honor very much for allowing me to have a fair trial. . . . I understand that you are trying to see that we defendants have a fair trial. . . . We also understand the necessity for peaceful decorum in the courtroom." Hilliard and Douglas were released that day.[53]

That evening, about forty-five hundred people—mostly white Yale students—gathered at Yale's Ingalls Rink to decide whether to call a strike. Kenneth Mills, a black assistant professor at the university, told the crowd that the plight of Bobby Seale and the accused Black Panthers symbolized the plight of blacks generally in "Racist America," and he called for action: "In recognition of the critical emergency, in recognition of the reality of oppression, in recognition of exploitation," he said, it was time to "close down" the university. "This is the time to say 'classroom space is not where it's happening.' The struggle for justice is much more important." The audience shouted and cheered, pumping clenched fists and chanting, "Strike, Strike, Strike!" Students organized meetings in all of Yale's undergraduate colleges and some of the graduate schools to mobilize support for the strike.[54]

The following morning, April 22, 1970, Yale students went on strike for the first time in the university's history. They set up picket lines surrounding classroom buildings and carried signs reading, "Don't go to class" and "Skip classes, talk politics." They handed out leaflets saying, "All academic commitments must be suspended so that we all may devote our full time and attention to the situation, educate ourselves, and act accordingly." The university canceled all intercollegiate sports events for the week. Students in Yale's undergraduate colleges passed referenda supporting the strike, and the undergraduate residence halls also voted to provide food, shelter, and first aid to Panther supporters who rallied on May 1. A university spokesperson estimated that between 50 and 75 percent of students were participating in the strike.[55]

On April 23, about four hundred Yale faculty members and administrators held a closed meeting to discuss the strike. A group of black professors called for faculty to support the student strike. The faculty rejected a proposal to cancel all classes but voted overwhelmingly to grant all professors the option to suspend normal academic activities and devote their class periods to discussions of race and politics. Further, they instructed all faculty to "take a tolerant position in regard to assignments and papers handed in late and they should make as much time as possible available for the discussion of immediate and pressing issues." The faculty also endorsed a proposal by the Black Students Alliance to hold a national conference of black organizations at Yale, as well as a proposal to establish a commission on "Yale involvement with the black community."[56]

With the trial scheduled to take place in New Haven, the May 1 mobilization at Yale promised to be significantly larger than the one at Harvard a few weeks earlier. Thousands of Yale students were mobilizing for the rally, and tens of thousands of supporters, many from out of town, were expected to join them. Eager to avoid disaster, Kingman Brewster Jr., the well-respected president of Yale, secretly met with friends from Harvard to learn from their experience. He decided that to protect Yale and his career, he would embrace the right to dissent, distinguish himself from Nixon, and distance Yale from the prosecution of the Panthers.

At the April 23 faculty meeting, Brewster pronounced that he was "skeptical of the ability of black revolutionaries to achieve a fair trial anywhere in the United States." Later that week, U.S. vice president Spiro Agnew called for Brewster's ouster, accusing him of pandering to students on the "criminal left that belong not in a dormitory but in a penitentiary" and of subverting the American judicial process. Yale students rallied to Brewster's defense, with more than three thousand of them signing a petition supporting his statement.[57]

Seeing the government's prosecution of Seale as an act to silence political dissent, thousands of Yale students had joined the Panther cause. By making the university a target and disrupting academic activities at Yale, the Panthers forced the university to take a position on the trial in New Haven. Initially, the administration responded with systematic repression, expelling students who disrupted regular academic activities in support of the Panthers. But as support for the Panthers grew, the administration changed course. Most of the Yale faculty and the broader New Haven community did not endorse the Panthers' politics but were strongly liberal. Few supported Nixon's Law and Order politics, and many felt threatened by it, seeing the repression of the Panthers as part of an overarching pattern of strong-arm repression. In this context, the administration was wary of heavily repressing Panther supporters and becoming a target of broader ire. To avoid that fate, Brewster publicly questioned the legitimacy of the U.S. judicial system and allowed the disruption of normal academic activities.

While Brewster sought to de-escalate the conflict, Connecticut governor John Dempsey—beholden to a more conservative electorate—expressed "shock" at Brewster's position and readied for May Day by dispatching two thousand state troopers to New Haven. Further, at the request of Governor Dempsey, U.S. attorney general Mitchell sent two thousand army paratroopers and two thousand marines to the region to assist the National Guard if necessary. Yale spokesperson Sam Chauncey said he was "surprised" and "upset" at the decision to deploy federal troops.[58] White House emissaries, including Assistant

Attorney General William Ruckelshaus, traveled to New Haven to monitor the situation.[59]

Yale's chaplain offered a refuge for people who wanted to retreat should the May Day protests turn into violent clashes with police.[60] John Hersey, college master at Yale and executive of the Connecticut Bar Association, established a "defense trust" to raise funds for the Panthers' legal expenses in the New Haven trial.[61]

Before May Day even arrived, the Panthers had won Yale. With Yale now supporting their right to dissent and Yale's own president questioning the fairness of the American judiciary, the Party knew that violence by its supporters would work against the defendants in the New Haven trial. The Panthers called a press conference, and Assistant Minister of Defense "Big Man" Howard urged protestors to stay nonviolent.[62] On behalf of the Black Panther Defense Committee, Ann Froines held several meetings with the New Haven chief of police to work out logistics of crowd control for the upcoming street mobilizations. She explained to the *New York Times* that violent protests "would not serve the interests of the defendants."[63] Panther allies Ann Froines, John Froines, David Dellinger, and Tom Hayden met with Kingman Brewster to coordinate strategy in order to avoid violence.[64] Working with the Panther supporters to stem potential violence, Kingman Brewster announced that Yale would open its gates to May Day protestors.[65]

The governor and U.S. attorney general, however, prepared for war. Marines, U.S. Army troops, and Connecticut Guardsmen—armed with rifles and bayonets, armored personnel carriers, and tanks—surrounded downtown New Haven. Officers instructed soldiers, "You will not be successfully prosecuted if you shoot someone while performing a duty. . . . There is nothing to fear concerning your individual actions."[66]

The next morning, about fifteen thousand people filled the New Haven Green for the May Day protests. The event was mostly peaceful and included marching, chanting, music, and speeches throughout the downtown and Yale's campus.[67] After a tense long day of protest in the face of police and heavily armed troops, someone pretending to be a Black Panther, later accused of working for the FBI, grabbed the microphone and falsely claimed that police had arrested three black people for walking on the green after dark. Protestors charged out to confront the police. Doug Miranda took the microphone and encouraged the audience to stay calm, explaining that the report was false. About fifteen hundred people confronted the police, a few throwing rocks. But the Black Panthers used their sound truck to urge rock throwers to disperse until peace was restored.[68]

The *Chicago Daily Defender* ran an editorial, "Yale U. and the Panthers," saying that the relatively peaceful New Haven rallies were likely to inspire similar protests at other campuses:

> The demonstrations were staged as evidence of a lack of trust in the integrity of the American courts and their capacity to conduct a fair trial, especially in cases where the Black Panthers are involved. . . . Yale has now become the focus for justice for the Black Panthers. With the singular exception of a few isolated incidents, the New Haven institution is going peacefully and serenely about the business of transforming a sick society into a healthy consortium. Other universities are sure to follow this lead and graft the Black Panther movement into the body of their own pleading for social change. Though a new force in the political horizon, the Panthers may provide the dynamism for the reformation of American society.[69]

NATIONAL STUDENT STRIKE

On the eve of the May Day protest at Yale, Nixon announced the U.S. invasion of Cambodia. The action was wrenching for the nation. Nixon's claims that he would promote "Vietnamization" of the war effort and gradually roll back the military draft appeased many, and the antiwar movement had become increasingly moderate by mid-1970. The anti-imperialist activists who built the student antiwar movement were gradually marginalized. But the Cambodia invasion threw into doubt Nixon's claims of de-escalation, shattering the fragile faith of many that the government would end the war and the draft without a fight.

Then on May 1, as Yale students mobilized support for the Panthers, Nixon denounced student activists in his strongest language to date. On the morning of May 2, the *New York Times* published the president's comments in a front-page story alongside coverage of the Yale May Day mobilizations: "You see these bums, you know, blowing up the campuses. Listen, the boys that are on the college campuses today are the luckiest people in the world, going to the greatest universities in the world, and here they are burning books and storming around."[70] Where the Panthers and their allies had won cautious acceptance from Yale, Nixon, in his pursuit of Law and Order politics, sought to strengthen his support by attacking the activists.

Later that day, about two thousand Panther supporters met in Yale's

Dwight Hall to build upon the successful New Haven mobilizations and respond to the invasion of Cambodia. They formed the National Student Strike Committee and drew up a plan for further national action. At an afternoon press conference on the New Haven Green, Tom Hayden announced the call for the nationwide strike. He said students across the country should boycott classes until three demands were met. The following day, the *New York Times* summarized the three demands in a front-page story about the Yale mobilizations:

- The United States must end its "systematic oppression" of all political dissidents, such as Bobby Seale, and all other Black Panthers.
- The United States must cease "aggression" in Vietnam, Laos and Cambodia, and unilaterally and immediately withdraw its force.
- Universities must end their "complicity" in war by ending war-related research and eliminating Reserve Officer Training Corps activities.[71]

In a survey of U.S. college students for the John D. Rockefeller Foundation at the time, 79 percent of respondents strongly or partially agreed that "the war in Vietnam is pure imperialism," and a full 71 percent of college students surveyed said they "Definitively believe" that Black Panthers "cannot be assured a fair trial."[72] With students across the country feeling betrayed and angered by Nixon's invasion of Cambodia and by his insults, and excited by the successful mobilizations at Yale, the call for a national student strike quickly spread. The Yale students, by targeting their own liberal university and making it take sides on the Panthers, had influenced national political debate. Others students sought to emulate their model. On May 3, editors from the student newspapers at eleven major eastern colleges—including six of the eight Ivy League universities—adopted the demands of the Panther allies in New Haven. Meeting at Columbia University in New York, the editors agreed to run a common editorial the following day calling for "the entire academic community of this country to engage in a nationwide university strike."[73]

Columbia University administrators attempted to undercut student support for the national strike by declaring a one-day moratorium on classes for Monday, May 4, and by holding a convocation to discuss possible responses to the invasion of Cambodia. At the convocation, Rich Reed, a black leader of the campus's Third World Coalition, accompanied by a Black Panther member, seized the microphone and declared that talk of peace in Vietnam would be meaningless unless people moved "to build a mass movement against the source of imperialism and racism which is closest to us—Columbia University."[74] Reed criticized the School of International Affairs for assisting in the development of oppressive foreign policy strategies and denounced the consignment of black and Latino workers to the lowest-paying and dirtiest jobs on campus. That afternoon, about three thousand students gathered in Wollman Auditorium and voted overwhelmingly to strike, taking up the three demands issued in New Haven. The following day, thirty-five hundred students and campus workers rallied. Featured speaker William Kunstler—a high-profile lawyer for the Panthers and the Chicago Seven—called for all charges against the New York Panther 21 to be dropped. Protestors marched from Columbia to the City College of New York behind a banner declaring, "No more racist attacks on third world people. US out of Southeast Asia; Free all political prisoners now." As the group marched through Harlem, members of the crowd chanted the Black Panther slogan, "Power to the people! Off the pig!"[75]

The call for a national student strike quickly gained steam, and by May 4, student activists had gone on strike at schools across the country, including Brandeis, the City University of New York, New York University, Notre Dame, Ohio State, Princeton, Rutgers, Sarah Lawrence, Stanford, the University of California at Berkeley, the University of Pennsylvania, and the University of Virginia.[76]

One of the most heated protests took place at Kent State University in Ohio, a campus with a history of SDS activism against the war in Vietnam and in solidarity with the Panthers.[77] On May 2, after the mayor of the city of Kent called in the Ohio National Guard, someone set fire to the ROTC (Reserve Officers' Training Corps) building there. The following afternoon, the conflict escalated. Students sat in at a downtown intersection, and the National Guard charged them, stabbing several with bayonets and arresting many others. Students pelted the guardsmen with stones. And then on May 4, guardsmen opened fire on the students, shooting thirteen students in a hail of bullets and killing four.[78]

The killing of the four student protesters fanned the flames of anti-imperialist fervor. On top of Nixon's Law and Order rule, the Cambodia invasion, the continued Vietnam War and draft, and the heavy repression of the Black Panthers, the killings undermined many people's faith in American democracy. The actions at Kent State showed that if students challenged the interests of those in power, they—like the Vietnamese and the Black Panthers—could be killed.

Inflamed by Nixon's invasion of Cambodia and the killings at Kent State, and bolstered by widespread outrage, students across the country took up the call of the anti-imperialist Panther supporters at Yale and went on strike. More than four million students at 1,300 colleges participated in campus protests that month. One and a half million went on strike, shutting down at least 536 college campuses—many for the remainder of the academic year. According to a survey of college presidents by the Carnegie Commission on Higher Education, 57 percent of the nation's colleges experienced a "significant impact" as a result of student protests in May 1970. More than 100 colleges reported that armed officers from outside the university, including city or state police, the National Guard, army troops or marines, came onto campus to quell student protests that month. At Mississippi's Jackson State College, a historically black institution, police shot eleven students on May 14, killing two of them, further fueling anti-imperialist rage.[79]

The political dynamics across three U.S. cities highlight the attraction of different constituencies to the Panthers' politics through 1969 and much of 1970. In Chicago, assassination of the charismatic Fred Hampton led to broad intervention by moderate blacks. In New Haven, repression catalyzed extensive mobilization by students and antiwar progressive allies. And in the Black Power ferment of Los Angeles, state repression of the Panthers made the Party stand out from the alternatives—militarizing activists, drawing financial support from affluent allies, and ultimately encouraging increased membership. The more the state took repressive action against the Black Panthers, the more the Party's membership, allied support, and political influence grew. Where would the cycle of insurgency lead?

PART FOUR

Revolution Has Come!

The sharpest struggles in the world today are those of the oppressed nations against imperialism and for national liberation. Within this country the sharpest struggle is that of the black colony for its liberation; it is a struggle which by its very nature is anti-imperialist and increasingly anti-capitalist. . . . Within the black liberation movement the vanguard force is the Black Panther Party. . . . We must keep in mind that the Black Panther Party is not fighting black people's struggles only but is in fact the vanguard in our common struggles against capitalism and imperialism.

—Students for a Democratic Society, National Council Resolution, April 4 1969

You are Black Panthers, We are Yellow Panthers!

—M. Hoang Minh Giam, North Vietnamese Minister of Culture, Hemispheric Conference to End the War in Vietnam, November 19, 1968

12

Black Studies and
Third World Liberation

In August 1968, George Mason Murray, the Black Panther minister of education, traveled to Cuba to represent the Black Panthers at a conference sponsored by the Organization of Solidarity with the People of Asia, Africa and Latin America (OSPAAAL). The oldest son of a Presbyterian minister, Murray had grown up poor, one of thirteen children in a religious family in rural Mississippi. He became a civil rights activist and left Mississippi. In 1963, he arrived in San Francisco and enrolled in San Francisco State College. Murray was a serious student who sported short-cropped hair and a tie. He soon gained admission to graduate school in English at SF State and became the first black director of the undergraduate tutorial program there, enthusiastically recruiting young blacks from San Francisco to take advantage of the university's educational resources. The program reached its peak enrollment under his direction. At SF State, the powerful tide of Black Power began to pull on Murray. He grew out his hair and began to wear a black leather jacket. He renounced Christianity and joined the Nation of Islam for a short period. He became active in the university's Black Student Union (BSU). Soon he joined the Black Panther Party.

Murray threw himself wholeheartedly into the Black Panthers. His fiery eloquence made him an important Party spokesman, and he was quickly promoted, joining the Central Committee as minister of education by April 1968.[1] He believed black liberation required a global revolution against imperialism, which in turn required a cultural revolution, new ways of being black. There was widespread debate within the Black Liberation Struggle at the time about the relative importance of black culture and black politics. Murray became an important voice in this debate, articulating a Black Panther position that black culture would have to be revolutionary if it was to liberate black people:

> The only culture worth keeping is the revolutionary culture. . . . Our culture must not be something that the enemy enjoys, appreciates, or says is attractive, it must be repelling to the slave master. It must smash, shatter and crack his skull, crack his eyeballs open and make water and gold dust run out. . . . We are changing, we are deciding that freedom means change, changing from the slaves, the cowards, the boys, the toms, the clowns, coons, spooks of the 50's, 40's, 30's, into the wild, courageous, freedom fighting, revolutionary black nationalists.[2]

When Murray traveled to Cuba in August 1968 to promote the "Free Huey!" campaign, leaders of anticolonial and revolutionary movements around the globe embraced the Panthers. "The genuine freedom of Huey Newton," declared the Executive Secretariat of OSPAAAL, "will be brought about as the result of the revolutionary action of the Afro-Americans and of the white people who are willing to run the same risks; as the result of new Watts, Newarks, Detroits and Clevelands. In this endeavor they will have the backing and the solidarity of the peoples and the revolutionary combatants of Africa, Asia and Latin America."[3] When Murray's turn came to speak at the OPAAAL conference, he affirmed the necessity of a global revolution against imperialism and the Black Panther Party's commitment to solidarity with revolutionary struggles throughout the Third World:

> We have vowed not to put down our guns or stop making Molotov cocktails until colonized Africans, Asians and Latin Americans in the United States and throughout the world have become free. . . . We want to tell the people who are struggling throughout the world that our collective struggle can only be victorious, and the defeat of the murderers of mankind will come as soon as we create a few more Vietnams, Cubas and Detroits. . . . The Black Panther Party recognizes the critical position of black people in the United States. We recognize that we are a colony within the imperialist domains of North America and that it is the historic duty of black people in the United States to bring about the complete, absolute and unconditional end of racism and neocolonialism by smashing, shattering and destroying the imperialist domains of North America. In order to bring humanity to a higher level, we will follow the example of Che Guevara, the Cuban people, the Vietnamese people and our leader and Minister of Defense, Huey P. Newton. If it means our lives, that is but a small price to pay for the freedom of humanity.

Illustrating his point, he argued that, "every time a Vietnamese guerilla knocks out a U.S. soldier, that means one less aggressor against those who fight for freedom in the U.S."[4]

Murray's speech in Cuba achieved his goal of being "repelling to the slave master." When he returned to SF State, he found himself at the center of a controversy. On September 26, perhaps emboldened by the national political climate in the buildup to the 1968 presidential election, the conservative Board of Trustees of the California State Colleges voted eight to five to ask President Smith of SF State to cancel Murray's teaching appointment and assign him to a nonteaching position. President Smith knew he would face strong protest from faculty and students if he canceled Murray's teaching appointment. Hoping to avoid this response, he denied the trustees' request that Murray be reassigned, arguing that as an instructor, Murray had a right to intellectual freedom.[5]

In 1968, more than half of San Francisco's youth were black, Latino, Asian American, or Native American, but SF State's student body was more than three-quarters white.[6] By the fall of 1968, black student activists at the university had developed a strong anti-imperialist perspective. As early as 1966, Black Student Union president James Garrett had said that the black student struggle was "no different from that of the Vietnamese. . . . We are struggling for self-determination . . . for our black communities; and self-determination for a black education."[7] A popular Black Student Union poster featured an Associated Press photo of an American soldier grabbing a Vietnamese woman by the hair and pressing his gun so hard against her temple that ridges of skin had formed around the muzzle. The caption read, "Today the Vietnamese, tomorrow the blacks."[8]

Earlier in 1968, despite opposition from the administration, the Black Student Union had obtained support from the Faculty Senate to create a black studies program, and it had hired Nathan Hare, a radical sociologist, to establish the program. In April 1968, Hare submitted "A Conceptual Proposal for Black Studies," in which he outlined an anti-imperialist framework and argued for more than a "mere blackening of white courses." He noted that successful development of a black studies curriculum required not only a substantive shift but also a significant increase in black student enrollment, methodological innovation, and community involvement. He took an activist approach that sought to position black studies as part of a transformation of the black condition rather than its perpetuation. "Black studies will be revolutionary or it will be useless if not detrimental," Hare wrote. As the black studies proposal gained steam in the spring of 1968, students formed the Third World Liberation Front (TWLF), which united the BSU with Latino and Asian American organizations. The TWLF called for "educational self-determination" and developed a proposal for an ethnic studies program that would include black, Latino and Asian American curricula to be developed along similar anti-imperialist lines. The TWLF and the predominantly white Students for a Democratic Society forged a strategic alliance to demand special admission of four hundred freshmen of color, the creation of nine minority faculty positions, and the elimination of ROTC (the Reserve Officers' Training Corps) training on campus. That spring brought sit-ins, confrontations with police, and some minor victories, including the firing of the college president, Smith's predecessor.[9]

The student movement at SF State looked to the Black Panther Party for leadership. The BSU office featured the "Free Huey!" poster and framed pictures of Kathleen Cleaver and Stokely Carmichael.[10] By the time George Murray returned from Cuba, the Black Panther Party was helping organize black student unions throughout the state and nationally to advance black university admissions and curricula. With the help of Virtual Murrell, who had worked with Bobby Seale and Huey Newton in their days at the Soul Students Advisory Committee at Merritt College, the Black Panther Party organized a Black Student Union Statewide Convention for October 26, 1968, to discuss the national organization of black students. The promotional materials for the conference emphasized point 5 of the Black Panther Party program: "We want education for our people that exposes the true nature of this decadent American society. We want education that teaches us our true history and our role in the present day society." The keynote speakers were Bobby Seale, Eldridge Cleaver, David Hilliard, and George Murray.[11] Out of the convention, the black student unions formed a statewide union and began to organize on the national level. They also adopted a ten-point program and platform that imitated the Ten Point Program and Platform of the Black Panther Party.[12]

Two days before the statewide convention, Murray spoke to an audience of two thousand at Fresno State College to promote anti-imperialist black student unions. He argued that black students' struggle was part of the global struggle against imperialism and compared it to the American Revolution. Murray blasted the trustees for trying to have him fired because of some so-called anti-American remarks that I was supposed to have made in Cuba, remarks like this: Every time an American mercenary is shot, that's one less cat that's going to be killing us in the United States. That's the truth. That's a fact. Dig this: in Detroit and in Newark (we can not deny it) the 101st airborne division and the 82nd airborne division of the infantry, soldiers from Viet Nam, were sent into the black community. Their ranks had been partially depleted by the victorious fighters of the National Liberation Front. So that when they came into the black community (it's sad to say because a lot of those soldiers were brothers) their ranks had been depleted because they were criminals fighting against another people of color.[13]

On October 28, 1968, the one-year anniversary of Huey Newton's incarceration, Donald Cox, field marshal of the Black Panther Party, and a contingent of five other Panthers visited San Francisco State. Murray called a BSU rally. Making circular motions in the air with his finger, he said, "I think we should have a demonstration for Huey today. He'd lay down his life for the people, and we should honor him."[14] As word spread, more than one hundred black students gathered on campus outside the BSU office. The crowd joined a call and response in support of Huey: "Black Is Beautiful!" "Free Huey!" "Set our warrior free!" "Free Huey!" The black students marched around campus. By the time they arrived at the cafeteria, the group was two hundred strong. Ben Stewart, chair of the Black Student Union, directed as BSU members cleared off four tables and pulled them together to create a platform for speakers.

Next George Murray called a student strike for November 6. He also spoke to the students about the need for black studies in revolutionary terms:

> Whether you Negroes recognize it or not, there is a revolution going on. There are people using guns to defend their communities. Your lunches are not only going to be disrupted, your whole lives are going to be disrupted, from today on. . . . Listen, you Motherfucker Smith [president of the university], we know you're lying. . . . The Black Studies Department is no department at all. There are four and one-half million black and brown people in California and they all pay taxes to pay for the racist departments here, but none of their taxes go to black and brown people. There are no full-time jobs for the brothers and sisters on the faculty here. The crackers still say they have the right to say how many black and brown people will come into this school and how many will not. There are four and one-half million black and brown people in California, so there should be five thousand black and brown people at this school.[15]

On the heels of the conflicts in Chicago, with the November elections right around the corner, Murray's anti-imperialist activities became the target of establishment politicians. Apparently attempting to outdo the right, San Francisco's Mayor Joseph Alioto, a Democrat, launched an investigation to see if criminal charges could be filed against Murray for encouraging students to bring guns to San Francisco State. On October 31, Chancellor Glenn Dumke, head of the Board of Trustees of the California State Colleges, ordered President Smith to suspend Murray, which he did that weekend.

Murray's dismissal added fuel to the fire. Uniting behind the revolutionary anti-imperialist perspective championed by the Black Panther Party, Murray attracted and consolidated support not only from radical black students but also from radical Latino, Asian American, and white students. Because of the political establishment's failure to address the draft, the war, and persistent racial inequality, the Panthers also received extensive support from faculty members, less radical students, antiwar liberals, and critically, moderate black leaders seeking expanded black educational access and curricula that encompassed black experiences and perspectives.

Building upon earlier demands for black and ethnic studies, the Third World Liberation Front issued a set of demands in the name of educational self-determination for Third World people. The list included not only the retention of George Murray and a full professorship for Dr. Hare, but creation of a full-fledged black studies department and school of ethnic studies with fifty faculty positions; control over the hiring, retention, and curricula for the departments; power to determine the administration of financial aid; and increased enrollment of students of color. Seeing racial oppression as an issue of internal colonialism distinct from the class exploitation experienced by poor whites, the TWLF also set up guidelines for white students' participation, casting them in a supportive rather than leadership role and creating a communications committee to coordinate white strike support.[16]

On Election Day, November 5, 1968, the night before the strike was set to begin, Stokely Carmichael, prime minister of the Black Panther Party, addressed more than seven hundred students and community members at a meeting called exclusively for nonwhites: "We must go now for the real control. . . . We want the right to hire and to fire teachers. We want the right to control . . . courses at San Francisco State, and once we get that then George Murray becomes irrelevant. Because George Murray is under our control, and Mayor Alioto has nothing to say about it. But if we fight over George Murray, even if we win next week, then they'll pick somebody else."[17]

The student strike at SF State and most of the critical campus rebellions that followed linked Black Power with a cross-race anti-imperialist perspective, often explicitly linking the fight for Black Power on campus to the Vietnam War and global anti-imperialism. Losing faith in the ability or commitment of the Democratic Party and the American system to address their needs, many young Americans of every race and class turned to the revolutionary anti-imperialist politics championed by the Black Panther Party. Student activists increasingly saw their struggle as larger than a fight about student enrollment or curricula. They defined the issue as one of global revolution against empire.

Barbara Williams, a black student at SF State, wrote about this idea of a shared Third World commitment to self-determination: "We are conscious of our blackness, brownness, redness, yellowness and are moving with that knowledge back into our communities. We intend to reveal to the world our own place in this world's history and to mark our place in space and time. For us, it is no 'privilege' to be a product of your racist universities and colleges from which emerge black men with white minds. We don't intend to reflect your destructive apathy and noninvolvement and inhumanity."[18]

George Murray further articulated this idea in an opinion piece he wrote for *Rolling Stone* magazine, where he talked about the struggle at San Francisco State in revolutionary anti-imperialist and Third World terms:

> To say you're Black and you're proud, and still go to Vietnam to fight our Vietnamese brothers or to go and entertain soldiers who are exterminating the Vietnamese people is a crime against all of us descendants of slaves in the U.S. It is reactionary and insane, and counter-revolutionary. . . . When we talk about becoming free, we have to talk about power, getting all the goods, services, and land, and returning them equally to the oppressed and enslaved Mexicans, Blacks, Indians, Puerto Ricans, and poor whites in the U.S. and to the rest of the oppressed and hungry people in the world. . . . A revolution will smash, shatter and destroy the oppressor and his oppressive system, return all the power, the milk, eggs, butter, and the guns to the people. . . . Listen to this: freedom is a state not limited to a particular culture, race or people, and therefore, the principles upon which a struggle for human rights is based must be all inclusive, must apply equally for all people. Freedom, equality is not relative. For example, the struggle at San Francisco State is based upon three principles: 1) a fight to the death against racism; 2) the right of all people to determine their economic, politi-

cal, social and educational destines; and 3) the right for the people to seize power, to carry out all their goals, and to answer all their needs. In short— *All Power to the People*. These are principles that all human beings can fight for, and the fight is being waged by Black, Brown, Red, and Yellow students, and workers, as well as progressive whites.[19]

Seeing themselves as engaged in a revolutionary war, the students increasingly turned to radically disruptive tactics. In the rally the night before the student strike, Benny Stewart, chairman of the BSU, told the audience that individual actions, seemingly small, would have great impact if applied persistently:

> From our analysis . . . we think we have developed a technique . . . for a prolonged struggle. We call it the war of the flea. What does the flea do? He bites, he slowly sucks blood from the dog. What happens when there are enough fleas on a dog? What will he do? He moves. He moves away. He moves on. . . . That's the philosophy we've got to get into. We've got to wear them down. . . . We are the majority and the pigs cannot be everywhere, everyplace all the time. And where they are not, we are. . . . Toilets are stopped up. Pipes are out. Water in the bathroom is just runnin' all over the place. Smoke is coming out of the bathroom. Trash cans are on fire. People are running in and out of the classrooms, letting the students know that school is out for the day. "I don't know nothin' about it. I'm on my way to take an exam. Don't look at me. . . ." When the pigs come runnin' on the campus, ain't nothin' happening. Everyone has split, so the pig don't have no heads to bust. When they split, it goes on and on and on. . . . We should fight the racist administration on our own grounds, you see; not theirs.[20]

THE WAR OF THE FLEA

While few students participated directly in the "war of the flea," those who did were highly disruptive and hard to repress because they enjoyed wide support for their demands among students, faculty, and important segments of the broader community, especially the black community and those disheartened by Nixon's election as president. Beginning the day after the election and continuing for five months, the San Francisco State strike made the college ungovernable.

During the first week of the strike, small groups of Latino, Asian American, and White students picketed on campus while members of the Black Student Union engaged in more disruptive tactics. BSU activists interrupted classes and asked teachers why they were not honoring the strike. They repeatedly stopped up campus toilets and left water running in bathroom sinks so that it overflowed into hallways.

A group of students targeted various administrative offices by cutting typewriter cords. The protestors set small fires in trashcans throughout campus. As excitement about the strike mounted, it became impossible for the college to conduct regular classes or activities, and by the end of the week, class attendance was down 50 percent.[21]

Students returned to school from a long weekend on November 12 to find the campus occupied by hundreds of San Francisco police officers in full riot gear, including a paramilitary tactical (tac) squad, while a police helicopter circled overhead. Subject to such close police scrutiny, the strikers transitioned away from destructive tactics and focused on strengthening the picket line. Roving groups of student activists became "educational teams," which calmly visited classes and conducted teach-ins, appealing to others to join them. Affronted first by the firing of George Murray and now the heavy police presence on campus, the faculty called an emergency meeting, and by the end of the day it had passed a motion calling for Chancellor Dumke's resignation.

The next day, many faculty members joined the picket line. George Murray told the press that the strike represented a historic moment, marking "the first time in the country that barriers have been dissolved between black, brown, yellow, and red people." Without warning, the paramilitary tac squad formed two columns and pushed into the picket line, beating and arresting several targeted members of the Black Student Union and the Third World Liberation Front. News spread across campus, and soon the student picket line grew from two hundred to about two thousand people. Tension escalated between the students and the tac squad, with students chanting "Pigs Off Campus!" and throwing rocks and bottles. The tac squad responded by repeatedly charging the crowd and indiscriminately beating students. As one officer pulled out his gun and began threatening to shoot students, faculty members intervened, stepping between the students and police. Eventually, the police left campus and President Smith, noting that the police presence "has moved us along farther and farther toward physical confrontation and injury," closed the campus, indicating that he would not reopen it until "reasonable stability" could be achieved.

While the liberal faculty largely supported President Smith's decision, conservative state politicians wanted to impose "Law and Order." Governor Ronald Reagan declared, "For a school administration to deliberately abandon the leadership invested in it by the people of this State . . . is an unprecedented act of irresponsibility. It is clear that the administration, in its obvious quest for what was considered an easy way out, ignored other options which were available to assure the orderly continuation of the educational process." A reporter asked what options were available, and Reagan responded, "If it's necessary we'll call out the National Guard, and if that's not sufficient, call in the federal troops."[22]

When Smith refused to immediately reopen the campus, the board of trustees held an emergency meeting Monday November 18 and voted to give Smith until that Wednesday to reopen the campus. The faculty voted to hold a three-day convocation where students and faculty could talk rationally about the issues and asked Smith to cancel classes. Smith attempted to compromise by opening classes but allowing those who wanted to attend the convocation to do that instead. For three days, almost no classes took place, and the auditorium where the convocation was held filled to overcapacity. Several members of the Black Student Union spoke about their objectives. Leroy Goodwin said that the struggle was an all-or-nothing battle. "The issues are not complex. The objective is seizure of power. Until we seize power, not visible power where a black man looks like he's running things—but real, actual power; everything else is bullshit. . . . Peace and order are bullshit; they are meaningless without justice." Nesbit Crutchfield said, "It is very important to realize that we are involved in a revolution. The revolution is the attempt of black people and Third World people to reject the old reality of going to an educational institution which denies them their own humanity as people."[23]

The students realized that Smith did not have the power to grant their demands for the creation of black and ethnic studies departments. The next morning, Crutchfield demanded an answer: "All I want to ask . . . is will classes be closed—yes or no?" When Smith refused to cancel classes, the students marched out of the convocation chanting "On Strike! Shut it down!" re-igniting the disruptive student strike. Police resumed their confrontations, beating and arresting students. One officer pulled a gun on protesting students and fired two shots over their heads. Smith canceled classes for the following day, Friday November 22, but confrontations between students and police continued. The following Monday, Governor Reagan held a press conference condemning Smith, and State Superintendent Max Rafferty declared, "If I were President of San Francisco State, there would be a lot less students, a lot less faculty, and a lot more Law and Order!" By noon Tuesday, under pressure from the Trustees, Smith had resigned.[24]

COMMUNITY SUPPORT AND THE LIMITS OF DIRECT REPRESSION

Emboldened by Nixon's victory, conservative California politicians called for "Law and Order" and forceful repression of dissent at San Francisco State. They found their ideal administrator in S. I. Hayakawa, a linguist and English professor of Japanese descent. Hayakawa was good at framing the issues and was eager to use any authoritarian measures at his disposal to subdue dissent.

Appointed interim president of San Francisco State on November 26, Hayakawa declared a state of emergency and said he would immediately suspend any faculty member who did not conduct class and any student who disrupted campus operations. He portrayed himself as the champion of racial equality while discrediting the students who had made racial equality an issue on campus, and he argued that most students did not support the strike. He distributed blue armbands to the "silent majority" and launched a campaign calling for "Racial Equality, Social Justice, Non-Violence, and the Resumption of Education." When the Third World Liberation Front continued to picket, Hayakawa promptly suspended student leaders and sent police to break up the picket lines.

Moderate black leaders were upset by this response. They supported the students' demands for increased minority enrollment, the development of black history curricula, and the creation of a black studies department. In September, black assemblyman Willie Brown had told the college administration, "If the black students on this campus are asking for something, they [s]hould get it. Period! Because our society is blowing up because black people have not gotten anything. And to sit here and go through these ponderous procedures really begs the question and asks for a confrontation."[25]

As repression of the students increased, black community leaders joined the student strike. On December 3, later called "Bloody Tuesday," the TWLF called a rally, assembling twenty-five hundred students and faculty and community members. Among the speakers expressing support for student demands were Dr. Carleton Goodlett, editor of the *Sun Reporter,* a black San Francisco newspaper; Willie Brown; Berkeley City Council member Ron Dellums; the Reverend Cecil Williams; and Hannibal Williams of the Western Addition Community organization. As the crowd marched toward the administration building, the paramilitary tac squad, armed with special four-foot-long clubs, surrounded the protestors and began beating them: community members, faculty, photographers, medics, campus staff, as well as students. The students fought back for an hour. By the end of the episode, countless protestors had injuries, and the police had arrested thirty-two people.

Hayakawa's repressive tactics backfired and galvanized black community support. The following morning, Hayakawa met with a group of more than two hundred black community leaders at the office of the *Sun Reporter* and tried to win their support; he failed in his appeal. Dr. Goodlett said the community would not allow black students to be isolated. Hayakawa retorted, "Those who call themselves representatives of the black community are in my opinion adding to the problem with their presence on the campus. If black leaders come on tomorrow and cause trouble they will be treated like anyone else who causes trouble."[26]

That afternoon, with widespread black support, more than six thousand people assembled to support the student demands. The National Association for the Advancement of Colored People, the Congress of Racial Equality, the black press, and several churches joined the Black Panther Party in supporting the student strike. They also adopted elements of the Panthers' rhetoric. Dr. Goodlett said that, if necessary, they would take up guns in self-defense to "protect our young people from the violence of the police." The students also received support from the San Francisco Central Labor Council.[27]

Hayakawa remained undeterred. He positioned police on rooftops to monitor every action on campus, and a police helicopter circled overhead. He addressed the picketers through the public address system: "Attention everybody! This is an order to disperse. . . . There are no innocent bystanders. . . . If you are found on campus in the next few minutes you can no longer be considered an innocent bystander."[28] The protestors dispersed but promised to return.

On December 5, the conflict escalated again, with police officers drawing their guns on students and community members as the picketers entered the administration building. In an effort to diffuse the situation, Dr. Goodlett surrendered outside, allowing himself to be arrested. After several dozen arrests and numerous injuries, the conflict subsided. Again on December 6, more than four thousand strike supporters assembled. Because of widespread support for the student demands, direct repression was clearly failing to subdue dissent. Hayakawa changed his approach and offered the black students concessions to many of their demands, but he refused to address any of the demands of the other, nonblack Third World students. Thus, in the name of Third World solidarity, the BSU rejected Hayakawa's offer outright. "He's offering us tidbits. He's trying to divide us," Nesbit Crutchfield said.[29]

Support for the student strike continued to grow. The American Federation of Teachers Local 1352, which represented SF State faculty, mobilized support for the TWLF. The newly formed Officers for Justice, a caucus of black San Francisco policemen, also came out in favor of the students, speaking publicly at TWLF rallies and endorsing the student demands.

Momentum built for a massive show of solidarity on December 16, which students dubbed Third World Community Day, expecting busloads of support from Latino, Filipino, Chinese, Japanese, and Native American as well as black residents of San Francisco. December 16 was also the strike deadline for Local 1352. To thwart such a gathering, Hayakawa closed campus early for the holidays.

On January 5, 1969, Governor Reagan told reporters that San Francisco State would reopen the following day and would remain open "at the point of a bayonet if necessary."[30] Hayakawa banned all public assembly and banned "all unauthorized persons" from entering campus. Faculty members in Local 1352 voted to hold a simultaneous strike of their own to put forth their contractual demands, and they received support from members of several unions, including the Painters Union; the International Longshore and Warehouse Union; the American Federation of State, County and Municipal Employees; the Social Workers Union, the Teamsters; and other American Federation of Teachers locals throughout the Bay Area.

When campus reopened on January 6, more than three thousand people joined a massive picket line that surrounded the campus. Fewer than one in five classes were held. Reagan and Hayakawa denounced the protestors and obtained an injunction against the American Federation of Teachers to prohibit picketing. But the faculty defied the injunction, and the statewide California Federation of Teachers declared that all California State College campuses would be shut down if even one striking faculty member was punished. With labor solidarity, the strike became comprehensive, as Teamsters refused to make deliveries to campus and custodial workers refused to pick up trash. The Third World Liberation Front even signed a mutual-aid pact with striking oil refinery workers in nearby Richmond and Martinez. The students continued to use occasional disruptive tactics such as "book-ins" at the library, during which a group of students would check out as many books as they could, then return them all, backing up the system and shutting down library circulation. But the combined student-faculty picket with broad support from both the black community and organized labor was extremely effective at shutting down campus, so the TWLF mostly supported the picketing at the perimeter of the university.

The standoff lasted for several weeks, with largely peaceful pickets effectively closing the campus. Then, on January 23, the TWLF called a massive on-campus rally, the first since early December. More than 1,000 students, faculty, and community members participated. The police responded with military precision. As the protestors chanted "All Power to the People!" the police drove a wedge through the crowd, splitting it in two; they surrounded one large group and proceeded to arrest every person in it, one by one. In all, 435 people were arrested, the largest mass arrest to date in San Francisco's history. The administration canceled final exams (which had been scheduled for later that month) and offered students a credit/no credit option for the fall semester.

THE END OF THE SAN FRANCISCO STATE STRIKE

Unable to end the strike through mass repression, Hayakawa turned to a more sophisticated approach that combined targeted repression with concessions designed to undermine the broad public support. He established a disciplinary panel to suspend and expel students involved in Third World Liberation Front activities and appointed his faculty allies to run it. Knowing that most of the TWLF students had to work on campus to fund their studies, he banned students who had been arrested from working on campus. He shut down the Equal Opportunity Program that facilitated such work-study arrangements for all students of color. He also shut down the student newspaper, the *Daily Gater,* and *Open Process,* another student publication that had supported the strike. He seized $400,000 in student funds controlled by the student government, which was friendly to the strike.[31]

Hayakawa and his allies spared no expense in making life difficult for the dissenting students. Conservative state assemblyman Donald Mulford held a special meeting with superior court judges to inform them that if they were lenient with student demonstrators, they would face "heavily financed opposition" when they ran for reelection. Instead of holding joint trials for arrested students as is customary in cases of civil disobedience, in the "S.F. State Trials," each student was tried individually leading to more than nine hundred civil jury cases. The trials lasted nearly a year, backlogging the entire civil court system. This approach cost the government a lot of money, but it also made it very difficult for the activists to mount effective defenses, tying up the movement's resources and serving as a significant deterrent to further action.

Prominent and effective student leaders were targeted for the heaviest repression. No one knows exactly what happened to George Murray in jail. But as TWLF leader Roger Alvarado reflected, "Once they got him in jail, I'm sure they really put the screw to him . . . I mean cause what was happening with the Panther Party at that time. . . . They were just out and out getting murdered." [32] As part of Murray's sentence, he was ordered to resign from the Black Panther Party and to refrain from ever appearing or enrolling in an educational institution again without explicit permission from the court. With his mother, wife, and newborn child with him in court, Murray agreed, and he dropped completely out of politics.

As more targeted repression of student leaders began to take its toll, Hayakawa offered concessions to the American Federation of Teachers, such as a reduced class load, and threatened to fire any faculty members who failed to return to work. By March 5, the American Federation of Teachers strike was over, and faculty members were back in their classrooms teaching.

On March 20, Hayakawa announced plans to establish the School of Ethnic Studies, which would contain a Department of Black Studies, a Department of Asian American Studies, and a Department of La Raza Studies. He also committed to taking measures to significantly increase minority student enrollment. Though Hayakawa's offer did not meet the protestors' demands for student participation in the hiring and firing of new faculty for the School of Ethnic Studies faculty or in setting the school's curricula, and it did not provide redress of Hayakawa's repression of George Murray and firing of Nathan Hare, the TWLF agreed, and the San Francisco State strike was over.

PROLIFERATION

As the San Francisco State strike developed, the student struggle spread across California and the country. "The spin-off from San Francisco State," predicted Ron Dellums, the black city council member from Berkeley, "will have implications for high schools, junior colleges, junior high schools, elementary schools as well as other colleges throughout the state and outside the state."[33] And he was right. From the example set at San Francisco State, black students and their allies learned that they could advance their demands for increased enrollment, ethnic studies curricula, and educational "self-determination" by forming broad anti-imperialist alliances and disrupting university functions.[34] They could expect harsh repression but also the widespread support necessary to endure it.

In early January 1969, SF State's Black Student Union and Third World Liberation Front convened a weeklong meeting attended by student representatives from more than thirty California colleges and high schools. They called this January 6–13 meeting a "National Week of Solidarity," during which they prepared a statement appealing for national action that read in part,

> The Third World Liberation Front and the Black Student Union demands stress our human rights to self-determination according to the needs of our community and not the military-industrial complex that controls the education of this nation. No longer must we or you put up with the psychological genocide that is called education. We must stop them from making us into "sophisticated slaves" with highly developed skills. We must attack from all levels those institutions and persons that have kept us fighting with each other and forgetting the real enemy. We must come back to our "grass roots" understanding that we are all brothers and sisters and extensions of our communities. We realize that the racist power structure has united to crush the strike at San Francisco State hoping to make it an exemplary defeat for Third World people as it has sought to repel the tide of Vietnamese self-determination. AN ATTACK ON ONE CAMPUS IS AN ATTACK AGAINST ALL CAMPUSES![35]

As the conflict at San Francisco State grew and word spread, students at other schools launched their own struggles. Black students at Balboa High School and Polytechnic High School in San Francisco organized a walkout, demanding the creation of classes in black history and culture. More than one thousand black students marched on the San Francisco Board of Education demanding the "right to determine our educational destiny." Black and Latino students at Mission High in San Francisco formed an alliance and went on strike with the support of parents and community activists. The city sent in the police tactical squad, and the conflict escalated as students were beaten and nearly three hundred were arrested. In the broader San Francisco Bay Area, black and Third World students launched student strikes and protests at the City College of San Francisco, Laney College in Oakland, Chabot College in Fremont, and California State College at Hayward demanding "educational self-determination." At the College of San Mateo, when students called a strike with demands similar to those at San Francisco State, the conflict escalated and the president of the college declared martial law, surrounding the school with armed police and limiting campus access to those with valid student IDs whose names did not appear on a "subversives" list. At UC Berkeley, the campus chapter of the Third World Liberation Front called for the creation of a Third World College and released a statement of demands: "The people must be given an effective voice in the educational apparatus which either prepares or fails to prepare their children for life as it actually is. WE MUST HAVE SELF DETERMINATION!! We can no longer afford to have our tax dollars used to finance private, privileged sanctuary for a group of backward, unrealistic colonialists while our needs go unmet. We must have change and change will come by any means the colonialists make necessary." Like those at San Francisco State, the Berkeley strikers successfully forced their concerns onto the statewide agenda. Governor Reagan declared an "extreme state of emergency," dropped tear gas on students from helicopters, and sent in the National Guard armed with bayonets.[36]

As word spread, so did mobilization by black and other Third World students. Throughout the spring of 1969, demands for increased black and Third World enrollment and curricula ripped through campuses across the country. About a third of all student protests that tumultuous year aimed to increase black studies curricula.[37] Many of the protests followed roughly the trajectory of those at San Francisco State: disruptive protests by a relatively radical minority could not be easily repressed because their demands spoke to the interests of a much broader constituency, including other marginalized students, black groups across the political spectrum, and liberals alienated by Law and Order politics. When college administrations attempted to repress the dissidents, public support for the student activists became overwhelming.

At the University of Wisconsin, Madison, which had only five hundred black students in its student body of thirty-two thousand, several hundred black and white radicals rallied on February 8 to call for a boycott of classes until the administration created a black studies department. A small-scale picket persisted until the mayor of Madison called in the National Guard to repress it. By noon, the picket had ballooned to two thousand students; conflicts with the Guard intensified, and the guardsmen used tear gas to disperse the students. By that evening, more than ten thousand students had joined the protest, and the crowd marched on the capitol, carrying lit torches, precipitating a major social crisis.[38]

Black students at Cornell University took over a campus building in April to demand the creation of a black college and to decry recent incidents of racism on campus. The conflict over redress of black concerns almost became an armed battle as students marched in front of news media bearing seventeen rifles and shotguns and bandoliers of bullets, refusing to back down until their demands were met.[39]

On May 21, protests by black students in Greensboro, North Carolina, developed into open warfare. The conflict started when a student with a Black Power platform was excluded from a ballot for student body president at the all-black Dudley High School. Police arrested student protestors, and students began throwing rocks and breaking windows. The conflict escalated. The mayor called a curfew. Angry black students took over several buildings and held them for two days at the historically black North Carolina Agricultural and Technical State University in Greensboro. The National Guard was called in with tanks and sharpshooters. The black students resisted and engaged in an extended shoot-out with police and the National Guard. At least five policemen were shot, and many students were injured. More than two hundred students were arrested, and sophomore honors student Willie B. Grimes was killed.[40]

All told, in the spring of 1969, major protests disrupted nearly three hundred colleges across the country. One-quarter involved strikes or building takeovers. One-quarter involved disruptions of classes or other school functions. About 20 percent of the protests involved bombs, fires, or destruction of property. At least eighty-four incidents of bombing or arson were reported on campuses that spring; the American Insurance Association estimated that these protests incurred at least $8,946,972 in property damage alone.[41]

In instigating the San Francisco State strike, the Black Panther Party forged broad alliances with community leaders, faculty, labor, and a multiracial coalition of radical students that would have been impossible to mobilize within the confines of a narrower black nationalism. While most faculty members did not agree with the political vision of the Panthers, as right-wing California politicians attempted to prevent the Panthers from organizing on campus, many of them believed that academic freedom had been undermined. Latino and Asian American students, opposed to the educational marginalization of their own communities, integrated their political agendas into an anti-imperialist "Third

World" alliance. Anti-imperialist white students mobilized in solidarity. And despite their political differences, black political, church, and civic leaders saw harsh repression of promising young black activists on campus as a threat to their own interests. In 1969 and 1970, the Black Panthers' resilient anti-imperialist politics propelled their Party into the center of an ever-widening resistance.

13

Vanguard of the New Left

Yolanda Lopez and Donna Amador, activists from the San Francisco State strike, were at the Free Huey rally on May 1, 1969, along with Ralph Ruiz when, as Amador recalls, "I was standing in the back of the crowd near a police motorcycle when I heard from a crackling radio that a police officer had just been shot in San Francisco's Mission District (my home). An all-points bulletin went out for a number of Latin men, and, coincidentally, one of the suspects [Ralph Ruiz] was standing right beside me! My priorities changed instantly. Education was important for the brothers and sisters, but the fight for freedom from the oppression and injustice of the real world suddenly took me away from SFSU [San Francisco State University]."[1]

Earlier that day, San Francisco police officers Joe Brodnik and Paul McGoran, both undercover, approached a group of young Latinos moving a television from their car into an apartment. Officer McGoran, who had been drinking that morning, called the youths "wetbacks" and a number of insults were exchanged. A fight broke out, and by the end, Brodnik had been killed with McGoran's gun. Despite evidence that four of the seven young Latino activists charged with the shooting were elsewhere at the time and with no clear argument about who had actually shot Brodnik, the prosecution charged all seven with first-degree murder and called for their execution. In response, San Francisco police raided more than 150 homes in the Mission District, claiming they were searching for the seven young men they said had shot Brodnik. The *Black Panther* asked rhetorically, "Was that pig

Brodnik shot by the many thousands of Brown people who live in San Francisco's Mission District?"[2]

The seven Latinos charged—Tony and Mario Martinez, Nelson Rodriquez, Jose Rios, George "Gio" Lopez, Gary Lescallet, and Danilo "Bebe" Melendez—were active in student efforts to force the administration to institute Third World curricula and enrollment at the College of San Mateo. They came to be known as Los Siete de la Raza (roughly, the seven Latinos). Many young Latinas and Latinos in San Francisco's Mission District had initially become politically active through the Mission Rebels, a federally funded program for low-income youth. Both the San Francisco State strike and conflicts with police had radicalized many young activists in the Mission District. When Los Siete were accused of murder, the charge gave young Mission District activists a focal point for their political energies.

Having gotten to know the Black Panthers during the SF State strike, Los Siete supporters Roger Alvarado and Donna Amador approached Bobby Seale for help, and the Panthers immediately came to their assistance. The Panthers offered Los Siete supporters publication assistance, shared the stage at rallies, introduced them to their lawyer Charles Garry, committed $25,000 to their legal defense, and mentioned Los Siete when they were interviewed on the evening news.

On June 28, 1969, the *Black Panther* headline was "Free the Latino Seven," and the newspaper featured a full-page cover graphic of Mexican revolutionary Emiliano Zapata and six photos of members of Los Siete de la Raza. The paper featured stories explaining the case and calling on readers to donate to the cause of Los Siete de la Raza, including one article that equated their struggle to the Panthers' own: "The Black Panther Party sees that these brothers are political prisoners the same as Huey P. Newton." Newton wrote a personal statement in support of Los Siete from prison, calling on Panthers to support them.[3]

Los Siete crafted a seven-point anti-imperialist program, "What We Want and What We Believe," that they modeled after the Panther's Ten Point Program:

1. We want self determination for all people of La Raza.
2. We support all revolutionary movements at home, in Latin America, and throughout the world.
3. We want an immediate end to police brutality and murder of La Raza people.
4. We want an end to exploitation of women, male chauvinism, male supremacy. We want freedom for women.

5. We want freedom for all La Raza men and women of all ages held in federal state, county, city prison, and youth detention centers.

6. We want all La Raza men to be exempt from military service.

7. We demand a free society where the needs of the people come first: free health care, free education, full employment, and decent housing.[4]

In August, the Black Panther Party provided pages in its newspaper for Los Siete de la Raza to launch its own news publication. Donna Amador was the editor, and Yolanda Lopez, after lessons from Emory Douglas, was in charge of layout. Three eight-page bilingual issues of *Basta Ya!* were published within the *Black Panther* newspaper, until Los Siete developed the capacity to publish independently in late September.[5]

RED GUARD

Another group that sought to emulate the Black Panthers was a Chinese-American group in San Francisco that grew out of Leway, a nonprofit organization serving low-income youths in Chinatown. After participating in the Stop the Draft Week and the San Francisco State strike, many Leway members came to believe that the government was not truly interested in their problems, and they sought more radical redress.

Alex Hing, Warren Mar, and others participated in Black Panther political education classes and helped recruit Chinese American youth to attend "Free Huey!" rallies. Soon, they left Leway and founded the Red Guard, named for Mao's army in China. They saw themselves as part of a global revolutionary struggle for self-determination, in solidarity with both the Chinese Revolution and the Black Panthers. The Red Guard emulated many of the Black Panthers' activities, including establishing community service programs and organizing against police brutality. They adopted a ten-point program very similar to that of the Panthers but with notable exceptions. For example, their tenth point read, "We demand that the United States government recognize the People's Republic of China. We believe that Mao Tse-Tung is the true leader of the Chinese people; not Chiang Kai Shek."[6]

YOUNG LORDS

In Chicago, as the Black Panthers developed a powerful presence in the black community, they pioneered strong alliances with nonblack anti-imperialist groups. One important ally of the Chicago Panthers was the Puerto Rican Young Lords Organization. The Young Lords originated in the 1950s as a Puerto Rican street gang in Chicago's Lincoln Park neighborhood. Jose "Cha Cha" Jimenez joined in 1959 and rose through the ranks to become leader of the gang in 1964. Jimenez used his position to advance a social service mission in the Puerto Rican community. The Young Lords started to give food and clothing to poor families, formed a social club, and began organizing community picnics. Eventually, Jimenez became dissatisfied with the giveaways as a means to effect real change. According to Jimenez, "The Young Lords Organization turned political because they found out that just giving gifts wasn't going to help their people, they had to deal with the system that was messing over them." In 1968, Cha Cha Jimenez met Fred Hampton in jail. After a long discussion about the divisions between blacks and Puerto Ricans, Jimenez embraced the Black Panther Party as the revolutionary vanguard and sought to emulate the Black Panther model. "We see and we recognize the Black Panther Party as a vanguard party, a vanguard revolutionary party. And we feel that as revolutionaries, we should follow the vanguard," Jimenez explained. When he got out of jail, he initiated a campaign to oppose Chicago's "urban renewal" policies that displaced many Puerto Ricans from their homes and transformed the Young Lords into the Young Lords Organization.[7]

The Young Lords wore purple berets, asserted their right to armed self-defense, and developed a thirteen-point platform and program modeled after the Black Panthers' program. The Young Lords were different from other domestic "Third World" organizations in that Puerto Rico was (and is still) a territory of the United States, subject to U.S. rule without full political representation. Led mostly by Puerto Rican youth born in the mainland United States, the Young Lords sought to link the liberation struggle in Puerto Rico to the social conditions they experienced in their urban neighborhoods in the United States. Like the Black Panthers, they saw problems in their communities as the result of imperialism, capitalism, and racism.[8]

On April 4, 1969, Chicago police killed the Young Lords' minister of defense, Manuel Ramos, and critically wounded the organization's minister of education, Ralph Rivera, shooting him in the head. Less than twenty hours later, the Young Lords turned out more than three thousand people for a protest at the police station. Allegedly, the police had tried to turn the black gangs in the area against the Young Lords. But on May 14, the Young Lords took over the McCormick Theological Seminary and invited the black gangs to talk. The Black

Panthers announced their support for the Young Lords and formally declared solidarity with the group: "Regarding you, the Young Lords as our true revolutionary brothers, as our comrades, as our allies, the Black Panther Party is working jointly with you to see that aggression is thwarted and suppression is ended." Jimenez talked about the class character of the struggle at the meeting and said, "We see the United States is our enemy. And we look out for allies, you know, we look at Cuba, we look at Mao, we look at all these other countries that have liberated themselves from the monsters."[9]

Recalling their earlier food and clothing giveaways and inspired by the Black Panther model, the Young Lords organized community service programs to address the basic needs of community members and to draw them to their organization. They organized joint free clothes distributions with the Black Panthers, handing out free new and used clothes to hundreds of families. The Young Lords also initiated a free breakfast program for children that served Chicago's Puerto Rican neighborhoods.[10]

In June 1969, the Chicago Black Panther Party announced the creation of a "Rainbow Coalition" with the Young Lords and the Young Patriots, a group of poor revolutionary white youths led by William "Preacherman" Fesperman, a white seminary student who had moved to Chicago from Appalachia, wore Black Panther buttons, and displayed the Confederate flag. Chicago's Black Panther deputy chairman, Fred Hampton, announced, "We got blacks, browns, and whites . . . we've got a Rainbow Coalition!" The national Black Panther Party promoted Chicago's revolutionary coalition as a national model, and speakers from the three groups were featured at events from Oakland to New York, such as a march on Fort Dix in New Jersey to protest alleged brutality against soldiers in the stockade there. Explaining the coalition, New York Black Panther leader Carlton Yearwood said that the groups shared a revolutionary commitment to class struggle across race. "We believe that racism comes out of a class struggle, it's just part of the divide-and-conquer tactics of the Establishment and a product of capitalism. When we provide free breakfasts for poor kids, we provide them for poor whites and poor blacks."[11]

As the Young Lords in Chicago emulated the Panthers, other Puerto Rican activists began to follow suit. On June 7, 1969, the *Black Panther* ran a story on the Young Lords in Chicago and the Rainbow Coalition. The article caught the eye of a group of Puerto Rican student activists in New York City who were looking for a way to address police violence, expand educational access for Puerto Ricans, transform educational curricula, and advance Puerto Rican independence. Pablo "Yoruba" Guzmán, as a student at Columbia University, and David Perez and Miguel "Mickey" Melendez, as students at Old Westbury College, had been involved in educational politics and social service programs. Guzmán had participated in the Columbia protests. By 1969, all three were moving toward revolutionary anti-imperialist politics. The students already looked to the Black Panthers for inspiration. When they heard about the Young Lords in Chicago, they decided to follow their example. In the words of Guzmán, "At first the only model we had to go on in this country was the Black Panther Party . . . [Then], in 1969 in the June 7 issue of the Black Panther newspaper there was an article about the Young Lords Organization in Chicago with Cha Cha Jimenez as their chairman. Cha Cha was talking about revolution and socialism and the liberation of Puerto Rico and the right to self-determination and all this stuff that I ain't *never* heard a spic say. I mean, I hadn't never heard no Puerto Rican talk like this—just Black people were talking this way, you know. And I said, 'Damn! Check this out.' That's what really got us started." [12]

After reading the Panther article on the Young Lords in June, Guzmán, Melendez, and Perez traveled to Chicago to ask Jimenez if their organization could become a formal chapter of the Young Lords. Jimenez told them they should merge with Juan "Fi" Ortiz and a group of New York high school students that was trying to get a chapter going. They recruited Fi to the Central Committee, and the New York Young Lords was formed. They decorated their office with posters of the Black Panthers, Pedro Albizu Campos (leader of the Puerto Rican independence movement in the mid-twentieth century), Ho Chi Minh, and Che Guevara. [13]

In October 1969, the Young Lords changed their name to the Young Lords Party and began publishing a mimeographed packet called *Palante,* which grew to a full-fledged newspaper by May of 1970. [14] Like the Panthers, they saw a need to create a revolutionary culture that would allow Puerto Ricans to liberate themselves from mental slavery and stand up to oppression. "The chains that have been taken off slaves' bodies are put back on their minds," explained Young Lord David Perez. "To support its economic exploitation of Puerto Rico, the United States instituted a new educational system whose purpose was to Americanize us. Specifically, that means that the school's principal job is to exalt the cultural values of the United States. . . . What all this does is to create severe problems for our people. First it creates a colonized mentality—that means that the people have a strong feeling of inferiority, they have a strong feeling of not being as worthy as the Americans because the structure tells them that to become American is always a goal they have to attain."[15]

The New York Young Lords used direct action tactics akin to those of organizer Saul Alinsky with an anti-imperialist edge to force confrontation with the city government of New York, seeking to gain concessions for their community. Many people complained about the mountains of piled-up garbage in the neighborhood because of the city's failure to clean the streets. In August 1969, the Young Lords went to the Department of Sanitation and requested the use of brooms to clean the streets. When the department staff refused their request, they took the brooms by force. They organized a community work day and swept the streets with the brooms they had "liberated." Hundreds of neighbors joined them, piling up a five-foot-high mountain of trash blocking off the six lanes of Third Avenue. As Juan González directed people away from the pile, Yoruba screamed "Burn the garbage!" and, to the cheers of the neighbors, the Young Lords doused the trash with gasoline and ignited the pile. As Yoruba explained to the *New York Times*, the Young Lords had organized the garbage-dumping demonstration to show people in "El Barrio," the Puerto Rican slums in East Harlem, that direct action was needed to force the city to meet community needs. Mayor John V. Lindsay, attempting to de-escalate the conflict and win support in his upcoming re-election campaign, reassigned Sanitation Department personnel to clean up the pervasive garbage problems in the neighborhood and keep it clean. The victory brought a tremendous outpouring of community support for the Young Lords.[16]

In the fall of 1969, the Young Lords in New York approached the Reverend Humberto Carranza of the local First Spanish Methodist Church on 111th Street in East Harlem. The church was not used during the week, and the Young Lords asked if they could use the basement of the church to run their free breakfast program for neighborhood children. Carranza refused, so about twenty Young Lords went to Sunday service to ask the parishioners directly. During the testimonial period, Young Lord chairman Felipe Luciano made a plea to the thirty parishioners who were present for the Young Lords to be able to use the space. But Reverend Carranza had warned the police, who proceeded to storm the front of the church and beat Luciano—breaking his arm and sending him to the hospital—and arrest all the Young Lords present. Melendez called the left-leaning National Lawyers Guild for help, and a brilliant young Latino lawyer, Jerry Rivers, was sent to help secure the Young Lords' release from jail. Rivers came to represent the Young Lords in most of their cases. He soon changed his name to Geraldo Rivera and eventually became a popular talk show host.[17]

The repression of the Young Lords brought them increased support from the community and for the following three months, Young Lords members regularly gave testimonials in Sunday services at the First Spanish Methodist Church, which were often attended by 80 parishioners and 150 Young Lords supporters. The Young Lords continued to ask permission to use the church space to conduct a "liberation school" and a day care center and to run a free breakfast program for children. But the Reverend Carranza continued to refuse their requests, and on December 28, after the Sunday service, the Young Lords and their Black Panther allies locked the doors of the church with chains and sealed them with six-inch railroad spikes. Yoruba told the press that the immediate plan was to feed hot breakfasts to fifty to seventy children at the church each morning and that the Young Lords would end the occupation if they were allowed to run the breakfast program. The Young Lords put up a sign proclaiming "La Iglesia de le Gente— People's Church." They served breakfasts of fruit juice, milk, and cookies in the mornings to seventy-five children and conducted classes on Latin American history for the community. The church takeover became a national story, and thousands visited the Young Lords to offer their support, including celebrities like Jane Fonda and Donald Sutherland. In the end, the National Council of Churches agreed to provide space in other churches in the neighborhood for the Young Lords' programs.[18]

In early October 1970, Young Lord Julio Roldán was sitting on a stoop and drinking a beer with friends when police pulled up. Roldán was arrested for drinking in public, and the next morning, he was found hung in his cell. Believing that Roldán had been killed by authorities, five thousand demonstrators carried his casket from the González funeral home on Madison Avenue and marched to the First Spanish Methodist Church on 111th Street. Again, the Young Lords took over the church, but this time, they were armed, and they refused to move. Fearing a disaster, the mayor negotiated with the Young Lords and granted a seat on the Board of Corrections to Young Lord ally and former light heavyweight boxing champion of the world José Torres. The mayor also granted amnesty for the church occupiers, given that no guns were found when they came out. The Young Lords agreed to the terms and then followed the example of the Algerian revolutionaries, sneaking their guns out in the bras of old women.[19]

On the strength of these successes, the Young Lords Party continued to grow. A Philadelphia office opened in August 1970. Others opened in Puerto Rico; Newark, New Jersey; and Hayward, California. Most of the members of the Philadelphia chapter were young Puerto Ricans involved with a Catholic service agency that had turned toward revolutionary politics through engagement with the Socialist Workers Party and then turned toward the model of the Young Lords, adopting their platform and achieved formal recognition as a chapter. The Philadelphia chapter focused on free breakfast for children and service programs for the community. When they began organizing for community control of the police, their offices were firebombed.[20]

Often working directly with the Black Panthers, the New York-based Young Lords created innovative campaigns, such as one to take over Lincoln Hospital, which had been housed in a condemned building for twenty-five years. In that campaign, they forced the City of New York to build a new hospital in the South Bronx. They took over a mobile X-ray truck to force the city administration to attend to a spreading tuberculosis epidemic in East Harlem and seized unused equipment to test for lead poisoning in children, whose exposure to peeling lead paint in substandard housing placed them at risk for brain damage. They challenged the Board of Corrections on prison conditions, conducted ongoing breakfast programs for children in four cities, and initiated bilingual education programs. They also turned out ten thousand people to demonstrate at the United Nations for an independent Puerto Rico and maintained direct alliances with independence movement organizations in Puerto Rico.[21]

THE WHITE NEW LEFT

Like the Panthers, the Young Lords, the Red Guards, and Los Siete de la Raza viewed their movements as struggles against racial oppression as well as against class exploitation. In emulating the Black Panther Party, they sought to devise policies and programs that addressed the distinctive forms of oppression they faced. Young white activists did not face racial oppression. And the Appalachian Young Patriots notwithstanding, many white New Left activists came from the middle class and did not personally suffer class exploitation either. Nonetheless, many looked to the Black Panther Party as a primary reference point for their own political activism.

In an interview with the *Movement* newspaper while he was in prison, Huey Newton explained the Black Panther position on the role of white allies in building a global revolution and emphasized the Panthers' commitment to socialism. In contrast with Stokely Carmichael and other separatist black nationalists, he reinforced the Panthers' openness to working with whites and advanced a sympathetic assessment of the white New Left:

> I personally think that there are many young white revolutionaries who are sincere in attempting to realign themselves with mankind, and to make a reality out of the high moral standards that their fathers and forefathers only expressed. In pressing for new heroes the young white revolutionaries found their heroes in the black colony at home and in the colonies throughout the world. The young white revolutionaries raised the cry for the troops to withdraw from Vietnam, hands off Latin America, withdraw from the Dominican Republic and also to withdraw from the black community or the black colony. So you have a situation in which the young white revolutionaries are attempting to identify with the oppressed people of the colonies and against the exploiter.[22]

Newton argued that because middle-class white revolutionaries had not experienced class exploitation or racial injustice, their oppression was "somewhat abstract." Nonetheless, he insisted that they had an important role to play in the global revolutionary struggle. White leftists, he said, needed to dedicate themselves to revolution and to align themselves with the anti-imperialist liberation struggles around the world and with the Black Panther Party: "[White revolutionaries] can aid the black revolutionaries first by simply turning away from the establishment, and secondly choosing their friends. For instance, they have a choice between whether they will be a friend of Lyndon Baines Johnson or a friend of Fidel Castro. A friend of Robert Kennedy or a friend of Ho Chi Minh. And these are direct Opposites. A friend of mine or a friend of Johnson's. After they make this choice then the white revolutionaries have a duty and a responsibility to act."[23]

Newton suggested that the abstract quality of white revolutionary struggle could be made real—that whites could prove their allegiance and become truly revolutionary—through support of the black struggle against oppression: "Black people are being oppressed in the colony by white police men, by white racists. We are saying they must withdraw. . . . When something happens in the black colony—when we're attacked and ambushed in the black colony—then the white revolutionary students and intellectuals and all the other whites who support the colony should respond by defending us." SDS published Newton's ideas about the white New Left as a pamphlet and distributed it nationwide that fall, in coordination with "Free Huey!" actions.[24]

Heeding the call to defense, in early 1969, the Students for a Democratic Society committed to work with the Panthers to organize a February 16–17 birthday celebration for Huey Newton in twenty cities nationwide to mobilize support for the "Free Huey!" campaign. Calling for SDS members across the country to participate, SDS interorganizational secretary Bernardine Dohrn explained the importance of doing whatever it took to defend the Panthers: "When an organization is rooted in the needs of the people, attacks on that organization or its leaders (frame-ups, jailing, assassination) are understood and resisted as a more visible form of the daily oppression of the entire people. The reaction is not just shock or indignation at the hypocrisy of the system, but more determined and conscious willingness to fight. The tactics of the fight are any means necessary." Dohrn ended her appeal by quoting Newton: "The racist dog oppressors have no rights which oppressed Black people are bound to respect. . . . The oppressor must be harassed until his doom. He must have no peace by day or night."[25]

By April 1969, SDS had embraced the Black Panther Party as central to its own struggle. On April 4, the one-year anniversary of Martin Luther King's assassination, SDS published a resolution passed by twelve hundred national representatives titled, "The Black Panther Party: Toward the Liberation of the Colony." The resolution linked the revolutionary core identity of SDS to the act of resisting the state's repression of the Panthers: "When the leading black revolutionary group is continually harassed, its leaders jailed, hounded out of the country and brutally assassinated, when Panther members daily face the provocations of the ruling class and its racist pigs, when their blood has been spilled and their list of revolutionary martyrs . . . increases daily, then the time has come for SDS to give total and complete support to their defense efforts. To do less would be a mockery of the word 'revolutionary.'"[26]

The SDS resolution called Newton the most important "political prisoner" in the United States and urged SDS members to form Newton-Cleaver defense committees to raise money for the legal defense of Newton and other Panthers facing charges. These committees would also serve an educational role, teaching people about the case and about the structural roots of racist oppression.

The resolution declared SDS's "total commitment to the fight for liberation in the colony and revolution in the mother country" and named the Black Panther Party the vanguard of all revolutionary struggle in the United States:

> The sharpest struggles in the world today are those of the oppressed nations against imperialism and for national liberation. Within this country the sharpest struggle is that of the black colony for its liberation; it is a struggle which by its very nature is anti-imperialist and increasingly anti-capitalist. . . . Within the black liberation movement the vanguard force is the Black Panther Party. . . . We must keep in mind that the Black Panther Party is not fighting black people's struggles only but is in fact the vanguard in our common struggles against capitalism and imperialism.[27]

UNITED FRONT AGAINST FASCISM

By the summer of 1969, the Black Panthers recognized that the broader New Left was turning toward their party for leadership. They seized the opportunity. In the May 31, 1969, issue of the *Black Panther*, the Party called for a "Revolutionary Conference for a United Front Against Fascism" (UFAF) to take place in Oakland in July. The issue featured a photo of nonblack New Left protestors on the cover next to a photo of Ericka Huggins with the caption "wife of the late John Jerome Huggins." The headline read "Fascism in America." Seven pages of the issue featured photos of crowds of nonblack New Leftists confronting bayonet-wielding National Guardsmen, a military helicopter gassing protestors, and graphic close-ups of wounded activists shot down by police. One photo caption featured Newton's dictum "Politics is war without bloodshed . . . War is politics with bloodshed." The centerfold, featuring a photo of a mob of police with shotguns and riot gear shutting down a street, declared, "The Black Panther Party Comes Forth. We Must Develop a United Front Against Fascism." The text called for a broad people's revolutionary alliance.[28]

The Panthers' conference announcement in late May linked the police killing of white Berkeley activist James Rector to the incarceration of Huey Newton. The conference would help develop a political program for all "poor, black, oppressed workers and people of America." It would also seek ways to advance community control of the police, free all political prisoners, expel the military from campus, and promote community self-defense. "People! Organizations! Groups! Yippies!" the flier announcing the conference beckoned, "Political

Parties! Workers! Students! Peasant-Farmers! You the Lumpen! Poor People, Black People, Mexican Americans, Puerto Ricans, Chinese . . . We Must Develop a United Front Against Fascism."[29]

In their move to take greater leadership in organizing a revolutionary movement across race, the Black Panthers sought to make their class and cross-race anti-imperialist politics more explicit. They began featuring nonblack liberation movements on the cover of their newspaper, starting with Ho Chi Minh and the North Vietnamese. They began widely using the word *fascism* to describe the policies of the U.S. government. Then in July 1969, two weeks before the United Front Against Fascism Conference, the Panthers changed point 3 of their Ten Point Program from "We want an end to the robbery by the white man of our Black Community" to "We want an end to the robbery by the CAPITALIST of our Black Community" [emphasis in original].[30]

The Black Panther Party held the United Front Against Fascism Conference in Oakland from July 18 to 21. Some events took place outdoors in west Oakland at "Bobby Hutton Park" (officially DeFremery Park); others took place in the Oakland Auditorium. At least four thousand young radicals from around the country attended the conference. The delegates included Latinos, Asian Americans, and other people of color, but the majority of delegates were white. More than three hundred organizations attended, representing a broad cross-section of the New Left. In addition to the Young Lords, Red Guard, Los Siete de la Raza, Young Patriots, and Third World Liberation Front, attendees included the Peace and Freedom Party, the International Socialist Club, Progressive Labor, Students for a Democratic Society, the Young Socialist Alliance, and various groups within the Women's Liberation Movement.[31]

Bobby Seale set the tone for the conference, reiterating his oft-stated challenge against black separatism: "Black racism is just as bad and dangerous as White racism." He more explicitly emphasized the importance of class to revolution, declaring simply, "It is a class struggle." Seale spoke against the ideological divisiveness among leftist organizations, arguing that such divisiveness would go nowhere. What was needed, he said, was a shared practical program. He called for the creation of a united "American Liberation Front" in which all communities and organizations struggling for self-determination in America could unite across race and ideology, demand community control of police, and secure legal support for political prisoners.[32]

Panther field marshal Don Cox talked about the necessity of armed self-defense. Elaine Brown, communications secretary for the Panthers from Southern California, presented a letter from Ericka Huggins, who at that time was in jail in New Haven, Connecticut, on conspiracy charges. Key Panther allies also spoke. Berkeley city councilman and future congressman Ron Dellums spoke about racism and politics. Father Earl Neil, pastor at St. Augustine Church, who had helped start the Panther's first breakfast program, gave a liberation theology perspective on revolution. Jeff Jones of Students for a Democratic Society spoke about the McClellan Committee in Congress that was seeking to impose harsher sentencing on student activists and undermine SDS's fight against fascism. Jones pointedly identified the Black Panther Party as the vanguard of revolution in the United States. William Kunstler spoke about community self-defense, pointing to the urban rebellions in Plainfield, New Jersey.[33]

A number of speakers drew parallels between their communities and the black community, seeking to show the applicability of various Black Panther political strategies across race. Roger Alvarado of the Third World Liberation Front at San Francisco State spoke about Los Siete de la Raza, as did Oscar Rios. The Parents of Adolfo Martinez, a member of Los Siete de la Raza, discussed the importance of the support of the Black Panthers and Third World alliance in furthering the struggle of Los Siete de la Raza. Penny Nakatsu from San Francisco State's Third World Liberation Front spoke about Japanese internment during World War II. Preacher Man, the field secretary of the white Young Patriot Party in Chicago, spoke about the need for armed self-defense against the police in the poor white neighborhoods of Chicago. At one point, a group of rank-and-file Black Panthers and Young Patriots, all in uniform, lined up on stage, alternating black and white to demonstrate their united stand against fascism.[34]

NATIONAL COMMITTEES TO COMBAT FASCISM

The main outcome of the conference was that the Panthers decided to organize National Committees to Combat Fascism (NCCFs) around the country. The NCCFs would operate under the Panther umbrella, but unlike official Black Panther Party chapters, they would allow membership of nonblacks. In this way, the Black Panther Party could maintain the integrity of its racial politics yet step into more formal leadership of a broader revolutionary movement across race. Initially, the NCCFs focused on two issues: local campaigns for community control of police and the development of legal teams to defend political prisoners.

One of the main issues facing the organizations at the conference was how to obtain adequate legal defense for charges stemming from radical political activities. Charles R. Garry of San Francisco and William M. Kunstler of New York, both prominent lawyers who worked with the Panthers, along with Bay Area lawyers Peter Frank and Robert Truehaft, put out a call to lawyers, legal secretaries, and law students to meet to develop a plan. The National Lawyers Guild agreed to help. When Garry had spoken at the UFAF conference, he had explained that the Nixon administration was seeking "more oppressive" measures against political radicals such as the Panthers. He said that Nixon was recommending that bail be eliminated in many political cases, and that in other cases, such as that of the New York 21—Black Panther activists facing dubious conspiracy charges—bail was being set impossibly high. He described wiretapping and other surveillance measures designed to repress radical politics and outlined a program to present seminars around the country over the next sixty days to enlist "a thousand lawyers to fight this fight against racism." The lawyers would work with the NCCFs on two hundred to three hundred test cases to defend Panthers and other "political prisoners" arrested for their radical political activities.[35]

Soon after the United Front Against Fascism Conference, leftist organizations around the world—including the Coordinating Committee of the Mexican Student Movement, the Tokyo Communist League, the Young Left League of Sweden, and the Left Wing Socialist Party of Denmark—sent the Panthers declarations of support for the UFAF.[36] The Black Panther Party was flooded with requests to open NCCFs throughout the country.[37] By April 1970, in addition to official Black Panther chapters, NCCFs were opened and operating in at least eighteen cities around the country.[38]

GENDER REVOLUTION

As the race and class insurgency in the United States broadened in 1969, young women and some men also sought to revolutionize gender relations. At the Panthers' United Front Against Fascism Conference, gender emerged as the most contentious issue. By that summer, the Women's

Liberation Movement was growing rapidly, and questions of gender were being seriously discussed nationally, especially in the New Left.

Women in the Black Panther Party organized a panel to discuss gender issues as part of the UFAF conference. Controversy erupted when the conference keynote speaker, renowned Communist historian Herbert Aptheker, spoke at great length. Some worried that the gender panel would not have an opportunity to present. One small group repeatedly interrupted Aptheker's speech and eventually stormed out of the conference.

Nonetheless, the gender panel did convene. Black Panther Roberta Alexander spoke at length about the problem of gender politics in the Party. She acknowledged that sexism in the Party was a problem. In particular, women had been denied equal access to power in the Party. She distinguished gender oppression from race and class oppression but pointed out that it compounded these problems. In conclusion, she chastised the people who had walked out of the conference because Aptheker's speech had dragged on. She said that men and women in the Party needed to address such problems collaboratively and find better ways of working together rather than tolerate male chauvinism and let it cause rifts.

Alexander first placed the issue of male chauvinism in its larger context, within the environment that had shaped the Party. Male supremacy, she explained, was "a true problem in our society and reflects capitalist society." In turn, she argued, it was important to acknowledge the persistence and depth of struggles over gender and sexuality within the Party: male supremacist culture demanded stalwart resistance. She spoke of the daily struggles within the Party over issues such as women's leadership within a male-dominated organization and the arming of women—namely, women's engagement in what some saw as the "male practice" of armed self-defense. The most explosive daily struggle, she explained, was the mistaken notion that one of women's revolutionary duties was to have sex with revolutionary men. She condemned some Panther men for seeking to use Party authority to demand sexual favors.[39]

Alexander argued, "Black women, interestingly enough, are oppressed as a class, part of the super-oppressed class of workers and unemployed in this country. Black women are oppressed because they are black, and then on top of that, black women are oppressed by black men. And that's got to go [applause]. Not only has it got to go, but it is going [applause]." Finally, she urged men and women in the Party to stay unified as they struggled over issues of gender and sexuality because "one of the most destructive aspects of male supremacy is how it divides people who should be united. . . . When we struggle against male supremacy, we struggle with the brothers in the party and the brothers struggle too. Cause it ain't the sisters that are doing all the struggle."[40]

All three members of the panel emphasized the centrality of gender and sexuality in the revolutionary struggle. Marlene Dixon, an assistant professor of sociology at the University of Chicago, criticized "bad faith" white male promises of equality. Black Panther Carol Henry lamented and urged resistance to a society wherein black women were victims of both mental and physical exploitation based "on the color of their skin and the shape of their breasts. . . . There cannot be a successful struggle against Fascism unless there is a broad front and women are drawn into it."[41]

Although the Black Panther Party started as a male organization, its expansion brought many female members, and by 1968, women permeated all levels of the organization. Beyond the famous Panther women leaders, like Kathleen Cleaver, Ericka Huggins, and Elaine Brown, and in addition to the thousands of rank-and-file women Panthers responsible for much of the daily work of the organization, numerous women played a key role in building and leading local Party chapters around the country. According to David Hilliard, unsung heroines like Lynn French in Chicago and Audrea Dunham in Boston were some of the Party's most influential and inspirational local leaders, commanding loyalty and respect from Panther men and women alike. Dunham, who organized the Boston chapter of the Black Panther Party, provided such effective leadership that the Party enlisted a number of the Panthers she had recruited and trained to lead high-priority campaigns around the country. For example, one of her recruits was Doug Miranda, the star organizer sent to New Haven to lead the Party's campaign in support of Bobby Seale and Ericka Huggins.[42]

Women's agitation for gender equality within the Party pushed the national Black Panther leadership to take a stand. Eldridge Cleaver in particular had to respond to criticism of the explicit misogyny and sexism in *Soul on Ice*. Two weeks before the UFAF conference, while women Panthers were organizing the gender panel, Cleaver released his first public statement from exile. In a statement dedicated to the revolutionary example set by Erika Huggins, the apparently reformed Eldridge Cleaver urged his fellow male Panthers to champion gender equality.

We must purge our ranks and our hearts, and our minds, and our understanding of any chauvinism, chauvinistic behavior of disrespectful behavior toward women. . . . We must too recognize that a woman can be just as revolutionary as a man and that she has equal stature, along with men, and that we cannot prejudice her in any manner, that we cannot relegate her to an inferior position. . . . The liberation of women is one of the most important issues facing the world today. Great efforts have been made in various parts of the world to do something about this, but I know from my own experience that the smoldering and the burning of the flame for liberation of women in Babylon is the issue that is going to explode, and if we're not careful its going to destroy our ranks, destroy our organization, because women want to be liberated just as all oppressed people want to be liberated. So if we go around and call ourselves a vanguard organization, then we've got to be the vanguard in all our behavior, and to be the vanguard also in the area of women's liberation and set an example in that area.[43]

Initially, Panther leadership rooted its calls for gender equality in a normative heterosexuality. In his statement, Cleaver wrote, "Women are our other half, they're not our weaker half, they're not our stronger half, but they are our other half."[44] This reliance on patriarchal social norms was common in the Party, and in black revolutionary circles more broadly. One focus, for example, was the idea of revolutionary motherhood: having babies for the revolution. Akua Njeri (Deborah Johnson), Fred Hampton's widow, remarked, "When you find your half that's for real, right on, go on and make those revolutionary babies, cause the youth make the revolution."[45] Panther Candi Robinson offered a similar argument: "Our men need, want and will love the beautiful children, that come from our fruitful wombs. . . . We are mothers of revolutionaries, with us is the future of our people." Indeed, "we are sisters, are mothers of revolution, and within our wombs is the army of the people.. . . . We my sisters are revolutionary women of revolutionary men! We are mothers of revolution!"[46] In this formulation of revolutionary motherhood, the revolutionary woman made babies not just for the revolutionary nation but for her revolutionary man. Revolutionary love, then, supported patriarchy, confirming conventional heterosexual gender norms. Malika Adams remembered, "I had three babies because I thought that it was my revolutionary duty to do that. I . . . wasn't thinking of what I wanted for me."[47]

In practice, such notions of revolutionary motherhood put severe burdens on some Panther women. The strains of state repression exacerbated these burdens, such as in the case of Akua Njeri, who lost the father of her child when the state assassinated Fred Hampton. Njeri later recalled the lack of support from the Party for her as a mother:

> I was in the first group of women to become pregnant and have babies within the context of the Black Panther Party. There was nothing set up after the birth of Fred Hampton, Jr. that spoke to the issue of childcare, of how we would continue to function in the structure of the Party and continue to provide for our children. Before, when you were in the Party, you were by yourself, you could really sleep anywhere and you could work all night. But when you have the responsibility of children, you can't do that. . . . There was no structure set up to work within the Party, to continue to work in the breakfast program, to continue to sell the newspaper. It was the demand to do it all or nothing. You would have to explain why you had to go take your child to the doctor, go through some struggle with that.[48]

In practice, through its heyday in the late 1960s, the Party often provided no more support for Panther mothers in handling the demands of child care and motherhood than most employers did at the time for their women employees.

As the Women's Liberation Movement and Gay Liberation Movement gained steam, the Black Panther Party leadership sought to deepen its commitment to gender and sexual liberation. A year after the UFAF conference, Huey Newton issued a formal Party position about the Women's Liberation and Gay Liberation Movements, challenging the heterosexual normativity and patriarchy in the Party. With Newton's public stance, the Black Panther Party became the first major national black organization to embrace gay rights. Newton identified "homosexuals and women as oppressed groups," noting that "homosexuals . . . might be the most oppressed people in the society" and arguing that a homosexual man "should have freedom to use his body in whatever way he wants to."[49]

The Black Panther Party saw black liberation as part of a global struggle against oppression, and Newton now identified women's and gay liberation as integral axes in that global struggle. He noted the importance of building alliances with women's liberation and gay liberation organizations: "When we have revolutionary conferences, rallies, and demonstrations there should be full participation of the gay liberation movement and the women's liberation movement."[50]

Finally, Newton acknowledged the need to confront ingrained gender and sexual values and language. In particular, he called for an end to Panthers' use of derogatory terms for homosexuals to disparage political enemies: "The terms 'faggot' and 'punk' should be deleted from our vocabulary, and especially we should not attach names normally designed for homosexuals to men who are enemies of the people, such as Nixon or Mitchell. Homosexuals are not enemies of the people."[51] Newton recognized that such language reflected basic social values, acknowledged that mere recognition of the problem of gender and sexual oppression was not enough to solve it, and suggested the need for a more complete transformation of social values: "We haven't established a revolutionary value system; we're only in the process of establishing it."[52]

Despite the Party's ideology, which at times reflected quite advanced thinking about gender and sexual liberation, deeply rooted sexism made the struggle for gender and sexual equality difficult. As with men in the broader world, changing Panther men's chauvinist attitudes and practices was a major challenge. Nationalism has historically been a gendered project, centered on patriarchy and male privilege.[53] The revolutionary black nationalism of the Black Panther Party began as part of that traditional project. Panther women and some Panther men fought heroically to break the Party out of that historical mold.

A critical element of the struggle was the development of feminist consciousness among Black Panther women. Looking back on her experiences as a Party member, Malika Adams noted, "Our consciousness about ourselves as women was very underdeveloped for the most part. . . . We didn't see ourselves as separate from the brothers. . . . I don't know that we really saw ourselves as women. . . . I think we saw ourselves in the eyes of men. The men defined pretty much what we were."[54]

The history of activism by revolutionary and radical women was relatively unknown at the time, which left women struggling with male interpretations of their role. As Angela Davis recalled, "Even those of us who were women did not know how to develop ways of being revolutionaries that were not informed by masculine definitions of the revolutionary. The revolutionaries were male. The women who became revolutionaries had to make themselves in those images."[55]

Given this masculinist context, women had to define for themselves their identities as women and revolutionaries. Rosemari Mealy later commented, "If you were . . . so male-identified, it was impossible for you to separate yourself as a woman and really internalize who you are as a woman and commit yourself as a woman to the struggle."[56]

Endemic and often intense Party struggles over issues of gender and sexuality yielded a richly varied, evolving, and at times highly contested gender and sexual consciousness within and beyond the Party. As Janet Cyril observed, this complex and uneven consciousness "developed by . . . fits and starts." "It grew out of . . . daily living and an evolving necessity in changing relationships . . . over a period of time." [57]

Given that the Black Panther Party's principal battle was against white supremacy and capitalist exploitation, male-female relationships and issues of gender and sexuality often took a back seat. Cyril remembered, "It was considered traitorous to deal with issues of gender in the context of the Black Revolution. I mean, people felt that strongly. . . . A lot of women felt like that also. . . . There was a lot of back and forth debate over that." As a result, innumerable women thought that "you were betraying brothers if you criticized what was going on with sisters in a general way." Tackling issues of gender and sexuality, especially from women's points of view, was to undermine race unity and thus impede the Black Liberation Struggle.[58]

The extreme repression the Party endured further intensified the common belief and feeling that the racial and class components of the struggle had to take priority. Elaine Brown recalled, "We clung to each other fiercely. We forgot cliques and chauvinism and any bit of internal strife."[59] Ericka Huggins expressed a similar feeling:

> In those days [we fought to] get rid of racism so we could stay alive. We didn't even think about sexism except when it reared its head. We didn't spend our time looking at what men and women did or didn't do because we didn't have time to think about it. We were too busy living so we didn't die. . . . A lot of people don't understand what that means in a day-to-day interaction. We were constantly looking over our shoulders. All I wanted to know about the person next to me, be it a man or woman, was would they back me up. If I needed to put my life in this person's hands, would it be all right. I didn't care whether they were man or woman, gay or straight, or any of that.[60]

Championing liberation struggle against all forms of oppression, the irrepressible Black Panther Party drove an ever-widening cycle of insurgency. How far would the revolutionary movement spread?

14

International Alliance

On Friday November 29, 1968, fifteen hundred delegates from through-out the Americas gathered in Montreal for the Hemispheric Conference to End the War in Vietnam. The delegates were political leaders from throughout the Americas who opposed U.S. intervention in Vietnam, including Salvador Allende, at that time president of the Chilean Senate (and later president of Chile); antiwar activists from a range of organizations; Quebeçois secessionists; and a delegation from North Vietnam led by the North Vietnamese minister of culture, M. Hoang Minh Giam. The Black Panther Party sent a delegation led by Bobby Seale and David Hilliard and including a dozen rank-and-file Panthers from various chapters.[1]

At the opening plenary at St. James Church in downtown Montreal, Seale argued that peace could not be achieved without justice. He said that the Vietnam War was a criminal act of U.S. aggression and called for a worldwide struggle against imperialism. On behalf of the Black Panther delegation, he put forth a long resolution stating in part, "Our purpose in attending this conference was a reaffirmation of our commitment to concrete support of the heroic struggles of the Vietnamese people and of all People's Liberation Struggles—it was not to hear vague resolutions passed in support of world peace." The conference focus, he said, "should be changed from supporting world peace to supporting Third-World Liberation Struggles and the title of this conference changed from Hemispheric Conference to End the War in Vietnam to

Hemispheric Conference to Defeat American Imperialism." The conference delegates gave him a standing ovation. Brother Zeke, a Black Panther from the Baltimore chapter, was elected chairman of the conference, and the program for the weekend was revised in keeping with the Panthers' proposed anti-imperialist theme. The French newspaper *Le Monde* reported that in speaking out about the fight against "imperialism in all its forms," the Panthers had captured the imagination of the international delegates and set the tone of the conference.[2]

Throughout the conference, various Black Panther speakers drew an analogy between their struggle and that of the National Liberation Front in Vietnam. They compared the rapid expansion of police departments and the brutalization of blacks in American ghettos with the occupation of Vietnam by the U.S. military. They asserted their right to self-defense and challenged the legitimacy of American authority in the ghettos. "We say that the oppressor has no laws and no rights that the oppressed are bound to respect. We cannot respect it." Further, they proclaimed the universal "right to self-determination." The Panthers said that they and the other delegates shared a common struggle to end the wars of repression being waged against those seeking self-determination throughout Latin America and the Third World and among the communities in the United States, "even against the white hippies and the leftists and those who are looking for much individual freedom."[3]

At the end of the conference, American delegates handed their draft cards to the Vietnamese representatives. Taking to the stage, the Vietnamese delegation built a small fire and burned the draft cards as the audience cheered. In solidarity with the Panthers, delegates in the audience raised their fists in the Black Panther salute and joined in the chant, "Panther Power to the Vanguard!" Their voices resonated throughout the church. Then, in front of the fifteen hundred delegates, the Minister M. Hoang Minh Giam turned toward David Hilliard and proclaimed, "You are Black Panthers, We are Yellow Panthers!"[4]

MARXISM AND ANTI-IMPERIALISM

The Black Panther Party's anti-imperialist politics were deeply inflected with Marxist thought. Evolving Marxist thinking underwrote the Panthers' class politics and helped them articulate alliances with a broad range of international as well as domestic actors. Primarily committed to advancing the interests of black people in the United States as part of a global struggle against imperialism, the Panthers' Marxist class analysis helped build common ground with other constituencies in the United States and internationally. The Party's embrace of Marxism was never rigid, sectarian, or dogmatic. Motivated by a vision of a universal and radically democratic struggle against oppression, ideology seldom got in the way of the Party's alliance building and practical politics.

In 1971, Huey Newton explained that the Black Panthers were "dialectical materialists," thereby drawing a dynamic and evolving method of political analysis from Marx rather than any stagnant set of ideas. He argued, "Marx himself said, 'I am not a Marxist'. . . . If you are a *dialectical materialist* . . . you do not believe in the conclusions of one person but in the validity of a mode of thought; and we in the Party, as dialectical materialists, recognize Karl Marx as one of the great contributors to that mode of thought."[5] Eldridge Cleaver made a similar point. Writing in the fall of 1969, Cleaver argued that independence struggles in Asia demonstrated that a foreign ideology should not be adopted wholesale. Specifically, any Marxist dogma notwithstanding, he asserted that unemployed blacks were a legitimate revolutionary group and that the Black Panther Party's version of Marxism transcended the idea that an industrial working class was the sole agent of revolution.[6]

From the start, the Black Panther Party drew upon Marxist thought, and Marxist theory imbued its political statements and actions. The Party's original Ten Point Program and Newton's essay "The Functional Definition of Politics," both published in the second issue of the *Black Panther*, on May 15, 1967, employed the foundational Marxist concept of "means of production."[7] However, the Party's use and incorporation of Marxist theory evolved greatly over time. Different Panther leaders used Marxist theory in different ways, to different degrees, and at different times. One important turning point in Marxist influence on Black Panther political theory was the rise of Ray "Masai" Hewitt to Party leadership. Coming into the Party from Los Angeles, Hewitt had read deeply in Mao and Marx. He proved to be a supreme educator and was soon brought to serve in the Party's national headquarters in Oakland.[8]

With Masai Hewitt's involvement, the cover of the *Black Panther* began featuring international nonblack liberation struggles. Ho Chi Minh and the North Vietnamese were the first such revolutionaries to be featured on the cover, appearing in the paper in March 1969. Such coverage was frequent thereafter. Hewitt visited Chicago, and soon the Party chapter there was teaching members to read Mao and Marx as well as Malcolm X. In July, Hewitt was appointed minister of education, and the Party's engagement with Marxist thought continued to deepen. That month, the Party further integrated race and class analysis into its Ten Point Program, changing point 3 from "We want an end to the robbery by the white man of our Black Community" to the Marx-inflected point "We want an end to the robbery by the CAPITALIST of our Black Community."[9]

Nondogmatic throughout its history, the Black Panther Party worked with a range of leftist organizations with very different political ideologies—a highlight being its hosting of the United Front Against Fascism Conference in July 1969.[10] The unchanging core of the Black Panther Party's political ideology was black anti-imperialism. The Party always saw its core constituency as "the black community," but it also made common cause between the struggle of the black community and the struggles of other peoples against oppression. Marxism and class analysis helped the Black Panthers understand the oppression of others and to make the analogy between the struggle for black liberation and other struggles for self-determination. While the Marxist content deepened and shifted over the Party's history, this basic idea held constant. The Black Panther Party saw itself as the revolutionary vanguard advancing the interests of the black community for self-determination within a larger global struggle against imperialism. Huey Newton sought to more fully articulate this theory as a theory of "revolutionary intercommunalism" in 1971.[11]

The Panthers' line of Marx-inflected anti-imperialist thinking drew on a long line of black anticolonialist thinkers going back at least to W. E. B. Du Bois.[12] This anti-imperialist perspective drove the world-changing Bandung Conference in 1955, was taken up by Malcolm X, and underwrote the Non-Aligned Movement, in which such international Panther allies as the postcolonial government of Algeria played important roles. The nondogmatic, Marx-inflected anti-imperialism of the Black Panthers allowed them to find common cause with many other movements around the world. It underwrote their practical political alliances with a wide range of international movements.

SCANDINAVIA

Drawn to the Black Panthers' synthesis of race and class politics, anti-imperialist movements from around the world came to see the Party as part of their own global cause. One of the Panthers' early sources of solidarity and support was the left-wing movements in Scandinavia. The lead organizer of this support was Connie Matthews, an energetic and articulate young Jamaican woman employed by the United Nations Educational, Scientific, and Cultural Organization in Copenhagen, Denmark. In early 1969, Matthews organized a tour for Bobby Seale and Masai Hewitt throughout Scandinavia to raise money and support for the "Free Huey!" campaign. She and Panther Skip Malone worked out the logistics of the trip with various left-wing Scandinavian organizations, enlisting their support by highlighting the class politics of the Black Panther Party. "I am only too willing time and time again to repeat to European audiences," Matthews told a reporter from *Land and Folk,* the Communist newspaper in Copenhagen, "that the BPP is speaking about a world proletarian revolution and recognize themselves as part of this. It is a question of the oppressor against the oppressed regardless of race."[13]

The tour took Bobby Seale and Masai Hewitt to Stockholm, Sweden; Oslo, Norway; Helsinki, Finland; and Copenhagen (with a brief stop in Germany), where they talked at each stop about the Black Panther program, the global anticolonial struggle, and the injustice of Newton's incarceration. In each city, the Panthers formed a solidarity committee. Seale and Hewitt's Scandinavia trip brought funding, the prestige of formal endorsements from European organizations, and a network of support for the "Free Huey!" campaign. After the Panthers returned to the United States, Chief of Staff David Hilliard and the Central Committee of the Black Panther Party commended Connie Matthews and Skip Malone for the work they were doing for the "Free Huey!" campaign, featuring their activities prominently in the *Black Panther* newspaper.

Matthews continued working with the solidarity committees in Stockholm, Oslo, and Helsinki, organizing contingents to join the May Day workers' demonstrations on May 1, where they passed out literature in support of the Black Panther Party and carried "Free Huey!" signs. In Copenhagen, the Left Wing Socialist Party was particularly active, organizing an independent march of more than six hundred people that broke off from the main May Day protest and rallied at the U.S. embassy to call for Huey Newton's release from prison. These Scandinavian solidarity committees also held a series of rallies linking the Black Panther cause to the Vietnam War, disrupting speeches by Hubert Humphrey in Copenhagen and calling for an end to Scandinavian complicity with American imperialism through membership in the North Atlantic Treaty Organization.

ALGIERS FESTIVAL

After Eldridge Cleaver went underground in the late fall of 1968, he clandestinely traveled to Cuba, arriving on Christmas day. Bay Area radical allies who had been involved in the "Free Huey!" campaign obtained a commitment from the Cuban mission at the United Nations in New York to help bring Cleaver back into the country and provide him with political asylum.[14]

The week of the United Front Against Fascism Conference in Oakland in July 1969, Eldridge Cleaver returned to public view at the Pan-African Cultural Festival in Algiers, Algeria. There the Black Panthers' anti-imperialist politics found fertile international ground. The Party posited, as had the venerable W. E. B. Du Bois twenty-five years earlier, that blacks in America were subjugated and oppressed and denied self-determination much like those in the colonies in Africa. By 1969, much of Africa had won independence from European colonialism. Yet important areas, such as South Africa, Zimbabwe, Guinea-Bissau, and Mozambique were still engaged in bloody struggles for independence.

In organizing the first-ever Pan-African Cultural Festival, Algeria sought to play a key role in advancing the interests of African independence. After a decade of bloody guerilla warfare, the Algerians had forced the French out of their country in 1962. The socialist Algerian government wanted to remain independent from Europe and the United States. Algeria had broken off formal diplomatic relations with the United States in 1967 during the Six-Day War involving Israel, Egypt, Syria and Jordan. Nevertheless, American companies had invested in the oil and natural gas industry there, providing staff and equipment.

President Houari Boumedienne, one of the leaders of the bloody military struggle for Algerian independence, was a fervent anticolonialist and sought to advance Algerian interests by promoting African unity, Arab unity, and the organization of nonaligned nations that pursued self-determination and resisted falling under the influence of either the United States or the Soviet Union during the Cold War. In 1968 and 1969, Boumedienne served as chairman of the Organization of African Unity (OAU). From this post, he sought to strengthen Algeria's hand in international affairs by building a Pan-African alliance for independence, supporting Pan-African unity generally, and specifically supporting the liberation struggles in African countries that had not yet gained independence. The Algerian government and the OAU organized the Pan-African Cultural Festival as part of this strategy. In particular, the Pan-Africanist leadership at the Algerian festival sought to transcend the racial, cultural, and political barriers that traditionally divided predominantly Arabic North Africa against predominantly black sub-Saharan Africa. The idea was to define the unity of Africa in geographic, class, and social terms. As Keita Mamadi, head of the Guinean delegation said, the conference sought to identify culture as an "arm of economic and social liberation."[15]

Each of the forty-one member nations of the OAU was invited to send a delegation to demonstrate its indigenous cultures, including poets, musicians, and dancers. Liberation movements from still-colonized countries in Africa such as South Africa, South-West Africa, Rhodesia, and Angola were also invited to send delegations, as were liberation struggles from certain countries outside Africa, such as Vietnam.[16] A contingent of black artists and political figures from the United States was also invited, including singer-pianist Nina Simone, jazz saxophonist Archie Shepp, playwright Ed Bullins, and Nathan Hare, former director of the Black Studies Program at San Francisco State.[17] The Algerians also invited Eldridge Cleaver, Bobby Seale, and a delegation from the Black Panther Party.[18]

Having only recently won independence from France, and with anti-colonial struggles sweeping the globe, the Algerian government took the liberation movements seriously. According to Cleaver, the Algerians related to the Black Panthers "as the nucleus of a future, American government."[19] The *New York Times* explained the Algerian commitment: "The Algerians, who are only eight years removed from the end of their own war of independence, feel it is natural to support other liberation movements throughout the world. . . . They expect to play a leadership role in a completely decolonized Africa. They are also willing to recognize any movement outside Africa, such as the Panthers, that is struggling against what they consider an imperialist or fascist state."[20]

In late May, Kathleen Cleaver, who was eight months pregnant, and Black Panther minister of culture Emory Douglas traveled to Algiers to meet Eldridge. In Paris, they were joined by Julia Hervé, the Pan-African activist and daughter of the eminent black author Richard Wright. Fluent in French and knowledgeable about African cultures and politics, Hervé served as a liaison and guide for the Panthers.[21] On July 15, the Algerian government reported that Eldridge Cleaver had arrived in Algiers as a government guest.[22] Black Panther chief of staff David Hilliard and minister of education Masai Hewitt also traveled to Algiers for the festival.[23]

The Black Panther delegation was put up in the government-run Hotel Aletti in the center of Algiers, which became a meeting place for all the political groups there. Kathleen Cleaver recalled, "Mealtimes in the enormous dining hall turned into a lively round of reunions, meetings, connections, and spontaneous gatherings, followed by further meetings in various parts of the sprawling hotel at all times of day and night."[24]

On July 21, Algerian desert horsemen galloped through the capital firing rifles to announce the beginning of the first-ever Pan-African Cultural Festival. Four thousand Africans from twenty-four countries helped kick off the twelve-day celebration and series of discussions. The independent revolutionary countries of Guinea, Tanzania, Mali, and the Congo sent large dance troupes. Museums throughout Europe and Africa lent spectacular exhibits of African painting and sculpture. Fourteen countries produced plays and sent acting troupes. Others sent poets, writers, and musicians. Black faces in Algiers were a rarity, and Algerian men, accustomed to veiled women, whistled at black Senegalese singers wearing flowing, strapless gowns. Guinean swordsmen performed tribal dances. Tunisian belly dancers and Moroccan tumblers lifted Algerian spirits. Drummers, jugglers, pipers, and dancers energized a two-hour-long parade through the capital. President Houari Boumedienne denounced the idea of a colonial "civilizing mission," which the French had promoted, and proclaimed that "culture is a weapon in our struggle for liberation."[25]

Algeria's minister of information, Mohammed Ben Yaya, assigned the Black Panthers a chic office on Rue de Duce Mariad, the main street in downtown Algiers.[26] Emory Douglas brought a colorful portfolio of revolutionary artwork to the festival, including posters of Huey Newton and Eldridge Cleaver and provocative graphics from the *Black Panther* newspaper, such as one of a black woman carrying a baby and wearing a rifle strapped on her back. He displayed the artwork in the window of the office, and crowds of Algerians gathered on the sidewalk to look at the pictures throughout the twelve days of the festival.[27] The Panther delegation held a formal opening of its Afro-American Information Center on July 22, 1969. Hervé introduced the Panthers to the audience in French, explaining that when Malcolm X came to Africa, he was only one man, but now the Black Panthers had come as a fully developed revolutionary organization representing the Black Liberation Struggle. Largely sharing the Panthers' view that American imperialism was their enemy, the Algerian audience responded enthusiastically, packing into the center to hear the speakers and asking lots of questions.[28]

The Pan-African Cultural Festival placed the Black Panthers amid representatives of anti-imperialist movements and governments from around the globe, and they immediately began networking on a new level internationally. Eldridge Cleaver met with the ambassador of the Democratic People's Republic of Korea (North Korea). The Koreans were particularly interested in the Black Panthers and invited Cleaver to attend the upcoming International Conference of Revolutionary Journalists in Pyongyang as a formal guest of the state. Cleaver also met with leaders of Al Fatah, the most powerful Palestinian liberation group led by Yasir Arafat, and he subsequently spoke in support of the Palestinian cause in his speech at the opening of the festival.[29]

During the festival, the Algerian government sponsored a meeting for representatives of all the liberation struggles there to discuss solidarity and opportunities for supporting each other. Attendees included leaders from the liberation struggles of Mozambique, Zimbabwe, Haiti, Angola, and South Africa, and Black Panther Party Central Committee members David Hilliard, Eldridge Cleaver, Emory Douglas, and Masai Hewitt. The discussion, moderated by a representative of the Algerian government, took place in the courtyard of the house in the Kasbah that had served as the headquarters of the National Liberation Front during the Algerian Revolution. In line with the theme of the festival, the conversation turned to the class character of the global liberation struggle. The representative from Haiti spoke about the rule of François Duvalier:

> I would like to say a few words about Duvalier who rules our country, who is Black, who has said that he is in favor of "Negritude" and is one of the worst oppressors that has been known. The experience with Duvalier shows clearly how "Negritude," which at one point of history, de-colonization, was effective and did achieve a certain amount of liberation and repersonalization of peoples, how this same concept of "Negritude" now turns back against the people. And in the case of Duvalier proves that we have to wage a class struggle. And that in the context of this class struggle, we Black people—if we begin to depend on the power of money, on the power structure and money—we also then become tyrants, dictators, or Tonton Macoutes as in the case in Haiti. And this is why one must destroy all the capitalist structures which create monsters, be they White, Black, or Yellow.[30]

Eldridge Cleaver maintained that the United States was "bankroll-ing and arming all of the oppressive regimes around the world. The people have an interest in any amount of pressure that we can put on that government because, if we can just slow it down and force it to have to deal with us, then the other people would be able to liberate themselves and then in return we would expect them to come to our rescue. . . . Like Chairman Bobby Seale always said the best care pack-age that we could send to the other liberation struggles around the world is the work we do at home."[31]

AMBASSADORS

In the fall of 1969, the *New York Times* reported that while in Algeria, Eldridge Cleaver had begun discussions with the Vietnamese delega-tion to the festival about an exchange of prisoners of war for the release of Bobby Seale and Huey Newton from prison.[32] These discussions were part of ongoing relations between antiwar groups and the North Vietnamese and were facilitated by the Panthers' relations with the Chicago Seven. According to the U.S. House Committee on Internal Security, "During 1968 and until August 1969, the North Vietnamese government released a total of nine American POWs [. . . as a] pro-paganda gambit," which also served to enhance the position of pro-Hanoi "peace groups in the U.S."[33] Unlike the North Vietnamese gov-ernment's unilateral release of POWs to antiwar groups, any exchange of POWs for the jailed Panthers would have required the participation of the U.S. government, and the U.S. never made such a deal. But the North Vietnamese did send 379 letters from prisoners of war home to their families in the United States through the Black Panther Party.[34]

In the year following the Pan-African festival, while the Algerian government allowed the Cleavers to stay in Algiers, it did not initially extend official status to the Black Panther Party. In the spring of 1970, the status of the Black Panthers in Algeria began to improve, in part through the intervention of Mohammed Yazid, a powerful Algerian diplomat whose wife was American. The Algerian government accred-ited the Black Panthers as one of twelve liberation movements that merited support in overthrowing the governments in their respective countries. Among the other liberation movements it cited were those in Guinea-Bissau, Mozambique, Angola, Palestine, Brazil, Rhodesia, South-West Africa, and South Africa.

The Black Panthers were the only Americans recognized by the

Algerian government since it had broken off diplomatic relations with the United States. An Algerian spokesman explained the rationale to a reporter: "These groups are generally involved in a clear-cut colonial situation. What right have the Portuguese got to be in Africa? It's as simple as that."[35] With the Black Panthers' new official status, the Algerian government granted entrance and exit visas for guests; official identity cards, which made it possible to register cars and open post office boxes; and a monthly stipend.[36]

That June, the Algerians presented the Panthers with an embassy building for the International Section of the Black Panther Party. The embassy was a beautiful Mediterranean-style white stucco and marble building with open, airy archways and whitewashed stairwells in El Biar, a suburb in the hills outside Algiers. It stood two stories aboveground, surrounding a courtyard garden, and a sublevel contained quarters for a maid and a cook.[37]

In the summer of 1970, a delegation of Panthers and their allies made a trip through Asia, during which they were welcomed as official guests of the governments in North Vietnam, North Korea, and China. The eleven members of the delegation were Eldridge Cleaver and Elaine Brown from the Black Panther Party; Robert Scheer and Jan Austin from *Ramparts;* Regina Blumenfeld and Randy Rappaport of the Women's Liberation Movement; Alex Hing of the Red Guard; Ann Froines of the Panther Defense Committee of New Haven; Patricia Sumi of the Movement for a Democratic Military; Andy Truskier of the Peace and Freedom Party; and Janet Kranzberg.[38]

The group arrived in Pyongyang, North Korea, on July 14, 1970, and was greeted at the airport by Kang Ryang Uk, vice president of the Presidium of the Supreme People's Assembly, and other dignitaries.[39] The delegation traveled the country meeting with local officials to discuss ways that anti-imperialist movements in North Korea and the United States could help each other. The official North Korean government newspaper printed a statement expressing solidarity with the Black Panther Party. The statement discussed the imprisonment and abuse of Bobby Seale, the repression of the Black Panther Party, and the plight of American blacks generally and ended with a pledge of solidarity:

> The Korean people send firm militant solidarity to the Black Panther Party of the U.S.A. and the American Negroes that have been shedding blood in their arduous but just struggle in the teeth of the brutal repression by the U.S. imperialists, the chieftain of world imperialism, the ring leader of

world reaction and the common enemy of the world people, and they will give them active support and encouragement in the future too. The Black Panther Party of the U.S.A and the Negroes that are commanding the support and encouragement of the progressive American people and the revolutionary people of the whole world are bound to be crowned with a final victory in their just struggle.[40]

After Korea, the delegation traveled to Hanoi, North Vietnam, as the government's official guests of honor for the "international day of solidarity with the black people of the United States" on August 18, 1970. In Hanoi, Phạm Văn Đồng, the prime minister of North Vietnam, gave a sake toast to the Black Panthers: "In the West, you are a black in the shadow. In Vietnam, you are a black in the Sun!"[41] Like the North Koreans, the North Vietnamese saw the Black Panther Party and its allies in the United States as freedom fighters waging a liberation struggle against a shared enemy—U.S. imperialism. The North Vietnamese government published an editorial in its official newspaper titled "An Inevitably Victorious Cause" celebrating the Black Liberation Struggle in the United States as a common cause:

> The Vietnamese people, who are now opposing the American imperialist aggressors with arms, consider the black people of the United States in the struggle for their emancipation as their natural companions in arms and allies. The more the Nixon group develops its aggression in Indochina, the more it develops its repression and terror against the black people and the forces of peace and progress in America. It sheds the blood of young blacks in Indochina while their compatriots have need of their arms and their brains to engage the struggle in the U.S.A. We follow with deep sympathy the progress realized by the black people in the United States on the difficult path of resistance and courage, similar to our own struggle against aggression.[42]

The North Vietnamese invited Cleaver to speak to black GIs fighting in Vietnam from the Voice of Vietnam radio station in Hanoi. He gladly accepted. After introducing himself and giving a historical overview of the war, Cleaver called on black GIs fighting in Vietnam to join the Black Liberation Struggle. He argued that the U.S. government had put them on the front line against their own interests: "What they're doing is programming this thing so that you cats are getting phased out on the battlefield. They're sticking you out front so that you'll get offed. And that way they'll solve two problems with one little move: they solve the problem of keeping a large number of troops in Vietnam; and they solve the problem of keeping young warriors off the streets of Babylon. And that's a dirty, vicious game that's being run on you. And I don't see how you can go for it."[43] From Vietnam, the delegation traveled to China for a government-sponsored tour of factories, hospitals, and new housing developments.[44] Finally, the delegation returned to Algiers.

On November 1, 1970, after seeing President Houari Boumedienne off at the airport, Wei Pao Chang, the Chinese ambassador to Algeria, made his way to the villa in El Biar for a reception at the Black Panther embassy. Two bronze plaques shone as he entered the gate, each emblazoned with the symbol of a crouching panther and the words "Black Panther Party—International Section" inscribed in Arabic. Upon entering the villa, Wei Pao Chang was greeted by Eldridge Cleaver, the towering Black Panther ambassador to Algeria, who was hosting the reception. Through translators provided by the Algerian government, Cleaver told Chang about his recent government-sponsored tour of China. The discussion turned to the United States. "We are enemies to the death with the American government," Chang told Cleaver, "because of its support of the puppet regime in Formosa [Taiwan]. But we have great sympathy for the American people. We hope you will overcome the American monopolies."[45] Representatives of the Vietnamese National Liberation Front, the government of North Korea, and members of other socialist governments and liberation movements from around the world also attended the reception.

Each of the movements represented at the reception had started out nonviolently but had eventually turned to armed struggle. Johnnie Makatini, ambassador to Algeria from South Africa's African National Congress, recalled, "It was the same year Albert Luthli won the Nobel Peace Prize that we opted for violence. On the day he came back from Stockholm, December 15, 1961, there were explosions all over the country." Joseph Turpin, the ambassador to Algeria from Guinea-Bissau recalled that it was after the strike in Pijiguiti, when police killed fifty longshoremen, that "we decided armed struggle was the only way." Cleaver explained the shift among American blacks: "With us it was the death of Martin Luther King." King's assassination, he explained, "exhausted the myth that you could get what you want without fighting, that when the plantation foreman cracks the whip you turn the other cheek." The conversation turned at a later point to the theories of Frantz Fanon, a key supporter and perceptive analyst of the Algerian revolution, and to the Cuban revolutionary leader Che Guevara. One of the guests said he was impressed by Cleaver's grasp of revolutionary theory. "I had nine years to study it," Cleaver said. The guest replied, "The French say that prisons are the antechambers of cabinet ministries." Cleaver smiled. "We're not there yet," he said.[46]

As the U.S. government sought to repress the Black Panthers, international political support continued to widen the revolutionary movement. Only concessions could break the insurgent cycle.

FIGURE 27. *(above)* On December 8, 1969, hundreds of officers from the Los Angeles police department, equipped with M16 rifles, military gear, and armored vehicles, raided the Black Panther office at 41st and Central Avenues. The Black Panthers held the officers at bay in a five-hour miniwar before surrendering. (Wally Fong/AP Photo)

FIGURE 28. *(below)* A few of the thousands of supporters who rallied December 11, 1969, in support of the Black Panther Party in Los Angeles express their anger about the police raid several days before. (Wally Fong/AP Photo)

FIGURE 29. Robert Bryan (*middle*), Lloyd Mims (*right*), and another member of the Black Panther Party, handcuffed and chained, await arraignment in Los Angeles after surrendering following the miniwar with police, December 11, 1969. (AP Photo)

FIGURE 30. *(above)* Fred Hampton was the charismatic leader of the Chicago Black Panther Party. (© Bettmann/Corbis/AP Images)

FIGURE 31. *(below)* Chicago police, working with federal agents and a paid infiltrator, shot Fred Hampton in the head as he lay in bed in the early morning of December 4, 1969, killing him and then dragging his corpse into the hallway to support the pretext that he had participated in a shoot-out. Police also killed Black Panther Mark Clark, wounded four others, and arrested all seven survivors on charges of attempted murder. When the federal conspiracy was uncovered and the case made its way to the U.S. Supreme Court, the state dropped the charges against the Panthers and eventually agreed to pay the estates of Hampton and Clark and the survivors of the raid $1.8 million to settle the case. (Chicago Police Department)

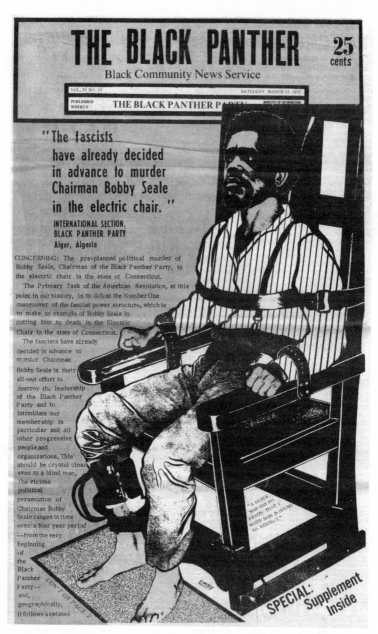

FIGURE 32. This graphic by Emory Douglas on the cover of the *Black Panther* illustrates the Party's view that the government wanted to vilify and kill Chairman Bobby Seale. The government first indicted Seale for causing a riot outside the 1968 Democratic Convention in Chicago, despite his minimal participation in the protests there, and then charged him with ordering the murder of a Black Panther member in New Haven. Courts found Seale not guilty on all charges. (© Dr. Huey P. Newton Foundation)

FIGURE 33. *(above)* A group of Seattle Black Panthers, led by Elmer Dixon, emulate the Black Panther action in Sacramento, standing on the steps of the state capitol in Olympia to protest a bill that would make it a crime to exhibit firearms in Washington, February 29, 1969. Seattle was one of the first cities outside of Oakland to open a Party chapter during the period of the Panthers' greatest repression and greatest growth from mid-1968 through 1970. (Governor Daniel J. Evans Photograph Collection, Washington State Archives)

FIGURE 34. *(below)* Vanetta Molson, head of the Black Panther free breakfast and free clinic programs in Seattle, talks with Aaron Dixon, leader of the city's Black Panther chapter, January 1971. Another Party member answers an incoming phone call. (© Bettmann/Corbis/AP Images)

FIGURE 35. *(above)* Allies rally in New York City's Central Park on April 8, 1969, to protest the repression of the Black Panther Party. (© J P Laffont / Sygma / Corbis)

FIGURE 36. *(below)* After the police shooting of a black woman sparked an urban rebellion in Lima, Ohio, on August 6, 1970, police and National Guardsmen armed with military equipment raided the office of the National Committee to Combat Fascism there. The Black Panther Party began opening committee offices in the summer of 1969, allowing nonblacks to join, whereas regular Black Panther Party chapters admitted only black members. (Gene Herrick / AP Photo)

FIGURE 37. Black Panther Party members surrender to Detroit police following an urban rebellion in the city on October 25, 1970, in which four police cars were set on fire, one police officer was killed, and another was wounded. Hundreds of police and two tanks surrounded the Black Panther Party office, and fifteen Black Panther party members—eight women and seven men—held the police at bay for nine hours. (Richard Sheinwald/AP Photo)

FIGURE 38. *(above)* Helmeted police wearing armored vests, carrying automatic rifles and carbines, and driving armored vehicles attempt to evict a group of Black Panthers occupying a unit in the Desire Housing Projects in New Orleans on November 19, 1970. When hundreds of neighbors came to the defense of the Panthers, the police withdrew. (© Bettmann/Corbis/AP Images)

FIGURE 39. *(below)* "Big Man" Elbert Howard *(speaking)*, deputy minister of defense, and Audrea Jones *(in white hat)*, leader of the Boston chapter of the Party, hold a press conference in front of the Black Panther Party office in Philadelphia in September 1970 during a national Party convention. (Stephen Shames/Polaris Images)

FIGURE 40. Black Panther Party members congregate in front of the Party's Community Information Center in Washington, DC, 1970. The banner over the window reads "Free Clothing; Free Bobby; Free Huey." The Black Panther standing on the steps in the black dress is Maria Edwards. (David Fenton/Getty Images)

FIGURE 41. Omaha Black Panther Party members *(left to right)* Robert Cecil, Robert Griffo, Frank Peate, Gary House, and William Peak leave the Omaha Central Police Station June 27, 1969, just after their release from questioning. (AP Photo)

FIGURE 42. *(above)* A speaker at a Black Panther Party rally in Philadelphia on September 6, 1970, lights up the crowd with the chant "Power to the People!" (© Bettmann/Corbis/AP Images)

FIGURE 43. *(below)* Black Panther minister of education George Murray started the student mobilization to demand black studies curricula and increased enrollment at San Francisco State College in the fall of 1968. The Third World Strike there drew broad participation of Latino, Asian American, and white students. Boldly confronting Nixon and Reagan's Law and Order politics, the strike made regular university operations impossible through much of the academic year and eventually led the administration to institute black and ethnic studies programs, inspiring similar mobilizations around the country. (Stephen Shames/Polaris Images)

FIGURE 44. Asian American and Latino activists rally in support of the Black Panther Party on the steps of the Alameda County courthouse in Oakland, where Huey Newton was incarcerated, 1969. The Black Panther Party saw the Black Liberation Struggle as part of the global struggle against oppression and drew strong allied support from many nonblacks. (© Roz Payne)

FIGURE 45. Members of the Puerto Rican Young Lords Organization are led out of an East Harlem church in New York on January 7, 1970, by members of the sheriff's office. More than one hundred policemen sealed off the area around the church in their effort to end the sit-in that began December 28. The Young Lords sought to use the church space in the morning to conduct their Free Breakfast for Children Program and were granted space by other churches in the neighborhood following the sit-in. (AP Photo)

FIGURE 46. *(above)* A group of feminists march in support of the Black Panther Party in New Haven, November 1969. The Black Panther Party embraced the ideals of gender equality and gay liberation and sought to forge alliances with women's and gay rights organizations. (David Fenton/Getty Images)

FIGURE 47. *(below)* Black Panther chief of staff David Hilliard speaks at Yale University on May 1, 1970. Tens of thousands of supporters mobilized in New Haven that day in advance of the trials of Bobby Seale and Ericka Huggins. Many believed that the government fabricated charges against the Panther leaders to repress the Party. Hilliard is accompanied by Elbert Howard *(in beret)* and New Left allies, including *(on left)* Tom Hayden and David Dellinger and *(to right of Howard)* Lee Weiner, Rennie Davis, and Abbie Hoffman. To avoid conflict with the Panthers, Yale president Kingman Brewster questioned the fairness of the judicial system, drawing outrage from President Nixon. The protest helped spark a nationwide wave of student protests in May 1970 and mobilized more than four million students, shutting down many campuses for the remainder of the year. (Fred W. McDarrah/Getty Images)

FIGURE 48. *(above)* Hundreds of people rally in Stockholm, Sweden, on September 21, 1969, in solidarity with the Black Panther Party. Portraying their struggle as part of a global revolution against imperialism, the Black Panthers generated strong support and powerful allies throughout the world. (© Dr. Huey P. Newton Foundation)

FIGURE 49. *(below)* Eldridge Cleaver, Black Panther minister of information, meets with representatives of the National Liberation Front for South Vietnam and a translator in the Vietnamese embassy in Algiers. A photograph of NLF Chairman Nguyễn Hữu Thọ is prominently displayed. Algeria hosted diplomatic exchanges with revolutionary independence movements and supportive governments throughout Africa and the world in the late 1960s and early 1970s. (H. K. Yuen Collection)

FIGURE 50. Huey Newton is welcomed as an honored guest by Zhou Enlai, premier of China, in late September 1971. On October 1, tens of thousands of Chinese gathered in Tiananmen Square, waving red flags and applauding the Panthers. Revolutionary theater groups, folk dancers, acrobats, and the revolutionary ballet performed. Huge red banners declared, "Peoples of the World, Unite to Destroy the American Aggressors and Their Lackeys." (© Dr. Huey P. Newton Foundation)

PART FIVE

Concessions and Unraveling

The Black Panther Party, as a national organization, is near disintegration. . . . The committee hearings document the steady decline in [party membership] during the last year. Furthermore, the feud between Eldridge Cleaver and Huey Newton threatens the start of a time of violence and terror within what remains of the Panther Party. Probably only remnants of the party will remain alive here and there to bedevil the police and enchant a few of the young, but its day as a national influence and influence in the black community seems over. It is hard to believe that only a little over a year ago the Panthers . . . ranked as the most celebrated ghetto militants. They fascinated the left, inflamed the police, terrified much of America, and had an extraordinary effect on the black community. Even moderate blacks, who disagreed with their violent tactics, felt that the Panthers served a purpose in focusing attention on ghetto problems and argued that they gave a sense of pride to the black community. . . . Liberals and idealists who once sympathized with the Panthers have . . . withdrawn their support.

—House Committee on Internal Security, August 1971

15

Rupture

On November 15, 1969, Black Panther chief of staff David Hilliard took the stage at Golden Gate Park in San Francisco at the West Coast Mobilization against the Vietnam War. As the senior Panther leader not in prison or exile, Hilliard was newly in charge of the national Party, having taken over when Bobby Seale was arrested in August. In the audience, more than one hundred thousand protestors rallied for peace—the largest protest ever held on the West Coast to date. Simultaneously, two hundred fifty thousand protestors gathered at the Washington Monument, which according to the *New York Times* was larger than any previous protest held in the U.S. capital—including the 1963 March on Washington for Jobs and Freedom. The crowds included plenty of the young radicals who had mobilized draft resistance and embraced anti-imperialism and revolution. But unlike the smaller and more radical antiwar actions of previous years, these crowds also included a large portion of moderates—waving American flags and politely expressing their desire for peace. A variety of Democratic elected officials participated in that day's mobilizations, including Senators Eugene McCarthy and George McGovern and San Francisco mayor Joseph Alioto.[1]

When Hilliard's time came to speak, he told his listeners that their American flags were symbols of fascism. Feeling out of his element, angry and defiant, he shouted, "We say down with the American fascist society! Later for Richard Milhous Nixon, the motherfucker." A segment of the audience booed, and Hilliard pushed further: "We will kill Richard Nixon. . . . We will kill any motherfucker that stands in the way of our freedom!" Much of the crowd reacted with chants of "Peace! Peace! Peace!" and Hilliard was eventually chanted and booed off stage, an experience that would undoubtedly shape his concerns as a Party leader in the months to follow.[2]

Underneath Hilliard's rough handling of the crowd that day lay a deeper contradiction that would eventually destroy the Black Panther Party. The Party's revolutionary politics of armed self-defense against the state had thrust it onto a national stage and won it significant political influence. But by late 1969, and increasingly into the 1970s, concessions by the political establishment to key constituencies eroded the bases of allied support for the Black Panthers' politics.

PURGES

Maintaining discipline and protecting the Party's reputation had always been a challenge. In the middle of the day on November 19, 1968, while using a Black Panther newspaper delivery truck clearly marked with large Black Panther logos painted on each side, William Lee Brent held up a gas station attendant in San Francisco at gunpoint, stealing eighty dollars. Seven other Black Panthers were in the vehicle at the time, but Brent acted alone. When police pulled over the vehicle, Brent jumped out and shot at the officers, injuring three.[3]

In noninsurgent organizations, established laws and customs are assumed and largely respected. Maintaining organizational coherence may be challenging, but transgressions of law and custom are generally outside of organizational responsibility. Within insurgent organizations like the Black Panther Party, law and custom are viewed as oppressive and illegitimate. Insurgents view their movement as above the law and custom, the embodiment of a greater morality. As a result, defining acceptable types of transgression of law and custom, and maintaining discipline within these constraints, often poses a serious challenge for insurgent organizations like the Black Panther Party. What sorts of violation of law and custom are consistent with the vision and aims of the insurgency? When William Lee Brent held up the gas station and shot three police, he was clearly breaking the law. But was he acting as a revolutionary or as a renegade from the revolution?

From early in the Party's history, the organization had tangled with these questions, issuing specific rules for member conduct that would serve the Panthers' political interests and threatening to expel anyone who defied these rules. Early in 1968, in response to politically embarrassing police raids of Black Panther homes without legal warrants, Newton issued Executive Order No. 3 mandating that members defend their homes against unlawful raids and that any member who fails to do so "be expelled from the Party for Life."[4]

By the fall of 1968, as the Party became a national organization, it had to manage the political ramifications of actions taken by loosely organized affiliates across the country. The Central Committee in Oakland codified ten Rules of the Black Panther Party and began publishing them in each issue of the *Black Panther*. These rules established basic disciplinary expectations, warning especially against haphazard violence that might be destabilizing or politically embarrassing. They prohibited the use of narcotics, alcohol, or marijuana while conducting Party activities or bearing arms. The Party insisted that Panthers use weapons only against "the enemy" and prohibited theft from other "Black people." But they permitted disciplined revolutionary violence and specifically allowed participation in the underground insurrectionary "Black Liberation Army."[5]

Brent's robbery attempt occurred about a month after the Central Committee first published these rules. Not only did he act without the blessing of Party leaders, but the robbery and shooting of police was also politically embarrassing to the Party because it appeared as if the Party was orchestrating apolitical crime—and executing it poorly. The Central Committee called a press conference to condemn Brent and purge him from the Party: "William Brent, who allegedly pulled an $80.00 holdup in our newspaper distribution truck, is considered to be either a provocateur agent or an insane man." The Central Committee argued more generally, "The Black Panther Party doesn't advocate roving gangs of bandits robbing service stations and taverns. Any member who violates the rules of the Black Panther Party is subject to summary expulsion."[6]

At the same time, the Central Committee expanded the Rules of the Black Panther Party and published the new set of twenty-six rules in the *Black Panther* on January 4, 1969. Most of the new rules emphasized organizational accountability, especially programmatic, ideological, and financial accountability to the Central Committee: "All chapters must adhere to the policy and the ideology laid down by the Central Committee of the Black Panther Party." They stipulated that "all Finance officers will operate under the jurisdiction of the Ministry of Finance." To keep abreast of local activities, the committee also mandated that "all chapters must submit weekly reports in writing to National Headquarters."[7]

In January 1969, to manage the rapid growth of the Party and constrain impolitic actions of the new members, the Central Committee froze membership. On January 12, Bobby Seale told the press, "We now have 45 [chapters]. . . . We aren't taking in any new members for the next three to six months. . . . We are turning inward to tighten security, [to] get rid of agents and provocateurs and to promote political education among those who have joined the Panthers but still don't understand what we're all about."[8]

The Black Panther Party derived its power largely from the insurgent threat it posed to the established order—its ability to attract members who were prepared to physically challenge the authority of the state. But this power also depended on the capacity to organize and discipline these members. When Panthers defied the authority of the Party, acted against its ideological position, or engaged in apolitical criminal activity, their actions undermined the Party, not least in the eyes of potential allies. The Panthers could not raise funds, garner legal aid, mobilize political support, or even sell newspapers to many of their allies if they were perceived as criminals, separatists, or aggressive and undisciplined incompetents. The survival of the Party depended on its political coherence and organizational discipline.

As the Party grew nationally and increasingly came into conflict with the state in 1969, maintaining discipline and a coherent political image became more challenging. The tension between the anti-authoritarianism of members in disparate chapters and the need for the Party to advance a coherent political vision grew. One of the principal tools for maintaining discipline—both of individual members and of local chapters expected to conform to directives from the Central Committee—was the threat of expulsion.

By the spring of 1969, the individual most responsible for tending to the political image of the Party was David Hilliard. With Huey Newton in jail, Eldridge Cleaver in exile, and Bobby Seale in high demand as a public speaker, Hilliard managed the Party's day-to-day operations. His responsibilities only increased when Seale was incarcerated in August. Hilliard personally carried much of the burden of maintaining Party discipline.

In an interview about the New York 21 in April 1969, Hilliard sought to protect the image of the New York chapter and the Party by challenging the notion that New York Panthers had planned to blow up department stores: "It is very absurd to think of an organization with the magnitude of the Black Panther Party, with some 40 chapters at this point, to risk the destruction of one of our most revolutionary chapters, one of our better organized chapters, by going around talking about blowing up department stores. It is something that our Central Committee does not endorse. It is just another lie."[9]

Hilliard explained the importance of the purge for maintaining Party discipline: "We relate to what Lenin said, 'that a party that purges itself grows to become stronger.' The purging is very good. You recognize that there is a diffusion within the rank and file of the party, within the internal structure of the party. So the very fact that you purge strengthens the party. . . . You will become stronger, more of a fortress. . . . Our doors are not open to anyone that decides that they want to join the party."[10] Later that year, in an interview from exile, Eldridge Cleaver echoed those ideas, explaining the need for purges:

> One thing that's important, a lot of people don't understand why a lot of people were purged from the Party. During the time when Huey Newton was going to trial . . . because of the necessity of mobilizing as many people as possible . . . we started just pulling people in. . . . In order to maximize the number of people we pulled in, we did not argue with people if they put on a black leather jacket or black berets, or said that they were Panthers. They just walked in and said they support Huey Newton and they wanted to join our organization. We didn't have time to conduct our political education classes. . . . They proved to be very undisciplined . . . so we just came down hard.[11]

As the Party continued to expand in 1969 and 1970, so did conflicts between the actions of members in local chapters across the country and the political identity of the Party—carefully groomed by the Central Committee. When members violated discipline, the Party leadership often expelled them and published these expulsions in the *Black Panther*. A sampling of a few of these purges provides a sense of the ongoing efforts of the national Party to restrain undisciplined, embarrassing, and "counterrevolutionary" actions by members in local chapters around the country:

- In February 1969, the Party published a statement by John Huggins after his death in which he declared, "The Black Panther Party, So. California chapter, in compliance with the directive of the Central Committee of the Black Panther, has moved to purge this chapter's ranks of provocateur agents, kooks, and avaricious fools."[12]

- In March, the Party expelled thirty-eight members of the east Oakland chapter, listing each by name. The Party purged twenty-six members of the Vallejo chapter, listing them by name and charging them with being "Renegade, Counter-Revolutionaries, and Traitors."[13]
- In April, shortly before the Rackley murder, the Party expelled a Connecticut Panther on suspicion of being a provocateur.[14]
- In May, the Party expelled a Chicago member for speaking in the name of the Party without authorization.[15]
- In June, the Party expelled two members for cooperating with a Senate investigation of the Panthers, and it purged three members of the Harlem branch.[16]
- In July, the Party purged Chico Neblett, a national field marshal of the Party, and sixteen other members of the Boston chapter. The Party gave the following rationale: "A bunch of cultural nationalist fools led by Chico Neblett attempted to undermine the people's revolution. These pea-brained counter-revolutionaries tried to go against the teachings of the Minister of Defense and take over the Boston Branch of the Black Panther Party. They failed in their attempt and were purged from the party. Chico joined the party with the other boot-licker Stokely Carmichael . . . talking about some madness he called Pan-Africanism. . . . By going against the teachings of Huey P. Newton, Chico has said 'fuck the people,' fuck the Party, and the complete and total liberation of blacks here in fascist America."[17]
- In August, the Party expelled a Denver Panther for threatening other Party members.[18]
- In the following months, the Party expelled three more members from east Oakland "because of their individualistic views and aversion to discipline." The Party also expelled a member from Chicago because he "refused to relate to organizational discipline," and ejected two members of the Harlem branch for "embezzling," and "showing a disregard for the principles which guide our party."[19]

CONCESSIONS

The resilience of the Black Panthers' politics depended heavily on support from three broad constituencies: blacks, opponents of the Vietnam War, and revolutionary governments internationally. Without the support of these allies, the Black Panther Party could not withstand repressive actions against them by the state. But beginning in 1969, and steadily increasing through 1970, political transformations undercut the self-interests that motivated these constituencies to support the Panthers' politics. As mainstream Democratic leaders opposed the war and Nixon scaled back the military draft, blacks won broader social access and political representation, and revolutionary governments entered diplomatic relations with the United States, the Panthers had greater difficulty sustaining allied support.

First, major concessions by the political establishment and the Nixon administration on the Vietnam War eroded the basis of war opponents' support for the Panthers politics. At the disastrous Chicago convention in August 1968, the Democratic Party leadership had pushed through a prowar candidate and prowar platform against the will of the Democratic Party base and lost the presidency as a result. But since then, the Democratic Party leadership had increasingly called for an end to the Vietnam War. In a party caucus organized by Democratic national chairman Fred Harris on September 26, 1969, about a dozen U.S. senators and a dozen U.S. representatives mapped out a strategy to "force a confrontation with the [Nixon] Administration that could lead to the withdrawal of all American troops from Vietnam." The caucus decided to push for a congressional resolution endorsing the nationwide antiwar "moratorium" protests organized for October 15 and considered attempting to prevent the U.S. Senate from meeting on that day as a gesture of solidarity with the protestors.[20] On October 6, in the buildup to the October 15 protests, a bipartisan committee unveiled a resolution cosponsored by 108 U.S. congressmen, about one-quarter of the House of Representatives, calling for withdrawal of troops from Vietnam.[21] On October 9, seventeen U.S. senators and 47 U.S. representatives sent an open letter to the Vietnam Moratorium Committee endorsing the upcoming national antiwar protest.[22]

Richard Nixon responded dramatically to the growing antiwar consensus. Elected president in 1968 on a Law and Order platform, he promised both to quell the antiwar rebellions in the streets and to quickly end the war in Vietnam and bring the troops home. In office, he promised "Vietnamization" of the war, shifting responsibility for the war to U.S. allies in Vietnam and allowing gradual withdrawal of U.S. troops. Even as Nixon increased repression of domestic activists, he made good on this promise to de-escalate. When he took office in January 1969, U.S. troop levels were at their peak, with over 540,000 military personnel in Vietnam. In the first year of his presidency, 12,214 U.S. soldiers were killed there. But by 1970, there were about 475,000 U.S. troops in Vietnam, and 4,221 U.S. soldiers were killed that year, about a third the number killed the previous year. By the end of 1971, troop levels had dipped below 160,000, with 1,381 U.S. troops killed, about one-ninth the number in 1969.[23]

Perhaps even more important, Nixon sharply reduced the military draft that had motivated many young people to embrace revolutionary anti-imperialism. Vietnam War draft inductions peaked in the late 1960s, with more than 225,000 soldiers inducted every year from 1965 through 1969. The Nixon administration inducted fewer than 165,000 new soldiers in 1970 and fewer than 95,000 new soldiers in 1971. By then, the majority of Americans embraced arguments against the war. Yet as long as Nixon followed through on his de-escalation of the war, people had less reason to embrace the anti-imperialist politics that had generated the antiwar movement—contributing to the moderation of the antiwar movement even as it grew.[24] Once it appeared the war would be ended through institutionalized political means, those principally committed to ending the draft and war no longer shared a personal stake in radically transforming political institutions. Many now increasingly saw the Panthers' call for revolution as unnecessary.

From 1969 onward, increasing electoral representation as well as affirmative action programs and growing access to government employment and elite education also weakened the basis of support for the Panthers' revolutionary politics among blacks. From the end of Reconstruction (1877) until 1969, no more than six black people had held a seat in the U.S. House of Representatives at once. But just two years later, black representation more than doubled, with thirteen black people holding seats in the U.S. House of Representatives by 1971. The number continued to grow throughout the decade, reaching eighteen seats in 1981 and more than forty seats today.[25] Following the disaster at the 1968 Democratic Party convention in Chicago, the Democratic Party reached out to black electoral activists and reformed the nomination process with the McGovern-Fraser Commission. Black representation among party delegates more than doubled by 1972, to about 15 percent.[26] Black electoral representation generally ballooned in the early 1970s. Whereas in March 1969, 1,125 black people held political offices across the United States, by May 1975, the number had more than tripled to 3,499. This figure included 281 black officeholders in state legislative or executive offices, 135 mayors, 305 county executives, 387 judges and elected law enforcement officers, 939 elected board of education members, and 1,438 people holding other elected positions in municipal government.[27] During this period, a variety of radical black organizations decided to work toward a unified black electoral program that would cross the political spectrum. This notion was promoted in the 1972 National Black Political Convention in Gary—what political scientist

Cedric Johnson called a "shotgun wedding of the radical aspirations of Black Power and conventional modes of politics." While the programmatic statements of the convention contained radical rhetoric, the principal political outcome was to help establish moderate black "politicos . . . as the chief race brokers in the post-segregation context."[28]

While the liberal establishment sought to redress black radicalism through social spending by extending Johnson's Great Society programs and facilitating the expansion of black electoral representation, President Nixon intensified the government's repression of black radicals. But even the right-wing Republican president sought to appeal to moderate blacks, bringing more into the middle class by expanding both civil service opportunities and official affirmative action outreach. Nixon had long advocated jobs programs as a way to redress black radicalism. In the summer of 1967, following the massive rebellions in Newark and Detroit, Nixon took the position that "jobs is the gut issue" in racial unrest.[29] In 1969, his first year in office, Nixon pushed through the first federal affirmative action policy, the "Philadelphia Plan," which established explicit, government-determined quotas for hiring blacks and other minorities on federally funded construction projects.[30]

Also during this period, many top predominantly white colleges and universities expanded their enrollment of blacks and other underrepresented students of color. These institutions also developed black studies programs in the wake of campus protests. Scholars have documented the crucial role of Black Panther Party activists at San Francisco State College in fomenting the national movement. They have also pointed to the important role of wealthy philanthropists—especially the Ford Foundation—in shaping black studies programs as a means of social control. While fewer than 5 percent of research universities offered black studies programs in 1967, by 1971, more than 35 percent did.[31]

Ballooning electoral representation, government hiring, affirmative action, and reform of college and university access and curricula granted blacks greater institutional channels for participating in American society and politics. This increasing access to mainstream institutions undercut the basis for blacks' support of the Panthers' politics.

At the same time that the domestic climate was shifting, the international basis of support for the Black Panther Party began to contract as the United States opened diplomatic relations with revolutionary governments around the world. Chinese state sponsorship of a Black Panther delegation in 1970 and then the high state honors shown Huey Newton during his visit in 1971 indicated the extent of global support for the Party. Yet underneath the surface symbolism, the 1971 visit also indicated that the foundations of global support for the Panthers' revolutionary politics were shaky at best. Earlier that spring, China had welcomed the professional U.S. table tennis team, giving rise to the popular term "ping-pong diplomacy." Newton's state-sponsored visit to China also followed the visit of Henry Kissinger and came amid planning for a visit by President Nixon himself. During an event honoring Newton and the Panthers, Premier Zhou Enlai revealed the importance of ping-pong diplomacy to the Chinese government by attributing it to Mao Zedong himself—chairman of the Chinese Communist Party and the top Chinese political leader. Zhou said China was ready to negotiate with the United States or to fight it, as the case may be.[32] Apparently Chinese sponsorship of the Panthers was part of a symbolic politics intended to send Zhou's message to the United States. As Sino-U.S. relations improved in the 1970s, China's support for the Panthers evaporated.

Algerian support for the Panthers also weakened as relations with the United States improved. The U.S. government had recognized Algerian independence in 1962 and established diplomatic relations. But Algeria severed diplomatic relations in 1967 following the Arab-Israeli War. While challenging U.S. geopolitical hegemony, Algeria became an important locus of support for independence movements throughout Africa and the world in the late 1960s. But economic relations with the United States continued and the U.S. government maintained an Interests Section through the Swiss embassy in Algiers. When Eldridge and Kathleen Cleaver arrived in Algeria in 1969, American oil companies and personnel were already heavily involved in the Algerian oil industry. The Panthers received support from the Algerian government but in the shifting geopolitical context, their status was never secure. Even before the Algerian government granted the Panthers formal diplomatic status and an embassy in Algiers, an Algerian official told the Cleavers that Algeria would eventually resume diplomatic relations with the United States. In the 1970s, Algerian relations with the United States improved, and support for the Panthers deteriorated. In 1972, Algeria terminated the Panthers' diplomatic status and expelled them from the country. So while the Panthers enjoyed strong support from Algeria as a foreign liberation movement from 1969 until 1971, the shifting geopolitical situation soon dissolved this relationship.[33]

Cuban support for the Black Panthers also shifted during the late 1960s. When Eldridge Cleaver fled to Cuba as a political exile in late

1968, Cuba not only provided safe passage and security but promised to create a military training facility for the Party on an abandoned farm outside Havana. This promise was consistent with the more active role Cuba had played in supporting the Black Liberation Struggle in the United States in the early 1960s, when it sponsored the broadcast of Robert Williams's insurrectionary radio program "Radio Free Dixie," as well as publication of his newspaper, the *Crusader,* and his book *Negroes with Guns.* But, as the tide of revolution shifted globally toward the end of the decade, security concerns took on higher priority in Cuban policy. Eager to avoid provoking retaliation from the United States, Cuba distanced itself from the Black Liberation Struggle, continuing to allow exiles but refraining from active support of black insurrection. The government never opened a military training ground for the Panthers, instead placing constraints on the political activities of Panther exiles.[34]

As the United States scaled back the war in Vietnam; reduced the military draft; improved political, educational, and employment access for blacks; and improved relations with former revolutionary governments around the world, the Black Panthers had difficulty maintaining support for politics involving armed confrontation with the state.

More comfortable and secure with the ability of mainstream political institutions to redress their concerns—especially the draft—liberals went on the attack, challenging the revolutionary politics of the Black Panther Party. On January 14, 1970, the Party held a fund-raiser at the Park Avenue duplex of Leonard Bernstein, the conductor laureate of the New York Philharmonic. The Panther delegation was led by Field Marshal Don Cox and included members of the New York Panthers, wives of the New York 21, and Party lawyers. About ninety members of New York's high society attended, including Cynthia Phipps, Otto Preminger, Mrs. August Heckscher, and of course Felicia and Leonard Bernstein. The guests discussed Panther ideology, and the Panthers collected $10,000 in donations. The next day, the *New York Times* published a devastating account of the event by women's-page editor Charlotte Curtis in which she ridiculed Bernstein for hosting the meeting.[35] Tom Wolfe took up the parody in a major feature—almost twenty-five thousand words long—published in *New York* magazine. In his semifictional account, "Radical Chic," Wolfe depoliticized the Party's support, portraying the Black Panthers as hustlers cashing in on their street credentials by catering to the exotic tastes of the super-aesthetic elite. In November, Wolfe republished the essay in book form, adding the related essay "Mau-Mauing the Flak Catchers."[36]

The following February, the *New Yorker* published a long article by Edward Jay Epstein questioning the veracity of some of the Panthers' claims of repression by police, specifically challenging the idea that Panther deaths "represent a pattern of systematic destruction." Reviewing the available evidence about violent confrontations in which Panthers had been killed, Epstein wrote, "The idea that the police have declared a sort of open season on the Black Panthers is based principally, as far as I can determine, on the assumption that all the Panther deaths . . . occurred under circumstances that were similar to the Hampton-Clark raid. This is an assumption that proves, on examination, to be false."[37] At that time, documentation of the FBI's role in the national repression of the Black Panther Party, particularly its COINTELPRO activities, was unavailable, so Epstein's detailed review of the circumstantial evidence and conclusion that there was no coordinated repression of the Party seemed convincing. Epstein's argument was widely quoted in the news media and did a lot to undermine allied support for the Black Panthers.[38] David Frost invited Panther lawyer Charles Garry to debate Edward Epstein on his show, where Frost and Epstein teamed up against Garry to attack his claims of coordinated repression of the Panthers.[39]

The liberal establishment avoided such attacks on the Panthers when the Party was a small local organization. And such jabs would have found less resonance in 1968 and 1969 as black rebellions swept U.S. cities and political leaders offered no credible redress to the draft. But liberal readers of the *New Yorker* and *New York* magazine were much more apt to embrace ridicule of the Black Panthers' anti-imperialism once their children were not likely to be drafted and killed in Vietnam.

Ironically, even as attacks on the Panthers by the liberal establishment gathered steam, the Party peaked both in notoriety and in the level of financial support it garnered from donors.[40] This created a political pressure cooker. At the same time that the Party was becoming increasingly dependent on allies, broad support for its revolutionary politics was becoming harder to maintain. The Party faced steadily increasing pressure from potential supporters to defend its image.

CONTRADICTIONS

The contradictory pressures of retaining the support of ever more complacent allies, on the one hand, and continuing the politics of armed self-defense against the police, on the other, came to a head when Huey Newton was set free. On August 5, 1970, Newton was released from prison on a technicality. By that time, the vast majority of current members of the Black Panthers had joined the Party while Newton was in prison, and almost all had worked for his release. The release was a hard-won victory, and ten thousand people gathered outside the Alameda County jail to celebrate. Surrounded by a sea of supporters, Newton climbed atop the Volkswagen of his lawyer Alex Hoffman—a makeshift stage in the hot sun. David Hilliard and Geronimo Pratt, the two most influential Panthers not in prison or exile at that time, flanked Huey. Chief of Staff Hilliard, wearing a long black trench coat and black sunglasses, stood behind Newton with outstretched arms and proudly announced Newton's freedom to the crowd. Geronimo Pratt did not have the formal rank that Hilliard did but was widely recognized and respected. He was the deputy minister of defense and the leader of the Los Angeles chapter that had successfully withstood the onslaught of the police and federal agents eight months earlier. Wearing a stylish brimmed hat, dark jacket, and black sunglasses, he surveyed the crowd for any threats to Newton's safety. In the heat of the sun and the enthusiasm of the crowd, Newton began to sweat. In a symbolic gesture, signifying his liberation won by the people, Huey stripped off his shirt, displaying his prison-buffed physique to awe-struck supporters.[41]

Many Panthers hoped that Huey would resolve the challenges the Party faced and lead them successfully to revolution. But his release had the opposite effect, exacerbating the tensions within the Party. Some rank-and-file Panthers took Huey's long-awaited release as a prelude to victory and a license to violence, and their aggressive militarism became harder to contain.[42] Organizationally, the Party had grown exponentially in Newton's name but was actually under the direction of other leaders. His release forced a reconfiguration of power in the Party.

Paradoxically, Newton's release also made it harder for the Party to maintain support from more moderate allies. It sent a strong message to many moderates that—contrary to Kingman Brewster's famous statement three months earlier—a black revolutionary *could* receive a fair trial in the United States. The radical Left saw revolutionary progress in winning Huey's freedom, but many moderate allies saw less cause for revolution.

When Newton first got out of prison, he presented a highly militarized and insurrectionary vision for the Party. In an interview about a week after his release, he stated,

> Our program is armed struggle. We have hooked up with the people who are rising up all over the world with arms, because we feel that only with the power of the gun will the bourgeoisie be destroyed and the world transformed. . . . I think that [the most important inspiration for the Black Panthers is] not only Fidel and Che, Ho Chi Minh and Mao and Kim Il Sung, but also all the guerilla bands that have been operating in Mozambique and Angola, and the Palestinian guerillas who are fighting for a socialist world. . . . The guerillas who are operating in South Africa and numerous other countries all have had great influence. We study and we follow their example. We are very interested in the strategy that's being used [by Carlos Marighella] in Brazil, which is an urban area, and we plan to draw on that.[43]

However romantic some may have found the analogy between the Black Panther Party and guerilla groups abroad, or the Party's advocacy of guerilla-type actions, the Party never directly organized guerilla warfare. Unlike the situation in Vietnam or Cuba, guerilla warfare was never politically practical in the United States. In the United States, the state capacity for violent repression was enormous, many constituencies had significant recourse through institutionalized politics and civil society, and only a very small portion of the populace supported guerilla warfare tactics. Within three months of his release, Newton had moderated his position considerably to fit the responsibilities of managing the national Panther organization and to maintain support from allies. In a November 18, 1970, speech at Boston College, Newton downplayed armed struggle and emphasized the role of the Party in providing community social service programs, which he now called "survival programs":

> Tonight, I would like to outline for you the Black Panther Party's program and also explain how we arrived at our ideological position and why we feel it necessary to institute a Ten Point Program. A Ten Point Program is not revolutionary in itself, nor is it reformist. It's a *survival program*. We feel that we, the people are threatened with genocide because racism and fascism is rampant. . . . We intend to change all of that. In order to change it, there must be a total transformation. But until such time that we can achieve that total transformation, we must exist. In order to exist, we must survive, so, therefore, we need a survival kit. The Ten Point Program is a survival kit, brothers and sisters. In other words, it is necessary for our children to grow up healthy, with minds that can be functional and cre-

ative. They cannot do this if they do not get the correct nutrition. That is why we have a breakfast program for children. We also have community health programs. We have a bussing program. . . . This too is a survival program.[44]

In the same speech, Newton also heralded the idea of "revolutionary suicide." Unlike guerilla warfare, which is an offensive strategy, the idea was basically defensive:

> We say that if we must die, then we will die the death of the *revolutionary suicide*. The revolutionary suicide that says that if I am put down, if I am driven out, I refuse to be swept out with a broom. I would much rather be driven out with a stick, because with the broom, when I am driven out, it will humiliate me and I will lose my self-respect. But if I am driven out with the stick, then at least I can remain with the dignity of a man and die the death of a man, rather than die the death of a dog. Of course, our real desire is to live, but we will not be cowed, we will not be intimidated.[45]

As Newton settled into leadership of the national Black Panther organization in late 1970, tensions between the Central Committee and some of the local chapters increased. Relations were especially charged between the New York chapter, one of the largest and best organized, and the national leadership. As mobilization for the New York Panther 21 became one of the Party's highest-profile campaigns, financial and ideological tensions widened this growing gulf.

The financial conflict centered around who should control the money raised for the Panthers in New York. The lead East Coast fund-raiser was a white Jewish New Left ally, Martin Kenner. Kenner became director of the Black Panther Defense Committee in mid-1969 and began soliciting funds from progressives, largely to support the legal defense of the New York 21. He organized the famous dinner party at Leonard Bernstein's house and reached out broadly to potential allies on the left. The money just trickled in at first. But with the publicity of the Chicago and New Haven trials, the murder of Fred Hampton and Mark Clark, and the raid on the L.A. office, the money started pouring in. Kenner later recalled, "Fred Hampton was murdered in Chicago. Four days later was the attack, on December 8, of the L.A. Panther[s]. . . . At that point . . . the money started coming in to our offices in unbelievable amounts. We just had some ads in the paper and we got unsolicited, huge amounts of money. Thousands and thousands of dollars. . . . We had people just opening envelopes all day long." In January 1970 alone, at least $100,000 came in small donations.

David Hilliard sent Masai Hewitt and Donald Cox to New York to help raise money. Soon some individuals were making single donations of $100,000 or more.[46]

According to Kenner, while donors contributed the funds because of the notoriety of the Black Panther Party generally, the New York Panthers thought they should be able to control the funds since most of the money was raised in their city:

> There . . . got to be bad blood because the Panther 21 said they felt neglected or something like this, and I just was horrified by this, because I knew how strongly David [Hilliard] had fought for them, and I also knew the origin of where their support came from, which wasn't from their own. Because later on, to jump ahead, it really pissed me off because they said "Hey, all of this was support for us." But I knew if it was the Panther 21 we wouldn't have been able to do anything. . . . If it wasn't for the chaining of Bobby and . . . the notoriety . . . none of these things would have happened. . . . They totally separated themselves, and they refused to acknowledge it.[47]

Further, according to Kenner, "part of this had to do also with the lawyers involved."[48] Some of the lawyers working on the New York 21 case were working in the background on a pro bono basis, while others were getting both pay and media attention. As a result, some of the lawyers who were not getting paid had hard feelings. When the Central Committee used some of the money raised in New York for other purposes, such as bailing out Panthers arrested in Los Angeles, the unpaid New York lawyers asked, "How could you do this?"[49]

On August 18, Geronimo Pratt skipped an appearance in Los Angeles Superior Court on charges of possession of a bomb, and the court issued a bench warrant for his arrest. Facing multiple trials, Geronimo went underground.[50] He later recalled that he had wanted to avoid spending time in court that he could be spending building guerilla cadres in the South and conducting paramilitary training for Panther members so they could better defend themselves.[51] On September 21, the L.A. Superior Court revoked Pratt's bail and issued a further bench warrant for his arrest for failing to appear in court on charges of conspiracy to commit murder in the December 8 shoot-out. The Party posted $30,000 bail, all forfeited when he failed to appear in court.[52]

At first, the Party continued to support Geronimo. In an August 29 article in the *Black Panther,* and again in a statement to the press on September 24, 1970, the Black Panther Party explained that Geronimo had gone underground. The statement explained that police were targeting Geronimo for extreme repression and that he had been unjustly jailed thirty-seven times, as well as beaten and shot at by police numerous times since January 1969, when he was appointed deputy minister of defense and placed in charge of the Southern California chapter of the Party. The Party emphasized Geronimo's illustrious military career—noting the thirteen medals he had received before his honorable discharge—and argued that "due to what the U.S. knew he could do with the very knowledge they had given him, and with his brilliant mind and devotion to his people, he suffered the severest attacks by the local and national police from that time on." Geronimo went underground, the statement said, so that he would be free "to continue his hard work for the people." [53]

But the harmony was not sustainable. Living underground cost money and raised political problems. Going underground was different from going into exile. When Geronimo went underground, he became an outlaw. Hiding out to avoid trial within the United States was a violation of the law, a declaration of war on the legitimacy of the United States within its own territory. This was a very different position from the denunciation of U.S. legitimacy by an exile. Exiles posed no immediate challenge to the law. Going underground also sacrificed the moral high ground of fighting in the courts—an activity that garnered much support from allies. Further, anyone who sheltered Geronimo was also breaking the law.

Moreover, living underground was expensive. Because of Geronimo's stature and support within the Party, he believed that the Party should financially sustain him underground. Huey Newton disagreed. Geronimo's friends recalled, "Newton stated that Geronimo demanded money. This is a half-truth. The leadership of the Panthers had refused to help him in his underground efforts while he and those with him were threatened with survival. . . . The refusal to support Geronimo made it more difficult for him to elude the pigs." [54]

On December 9, 1970, the FBI and local police arrested Geronimo in Dallas, Texas, on the charges stemming from the December 8, 1969, siege. Along with Geronimo, they arrested Panthers Melvin "Cotton" Smith, Ellie Stafford, and Roland Freeman. [55] David Hilliard later recalled, "G.'s underground unit self-destructs. The guys call, complaining they need money, they're bored, they're in trouble. They have stupid shoot-outs, lack any self-discipline, and Geronimo can't control them. We create a telephone tree to avoid speaking to them on the bugged Central HQ lines. They use the wrong numbers anyway, saying adventuristic, incriminating things. Even when we chastise them, they

continue in their unrestrained ways. In early December the police capture Geronimo in Dallas."[56] The underground activities plus the lack
of discipline, possibly instigated by agent provocateurs, threatened to
seriously damage the image of the Party.[57]

Meanwhile, from their refuge in Algeria, members of the International Section of the Party promoted immediate guerilla warfare against
the U.S. government. Eldridge Cleaver and Field Marshal Donald Cox
regularly exhorted young blacks to violence in the pages of the *Black
Panther*. In January 1971, Cox argued, "When a guerilla unit moves
against this oppressive system by executing a pig or by attacking its institutions, by any means—sniping, stabbing, bombing, etc.—in defense
against the 400 years of racist brutality, murder, and exploitation, this
can only be defined correctly as self-defense." He quoted Brazilian guerilla Carlos Marighella: "Today, to be an assailant or terrorist is a quality that ennobles any honorable man because it is an act worthy of a
revolutionary engaged in armed struggle against the shameful military
dictatorship and its monstrosities. . . . GUERILLA UNITS (self-defense
groups) must be formed and blows must be struck against the slavemas-
ter until we have secured our survival as a people."[58]

MUTINY

Over time, as developments outside the Party made it harder to sustain
allied support, the demands upon the national organization to maintain Party discipline increased. A swelling Party budget only exacerbated
these tensions, heightening the need for Party discipline to please increasingly influential donors. Allocation of funding increasingly became a
point of contention within the Party. Local leaders chafed at national
Party discipline and the Party began to unravel. In the first two months
of 1971, three of the most important Panther groups broke with the
national organization.

David Hilliard later recalled tensions during that period between
some Panthers' call for immediate revolutionary war and the limits of
allied support: "I speak to Eldridge every day and am mindful of the
cadre who want to pick up the gun. But the concept of the Party as a
liberation army overthrowing the American government is not realistic.
When we begin our attack who's going to join us? Party comrades will
jump off the moon if Huey tells them to. Our allies won't."[59]

On January 19, 1971, the New York Panther 21 published an open letter to the Weather Underground in the *East Village Other,* not so subtly denouncing their own Black Panther Party national leadership. The Weather Underground was a splinter group that had broken off from the Students for a Democratic Society to engage in bombings and other acts of war. They believed that they would attract a large following and help lead a revolutionary overthrow of the state, but they never attracted more than a handful of members willing to participate in guerilla warfare. Alongside a cartoonish graphic of a souped-up jeep with a semipornographic depiction of a woman blasting a top-mounted machine gun and the words "Instant Proletarian Vengeance" stenciled on the side, the New York Panthers praised the Weather Underground for embracing guerilla warfare and decried their own Party's restraint.

The Panther 21 asserted that the Black Panther Party was not the true revolutionary vanguard in the United States and hailed the Weather Underground as one of, if not "the true vanguard." In line with the vanguardist ideology of the Weather Underground, the Panther 21 argued that it was now time for all-out revolutionary violence that they believed would attract a broad following and eventually topple the capitalist economy and the state:

> The only thing that will deal with reactionary force and violence is revolutionary counter-force and counter-violence. . . . The Amerikkkan machine and its economy must be destroyed—and it can only be done with intelligent political awareness and armed struggle—revolution. . . . as Che stated—"Armed struggle is the only solution for people who fight to free themselves". . . . Revolution is—in the final analysis—ARMED STRUGGLE—revolution is VIOLENCE—revolution is WAR—revolution is BLOODSHED! How long have different successful national liberation fronts fought before they have won large popular support? Che stated—"A revolution is a handful of men and women with no other alternative but death or victory. At moments when death is a concept a thousand times more real and victory a myth that only a revolutionary can dream of." Are you hip to Marighella—Carlos Marighella? . . . "Revolutionary organization usually grows by two important methods: 1) grouping and training of political cadres to hold meetings and discuss documents and programs; 2) revolutionary action—its method is extreme violence and radicalization. We chose the latter because we feel it is the most convincing method and that the former leads—if not combined with the latter—to bourgeois tactics and loses initiative.". . . . The object is to 1) destroy the economy—like bombing sites which will affect the economy the most; 2) rip-off money, weapons, and etc; 3) sniping attacks. Bomb factories, mine factories, gun factories, and bullet factories are needed. Let's talk about "Large scale material damage"—this economy must fall—There is a war on.[60]

The New York Panther 21 also criticized the gradualist approach of the Black Panther Party Central Committee:

> We realize that this will be a protracted struggle—but when does protracted become non-movement—escapism isolation and retrogression?. . . . For instance, take a group, a party and its supporters with a few activists—it can move in a revolutionary manner against the pigs OR it can function— have a newspaper, hold rallies, conventions, congresses, etc.—then rhetoricians rhetoric, functionaries function, printing presses print, delegates travel, international friendships grow, "leaders" become overwhelmed with "work"—then the prospects of armed struggle—real revolution—diminish. It gets lost in the "works"—it comes to be looked upon as adventurism— always premature—it might "sabotage" the legality of the party—(which if it was effective would be illegal anyway)—it might bring down too much repression—meanwhile, the fascists snatch out the activists who are not so noisy—but deemed more dangerous. Does this not sound familiar?[61]

Meanwhile, as the New York Panthers denounced their own Party's gradualism, Geronimo Pratt was still in prison in Dallas fighting his extradition to California. He tried calling Huey Newton and members of the Black Panther Party Central Committee but could not get through.[62] Then, on January 23, four days after the New York Panthers published their open letter, Huey Newton published a letter in the *Black Panther* purging from the Black Panther Party Geronimo Pratt— one of the most famous and well respected Black Panthers—along with his close allies Saundra Lee, Will Stafford, Wilfred "Crutch" Holiday, and George Lloyd. Newton claimed that while trying to survive underground, Geronimo had demanded money from the Party and threatened to kill David Hilliard if the Party did not provide it.[63]

After learning that he had been purged, Geronimo signed the California extradition papers and was sent to face trial in Los Angeles. He desperately tried to reach someone in the Party headquarters to find out what was going on, but he was shut out. But when he spoke to Eldridge Cleaver in Algeria he found a welcome reception. Geronimo told an interviewer later that year, "I tried to contact David, somebody to lend an ear. It was like I was already tried and convicted. When Papa [Eldridge Cleaver] contacted me, it was like a fresh breath of life. Eldridge told me that he knew what was going on, that the brothers were not expelled, that he would talk to Huey."[64]

About two weeks later, on February 8, two of the leading New York Panthers—Dhoruba Bin Wahad (Richard Moore) and Cetawayo Tabor—did not appear for their scheduled court date as part of the

New York 21 trial. In failing to appear, they forfeited $150,000 in bail money raised from Panther supporters. The judge ordered a warrant for their arrest. He also revoked the $200,000 bail of Joan Bird and Afeni Shakur, the only two other New York Panthers who were out free on bail, and returned them to prison.[65]

At the same time, Huey Newton's secretary, Connie Matthews, also disappeared, taking important Party records, including contact information for Black Panther allies in Europe. New York assistant district attorney Phillips, one of the prosecutors in the Panther 21 case, announced in court that Cetawayo Tabor had married Connie Mathews in California several months earlier and that Matthews had Algerian citizenship. He speculated that Matthews had obtained passports for Tabor and Dhoruba and that they had fled with her to Algeria.[66]

Dhoruba Bin Wahad explained his decision to desert the Black Panther Party as a response to the increasing moderation of Newton, Hilliard, and the Central Committee and their efforts to appease wealthy donors. In a public statement in May 1971, Dhoruba wrote,

> We were aware of the Plots emanating from the co-opted Fearful minds of Huey Newton and the Arch Revisionist, David Hilliard. We knew of their desires to destroy, with their fear-oriented plans and bourgeois dreams, the only truly revolutionary organ of social change that Black People possessed [the Black Panther Party]. . . . We therefore took up completely the war against our People's oppressor—to either win or die. . . . It became clear almost a year ago that David Hilliard was destroying the desire in comrades to wage resolute struggle by confining the Party to mass rallies and "fund raising benefits." Of course mass mobilization is important and money is necessary to function, but the effects that these restrictions have upon the mentality of a Brother or Sister is horrifying. . . . Obsession with fund raising leads to dependency upon the very class enemies of our People. . . . These internal contradictions have naturally developed to the Point where those within the Party found themselves in an organization fastly approaching the likes of the N.A.A.C.P.—dedicated to modified slavery instead of putting an end to all forms of slavery.[67]

On February 9, the day after Dhoruba and Tabor failed to appear in court and forfeited their $150,000 bail, the Central Committee expelled most of the New York 21 from the Black Panther Party. In a mimeographed statement signed by Newton and distributed outside the courtroom at 100 Centre Street, the Central Committee called the New York renegades "enemies of the people." The statement charged that by skipping bail, Dhoruba and Tabor "gave the pigs an excuse to throw Joan Bird and Afeni Shakur, four months pregnant, back into maximum security," jeopardized the possibility of bail for their co-defendants, and "propped up the dying case" of the prosecution.[68]

The cover of the February 13, 1971, issue of the *Black Panther,* under the headline "Enemies of the People," featured photographs of Michael Cetawayo Tabor, Connie Matthews Tabor, and Dhoruba Bin Wahad and reproduced the mimeographed statement distributed outside the New York courtroom that expelled most of the New York Panthers from the Party.[69] The statement explained that nine imprisoned New York Panthers had already been expelled for their "Open Letter to the Weathermen" in January but that the leaders had kept the expulsion quiet as an intraparty matter until the trial was over. The disappearance of Tabor and Dhoruba had forced the Party to reveal the split.

This sequence suggests that the Central Committee was concerned about how the Party's allies and supporters, especially funders, would perceive the expulsions. The committee's quick and high-profile expulsion of the underground New York Panthers signaled that the leadership wanted to distance itself from any underground activities Dhoruba and Tabor might undertake and to make clear its disapproval of their forfeit of the bail money that Party donors had provided. The Central Committee still was willing to advocate revolution, but it would also try to further its cause in court—not in immediate armed struggle. And it wanted allies, supporters, and donors to know that.[70]

On February 26, on the Jim Dunbar "A.M. Show" aired live on San Francisco's ABC-TV affiliate, tensions in the Party exploded. From the studio, Huey Newton spoke with Eldridge Cleaver in Algiers via telephone. Cleaver demanded that Newton reinstate the New York 21 and that Newton expel Hilliard from the Party. Newton refused to continue the discussion.[71] After the program, in a private phone call that Cleaver secretly recorded, Newton blasted Cleaver for airing Party business publicly and expelled him and the entire International Section from the Party. He told Cleaver he would have him cut off from the Party's international allies: "I'm going to write the Koreans, the Chinese, and the Algerians and tell them to kick you out of our embassy, and to put you in jail."[72]

FACTIONAL NASTINESS

The factional dispute quickly intensified. Two days after the televised flare-up, Eldridge Cleaver and Donald Cox released videotapes to the U.S. press accusing Hilliard of turning the Panther organization into a

top-heavy and undemocratic bureaucracy that served his personal purposes and of purging those he did not favor. Cox called for the removal
of David and June Hilliard from Party leadership by force: "Conditions
should be created so they can't even walk the streets. . . . They must not
be allowed to go to any office of the Black Panther Party. This machinery that they are now using was built on the blood of our comrades,
like Bobby and Bunchy. . . . And if Huey can't understand this and
relate to this then he's got to go too."[73]

The cover of the March 6, 1971, issue of the *Black Panther* featured an image of Kathleen Cleaver wearing shades and the headline
"Free Kathleen Cleaver and All Political Prisoners." Inside the issue,
an article by Elaine Brown alleged that Eldridge Cleaver was beating
Kathleen, preventing her from leaving Algiers, and not allowing her
to talk with her fellow members of the Central Committee. Brown
claimed that Kathleen was scheduled to speak on behalf of Bobby Seale
on March 5 but Eldridge would not let her come. She also said that
Eldridge had isolated Kathleen in North Korea and confiscated letters she tried to send to Oakland. She asserted that Eldridge was having multiple affairs but that he forbade Kathleen from doing the same.
And she charged that Eldridge murdered Clinton "Rahim" Smith in
Algiers for having an affair with Kathleen. She wrote, "Even though, if
Kathleen is allowed to speak for herself, she will probably support the
ravings of her personal, mad oppressor, we know that to speak otherwise at this time would be a death warrant for her."[74]

Two days later, on Monday March 8, Black Panther Robert Webb
was shot in the head and killed at 125th Street and Seventh Avenue in
New York. In a press conference the following day, Zayd Shakur of
the Cleaver-aligned New York Panthers asserted that Webb was shot
while trying to "confiscate the reactionary rag sheet from two fools."
In other words, Shakur said that Webb was killed when he attempted
to seize copies of the *Black Panther* that described Kathleen Cleaver
as a political prisoner from two Newton allies who were distributing
the newspaper on the street. Shakur also alleged that Webb had been
killed because he had joined the call to dismiss or force the resignation of David Hilliard, and he referred to the Newton faction as "revi-
sionist" or "right wing."[75] In another account of the killing, Shakur
said, "The six or seven mad dog assassins who took the life of our
brother Robert Webb were the first ones to arrive [in New York]."[76]
The Panther Central Committee called this charge that they had sent
someone to Harlem to kill Webb "ridiculous."[77] No one was ever con-

victed of killing Webb.[78] Nevertheless, the killing was widely alleged to be a result of the factional dispute.[79]

Samuel Napier was the national distribution manager for the *Black Panther*. Aligned with the Party's national leadership, he worked out of New York City. On the afternoon of April 17, 1971, assailants shot Napier three times in the back, tied him to a bed in the headquarters of the Oakland-aligned Corona Queens Black Panther chapter, gagged him, shot him three times in the head, and then set the building on fire. Burned beyond recognition, Napier's body was identified through his fingerprints. Following a murder trial and a hung jury, New York Panthers Dhoruba Bin Wahad, Michael Hill, Eddie Jamal Joseph, and Irving Mason pled guilty to a reduced charge of attempted manslaughter.[80]

IDEOLOGICAL SPLIT

Overall, relatively few Black Panther chapters challenged the national Party leadership.[81] Most of the local Panther leadership across the country stuck with the Party. On March 20, 1971, alongside a notice that the International Section had "defected from the Black Panther Party," the *Black Panther* published letters in which crucial national leaders proclaimed their loyalty.[82] One letter was cosigned by Doug Miranda, leader of the New Haven mobilizations; Masai Hewitt, minister of education; "Big Man" Howard, editor of the *Black Panther*; Emory Douglas, minister of culture; and Bobby Rush, leader of the Chicago chapter. They declared their unequivocal support for Huey Newton and claimed that the "defection" of some Panthers actually strengthened the Party: "Corrosive elements of our Party . . . are falling off and purging themselves. Thus, they are cleansing our Party, so that we remain the strong invincible force we always were."[83]

On trial for his life in New Haven, Bobby Seale wrote a letter condemning Cleaver: "The Party accepts constructive criticism. . . . But the divisionary, counter-revolutionary actions and jive tactics of Eldridge Cleaver are doing nothing but aiding the pig power structure in their attempt to put in gas chambers and jails over 130 political prisoners, who are presently, like myself and Ericka, caught up in these jails, and are being railroaded to the gas chamber, where we're fighting for our lives in these trials. . . . There is no split in the Black Panther Party."[84] Another letter, from the San Quentin branch of the Black Panther Party, headed by George Jackson, derided Cleaver and declared strong support for Newton. On August 7, 1970, George Jackson's younger brother Jonathan Jackson, attempting to free George, was killed when he stormed into a court and kidnapped a judge. The support of the San Quentin branch was important for Newton because Eldridge Cleaver had widely heralded Jonathan Jackson as a martyr and lauded his insurrectionary act the previous August as emblematic of the kind of action that was needed. The San Quentin branch's endorsement of Newton did a lot to undermine Cleaver's credibility.[85]

The number of recognized leaders who turned against Huey Newton and the national Party leadership in early 1971 remained small. But with the killings of Robert Webb and Sam Napier, the mutiny became the basis of a catastrophic ideological split. The split brought an end to the politics of the Black Panther Party that had enabled its growth from a local organization in the beginning of 1968 to a considerable national political power by the end of 1970.

For these three years, the Panthers had had a winning recipe. Their politics of armed self-defense had tapped the wells of resistance among black youth, and the national organization had mobilized broad support from a spectrum of black, antiwar, and international allies. This support in turn allowed the Party to flourish in the face of government repression and to sustain its anti-imperialist movement. In comparison, most other Black Power organizations were politically impotent and did not come close to the Panthers in their effectiveness or influence. Some, like Karenga's US organization, remained small, tight-knit organizations, delivered no political consequences, and garnered a limited national following. Others, like the Republic of New Afrika, challenged the state and suffered heavy repression as a result, but—drawing little allied support—were unable to sustain or expand their struggle.

While the Panthers' strategy proved highly effective for three years, it eventually created significant organizational tensions. The Central Committee had an organization to run and a public face to maintain. As a consequence, it focused primarily on maintaining organizational coherence and allied support. Conversely, many members and local chapters participated in the Party because they wanted to challenge the status quo. They wanted to stand up to the police and to the system that oppressed them. But the boundaries between revolutionary action, adventurism, and criminal activity were not always clear. As a result, tensions developed between the necessarily independent activities of the local chapters, some of which bordered on open insurrection, and the Central Committee's efforts to maintain allied support.

Between 1968 through 1970, three factors exacerbated these tensions. First, counterintelligence activities by the federal government worked to vilify the Party. The government recognized that raids and other forms of direct repression of the Panthers tended to legitimize their claims and increase allied support for the Party. Thus, it sought to discredit the Party by sowing internal conflict through agent provocateurs who fostered unpalatable and impolitic violence. The FBI masterminded campaigns to destroy the reputations of Black Panther leaders, such as the effort to pin the murder of Alex Rackley on Bobby Seale.

Second, the success of the Party created a conflict between promoting insurrection and maintaining the Party's image. For example, Huey Newton's release from prison suggested to many potential allies that the Panthers could get justice in court but suggested to many rank-and-file members that they could get justice through armed resistance to police. And the increased influence and budget of the Party gave Panther leaders something to lose and something to fight over. But neither of these first two factors—repression nor success—could on its own undermine the Party's politics, and the Black Panthers continued to grow through 1969 and 1970, when it experienced both its greatest repression and its greatest success.

The third factor that made Black Panther politics unsustainable was the establishment's decision to offer political concessions to Panther allies, thereby shifting the political context and cutting into the Panthers' ability to maintain allied support. As many of the Panthers' potential allies among antiwar activists, black moderates, and others saw their interests addressed by government policy and rhetoric, they became less willing to support revolutionary activities. At the same time, normalization of diplomatic relations between the United States and the Panthers' international allies made it ever more difficult for the Party to sustain international support. The times were changing, and the Black Panthers' revolutionary politics of armed self-defense began to lose resonance.

As the tension increased between the need to please potential allies and the commitment to the Panthers' politics of armed self-defense, so did the tension between some chapters of the Party and the national leadership in Oakland. This tension was evident in the growing strife between the New York Panthers, the Cleavers, and Geronimo Pratt, on one side, and national Party leaders David Hilliard and Huey Newton, on the other. In each case, local leaders chafed against management by the national organization.

As internal and external pressures mounted, ideological differences began to solidify, pitting the Central Committee's social democratic emphasis against the breakaway Party elements' emphasis on guerilla warfare. With the mutiny, and especially with the deaths of Webb and Napier, this ideological split hardened.

The killings of Webb and Napier may have had nothing to do with ideological differences. They could have resulted from simple factional power struggles, and it is hard to establish with certainty who committed these murders. Nevertheless, the killings rendered insurrectionary rhetoric untenable for the Party and crystallized a sharp ideological division.

In previous cases in which Panthers were accused of killing a police officer or suspected informant, the Party could recast the charges as state repression.

For example, the Party had argued that Huey was defending himself against police brutality when Officer Frey was killed and that the FBI had likely ordered Rackley's murder as a means of framing Bobby Seale and sending him to the gas chamber. The aggressive and often explicit repressive actions by the state in these cases and others, such as the killing of Fred Hampton while he slept in his bed, lent credibility to the Panther perspective and allowed the Party to continue advancing insurrectionary rhetoric and still appeal to potential allies as victims of oppression.

But with heavy media coverage of vicious factionalism, the brutal murders of representatives of each faction, and the subsequent widespread accusations that the rival factions were responsible, the Panthers could not simultaneously maintain broad support and insurrectionary rhetoric. The Central Committee could not denounce Cleaver, the New York 21, and Geronimo—some of the most important former members of the Party—deny any role in the killing of Webb; credibly appeal to black, antiwar, and international allies for support against state repression; and at the same time glorify armed resistance against the state.

Instead, the Central Committee renounced immediate insurrection, denounced the "defecting" rival faction for its reckless embrace of insurrection, and insisted that the Panthers focus exclusively on social democratic programs until a sufficient mass of people was ready for revolution. This stance was a sharp departure from the rhetoric of armed resistance and the practical politics of armed self-defense against the police that had fed the Party's explosive growth.

The dissidents faced the same dilemma, unable to promote insurrectionary rhetoric and expect to appeal to a broad base of potential allies. But whereas the Central Committee had been managing relations with allies all along, the rival faction had been chafing at the demands of its leadership. The New York 21 had already called for immediate insurrection in their open letter to the Weather Underground in January, and the deaths of Webb and Napier only cemented this position. Abroad in Algiers, the Cleavers and their group yearned for action and felt cut off and restrained by the Oakland leadership. Eldridge Cleaver had been the main architect of the Party's insurrectionary rhetoric. For him, a pacified call for social democracy held no appeal. Geronimo had gone underground and been arrested for illegal activities, and then was exiled by the Central Committee. Joining up with the Cleaverites and the call for immediate insurrection was his best—if not only—option.

The politics of immediate insurrection was not completely without allied support. An extreme Left best exemplified by the Weather Underground—but also by some of the lawyers who continued to defend the New York 21 and Geronimo in court, some of the alternative press, and a few wealthy funders—agreed fully and explicitly that immediate insurrection was essential. But the much broader base of allies that supported the national Panther organization in 1969 and 1970 did not support this position.

In the March 20, 1971, issue of the *Black Panther,* alongside demonstrations of support for the national Party leadership, the back cover featured the banner headline "Survival Pending Revolution" and a graphic of a woman carrying items labeled for the "People's" programs: a bag of food labeled "Free Food Program," shoes labeled "Free Shoes Program," a blouse labeled "Free Clothing Program," and a book labeled "Liberation Schools." The woman wore a nurse's cap labeled "free health clinics," and a bus in the backgrounds bears the sign "free busing program." The graphic included a quote by Huey Newton: "There must be total transformation. But until that time that we can achieve that total transformation, we must exist. In order to exist, we must survive; so therefore we need a survival kit."[86]

On March 27, following the heavy denunciations of the Cleaver faction and statements of allegiance to Huey Newton, the cover of the *Black Panther* featured photos of preschool and elementary-school children dressed in Panther uniforms and standing in formation. A large caption read, "The world is yours as well as ours, but in the last analysis, it is yours. You young people, full of vigour and vitality, are in the bloom of life, like the sun at eight or nine in the morning. Our hope is placed in you." The paper featured stories about the Panther school and social programs and included many photos of Panther children reading, marching, playing, studying in class, and eating breakfast.[87]

With this issue, the Black Panther Party implemented a sweeping demilitarization of its image, a shift documented in the *Black Panther* issues for the first half of 1971. The first twelve issues of the *Black Panther* in 1971, through March 20, included 225 graphic images of weapons, an average of more than eighteen images of weapons per issue. In sharp contrast, the twelve issues published March 27 and thereafter contained only five portrayals of weapons, an average of less than one image every other issue.[88]

In most issues of the *Black Panther,* the Party printed its Ten Point Program near the back of the paper. Until March 1971, the Ten Point Program layout prominently featured a photo of Huey carrying a shotgun and bandolier with the caption "Huey P. Newton, Minister of Defense, Black Panther Party"; the top of the layout featured the Ten Point Program, and the bottom featured a photo of a machine gun. On March 13, the photos were removed and from March 27 onward, the Ten Point Program layout featured the large bold caption, "Serving the People Body and Soul" alongside Newton's new title, "Servant of the People."[89]

This graphic change was emblematic of a sea change in Party rhetoric. From 1967 to 1969, 45 percent of political editorial articles in the *Black Panther* advocated "revolution now." In 1970, that share jumped to 65 percent. But in 1971, it fell to 16 percent, and in 1972–73, it dropped below 1 percent. Conversely, advocacy of "traditional politics" in political editorial articles in the *Black Panther* greatly increased after the split. From 1967 to 1969, only 7 percent of such articles advocated "traditional politics," and less than 4 percent in 1970, compared with 32 percent in 1971 and almost 67 percent in 1972–73.[90]

As the national Party leadership moved toward social democratic rhetoric and away from talk of insurrection, the Cleaverite faction took an insurrectionary turn. On April 3, 1971, it began publishing its own newspaper, *Right On!,* advocating full and immediate insurrection. The paper was published with support from the Weathermen via an aboveground ally—the Independent Caucus of SDS at the State University of New York. The paper featured articles by Eldridge Cleaver and the New York 21. At the bottom of the front page, a quote summarized the Cleaverite position: "The best example that we have of an alternative way of dealing with the courts is the case of Jonathan Jackson."[91]

In early April, a reporter from the independent leftist newspaper the *Guardian* interviewed Kathleen Cleaver in Algiers about the rift. Cleaver railed against David Hilliard for his "right opportunism," his "lack of militancy," and his "bureaucratic methods" in running the Party since her husband had gone into exile.[92] Kathleen claimed that David reoriented the party from "organizing violence against the pigs" to "concentrating on legal action and defending people in court," and "consciously set about to destroy the armed underground." She said, "He even ordered that guns be taken out of some Panther offices! . . . The phase of legal defense is over. . . . Jonathan Jackson ended all that. . . . Now we got to break them all out." Kathleen Cleaver asserted that the conflict between the "Hilliard clique" and the Cleaver faction had long been simmering but that the International Section had hoped that Newton "would put the party back on the right course when he got out of jail last year." Instead he endorsed Hilliard's stewardship.[93]

Kathleen Cleaver noted that the International Section had opened a U.S. headquarters in the Bronx and that its main focus would be armed action, sabotage, and support for a military underground. She declared, "We are through with legal action. . . . What is necessary now is a party to advance and expedite the armed struggle. . . . There's a revolutionary war going on. The people are ready for a real vanguard, for military action. . . . We need a people's army and the Black Panther party vanguard will bring that about. . . . The people are ready."[94]

On April 17, 1971, the same day that Kathleen Cleaver's interview appeared in the *Guardian,* Huey Newton published an essay in the *Black Panther* titled "On the Defection of Eldridge Cleaver from the Black Panther Party and the Defection of the Black Panther Party from the Black Community." Newton described the conflict as an ideological one. He claimed that the roots of the Party were solidly social democratic (pending sufficient support for a revolution) and criticized Eldridge Cleaver's advocacy of insurrection:

> You have to set up a program of practical action and be a model for the community to follow and appreciate. The original vision of the Party was to develop a lifeline to the people, by serving their needs. . . . Many times people say that our Ten Point Program is reformist; but they ignore the fact that revolution is a process. . . . The people see things as moving from A to B to C; they do not see things as moving from A to Z. In other words they have to see first some basic accomplishments, in order to realize that major successes are possible. . . . The Black Panther Party has reached a contradiction with Eldridge Cleaver and he has defected from the Party, because we would not order everyone into the streets tomorrow to make a revolution.

We recognize that this is impossible . . . because the people are not at that point now. This contradiction and conflict may seem unfortunate to some, but. . . . we are now free to move toward the building of a community structure which will become a true voice of the people, promoting their interests in many ways. We can continue to push our basic survival program. We can continue to serve the people as advocates of their true interests. We can truly become a political revolutionary vehicle which will lead the people to a higher level of consciousness, so that they will know what they must really do in their quest for freedom.[95]

The politics of the Black Panther Party contained a tension. On the one hand, much of the Party's political leverage and appeal to members derived from armed resistance to the police. On the other hand, its ability to withstand repression by the state depended largely on support from more moderate allies. Through 1969 and much of 1970, the national Party was able to contain this tension, shaping its public image through its service programs and maintaining internal discipline through purges. But over time, concessions exacerbated the contradiction the Party faced between practicing armed self-defense against the state and maintaining allied support. These tensions came to a head when key factions challenged the national Party leadership. As the intra-organizational struggle became violent, the Panthers split along ideological lines. The national organization called upon members to put down the gun and emphasize community programs, and the dissident faction called for immediate guerilla warfare against the state. Stripped of the viability of the politics of armed self-defense against the police, how would these new Panther politics fare in the 1970s?

16

The Limits of Heroism

In the months following the Panther rift in early 1971, sustained pressure from the state kept the Black Panther Party in the national spotlight. This pressure only exacerbated the tensions inside the Party as the national headquarters sought to distance itself from insurrectionary activities in order to hold on to allied support. Newspapers widely reported the trial of the New York Panthers charged with conspiracies to kill police and bomb public buildings. The state opened its criminal case against Bobby Seale and Ericka Huggins on March 18, charging that the Panther leaders were responsible for the murder of Alex Rackley in New Haven. In June, the State of California began a retrial of Huey Newton on charges of manslaughter in the 1968 killing of Officer John Frey. That month, the trial of David Hilliard also began for charges stemming from the shoot-out in which Bobby Hutton was killed.[1]

At the same time, Panther members in chapters around the country continued to engage in insurrectionary acts, or at least to be accused of them. Juxtaposed with the national Party's proclamations of its commitment to nonviolent service of the people pending future revolution, these actions—and accusations that the Party was responsible—were embarrassing to the Party, especially to its national leadership.

EMBARRASSMENTS

On April 2, 1971, police raided the Black Panther headquarters in Jersey City, New Jersey, and arrested five Panthers. The police claimed they found an underground rifle range, sandbagging, rifles, pistols, ammunition, and various preparations for a battle with authorities.[2] Also in April, police arrested and charged four Detroit Black Panthers—Ronald Irwin, Larry Powell, Anthony Norman, and Ronald Smith—with stealing drugs and money from residents of a "student commune" and killing one student in the process.[3] On April 20, police announced they had found the charred, scattered remains of Fred Bennett, a Black Panther Party captain, near what they claimed was a Panther "bomb factory" replete with "149 sticks of dynamite, quantities of nitroglycerin, fuses, timing devices, and dynamite caps."[4] On May 13, in a Chicago apartment "regarded as a Panther hangout" and "stocked with Black Panther literature," gunmen shot three police dispatched to investigate a domestic dispute.[5] On May 21, two New York police officers were ambushed and killed in Harlem. People claiming to be members of the Black Panther–affiliated Black Liberation Army notified the press, taking responsibility for the murders.[6]

In early June, Dhoruba Bin Wahad and Eddie Jamal Joseph—previously acquitted of all charges in the high-profile New York 21 case—were again arrested and charged with holding up a Bronx social club. Police claimed that the submachine gun the two men had used in the holdup had been "positively identified" as the weapon used in May to shoot two police officers.[7] In July, former Panther Melvin "Cotton" Smith testified in the trial of Geronimo Pratt and other L.A. Panthers for charges stemming from the December 1969 siege in which the Panthers had attempted unsuccessfully to bomb a Los Angeles police station. He also claimed that one of the guns seized during the siege had been used by Panthers to kill three people.[8] Various sources claim that Melvin Smith was working as a paid police agent both while he was a member of the L.A. Panthers and when he gave his testimony.[9] In late July, a New York grand jury indicted seven New York Panthers—including Moore and Josephs—in the brutal murder of the national distribution captain of the *Black Panther,* Samuel Napier.[10]

Wracked by internal divisions, the Party was disintegrating and rapidly losing members and allied support. The *New York Times* reported in March 1971 that the Party was falling apart: "A check of the Party's chapters across the country suggests that the operation is now only a shell of what it was a year ago."[11] Black Panther chairman Bobby Seale later recalled that immediately after the killings of Robert Webb and Samuel Napier, 30 to 40 percent of Black Panther members left the organization.[12] Even the federal government recognized that the Party was no longer a serious threat. The House Committee on Internal Security reported in August 1971,

> The Black Panther Party, as a national organization, is near disintegration. . . . The committee hearings document the steady decline in [party membership] during the last year. Furthermore, the feud between Eldridge Cleaver and Huey Newton threatens the start of a time of violence and terror within what remains of the Panther Party. Probably only remnants of the party will remain alive here and there to bedevil the police and enchant a few of the young, but its day as a national influence and influence in the black community seems over. It is hard to believe that only a little over a year ago the Panthers . . . ranked as the most celebrated ghetto militants. They fascinated the left, inflamed the police, terrified much of America, and had an extraordinary effect on the black community. Even moderate blacks, who disagreed with their violent tactics, felt that the Panthers served a purpose in focusing attention on ghetto problems and argued that they gave a sense of pride to the black community. . . . Liberals and idealists who once sympathized with the Panthers have . . . withdrawn their support.[13]

MARTYRS WITHOUT A MOVEMENT

On August 21, 1971, guards at San Quentin State Prison in Marin County, California, shot and killed Panther leader, author, and prison activist George Jackson. Three prison guards and two white inmates were also killed in the incident, their throats slashed. Prison authorities claimed that Jackson had smuggled a gun into the prison, killed the guards with help from other inmates, and was attempting to escape when he was shot.[14] The "truth" of what actually happened is still contested.

George Jackson had been an important and influential Black Panther leader. Sent to prison at the age of eighteen for the theft of seventy dollars, he organized prisoners against repression. His leadership was transracial, overriding the racial divisions that set black, white, and Latino prisoners against one another and kept them under control. In prison, he learned to write well and became a noteworthy Marxist political theorist. His compelling collection of letters, *Soledad Brother,* was widely read and quite influential, particularly in certain circles of the U.S. and international Left.[15] *Soledad Brother* confirmed Jackson's growing influence not only as a Marxist theorist but also as a vital spokesman for political prisoners everywhere. Jackson founded and led the Black Panther chapter at San Quentin Prison and organized a strong revolutionary movement among prison inmates. His writings and leadership garnered an impressive international as well as domestic audience. In effect, he became a powerful symbol for the Black Panther Party, the international human rights movement to free political prisoners, and the convergence of their causes.[16]

Jackson's death put the Black Panther Party in a difficult dilemma that revealed how much the times had changed. A year earlier, the Party would have heralded Jackson as a martyr for revolution. In fact, the Party had heralded the efforts of his brother, Jonathan Jackson, to break him out of the Marin County courthouse in August 1970. If George had met death at that moment, the Party would have touted his death as a great injustice perpetrated by the "pigs" and would have called for revenge, encouraging its supporters to take insurrectionary actions against the state, as it had when John Huggins and Bunchy Clark were murdered in Los Angeles in January 1969 and Fred Hampton and Mark Clark were murdered in Chicago in December 1969.

A week after the killings of John Huggins and Bunchy Carter, the January 25, 1969, issue of the *Black Panther* had been filled with graphics of weapons and violent confrontations with the state, as well as calls to revolutionary violence. The cover headline called the killings "Political Assassination" and featured a photo of John Huggins holding up the poster of Huey Newton with a spear in one hand and a rifle in the other. The top story argued that the state and its stooges had assassinated Huggins and Carter because of the revolutionary threat they posed.[17] Under a series of photos of an armed Huey Newton and a photo of a submachine gun was the caption "Free Huey Now—Guns, Baby, Guns!" Under a photo of Vietnamese women carrying rifles and participating in military training, a caption read "Hanoi's militiawomen learn techniques for shooting down American planes." One page featured an image of a young black man carrying a submachine gun in one hand and a "Black Studies" book in the other. Another page featured a drawing of a policeman with a bloodied head. The caption read "This pig will be back. Don't let this happen. Shoot to kill."[18]

Similarly, the December 13, 1969, issue of the *Black Panther* had argued that the December 4 killing of Panther leaders Fred Hampton and Mark Clark in Chicago was state-sponsored assassination and demanded revenge. The front page featured a photo of Fred Hampton in red with the caption, "He stood up in the midst of fascist gestapo forces and declared, 'I am a revolutionary.' Fred Hampton, Deputy Chairman Illinois Chapter Black Panther Party, Murdered by Fascist Pigs, December 4, 1969." The article explained that Hampton was a martyr and called on readers to take up his revolutionary struggle:

Deputy Chairman Fred Hampton . . . has joined the ranks of martyrs, revolutionary heroes: Lumumba, Malcolm X, Little Bobby Hutton, Bunchy Carter, John Huggins, Che, Toure, Jake Winters and the countless other revolutionaries who have given the most precious gift that they could give in the name of the people. . . . These brothers and sisters gave their lives in order that you and yours may one day enjoy true freedom. . . . Eldridge Cleaver, Minister of Information, has stated that "it is time to intensify the struggle," and that now is the time for "mad men." Deputy Chairman Fred Hampton was just such a "mad man." Reactionaries wondered why Deputy Chairman Fred waged such a resolute struggle seemingly against the greatest of "odds". . . . [In] Malcolm's words . . . we are a generation that don't give a f—k about the "odds." . . . Deputy Chairman Fred dug that vulturistic capitalists were growing fat off the flesh and blood of the toiling masses of the world. So Deputy Chairman dedicated his life to destroying the number one enemy of mankind. . . . By raising their hands against Deputy Chairman Fred Hampton, they lifted their hands against the best that humanity possesses. AND ALREADY OTHER HANDS ARE REACHING OUT, PICKING UP THE GUNS!!! . . . The arm of the people is long and their vengeance TERRIFYING!!![19]

Illustrations further advocating armed confrontation with the state filled the rest of the issue. A full-page color graphic depicted a black man wearing a bandolier. In one hand, he held a military rifle equipped with a bayonet dripping blood, and he thrust a grenade into the air with the other hand while yelling out. Pigs in the distance fled as a grenade flew through the air after them. The large caption quoted Huey Newton: "The racist dog policemen must withdraw immediately from our communities, cease their wonton murder, brutality and torture of Black People, or face the wrath of the armed people." Beneath a photo of armed police surrounding the Southern California office after the December 8 siege, a caption read, "Fascist troops mill around after attempted massacre." Another picture on the same page showed young, bare-chested Panthers handcuffed and held by police with the caption "Youthful Panther Warriors." A beautiful graphic of a black mother carrying her baby and a rifle bore the caption "If I should return, I shall kiss you. If I should fall on the way, I shall ask you to do as I have in the name of the revolution."[20]

By the time of George Jackson's death in August 1971, such a response was no longer tenable. If the leadership was to hold onto the Party's dwindling allied support, it could not advocate revenge killings of police. Since early that year, the Party had moved definitively away from advocating insurrection.

The issue of the *Black Panther* published immediately after George Jackson's death heralded and mourned him. But the Party's message was essentially nonviolent. The cover of the paper featured a photo of Jackson sitting contemplatively by a sunny window under the headline "George Jackson Lives!" Commemorative writings by Jackson himself, some of it promoting violence, filled the issue. Yet the Party issued no calls to insurrection and made no suggestions that violent revenge was appropriate. The Party celebrated and supported Jackson, but it did not agitate for immediate violent retribution. The newspaper contained not a single image of a weapon or violent action by a revolutionary against any agent of the state. Jackson was a martyr, but without an insurrectionary movement. Stripped of its insurrectionary rhetoric and the politics of armed self-defense against the state, the Party no longer offered a practical outlet for the anger that Panther members and supporters felt about Jackson's killing.

While the editorial policy of the *Black Panther* was tightly controlled, the political views of Black Panther members and supporters were not. Many of George Jackson's admirers took his insurrectionary writings to heart and wanted vengeance for his death. A group of Black Panthers incarcerated at Folsom State Prison in California wrote to Jackson's parents to commiserate:

> We know, Father and Mother Jackson, that our pitifully few words fall far short in filling that vacuum created by George's murderers; you see we feel that vacuum also. You must be strong and take consolation in the reality that George lives in all of us and we all therefore are your sons. Take pride in the fact that you have a large strong revolutionary family of budding warriors—we will not let you down. Comrade George, the battleground is defined and that split between the enemy and ourselves has become a chasm. This cruel cut can never heal; the pain is too intense.[21]

Given the calls by the Cleaver faction for immediate armed action, the Black Panther Party national leadership could not afford to alienate those Jackson supporters who were deeply angered by Jackson's killing and wanted revenge. To manage the complex and vast outpouring of emotions from members and supporters after Jackson's murder, the leaders organized a massive funeral. Thousands participated. Huey Newton gave a long, philosophical eulogy emphasizing the strength and beauty of George Jackson's character. "He lived the life that we must praise. It was a life, no matter how he was oppressed, no matter how wrongly he was done, he still kept the love for the people."[22]

Bobby Seale read letters from Panther members and supporters representing a range of perspectives on Jackson's death, giving voice to those who wanted revenge as well as those who simply wanted to express sadness about the loss.[23]

The next issue of the *Black Panther,* on September 4, was dedicated to Jackson's funeral, and the editors reproduced many of the letters read by Seale along with statements from notables such as scholar-activist Angela Davis (a close comrade and love of George Jackson), French writer Jean Genet, and author James Baldwin, as well as a transcript of Newton's speech. Consistent with its new editorial policy, the newspaper presented not a single drawing or photo of violent confrontation, though it did contain a number of photos of the funeral, including images of members of an honor guard standing by holding rifles to their chests. Dressed in fancy suits, they looked ceremonial, not at all aggressive. Aside from the guards, the issue contained no images of weapons. The overriding message was one of mourning and loss: Jackson was a hero, and he had been unjustly taken away. The last article in the issue was a statement by Genet, which ended, "In these 11 years, Jackson learned to write and think. The American police shot him down."[24] As the *Black Panther* reported it, Jackson's death was a tragic loss but not a call to arms.

The following week, on September 9, inmates took over Attica prison in New York. They called in the Panthers to help negotiate their demands but achieved no resolution. On September 13, Governor Rockefeller responded with force, sending in a thousand National Guardsmen, prison guards, and police to take back the prison. The troops killed twenty-eight prisoners, while nine hostages died in the battle.[25] The *New York Times* reported on its front page that the prisoners had slit the throats of the nine hostages.[26] An editorial emphasized the brutality of the killing and suggested that Bobby Seale and the Black Panthers were partly to blame:

> The deaths of these persons by knives . . . reflect a barbarism wholly alien to civilized society. Prisoners slashed the throats of utterly helpless, unarmed guards whom they had held captive through the around-the-clock negotiations, in which inmates held out for an increasingly revolutionary set of demands. . . . What began last Thursday as a long-foreseeable protest against inhuman prison conditions, with an initial list of grievances that many citizens could support, degenerated into a bloodbath that can only bring sorrow to all Americans. . . . The contribution of Black Panther Bobby Seale seems to have been particularly negative, that of an incendiary, not a peacemaker.[27]

The charge that the Panthers had contributed to the violence at Attica had potential to alienate many of the Black Panther Party's more moderate allies.

The next day, the *Times* reported on page one that the hostages had actually been killed by gunfire and that the prisoners had no guns—implying that state troopers had killed the hostages as well as the prisoners.[28] Several elected officials, including New York congressman Herman Badillo and Assemblyman Arthur Eve from Buffalo, charged that Governor Rockefeller's administration had fabricated the story that the prisoners had killed the hostages.[29]

The false story that prisoners had brutally killed hostages and that the Panthers had helped instigate the killing vilified the Attica insurgents and the Black Panthers. In response, the Panthers shied away from insurgent rhetoric. Rather than call for resistance to prison authorities in the spirit of Attica, the Panthers advanced a moderate stance. They dedicated the next issue of their newspaper to the uprising, with the title "Massacre at Attica" across the cover. Again, as with the killing of George Jackson, the Party's rhetoric stopped short of advocating insurrection, instead mourning the loss of the prison rebels and decrying their oppression. The issue contained no photos or images of revolutionary violence and no calls to armed action.[30] This treatment of the event stood in stark contrast to the rhetoric of the Party before the ideological split. Strategically, the Panthers were trying to hold onto allied support in the shifting political environment. At the behest of the Panthers, a committee of eighteen official observers who had been allowed into Attica as negotiators during the rebellion, including Seale, issued a statement supporting Seale against the charges in the *New York Times* editorial that he had inflamed the Attica rebels from within: "No individual on the observer committee adopted any position which prevented or hindered a peaceful resolution of the crisis."[31]

RETREAT

No longer advocating armed insurrection, the Black Panthers sought to build power through other means. In addition to their service programs, the Oakland Panthers launched an extended boycott of Bill Boyette, a local black businessman who owned markets in black neighborhoods and ran a black business association called Cal-Pak but refused to donate to the Black Panther Party. In January 1972, the Party announced it had reached an agreement with Boyette. His stores would now donate regularly to the Party's programs, and the Party would call off the boycott.[32] The Party deepened relationships with black elected politicians, including Congressman Ron Dellums and Congresswoman Shirley Chisholm.[33]

On May 20, 1972, the Black Panther Party announced that it was running Chairman Bobby Seale for mayor of Oakland, and Minister of Information Elaine Brown for a seat on the Oakland City Council.[34] The Party had earlier participated in electoral politics with Eldridge Cleaver's 1968 presidential candidacy on the Peace and Freedom Party ticket, but it had never actually sought to win. Now, the Party turned all of its national notoriety and resources to winning the Oakland elections.

Facing dwindling public support, and embarrassing violent activity by rank-and-file members in chapters across the country, Newton and the national Party leadership decided to cut their losses and consolidate their political strength in Oakland. Since they could not expect to win violent confrontations with the state and could no longer win politically either, the Party decided to use its still considerable national clout to win electoral political power in Oakland. The leadership put out the message in July 1972, declaring Oakland a "base of operation" and calling on Party members to close down their local Panther chapters and bring all Party resources back to Oakland.

Instead of pursuing immediate insurrectionary activity, now the Party would consolidate its power to take over the city of Oakland, including its strategically and economically important port, through electoral struggle. Once Oakland was liberated through electoral victory, the Party would expand the revolution by taking over other cities. "In this interest, each week the Black Panther Intercommunal News Service will publish a supplement examining one aspect of the city of Oakland in the hope that this information can be used to turn a reactionary base into a revolutionary base."[35]

On the campaign trail, Elaine Brown explained the strategy to a supportive audience at Merritt College in Oakland, where the Panthers got their start in 1966:

> We're talking about liberating the territory of Oakland. . . . Are we ready to defend at this moment? I don't think we are. The Oakland Police Department has got all the guns. There's a practical problem, when you talk about liberating territory, or establishing a provisional revolutionary government. Think about those issues when you start talking about implementing a revolutionary process in the United States of America, with its

super-technological weapons, where they do not have to commit a troop to take out the whole city, because they have "smart" bombs, helicopters, and all kinds of things so that it doesn't even require the entrance of one troop. Think about that. We have to start talking about how to win, not how to get killed. We can begin by talking about voting in the city of Oakland, the Oakland elections, in April 1973, for Bobby Seale, for Elaine Brown.[36]

Bobby Seale forced a runoff election in the mayoral election, and Elaine Brown came in a close second for city council, but both lost their political bids in April 1973.[37]

UNRAVELING

A few Party chapters did persist. But for most practical purposes, the Black Panther Party ceased to be a national organization and once again became a local Oakland organization. Rather than move to Oakland, many Panthers simply left the Party. Bobby Rush, who inherited leadership of the Chicago chapter when Fred Hampton was murdered, later recalled the response of Chicago Panthers: "Most people in Chicago didn't want to go [to Oakland] because they were pretty practical folks. . . . They began to resent things: I remember when I sent our bus and the printing press we had acquired out to Oakland. . . . People just wanted to move on, wanted to do something. So they said, 'Rather than go out to Oakland, we're just gonna disband. We're just gonna leave.' One by one they began to peter out."[38]

No longer able to sustain allied support for insurgent politics and lacking other sources of political leverage, the Party unraveled. Once Newton closed the Party chapters across the nation and called members back to Oakland, the Panthers no longer advanced effective and replicable politics. The greatest strengths of the Party after 1971 were its notoriety and its concentration of relationships and resources in Oakland. It continued to draw members, donations, and support on a local scale because of its past actions. But despite the best aspirations of its leadership, the Panthers never again were able to advance insurgent practices that others could emulate. Now drawing power from reputation rather than from the ability to mobilize insurgency, the Oakland Black Panther Party became increasingly cultish, resembling a social service organization, motivated by revolutionary ideology, with a mafioso bent.

In late 1971, Newton told David Hilliard that "the Party is over." Hilliard recalls that Newton was surrounded by loyalists who applauded

Newton's every action, challenged nothing, and would do anything to win his approval.[39] As the Party unraveled, so did Newton's mental health. According to those closest to him, in the years that followed, Newton was governed by despair, untreated bipolar disorder, and clinical depression. Newton became severely addicted to cocaine.[40]

Accusations abound about Newton's alleged criminal activities during this period. Few people agree on the specifics, and few of the accusations have been verified: Newton eventually defeated every one of the major criminal charges in court. Some of the most widely touted accusations come from right-wing activists such as David Horowitz and Kate Coleman, who seek to vilify the Black Panther Party. Yet retrospective accounts from a range of sources add some credence to these accusations.

According to these stories, for much of the 1970s, Newton ruled the Party through force and fear and began behaving like a strung-out gangster. According to Elaine Brown, "Huey and his entourage of restless gunmen were prowling the after-hours clubs nightly."[41] According to Kate Coleman, Newton had various after-hours-club operators, drug dealers, and pimps beaten, shot, and killed in his zeal to enforce an extortion scheme and control Oakland's underworld.[42] Coleman writes that Newton pistol-whipped Preston Callins, a "tailor" who came to his apartment to "measure him for a suit," fracturing his skull four times.[43] Elaine Brown recounts the same story and testifies that she personally cleaned up the blood.[44] The Alameda County District Attorney's office attempted to prosecute Newton for the 1974 murder of Kathleen Smith, a seventeen-year-old prostitute, claiming that Newton shot her in the head because of a perceived slight as she worked the street corner.[45] Flores Forbes, who was a member of the Black Panther Central Committee in the mid-1970s, testifies in his autobiography that he attempted to assassinate the star witness against Newton in Smith's murder trial in 1977.[46] Elaine Brown, who had been chairwoman of the Party at the time of this attempted assassination, prominently endorsed Forbes's book, writing, "This is our story . . . an unadulterated truth, told in a pure voice."[47] Newton was eventually killed on August 23, 1989, by a petty crack dealer from whom he was likely trying to steal drugs.[48]

Lore about Newton and the Party's criminality, widely broadcast in the media, eroded the Black Panther legacy. To what extent federal counterintelligence measures may have contributed to the unraveling of Newton and the Oakland Party in the 1970s is difficult to determine. But the spirit of J. Edgar Hoover would have been proud of the results.

Hoover had recognized by 1969 that criminalization was the best way to diminish public support for the Black Panthers and the political challenge they posed. Nothing did more to criminalize the Party in the public imagination than the allegations about Newton's actions in the years following the ideological split.[49]

THE LIMITS OF HEROISM: SOCIAL DEMOCRACY

By 1971, the Black Panther Party was quickly unraveling, but even as the Party's national influence declined, a new leadership emerged that struggled to advance revolutionary aims through a social democratic politics. Under the leadership of Elaine Brown, the Party showed impressive development of this brand of politics.

Following her trip to China, North Vietnam, and North Korea with the Black Panther delegation in the summer of 1970, Elaine Brown had quickly risen to national leadership in the Party. Upon her return to the United States, she was greeted at the airport by Huey Newton—newly released from prison—and that evening became his lover and soon his close collaborator. Following the split in early 1971, Brown became editor of the *Black Panther,* the Party's main voice. In October that year, she became minister of information, replacing Eldridge Cleaver. In late 1972 and early 1973, Brown was at the center of Black Panther activities, running for political office with Bobby Seale in Oakland. And later in 1973, when Newton expelled Seale from the Party, he appointed Elaine Brown chairwoman—the number two position in the Party after his. When Newton fled to Cuba following his indictment for charges that he killed Kathleen Smith and pistol-whipped Preston Callins, Brown took charge of the Black Panther Party operations.[50]

Under Elaine Brown's leadership from August 1974 through June 1977, the Party experienced something of a local renaissance as a social democratic organization.[51] Elaine Brown supported the candidacy of Democrat Jerry Brown for governor of California that year and helped bring in strong support from Oakland's black voters, which helped Jerry Brown win the election. Governor Brown appointed his longtime friend and former Panther lawyer and ally J. Anthony Kline to an important post in his administration, cementing Elaine Brown's access to the governor's office. Despite long electoral dominance by white Republicans in Oakland, Elaine Brown ran a formidable campaign for Oakland City Council in 1975. She developed strong ties to black political networks, including Congressman Ron Dellums's political machine. These ties brought endorsements from every local Democrat and many black businesses, including Cal-Pak. She garnered wide support from organized labor, including endorsements from the Alameda County Central Labor Council, the United Auto Workers, the United Farm Workers, and the Teamsters. She won 44 percent of the vote against the Republican candidate.[52]

Under Brown's leadership, the Oakland Panthers took community service to new heights. The cornerstone of the Party's program was the Oakland Community School, an elementary school directed by Ericka Huggins with the help of Panther Regina Davis. Through their efforts, the school eventually offered a top-notch education, enrolling about two hundred kids, with twice that many on the waiting list. The Party began competing for and winning public funding to run service programs, such as crime prevention for Oakland teenagers.[53]

In the 1976 Democratic presidential primaries, Jimmy Carter benefited from the backlash against the Republican Party after Nixon's impeachment for the Watergate scandal and emerged as an early favorite for the Democratic Party nomination. Late in the game, when Governor Brown entered the race to challenge Carter, Elaine Brown helped him win the black vote in Baltimore, which in turn was the key to winning the state of Maryland. Her efforts also contributed to his sweeping victory in the California primary. Jerry Brown went to the Democratic Convention in July with the second-highest number of delegates of any candidate, but he was handily defeated by Carter in the first round of voting.

Leveraging her support, Elaine Brown elicited Governor Brown's approval of $33 million to extend the freeway in Oakland in exchange for a commitment from Clorox, Hyatt, Wells Fargo, Sears, and other multinational corporations to develop Oakland City Center—bringing ten thousand new jobs to Oakland. The companies wanted to develop Oakland and had proposed the freeway extension when Reagan was governor, but the project had been blocked. Brown used her influence with the governor to move the deal forward with the idea that the political prestige garnered could help Lionel Wilson, a black Oakland judge and Panther ally, become mayor. In return, the Black Panthers would gain significant influence over the distribution of the new jobs.[54]

Astonishingly, the strategy worked. The Black Panther Party did its best to keep its relationship with Lionel Wilson out of the public eye. But according to Elaine Brown's account, the Black Panthers played a crucial role behind the scenes. Not only did she get the governor to agree to the freeway extension, unblocking plans for Oakland development and greatly expanding her cachet in Oakland politics, but she also obtained his endorsement, and that of much of the state Democratic machine, for Lionel Wilson for mayor of Oakland. The Black Panther Party fielded its entire membership to work on Wilson's mayoral campaign, registering ninety thousand new black voters. When Wilson became the first black elected mayor of Oakland in May 1977, he owed much of his success to the efforts of Elaine Brown and the Black Panther Party.[55]

Elaine Brown endured great personal costs to advance the Black Panther revolution through social democratic politics. She was also very effective in developing conventional political power for blacks in Oakland. Yet her hard work did little to advance the Black Panther Party as a radical movement organization. The politics of armed self-defense was no longer viable, and the Panthers had no alternate insurgent strategy for building power.

The month after Lionel Wilson's election as mayor, with Oakland safely in the hands of friends, Newton returned from Cuba.[56] Brown had considered her efforts to be preparing Oakland for his return all along. However, it soon became clear that his leadership and Brown's continued management of the Black Panther Party were incompatible. Brown soon left the Party, and the foothold the Panthers had gained in conventional Oakland politics was lost.[57]

The limits of Elaine Brown's heroism went well beyond the problems with Newton and the particularities of Oakland politics. The source of the Party's power under her leadership was conventional political savvy coupled with community service—an approach to grassroots politics adopted by thousands of community activists in hundreds of cities throughout the country. These political actors made inroads into political power and reform well before the Black Panther Party began and continue to do so today. Black electoral representation, in particular, mushroomed in the 1970s during the period Elaine Brown chaired the Black Panther Party. But conventional political savvy and community service alone have never been able to mobilize a serious radical challenge to status quo arrangements of power. For insurgent social movements to expand and proliferate, they must offer activists a set of insurgent practices that disrupt established social relations in ways that are difficult to repress.[58]

The Panthers' stated objective in using Oakland as a "base of operations" was to create a revolutionary stronghold—and a model of revolutionary practice—that could eventually be expanded throughout the

United States and the world. But despite the revolutionary rhetoric, the political practices of the social democratic Panthers were very similar to the conventional politics that engaged black people nationwide in the 1970s. Unlike the Black Panther Party before the ideological split, the Oakland Black Panthers in the 1970s never provided a model for disrupting established relations of domination. They never provided political leverage or a replicable source of political power. And so, despite Elaine Brown's savvy and exceptional talent, the social democratic Black Panther Party never proliferated.

THE LIMITS OF HEROISM: GUERILLA WARFARE

Many treatments—both mainstream and radical—of the insurrectionary practices of revolutionary black nationalists seek to evaluate insurgents in ethical terms, judging them by who they hurt and whether their actions are good or bad. Unfortunately, most accounts fail to analyze the crucial political questions. How do insurgents see themselves? Who is attracted to participate, and why? What political leverage do the practices create for insurgents in a particular historical context?

From this vantage, it is clear that the armed, insurrectionary practices of the Black Panther Party were critical to its power and growth between 1968 and 1970. Huey Newton theorized in "The Functional Definition of Politics" in 1967 that poor and politically marginalized blacks could tap a source of power through armed insurrection. By taking up arms and organizing, they could create the capacity to deliver a violent consequence and thereby gain political influence.[59] The Black Panther Party did in fact garner extensive political leverage through its armed challenges to state authority.

But key to the success of the Panther's politics of armed self-defense was Newton's insistence that the Party—while advocating armed resistance—stay aboveground as long as possible, avoiding direct and explicit organization of insurrection. As a result, the Panthers had to navigate a narrow boundary between legal participation in U.S. politics and full-out war. The Party's capacity to sustain an insurgent challenge depended on its ability to stay largely within the law despite the armed resistance mounted by members. Most Party activities were incompatible with armed insurrection. Panthers who explicitly participated in armed insurrection could not participate in community programs, produce or distribute the Party newspaper, engage overtly in local organizing, work aboveground with allies, raise funds legally, live or work in known locations, or organize street mobilizations. Had the Party explicitly organized and directed armed insurrection, rather than simply advocating it, the state would have readily crushed it.

From 1971 on, as the political context shifted and the Black Panther Party stopped advocating insurrectionary activity, a significant number of former members sought to take armed politics to a "higher" level and engage the United States in guerilla warfare. Asserting that the imperialist domination of black people in the United States persisted, these dissidents believed that guerilla warfare was the best route to free black communities from oppression and that committing their lives to overthrowing the imperialist system through violence was the most heroic contribution they could make to freedom. Many of these guerilla warriors identified themselves as part of the revolutionary underground network called the Black Liberation Army (BLA).

Assata Shakur, a member of the BLA who had been convicted of killing a New Jersey State Police officer in 1972 and escaped to Cuba with comrades' help in 1979, described the BLA as follows:

> The Black Liberation Army is not an organization: it goes beyond that. It is a concept, a people's movement, an idea. Many different people have said and done many different things in the name of the Black Liberation Army. The idea of a Black Liberation Army emerged from conditions in Black communities: conditions of poverty, indecent housing, massive unemployment, poor medical care, and inferior education. The idea came about because Black people are not free or equal in this country. Because ninety percent of the men and women in this country's prisons are Black and Third World. Because ten-year-old children are shot down in our streets. Because dope has saturated our communities, preying on the disillusionment and frustration of our children. The concept of the BLA arose because of the political, social, and economic oppression of Black people in this country. And where there is oppression, there will be resistance.[60]

According to BLA member Sundiata Acoli, the purpose of the Black Liberation Army was to "defend Black people, and to organize Black people militarily, so they can defend themselves through a people's army and people's war."[61] Writing from prison in 1979, BLA member Jalil Muntaqim described the BLA as "a politico-military organization, whose primary objective is to fight for the independence and self-determination of Afrikan people in the United States. The . . . BLA evolved out of the now defunct Black Panther Party."[62]

A more theoretical statement by the Coordinating Committee of the Black Liberation Army in 1975 argued that for colonized and oppressed blacks, American law was unfair and thus illegitimate:

> The BLA has undertaken armed struggle as a means by which the social psychosis of fear, awe, and love of everything white people define as being of value, is purged from our peoples' minds. . . . We must clarify revolutionary violence in relationship to our actual condition, because many of our people believe in the "law". . . . In a society such as exists here today, law is never impartial, never divorced from the economic relationships that brought it about. History clearly shows that in the course of the development of modern western society, the code of law is the code of the dominant and most powerful class, made into laws for everyone. It is implemented by establishing "special" armed organs, that are obliged to enforce the prevailing class laws.[63]

Members of the Black Liberation Army participated in a range of insurrectionary actions, mostly against police, through the early 1970s. In a 1979 pamphlet, Jalil Muntaqim listed at least sixty violent confrontations with police for which he claimed BLA members were either responsible or under suspicion. A few from 1971 alone included ambushing and killing two police officers and attacking another group of police officers with a hand grenade in New York; robbing a bank and killing a policeman in Atlanta; firing on a police car with a machine gun and killing a police sergeant in an attack on a police station in San Francisco; and robbing a bank, shooting a police officer in his patrol car, and breaking three BLA members out of prison in Atlanta.[64]

In principle, these guerilla activities were not so different from the kinds of armed resistance to the police that the Black Panther Party had advocated all along. Most members of the Party agreed that the U.S. government was imperialist and oppressive and should be overthrown through violence. They sought to liberate black communities to govern themselves without intervention. They saw police, government officials, and capitalists alike as "pigs" and agents of oppression. Many Panthers were prepared to kill the "pigs" for their freedom.

But politically, direct organization of guerilla warfare was a world apart from the politics of armed self-defense upon which the Black Panther Party had thrived. Unlike the practices of the Black Panther Party of the late 1960s, guerilla warfare in the United States never attracted broad allied support. Most moderate blacks and antiwar activists viewed such activity as criminal. Guerillas were highly isolated, and they could not easily avoid capture and sometimes fatal encounters with police; when arrested, they received little legal or political support from allies in court. They had difficulty obtaining financial support for their activities, let alone for their basic survival. They had little means of communicating their perspective to a broad public other than through acts of violence.

Thus, while in principle many Panthers and former Panthers saw the BLA guerillas as heroic, most recognized that guerilla warfare was a doomed political strategy. Most stayed away. The few that did go underground and attempt to wage guerilla warfare were heavily repressed with intensive, direct state violence that most U.S. observers believed to be warranted. "By 1974–75," Muntaqim acknowledged, "the fighting capacity of the Black Liberation Army had been destroyed."[65]

Some black revolutionary nationalist guerilla activity persisted on a small scale after the demise of the BLA, and it continues even to this day. Despite the heroism of its proponents in the eyes of its adherents, the impact of this activity has remained negligible at best. Contrary to the experiences of revolutionary African anticolonial struggles, in which a black majority sought to overcome political domination by a white minority, in the United States, guerilla warfare by revolutionary black nationalists has never achieved broad participation or significant political support.[66]

Despite the heroism of members of both the social democratic and guerilla warfare wings, the Black Panther Party no longer offered a viable pathway to political power. As a result, the organization suffered a long and painful demise, finally closing its last office in 1982.

Conclusion

When Civil Rights practices proved incapable of redressing the grievances of young urban blacks in the late 1960s, the Black Panthers armed themselves and promised to overcome poverty and oppression through revolution. They organized the rage of ghetto youth by confronting the police and resisted repression by winning the support of moderate black, antiwar, and international allies. These allies, like the Party, recognized the limited recourse available for real change through traditional political channels. But as blacks won greater electoral representation, government employment, affirmative action opportunities, as well as elite college and university access; the Vietnam War and military draft wound down; and the United States normalized relations with revolutionary governments abroad, it became impossible for the Panthers to continue advocating armed confrontation with the state and still maintain allied support. The Party, racked by external repression and internal fissures, quickly and disastrously unraveled.

There can be no doubt that individual and organizational contingencies—not least the personal flaws of Newton and Cleaver and the power struggle between them—contributed to the demise of the Black Panthers. But the Black Panther Party was not the only group to die out in the 1970s. All revolutionary black organizations in the United States declined at the same time.

These revolutionary nationalist organizations drew on deep roots. Without the Universal Negro Improvement Association of the 1920s, the Nation of Islam, or the Communist Party, it is hard to imagine the emergence of the Revolutionary Action Movement, the Republic of New Afrika, or the League of Revolutionary Black Workers, let alone the Black Panther Party. And yet widespread mobilization along revolutionary black nationalist lines was unique to the late 1960s. In every city with a significant black population, hundreds of young blacks took up arms and committed their lives to revolutionary struggle. That had never happened in the United States before. And it has not happened since.

To this day, small cadres in the United States dedicate their lives to a revolutionary vision. Not unlike the tenets of a religion, a secular revolutionary vision provides these communities with purpose and a moral compass. Some of these revolutionary communities publish periodicals, maintain websites, collectively feed and school their children, and share housing. But none wields the power to disrupt the status quo on a national scale. None is viewed as a serious threat by the federal government. And none today compares in scope or political influence to the Black Panther Party during its heyday.

The power the Black Panthers achieved grew out of their politics of armed self-defense. While they had little economic capital or institutionalized political power, they were able to forcibly assert their political agenda through their armed confrontations with the state. They obstructed the customary (and brutal) policing of black ghettos, creating a social crisis. Drawing broad legal, political, and financial support from allies, the Party was difficult to repress. The Black Panthers' capacity to sustain disruption legitimized their revolutionary vision and attracted members looking to make a real impact.

The Black Panther Party did not spring onto the historical stage fully formed; it grew in stages. Newton and Seale wove together their revolutionary vision from disparate strands. By standing up to police, they found they could organize the rage of young blacks fueled by brutal containment policing and persistent ghettoization. Through their tactic of deploying armed patrols of the police, they generated a local base of support in the Bay Area by May 1967. When the California Assembly outlawed these tactics, the Panthers reconceived themselves as a vanguard party and began advocating violent confrontation with the state. The Detroit and Newark rebellions revealed the depth of rage at ghetto conditions and showed that many young blacks were ready to pick up arms against the state to redress them. The Panthers had the pulse of the streets. When Newton was arrested on charges of killing a police officer in a late-night confrontation in October 1967, the call to Free Huey! became a national and eventually international cause. When Martin Luther King Jr. was assassinated the following spring, young people from around the country flooded the Black Panther Party with requests to open new chapters.

The Federal Bureau of Investigation, the Central Intelligence Agency, the Justice Department, and the House Committee on Internal Security all saw the Black Panther Party as a serious threat to "internal security." Starting in late 1968, the federal government, in coordination with local police departments throughout the country, waged a campaign of brutal repression against the Party.

In 1969, the Panthers made social service, notably feeding free breakfasts to children, the focus of their activities nationally. The Party's programs met real needs, strengthened community support, and gave members meaningful work. They exposed the failures of the federal War on Poverty and burnished the public image of the Party. In the face of repression, allied support for the Panthers increased.

Nixon won the White House on his Law and Order platform, inaugurating the year of the most intense direct repression of the Panthers. But the Party continued to grow in scope and influence. By 1970, it had opened offices in sixty-eight cities. That year, the *New York Times* published 1,217 articles on the Party, more than twice as many as in any other year.[1] The Party's annual budget reached about $1.2 million (in 1970 dollars).[2] And circulation of the Party's newspaper, the *Black Panther,* reached 150,000.[3]

The resonance of Panther practices was specific to the times. Many blacks believed conventional methods were insufficient to redress persistent exclusion from municipal hiring, decent education, and political power. Inspired by civil rights victories, young blacks wanted to extend the Black Liberation Struggle to challenge black poverty and ghettoization. As Panthers, they could stand up to police brutality, economic exploitation, and political exclusion. As Panthers, they extended the struggle to break continuing patterns of racial submissiveness. Panthers would not kowtow to anyone, not even police. As a result, they inspired blacks' self-esteem. In an impressive show of racial unity and pride, most black political organizations fiercely opposed the brutal repression of the Panthers. Even mainstream organizations like the Urban League and the National Association for the Advancement of Colored People mobilized against state repression of the Panthers.

Young men of every race, drafted to fight an unpopular war in Vietnam, found common purpose in the Panthers' global anti-imperialism. The Panthers drew a line dividing the world in two. They argued that the oppression of draft resisters by the National Guard was the same as oppression of blacks by the police and the same as the oppression of the Vietnamese by the marines. Forced to choose sides by the state, many young draftees chose the side of the oppressed. Alienated from the mainstream political leadership that had pursued the war despite popular opposition, many of their friends and family members supported their choice.

The Panthers helped foment a widespread radical challenge in the late 1960s. From riots in the streets to the closing of campuses, the questioning of traditional gender and sexual roles, and widespread defiance of the draft, radicals destabilized established rule. The Democratic Party responded by seeking to reconsolidate its liberal base by pushing initiatives advocating an end to the war and championing black electoral representation. The Nixon administration responded by attempting to repress the radicals, on the one hand, and making broad concessions to moderates, on the other. Nixon was the one who rolled back the draft, wound down the war, and advanced affirmative action. In the 1970s, black electoral representation and government hiring ballooned. As a result of these changes, the Panthers had difficulty sustaining broad support among blacks and antiwar activists.

By 1970, the Panthers had reached the pinnacle of their influence. The national headquarters worked hard to maintain the flow of allied support. What was once a scrappy local organization was now a major international political force, constantly in the news, with chapters in almost every major city. The thousands of recruits who flocked to the Party in 1968 and 1969 did not all share the national leadership's concern with Party discipline. The federal government infiltrated the Party with agent provocateurs, attempting to undermine Party discipline and alienate allies whenever it could. The countervailing pressures became ever more difficult for the national Party leadership to manage as the Party grew in influence. The eroding bases of allied support made managing these pressures untenable.

The hard-core right wing was not the main threat to the Party. Rather concessions to blacks and opponents of the war reestablished the credibility of liberalism to key constituencies.[4] It was much easier for the parents of young adults to find Tom Wolfe's parody of Leonard and Felicia Bernstein's Panther fund-raiser funny when they believed their children would not be drafted to die in Vietnam. When the government had pursued the war irrespective of the public will, killing countless young Americans, the Panthers' concerns were not so far afield. But when the Democratic Party began fighting to end the war, the Nixon administration rolled back the draft and created affirmative action programs, the United States normalized relations with revolutionary governments abroad, and black electoral representation ballooned, the Party had to work harder to maintain allied support. Eventually, the politics of armed self-defense became impossible to sustain.

Without the politics of armed self-defense that had driven the explosive growth of the Black Panther Party for three short years, from 1968 to 1970, dedicated revolutionaries in the Party were left with a creed and mission—to overthrow capitalism and advance self-governance in communities throughout the world—but they had no practical avenue to pursue these ends. Despite the heroism of their advocates, neither guerilla warfare nor social democratic practices provided a viable foundation for insurgent politics in the United States of the 1970s.

On the one hand, those who attempted to wage guerilla warfare were unrealistic politically. Unlike the Black Panther Party leadership during the peak years, they did not hold a coherent grasp of the political realities and possibilities of the times, nor practical means to build power. It is not difficult to see why some turned to guerilla warfare in the 1970s. The Panthers had built power and organization by standing up to the state and challenging the legitimacy of police violence. While the Party stopped advocating armed challenge of the police in 1971, most Panthers still considered the state and police to be brutal, unjust, and illegitimate oppressors. Many of them were still ready to die fighting for their liberation. As allies deserted the Panthers, the guerilla faction naively sought to advance its cause through armed struggle despite the slim chance of success. After several years of losses, most were either dead or in prison.

The social democratic practices of Elaine Brown and others were more realistic and more attuned to the political possibilities. In Oakland, the Panthers did succeed in using the political clout they had garnered in the Party's heyday to build local electoral power. But the Party no longer had any practical basis for building a broad insurgent movement. Unlike the viable insurgent politics of the Party's earlier days, the social democratic Panthers could deliver no consequence. They had limited institutionalized power and no longer wielded the capacity to disrupt on a large scale, so they advanced no practical basis for a national movement.

The vast literature on the Black Liberation Struggle in the postwar decades concentrates largely on the southern Civil Rights Movement. Our analysis is indebted to that literature as well as to more recent historical scholarship that enlarges both the geographic and temporal scope of analysis.[5] Thomas Sugrue in particular makes important advances, calling attention to the black insurgent mobilizations in the North and West, and to their *longue durée*.[6] This work, however, fails to analyze these mobilizations on their own terms, instead seeking to assimilate these black insurgencies to a civil rights perspective by presenting the range of black insurgent mobilizations as claims for black citizenship, appeals to the state—for full and equal participation. This perspective obscures the revolutionary character and radical economic focus of the Black Panther Party.

A newer generation of Black Power scholars, most compellingly Peniel Joseph, challenges this conflation by distinguishing Black Power activism and thought from civil rights activism and thought.[7] Joseph argues that the Black Power movement, perhaps epitomized by the Black Panther Party, was distinct in crucial ways from, ran parallel to, and at times intersected with the Civil Rights Movement throughout the twentieth century.[8] We agree that Black Power—and the revolutionary black politics of the Panthers in particular—followed a distinct and coherent logic and in fundamental ways is best understood as separate from the Civil Rights Movement. Ideologically and practically, revolutionary black nationalism has long ties to previous mobilizations.

Ultimately, however, both of these perspectives fail to answer important political questions. Why did revolutionary black nationalism—and Black Power mobilization generally—become so influential in the late 1960s, and why did it unravel so disastrously in the 1970s? The Sugrue approach bypasses this question by conflating radical Black Power mobilization with the Civil Rights Movement. While Joseph's important corrective acknowledges that Black Power was different in significant ways from civil rights activism, by emphasizing the roots and *longue durée* of Black Power, his approach obscures and does not adequately explain why Black Power as exemplified by the Black Panther Party became the center of black politics in the late 1960s, influencing the world around it in ways it never had before and hasn't since.

Our analysis shows that, even as Jim Crow was defeated and civil rights practices lost their political salience, the revolutionary practices of the Black Panther Party tapped into the rage of young blacks. The Panthers provided an insurgent channel for influence, drawing broad support from blacks, opponents of the war, and international revolutionary movements. The ideological and practical roots of Black Power politics had long been present on the political stage. But to the extent that Panther-like practices may have appealed to young blacks throughout the twentieth century, Panther politics were impractical both before and after the late 1960s. Panther practices could receive broad political support only while the majority of Americans opposed to the Vietnam War and draft had no recourse through institutionalized political channels and while most blacks continued to face economic and political exclusion.

The history of the Black Panther Party holds important implications for two more general theoretical debates. First, this history suggests a way out of dead-end debates about how the severity of repression affects social movement mobilization. One common perspective, supported by a rich scholarly literature covering various times and places, is that "repression breeds resistance": When authorities repress insurgency, the repression encourages further resistance.[9] But others pose the opposite argument, with equally rich scholarly support, suggesting that repression discourages and diminishes insurgency.[10] A classic sociological position that seeks to reconcile this apparent contradiction is that the relationship between repression and insurgency is shaped like an "inverse U": When repression is light, people tend to cooperate with established political authorities and take less disruptive action; when repression is heavy, the costs of insurgency are too large, causing people to shy away from radical acts. But, according to this view, it is when authorities are moderately repressive—too repressive to steer dissenters toward institutional channels of political participation but not repressive enough to quell dissent—that people widely mobilize disruptive challenges to authority.[11]

The history of the Panthers defies the basic premise of this debate: that the level of repression independently explains the level of resistance. The Black Panther Party faced heavy federally coordinated state repression at least from 1968 through 1971. Our analysis shows that for the first two years, from 1968 through 1969, brutal state repression helped legitimate the Panthers in the eyes of many supporters and fostered increased mobilization.[12] Taken alone, this finding would appear to support the idea that repression breeds resistance. But during the second two years, 1970 and 1971, the dynamic gradually shifted. The Panthers maintained the same types of practices they had embraced in the previous two years, and the state maintained a similar level and type of repressive practices. But in this later period, as the political context shifted—increasing the difficulty of winning support for the Panthers' revolutionary position—repression made the core Panther practices difficult to sustain and quickly led to the Party's demise.

The level of repression did not independently affect the level of mobilization in a consistent way across the four years. Instead, the level of repression interacted with the political reception of insurgent practices to affect the level of mobilization. In other words, potential allies' political reception of Panther insurgent practices determined the effects of repression on mobilization. During the time that Panther practices were well received by potential allies, in 1968 and 1969, repressive measures fostered further mobilization. But as these allies became less open to the Panthers' revolutionary position in 1970 and 1971, repressive actions by the state became increasingly effective.[13]

Our analysis also suggests a way forward in stalled debates of the political opportunity thesis that broad structural opportunities, by conferring political advantage on a social group, generate mobilization. The political opportunity thesis has made a crucial contribution to the sociological study of social movements in recent decades by emphasizing the importance of political context for explaining mobilization.[14] But attention to political context in isolation does not provide much explanatory power in the case of the Black Panther Party. From the classic political opportunity perspective, the late 1960s were the period in which the civil rights movement declined and thus a period of contracting political opportunities for blacks generally. That perspective makes it hard to understand why, even as the insurgent Civil Rights Movement fell apart, revolutionary black nationalism developed and thrived.

Recovering lost insights from early political process writings by Doug McAdam and Aldon Morris about the importance of tactical innovation for explaining mobilization, we designed this study to focus on the development of Panther political practice and influence.[15] We have found that political context, rather than independently determining the extent of mobilization, determines the efficacy of particular insurgent practices. The stepwise history of the Black Panther Party's mobilization and influence demonstrates that the relative effectiveness of its practices depended on the political context. Panther insurgent practices—specifically armed self-defense—generated both influence and following when they were both disruptive and difficult to repress. But the Panthers became much more repressible when the political context shifted, making it harder for the Party to practice armed self-defense and sustain allied support. This history suggests that insurgent movements proliferate when activists develop practices that simultaneously garner leverage by threatening the interests of powerful authorities and draw allied support in resistance to repression. Conversely, when concessions undermine the support of potential allies for those practices, the insurgency dies out.[16]

There is no movement like the Panthers in the United States today because the political context is so different from that in the late 1960s. This is not to say that the core grievances around which the Panthers mobilized have disappeared. To the contrary, large segments of the black population continue to live impoverished in ghettos, subject to containment policing, and send more sons to prison than to college. Many young people in these neighborhoods might well embrace a revolutionary political practice today if it could be sustained. But crucially, the conditions for rallying potential allies have changed.

The black middle class has greatly expanded since the Panthers' heyday. Its sons and daughters have access to the nation's elite colleges and universities. Black public sector employment has expanded dramatically: city governments and municipal police and fire departments hire many blacks. Blacks have won and institutionalized electoral power both locally and nationally. Most blacks in the United States today, especially the black middle class, believe their grievances can be redressed through traditional political and economic channels. Most view insurgency as no longer necessary and do not feel threatened by state repression of insurgent challengers.

No less important, the United States has no military draft today, and no draft resistance. The wars in Iraq and Afghanistan may be unpopular, but few people will risk years in jail to oppose them. No New Left exists today to embrace a Black Panther Party as its vanguard. Internationally, the struggles for national independence have almost all been won: the vast majority of the world's population is no longer colonized, if not yet truly free. Today, with few potential allies for a revolutionary black organization, the state could easily repress any Panther-like organization, no matter how disciplined and organized.

The broader question is why no revolutionary movement of any kind exists in the United States today. To untangle this question, we need to consider what makes a movement revolutionary. Here, the writings of the Italian theorist and revolutionary Antonio Gramsci are instructive: "A theory is 'revolutionary' precisely to the extent that it is an element of conscious separation and distinction into two camps and is a peak inaccessible to the enemy camp."[17] In other words, a revolutionary theory splits the world in two. It says that the people in power and the institutions they manage are the cause of oppression and injustice. A revolutionary theory purports to explain how to overcome those iniquities. It claims that oppression is inherent in the dominant social institutions. Further, it asserts that nothing can be done from within the dominant social institutions to rectify the problem—that the dominant social institutions must be overthrown. In this sense, any revolutionary theory consciously separates the world into two camps: those who seek to reproduce the existing social arrangements and those who seek to overthrow them.

In this first, ideational sense, many insurgent revolutionary movements do exist in the United States today, albeit on a very small scale. From sectarian socialist groups to nationalist separatists, these revolutionary minimovements have two things in common: a theory that calls for destroying the existing social world and advances an alternative trajectory; and cadres of members who have dedicated their lives to advance this alternative, see the revolutionary community as their moral reference point, and see themselves as categorically different from everyone who does not.

More broadly, in Gramsci's view, a movement is revolutionary *politically* to the extent that it poses an effective challenge. He suggests that such a revolutionary movement must first be creative rather than arbitrary. It must seize the political imagination and offer credible proposals to address the grievances of large segments of the population, creating a "concrete phantasy which acts on a dispersed and shattered people to arouse and organise its collective will."[18] But when a movement succeeds in this task, the dominant political coalition usually defeats the challenge through the twin means of repression and concession. The ruling alliance does not simply crush political challenges directly through the coercive power of the state but makes concessions that reconsolidate its political power without undermining its basic interests.[19] A revolutionary movement becomes significant politically only when it is able to win the loyalty of allies, articulating a broader insurgency.[20]

In this second, political sense, there are no revolutionary movements in the United States today. The country has seen moments of large-scale popular mobilization, and some of these recent movements, such as the mass mobilizations for immigrant rights in 2006, have been "creative," seizing the imagination of large segments of the population. One would think that the 2008 housing collapse, economic recession, subsequent insolvency of local governments, and bailout of the wealthy institutions and individuals most responsible for creating the financial crisis at the expense of almost everyone else provide fertile conditions for a broad insurgent politics. But as of this writing, it is an open question whether a broad, let alone revolutionary, challenge will develop. Recent movements have not sustained insurgency, advanced a revolutionary vision, or articulated a broader alliance to challenge established political power.

In our assessment, for the years 1968 to 1970, the Black Panther Party was revolutionary in Gramsci's sense, both ideationally and politically. Ideationally, young Panthers dedicated their lives to the revolution because—as part of a global revolution against empire—they believed that they could transform the world. The revolutionary vision of the Party became the moral center of the Panther community. To stand on the sidelines or die an enemy of the Panther revolution was to be "lighter than a feather"—to be on the wrong side of history. To die for the Panther revolution was to be "heavier than a mountain"—to be the vanguard of the future.[21] The Black Panther Party stood out from countless politically insignificant revolutionary cadres because it was creative politically. For a few years, the Party seized the political imagination of a large constituency of young black people. Even more, it articulated this revolutionary movement of young blacks to a broader oppositional movement, drawing allied support from more moderate blacks and opponents of the Vietnam War of every race.

When expanding political and economic opportunities for blacks and the growing consensus among mainstream politicians to wind down the Vietnam War opened institutionalized channels for redressing the interests of key Panther supporters, Panther practices lost their political salience. When the political foundation of the Black Panther Party collapsed in early 1971, the practices that had won the Panthers so much influence became futile. No Panther faction was able to effectively reinvent itself.

Even as concessions siphoned off allied support, the state sought to vilify the Party, driving a wedge between Panthers and their allies. Ultimately, nothing did more to vilify the Panthers than the widely publicized evidence of intraorganizational violence and corruption as the Party unraveled. Any attempt to replicate the earlier Panther revolutionary nationalism was now vulnerable to provocation and vilification. The political "system" had been inoculated against the Panthers' politics.[22]

While minimovements with revolutionary ideologies abound, there is no politically significant revolutionary movement in the United States today because no cadre of revolutionaries has developed ideas and practices that credibly advance the interests of a large segment of the people. Members of revolutionary sects can hawk their newspapers and proselytize on college campuses until they are blue in the face, but they remain politically irrelevant. Islamist insurgencies, with deep political roots abroad, are politically significant, but they lack potential constituencies in the United States. And ironically, at least in the terrorist variant, they tend to reinforce rather than challenge state power domestically because their practices threaten—rather than build common cause with—alienated constituencies within the United States.

No revolutionary movement of political significance will gain a foothold in the United States again until a group of revolutionaries develops insurgent practices that seize the political imagination of a large segment of the people and successively draw support from other constituencies, creating a broad insurgent alliance that is difficult to repress or appease. This has not happened in the United States since the heyday of the Black Panther Party and may not happen again for a very long time.

Notes

INTRODUCTION

1. Albin Krebs, "Newton Visits China," *New York Times*, September 29, 1971, 30; "Huey Newton in Peking," *New York Times*, September 30, 1971, 6; Huey P. Newton, *Revolutionary Suicide* (New York: Writers and Readers, 1995), 324–26. One of Newton's companions on the trip was Elaine Brown, his lover and the future chairwoman of the Black Panther Party. The other was Robert Bay, his bodyguard.

2. Newton, *Revolutionary Suicide*, 324; Elaine Brown, *A Taste of Power: A Black Woman's Story* (New York: Pantheon Books, 1992), 295–96.

3. The petition is reproduced in a supplement to the October 16, 1971, issue of the *Black Panther*, and a photo of the meeting appears on the front page of this issue. Brown, *A Taste of Power*, 303; Newton, *Revolutionary Suicide*, 325; "Huey Newton Returns from China," *Los Angeles Times*, October 9, 1971, 3.

4. Agence France-Presse, "Chou and Other Officials Attend National Day Rites," *New York Times*, October 2, 1971, 1.

5. Newton, *Revolutionary Suicide*, 326.

6. "Revisit to Peking," editorial, *New York Times*, October 6, 1971, 46.

7. Huey P. Newton, "The Functional Definition of Politics," *Black Panther*, May 15, 1967, 4.

8. For the approximate date when the Black Panther Party opened offices in various cities, see House Committee on Internal Security, *Gun-Barrel Politics: The Black Panther Party, 1966–1971*, part 470, 92d Cong., 1st sess. (Washington, DC: Government Printing Office, 1971), 88–89.

9. We follow Gramsci in our conception of revolutionary movements and further discuss the Panthers in this context in our final chapter. Antonio Gramsci, *Prison Notebooks* (New York: International Publishers, 1971).

10. Interagency Committee on Intelligence (Ad Hoc), Special Report [Huston Report], June 25, 1970, 9–10.

11. Students for a Democratic Society resolution at the Austin National Council, "The Black Panther Party: Toward the Liberation of the Colony," *New Left Notes,* April 4, 1969, 1, 3. The best collection of surviving copies of *New Left Notes* resides in the Wisconsin State Historical Society Archives in Madison.

12. J. Edgar Hoover quoted in "FBI Director Blacks Black Panthers," *Oakland Tribune,* July 15, 1969, 17.

13. We measured the degree of repression by the annual number of Panthers killed in direct confrontations with the state.

14. David Garrow, "Picking Up the Books: The New Historiography of the Black Panther Party," *Reviews in American History* 35, no. 4 (2007): 650.

15. Robert Blauner, "The Outlaw Huey Newton: A Former Admirer Paints an Unromantic Portrait of the Black Panther Leader," *New York Times,* July 10, 1994, BR1.

16. Garrow, "Picking Up the Books"; Judson L. Jeffries and Ryan Nissim-Sabat, introduction to *On the Ground: The Black Panther Party in Communities Across America,* ed. Judson Jeffries (Jackson: University Press of Mississippi, 2010); Elaine Brown, foreword to *To Die for the People,* by Huey Newton (San Francisco: City Lights Press, 2009); Charles E. Jones, introduction to *The Black Panther Party [Reconsidered],* ed. Charles E, Jones (Baltimore: Black Classic Press, 1998).

17. This quote is variously attributed to Niccolo Machiavelli, Napoleon Bonaparte, Winston Churchill, and others.

18. For an overview of the FBI counterintelligence program against the Panthers, see Select Committee to Study Governmental Operations with Respect to Intelligence Activities [Church Committee], *Supplementary Detailed Staff Reports on Intelligence Activities and the Rights of Americans,* book 3, Final Report, S. Doc. No. 94–755 (April 1976). For details on raids and the assassination of Fred Hampton, see chapter 10, "Hampton and Clark."

19. Airtel [a high-priority FBI memo sent via airmail], FBI Director [J. Edgar Hoover] to SAC [Special Agent in Charge], Sacramento [and FBI field offices throughout the country], March 4, 1968, "Counterintelligence Program—Black Nationalist-Hate Groups—Racial Intelligence." This and all other FBI memos cited in this chapter are available in the FBI Reading Room, FBI Headquarters, Washington, DC. As of May 2, 2012, many of the COINTELPRO documents cited in this book became available online at http://vault .fbi.gov/cointel-pro/cointel-pro-black-extremists. See also memo, G. C. Moore to W. C. Sullivan, February 29, 1968, "Counterintelligence Program—Black Nationalist-Hate Groups—Racial Intelligence."

20. Airtel, FBI Director [J. Edgar Hoover], to Special Agent in Charge, San Francisco, May 27, 1969.

21. Memo, G. C. Moore to W. C. Sullivan, September 27, 1968.

22. Ibid.

23. Provocateur actions such as the case of the New York 21 are well documented and known; see Select Committee to Study Governmental Opera-

tions, *Supplementary Detailed Staff Reports on Intelligence Activities and the Rights of Americans.* For promotion of kangaroo courts and torture by a documented agent provocateur, see William O'Neal, Captain of Security, "FBI Informer," *Black Panther,* February 17, 1969, 9.

24. Kate Coleman and Paul Avery, "The Party's Over," *New Times,* July 10, 1978, 1.

25. David Horowitz, "Vicious Criminals," *San Jose Mercury News,* October 5, 1994. See also Peter Collier and David Horowitz, "Baddest," in *Destructive Generation: Second Thoughts about the Sixties* (New York: Summit Books, 1989); and David Horowitz in Doris Tourmarkine, "'Panther' Labeled a 'Lie'," *Hollywood Reporter,* April 29, 1995.

26. Hugh Pearson, *The Shadow of the Panther: Huey Newton and the Price of Black Power in America* (Boston: Addison-Wesley, 1994).

27. Christopher Lehmann-Haupt, "On the Rise and Fall of Huey Newton," *New York Times,* June 30, 1994, C18. "Notable Books of the Year 1994," *New York Times,* December 4, 1994, BR65.

28. See, for example, a comment on the original Black Panther Party posted on Yahoo Answers on May 12, 2011: "It was a black version of the KKK."

29. "Envoy from the '60s," editorial, *Providence Journal-Bulletin,* September 20, 2000, 6B.

30. Michele Wallace, *Black Macho and the Myth of the Superwoman* (New York: Dial Press, 1978), 73, 160, 167.

31. June Jordan, "To Be Black and Female," review of *Black Macho and the Myth of the Superwoman,* by Michele Wallace, *New York Times Book Review,* March 18, 1979, BR4.

32. Among the authors who discuss the Black Panthers within broader histories are Nikhil Pal Singh, Robin D. G. Kelley, Rod Bush, Laura Pulido, Robert Self, Chris Rhomberg, and Jeffrey Ogbar.

33. As of May 23, 2011, ProQuest Digital Dissertations listed ninety abstracts of dissertations and master's theses that contain the phrase *Black Panther Party;* www.proquest.com/en-US/catalogs/databases/detail/pqdt.shtml.

34. One of our guiding theoretical propositions is that as people find effective ways of struggling for political power, others join them. As social movements develop in this way, they tend to leave a "strategic trace." In other words, a history of the genesis of movement strategy ought to reveal increased adoption (and evolution) of demands and tactics of struggle as these demands and tactics meet with success. For a more extended discussion of strategic genealogy, see the original book proposal, Joshua Bloom, "Power of the Panther: The History and Politics of the Black Panther Party," unpublished manuscript, 2000, in possession of the author.

35. Joshua Bloom, collection editor, Black Panther Newspaper Collection, Black Thought and Culture database, Alexander Street Press, 2009; http://solomon.bltc.alexanderstreet.com/cgi-bin/asp/philo/bltc/bltc.bpp.pl?year=1967. With some twelve thousand pages, this collection of the *Black Panther* contains more than twice as many issues as the next most complete collection.

36. We are, of course, fully aware that some Civil Rights Movement scholars will disagree with this characterization. Our analysis here, and through-

out this book, is guided by a conception and theory of social movements that is not yet standard among historians or sociologists. We conceptualize an insurgent social movement as the proliferation of a set of practices—including a relatively consistent set of targets, frames, and repertoires—that are immediately disruptive to established social practices. Our main theoretical argument is that when, given a particular political context, a set of insurgent practices draws broad allied support in resistance to repression by authorities, it provides insurgents with a sustainable source of political leverage, and the insurgency proliferates. We argue that insurgent social movements can best be understood in these terms.

So in this sense, the Civil Rights Movement can best be understood as the wide proliferation of a particular set of insurgent practices. The bus boycotts, the sit-ins, the freedom rides, the community campaigns, and the voting rights campaigns all entailed similar practices: nonviolent civil disobedience that disrupted legal segregation and de facto disenfranchisement, coupled with claims for full citizenship rights and equal participation in American society. Following closely upon the heels of its extraordinary victories in the mid-1960s, the Civil Rights Movement did not just shift gears, it ended as an insurgent movement. Some of the organizations and individuals continued to pursue similar goals. And the broader Black Liberation Struggle continued in the sense of a multimovement amalgam of many waves of activists seeking liberation from racial oppression in different ways. But nonviolent civil disobedience against legal segregation was no longer a source of powerful political leverage, its practice ebbed, and the insurgent Civil Rights Movement ended. For further discussion see the conclusion, and especially Joshua Bloom, "Pathways of Insurgency: Black Liberation Struggle and the Second Reconstruction, 1945–1975," unpublished manuscript.

37. In this sense, there are many parallels with the immigrant rights campaigns today. A wide spectrum of organizations and forms of activism share the basic premise that undocumented immigrants are economically exploited and politically oppressed. But they have no movement that provides a coherent and powerful practical avenue for redress.

1. HUEY AND BOBBY

Epigraph, part 1: Alprentice "Bunchy" Carter, *Black Panther*, March 3, 1969.

1. The description of Huey Newton's family and childhood is drawn from Huey P. Newton, *Revolutionary Suicide* (New York: Writers and Readers, 1995), and David Hilliard and Lewis Cole, *This Side of Glory: The Autobiography of David Hilliard and the Story of the Black Panthers* (New York: Little, Brown, 1993).

2. Armelia Johnson paraphrased by Newton in *Revolutionary Suicide*, 12.

3. Walter Newton quoted by Melvin Newton in Hilliard and Cole, *This Side of Glory*, 71; Walter Newton paraphrased in Huey Newton, *Revolutionary Suicide*, 30.

4. Newton, *Revolutionary Suicide*, 11, 32.

5. Ibid., 24.

6. Ibid., 33–44.

7. Ibid., 45–55, 60.

8. Bobby Seale, *Seize the Time: The Story of the Black Panther Party and Huey P. Newton* (1971; repr. Baltimore: Black Classic Press, 1990), 13–21; Newton, *Revolutionary Suicide*, 105–6.

9. This account of Bobby Seale's early life draws from four sources: Bobby Seale, *Lonely Rage: The Autobiography of Bobby Seale* (New York: Times Books, 1978); Seale, *Seize the Time*; Bobby Seale, interview by Joshua Bloom, April 25, 1999; Joshua Bloom, "Bobby Seale," in *Civil Rights in the United States*, vol. 2, ed. Waldo E. Martin Jr. and Patricia Sullivan (New York: Macmillan, 2000), 677.

10. Seale, *Lonely Rage*, 19.

11. Ibid., 26.

12. Ibid., part 3.

13. Ibid., 91 and part 4.

14. Seale, *Seize the Time*, 13–21; Robin D. G. Kelley, *Freedom Dreams: The Black Radical Imagination* (Boston: Beacon Press, 2002), 74–77. For detailed treatment of Warden at Berkeley, see especially Donna Jean Murch, *Living for the City* (Chapel Hill: University of North Carolina Press, 2010), 75–95.

15. Thomas Barry, "Soul Brother No.1," *New Dawn*, November 1970, 3. See chapter 6 for more on Karenga.

16. Spence Conley, "Clay Here—'Ugly Bear to Fall,'" *Oakland Tribune*, September 28, 1963, B-11; "Rally Will End Rights Meet Here," *Oakland Tribune*, September 28, 1963, 1; George Draper, "The World's Greatest: Cassius Clay in East Bay," *San Francisco Chronicle*, September 28, 1963, 9; Newton, *Revolutionary Suicide*, 63, 71; Kelley, *Freedom Dreams*, 74–77; Murch, *Living for the City*, 90–92; Donald Warden interview by James M. Mosby Jr., July 22, 1970, Ralph J. Bunche Oral History Collection, item 426, Moorland-Springarn Library, Howard University. Some sources mistakenly claim that Malcolm X spoke at this conference and that Clay was already publicly a Muslim. But none of the press accounts support these claims. These accounts list many speakers who participated in the conference but not the famous Malcolm X, and they make no mention of Clay's participation in the Nation of Islam (NOI), which would have been big and highly controversial news. Clay's championship fight with Liston in February 1964 was almost canceled over rumors that he was associated with Malcolm X, and Clay only announced his membership in the NOI and his relationship with Malcolm X after beating Liston for the championship in February of 1964. Moreover, a second association conference at McClymonds could not have taken place involving both Malcolm X and Newton because Newton left the Afro-American Association not long after the 1963 conference. Any such appearance would have been big news, and we could find no news reports of such a conference. There were only about four weeks in February and March of 1964 when Ali was publicly associated with Malcolm X before Malcolm X was expelled from the NOI.

17. Newton, *Revolutionary Suicide*, 64–65.

18. Seale, *Lonely Rage*, 133–36; Seale, *Seize the Time*, 3.

19. The account of the MFDP and Atlantic City Convention draws from seven sources: Clayborne Carson, *In Struggle: SNCC and the Black Awakening of the 1960s* (Cambridge, MA: Harvard University Press, 1981), 121–28; Charles Payne, *I've Got the Light of Freedom: The Organizing Tradition and the Mississippi Freedom Struggle* (Berkeley: University of California Press, 1995); Robert P. Moses and Charles E. Cobb Jr., *Radical Equations* (Boston: Beacon Press, 2001), 78–83; James Forman, *The Making of Black Revolutionaries* (Washington, DC: Open Hand Publishing, 1985), 371–407; Stokely Carmichael with Ekwueme Michael Thelwell, *Ready for Revolution: The Life and Struggles of Stokely Carmichael (Kwame Ture)* (New York: Scribner, 2003); Taylor Branch, *Pillar of Fire: America in the King Years 1963–65* (New York: Simon & Schuster, 1998), 456–76; John Dittmer, "Politics of the Mississippi Movement, 1954–1964," in *The Civil Rights Era in America*, ed. Charles W. Eagles (Jackson: University Press of Mississippi, 1986).

20. Hamer quoted in Carson, *In Struggle*, 125.

21. Humphrey quoted in Moses and Cobb, *Radical Equations*, 82.

22. Moses and Cobb, *Radical Equations*, 82.

23. *Malcolm X Speaks*, ed. George Breitman (New York: Grove Press, 1965), 106.

24. Ibid., 35. See also William W. Sales Jr., *From Civil Rights to Black Liberation: Malcolm X and the Organization of Afro-American Unity* (Boston: South End Press, 1994).

25. *Malcolm X Speaks*, 31–32.

26. William L. Van Deburg, *New Day in Babylon: The Black Power Movement and American Culture, 1965–1975* (Chicago: University of Chicago Press, 1992), 2.

27. Gerald Horne, *Fire This Time: The Watts Uprising and the 1960s* (New York: Da Capo, 1997), 35.

28. Ibid.

29. McCone Commission Report in Anthony M. Platt, *The Politics of Riot Commissions* (New York: Collier Books, 1971), 279.

30. Parker quoted in Tracy Tullis, "A Vietnam at Home: Policing the Ghettos in the Counterinsurgency Era" (PhD diss., New York University, 1999), 208.

31. Tullis, "A Vietnam at Home," 208–9.

32. Horne, *Fire This Time*, 68.

33. Ibid., 54–55.

34. Ibid., 58, 66.

35. Jack McCurdy and Art Berman, "New Rioting: Stores Looted, Cars Destroyed, Many Fires Started; 75 Reported Injured in 2nd Violent Night," *Los Angeles Times*, August 13, 1965, 1.

36. Horne, *Fire This Time*, 64, 67.

37. Ibid., 36–38.

38. McCone Commission Report in Platt, *The Politics of Riot Commissions*, 264–71.

39. Horne, *Fire This Time*, 183–84.

40. Paul Jacobs and Saul Landau, *The New Radicals: A Report with Documents* (New York: Random House, 1966), 26.

41. Newton, *Revolutionary Suicide.*

42. Timothy Tyson, *Radio Free Dixie: Robert F. Williams and the Roots of Black Power* (Chapel Hill: University of North Carolina Press, 1999).

43. Kelley, *Freedom Dreams,* 75–76.

44. *Soulbook,* nos. 4–7 (Winter 1965–66 through Summer/Fall 1967), a publication of the AfroAmerican Research Institution, Berkeley, CA; Newton, *Revolutionary Suicide,* 108; Kelley, *Freedom Dreams,* 76.

45. Seale, *Seize the Time,* 24–27; Newton, *Revolutionary Suicide,* 108. See Murch, *Living for the City,* chapter 4 for more on SSAC.

46. For Newton's introduction to Fanon, see Seale, *Seize the Time,* 25. Newton discusses reading Fanon, Mao, and Che during this period in *Revolutionary Suicide,* 111. Explicit references to Fanon, Mao, and Che are common in the earliest issues of the *Black Panther.*

47. See Penny Von Eschen, *Race against Empire: Black Americans and Anticolonialism 1937–1957* (Ithaca, NY: Cornell University Press, 1997).

48. Max Stanford, "Revolutionary Nationalism and the Afroamerican Student," in *Liberator,* January 1965, 15. These ideas permeate the writings of RAM during this period. For example, see also Revolutionary Action Movement, "In Summary: A New Philosophy," *Black America,* Summer–Fall 1965, 20; Revolutionary Action Movement, "The Relationship of Revolutionary Afro-American Movement to the Bandung Revolution," *Black America,* Summer–Fall 1965, 11;

49. Revolutionary Action Movement letter, "Greetings to Our Militant Vietnamese Brothers," July 4, 1965, reel 6, frame 0228, Black Power Movement collection, Part 3: Papers of the Revolutionary Action Movement, 1962–1966, UC Santa Barbara Library.

50. "Message from RAM (Revolutionary Action Movement), the Black Liberation Front of the U.S.A. to Afro-Americans in the United States Racist Imperialist Army," July 4, 1965, reel 6, frame 0229, Black Power Movement collection, Part 3, Papers of the Revolutionary Action Movement, 1962–1966, UC Santa Barbara Library.

51. Rally to Oppose the Drafting of Black Men, flier 313–660426–000, H.K. Yuen Collection, Bancroft Library, University of California, Berkeley (hereafter Yuen Collection).

52. Timothy B. Tyson. *Radio Free Dixie: Robert F. Williams and the Roots of Black Power.* (Chapel Hill: University of North Carolina Press, 1999).

53. Mao Zedong, "Statement calling on the people of the world to unite to oppose racial discrimination in the U.S. and support the American Negroes in their struggle against racial discrimination," August 8, 1963, RAM archive, reel 6, frame 0195. The statement read in part,

> The speedy development of the struggle of the American Negroes is a manifestation of the sharpening of class struggle and national struggle within the United States; it has been causing increasing anxiety to U.S. ruling circles. The Kennedy Administration has resorted to cunning two-faced tactics. On the one hand, it continues to connive at and take part in the discrimination against Negroes and their persecution; it even sends troops to suppress them. On the other hand, in its attempt to lull the fighting will of the Negro people and deceive the masses throughout the country, the Kennedy

Administration is parading as an advocate of the "defense of human rights" and "the protection of the civil rights of Negroes," is calling upon the Negro people to exercise "restraint," and is proposing the "civil rights legislation" to Congress. But more and more Negroes are seeing through these tactics of the Kennedy Administration. The fascist atrocities committed by the U.S. imperialists against the Negro people have laid bare the true nature of the so-called democracy and freedom of the United States and revealed the inner link between the reactionary policies pursued by the U.S. government at home and its policies of aggression abroad.

I call on the workers, peasants, revolutionary intellectuals, enlightened elements of the bourgeoisies and other enlightened persons of all colours in the world, whether white, black, yellow or brown, to unite to oppose the racial discrimination practiced by U.S. imperialism and support the American Negroes in their struggle against racial discrimination. In the final analysis, a national struggle is a question of class struggle. In the United States, it is only the reactionary ruling circles among the whites who oppress the Negro people. They can in no way represent the workers, farmers, revolutionary intellectuals and other enlightened persons who comprise the overwhelming majority of the white people. At present, it is the handful of imperialists headed by the United States, and their supporters, the reactionaries in different countries, who are inflicting oppression, aggression and intimidation on the overwhelming majority of the nations and peoples of the world. We are in the majority and they are in the minority. At most, they make up less than 10 percent of the 3,000 million population of the world. I am firmly convinced that, with the support of more than 90 per cent of the people of the world, the American Negroes will be victorious in their just struggle. The evil system of colonialism and imperialism grew up along with enslavement of Negroes, and it will surely come to its end with the thorough emancipation of the black people.

54. Robert F. Williams, Negroes with Guns (New York: Marzani & Munsell, 1962).

55. Newton, *Revolutionary Suicide*, 108–12.

56. For example, RAM members allegedly conspired to blow up the Statue of Liberty, *Chicago Sun Times*, February 17, 1965.

57. Amory Bradford, *Oakland's Not for Burning* (New York: D. McKay Co., 1968), 6; and Daniel Edward Crowe, "The Origins of the Black Revolution: The Transformation of San Francisco Bay Area Black Communities, 1945–1969" (PhD diss., University of Kentucky, 1998), 199–202. Curtis Lee Baker served as the director of the West End Help Center in west Oakland and helped found Justice on Bay Area Rapid Transit, an effort to win employment for blacks on BART. Mark Comfort organized protests in 1964 with the Congress of Racial Equality to challenge discriminatory hiring practices at the *Oakland Tribune* and went on to form the Oakland Direct Action Committee.

58. "Oakland Mayor's Angry Orders on Racial Crisis," *Oakland Tribune*, April 22, 1966, 1; Crowe, "Origins of the Black Revolution," 199–200; Bradford, *Oakland's Not for Burning*, 6, 19. In 1966, Comfort and Baker collaborated to bring Chicago-based radical community organizer and writer Saul Alinsky to Oakland for a series of talks and attempted to get the Oakland Council of Churches to bring Alinsky to Oakland for an extended stay.

59. "Youths Protest 'Police Brutality,'" *San Francisco Chronicle*, February 20, 1965, 4.

60. "Negro Area Cops Blasted in Oakland," *San Francisco Chronicle*, August 26, 1965, 6.

61. "Conditions in the Oakland Ghetto: Mark Comfort interviewed by Elsa Knight Thompson," 1967, cassette E2BB1309, Pacifica Radio Archive, North Hollywood, CA, cited in Crowe, "Origins of the Black Revolution," 202.

62. Seale, *Seize the Time*, 27–28.

63. The People of the State of California v. Bobby Seale, case #38842; Seale, *Seize the Time*, 27–28. Megan Miladinov, "Former Black Panther Leader," *Athens News*, February 12, 2004.

64. Seale, *Seize the Time*, 28–29, 33.

65. Ibid., 29.

66. Seale, *Lonely Rage*, 151.

67. Newton, *Revolutionary Suicide*, 108–9; Seale, *Seize the Time*, 30–34.

68. Seale, *Seize the Time*, 33.

69. Ibid., 35–56.

70. Martin Luther King Jr., *Where Do We Go from Here: Chaos or Community?* (New York: Harper, 1958), 27–37.

71. Manning Marable, *Race, Reform, and Rebellion: The Second Reconstruction in Black America, 1945–1982* (Jackson: University Press of Mississippi, 1984), 94.

72. Martin Luther King Jr. quoted in Carson, *In Struggle*, 210.

73. "Oakland Mayor's Angry Orders on Racial Crisis," *San Francisco Chronicle*, April 22, 1966, 1.

74. Bradford, *Oakland's Not for Burning*, 2.

75. Quoted in Crowe, "The Origins of the Black Revolution," 139.

76. Flier reproduced in Bradford, *Oakland's Not for Burning*, 16.

77. Thomas C. Fleming, "Wild Rioting by Oakland Youths," *Sun Reporter*, October 22, 1966, in Crowe, "The Origins of the Black Revolution," 196.

78. *Sun Reporter* in Crowe, "The Origins of the Black Revolution," 193n10. Also Bradford, *Oakland's Not for Burning*, 194.

79. Sol Stern, "The Call of the Black Panthers," *New York Times Magazine*, August 6, 1967, 10. Newton and Seale were not the only ones enraged by the incident. On September 29, the predominantly white chapter of the Students for a Democratic Society at UC Berkeley held a protest on the steps of San Francisco City Hall to demand the policeman be tried for murder. In a press statement endorsing the student demonstration, Community for New Politics argued that in the twenty years since the black neighborhood of Hunters Point had been established, "the white power structure in San Francisco has done nothing about the worsening conditions of the area. And when the residents finally rebel against these conditions they are met with a policeman and a gun." SDS identified the National Guard as an "alien occupying force" in the ghetto and called for its immediate withdrawal from Hunters Point. "In the ghetto, too often police are protecting white property and serve white interests, while treating the people who live in the area as the enemy," explained an SDS spokesperson. Picketers at the rally also expressed opposition to the government policy in Vietnam. The rally became a march as sev-

eral hundred students and community members shouted "Cops must go!" and "Jobs not cops!" Soon, truckloads of National Guardsmen and police pulled up, and the officers, carrying rifles with bayonets, jumped out and surrounded the marchers. Without giving an order to disperse, the police started to pull protestors out of the march and beat them. More than seventy protestors were arrested, many charged with "inciting to riot." Bill Crosby, "SDS: 'Aliens' Occupy SF Ghetto," *Daily Californian,* September 30, 1966, 6; "SDS Rally: 'White Power' Hit," *Daily Californian,* October 3, 1966, 3; "In Support of the People of the Ghetto," flier 313–660930–000, Yuen Collection; "Eighty Arrested on Protest March," flier 313–660930–001, Yuen Collection.

80. Terence Cannon, "A Night with the Watts Community Alert Patrol," *Movement,* August 1966, 1, article in Huey Newton's possession, Huey P. Newton Collection, series 7, flat box 9, folder 13, Stanford University; Horne, *Fire This Time,* 54.

81. Newton, *Revolutionary Suicide,* 115; Seale, *Seize the Time,* 73, 89.

82. See *Daily Californian,* October 1966, multiple articles.

83. Associated Press, "Reagan Hits Campus Meets: Cites Fear of Riot," *Daily Californian,* October 21, 1966, 1; Associated Press, "Brown First on Stokely," *Daily Californian,* October 27, 1966; Bill Crosby, "Oakland Visit: Brown on Black Power," *Daily Californian,* October 28, 1966.

84. "Black Power and Its Challenges," flier 313–661030–000.

85. Original footage of the Conference on Black Power and Its Challenges held in Berkeley, October 29, 1966, in *The Frog in the Well: The Life and Work of Hoh-Kun Yuen,* a film produced by Cervando David Martinez, Yuen Collection. Bill Crosby, "Afro-Students Tongue Lash SDS," *Daily Californian,* October 27, 1966, 1; Rich Weinhold, "'Power' Aftermath," *Daily Californian,* October 31, 1966, 1.

86. Footage of the Black Power conference in *The Frog in the Well.* Ivanhoe Donaldson in "Stokely Carmichael," audio reel 044–661029–000, Yuen Collection; Gary Plotkin, "Black Power Meet," *Daily Californian,* October 31, 1966, 16.

87. "Stokely Carmichael," audio reel 044–661029–000, Yuen Collection.

88. Ibid.

89. Ibid.

90. Committee for Lowndes County, *Support the Lowndes County Freedom Organization,* pamphlet 313–661108–006, Yuen Collection; Stokely Carmichael, "What We Want," *New York Review of Books,* September 22, 1966; Roy Reed, "Alabama Negro Candidates Lead in 2 Legislative, 3 Sheriff's Votes," *New York Times,* May 4, 1966, 28; Gene Robers, "The Story of Snick: From 'Freedom High' to 'Black Power,'" *New York Times,* September 25, 1966, 242; Jonathan L. Foster, "Radical Loss: The First Black Panthers and the Lowndes County Election of 1966," *Vulcan Historical Review,* Spring 2001; Carson, *In Struggle,* 162–66; John Hulett quoted in Frank Miles, "Lowndes County Freedom Organization Leaders Talk about Their Party," *Movement,* June 1966, 3, cited in Carson, *In Struggle;* Hasan Jeffries, *Bloody Lowndes: Civil Rights and Black Power in Alabama's Black Belt* (New York: New York University Press, 2009).

91. "Black Panthers Open Harlem Drive," *New York Amsterdam News,* September 3, 1966, 1; "Negro Leaders Show Differences," *New York Amsterdam News,* September 3, 1966, 30.

92. Carmichael, "What We Want."

93. "Black Power and Its Challenges," flier 313–661030–000; *Support the Lowndes County Freedom Organization,* pamphlet 313–661108–006; "Support the Black Panther!" flier 313–661108–007; all in the Yuen Collection.

94. Newton, *Revolutionary Suicide,* 113.

95. Some have suggested that contrary to Newton and Seale's assertions in their memoirs, there was originally only one Black Panther Party in the Bay Area and that Newton and Seale split off from RAM's Black Panther Party of Northern California at the time of their conflict during the Shabazz incident in February 1967, or even later, after the action in Sacramento in May 1967, both discussed in chapter 2. These suggestions are incorrect. The evidence clearly supports Newton and Seale's claims that they founded the Black Panther Party for Self-Defense as a separate organization from RAM well in advance of either the Shabazz incident or the Sacramento action. See, for example, "Black Panther Close," *Berkeley Barb,* February 17, 1967; and "Oakland's Black Panthers Wear Guns, Talk Revolution," *San Francisco Chronicle,* April 30, 1967. It is hard to pin down a precise date for the Party's founding. Some have claimed that the Party was founded on October 15, 1966, and suggested that Huey Newton and Bobby Seale decided to start their own organization, chose to adopt the name and logo of the Black Panther Party from the Lowndes County effort, and drafted their Ten Point Program all on that day. The evidence does not support this conclusion. Newton and Seale likely adopted the name and logo sometime after the October 29, 1966, Black Power Conference at Berkeley, and they likely drafted the Ten Point Program in 1967. See chapter 3 for more on the development of the Ten Point Program.

2. POLICING THE POLICE

1. The description of the event comes from Bobby Seale, *Seize the Time: The Story of the Black Panther Party and Huey P. Newton* (1971; repr. Baltimore: Black Classic Press, 1990), 93–98; and from Joshua Bloom's tour of the site of the incident with Bobby Seale, January 19, 1999.

2. Seale, *Seize the Time,* 97. While numerous firsthand news accounts attest to the general character of the Panthers' early armed confrontations with police, the thickest descriptions are in retrospective accounts, especially Bobby Seale's 1970 *Seize the Time.* Published during the height of the "Free Huey!" campaign, the text portrays Huey as the main person speaking to the crowd in this confrontation. But this portrayal is inconsistent with Huey Newton's character. By many accounts, Newton was neither comfortable nor skilled at rousing public audiences. Although Newton likely developed the tactic of legal armed confrontation with the police and led the confrontations with the police in practice, Bobby Seale probably did most of the public speaking to crowds during these confrontations, as elsewhere. In a discussion of a draft manuscript with Joshua Bloom at the East Side Arts Alliance in Oakland on June 3,

2011, Seale asserted that this was the case and that he originally credited Newton with speaking to the crowds to support the Free Huey! campaign but that he was really the one who did most of the rallying.

3. The description of Aoki is based on Joshua Bloom's impressions during several informal meetings with him. Bobby Seale, interview by Joshua Bloom, April 25, 1999; and interview by Robyn Spencer, October 13, 1997, quoted in Robyn Ceanne Spencer, "Repression Breeds Resistance: The Rise and Fall of the Black Panther Party in Oakland, CA, 1966–1982" (PhD diss., Columbia University, 2001), 24; Seale, *Seize the Time*, 73.

4. Seale, *Seize the Time*, 79–85. For the timing of the publicity for the sale of Mao's Little Red Book, see "World Sale of 'Quotations' Brisk," *New York Times*, February 17, 1967, 3.

5. Seale, *Seize the Time*, 77.

6. This treatment of the Shabazz escort, the buildup to it, the confrontation at *Ramparts*, and the aftermath is taken from five firsthand accounts: Eldridge Cleaver, "The Courage to Kill: Meeting the Panthers," June 1968, in *Eldridge Cleaver: Post-Prison Writings and Speeches*, ed. Robert Scheer (New York: Random House, 1969); Gene Marine, *The Black Panthers: Eldridge Cleaver, Huey Newton, Bobby Seale—A Compelling Study of the Angry Young Revolutionaries Who Have Shaken a Black Fist at White America* (New York: Signet, 1969), 52–56; Earl Anthony, *Spitting in the Wind: The True Story behind the Violent Legacy of the Black Panther Party* (Santa Monica, CA: Roundtable Publishing, 1990), 22–23; Seale, *Seize the Time*, 113–32; "Frightening 'Army' Hits the Airport," *San Francisco Chronicle*, February 22, 1967, 1.

7. Nessel quoted in "Frightening 'Army' Hits the Airport," 1.

8. Ibid.

9. Cleaver, "The Courage to Kill," 36.

10. *Black Panther*, April 25, 1967, 1–2.

11. "Sudden Death: Suspect in Robbery Shot Down," *Oakland Tribune*, April 1, 1967, 1.

12. Marine, *The Black Panthers*, 57–59; Anthony, *Spitting in the Wind*, 28; *Black Panther*, April 25, 1967, 1–2.

13. Marine, *The Black Panthers*, 57; Huey P. Newton, *Revolutionary Suicide* (1973; repr. New York: Writers and Readers, 1995), 137–38.

14. *Black Panther*, April 25, 1967, 2; "Youth Sought in Slaying Investigation," *Oakland Tribune*, December 11, 1966, 1B.

15. Marine, *The Black Panthers*, 57–59; *Black Panther*, April 25, 1967, 1–2; Newton, *Revolutionary Suicide*, 138.

16. George Dowell, interview published in the *Black Panther*, May 15, 1967, 2; Marine, *The Black Panthers*, 58.

17. Newton, *Revolutionary Suicide*, 139.

18. Marine, *The Black Panthers*, 60.

19. Newton, *Revolutionary Suicide*, 139.

20. Ibid.

21. Seale, *Seize the Time*, 141–42.

22. Jerry Belcher, "It's All Legal: Oakland's Black Panthers Wear Guns,

Talk Revolution," *San Francisco Chronicle,* April 30, 1967, 1; Seale, *Seize the Time,* 141–42.

23. Marine, *The Black Panthers,* 61; Seale, *Seize the Time,* 145–47; Belcher, "It's All Legal," 1; *Black Panther,* April 25, 1967, 2.

24. Newton, *Revolutionary Suicide,* 142.

25. Seale, *Seize the Time,* 138–39; *Black Panther,* April 25, 1967, 3.

26. Gilbert Moore, *A Special Rage* (New York: Harper & Row, 1971), 58; *Black Panther,* April 25, 1967; Anthony, *Spitting in the Wind,* 31; Marine, *The Black Panthers,* 62; Newton, *Revolutionary Suicide,* 142–43.

27. Belcher, "It's All Legal," 1; *Black Panther,* April 25, 1967, 1; Anthony, *Spitting in the Wind,* 29.

28. Oakland police officer Richard Jensen interviewed for *Eyes on the Prize II: America at the Racial Crossroads 1965–1985,* episode 3, "Power!" (1967–1968), produced and directed by Henry Hampton, aired 1987 (Washington, DC: PBS, 2010), DVD.

29. For details about the passage of AB 1591, see California Legislature, *Final Calendar of Legislative Business,* 1967, part 2,506.

30. Statutes of California, 1967 Regular Session, Chapter 960.

31. Belcher, "It's All Legal," 1.

32. Seale, *Seize the Time,* 153–63; Marine, *The Black Panthers,* 63–64; *Eyes on the Prize II;* Newton, *Revolutionary Suicide,* 149.

33. Seale, *Seize the Time,* 153–63.

34. Marine, *The Black Panthers,* 63–64.

35. "Black Panthers Disrupt Assembly," *San Francisco Chronicle,* May 3, 1967, 1.

36. Seale, *Seize the Time,* 153–63; "Black Panthers Disrupt Assembly," 1.

37. "Black Panthers Disrupt Assembly," 1; Sacramento footage in *Eyes on the Prize II,* part 3.

38. Executive Mandate No. 1 as quoted in Philip S. Foner, ed., *The Black Panthers Speak* (Philadelphia: Lippincott, 1970; repr. New York: Da Capo, 1995), 40.

39. "Black Panthers Disrupt Assembly," 1.

40. TV footage from *Eyes on the Prize II;* on the concealed weapon charges, see Marine, *The Black Panthers,* 65; on the Forte arrest, see Seale, *Seize the Time;* on the Fish and Game Code booking, see "Black Panthers Disrupt Assembly," 1.

41. On the conspiracy charges, see "Black Panthers Disrupt Assembly"; Cleaver situation from Moore, *A Special Rage,* 63; unknown black woman from Marine, *The Black Panthers,* 65.

42. On the press conference, see Marine, *The Black Panthers,* 65.

43. See San Francisco Chronicle Index, "Negroes, Black Panthers Armed with Firearms, Invade State Capitol."

44. Sol Stern, "The Call of the Black Panthers," *New York Times Magazine,* August 6, 1967. The magazine gave the story a full two-page spread, with large photos, and the article took up three columns on three additional pages.

45. Belcher, "It's All Legal," 1.

46. Seale made this point in a speech in February 1968 that was printed

in the *Black Panther:* "Now I'm gonna show you how smart Brother Huey is when he planned Sacramento. He said, now, the papers gon call us thugs and hoodlums. A lot of people ain't gon know what's happening. But the brothers on the block, who the man's been calling thugs and hoodlums for four hundred years, gon say, 'Them some out of sight thugs and hoodlums up there!' The bothers on the block gon say, 'Who *is* these thugs and hoodlums?' In other words, when the man calls us 'nigger' for four hundred years with all its derogatory connotations, Huey was smart enough to know that the Black people were going to say, 'Well, they've been calling us niggers, thugs, and hoodlums for four hundred years, that ain't gon hurn *me,* I'm going to check out what these brothers is doing!'"

47. Billy John Carr quoted in Stern, "The Call of the Black Panthers," August 6, 1967.

48. Emory Douglas interview in *Eyes on the Prize.*

49. George Dowell interview in *Black Panther,* May 15, 1967, 2, 4.

3. THE CORRECT HANDLING OF A REVOLUTION

Epigraph, part 2: Césaire excerpted by Frantz Fanon in *Wretched of the Earth* (New York: Grove Press, 1963), 88. For the Black Panther Party booklist, see, for example, *Black Panther,* October 26, 1968, 18.

1. Newton's analysis in "Fear and Doubt" (*Black Panther,* May 15, 1967) is foreshadowed in an article in the first issue of the *Black Panther:* "The White man has instilled fear into the very hearts of our people. We must act to remove this fear. The only way to remove this fear is to stand up and look the white man in his blue eyes. Many Black people are able nowadays to look the white man in the eyes—but the line thins out when it comes to looking the white cops in the eye. But the white cop is the instrument sent into our community by the Power Structure to keep Black People quiet and under control.... The BLACK PANTHER PARTY FOR SELF DEFENSE has worked out a program that is carefully designed to cope with this situation" ("Armed Black Brothers in Richmond Community," *Black Panther,* April 25, 1967, 4). Though this earlier article reflects Huey Newton's tactic and thinking, the author is unlisted, and its style and tone indicate that it was probably written by Eldridge Cleaver, particularly because Cleaver was principally responsible for assembling the first issue of the paper.

2. Huey P. Newton, "The Functional Definition of Politics," *Black Panther,* May 15, 1967, 4.

3. Huey P. Newton, "In Defense of Self-Defense," *Black Panther,* June 20, 1967, 3–4.

4. Huey P. Newton, "The Functional Definition of Politics," *Black Panther,* May 15, 1967, 4.

5. Huey P. Newton, "The Correct Handling of a Revolution," *Black Panther,* July 20, 1967, 3.

6. For a related discussion, see letter from S. C. Anderson in "S. C. Anderson Writing from New York Concerning (R.A.M.) Revolutionary Action Movement and B.P.S.D. Possibly Being the Same," *Black Panther,* July 3, 1967, 10.

7. "What the Muslims Want, What the Muslims Believe," *Muhammad Speaks,* August 16, 1963.

8. *Black Panther,* May 15, 1967, 3, original was published in all caps. Despite many later issues of the *Black Panther* that labeled other versions of the Ten Point Program the "October 1966" version, this is the earliest surviving print version. Versions printed in subsequent issues, often under the header "October 1966 Platform and Program," added the demand for a United Nations–supervised plebiscite, changed point 3 to identify the capitalist rather than the white man as the robber of the black community, interspersed the sections on wants and beliefs rather than presenting them sequentially, removed the introductory paragraph, and corrected the typos. These changes took place well before the 1972 overhaul of the platform and were reproduced as the original platform by others. Almost all previous renditions of the Ten Point Program actually reproduce much later versions and date them to October 1966. For example, even the great historian Phillip S. Foner, in his edited *Black Panthers Speak* of 1970 (reissued by Da Capo Press in 1995), makes this mistake. On the first page, he gives October 1966 as the date for a reproduction of the Ten Point Program that mentions the U.N. plebiscite and contains other changes that did not appear until the October 1968 issue of *Black Panther,* after the Panthers sent a delegation to the United Nations. Indeed, there is no evidence that the Ten Point Program was even written before late April 1967. The earliest evidence we could find, suggesting the points had been drafted by the time of the Dowell mobilizations in late April 1967, was a brief mention of the Party's program in the first issue of the *Black Panther,* on April 25, 1967, 2. While the Ten Point Program could have been drafted earlier, only when the Black Panther Party sought to promote a broader political program after the Sacramento incident did it distribute the Ten Point Program broadly to the public. The program is not mentioned in news accounts for which Huey and Bobby were interviewed at the time and in which they describe the philosophy and program of the Party. For example, in Jerry Belcher, "It's All Legal: Oakland's Black Panthers Wear Guns, Talk Revolution" (*San Francisco Examiner,* April 30, 1967, 1), Huey identifies some concerns that are generally similar to a couple of the points in the Ten Point Program, but he does not mention an overarching program and he uses different language from that in the published program. It is striking that, after the Sacramento action on May 3, the version of the Ten Point Program printed in the May 15, 1967, *Black Panther* was distributed in different forms—for example, as a flier handed out on the University of California, Berkeley, campus on May 5, three days after the Sacramento action. Black Panther Party for Self-Defense, "What We Want, What We Believe," flier 329–670505–000B, H.K. Yuen Collection, Bancroft Library, University of California, Berkeley. The long quotation from the Declaration of Independence provided a classical political justification for the Party's revolutionary demands and situated its revolutionary politics in the democratic tradition of the American Revolution.

9. Lauren Araiza and Joshua Bloom, "Eldridge Cleaver," in Mark Carnes, ed., *American National Biography* (New York: Oxford University Press, 2001).

10. Eldridge Cleaver, *Soul on Ice* (New York: McGraw-Hill, 1967), 3–4.

11. Ibid., 7–11.

12. Stephen J. Whitfield. *A Death in the Delta: The Story of Emmett Till* (New York: Free Press, 1988)

13. Frantz Fanon, "The Man of Color and the White Woman," in *Black Skin, White Masks* (New York: Grove Press, 1967), 63.

14. Cleaver, *Soul on Ice,* 6–12.

15. Ibid., 14.

16. Eldridge Cleaver, interview by Henry Louis Gates Jr. in Paris, winter 1975, transcript in possession of author.

17. For copies of early love letters between Eldridge Cleaver and Beverly Axelrod, see Cleaver, *Soul on Ice,* 141–51, and also commentary, 18–25.

18. Ibid., 143–44.

19. Beverly Axelrod in Cleaver, *Soul on Ice,* 145–46.

20. Cleaver, *Soul on Ice,* 150.

21. Gene Marine, *The Black Panthers: Eldridge Cleaver, Huey Newton, Bobby Seale—A Compelling Study of the Angry Young Revolutionaries Who Have Shaken a Black Fist at White America* (New York: Signet, 1969), 52–53; Wyatt Buchanan, "Edward Keating, Ramparts Founder," *San Francisco Chronicle,* April 10, 2003.

22. Cleaver, interview in Paris.

23. Marine, *The Black Panthers,* 52–53; Wyatt Buchanan, "Edward Keating, Ramparts Founder," *San Francisco Chronicle,* April 10, 2003.

24. Kathleen Rout, *Eldridge Cleaver* (Boston: Twayne Publishers, 1991), 23.

25. Cleaver, *Soul on Ice,* 21.

26. Ibid., 14.

27. Bobby Seale, *Seize the Time: The Story of the Black Panther Party and Huey P. Newton* (1971; repr. Baltimore: Black Classic Press, 1990), 172–73.

28. Maitland Zane, "Ugly Words at S.F. State—A Pro-Panther Rally," *San Francisco Chronicle,* May 5, 1967, 8.

29. Seale, *Seize the Time,* 177.

30. Ibid., 181–82. Previous accounts have mistakenly identified Stephen Shames as the photographer. The confusion likely stems from the image of Huey in the wicker throne published on the cover of Huey P. Newton, *Revolutionary Suicide* (1973; repr. New York: Writers and Readers, 1995), which is correctly attributed to Shames. But that cover image is actually a photo Shames took of the poster hanging in the window of the Black Panther office in 1968, not the original photo of Newton taken during the summer of 1967. Shames did not start working with the Party until 1968. Joshua Bloom telephone conversation with Stephen Shames, March 10, 2012.

31. After Sacramento, the Party made a deal. Bobby Seale and a few others who didn't have records would serve time for "disturbing the peace," and the others would be let off. Seale and Warren Tucker would serve the most time, six months each. Seale, *Seize the Time,* 187. The rally took place on Wednesday, May 10, after the Young Socialist Alliance had overcome the objections by the university administration.

32. Seale quoted in Jim Hyde, "Protest Police Brutality: Black Panthers Defend Negro," *Daily Californian,* May 11, 1967, 3.

33. Barbara Arthur in Jim Hyde, "Protest Police Brutality: Black Panthers Defend Negro," *Daily Californian,* May 11, 1967, 3; "Panther Rally Postponed," *Daily Californian,* May 5, 1967, 1; "Black Panthers at UC—Friendly, Unarmed Visit," *San Francisco Chronicle,* May 11, 1967, 2.

34. Zane, "Ugly Words at S.F. State," 8

35. Newton, *Revolutionary Suicide,* 150.

36. For details on the Community for a New Politics, see David Mundstock, "Chapter 1—Before 1971," in "Berkeley in the 70s: A History of Progressive Electoral Politics," unpublished manuscript, 1985, in possession of the author.

37. [Minister of Information Eldridge Cleaver], "White 'Mother Country' Radicals," *Black Panther,* July 20, 1967, 1; [Bob Avakian], "White 'Mother Country' Radical Responds to Editorial," *Black Panther,* July 20, 1967, 6. In the first article, Cleaver is identified only by his title. In the second, Avakian is not identified in a byline, but he explains his role in such a way that only he could be the author. See also Bob Avakian, "L.A. Gestapo Attacks Anti-War Demonstrators," *Black Panther,* July 20, 1967, 16.

38. Bobby Seale, "The Coming Long Hot Summer," *Black Panther,* June 20, 1967, 4, 7. The phrase "long hot summer" is a reference to Malcolm X's discussion of the Harlem rebellion.

39. The statistics in this paragraph come from the city's application for Model City funding.

40. The account of the Newark rebellion draws from five sources: U.S. Riot Commission, *Report of the National Advisory Commission on Civil Disorders* (New York: Bantam, 1968); Robert L. Allen, *Black Awakening in Capitalist America: An Analytic History* (Garden City, NY: Anchor Books, 1969); Komozi Woodard, *A Nation within a Nation* (Chapel Hill: University of North Carolina Press, 1999); Tom Hayden, *Rebellion in Newark* (New York: Vintage, 1967); and Kevin Mumford, *Newark: A History of Race, Rights, and Riots in America* (New York: New York University Press, 2007).

41. LeRoi Jones quoted in Allen, *Black Awakening in Capitalist America,* 135.

42. *Black Panther,* July 20, 1967, 1.

43. Ibid., 12–13.

44. The formal name of the eleven-member commission was the National Advisory Commission on Civil Disorders, but it became known as the Kerner Commission, after its chair, Governor Otto Kerner Jr. of Illinois.

45. Andrew Kopkind, "White on Black: The Riot Commission and the Rhetoric of Reform," in *The Politics of Riot Commissions,* ed. Anthony M. Platt (New York: Collier, 1971), 380.

46. Robert Shellow et al., "The Harvest of American Racism," unpublished report quoted in ibid, 387.

47. Campbell-Schumann survey in Sidney Fine, *Violence in the Model City: The Cavanagh Administration, Race Relations, and the Detroit Riot of 1967* (Ann Arbor: University of Michigan Press, 1989), 351. There is some evidence that this more political interpretation of the incident was not so widely held initially but that it developed in the weeks following the rebellion as the black community sought to make sense of the conflict.

48. Fine, *Violence in the Model City,* 249, 294; U.S. Riot Commission, *Report of the National Advisory Commission on Civil Disorders,* 107.

49. For details of the Detroit rebellion in this section, see Fine, *Violence in the Model City,* except where otherwise noted.

50. Ibid., 160.

51. Ibid., 148.

52. Ibid., 183.

53. Sol Stern, "America's Black Guerillas," *Ramparts,* September 2, 1967, 26; Fine, *Violence in the Model City,* 191–201.

54. Fine, *Violence in the Model City,* 177.

55. Ibid., 170, 180, 181, 194, 206, 207, 224–25; U.S. Riot Commission, *Report of the National Advisory Committee on Civil Disorders,* 101.

56. U.S. Riot Commission, *Report of the National Advisory Commission on Civil Disorders,* ch. 2.

57. Ibid., 16.

58. Ibid., 10–11.

59. Ibid., 120, 206.

60. *Black Panther,* May 15, 1967, 3.

61. Ibid., July 3, 1967, various articles, 1, 6, 7; "Carmichael 'Drafted' by Panthers," *San Francisco Chronicle,* June 30, 1967, 48. Carmichael was later appointed "Prime Minister" of the Black Panther Party. See the discussion of the February 1968 Huey birthday rallies and exploration of the merger with SNCC in chapter 4.

62. *Black Panther,* July 3, 1967, various articles, 1, 6, 7.

63. Ibid., 3.

64. "Core Convention Fallout," *Black Panther,* July 20, 1967, 2.

65. See "Bootlickers Gallery," 19; "Long Tongue Ussery," 19; "Bootlicker Tshombe Captured," 2; "Core Convention Fallout," 2; "Good Beggin' Willie Goofs," 5; "Old Toms Never Die Unless They're Blown Away," 7; "Bedfellows: NAACP and Others," 7; all in *Black Panther,* July 20, 1967.

66. On David Hilliard's coining of the phrase "Paper Panthers," see Seale, *Seize the Time,* 113; Paper Panther graphic by Emory Douglas, *Black Panther,* July 20, 1967, 5.

67. Newton, *Revolutionary Suicide,* 132.

68. Newton, "Fear and Doubt," 3.

69. Tracye Matthews, while making an important contribution to understanding the Black Panthers based in rich research and sophisticated analysis, like Michelle Wallace, argues that Newton's concern with society's social castration of black males parallels the argument in the Moynihan Report (formally titled *The Negro Family: The Case for National Action*), which had been spearheaded by the assistant secretary of labor, Daniel P. Moynihan. See Matthews, "No One Ever Asks What a Man's Place in the Revolution Is," in *Black Panther Party [Reconsidered],* ed. Charles E. Jones (Baltimore: Black Classic Press, 1998), 267–304. But despite some mild parallels, Newton sharply departs from Moynihan, both in his analysis and proposed redress. For Newton, like Fanon, the social castration of black men is the result of imposed structural oppression rather than an internal cultural pathology. And

for Newton, like Fanon, black men can regain their humanity only by destroying the society that oppresses them.

70. Barbara Arthur, "Sisters Unite," *Black Panther,* May 15, 1967, 6.

71. Sister Williams, "Sister Williams Says," *Black Panther,* May 15, 1967, 6.

72. *Black Panther,* July 3, 1967, 4.

73. Judy Hart, "Black Womanhood," *Black Panther,* July 20, 1967, 11.

74. Ibid.

75. Tracye Ann Matthews, "'No One Ever Asks What a Man's Role in the Revolution Is': Gender and Sexual Politics in the Black Panther Party, 1966–1971" (PhD diss., University of Michigan, 1998).

4. FREE HUEY!

1. The account of the lead-up to the incident on October 28, 1967, draws from five sources except where otherwise noted: the transcript of the trial "The People of the State of California vs. Huey P. Newton, No. 41266," copy in possession of author; Edward M. Keating, *Free Huey!* (1970; repr. Berkeley: Ramparts Press, 1971); Gene Marine, *The Black Panthers: Eldridge Cleaver, Huey Newton, Bobby Seale—A Compelling Study of the Angry Young Revolutionaries Who Have Shaken a Black Fist at White America* (New York: Signet, 1969), ch. 9; Michael Newton, *Bitter Grain* (Los Angeles: Holloway House, 1980), ch. 4; Huey P. Newton, *Revolutionary Suicide* (1973; repr. New York: Writers and Readers, 1995), ch. 23.

2. Marine, *The Black Panthers,* 100–101.

3. Mary Jane Aguilar, M.D., "Doctor Apologizes to Huey," *Black Panther,* November 23, 1967, 6.

4. On Hilliard transporting Newton to the hospital, see David Hilliard and Lewis Cole, *This Side of Glory: The Autobiography of David Hilliard and the Story of the Black Panther Party* (New York: Little, Brown, 1993), 131. On the ambiguous account by the jury, see Marine, *The Black Panthers,* 104.

5. Keating, *Free Huey!* 47–48; Newton, *Revolutionary Suicide,* 182–91; Charles Garry and Art Goldberg, *Streetfighter in the Courtroom* (New York: E.P. Dutton, 1977).

6. Eldridge Cleaver, "Huey Must Be Set Free!"*Black Panther,* November 23, 1967, 1.

7. Michael Ferber and Staughton Lynd, *The Resistance* (Boston: Beacon Press, 1971), 103.

8. Ibid., 145.

9. Hal Jacobs quoted by H.K. Yuen in his notes on the back of flier 329–671013–000, H.K. Yuen Collection, Bancroft Library, University of California, Berkeley (hereafter Yuen Collection).

10. Fliers 329–671016–007, 329–671016–008, 329–671013–001 (oversize), and 329–1016–004, Yuen Collection. Many other fliers in box 329 of the collection also provide important insights into Stop the Draft Week in Oakland. For example, in an attempt to stop the induction center actions planned for Tuesday October 17, Judge Lercara issued an injunction requiring UC Berkeley to prohibit the use of campus facilities to organize draft resistance activi-

ties. Chancellor Haynes's overzealous enforcement of the injunction reminded the students of the previous struggle for free speech and reinforced their idea that they were being subjected to the demands of empire and that their struggle was one for self-determination much like that of the Vietnamese or the ghetto residents who had rebelled in America's cities. See fliers 329–671017–000 and 329–671026–000 in the Yuen Collection; Charles DeBenedetti and Charles Chatfield, *An American Ordeal: The Antiwar Movement of the Vietnam Era* (Syracuse, NY: Syracuse University Press, 1990), 196; Tom Wells, *The War Within: America's Battle over Vietnam* (Berkeley: University of California Press, 1994), 191–95; "Cops Beat Pickets," *San Francisco Chronicle,* October 17, 1967, 1.

11. Marine, *The Black Panthers,* 106.

12. SNCC, Western Union telegram, October 28, 1967, reproduced in *Black Panther,* November 23, 1967, 5 (punctuation and capitalization added for readability).

13. Progressive Labor Party, Western Union telegram, October 28, 1967, reproduced in *Black Panther,* November 23, 1967, 10; Bob Avakian, "White 'Mother Country' Radical Supports Huey," *Black Panther,* November 23, 1967, 3.

14. Marine, *The Black Panthers,* 93; Newton, *Revolutionary Suicide,* 189.

15. Newton and Garry would use the phrase "exhaust all legal means" after the announcement of the involuntary manslaughter verdict in the trial. See ABC News coverage, "Huey Newton Decision/Black Panthers," September 8, 1968.

16. Kathleen Cleaver and George Katsiaficas, *Liberation, Imagination, and the Black Panther Party* (New York: Routledge, 2001), 124.

17. Marine, *The Black Panthers* , 128–29.

18. Cleaver and Katsiaficas, *Liberation, Imagination, and the Black Panther Party,* 123.

19. Marine, *The Black Panthers,* 128–29.

20. Kathleen Cleaver, "On Eldridge Cleaver," *Ramparts,* June 1969, 4.

21. Ibid.

22. Ibid.

23. Cleaver and Katsiaficas, *Liberation, Imagination, and the Black Panther Party,* 124, 227.

24. Ibid., 124.

25. Interview with Kathleen Cleaver in the *Washington Post,* February 1970, cited in Philip S. Foner, ed., *The Black Panthers Speak* (Philadelphia: Lippincott, 1970; repr. New York: Da Capo Press, 1995), 145.

26. Marine, *The Black Panthers,* 129.

27. Huey Newton, "Executive Mandate No.3," *Black Panther,* March 16, 1968, 1.

28. For the photo of Kathleen Cleaver, taken to illustrate Executive Mandate No.3 and published later, see *Black Panther,* September 28, 1968, 20.

29. Cleaver, "On Eldridge Cleaver," 6.

30. Joel R. Wilson, "'Free Huey': The Black Panther Party, the Peace and Freedom Party, and the Politics of Race in 1968" (PhD diss., University of California, Santa Cruz, June 2002), 83, 98.

31. Ibid., 102–3.

32. Ibid., 105–6.

33. For James Forman's thoughts on the Peace and Freedom Party, see his *The Making of Black Revolutionaries* (1972; repr. Washington, DC: Open Hand Publishing, 1985), 525–26.

34. December 3, 1967, Meeting Notes, box 17, folder 1, P&F Collection; and "Peace and Freedom Party to Press On," *People's World*, December 9, 1967, 2; both in Wilson, "Free Huey," 122. "Peace/Freedom: Blacks to Aid as Court Rebuffs," *Berkeley Barb*, December 29, 1967, quoted in ibid., 135.

35. Mike Parker, KPFA Radio, February 15, 1968, recording BB1632, 18:30, Pacifica Radio Archives, North Hollywood, California.

36. "Common Cause," *Berkeley Barb*, December 22, 1967, quoted in Wilson, "Free Huey," 127.

37. Bobby Seale, *Seize the Time: The Story of the Black Panther Party and Huey P. Newton* (1971; repr. Baltimore: Black Classic Press, 1990), 208.

38. Wilson, "Free Huey," 138–40.

39. "B.P.P. and P.F.P.," editorial, *Black Panther*, March 16, 1968, 3.

40. Ibid.

41. Ibid.

42. Bobby Seale at a rally in support of the Oakland Seven facing criminal charges for their leadership role in organizing Stop the Draft Week, with Bettina Aptheker, Bob Avakian of the Peace and Freedom Party, and Robert Scheer of *Ramparts*. KPFA Radio, February 20, 1968, recording BB1783, Pacifica Radio Archives.

43. Bettina Aptheker, ibid., 13:30.

44. Bob Avakian, ibid., 36:40.

45. *Black Panther*, March 16, 1968, 6; Peace and Freedom Party, "Know Your Enemy!" flier 334–680517–003, Yuen Collection; Newark photo reproduced in flier 321–670906–000, Yuen Collection. White antiwar activists' use of Black Power to legitimate their struggle against imperialism was not new. In September 1967, before Newton was arrested, the Progressive Labor Party had issued a flier in support of antiwar protestors arrested in San Francisco. Under the title "How Much Political Freedom Do We Have?" the flier reproduced a photo of blacks confronting soldiers in the Newark rebellion from the July 20, 1967, *Black Panther* next to a photo of unarmed citizens confronting soldiers in Vietnam. The implication was clear: the antiwar protestors were part of the global struggle against imperialism. Newark photo reproduced in flier 321–670906–000, Yuen Collection.

46. Bobby Seale, February 17, 1968, recording BB 5471, Pacifica Radio Archives.

47. H. Rap Brown, ibid., recording BB 1708.

48. Stokely Carmichael, ibid.

49. *Black Panther*, March 16, 1968, 1.

50. One of the many actions spurred by the birthday rally was a resolution that Councilman Ron Dellums (later a U.S. congressman and Oakland mayor) introduced to the Berkeley City Council calling for the freeing of Huey Newton and dismissal of the murder charges against him. The resolution argued

that the indictment had been passed down by a grand jury not composed of Newton's peers. KPFA Radio, February 20, 1968, recording BB1633, Pacifica Radio Archives.

5. MARTYRS

1. Earl Caldwell, "Guard Called Out," *New York Times,* April 5, 1968, 1; Walter Rugaber, "A Negro Is Killed in Memphis March," *New York Times,* March 29, 1968, 1.

2. King Papers Project, Martin Luther King, Jr., Research and Education Institute, Stanford University; on the Memphis rebellion, see Caldwell, "Guard Called Out," 1.

3. The NAACP in particular did much of the foundational work upon which the Civil Rights Movement built and provided crucial legal and political support for the insurgents throughout.

4. Martin Luther King Jr. quoted in Jose Yglesias, "It May Be a Long, Hot Spring in the Capital," *New York Times,* March 31, 1968, SM30.

5. Yglesias, "It May Be a Long, Hot Spring," SM30.

6. Martin Luther King Jr. quoted in Ben A. Franklin, "Dr. King Hints He'd Cancel March If Aid Is Offered," *New York Times,* April 1, 1968, 20.

7. Max Frankel, "President Offers U.S. Aid to Cities in Curbing Riots," *New York Times,* March 30, 1968, 1, quote from 30. For a detailed exploration of King's and Johnson's complex working relationship, see Nick Kotz, *Judgment Days: Lyndon Baines Johnson, Martin Luther King Jr., and the Laws That Changed America* (New York: Mariner Books, 2006).

8. Senator Robert Byrd in Max Frankel, "President Offers U.S. Aid to Cities," 30.

9. Martin Luther King Jr. in Earl Caldwell, "Court Bars March in Memphis; Dr. King Calls Order 'Illegal,'" *New York Times,* April 4, 1968, 30.

10. "President's Plea," *New York Times,* April 5, 1968, 1.

11. Nan Robertson, "Johnson Leads U.S. in Mourning," *New York Times,* April 6, 1968, 25.

12. Homer Bigart, "Leaders at Rites," *New York Times,* April 10, 1968, 1.

13. John Kifner, "Followers Sing on Final March," *New York Times,* April 10, 1968, 33.

14. According to sociologist Doug McAdam, the Southern Christian Leadership Conference initiated about a quarter of all black insurgent events during the 1960s through 1968, the year of King's death. That year, SCLC was responsible for fully 36 percent of all black insurgent events initiated by formal movement organizations. But in 1969, the percentage fell by half, to only 18 percent, and in 1970, to only 8 percent. McAdam's statistics likely underestimate SCLC's precipitous decline as they do not account for the rise of spontaneous actions of black urban rebellion. Similarly, he estimates that while SCLC attracted more than $1 million annually in external income between 1965 and 1968, while King was still alive, external income plummeted to $500,000 in 1969 and $400,000 in 1970. See Doug McAdam, *Political Process and the Development of Black Insurgency, 1930–1970* (Chicago: University of Chicago, 1982).

15. Andrew Young in Earl Caldwell, "Nonviolent Rights Movement Faces Uncertain Future as Doubts Rise It Can Survive Loss of Dr. King," *New York Times,* July 1, 1968, 17.

16. Stokely Carmichael, "Stokely on King," transcript of press announcement via the Liberation News Service, republished in *Black Panther,* May 4, 1968, 10.

17. The other Panthers in the entourage were Wendell Wade, Terry Cotton, Charles Bursey, Donnell Lankford, Warren Wells, and John L. Scott—all in their late teens or early twenties.

18. Eight Panthers were arrested, and six Panthers and two policemen were wounded, none critically. Accounts differ about how the shoot-out began and what the Panthers were doing there. There is also conflicting evidence about the conditions under which Hutton was killed. Two black Oakland police officers involved in the conflict, Gwynne Peirson and Eugene Jennings, testified that Hutton was outright murdered by white police officers after surrendering to them. This testimony was repressed, and the grand jury found the killing of Hutton justified. Gwynne Peirson left the police force and completed a PhD at Berkeley. His 1977 doctoral dissertation, "An Introductory Study of Institutional Racism in Police Law Enforcement," discusses the incident, 169–171. Officer Jennings's April 10, 1968, testimony, also describing Hutton's death as a murder by white police, was secret until thirty-seven years later when he released a copy of the original testimony transcript. David Hilliard and Lewis Cole, *This Side of Glory: The Autobiography of David Hilliard and the Story of the Black Panther Party* (New York: Little, Brown, 1993), 182–93; Eldridge Cleaver, "Affidavit #2: Shoot-out in Oakland," in *Eldridge Cleaver: Post-Prison Writings and Speeches,* ed. Robert Scheer (New York: Random House, 1969), 80; Daryl E. Lembke, "Oakland Tense in Wake of Police, Panthers Battle," *Los Angeles Times,* April 8, 1968, 3; "Black Panther Chief Demands Indictment," *Los Angeles Times,* April 13, 1968, A16; "Panthers Ambushed, One Murdered," *Black Panther,* May 4, 1968, 4; "Oakland Police Attack Panthers," *New Left Notes,* April 15, 1968, 1.

19. Bobby Seale, press conference at Oakland Hall of Justice, recording BB 5543, Pacifica Radio Archives, North Hollywood, California.

20. Lawrence E. Davies, "Black Panthers Denounce Policemen," *New York Times,* April 13, 1968, 12; "Brando at Oakland Funeral for Slain Black Panther, 17," *Los Angeles Times,* April 13, 1968, B1.

21. Cleaver, "Affidavit #2," 92.

22. Lawrence E. Davies, "Black Panthers Denounce Policemen," *New York Times,* April 13, 1968, 12.

23. Harry Edwards quoted in Dick Halgren, "San Jose Professor Joins Black Panthers," *San Francisco Chronicle,* April 12, 1968, cited in Hugh Pearson, *The Shadow of the Panther: Huey Newton and the Price of Black Power in America* (Reading, MA: Addison-Wesley, 1994), 157.

24. Shabazz, Carmichael, and Brando in "Brando at Oakland Funeral," B1.

25. "Letter from New York," *San Francisco Chronicle,* May 17, 1968, cited in Pearson, *Shadow of the Panther,* 156.

26. See Hasan Kwame Jeffries, *Bloody Lowndes* (New York: New York University Press, 2009).

27. See Joshua Bloom, "Opportunities for Practices" unpublished manuscript.

28. Eldridge Cleaver, "On Meeting the Needs of the People," *Ramparts,* September 8, 1969.

29. For Cleaver's description of the purpose of the plebiscite and the early role of James Forman, see Eldridge Cleaver, "Black Paper by the Minister of Information," *Black Panther,* May 4, 1968, 12.

30. Point 10 of Ten Point Program as amended in the *Black Panther,* May 4, 1968, 7. Previous versions of point 10 read only "We want land, bread, housing, education, clothing, justice and peace" (as published in the *Black Panther* through the last issue before King's assassination, *Black Panther,* March 16, 1968, 4). Philip Foner and other historians have been somewhat confused about this timing because some later issues of the *Black Panther* published amended versions of the Ten Point Program and Platform under the header "October 1966 Black Panther Party Platform and Program."

31. Gerald C. Fraser, "S.N.C.C. in Decline after 8 Years in Lead: Pace-Setter in Civil Rights Displaced by Panthers," *New York Times,* October 7, 1968.

32. James Forman, *The Making of Black Revolutionaries* (1972; repr. Washington, DC: Open Hand Publishing, 1985), 534.

33. "Free Huey at the U.N.," *Black Panther,* September 14, 1968, 3; John Leo, "Black Panthers," *New York Times,* July 28, 1968, 41; Forman, *The Making of Black Revolutionaries,* 534–38.

34. Fraser, "S.N.C.C. in Decline"; Forman, *The Making of Black Revolutionaries,* 522–43.

35. Fraser, "S.N.C.C. in Decline."

36. Ella Baker quoted in ibid."

37. Ibid.

38. "Cleaver of the Panthers Is Nominee of Leftists," *New York Times,* August 19, 1968, 32; Eldridge Cleaver, "Black Paper by the Minister of Information," *Black Panther,* May 4, 1968, 12; "Eldridge Cleaver for President," *Black Panther,* May 18, 1968, 17; "Kathleen Cleaver for Assemblywoman," *Black Panther,* May 18, 1968, 18; "Imprisoned Black Panther Enters Race for President," May 14, 1968, 31.

39. "Black-Brown Caucus of the Peace and Freedom Party," audiotape 018–680702–000A, H.K. Yuen Collection, Bancroft Library, University of California, Berkeley (hereafter Yuen Collection); Daryl E. Lembke, "Negro, Latin Delegates in Peace Party Accord," *Los Angeles Times,* March 18, 1968, 3; John Kifner, "Freedom Party Endorses Candidates," *New York Times,* July 22, 1968, 27; Dorothy Townsend and William Tully, "California Peace Party Favors Panther Leader for President," *Los Angeles Times,* August 4, 1968, EB; "Cleaver of Black Panthers Is Nominee of Leftists," *New York Times,* August 19, 1968, 32; Joel R. Wilson, "'Free Huey': The Black Panther Party, The Peace and Freedom Party, and the Politics of Race in 1968" (PhD diss., University of California, Santa Cruz, 2002), 347. Interestingly, Cleaver attempted to recruit Carl Oglesby of SDS as the vice presidential candidate.

Oglesby deferred to SDS authority, and SDS declined the nomination. SDS had several concrete political reasons for making this decision. SNCC's relationship with the Panthers was new, the Panthers and SNCC were in a dispute at the time, and many SDS chapters still had strong relationships with SNCC; SDS had political differences with the Peace and Freedom Party. See [Mike Klonsky], "Why Oglesby Won't Run," *New Left Notes*, September 9, 1968, 8 (the editorial is unsigned, but authorship can be inferred from *New Left Notes*, September 16, 1968, 3); and Bernardine Dohrn, "White Mother Country Radicals," *New Left Notes*, July 29, 1968, 1. According to Oglesby's later account, he wanted to accept the nomination but was blocked because of interpersonal power struggles within SDS at the time; see Carl Oglesby, *Ravens in the Storm: A Personal History of the 1960s Antiwar Movement* (New York: Scribner, 2008), 202.

40. The description of the August 25, 1968, rally in Bobby Hutton Memorial Park draws from four sources: Gilbert Moore, *A Special Rage* (New York: Harper & Row, 1971), 94–95; Ruth-Marion Baruch and Pirkle Jones, *Black Panthers 1968* (Los Angeles: Greybull Press, 2002); Stephen Shames, *The Black Panthers* (New York: Aperture, 2006); Howard Bingham, *Black Panthers 1968* (Pasadena, CA: AMMO Books, 2009). Some of the photographic images described here may depict similar rallies held by the Panthers in Hutton Park that summer, not specifically the August 25 rally.

41. Cleaver quoted in Moore, *A Special Rage*, 95.

42. Kirkpatrick Sale, *SDS* (New York: Random House, 1973), 663–64 (membership figures are listed chronologically on these pages).

43. Draft induction statistics are from the Selective Service System, History and Records Division. The Selective Service defines World War II inductions as those occurring between November 1940 and October 1946; Korean War inductions, between June 1950 and June 1953; and Vietnam War inductions, between August 1964 and February 1973.

44. "The Nation—Conchies to China," *New York Times*, April 18, 1943, E2.

45. Michael S. Foley, *Confronting the War Machine: Draft Resistance during the Vietnam War* (Chapel Hill: University of North Carolina Press, 2003), 19–20, 28.

46. Clayborne Carson, *In Struggle: SNCC and the Black Awakening of the 1960s* (Cambridge, MA: Harvard University Press, 1981), 183.

47. Ted Sell, "Ratio of Negroes Killed in Vietnam Tops Whites," *Los Angeles Times*, March 10, 1966, 16.

48. See Staughton Lynd, "A Radical Speaks in Defense of S.N.C.C.," *New York Times Magazine*, September 10, 1967, 271; Carson, *In Struggle*, 184.

49. Michael Ferber and Staughton Lynd, *The Resistance* (Boston: Beacon Press, 1971), 33.

50. SDS often supported and emulated SNCC throughout the first half of the decade. In the words of the SDS National Office at the time, "We have followed SNCC's evolution for years, learning from it, adapting its approaches in our own organizing efforts, and acting as allies when called upon to assist." So the turn toward draft resistance at SNCC's behest was not surprising. Paul R. Booth, "Letter to SNCC" from SDS National Office, *New Left Notes*, June 10, 1966, 3.

51. Stokely Carmichael, Chairman of SNCC and Carl Oglesby, President of SDS, "Joint Statement of the Student Non-Violent Coordinating Committee and the Students for a Democratic Society on the Conscription Laws before the House Committee on the Armed Services," reprinted in *New Left Notes,* July 8, 1966, 1.

52. Ferber and Lynd, *The Resistance,* 34–35.

53. Stokely Carmichael, audio reel 044–661029–000, Yuen Collection.

54. In a sampling of nineteen antiwar fliers distributed on the UC Berkeley campus from August through October 1966, none emphasized the draft or resistance to it; box 313, Yuen Collection. While there is no way to construct a complete universe of antiwar fliers distributed on campus during this period, we have good reason to believe this sampling is representative. H.K. Yuen's collection was near comprehensive, and he put most of the antiwar fliers for this period in box 313. The pre– and post–October 1966 variation within the fliers in this box is striking.

55. SDS flier, 313–661119–000, Yuen Collection.

56. See, for example, the following fliers in the Yuen Collection: "The Resistance," flier 329–670425–000; "Tonight—Forum—Draft Refusal," flier 329–670428–000; "We Won't Go," flier 329–670428–000; "Conference on Draft Refusal," flier 329–670514–001; "Protest Congressional Draft Hearings," flier 329–670508; "Picket Oakland Induction Center," flier 329–670515–000.

57. Carl Davidson, "Anti-Draft Resolution: Adopted by the National Council, Students for a Democratic Society, December 28, 1966, Berkeley, California," *New Left Notes,* January 13, 1967, 1.

58. Greg Calvert, "Protest to Resistance," *New Left Notes,* January 13, 1967, 1; see also Sale, *SDS,* ch. 16.

59. SDS argued that students did not have to be drafted to be subjected to imperial imposition. Having called for nationwide draft resistance, in January 1967 SDS published extensive quotes from a Selective Service System memorandum on the concept of "channeling manpower." The idea was that the draft functioned not only to obtain soldiers for the military but to manage human resources society wide. In short, SDS argued, whether or not students were actually drafted, the Selective Service System was subjecting them to the interests of empire. Freedom required resistance. Even those exempted from the draft because of student deferments could resist by refusing their deferment, signing "We Won't Go" statements, joining antidraft unions, joining sit-ins at induction centers, or burning their draft cards. Selective Service System memo quoted in *New Left Notes,* January 20, 1967.

60. Greg Calvert, "In White America," speech, reprinted in *Guardian,* March 25, 1967.

61. Sale, *SDS,* 319.

62. Ferber and Lynd, *The Resistance,* 62.

63. Douglas Robinson, "100,000 Rally at U.N. against Vietnam War," *New York Times,* April 16, 1967, 1.

64. Paul Hofmann, "50,000 at San Francisco Peace Rally," *New York Times,* April 16, 1967; Daryl E. Lembke, "40,000 Parade in San Francisco for Viet Peace," *Los Angeles Times,* April 16, 1967; on Cleaver at the Spring

Mobilization in San Francisco, see Mike Culbert, "War Protest Marchers Filled Kezar Stadium," *Berkeley Daily Gazette,* April 17, 1967, 1.

65. Robinson, "100,000 Rally at U.N. against Vietnam War," 1; Ferber and Lynd, *The Resistance,* 72–75.

66. See David Remnick, *King of the World* (New York: Vintage, 1998).

67. Foley, *Confronting the War Machine,* 10.

68. "License for Bout Is Called Illegal: Attorney General in Illinois Seeks to Bar Fight after Clay Balks at Hearing," *New York Times,* February 26, 1966.

69. Herman Graham III, "Muhammad Ali and Draft Resistance," in *The Brothers' Vietnam War: Black Power, Manhood, and the Military Experience* (Gainesville: University Press of Florida, 2003), 5:74.

70. "License for Bout Is Called Illegal; "Clay Plans to Apologize in Chicago for Remarks about Draft Classification," *New York Times,* February 22, 1966.

71. "TV of Clay Fight Banned in 3 Cities," *New York Times,* March 19, 1966, 22.

72. Remnick, *King of the World,* 288.

73. Graham, "Muhammad Ali and Draft Resistance," 73 and 78.

74. Charles DeBenedetti and Charles Chatfield, *An American Ordeal: The Antiwar Movement of the Vietnam Era* (Syracuse, NY: Syracuse University Press, 1990), 186.

75. Tom Wicker, "In the Nation: Muhammad Ali and Dissent," *New York Times,* May 2, 1967, 46.

76. "The Resistance Now," flier 329–671016–005 (oversize), Yuen Collection.

77. DeBenedetti and Chatfield, *An American Ordeal,* 187–88.

78. Ferber and Lynd, *The Resistance,* 103.

79. Paul Lauter and Florence Howe quoted in ibid., 136.

80. Tom Wells, *The War Within: America's Battle over Vietnam* (Berkeley: University of California Press, 1994), 194–97. DeBenedetti and Chatfield, *An American Ordeal,* 196–98.

81. On SDS membership estimates for April 1968, see SDS telegram, April 12, 1968, reproduced in *New Left Notes,* April 15, 1968, 7; see also Sale, *SDS.* On the previous lack of relations between SDS and the Panthers, see Bernardine Dohrn [the interorganizational secretary of SDS], "White Mother Country Radicals," *New Left Notes,* July 29, 1968, 1.

82. We went through all the issues of the *New Left Notes* from its founding in January 1966 through April 1968 (108 issues) and found no mention of the Black Panther Party—no discussion of the May 1967 event in Sacramento, no discussion of Huey's confrontation with Frey or his arrest, no discussion of the "Free Huey!" campaign or the birthday mobilizations in February or the merger with SNCC. The publication contained numerous stories about SNCC, Black Power, race and racism, and the role of whites in mobilization throughout this period. But only starting in April 1968 did it begin covering the Black Panther Party, and this coverage was extensive.

83. "We Made the News Today, Oh Boy," *New Left Notes,* April 15, 1968, 3, cited in Lawrence David Barber, "'The Price of the Liberation': The New Left's Dissolution, 1965–1970" (PhD diss., University of California, Davis, 2003), 1:36; Sale, *SDS,* 428–29.

84. SDS telegram, April 12, 1968, reproduced in *New Left Notes*, April 15, 1968, 7.

85. "Oakland Police Attack Panthers," *New Left Notes*, April 15, 1968, 1.

86. Ibid.

87. "Convention Statement on Huey and the Panthers," *New Left Notes*, July 8, 1968.

88. Our discussion of the "Free Huey!" rally in front of the Alameda County courthouse in Oakland on July 15, 1968, draws from four sources: original film and audio footage in Roz Payne and Newsreel Films, *Off the Pig*, [1968] in video collection *What We Want, What We Believe* (Oakland: AK Press, 2006); Gilbert Moore's personal account in *A Special Rage*, 118–21; Daryl E. Lembke and Ray Rogers, "Black Panthers Chant at Start of Newton Trial," *Los Angeles Times*, July 16, 1968, 3; "2,500 in a March at Trial on Coast: Protest as Panther Leader Appears on Murder Count," *New York Times*, July 16, 1968, 14.

89. The press contingent included reporters from the *Boston Globe*, the *New York Times*, the *Los Angeles Times*, the *San Francisco Chronicle*, the *San Francisco Examiner*, the *Oakland Tribune*, multiple television and radio stations, the *Berkeley Barb*, the *National Guardian*, the *San Francisco Guardian*, the *Mid Peninsula Observer*, *People's World*, the *Sun Reporter*, the *Berkeley Gazette, and Time, Newsweek*, and *Life* magazines.

90. Bingham, *Black Panthers 1968*, 148–49.

91. Mike Klonsky, "Free Huey! . . . Or the Sky Is the Limit," *New Left Notes*, July 29, 1968, 6. See also "Huey in Court," *New Left Notes*, August 5, 1968, 7.

92. See William J. Drummond, "Cleaver Dispute," *Los Angeles Times*, September 18, 1968, 1.

93. Ronald Reagan quoted in "Reagan Demands Appointment of Cleaver Be Rescinded by UC," *Los Angeles Times*, September 14, 1968, B1. See also "Eldridge Cleaver, UC Lecturer," *Los Angeles Times*, September 16, 1968; "Bid to Cleaver Scored by Reagan and Unruh," *New York Times*, September 18, 1968; "Assembly All but Kills UC Censure on Cleaver," *Los Angeles Times*, September 19, 1968; "Campus Can't Be Springboard of Revolt—Reagan," *Los Angeles Times*, October 10, 1968; "Reagan Accuses UC Regents of Showing Disdain for Public," *Los Angeles Times*, October 22, 1968; and extensive coverage in the *Los Angeles Times*.

94. See "Reaction Varies Widely: Cleaver-UC Controversy," *Los Angeles Times* September 21, 1968, B4; "'Necessary,' 'Disturbing': UC Regents and Cleaver," *Los Angeles Times*, September 28, 1968, B4.

95. Cleaver at Sacramento State College, October, 1968, audio reel 003–690217–000, Yuen Collection. See also "Cleaver Derides Reagan and 3 Candidates in Lecture at Stanford," *New York Times*, October 3, 1968, 22; "Cleaver Assails Johnson and Reagan at UCI Racism Panel," *Los Angeles Times*, September 27, 1968, H1.

96. "Black Conference Threatens Campaign against University," *Daily Californian*, October 3, 1968, 3.

97. "Students Map Fight over Cleaver Ban," *Daily Californian*, Septem-

ber 24, 1968, 1; Sharon Frumkin, "6 Campuses Decry Ruling on Courses," *Daily Californian*, October 3, 1968, 1; John Dreyfuss, "Student Body at UC Demands Regents Rescind Cleaver Ruling," *Los Angeles Times*, September 24, 1968; "California Students Back Lecture Series by Cleaver," *New York Times*, September 25, 1968, 17; "Demonstrators Disrupt UC Regents Meeting," *Los Angeles Times*, October 18, 1968, 2; "Jeering Reception for Reagan," *Los Angeles Times*, October 20, 1968; "Students Seize Berkeley Office," *New York Times*, October 24, 1968, 32; "New Cleaver Issue Eruptions," *Los Angeles Times*, October 27, 1968, K5.

98. "Cleaver Omits Obscenities in 'Scholarly' First UC Lecture," *Los Angeles Times*, October 9, 1968; "6 Campuses Decry Ruling on Courses" 1; "Students Map Fight Over Cleaver Ban" 1; John Dreyfuss, "Limit on Cleaver," *Los Angeles Times*, September 21, 1968, 1; William Drummond, "UC Academic Senate Rejects Regents' Censure over Cleaver," *Los Angeles Times*, October 4, 1968, 1.

6. NATIONAL UPRISING

1. Michele Russell, "Conversation with Ericka Huggins. Oakland, California, 4/20/77," 10, box 1, Huey P. Newton Papers, cited in Robyn Ceanne Spencer, "Repression Breeds Resistance: The Rise and Fall of the Black Panther Party in Oakland, CA, 1966–1982" (PhD diss., Columbia University, 2001), 105.

2. Biographical information on Ericka and John Huggins comes from Donald Freed, *Agony in New Haven: The Trial of Bobby Seale, Ericka Huggins, and the Black Panther Party* (New York: Simon & Schuster, 1973), 62–64; Elaine Brown, *A Taste of Power: A Black Woman's Story* (New York: Pantheon Books, 1992), 131, 138.

3. Elaine Brown, *A Taste of Power*, chs. 2–5. Of Elaine Brown's white lovers, Jay Kennedy stands out as having an especially strong influence on her life and her political development; see ibid., 76–104. Kennedy was a former socialist known for working with the CIA to expose Martin Luther King's ties to the Communist Party. According to CIA documents, "Kennedy's position is one of complete sympathy with the Negro and the Civil Rights Movement, but holds that only through legal means and peaceful means should the Negro aims be accomplished"; quoted in David Garrow, *The FBI and Martin Luther King, Jr: From "Solo" to Memphis* (New York: Norton, 1981), 142, and see 139–44.

4. Ray Rogers, "Alert Patrol Chairman Quits under Pressure," *Los Angeles Times*, August 12, 1967, 3; Terence Cannon, "A Night with the Watts Community Alert Patrol," *Movement*, August 1966.

5. "Partial List of Black Congress," *Harambee*, November 17, 1967, 8, cited in Scot Brown, "The US Organization: African-American Cultural Nationalism in the Era of Black Power, 1965 to the 1970s" (PhD diss., Cornell University, 1999), 156; In chapter 6 of *Taste of Power*, Elaine Brown gives a rich personal description of Harry Truly and her experiences in the Black Congress. See also *Angela Davis: An Autobiography* (New York: Random House, 1974).

6. Scot Brown, *Fighting for US: Maulana Karenga, the US Organization,*

and Black Cultural Nationalism (New York: New York University Press, 2003), and Brown, "The US Organization," quote from 135.

7. "The Black Panther Moves in Alabama," *Harambee,* November 3, 1966, 1; "Speech by John Hylett *[sic],*" *Harambee,* November 3, 1966, 3; "From the White House to the Courthouse," flier reproduced in *Harambee,* November 3, 1966, 8; "Panthers to Enter Politics," *San Francisco Chronicle,* June 18,1967, 9; Rogers, "Alert Patrol Chairman Quits under Pressure," 3; Davis, *Autobiography,* 162–67.

8. Elaine Brown, *A Taste of Power,* ch. 6.

9. This idea is supported by Elaine Brown's account of fights about what posters to hang on the walls (Taste of Power, ch. 6), and Scot Brown, in "The US Organization," also suggests that shared physical space contributed to the tension (172).

10. Davis, *Autobiography,* 158–59.

11. Scot Brown, "The US Organization," 173.

12. Scot Brown, *Fighting for US,* 74.

13. Elaine Brown, *A Taste of Power,* 118.

14. Jack Olsen, *Last Man Standing: The Tragedy and Triumph of Geronimo Pratt* (New York: Doubleday, 2000), 37–38; Earl Anthony, *Spitting in the Wind: The True Story behind the Violent Legacy of the Black Panther Party* (Santa Monica, CA: Roundtable Publishing, 1990), 44–45; Elaine Brown, *A Taste of Power,* ch. 6.

15. See Elaine Brown, *A Taste of Power,* 120. for one account of Carter's attraction to the Party.

16. Olsen, *Last Man Standing,* 37–38; Anthony, *Spitting in the Wind,* 44–45; Elaine Brown, *A Taste of Power,* 118–20 and ch. 6.

17. Alprentice "Bunchy" Carter quoted and event described in Elaine Brown, *A Taste of Power,* 125. Given how many years later the account was published and the fact that Brown cites no source other than her memory, this extract may be more of a paraphrase of Carter than a direct quote.

18. Davis, *Autobiography,* 162–67.

19. For US and wide Black Congress support of the "Free Huey!" campaign, see Scot Brown, "The US Organization," 160.

20. Clayborne Carson, *In Struggle: SNCC and the Black Awakening of the 1960s* (Cambridge, MA: Harvard University Press, 1981), 282–83; Scot Brown, "The US Organization," 163–64.

21. Davis, *Autobiography,* 162–67; Elaine Brown, *A Taste of Power,* 126; Scot Brown, "The US Organization," 160–63.

22. Freed, *Agony in New Haven,* 62–64.

23. Scot Brown, "The US Organization," 176.

24. *Eldridge Cleaver: Post-Prison Writings and Speeches,* ed. Robert Scheer (New York: Random House, 1969), 38.

25. "Watts Festival," *Los Angeles Times,* August 11, 1968, L5; "25,000 Witness Parade as Watts Festival Closes," *Los Angeles Times,* August 12, 1968, 3.

26. Phil Fradkin and Dial Torgerson, "Negro Leaders Urge Suspect in Police Shootout to Give Up," *Los Angeles Times,* August 7, 1968, 1.

27. Ibid. See also "Three L.A. Panthers Murdered by Pigs," *Black Panther,* September 7, 1968, 6. On the funeral, including the alliance with Chicanos, see William Drummond and Ray Rogers, "Negroes, Mexican-Americans Drill at Funeral of Panther," *Los Angeles Times,* August 11, 1968, FB; and *Black Panther,* September 7, 1968, .6. On further police violence at the Watts festival, see Jack Jones, "Watts Violence Takes Toll of 3 Dead, 41 Hurt," *Los Angeles Times,* August 13, 1968, 1; and "Watts Festival Revolt," *Black Panther,* September 7, 1968, 6. According to Elaine Brown, the young Panthers had taken Newton's Executive Mandate No. 3 to heart and extended its scope to include their car. The mandate required Panthers to defend their homes, by force, against unwarranted search. Elaine Brown, interview by Joshua Bloom, June 15, 2008.

28. Fradkin and Torgerson, "Negro Leaders Urge Suspect."

29. Aaron Dixon, *My People Are Rising: Memoir of a Black Panther Party Captain* (Chicago: Haymarket Books, forthcoming).

30. Ibid.

31. Ibid., 110–19.

32. *Black Panther,* special issue cataloguing conflicts with the police, February 21, 1970.

33. "Welton Armstead Murdered by Seattle Pigs," *Black Panther Party Seattle Chapter Ministry of Information Bulletin #2,* November 1969, 1, Vietnam War Era Ephemera Collection, University of Washington Libraries, Seattle; Earl Caldwell, "Lawyer Names 19 Panthers He Says Were Slain," *New York Times,* December 21, 1969, 47; "Seattle Pigs Murder Panther," *Black Panther,* October 19, 1968, 6.

34. See, for example, Thomas A. Johnson, "Black Panthers Picket a School," *New York Times* September 13, 1966, 38; Leonard Buder, "Schools in City Open Smoothly Despite Protests," *New York Times* September 13, 1966, 1. Contrary to the national Black Panther Party headquarters in Oakland, the Party chapter in Harlem, drawing on the neighborhood's deep historical roots of black nationalism, maintained strong cultural nationalist tendencies. New York Panther members adopted African names, wore dashikis, and spoke in Swahili. See Murray Kempton, *The Briar Patch: The Trial of the Panther 21* (1973; repr. New York: Da Capo Press, 1997), 54.

35. Kempton, *The Briar Patch,* 43.

36. Joudon Ford quoted in ibid., 44; age on 43.

37. In the Black Panther Party, the civilian titles were subordinate to the military ones. So Newton, as minister of defense, held the top position in the Party, whereas Seale, as chairman, was second in command. Similarly, chapter chairmen were usually subordinate to captains. But such titles were not systematic, and this hierarchy was not universally imposed; for example, Deputy Chairman Fred Hampton was the top Panther leader in Chicago.

38. Kempton, *The Briar Patch,* 54.

39. Ibid., 56.

40. Dan Sullivan, "Black Panther Benefit Is Held in East Village. 2,600 at Program to Raise Funds for 7 Jailed Members," *New York Times,* May 21, 1968, 42; "Rap Brown to Speak at Panther Benefit," *New York Times,* May 16, 1968, 54.

41. Lumumba Shakur in Kuwasi Balagoon, Joan Bird, Cetewayo, Robert Collier, Dhoruba, Richard Harris, Ali Bey Hassan, Jamal, Abayama Katara, Kwando Kinshasa, Baba Odinga, Shaba Ogun Om, Curtis Powell, Afeni Shakur, Lumumba Shakur, and Clark Squire, *Look for Me in the Whirlwind: The Collective Autobiography of the New York 21* (New York: Random House, 1971), 295; Kempton, *The Briar Patch,* 45–46.

42. Ibid., 89.

43. Ibid., 175.

44. Balagoon et al., *Look for Me in the Whirlwind,* 176–79.

45. Lumumba Shakur in ibid., 179.

46. Balagoon et al., *Look for Me in the Whirlwind,* 180–83.

47. "Prison Racial Fight Injures 23 Upstate; 450 Join in Melee," *New York Times,* September 28, 1963, 22; Balagoon et al., *Look for Me in the Whirlwind,* 183, 260–63. Sekou Odinga chapter in *Can't Jail the Spirit: Political Prisoners in the U.S.: A Collection of Biographies,* 4th ed. (Chicago: Committee to End the Marion Lockdown, March 1998).

48. Lumumba Shakur in Balagoon et al., *Look for Me in the Whirlwind,* 264–65 (quote on 265).

49. Odinga in *Can't Jail the Spirit.*

50. Balagoon et al., *Look for Me in the Whirlwind,* 257–60.

51. Ibid., 270–71.

52. Afeni Shakur is known today not only as a key leader of the New York 21, but also as the mother of the late rap artist Tupac Shakur. Afeni married Lumumba Shakur and took his name, but Tupac was born in 1971, and Lumumba was not his father.

53. Afeni Shakur in Balagoon et al., *Look for Me in the Whirlwind,* 287–88.

54. Ibid., 288–89.

55. Earl Caldwell, "Black Panthers: 'Young Revolutionaries at War,'" *New York Times,* September 6, 1968, 49.

56. Abayama Katara in Balagoon et al., *Look for Me in the Whirlwind,* 90–91.

57. Ibid., 273.

58. Balagoon et al., *Look for Me in the Whirlwind,* 277–78, 295–96. See also McCandlish Phillips, "4 Pupils Arrested at Brandeis High: Brown Appearance Barred before Trouble Erupts," *New York Times,* June 6, 1968, 58; David K. Shipler, "Classes Go On Despite District Woes," *New York Times,* June 11, 1968, 49; Sidney E. Zion, "5 Black Panthers Held in Brooklyn," *New York Times,* September 13, 1968, 93; David Bird, "Judge Forbids Slogan Buttons at Panther Hearing in Brooklyn," *New York Times,* September 19, 1968, 32; Steven Roberts, "Race: The Third Party in the School Crisis," *New York Times,* September 22, 1968, 182; Leonard Buder, "Shanker Rejects Offer to Protect Ocean Hill Staff," *New York Times,* September 25, 1968, 1; Peter Kihiss, "Open Schools, Galamison Tells Rally," September 26, 1968, 56; "20,000 in N.Y. March for Black Control," *Black Panther,* October 26, 1968, 15.

59. Robert D. McFadden, "Police-Black Panther Scuffles Mark Brooklyn

Street Rally," *New York Times,* August 2, 1968, 31; "Panthers' Account of N.Y. Incident," *Black Panther,* October 5, 1968, 3.

60. Furey quoted in Joseph Novitski, "Judge's Ouster Sought," *New York Times,* August 5, 1968, 1.

61. Martin Tolchin, "150 Hunt Ambusheers Who Shot Policemen," *New York Times,* August 3, 1968, 1.

62. Joudon Ford quoted in David Burnham, "Panthers to Seek Voice Over Police," *New York Times,* September 11, 1968, 56. The district attorney later said that Panthers were suspects in the case; see David Burnham, "Black Panthers Sought in West in Ambush of Brooklyn Police," *New York Times,* September 4, 1968, 38.

63. Novitski, "Judge's Ouster Sought," 1.

64. Martin Arnold, "Bar Group Urges Inquiry on Judge," *New York Times,* August 6, 1968, 40.

65. Joseph Novitski, "Brooklyn Police Set Up Group to Back 'Vigorous' Enforcement," *New York Times,* August 8, 1968, 18. "Warren Court" refers to the common view of the Supreme Court under Chief Justice Earl Warren (1953–1969) as liberal.

66. Ira Glasser quoted in Sidney E. Zion, "Rights Groups Assail Demands of New Police Unit," *New York Times,* August 9, 1968, 16. For other responses, see Irving Spiegel, "P.B.A. Will Issue 'Get Tough' Advice," *New York Times,* August 12, 1968, 1; Sylvan Fox, "P.B.A. Directives Held Sop to Right," *New York Times,* August 16, 1968, 38. The Fox article agrees with our assessment that the PBA head was playing politics, attempting to stay in front of his union membership by taking a strong rhetorical stand while staying within the law. David Burnham, "Leary Declares He Alone Makes Police Decisions," *New York Times,* August 14, 1968, 1; "Inquiry Planned on Judge Furey," *New York Times,* August 27, 1968, 82; "Bar Group Cancels Hearings on Charges against Judge Furey," *New York Times,* September 10, 1968, 31.

67. John Sibley, "100 Police Guard 7 Negro Suspects," *New York Times,* August 22, 1968, 48.

68. Kunstler quoted in David Burnham, "3 in Black Panther Party Win Hearing Over Bail," *New York Times,* August 24, 1968, 30; David Burnham, "3 Black Panthers Win Bail Cut in Assault Case," *New York Times,* August 28, 1968, 23; David Burnham, "Black Panthers Sought in West in Ambush of Brooklyn Police," *New York Times,* September 4, 1968, 38.

69. David Burnham, "Off-Duty Police Here Join in Beating Black Panthers," *New York Times,* September 5, 1968, 1; "Brutality, New York Style," editorial, *New York Times,* September 5, 1968, 46; "New Flash . . . New York Pigs Use New Tactic to Vamp on 12 Panthers," *Black Panther,* September 7, 1968, 10; Balagoon et al., *Look for Me in the Whirlwind,* 275–77.

70. Katara in Balagoon et al., *Look for Me in the Whirlwind,* 275–77.

71. David Burnham, "Mayor and Leary Warn Policemen in Panther Melee," *New York Times,* September 6, 1968, 1.

72. David Burnham, "Black Panthers Give Grievances," *New York Times,* September 7, 1968, 1.

73. Emanuel Perlmutter, "N.A.A.C.P. Urges Inquiry on Police," *New York Times,* September 8, 1968, 38.

74. "Jury Study Ordered in Attack by Police on Black Panthers," *New York Times,* September 21, 1968, 28.

75. David Burnham, "Panthers to Seek Voice Over Police," *New York Times,* September 11, 1968, 56; "Press Conference of N.Y. Panthers," *Black Panther,* October 5, 1968, 3.

76. Albin Krebs, "Two Policemen Shot in Brooklyn Ambush," *New York Times,* September 12, 1968, 1; Murray Schumach, "50 Police Join Hunt in Brooklyn Sniping," *New York Times,* September 13, 1968.

77. Kathleen Cleaver in Henry Hampton and Steve Fayer, *Voices of Freedom: An Oral History of the Civil Rights Movement from the 1950s through the 1980s* (New York: Bantam Books, 1990), 514.

78. Local law enforcement officials reported openings of Black Panther chapters, branches or National Committee to Combat Fascism offices (local interracial organizations that did not have the full status of Party chapters) to the House Committee on Internal Security, *Gun-Barrel Politics: The Black Panther Party, 1966–1971,* part 470, 92d Congress, 1ˢᵗ session (Washington, DC: Government Printing Office, 1971), 88. These twenty cities comprise more than half of the Panther chapter openings for which the committee report provides dates. The report lists many Black Panther Party chapters for which the date of opening is unknown. So there were probably well over thirty chapter openings by the end of 1968. For additional coverage of Black Panther Party growth in 1968 outside Oakland, New York, Los Angeles, and Seattle, including the opening of offices in San Francisco and Long Beach, see the following articles in the *Black Panther.* October 5, 1968: "Two Strikeouts of Nebraska Power Structure," 4. October 19, 1968: "A Message to the Ghetto" [on Long Beach chapter], 2; "Denver Pigs Incite Riot," 6. October 26, 1968: Sacramento Black Panther Party, "The Pig, the Hog, and the Boar," 6. November 16, 1968: "Panthers-B.S.U. Close S.F. State College," 8; "Mafia Pigs of Alioto," 8; "S.F. Gun Suit," 17. December 7, 1968: "Pigs Uptight: Bomb N.J. Panther Office," 3. November 21, 1968: "Panthers-B.S.U. Get It Together" [on San Francisco office], 3; "New Jersey Panthers Go Underground," 16; "Denver Pigs Raid and Ransack Panther H.Q.," 22. January 4, 1969: "San Francisco State Strike Spreads," 2; "B.S.U. Mexican Students Revolt in L.A. Schools," 2; "Denver Pigs," 4. January 15, 1969: "Nationwide Harassment of Panthers by Pig Power Structure," 1; "Sign Petition: Control Your Local Pigs," 6 concerning Black Panther Party chapters in Northern California; "Pigs Raid Des Moines Panthers," 9; "Pigs Uptight: Bomb N.J. Panther Office," 9; "Indianapolis Panthers Target of Pig Attack," 9; "Denver Pigs Incite Riot," 10; "Denver Pigs Attack Panthers," 11. See also the following articles in the *New York Times:* Wallace Turner, "Oakland Streets Have Led to Two Deaths—Group's Backing Grows," July 20, 1968; "Black Panther Says Police in Newark Planted Pistol," September 19, 1968; "3 Black Panthers Arrested in Fight with Jersey Police," September 25, 1968.

7. BREAKFAST

Epigraphs, part 3: Hampton quoted in David Hilliard and Lewis Cole, *This Side of Glory: The Autobiography of David Hilliard and the Story of the Black Panther Party* (New York: Little, Brown, 1993), 227; Hoover memo reproduced in Ward Churchill and Jim Vander Wall, *The COINTELPRO Papers: Documents from the FBI's Secret Wars against Dissent in the United States* (Boston: South End Press, 1990), 144; Hampton quoted in Masai Hewitt, "Seize the Time—Submit or Fight," *Black Panther*, December 13, 1969, 3.

1. Episode recounted in Devin Fergus, *Liberalism, Black Power, and the Making of American Politics 1965–1980* (Athens: University of Georgia Press, 2009), 103–5; Benjamin R. Friedman, "Picking Up Where Robert F. Williams Left Off: The Winston-Salem Branch of the Black Panther Party," in *Comrades: A Local History of the Black Panther Party*, ed. Judson L. Jeffries (Bloomington: Indiana University Press, 2007), 7; Benjamin Friedman, "Fighting Back: The North Carolina Chapter of the Black Panther Party" (master's thesis, George Washington University, 1994), 57–58.

2. Friedman, "Picking Up Where Robert F. Williams Left Off," 64.

3. Mumia Abu-Jamal, *We Want Freedom* (Cambridge, MA: South End Press, 2004), 197.

4. *Black Panther*, April 6, 1969, 14

5. Hilliard and Cole, *This Side of Glory*, 159.

6. Earl Caldwell, "Cleaver Is Sought As Coast Fugitive for Defying Order," *New York Times*, November 28, 1968, 1.

7. Paul Alkebulan, *Survival Pending Revolution*, ch. 2. Alkebulan provides the most insightful and thoroughly documented treatment of the founding of the community programs. For additional contributions, see Andrew Witt, "'Picking Up the Hammer': The Community Programs and Services of the Black Panther Party with Emphasis on the Milwaukee Branch, 1966–1977" (PhD diss., Loyola University, 2005); and Ashley Chaifetz, "Introducing the American Dream: The Black Panther Party Survival Programs, 1966–1982" (master's thesis, Sarah Lawrence College, 2005).

8. Huey Newton, Bobby Seale, Eldridge Cleaver, and David Hilliard, "Breakfast for Black Children," *Black Panther*, September 7, 1968, 7; "Volunteers Needed to Help Prepare and Serve Breakfast for School Children," *Black Panther*, October 19, 1968, 2; "Volunteers Needed to Help Prepare and Serve Breakfast for School Children," *Black Panther*, November 2, 1968, 7; "Breakfast for School Children," *Black Panther*, December 21, 1968, 15. These notices announce the breakfast program but imply that the program had not yet begun ("The first of these programs *will* exist at Downs Memorial Church" in Oakland and Concord Baptist Church in Berkeley—emphasis mine). We could find no credible evidence that such programs were actually started in 1968, or ever at the sites mentioned in the articles.

9. "Breakfast for School Children," 15. The announcement giving Beckford-Smith as a contact also appears in three other issues of the *Black Panther*: January 4, 1969, 16; January 25, 1969, 21; and March 23, 1969, 23. For the date of the first Black Panther breakfast program, see also Father Earl A. Neil, "The Role of the Church and the Survival Program," *Black Panther*, May 15,

1971: "In January, 1969, St. Augustine's co-sponsored the first Free Breakfast Program with the Black Panther Party." For early news coverage, see Tim Findley, "School Kids: The Panther Breakfast Club," *San Francisco Chronicle,* January 31, 1969 (quote in text from this article. For further details on Beckford-Smith's role, see Father Earl A. Neil, "Black Panther Party and Father Neil," personal statement produced in preparation for a 2002 Black Panther reunion, copy in Joshua Bloom's possession.

10. "Black Panthers Serve Free Breakfasts to Youngsters," *Berkeley Gazette,* March 11, 1969; "Breakfast for Schoolchildren in Double Rock and Hunters Point" and "Richmond Breakfast for School Children," *Black Panther,* March 31, 1969, 9; "Black Panthers Serve Free Breakfasts to Youngsters," *Berkeley Gazette,* March 11, 1969.

11. "Some Chapters and Branches of the Black Panther Party with Breakfast Programs," *Black Panther,* April 27, 1969, 3. For an early programmatic statement, see Bobby Seale interview in *Movement* newspaper, March 1969, republished as "Chairman Bobby Seale," *Black Panther,* March 3, 1969, 10.

12. In addition to Hilliard's own account in *This Side of Glory* (211–12, 227), Father Earl A. Neil testifies to David Hilliard's important and early role in building the Party relationship with St. Augustine Church, even before the creation of the first breakfast program there; Neil, "Black Panther Party and Father Neil," personal statement produced in preparation for a 2002 Black Panther reunion.

13. The twenty-three cities are Berkeley, San Francisco, Richmond, Oakland, Los Angeles, Watts, and San Diego in California; Seattle, Washington; Eugene, Oregon; Denver, Colorado; Indianapolis, Indiana; Kansas City, Missouri; Milwaukee, Wisconsin; Chicago, Illinois; Boston, Massachusetts; New York City, Queens, Peekskill, White Plains, and Brooklyn in New York; Philadelphia, Pennsylvania; Baltimore, Maryland; and New Haven, Connecticut; "List of Chapters and Branches with Breakfast Programs," *Black Panther,* November 15, 1969, 17. Beginning in July 1969, almost every weekly issue of the *Black Panther* carried coverage of Panther community service programs around the country. The *Black Panther* carried no coverage of actual Panther community service programs before January 1969 and very little before July 1969.

14. See Andrew Witt, "A Sampling of Locations of Black Panther Party Community Programs Nationwide," appendix E in *The Black Panthers in the Midwest: The Community Programs and Services of the Black Panther Party in Milwaukee, 1966–1977* (New York: Routledge, 2007), 111–13.

15. Except where otherwise noted, this biographical information is drawn from Hilliard and Cole, *This Side of Glory,* and Joshua Bloom's discussions with Hilliard.

16. Hilliard and Cole, *This Side of Glory,* 114.

17. Ibid., 27.

18. Charles E. Jones and Judson L. Jeffries, "'Don't Believe the Hype': Debunking the Panther Mythology," in *The Black Panther Party [Reconsidered],* ed. Charles E. Jones (Baltimore: Black Classic Press, 1998), table 1, 30; "Breakfast Programs Being Initiated," *Black Panther,* May 25, 1969, 8.

19. *Black Panther,* October 4, 1969, 7.

20. JoNina M. Abron, "'Serving the People': The Survival Programs of the Black Panther Party," in Jones, *Black Panther Party [Reconsidered],* 182; see also Flores Forbes, *Will You Die with Me? My Life and the Black Panther Party* (New York, Atria, 2006), 50; and Judson L. Jeffries, "Revising Panther History in Baltimore," in his *Comrades,* 23, for similar points.

21. Miriam Ma'at-Ka-Re Monges, "'I Got A Right to the Tree of Life': Afrocentric Reflections of a Former Community Worker," in Jones, *The Black Panther Party [Reconsidered],* 139.

22. Forbes, *Will You Die with Me?* 50.

23. "Capitalist Attacks Breakfast for Children," *Black Panther,* April 20, 1969, 15; "Vallejo Chapter Starts Breakfast for Children," *Black Panther,* March 31, 1969, 9; "Indiana Breakfast," and "Boston Breakfast," *Black Panther,* July 19, 1969, 16.

24. Abron, "Serving the People," 184.

25. Andrew Witt, "Picking Up the Hammer: The Milwaukee Branch of the Black Panther Party," in Jeffries, *Comrades,* 180.

26. Forbes, *Will You Die with Me?* 50.

27. Jeffries, "Revising Panther History in Baltimore," 23; Safiya A. Bukhari quoted in Abu-Jamal, *We Want Freedom,* 169–70; Joe Cuba, "Breakfast Sabotage," *Black Panther,* November 15, 1969, 17.

28. Jeffries, "Revising Panther History in Baltimore," 32, 43; "Report Concerning an Attempted Vamp on Baltimore Chapter," *Black Panther,* May 19, 1970.

29. Alondra Nelson, "Black Power, Biomedicine, and the Politics of Knowledge," (PhD diss., New York University, 2003), 103–206; Karen Davis and Cathy Schoen, *Health and the War on Poverty: A Ten-Year Appraisal* (Washington, DC: Brookings Institution, 1978); Alondra Nelson, *Body and Soul: The Black Panther Party and the Fight against Medical Discrimination* (Minneapolis: University of Minnesota Press, 2011).

30. Jeffries," Revising Panther History in Baltimore," 22.

31. Nelson, "Black Power," 103–206; Abron, "Serving the People," 184; Witt, *The Black Panthers in the Midwest,* 63.

32. This statistic comes from the National Institutes of Health, Bethesda, MD.

33. Nelson, "Black Power," 144–206.

34. "Revolutionary Drug Program Serves the People," *Black Panther,* October 31, 1970; "People for the People," *Black Panther,* November 28, 1970, 6.

35. Charles E. Jones, "'Talkin' the Talk and Walkin' the Walk': An Interview With Panther Jimmy Slater," in Jones, *Black Panther Party [Reconsidered],* 148.

36. "Racist Bandits Attack People's Free Health Center," *Black Panther,* July 18, 1970.

37. Friedman, "Fighting Back," 84–85.

38. Ibid., 80–81.

39. Ibid., 81; Friedman, "Picking Up Where Robert F. Williams Left Off," 74–76.

40. "Excerpts from an Interview with Huey," *Black Panther,* August 1, 1970, 10–11; "The National Committee to Combat Fascism Opens in Denver, Colorado," *Black Panther,* September 5, 1970; "Free Bussing Program in Boston," *Black Panther,* November 21, 1970, 2; Ryan Nissim-Sabat, "Panthers Set Up Shop in Cleveland," in Jeffries, *Comrades,* 126–27; Witt, "The Milwaukee Branch," in ibid., 181, 196–97; Judson L. Jeffries and Malcolm Foley," To Live and Die in L.A.," in ibid., 270.

41. Ronald Stark, cited in Witt, "The Milwaukee Branch," 198.

42. Abron, "Serving the People," 186–87.

43. Ibid., 187.

44. JoAnn Bray quoted in Nissim-Sabat, "Panthers Set Up Shop in Cleveland," 126–27.

45. Katherine M. Charron, *Freedom's Teacher: The Life of Septima Clark* (Chapel Hill: University of North Carolina Press, 2009); Daniel Perlstein, "SNCC and the Creation of the Mississippi Freedom Schools," *History of Education Quarterly* 30, no. 3 (Fall 1990): 297–324; Sandra E. Adickes, *Legacy of a Freedom School* (New York: Palgrave Macmillan, 2005).

46. Witt, *The Black Panthers in the Midwest,* appendix E, 113–14; Abron, "Serving the People," 185.

47. Omari L. Dyson, Kevin L. Brooks, Judson L. Jeffries, "'Brotherly Love Can Kill You': The Philadelphia Branch of the Black Panther Party," in Jeffries, *Comrades,* 223; Nissim-Sabat, "Panthers Set Up Shop in Cleveland," 119; Monges, "I Got a Right to the Tree of Life," 140.

48. Douglas Corbin, "The Oakland Black Panther Party School" (senior honors thesis, University of California, Berkeley, 2004); Abron, "Serving the People," 185–86.

49. Corbin, "The Oakland Black Panther Party School"; Abron, "Serving the People," 185–86.

50. "Breakfast for School Children," *Black Panther,* April 27, 1969, 4; "Breakfast for School Children," *Black Panther,* May 19, 1969, 7; "Breakfast for School Children: Peekskill, NY," *Black Panther,* July 5, 1969, 15; "San Diego Breakfast Moves Ahead Despite Continued Harassment," *Black Panther,* July 26, 1969, 15; "Breakfast for School Children Programs," *Black Panther,* December 27, 1969, 4.

51. Tracye Matthews, "'No One Ever Asks, What a Man's Role in the Revolution Is'; Gender and the Politics of the Black Panther Party, 1966–1971," in Jones, *Black Panther Party [Reconsidered],* 270.

52. Ibid.; Frankye Malika Adams quoted in Abu-Jamal, *We Want Freedom,* 164.

53. Ericka Huggins, public lecture, Marcus Books, Oakland, California.

54. *To Die for the People: The Writings of Huey P. Newton* (New York: Random House, 1972), 81.

55. Matthews, "No One Ever Asks," 206–71.

56. Bobby Seale, *Seize the Time: The Story of the Black Panther Party and Huey P. Newton* (1971; repr. Baltimore: Black Classic Press, 1990), 412–13.

57. Monges, "I Got a Right to the Tree of Life," 137.

58. Patricia A. Sullivan, *Lift Every Voice: The NAACP and the Making of the Civil Rights Movement* (New York: New Press, 2009); Jesse T. Moore Jr., *A Search for Equality: The National Urban League, 1910–1961* (University Park: Pennsylvania State University Press, 1981); Steven Hahn, *A Nation under Our Feet: Black Political Struggles in the Rural South from Slavery to the Great Migration* (Cambridge, MA: Harvard University Press, 2003).

59. Nissim-Sabat, "Panthers Set Up Shop in Cleveland," 128.

60. *Black Panther,* May 2, 1969, 14.

61. Clayborne Carson, *In Struggle: SNCC and the Black Awakening of the 1960s* (Cambridge, MA: Harvard University Press, 1981); Thomas J. Sugrue, *Sweet Land of Liberty: The Forgotten Struggle for Civil Rights in the North* (New York: Random House, 2008).

62. Malcolm X and Alex Haley, *The Autobiography of Malcolm X* (New York: Grove Press, 1965); Manning Marable, *Malcolm X: A Life of Reinvention* (New York: Penguin, 2011).

63. Jones, "Talkin' the Talk and Walkin' the Walk," 148.

64. Forbes, *Will You Die With Me?* 50.

65. Clarence Peterson cited in Dyson, Brooks, and Jeffries, "Brotherly Love Can Kill You," 243.

8. LAW AND ORDER

1. Wallace Turner, "Coast Police Fire at Panther Camp," *New York Times,* September 11, 1968, 37; "2 Officers Accused of Firing at Newton Office," *Los Angeles Times,* September 11, 1968, 3.

2. Kenneth O'Reilly, *"Racial Matters": The FBI's Secret File on Black America, 1960–1972* (New York: Free Press, 1991), ch. 1.

3. David Cunningham, *There's Something Happening Here* (Berkeley: University of California Press, 2004), 6.

4. O'Reilly, *"Racial Matters,"* chs. 2 and 3.

5. Select Committee to Study Governmental Operations with Respect to Intelligence Activities [Church Committee], *Supplementary Detailed Staff Reports on Intelligence Activities and the Rights of Americans*, Final Report, S. Doc. No. 94–755 (April 1976), book 3, 79–184 (hereafter Church Committee Report).

6. Martin Luther King Jr., "Beyond Vietnam," in *Call to Conscience,* ed. Clayborne Carson and Kris Shepard (New York: Warner Books, 2001), 133–64.

7. Memo, J. Edgar Hoover, FBI Director, to Field Offices, August 25, 1967. All FBI memos cited in this chapter are available in the FBI Reading Room, FBI Headquarters, Washington, DC.

8. Ibid. The other five organizations listed in the memo are the Student Nonviolent Coordinating Committee and Congress of Racial Equality, both leading civil rights organizations that turned nationalist after 1966; the Revolutionary Action Movement and the Deacons for Defense, both proponents of armed black struggle with significant influence on the Black Panthers (see ch. 1 in this book); and the Nation of Islam.

9. Memo, J. Edgar Hoover to Field Offices, March 4, 1968; see also memo, G.C. Moore to W.C. Sullivan, February 29, 1968.

10. Memo, G.C. Moore to W.C. Sullivan, September 27, 1968.

11. Poll result reported in Melvin Small, *Johnson, Nixon, and the Doves* (New Brunswick, NJ: Rutgers University Press, 1988), 130.

12. Ibid., 103, 110–13, 117.

13. Ibid., 94. Except where otherwise noted, most of the events in this section are drawn from Small's *Johnson, Nixon, and the Doves* and Charles DeBenedetti and Charles Chatfield, *An American Ordeal: The Antiwar Movement of the Vietnam Era* (Syracuse, NY: Syracuse University Press, 1990).

14. Small, *Johnson, Nixon, and the Doves,* 118–19; DeBenedetti and Chatfield, *An American Ordeal,* 200–202.

15. Small, *Johnson, Nixon, and the Doves,* 120–23.

16. "Bloody Path to Peace?" *New York Times,* February 1, 1968; "More Than a Diversion," *New York Times,* February 2, 1968; "After the Tet Offensive," *New York Times,* February 8, 1968; David Caute, *The Year of the Barricades* (New York: Harper & Row, 1988), 11–12; George Katsiaficas, *The Imagination of the New Left: A Global Analysis of 1968* (Boston: South End Press, 1987), 29–30; DeBenedetti and Chatfield, *An American Ordeal,* 209–10.

17. Captured NLF officer quoted by Bernard Weintraub, "Questioning of Captured Vietcong Yields Picture of a Determined Enemy," *New York Times,* February 15, 1968, 4.

18. Small, *Johnson, Nixon, and the Doves,* 135.

19. DeBenedetti and Chatfield, *An American Ordeal,* 211.

20. Small, *Johnson, Nixon, and the Doves,* 138.

21. Ibid., 137; DeBenedetti and Chatfield, *An American Ordeal,* 212.

22. Small, *Johnson, Nixon, and the Doves,* 147.

23. Ibid., 132; DeBenedetti and Chatfield, *An American Ordeal,* 214.

24. In 1964, Johnson won every state except those in the Deep South (Louisiana, Mississippi, Alabama, Georgia, and South Carolina) that had been alienated by his civil rights policies and turned toward the Republican Party for the first time, and his opponent's home state of Arizona.

25. Small, *Johnson, Nixon, and the Doves,* 158.

26. Tom Wells, *The War Within: America's Battle over Vietnam* (Berkeley: University of California Press, 1994), 237–40; Kirkpatrick Sale, *SDS* (New York: Random House, 1973), 473.

27. "Chairman Bobby Seale and Chief of Staff David Hilliard in Chicago," *Black Panther,* September 7, 1968, 3.

28. Todd Gitlin, *The Sixties: Years of Hope, Days of Rage* (New York: Bantam Books, 1987), 321–23; *New York Times,* August 29, 1968. Sixty black soldiers in Fort Hood, Texas, refused to help put down protests against the war in Chicago, and forty-three of them were taken to the stockades as a result: "60 Negro GIs Balk at Possible Riot Control," *Los Angeles Times,* August 25, 1968, F9.

29. Wells, *The War Within,* 277–78; DeBenedetti and Chatfield, *An American Ordeal,* 227; *New York Times,* August 26, 1968; Earl Caldwell, "Chicago

Negroes Stirred by Clashes between Whites and Police, Not Convention," *New York Times,* August 29, 1968, 22.

30. Caldwell, "Chicago Negroes"; Sale, *SDS,* 475.

31. J. Anthony Lukas, "War Critics Liken Chicago to Prague," *New York Times,* August 25, 1968, 62.

32. DeBenedetti and Chatfield, *An American Ordeal,* 227–28; Gitlin, *The Sixties,* 332; Wells, *The War Within,* 279.

33. "Chairman Bobby Seale and Chief of Staff David Hilliard in Chicago," *Black Panther,* September 7, 1968, 3; see also "White Radicals vs. Pigs at Chicago," *Black Panther,* October 5, 1968.

34. Gitlin, *The Sixties,* 332–34; Wells, *The War Within,* 279–80.

35. Ibid. The "Battle of Algiers" refers to the bloody urban warfare in 1957 between the National Liberation Front and the French Army during the Algerian struggle for independence, famously depicted in the 1966 film by the same name by Italian director Gillo Pontecorvo.

36. DeBenedetti and Chatfield, *An American Ordeal,* 228.

37. "Opening Salvos from a Black/White Gun," *Black Panther,* October 5, 1968.

38. Sale, *SDS,* 475; DeBenedetti and Chatfield, *An American Ordeal,* 228.

39. Sale, *SDS,* 478–79. Sale also cites the Liberation News Service, "SDS Membership Mushrooms," October 18, 1968, part reprinted in *Guardian,* October 26, 1968; *Guardian,* November 16, 1968, and January 4, 1969; Jack Gerson, "Go Go Stanford," *Movement,* November 1968; *Newsweek,* September 30, 1968; "Across the Country," *New Left Notes,* October 7, 1968; Carl Davidson, *Guardian,* November 16, 1968.

40. "Pledges End of War, Toughness on Crime," *New York Times,* August 9, 1968, 1.

41. John W. Finney, "Nixon and Reagan Ask War on Crime," *New York Times,* August 1, 1968, 1.

42. White supremacist George Wallace ran as a third-party candidate, eventually winning 13 percent of the popular vote and most of the electoral votes in the Deep South. Many on the left refused to vote. Of those in the left wing of the Democratic Party who did vote for Hubert Humphrey, most were disgusted by the party leadership and declined to help the campaign with time or money. Humphrey was lagging far behind in the polls until, desperate to bring the Democratic base back into the election in the last few weeks of the campaign, he became critical of President Johnson's war policy and called for a halt to bombing. When Johnson announced he would stop the bombing, Humphrey surged ahead in the polls, closing in on Nixon. But the comeback surge was not enough.

43. Nixon and Hoover conversation reported in memos by FBI Assistant Director Tolson, cited in O'Reilly, *"Racial Matters,"* 298. Nixon also eventually placed the Black Panther Party on his infamous list of "enemies," which was revealed in the Watergate scandal; see David E. Rosenbaum, "Scores of Names," *New York Times,* June 28, 1973, 1; and "Opponents List," in Edward W. Knappman, ed., *Watergate and the White House* (New York: Facts on File, 1973), 1: 96–97.

44. "The Panthers and the Law," *Newsweek,* February 23, 1970, 26. Some sources have quoted Mitchell telling *Newsweek* in February 1969 that the Department of Justice would "wipe out the Black Panther Party by the end of 1969." But that is incorrect. Public statements by the Justice Department about the program against the Panthers came a year after Nixon took office, not right away. Even Hoover did not make broad public statements about the threat the Panthers posed until the summer of 1969. And we could find no quote from Justice Department officials promising the eradication of the Panthers and no quotation in *Newsweek* of any direct statement by Mitchell about the Black Panthers. See also "Too Late for the Panthers?" *Newsweek,* December 22, 1969, 26; "Order in the Court," *Newsweek,* February 16, 1970, 27; "Gentlemen Songsters Off on a Spree," *Newsweek,* May 11, 1970; "The Revolutionaries," *Newsweek,* May 11, 1970, 34; "Mr. Nixon's Home Front," *Newsweek,* May 18, 1970, 26–28.

45. J. Edgar Hoover quoted by United Press International (UPI) in "FBI Director Blacks Black Panthers," *Oakland Tribune,* July 15, 1969, 17. This is perhaps the most famous quote Hoover made about the Panthers. Usually, the 1976 Church Committee Report is cited as a source, but the report cites a *New York Times* article on September 8, 1968, that doesn't exist, and the timing is wrong. Hoover took no such public position on the Panthers in 1968. The UPI story ran on July 15, 1969, in dozens of newspapers, including the *San Mateo Times, Washington Court House* [Ohio] *Record Herald, Tucson Daily Citizen, Hayward Daily Review, Long Beach Independent,* and *Ukiah Daily Journal.* It was also reported that day on the *CBS Evening News* (retrieved from the Vanderbilt News Archive). But interestingly, the report and the statement were not mentioned independently in any of the major newspapers in July 1969. The first major newspaper report of the quote that we could find was David McClintick, "Black Panthers: Negro Militants Use Free Food, Medical Aid, to Promote Revolution," *Wall Street Journal,* August 29, 1969, 1.

Of further interest, UPI (July 15, 1969), CBS (July 15, 1969), and the *Wall Street Journal* (August 29, 1969) all attributed the quote to the FBI fiscal report for 1969. But that is not correct. The formal FBI fiscal report for 1969 was not released until October 29, 1969, and it contains milder language. Subsequent quotes from Hoover were similar and provide one clue to the context in which Hoover may have made the statement. See, for example, Hoover in Earl Caldwell, "Declining Black Panthers Gather New Support from Repeated Clashes with Police," *New York Times,* December 14, 1969, 64; "F.B.I. Brands Black Panthers 'Most Dangerous' of Extremists," *New York Times,* July 14, 1970, 21; Interagency Committee on Intelligence (Ad Hoc), Special Report [Huston Report], June 25, 1970, 9 [hereafter Huston Report]. The July 14, 1970, article in the *New York Times* cites an annual report released in July for fiscal 1970. We found a July 14, 1970, press release from the Office of the Director of the FBI from which that article quoted. The tone of that press release was much stronger and more similar to the famous "greatest threat" quote than the formal FBI annual reports (1968, 1969, 1970, etc.) and had a similar release date as the June 15, 1969, reports by UPI and CBS. There may have been a similar July 15, 1969, press release by J. Edgar Hoover that was presented as an annual report, apart from the formal report. If so, this begs the question why the release was reported only by UPI and CBS and whether Hoover ever sent the press release to the major papers. One possible explanation is that Hoover wanted a more limited and less traceable release of the provocative quote. The release to UPI (which CBS may have reported) gave public exposure of the quote while making it hard to trace. To date, we have not been able to recover the precise context of the quote, but at least the UPI stories date it precisely.

46. The following is the only mention of the Panthers in the report: "Another such organization is the Black Panther Party, which was founded as the Black Panther Party for Self-Defense at Oakland, California in December, 1966, for the alleged purpose of combating police brutality and uniting militant black youth. The political philosophy of its leaders is based on the writings of Mao Zedong and black revolutionary writers. They advocate the use of guns and guerrilla tactics to end their alleged oppression." Office of John Edgar Hoover, *FBI Annual Report: Fiscal Year 1968*, October 1, 1968, 24.

47. Church Committee Report, book 3, 188. The program was initiated in 1967; see Memo, J. Edgar Hoover, FBI Director, to Field Offices, August 25, 1967 for initiation of the COINTELPRO against black nationalist groups. The COINTELPRO was terminated in 1971; see David Cunningham, *There's Something Happening Here* (Berkeley: University of California Press, 2004), 13.

48. Airtel, Director, FBI, to SAC [Special Agent in Charge], San Francisco, May 27, 1969. Reproduced in Ward Churchill and Jim Vander Wall, *The COINTELPRO Papers: Documents from the FBI's Secret Wars against Dissent in the United States* (Boston: South End Press, 1990), 145.

49. Church Committee Report, book 3, 210–11. See also assorted news coverage of these revelations, such as Richard Philbrick, "Panther Free Meals 'Threat' to Hoover," *Chicago Tribune*, May 8, 1976, 5.

50. Memo, Internal Revenue Service Assistant Commissioner D. W. Bacon to chief counsel and other officers, "Re: Activist Organizations Committee," July 24, 1969; "Internal Revenue Service: An Intelligence Resource and Collector," in Church Committee Report, book 3, 876–90.

51. Huston Report, 9–10.

52. "Denver Pigs Incite Riot," *Black Panther*, October 19, 1968, 6; "Panthers Account of NY Incident," *Black Panther*, October 5, 1968, 3; "Review of Panther Growth and Harassment," *Black Panther*, January 4, 1969, 14; "Nationwide Harassment of Panthers by Pig Power Structure," *Black Panther*, January 15, 1969, 8.

53. "Indianapolis Panthers Target of Pig Attack," *Black Panther*, January 15, 1969, 8; "Pigs Raid Indianapolis Panthers," *Black Panther*, January 25, 1969, 6.

54. Ronnell Steward, "Denver Pigs Raid and Ransack Panther H.Q.," *Black Panther*, December 21, 1968, 22; Melvin D. Briscoe, "Rap Denver Cops for Wrecking Center," *Chicago Daily Defender*, December 21, 1968, 28.

55. "Des Moines Panthers," *Black Panther*, February 17, 1969, 9; "Pigs Raid Des Moines Panthers," *Black Panther*, January 15, 1969, 8.

56. Charles Buesey, "Pigs Uptight: Bomb New Jersey Panther Office,"

Black Panther, December 7, 1968, 3; "Panther Offices in Newark Bombed," *New York Times,* December 2, 1968, 29.

57. Murray Kempton, *The Briar Patch: The Trial of the Panther 21* (1973; repr. New York: Da Capo, 1997), ch. 1 (arrests), ch. 3 (history), 162 (conspiracy allegations), 277 (acquittal). Kuwasi Balagoon, Joan Bird, Cetewayo, Robert Collier, Dhoruba, Richard Harris, Ali Bey Hassan, Jamal, Abayama Katara, Kwando Kinshasa, Baba Odinga, Shaba Ogun Om, Curtis Powell, Afeni Shakur, Lumumba Shakur, and Clark Squire, *Look for Me in the Whirlwind: The Collective Autobiography of the New York 21* (New York: Random House, 1971); Zayd-Malik Shakur, "Pig Conspiracy against NY Panther Twenty-One," *Black Panther,* April 20, 1969, 10; Olaywah, "NY Pigs Move to Destroy Panthers," *Black Panther,* April 20, 1969, 11; "Statement by the Central Committee of the Black Panther Party," *Black Panther,* April 27, 1969, 14; Morris Kaplan, "Bomb Plot Is Laid to 21 Panthers," *New York Times,* April 3, 1969, 1; Edith Evans Asbury, "Black Panther Party Members Freed after Being Cleared of Charges," *New York Times,* May 14, 1971, 1.

58. "Pigs Bomb Des Moines Panther Headquarters," *Black Panther,* May 11, 1969, 2; "Des Moines Pigs Try to Halt Free Breakfast Program through Terror," *Black Panther,* May 11, 1969, 3; "Des Moines Panther Bombing," *Black Panther,* May 19, 1969, 15; "Iowa Panther Headquarters Hit by Blast," *Los Angeles Times,* April 28, 1969, A16.

59. Donald Cox, "Pigs Vamp on SF Panther Office," *Black Panther,* May 4, 1969, 5; "Frisco Cops Put Lid on Disorder," *Chicago Daily Defender,* April 30, 1969, 5; "10 Seized on Coast in Raid on Panthers," *New York Times,* April 29, 1969, 9.

60. "Fascist Milwaukee Pigs Attempt to Bait Panthers into Shootout," *Black Panther,* July 5, 1969, 1; "Panther Struck Down in Milwaukee," *Black Panther,* July 5, 1969, 16.

61. "Fascist Actions against the People of Sacramento," *Black Panther,* June 21, 1969, 12; Carl Ingram, "A Score Wounded, 37 Arrested in Calif. Shooting," *Chicago Daily Defender,* June 17, 1969, 2; "37 Arrested, 13 Policemen Wounded in Sacramento," *New York Times,* June 17, 1969, 28.

62. "Fascist Pigs Vamp on San Diego Panther Office," *Black Panther,* July 19, 1969, 3.

63. "Attempted Murder by the Fascist Pigs of Richmond Calif," *Black Panther,* August 16, 1969, 21.

64. "Press Release: San Diego Branch," *Black Panther,* September 20, 1969, 3; "40 San Diego Police Storm Panther Office," *Los Angeles Times,* September 4, 1969, 31.

65. "FBI's Philly Frame-Up," *Black Panther,* October 4, 1969, 4.

9. 41ST AND CENTRAL

1. Pratt citation quoted in Jack Olsen, *Last Man Standing: The Tragedy and Triumph of Geronimo Pratt* (New York, Doubleday, 2000), 31.

2. Pratt in ibid., 32; 33.

3. Ibid., 4.

4. Ibid., 38–39.

5. Elaine Brown, *A Taste of Power: A Black Woman's Story* (New York: Pantheon Books, 1992), 153–55.

6. Memo, J. Edgar Hoover to Field Offices, "Counter Intelligence Program, Black Nationalist Hate Groups, Racial Intelligence (Black Panther Party)," November 25, 1968. All FBI memos cited in this chapter are available in the FBI Reading Room, FBI Headquarters, Washington, DC.

7. Memo, Special Agent in Charge, Los Angeles, to J. Edgar Hoover, "Counterintelligence Program, Black Nationalist—Hate Groups, Racial Intelligence, Re Los Angeles letter to Bureau dated 9/25/68," November 29, 1968.

8. William J. Drummond and Kenneth Reich, "Two Black Panthers Slain in UCLA Hall," *Los Angeles Times,* January 18, 1969; Douglas Kneeland, "17 Black Panther Members Are Arrested at the Home of Slain Youth in Los Angeles," *New York Times,* January 19, 1969, 45; William J. Drummond, "Black Panther Aide Lauds 2 Who Were Slain in UCLA Hall," *Los Angeles Times,* January 19, 1969, B; "Brothers Arraigned in UCLA Slayings," *Los Angeles Times,* January 24, 1969; Ron Einstoss, "5 Negroes Indicted in 2 UCLA Slayings: All Ranking Members of US," *Los Angeles Times,* February 18, 1969; Ron Einstoss, "Three Found Guilty in UCLA Panther Killings," *Los Angeles Times,* September 11, 1969; "Stiner Brothers Get Life Prison Terms," *Los Angeles Times,* October 28, 1969; Scot Brown, *Fighting for US: Maulana Karenga, the US Organization, and Black Cultural Nationalism* (New York: New York University Press, 2003), 95–97; Elaine Brown, *A Taste of Power,* 153–67; Gene Marine, *The Black Panthers: Eldridge Cleaver, Huey Newton, Bobby Seale—A Compelling Study of the Angry Young Revolutionaries Who Have Shaken a Black Fist at White America* (New York: Signet, 1969), 208–9. Although some authors dispute the specific immediate motives of the shooting, most are in basic agreement about the events as we present them in this chapter. In a February 13, 1971, article in the *New Yorker* titled "Black Panthers and the Police," Edward Jay Epstein argued that the fact that the conflict was between members of rival black organizations shows that there was no government conspiracy; but the FBI memos quoted here show that while the extent of FBI involvement in planning the confrontation is not clear, the agency certainly conspired to escalate the conflict with the specific intention of undermining the Black Panther Party.

9. Elaine Brown, *A Taste of Power,* 167–70; Kneeland, "17 Black Panther Members Are Arrested," 45.

10. Bobby Seale quoted in William Drummond, "2 Black Panther Students Slain in UCLA Hall," *Los Angeles Times,* January 18, 1969, A1; Elaine Brown, *A Taste of Power,* 167–74; Ray Rogers, "Accusations Hurled at Slain Panther's Rites," *Los Angeles Times,* January 25, 1969, B10; Kneeland, "17 Black Panther Members Are Arrested," 45;

11. "A Political Assassination," *Black Panther,* January 25, 1969, 3.

12. Scot Brown, *Fighting for US,* 97.

13. Donald Freed, "Breakfast for Children," *Black Panther,* March 16, 1969, 6; Elaine Brown, *A Taste of Power,* 181; "L.A. Panthers Begin Free Breakfast Program," *Black Panther,* June 14, 1969, 3.

14. Elaine Brown, *A Taste of Power,* 208–10. Panther allies such as Seberg and Freed became the targets of FBI counterintelligence measures because of their support of the Panthers. See Judson Jeffries and Malcolm Foley "To Live and Die in L.A.," in *Comrades: A Local History of the Black Panther Party,* ed. Judson Jeffries (Bloomington: Indiana University Press, 2007), 283–86.

15. "L.A. Opens First Community Center," *Black Panther,* November 22, 1969, 2; Elaine Brown, *A Taste of Power,* 197.

16. Los Siete de la Raza Los Angeles Chapter, "Free Breakfast," *Black Panther,* October 25, 1969, 8. This effort grew out of the Los Siete de la Raza campaign in San Francisco discussed in chapter 13.

17. "L.A. Oppression," *Black Panther,* November 22, 1969, 2.

18. "Repression and Harassment of L.A. Panthers Stepped Up," *Black Panther,* May 31, 1969, 20; "News of the Day: Metropolitan," *Los Angeles Times,* May 2, 1969, A2.

19. Select Committee to Study Governmental Operations with Respect to Intelligence Activities [Church Committee], *Supplementary Detailed Staff Reports on Intelligence Activities and the Rights of Americans,* Final Report, S. Doc. No. 94-755 (April 1976), book 3, 190–92.

20. "Black Panther Shot to Death in San Diego," *Los Angeles Times,* August 16, 1969, 16; "Southland," *Los Angeles Times,* August 19, 1969, OC2; "3 US Members Go on Trial in Panther Slaying," *Los Angeles Times,* January 23, 1970, A32; "Southland," *Los Angeles Times,* April 29, 1970, 2.

21. Memo, Special Agent in Charge, San Diego, to J. Edgar Hoover, August 20, 1969.

22. Geronimo Pratt in Olsen, *Last Man Standing,* quote on 59, discussion of Pratt's appointment on 53.

23. "L.A. Oppression," *Black Panther,* November 22, 1969, 2; Elaine Brown, *A Taste of Power,* 201–2.

24. Renee Moore quoted in Dial Torgerson, "Police Seize Panther Fortress in 4-Hour Gunfight, Arrest 13," *Los Angeles Times,* December 9, 1969, 1. The account of the December 8 events also draws from: "Pigs Attack Southern California Chapter of Black Panther Party," *Black Panther,* December 13, 1969, 10; "Statement by Witnesses of Attack at Black Panther Headquarters," *Black Panther,* December 13, 1969, 10; Olsen, *Last Man Standing,* 63–64; Kenneth Reich, "National Pattern Followed in Raid on Panthers Here," *Los Angeles Times,* December 9, 1969, 1; Philip Fradkin, "Bombs, Gunfire Shatter Quiet of Central Ave," *Los Angeles Times,* December 9, 1969, 3.

25. Bunchy Carter quoted in "What Really Happened in Los Angeles," *Black Panther,* December 20, 1969, 12.

26. Mervin Dymally quoted in Dial Torgerson, "Police Seize Panther Fortress in 4-Hour Gunfight, Arrest 13," *Los Angeles Times,* December 9, 1969, 1.

27. This suggests how resilience works. The moderate leaders' statements show that they understood the repression experienced by the Panthers, and because they felt themselves to be in the same boat, they believed they were under threat whenever the Panthers were repressed. The later repeal of the draft and development of affirmative action programs eroded that sense of identity with the Panther cause for many middle-class blacks and antiwar lib-

erals, so they no longer felt themselves to be in the same boat: repression of the Panthers was no longer threatening to them.

28. Art Berman and Roy Haynes, "Negro Leaders Call for City Hall Mass Rally," *Los Angeles Times,* December 11, 1969, 3.

29. Art Berman, "Thousands Protest Panther Raid in City Hall," *Los Angeles Times,* December 12, 1969, 1.

10. HAMPTON AND CLARK

1. Bobby Rush in David Hilliard and Lewis Cole, *This Side of Glory: The Autobiography of David Hilliard and the Story of the Black Panther Party* (New York: Little, Brown, 1993), 214–15. The description of Fred Hampton also draws from the documentary film *The Murder of Fred Hampton,* directed by Howard Alk (Chicago: Film Group, 1971), DVD, 88 min.; and from Jesse Jackson, "On Fred Hampton," *Chicago Daily Defender,* December 13, 1969, 1.

2. Dave Potter, "Martial Law in Maywood Provokes More Boycotts," *Chicago Daily Defender,* September 27, 1967, 3; some of the biographical details about Hampton come from Akua Njeri, *My Life with the Black Panther Party* (St. Petersburg, FL: Burning Spear Publications, 1991), 29.

3. Bobby Rush in Hilliard and Cole, *This Side of Glory,* 214–15.

4. Jon Rice, "Black Radicalism on Chicago's West Side: A History of the Illinois Black Panther Party (PhD diss., Northern Illinois University, 1998), 71–72; Bobby Rush in Hilliard and Cole, *This Side of Glory,* 214–15. Former members of the Disciples gang had set up a Panther chapter in Chicago earlier, but it was not very active and merged with Hampton and Rush's group. In *This Side of Glory,* Hilliard recalls that Masai Hewitt, as acting minister of education, accidentally ended up in Chicago and helped Rush start the new chapter. But the details of the story don't quite make sense. The chapter must have been started in 1968, because the FBI documented plans for it in late 1968, which is why it began monitoring the Blackstone Rangers under COINTELPRO. But Hewitt was not appointed minister of education until after the strike at San Francisco State and is first listed as such in the *Black Panther,* July 12, 1969, 23. On Hewitt's involvement in Chicago, see Clark Kissenger, *Guardian* Midwest Bureau, "Chicago Panthers Busted," reprinted in *Black Panther,* May 4, 1969, 6; and "Chicago Panthers Serve the People," *Black Panther,* May 31, 1969, 4. Hewitt may have played an important role in the chapter's development after it was established.

5. James Alan McPherson, "Chicago's Blackstone Rangers," *Atlantic Monthly,* May 1969 (part 1) and June 1969 (part 2).

6. FBI memo, December 20, 1968, quoted in Select Committee to Study Governmental Operations with Respect to Intelligence Activities [Church Committee], *Supplementary Detailed Staff Reports on Intelligence Activities and the Rights of Americans,* Final Report, S. Doc. No. 94–755 (April 1976), book 3, 196 [hereafter Church Committee Report].

7. Memo, Chicago Field Office to FBI Headquarters, January 10, 1969, quoted in Church Committee Report, book 3, 197 (emphasis added in report).

8. Memo, Chicago Field Office to FBI Headquarters, January 13, 1969, quoted in Church Committee Report, book 3, 197.

9. Church Committee Report, book 3, 198.

10. At a press conference in April, Hampton said, "Any enemies of the people will never be able to divide and create hostilities between class brothers, just like they tried to create conflict between the Panthers and the Stones [Blackstone Rangers] but there is no fighting between us." This statement shows that Hampton knew that infiltrators were responsible for provoking the conflict years before full exposure of the COINTELPRO. Hampton quoted in Faith C. Christmas, "Black Panthers Cite 'Persecution,'" *Chicago Daily Defender*, April 14, 1969, 3

11. "Panther Official Convicted, Freed By Judge Jones," *Chicago Daily Defender*, April 9, 1969, 1; Clark Kissenger, *Guardian* Midwest Bureau, "Chicago Panthers Busted," reprinted in *Black Panther*, May 4, 1969, 6.

12. Christmas, "Black Panthers Cite 'Persecution,'" 3

13. "Panther Official Convicted, Freed By Judge Jones," 1.

14. Williams had defended notables such as black civil rights activist and comedian Dick Gregory, and in 1972, she would become the first black female judge in the state of Arizona.

15. "Panther Official Convicted, Freed By Judge Jones," 1.

16. Hampton quoted in Christmas, "Black Panthers Cite 'Persecution,'" 3

17. *Murder of Fred Hampton*, 29:40.

18. Bobby Seale in ibid., 6:08.

19. "Black Alliance Sides with Panthers Here," *Chicago Daily Defender*, May 29, 1969. See also "Panther Official Convicted, Freed by Judge Jones," 1, on Hanrahan's efforts to pressure the judge; and *Murder of Fred Hampton*, 40:30, for footage of Bobby Rush at the May 27, 1969, press conference.

20. "Chicago Panthers Serve the People," *Black Panther*, May 31, 1969, 4.

21. Kissenger, "Chicago Panthers Busted," 6.

22. Ibid. This first article to cover the Chicago Panthers in the *Black Panther* features a photo of Chairman Bobby Seale, Field Marshal Donald Cox, and future Minister of Education Masai Hewitt meeting in the Chicago office with Hampton and Rush.

23. Kissenger, "Chicago Panthers Busted," 6.

24. "Chicago Panthers Serve the People," 4.

25. David Hilliard, "Statement from Chief of Staff: Attack on Chicago Office," *Black Panther*, October 11, 1969, 3.

26. "Panthers, FBI Tell Views," *Chicago Daily Defender*, June 5, 1969, 1; Tommy Picou, "Rush Says U.S. Bent on Panther Extermination," *Chicago Daily Defender*, June 7, 1969, 1. The FBI's pretext for the raid was that it was searching for fugitive George Sams, a key figure in the torture and killing of Alex Rackley in New Haven, who many authors have subsequently suggested was himself working for the FBI.

27. Donald Mosby, "Tighten Noose on Panthers, Grand Jury Hits Leaders," *Chicago Daily Defender*, June 11, 1969, 1; "16 Chicago Panthers Indicted—Face Electric Chair," *Black Panther*, June 28, 1969, 16. On O'Neal's secret employment by the FBI, see Kenneth O'Reilly, *"Racial Matters": The FBI's Secret File on Black America, 1960–1972* (New York: Free Press, 1998), 310–11.

28. Donald Mosby, "2 Arrested after Shoot-Out," *Chicago Daily Defender,* July 17, 1969, 3; Cheryl Peterson, "Mystery Surrounds the Attack on Chicago Panthers," *Black Panther,* August 9, 1969, 20; [FBI infiltrator William] O'Neal, "Chicago Panthers Shot by Fascist Pigs," *Black Panther,* August 9, 1969, 22; "Revolutionary Murdered," *Black Panther,* September 20, 1969, 5.

29. "What Really Happened in Chicago from an Interview with Bobby Rush," *Black Panther,* August 9, 1969, 20; "Chicago Panther Office Vamped on by Pigs," *Black Panther,* August 16, 1969, 16–17; *Murder of Fred Hampton,* about 43:00.

30. *Murder of Fred Hampton,* about 35:00.

31. "Panthers Raid Was Smear," *Chicago Daily Defender,* October 6, 1969, 1; "Illinois Office Ambushed No. 3," *Black Panther,* October 11, 1969, 4; Hilliard, "Statement from Chief of Staff," 3.

32. Hilliard, "Statement from Chief of Staff," 3.

33. John P. Vasilopoulos, "Joint Coalition, Black Panther Rally Set Today," *Chicago Daily Defender,* November 3, 1969, 4. The group held a joint press conference at the Urban Training Center on Ashland Avenue.

34. "Revolutionary Murdered," 5.

35. Thomas M. Gray, "Order FBI to Probe Slayings of 2 Brothers Here," *Chicago Sun-Times,* January 7, 1970; Sam Washington, "Nightmare to Reality: How Brothers Died in Ghetto," *Chicago Sun-Times,* March 2, 1970; Michael Soto and John Soto, appendix to *The Police and Their Use of Fatal Force in Chicago,* by Ralph Knoohuizen, Richard P. Fahey, and Deborah J. Palmer (Chicago: Chicago Law Enforcement Study Group, 1972).

36. News clippings reproduced in Linda Anderson, appendix to Knoohuizen, Fahey, and Palmer, *The Police and Their Use of Fatal Force in Chicago.*

37. Knoohuizen, Fahey, and Palmer, *The Police and Their Use of Fatal Force in Chicago,* 20.

38. This account of Spurgeon Jake Winters's stand against the Chicago police draws from Rice, "Black Radicalism on Chicago's West Side," 157–62. Rice cites newspaper articles from the November 14, 1969, *Chicago Tribune* and *Chicago Sun-Times,* as well as from the *Chicago Daily Defender,* November 22–28, 1969. He also interviewed former Panthers Henry English, Locket Dibbs, and Bobby Rush. See also the photo of Winters in *Black Panther,* January 10, 1970, 7; and the news clippings reproduced in Spurgeon Winters, appendix to Knoohuizen, Fahey, and Palmer, *The Police and Their Use of Fatal Force in Chicago.*

39. Hampton v. Hanrahan, 600 F.2d 600 (7th Cir. 1970), §§ 47–49; on warrantless wiretap authorization, see §§ 52.

40. Ibid., §§ 53–54.

41. Ibid., §§ 56–65.

42. Fred P. Graham, "U.S. Jury Assails Police in Chicago on Panther Raid," *New York Times,* May 16, 1970, 1; Hampton v. Hanrahan, §§ 66–81. For the specific weapons carried by the officers, see Roy Wilkins and Ramsey Clark, *Search and Destroy: A Report by the Commission of Inquiry into the Black Panthers and the Police* (New York: Metropolitan Applied Research Center, 1973), 35–36.

43. Hanrahan quote from television coverage in *Murder of Fred Hampton*, 53:55. See also John Kifner, "State's Attorney in Chicago Makes Photographs of Black Panther Apartment Available," *New York Times*, December 12, 1969, 46.

44. Memo, Chicago Field Office to FBI Headquarters, December 8, 1969, quoted in Church Committee Report, book 3, 223. On the approval of the bonus, see John Kifner, "F.B.I. Files Say Informer Got Data for Panther Raid," *New York Times*, May 7, 1976, 14.

45. Faith C. Christmas, "Bobby Rush Surrenders before 5,000," *Chicago Daily Defender*, December 8, 1969, 2.

46. Faith C. Christmas, "'It Was Murder,' Rush," *Chicago Daily Defender*, December 6, 1969, 1; John Kifner, "Inquiry into Slaying of 2 Panthers Urged in Chicago," *New York Times*, December 6, 1969.

47. Kifner, "Inquiry into Slaying of 2 Panthers Urged in Chicago."

48. See extensive historical footage of Francis Andrew in *The Murder of Fred Hampton*. John Kifner, "Panthers Say an Autopsy Shows Party Official Was 'Murdered,'" *New York Times*, December 7, 1969, 68; John Kifner, "Policeman Who Led Chicago Panther Raid Testifies at Boycotted Inquest," *New York Times*, January 8, 1970, 27.

49. Kifner, "Panthers Say an Autopsy Shows Party Official was 'Murdered,'" 68.

50. "Pigs Assassinate People's Servants," *Black Panther*, December 20, 1969, 8; "Fred Hampton—Mark Clark Inquest," *Black Panther*, January 17, 1969, 3; see also "Deputy Chairman Fred Hampton Drugged Then Murdered," *Black Panther*, January 17, 1969, 3.

51. Kifner, "Panthers Say an Autopsy Shows Party Official was 'Murdered,'" 68; John Kifner, "Inquiry Is Urged in Slaying of Chicago Black Panther," *New York Times*, December 9, 1969, 40; John Kifner, "Black Panthers Lose Plea to Bar a Subpoena for Three Doctors," *New York Times*, January 14, 1970, 18.

52. Christmas, "Bobby Rush Surrenders before 5,000," 2.

53. Ibid..

54. Ibid.

55. Faith C. Christmas, "Hampton's Brother Tells Audience, 'Maintain Peace,'"*Chicago Daily Defender*, December 8, 1969, 3.

56. John Kifner, "Chicago Panther Mourned," *New York Times*, December 10, 1969, 37; John Kifner, "Coroner Seals Panther Slaying Site," *New York Times*, December 18, 1969, 66; see also historical footage of the tours in *The Murder of Fred Hampton*, 55:00 and throughout.

57. Charles Garry statement in John Kifner, "Police in Chicago Slay 2 Panthers," *New York Times*, December 5, 1969, 5.

58. David Hilliard statement quoted on front page, *Black Panther*, January 3, 1969. We slightly modified the transcriber's punctuation for clarity.

59. Kifner, "Inquiry Is Urged," 40; Kifner, "Panthers Say an Autopsy Shows Party Official was 'Murdered,'" 68; John D. Vasilopoulos, "Rights Groups Unite in Probe Demand," *Chicago Daily Defender*, December 9, 1969, 5.

60. Vasilopoulos, "Rights Groups Unite in Probe Demand," 5.

61. "Was It Murder?" *Chicago Daily Defender*, December 8, 1969, 13.

62. Morris Kaplan, "25 Are Arraigned in Protest Here," *New York Times,* December 11, 1969, 24.

63. Earl Caldwell, "Declining Black Panthers Gather New Support from Repeated Clashes with Police," *New York Times,* December 14, 1969, 64.

64. "Fred Hampton Rites: An Epitaph to a Revolutionary," *Chicago Daily Defender,* December 11, 1969, 1; "Inquiry in Chicago," *New York Times,* December 11, 1969, 50.

65. Bobby Rush, historical footage in *Murder of Fred Hampton,* 53:00.

66. Kifner, "Chicago Panther Mourned," 37; Jeffrey Hass, *The Assassination of Fred Hampton: How the FBI and the Chicago Police Murdered a Black Panther* (Chicago: Lawrence Hill Books, 2010).

67. John D. Vasilopoulos, "Black Politicians Ask Death Probe," *Chicago Daily Defender,* December 10, 1969.

68. "Afro Cops Begin Own Death Quiz," *Chicago Daily Defender,* December 10, 1969, 3.

69. "Conference on Religion, Race Seeks Investigation," *Chicago Daily Defender,* December 10, 1969, 2.

70. Carter Gilmore, NAACP statement on December 11, 1969, reprinted as "N.A.A.C.P. against Pig Repression of Black Panthers," *Black Panther,* January 3, 1970, 3.

71. Kifner, "State's Attorney in Chicago," 46.

72. John Kifner, "Negroes in Chicago Impose a Curfew on Whites," *New York Times,* December 16, 1969, 21.

73. John Kifner, "Chicago Negroes Back Off on Curfew," *New York Times,* December 17, 1969, 42.

74. Ibid.

75. Jackson, "On Fred Hampton," 1.

76. "Robert Williams Speaks at NCCF Panther Benefit; Detroit, Michigan," transcript of speech, *Black Panther,* January 3, 1970, 20.

77. "National Urban League Backs Hampton Probe," *Chicago Daily Defender,* December 17, 1969, 3.

78. John Kifner, "Coroner Seals Panther Slaying Site," *New York Times,* December 18, 1969, 66.

79. Earl Caldwell, "Declining Black Panthers Gather New Support from Repeated Clashes with Police," *New York Times,* December 14, 1969, 64.

80. Chaka Walls, "Black Representatives Investigate Government Conspiracy," *Black Panther,* December 27, 1969, 7; John Kifner, "5 Negroes Start Panther Inquiry," *New York Times,* December 21, 1969, 47.

81. John Kifner, "The 'War' Between Panthers and Police," *New York Times,* December 21, 1969, E3.

82. "No Misconduct," *New York Times,* December 20, 1969, 20; John Kifner, "2 Panther Deaths in Raid in Chicago Ruled 'Justifiable,'" *New York Times,* January 22, 1970, 1.

83. Fred P. Graham, "Special U.S. Jury to Examine Deaths of Black Panthers," *New York Times,* December 20, 1969, 1.

84. John Kifner, "3 Panthers Snub Hampton Inquest," *New York Times,* January 7, 1970, 30.

85. Deborah Johnson, historical footage in *Murder of Fred Hampton,* about 1:10:00.

86. Paul L. Montgomery, "Militants Occupy Columbia School," *New York Times,* March 14, 1970, 35.

87. Seth King, "7 Panthers Freed in Chicago Clash," *New York Times,* May 9, 1970, 1.

88. Fred P. Graham, "U.S. Jury Assails Police in Chicago on Panther Raid," *New York Times,* May 16, 1970, 1.

89. "Settlement Near in a Panther Suit: Government Reports Progress in 10-Year-Old Rights Suit over Raid in Chicago," *New York Times,* October 26, 1982, A18; "$1.85 Million Settlement Ends Black Panther Suit," *New York Times,* March 2, 1983, 16. For the legal wrangling, see also Seth King, "Long-Delayed Chicago Civil Suit on Black Panther Raid Is Begun," *New York Times,* January 23, 1976, 12; Seth King, "Ex-Head of Chicago F.B.I. Office Says Agency Sought to Discredit Panthers," *New York Times,* February 22, 1976, 40; "Around the Nation," *New York Times,* April 17, 1977, and April 24, 1979, A16; Seth King, "Black Panther Suit Dismissed in Chicago," *New York Times,* June 21, 1977, 16; Nathaniel Sheppard Jr., "F.B.I. Assailed by U.S. Court in Black Panther Case," *New York Times,* May 6, 1979, 20; "Rehnquist to Hear Black Panther Case," *New York Times,* May 1, 1980, A21.

11. BOBBY AND ERICKA

1. *State v. Seale and Huggins* transcript, excerpted in Donald Freed, *Agony in New Haven* (New York: Simon and Shuster, 1973), 284. On the Connecticut Panthers pre-May 1969, see also Yohuru Williams, *Black Politics/White Power: Civil Rights, Black Power, and the Black Panthers in New Haven* (St. James, NY: Brandywine Press, 2000), 127–35; Paul Bass and Douglas W. Rae, *Murder in the Model City: The Black Panthers, Yale, and the Redemption of a Killer* (New York: Basic Books, 2006), 59–65.

2. Bass and Rae, *Murder in the Model City,* 59–65; for Kimbro's age, see John Darnton, "8 Black Panthers Seized in Torture-Murder Case," *New York Times,* May 23, 1969, 24.

3. New Haven Panther flier quoted in Williams, *Black Politics/White Power,* 131.

4. Memo, J. Edgar Hoover to Special Agent in Charge, New Haven, March 28, 1969, quoted in Williams, *Black Politics/White Power,* 135.

5. Memo, Special Agent in Charge, New Haven, to Director of FBI, Washington, D.C., May 9, 1969; and memo, Director of FBI, Washington, D.C., to Special Agent in Charge, New Haven, "Re: SF Airtel 9 May, 1969 'Black Panther Party New Haven Division, RM-BPP,'" cited in Williams, *Black Politics/White Power,* 137.

6. On Sams's stabbing of another Panther and his expulsion from the Party, see quote from Bobby Seale and Ericka Huggins defense brief in Freed, *Agony in New Haven,* 250; Bass and Rae, *Murder in the Model City,* 22–26.

7. Sams quoted in "The Enforcer," *Newsweek,* August 17, 1970, 33.

8. Williams, *Black Politics/White Power,* 140.

9. Carter quoted in David Hilliard and Lewis Cole, *This Side of Glory: The Autobiography of David Hilliard and the Story of the Black Panther Party* (New York: Little, Brown, 1993), 249; Bass and Rae, *Murder in the Model City*, 27.

10. Bass and Rae, *Murder in the Model City*, 28–33; Williams, *Black Politics/White Power*, 140–41; Freed, *Agony in New Haven*.

11. Bass and Rae, *Murder in the Model City*, 8–10.

12. James F. Ahern, *Police in Trouble: Our Frightening Crisis of Law Enforcement* (New York: Hawthorn Books, 1972), 32–34; Bass and Rae, *Murder in the Model City*, 4–5.

13. Darnton, "8 Black Panthers Seized in Torture-Murder Case," 24.

14. Jennifer Smith, *An International History of the Black Panther Party* (New York: Garland, 1999), 98–99; "Canada Turns Over Panther," *New York Times*, August 22, 1969, 33.

15. Justice Department quoted in Bass and Rae, *Murder in the Model City*, 68–69, citing an "urgent" teletype on August 12, 1969, to the special agent in charge in New Haven from the FBI director; and a memo from the assistant attorney general, September 9, 1969.

16. "Black Panther Chief Seized in Berkeley in Torture-Slaying," *New York Times*, August 20, 1969, 15.

17. Williams, *Black Politics/White Power*, 164; Bass and Rae, *Murder in the Model City*, 218; "Notes on People . . . George Sams," *New York Times*, September 19, 1974, 49.

18. Joseph Lelyveld, "Role in Murder Laid to Panther," *New York Times*, August 1, 1970, 26; "New Haven Judge Ends Panther Case," *New York Times*, November 20, 1971, 35.

19. "New Haven Judge Ends Panther Case," 35.

20. Diane Henry, "Wiretap Case," *New York Times*, December 4, 1977, 520.

21. Ward Churchill and Jim Vander Wall, *The COINTELPRO Papers: Documents from the FBI's Secret Wars against Dissent in the United States* (Boston: South End Press, 1990), 360.

22. Beyond the possibilities that Sams was taking orders from the FBI or from the Panther leadership in killing Rackley, it is also possible that he was acting on his own sadistic impulses. But circumstantial evidence makes this explanation highly improbable. The FBI later charged that, under the direction of the Black Panther national office, Black Panthers tortured and murdered a suspected informant in Baltimore in July 1969. While the FBI informed the Baltimore police of these charges in November, the police waited until April 30, 1970—the eve of the major mobilization in support of Bobby Seale in New Haven—to act on them. As Yale students and other Panther supporters prepared to rally on the New Haven Green, Baltimore SWAT teams working with the FBI raided seventeen Baltimore homes, offices, and bars. Equipped with bulletproof vests and combat firearms, they broke down doors and arrested six Panthers on charges of murder. Some of the local Panthers were acquitted and others convicted, but the prosecution never established any involvement by the national leadership of the Panthers. That multiple torture-murders of rank-and-file Pan-

thers would have occurred coincidentally within weeks of each other is unlikely. On the events in Baltimore, see Judson L. Jeffries, "Revising Panther History in Baltimore," in *Comrades: A Local History of the Black Panther Party* (Bloomington: Indiana University Press, 2007), 18–35; "Free Breakfast in Baltimore," *Black Panther,* June 21, 1969, 15; "Baltimore Police Hold 10 Panthers," *New York Times,* May 1, 1970, 42; "Baltimore Seeks to Extradite Man Wanted in Killing," *New York Times,* October 25, 1970, 41; "Man Is Acquitted in Torture Killing," *New York Times,* April 14, 1971, 5. See also Steve McCutchen, "Selections from a Panther Diary," in *The Black Panther Party [Reconsidered],* ed. Charles E. Jones (Baltimore: Black Classic Press, 1998), 115–35.

23. William O'Neal, Captain of Security, "FBI Informer," *Black Panther,* February 17, 1969, 9.

24. "Panthers on Trial," *Time,* May 11, 1970.

25. Freed, *Agony in New Haven,* 25.

26. "Chicago F.B.I. Raids Office of Panthers," *New York Times,* June 5, 1969, 94.

27. Smith, *An International History of the Black Panther Party.*

28. *The "Trial" of Bobby Seale,* edited transcript of the trial (New York: Priam Books, 1970), 90.

29. Ibid.; J. Anthony Lukas, "Seale Put in Chains at Chicago 8 Trial," *New York Times,* October 30, 1969, 1; J. Anthony Lukas, "Seale Found in Contempt, Sentenced to Four Years," *New York Times,* November 6, 1969, 1. After Seale's case was severed from the other seven, the defendants made a mockery of the proceedings and turned the trial into a political circus, attracting continued international attention and support.

30. "Clergy in Support of Chairman Bobby," *Black Panther,* November 8, 1969, 4.

31. Telegram, Staff and Steering Committee of the New Mobilization to End the War in Vietnam Telegram, October 30, 1969, reproduced in *Black Panther,* November 8, 1969, 8.

32. Black Panther Party Solidarity Committee Stockholm, "People in Scandinavia Getting Hip to U.S. Fascism: Demand Release of Bobby Seale," *Black Panther,* October 25, 1969, 21; "Big Man" Howard, "Big Man Speaks to NLF in Stockholm, Sweden," transcript in *Black Panther,* November 18, 1969, 2.

33. M.P. Naicker, director of publicity and information, African National Congress, letter reprinted in *Black Panther,* November 22, 1969, 7.

34. David Hilliard, conversation with Joshua Bloom, May 3, 2011, on the Panther leaders' view of Miranda; Bass and Rae, *Murder in the Model City,* 88–90, for biographical details on Miranda; Michael T. Kaufman, "Yale Rally Cry: 'Bulldog and Panther," *New York Times,* May 1, 1970, 40; New Haven FBI office, "Urgent" teletype, September 25, 1969, in John R. Williams Papers, cited in Bass and Rae, *Murder in the Model City,* 88 (end note). The date on the FBI teletype shows that the appointment was made after Seale's indictment in August.

35. "Defense of the New Haven Panther 14," *Black Panther,* October 25, 1969, 6.

36. Ibid. See also "Connecticut Prisoners," *Black Panther,* October 25,

1969, 6, for an example of the public relations work of these allies; and "New Haven Coalition to Support B.P.P.," *Black Panther,* November 1, 1969, 4, for several organizations' statements of support.

37. "Defense of the New Haven Panther 14," 6; Bass and Rae, *Murder in the Model City,* 89; "Mothers Support Breakfast Program," *Black Panther,* November 1, 1969, 21; "Open House at the New Haven Community Information Center," *Black Panther,* April 6, 1970, 9.

38. "Womens Liberation Group Up—Tight," *Black Panther,* November 8, 1969, 8; Charles "Cappy" Pinderhughes, Lt. of Information, New Haven Chapter, Black Panther Party, "Free Our Sisters," *Black Panther,* December 6, 1969, 2. Cathy Forman provided an unpublished account of and various organizational materials from Women's Liberation in New Haven about the Black Panthers; copies in Joshua Bloom's possession. The group grew out of New Haven's American Independent Movement.

39. Hoover in Bass and Rae, *Murder in the Model City,* 95.

40. Bass and Rae, *Murder in the Model City,* 89.

41. "Yale Suspends 5 on Charges of Disrupting a Lecture," *New York Times,* December 19, 1969, 36.

42. Women's International League of Peace and Freedom, "Statement of Repression," February 15, 1970, reprinted in *Black Panther,* March 15, 1970, 5.

43. Eric Desmond, National Secretary, "Letter from British Tricontinental Organization"; and Afro Ogun Olaudah, Minister of Education, Malcolmites, "An Open Letter to Huey Newton and Bobby Seale," *Black Panther,* March 28, 1970, 7; Union Nationale des Etudiants du Kamerun (National Union of Kamerun Students), *Black Panther* April 6, 1970, 9; "British Solidarity with the Movement to Free Bobby Seale," *Black Panther,* April 25, 1970, 16.

44. Jean Genet, "Bobby Seale, The Black Panthers and Us White People," *Black Panther,* March 28, 1970, 7; Jean Luc Godard statement transcribed in *Black Panther,* April 25, 1970, 4.

45. Kaufman, "Yale Rally Cry," 40; Homer Bigart, "Yale to Open Gates This Weekend to Protesters Assembling to Support Black Panthers," *New York Times,* April 30, 1970, 39.

46. Bass and Rae, *Murder in the Model City,* 117–18.

47. Ibid., 118.

48. "Moratorium Urged at Yale," *New York Times,* April 17, 1970, 35.

49. Miranda in Taft, *Mayday at Yale: A Case Study in Student Radicalism* (Boulder, CO: Westview Press, 1976), 25.

50. Donald Janson, "Damage Estimated at $100,000 after Harvard Riot," *New York Times,* April 17, 1970, 35; Bass and Rae, *Murder in the Model City,* 119.

51. Miranda quoted in Bass and Rae, *Murder in the Model City,* 132–33; Kaufman, "Yale Rally Cry," 40.

52. "Yale Strike Urged to Back Panthers," *New York Times,* April 21, 1970, 1.

53. Bass and Rae, *Murder in the Model City,* 135.

54. Joseph B. Treaster, "Strike Rally at Yale," *New York Times,* April 22, 1970, 1.

55. Joseph B. Treaster, "Attendance at Yale Is Cut '50% to 75%' by Pickets Supporting Black Panthers," *New York Times,* April 23, 1970, 29; Treaster, "Strike Rally at Yale," 1.

56. Joseph B. Treaster, "Yale Faculty Rejects Proposal to Cancel All Classes to Support Panthers," *New York Times,* April 24, 1970, 23; Joseph B. Treaster, "Brewster Doubts Fair Black Trials," *New York Times,* April 25, 1970, 1.

57. Treaster, "Yale Faculty Rejects Proposal," 23; Treaster, "Brewster Doubts Fair Black Trials," 1; "Yale Student Petition Supports Brewster's Stand on the Panthers," *New York Times,* April 30, 1970, 1; Roy Reed, "Agnew Says White House Is Neutral in Florida Race," *New York Times,* April 29, 1970, 1.

58. Homer Bigart, "U.S. Troops Flown In for Panther Rally; New Haven Braces for Protest by 20,000," *New York Times,* May 1, 1970, 1.

59. Bass and Rae, *Murder in the Model City,* 145.

60. "Yale Chapel Offered as Haven if Panther Rally becomes Riot," *New York Times,* April 27, 1970, 39. Yale's chaplain at the time was Reverend William Sloane Coffin.

61. Joseph B. Treaster, "National Guard Alerted for Panther Rally Duty," *New York Times* April 29, 1970, 1.

62. "Big Man" Howard in "Yale Student Petition Supports Brewster's Stand on Panthers," *New York Times,* April 30, 1970, 1.

63. Kaufman, "Yale Rally Cry," 40; Bigart, "Yale to Open Gates," 39.

64. Taft, *Mayday at Yale,* 29.

65. Bigart, "Yale to Open Gates," 39.

66. Homer Bigart, "U.S. Troops Flown In for Panther Rally," 1; Bass and Rae, *Murder in the Model City,* 152.

67. Homer Bigart, "New Haven Police Set Off Tear Gas at Panther Rally," *New York Times,* May 2, 1970, 1.

68. Ibid.; Bass and Rae, *Murder in the Model City,* 157.

69. "Yale U. and the Panthers," *Chicago Daily Defender,* May 7, 1970, 19.

70. Richard Nixon quoted in Juan de Onis, "Nixon Puts 'Bums' Label on Some College Radicals," *New York Times,* May 2, 1970, 1.

71. Homer Bigart, "New Haven Rally," *New York Times,* May 3, 1970, 1.

72. 1970 Rockefeller Foundation survey in Daniel Yankelovich, *The Changing Values on Campus: Political and Personal Attitudes of Today's College Students* (New York: Washington Square Press, 1972), 62, 64, 70.

73. Joint editorial quoted in Michael T. Kaufman, "Campus Unrest over War Spreads with Strike Calls," *New York Times,* May 4, 1970, 1; "Columbia Agrees to Halt Classes," *New York Times,* May 3, 1970, 5.

74. Reed quoted in Alan Adelson, *SDS* (New York: Charles Scribner's, 1972), 33.

75. Ibid., 48–67; Linda Charlton, "Antiwar Strike Plans in the Colleges Pick Up Student and Faculty Support," *New York Times,* May 5, 1970, 18; Michael T. Kaufman, "3,500 Columbia Protesters March to City College," *New York Times,* May 6, 1970, 20.

76. Kaufman, "Campus Unrest over War," 1; Charlton, "Antiwar Strike Plans," 18; Richard E. Peterson and John A. Bilorusky, *May 1970: The Campus Aftermath of Cambodia and Kent State* (Berkeley: Carnegie Commission

on Higher Education, 1971), 15–19; Nancy Zaroulis and Gerald Sullivan, *Who Spoke Up? American Protest against the War in Vietnam* (New York: Doubleday, 1984), 319.

77. See Joe Eszterhas and Michael Roberts, *Thirteen Seconds: Confrontation at Kent State* (New York: Dodd, Mead, 1970), 57, 68.

78. Irwin Unger, *The Movement: A History of the American New Left, 1959–1972* (New York: Dodd, Mead, 1975), 183–86.

79. Richard E. Peterson and John A. Bilorusky, *May 1970: The Campus Aftermath of Cambodia and Kent State* (Berkeley: Carnegie Commission on Higher Education, 1971), 15–19; Charles DeBenedetti and Charles Chatfield, *An American Ordeal: The Antiwar Movement of the Vietnam Era* (Syracuse, NY: Syracuse University Press, 1990), 279–80; Todd Gitlin, *The Sixties: Years of Hope, Days of Rage* (New York: Bantam Books, 1987), 409–10; Jeffrey P. Kimball, *Nixon's Vietnam War* (Lawrence: University Press of Kansas, 1998), 215–16.

12. BLACK STUDIES AND THIRD WORLD LIBERATION

Epigraphs, part 4: SDS resolution, *New Left Notes*, April 4, 1969, 1, 3; Giam statement in Raymond Lewis, "Montreal: Bobby Seale—Panthers Take Control," *Black Panther*, December 21, 1968, 3.

General note on this chapter: Of all the treatments of the San Francisco State strike, one source stands out as especially detailed and insightful: Jason Michael Ferreira, "All Power to the People: A Comparative History of Third World Radicalism in San Francisco, 1968–1974" (PhD diss., University of California, Berkeley, 2003). We also drew heavily on three other sources: William H. Orrick Jr., *Shut It Down! A College in Crisis, San Francisco State College, October 1968–April 1969: A Staff Report to the National Commission on the Causes and Prevention of Violence* (Washington, DC: Government Printing Office, June 1969); William Barlow and Peter Shapiro, *An End to Silence: The San Francisco State College Student Movement in the '60s*, (New York: Pegasus, 1971); and Dikran Karagueuzian, *Blow It Up! The Black Student Revolt at San Francisco State College and the Emergence of Dr. Hayakawa* (Boston: Gambit, 1971). The analyses, and any errors, are our own.

1. For Murray's appointment as minister of education by April 1968, see "Over 2500 Attend Funeral," *Black Panther*, May 4, 1968, 16. As a newly appointed member of the Central Committee, Murray served as a pallbearer at Lil' Bobby Hutton's funeral. Barlow and Shapiro, *An End to Silence*, 206–7; Karagueuzian, *Blow It Up!* 32–33.

2. George Murray "For a Revolutionary Culture," *Black Panther*, September 7, 1968, 12.

3. Executive Secretariat of the OSPAAAL, "OSPAAAL on Black American Revolution," reprinted in *Black Panther*, September 7, 1968, 10; see also "Minister of Education Returns from Cuba," *Black Panther*, September 14, 1968, 5.

4. Transcript of George Mason Murray speech, *Gramma News*, Cuba, reprinted in *Black Panther*, October 12, 1968, 14.

5. Mike Hall, "SF State Head Resists Panther Removal," *Daily Californian*, September 30, 1968, 6; Smith quoted in Barlow and Shapiro, *An End to Silence*, 208.

6. Student body composition in Ferreira, "All Power to the People," 116.

7. James Garrett quoted in ibid., 80.

8. Orrick, *Shut It Down!* 96.

9. Ferreira, "All Power to the People," 105–11, Hare quotes on 107, 110.

10. Karagueuzian, *Blow It Up!* 30, 31.

11. "Black Students Union," *Black Panther*, October 12, 1968, 9.

12. "Black Student Union News Service," *Black Panther*, December 21, 1968, 11; "10 Point Program and Platform of the Black Student Unions" and "Important" Black Student Unions," *Black Panther*, February 2, 1969, 22; SF State BSU demands, reprinted in *Black Panther*, January 25, 1969, 10.

13. "The Necessity of Black Revolution," transcript of Murray's speech at Fresno State College, *Black Panther*, November 16, 1968, 13, 24.

14. Karagueuzian, *Blow It Up!* 33–36.

15. Ibid., Murray quote on 38–39.

16. Barlow and Shapiro, *An End to Silence*, 217, 224.

17. Carmichael quoted in Ferreira, "All Power to the People," 121.

18. Barbara Williams, "Our Survival Is Non-Negotiable!" *Black Panther*, January 25, 1969, 11.

19. George Mason Murray, "Panthers' Fight to the Death against Racism," *Rolling Stone*, April 5, 1969, 14.

20. Stewart in Ferreira, "All Power to the People," 123.

21. Ibid., 124.

22. Ibid., 127.

23. Ibid., 130.

24. Ibid., 132.

25. Brown quoted in Karagueuzian, *Blow It Up!* 72.

26. Ferreira, "All Power to the People," 141–42.

27. In addition to supporting the students directly, the Black Panthers maintained ongoing news, editorial, and graphic coverage of the developments at San Francisco State in the *Black Panther* and encouraged readers to support strike activities. See, for example, the following stories in the newspaper: "Panthers/B.S.U. Close S.F. State College," November 16, 1968, 8; "Riots Continue at San Francisco State College," December 7, 1968, 4; "Panthers-B.S.U. Get It Together: Demands for George Murray's Return Sparks San Francisco State College Violent Chaos," December 21, 1968, 3; "San Francisco State Strike Spreads," January 4, 1968, 2; "Panthers and B.S.U. Face 'Racist Kangaroo Court System,'" January 25, 1968. Goodlett quote from Ferreira, "All Power to the People," 142.

28. Ferreira, "All Power to the People," 142.

29. Crutchfield quoted in Orrick, *Shut It Down!* 60.

30. Ferreira, "All Power to the People," 147.

31. Ibid., 166–67.

32. Ibid., 168.

33. Dellums quoted in Orrick, *Shut It Down!* 73.

34. Many anti-imperialist student activists demanded "Third World studies" but eventually settled for "ethnic studies."

35. Statement quoted in Ferreira, "All Power to the People," 154.

36. Ibid., 154–60, quote on 160.

37. Urban Research Corporation study cited in the *Report of the President's Commission on Campus Unrest* (Washington, DC: Government Printing Office, 1970), 109.

38. Rodney Stark, "Protest + Police = Riot," in *Black Power and Student Rebellion: Conflict on the American Campus,* ed. James McEvoy and Abraham Miller (Belmont, CA: Wadsworth, 1969), 170.

39. Homer Bigart, "Cornell Faculty Votes Down Pact Ending Take-Over," *New York Times,* April 22, 1969, 1; John J. Goldman, "Faculty at Cornell Bows, Will Drop Charges on Negroes," *Los Angeles Times,* April 24, 1969, A1.

40. "5 Policemen Wounded at North Carolina A. & T.," *New York Times,* May 23, 1969, 28; James T. Wooten, "Cops Disperse Carolina Snipers," *New York Times,* May 24, 1969, 1; "Copter Breaks Up Berkeley Crowd," *New York Times,* May 21, 1969, 1; John Kendall and William Endicott, "Berkeley: Birth, Growth of 'War,'" *Los Angeles Times,* May 30, 1969, A1.

41. Kirkpatrick Sale, *SDS* (New York: Random House, 1973), 512–14.

13. VANGUARD OF THE NEW LEFT

1. The treatment of Los Siete de la Raza in this chapter draws from coverage in the *Black Panther,* various issues 1969; and Jason Michael Ferreira, "All Power to the People: A Comparative History of Third World Radicalism in San Francisco, 1968–1974" (PhD diss., University of California, Berkeley, 2003).

2. "S.F. Pigs Attempt to Arrest Entire Brown Community," *Black Panther,* May 19, 1969, 14.

3. "Los Siete de la Raza and the Black Panther Party," *Black Panther,* June 28, 1969, 2; Huey P. Newton, "Los Siete de la Raza," *Black Panther,* June 28, 1969, 2; see also "Free Los Siete," *Black Panther,* November 1, 1969, 8.

4. La Raza's seven points are reprinted in Ferreira, "All Power to the People," 307.

5. See *Basta Ya!* in the back eight pages of the following issues of the *Black Panther*: August 16, 1969; September 6, 1969; and September 20, 1969. On the roles of Lopez and Amador, see Ferreira, "All Power to the People," 301.

6. For the Red Guard's ten-point program, see "Red Guard," *Black Panther,* March 23, 1969, 9; for the genesis of the Red Guard, see Jason Luna Gavilan, "The Right Place at the Right Time: The Making of an Afro-Asian American Coalition—A Strategic Genealogy behind the Black Panther Party's Alliance with the Yellow Power Movement," 2001, unpublished manuscript in Joshua Bloom's possession. See also Steve Louie and Glenn Omatsu, eds., *Asian Americans: The Movement and the Moment* (Los Angeles: UCLA Asian American Studies Center Press, 2001); Fred Ho, *Legacy to Liberation: Politics and Culture of Revolutionary Asian Pacific America* (N.p.: Big Red Media, 2000); William Wei, *The Asian American Movement* (Philadelphia: Temple University Press, 1993).

7. Iris Morales, "¡Palante, Siempre Palante!: The Young Lords," in Andrés Torres and José E. Velásquez, eds., *The Puerto Rican Movement: Voices from the Diaspora* (Philadelphia: Temple University Press, 1998), 212; Jimenez quoted in "Interview with Cha Cha Jimenez, Chairman—Young Lords Organization," *Black Panther,* June 7, 1969, 17. See also "Cha Cha Jimenez Accused of Kidnapping Own Child," *Black Panther,* June 7, 1969, 17; "Pigs Block Cha Cha Jimenez," *Black Panther,* October 18, 1969, 3. Archival materials on the Chicago Young Lords, including oral histories conducted by the Lincoln Park Project and the Center for Latino Research, are available in the Young Lords Collection, DePaul University Archives, Chicago.

8. David Perez, in Young Lords Party and Michael Abramson, *Palante: Young Lords Party* (New York: McGraw-Hill, 1971), 65. See Carmen Teresa Whalen, "Bridging Homeland and Barrio Politics: The Young Lords in Philadelphia," in Torres and Velásquez, *The Puerto Rican Movement,* 107. They coined the phrase *"Tengo Puerto Rico en Mi Corazón"* (I Have Puerto Rico in My Heart), which spread quickly through Puerto Rican communities across the United States. Pablo Guzmán, "La Vida Pura: A Lord of the Barrio," in Torres and Velásquez, *The Puerto Rican Movement,* 157.

9. Black Panther position in Carletta Fields, "Persecution of the Young Lords," *Black Panther,* May 19, 1969, 14; "Interview with Cha Cha Jimenez," 17; see also "Cha Cha Jimenez Accused of Kidnapping Own Child," 17; "Pigs Block Cha Cha Jimenez," 3; for the date of the seminary takeover, see George Dugan, "Church Assembly Applauds Forman," *New York Times,* May 16, 1969.

10. Morales, "¡Palante, Siempre Palante! 212; Liberation News Service, "Panthers and Young Lords Serve the People," reprinted in *Black Panther,* October 11, 1969, 5.

11. Carlton Yearwood quoted in Michael T. Kaufman, "Black Panthers Join Coalition with Puerto Rican and Appalachian Groups," *New York Times,* November 9, 1969, 83; photo caption above "Pigs Bust Nine Young Patriots," *Black Panther,* June 7, 1969, 15; for a picture of the Young Patriots' surprising mix of symbols, see "The Patriot Party Speaks to the Movement," *Black Panther,* February 17, 1970, 12. Hampton quoted in David Hilliard and Lewis Cole, *This Side of Glory: The Autobiography of David Hilliard and the Story of the Black Panther Party* (New York: Little, Brown, 1993), 229–30. According to Hilliard, a lot of Jesse Jackson's best lines are taken from Fred Hampton.

12. Yoruba in Young Lords and Abramson, *Palante,* 74–75.

13. Miguel "Mickey" Melendez, *We Took the Streets: Fighting for Latino Rights with the Young Lords* (New York: St. Martin's Press, 2003), 77–86, 103.

14. Central Committee of the Young Lords Party, "History of the Young Lords Party," in Young Lords and Abramson, *Palante;* for the thirteen-point program, see 150.

15. David Perez in Young Lords and Abramson, *Palante,* 65–66.

16. Joseph P. Fried, "East Harlem Youths Explain Garbage-Dumping Demonstration," *New York Times,* August 19, 1969, 86; Melendez, *We Took the Streets,* 100–108.

17. Morales, "¡Palante, Siempre Palante!" 214; Melendez, *We Took the Streets,* 113–16.

18. Michael T. Kaufman, "Puerto Rican Group Seizes Church in East Harlem in Demand for Space," *New York Times,* December 29, 1969, 26; Arnold H. Lubasch, "Young Lords Give Food and Care at Seized Church," *New York Times,* December 30, 1969, 30; Melendez, *We Took the Streets,* 126, 129.

19. Guzmán, "La Vida Pura," 164–65.

20. Whalen, "Bridging Homeland and Barrio Politics," 112, 117–18; "The Young Lords Organization on the Move," interview with Rafael Viera, chief medical cadre, *Black Panther,* February 17, 1970, 6; Central Committee of the Young Lords Party, "History of the Young Lords Party."

21. "The Young Lords Organization on the Move," 6; Young Lords and Abramson, *Palante,* 101; Guzmán, "La Vida Pura," 158; Melendez, *We Took the Streets,* 150.

22. Huey Newton in *Huey Newton Talks to the Movement about the Black Panther Party, Cultural Nationalism, SNCC, Liberals and White Revolutionaries* (Chicago: Students for a Democratic Society, 1968). This pamphlet reproduces an interview, "Huey Newton Talks to the Movement," originally published in *Movement,* August 1968. The pamphlet was reprinted by Students for a Democratic Society in August 1968. SDS distributed the pamphlet nationwide in coordination with "Free Huey!" actions; see *New Left Notes,* November 19, 1968, 8. Philip Foner also included a reprint of Newton's statement in *The Black Panthers Speak* (Philadelphia: Lippincott, 1970; repr. New York: Da Capo, 1995), 50–66 (quote on 54).

23. Foner, *Black Panthers Speak,* 54.

24. Ibid, 55.

25. Bernardine Dohrn, SDS Inter-Organizational Secretary, "SDS & Panthers to Celebrate Huey's Birthday," *New Left Notes,* February 15 1969, 1.

26. SDS resolution at the Austin National Council, "The Black Panther Party: Toward the Liberation of the Colony," *New Left Notes*, April 4, 1969, 1, 3.

27. Foner, *Black Panthers Speak,* 54. Although about two-thirds of the attendees at the SDS National Convention supported the resolution, the fact that one-third did not is telling. Against the tenuous alliance of SDS's dominant leadership bloc, which was ideologically diverse but in agreement about supporting the Panthers, the opposition to the resolution came from a bloc of ideologically unified and disciplined Progressive Labor Party activists, who at this time argued for the importance of class over race and other considerations. Ironically, readers may recall that the Progressive Labor Party sent members of the Revolutionary Action Movement to Cuba in the early 1960s and helped black revolutionary nationalism build a foundation in the United States. But by 1969, the Progressive Labor Party had turned against the North Vietnamese and also against the Black Panther Party, arguing that the Left in the United States should focus on organizing workers and de-emphasize questions of race. This was a highly ironic turn of position at a time when draft resistance and the Black Panther Party and its anti-imperialist politics were the core of a greatly expanding and influential New Left. Progressive Labor did

not walk away from the anti-imperialist New Left but sought to undermine it by fighting tooth and nail for the completely unrealistic notion that the newly politicized students of the New Left, who had found their identity as revolutionary actors in draft resistance and in support of the Panthers, ought to stop organizing around the Vietnam War and against racism and instead seek to organize workers. It is quite possible that this obstructionist position was due, in part, to the manipulations of the FBI. A serious study of the causes of Progressive Labor's obstructionist turn would be invaluable for understanding the late 1960s and its repercussions. Progressive Labor's obstructionist turn fragmented SDS and contributed significantly to the demise of the New Left. But the important thing about SDS's endorsement of the Panthers as the "vanguard" is exactly that the New Left could not desert the Panthers any more than it could desert the Vietnamese and still be the New Left, because the alliance linking the New Left, rooted in the practices of draft resistance, to the political activities of the Panthers was the practical foundation for the New Left's revolutionary morality, the basis for its identity. This was not a class basis for a superstructure in orthodox Marxist terms as much as a practical political basis for a political ideology.

28. *Black Panther,* May 31, 1969. Most of these images depict the People's Park campaign in Berkeley.

29. Ibid.; flier announcing United Front Against Fascism conference 323–690721–000, H.K Yuen Collection, Bancroft Library, University of California, Berkeley.

30. To see the change in the Ten Point Program, compare the old version in *Black Panther,* June 28, 1969, 21, to the new version in *Black Panther,* July 5, 1969, 22. For use of the word *fascism,* see, for example, "Capitalism Plus Racism Breeds Fascism," *Black Panther,* June 14, 1969, cover story and articles on 2 and 17. On March 3, 1969, the *Black Panther* featured coverage of the Vietnamese resistance, publishing a photo of North Vietnamese president Ho Chi Minh on the cover. This was the first time the *Black Panther* featured a nonblack liberation struggle on its cover. Such coverage of various nonblack international and domestic liberation struggles was frequent thereafter.

31. Earl Caldwell, "'Fascism' Decried at Black Panther Conference," *New York Times,* July 21, 1969, 48; Earl Caldwell, "Panthers' Meeting Shifts Aims from Racial Confrontation to Class Struggle," *New York Times,* July 22, 1969, 21; Earl Caldwell, "Panthers," *New York Times,* July 27, 1969, E6; Earl Caldwell, "3,000 Radicals, Mostly Whites, Open Panther-Led Unity Parley," *New York Times,* July 20, 1969, 43. Names of other participating organizations come from articles in the *Black Panther.*

32. Bobby Seale quoted in Earl Caldwell, "'Fascism' Decried at Black Panther Conference," 48. "Chairman Seale Sums Up Conference," transcript of speech, *Black Panther,* July 26, 1969, 4.

33. "Elaine Brown Presents a Letter from Sister Ericka Huggins," transcript, *Black Panther,* August 2, 1969, 5; "Field Marshal Don Cox at the Conference," transcript, *Black Panther,* July 26, 1969, 11; "Ron Dellums at UFAF Conference," transcript, *Black Panther,* July 26, 1969, 11; Father Earl Neal, "U.F.A.F. Conference: Religion Versus Fascism," transcript of speech, *Black*

Panther, August 9, 1969, 16; "Jeff Jones at the Conference," transcript, *Black Panther,* July 26, 1969, 9; "Atty Bill Kunstler Speaks at UFAF Conference," transcript, *Black Panther,* July 26, 1969, 10.

34. "Roger Alvarado Speaks to Intellectuals," transcript, *Black Panther,* July 26, 1969, 5; " Oscar Rios of Los Siete Speaks at UFAF Conference," transcript, *Black Panther,* August 2, 1969, 8; "Habla Señor Martinez," transcript, *Black Panther,* August 2, 1969, 6; "Young Patriots at UFAF Conference," transcript, *Black Panther,* July 26, 1969, 8; "Penny Nakatsu, A Japanese American Speaks Out against Fascism," transcript, *Black Panther,* August 2, 1969, 8; photo of Panther/Patriot lineup captioned "Patriots and Panthers Stand United against Fascism," *Black Panther,* July 26, 1969, 11. Preacherman wore a beret displaying one pin of Huey P. Newton and another of a Confederate flag. In his remarks, he suggested that racially specific groups represent their own racially specific communities as part of a broader revolutionary alliance. The Panthers highlighted the Young Patriot Party at the conference because they wanted to send New Left groups like SDS the message that the proper role of revolutionary whites is to organize in poor white communities.

35. Charles R. Garry, "Defender of Political Prisoners and Human Rights," transcript, *Black Panther,* July 26, 1969, 12; Caldwell, "Panthers' Meeting Shifts Aims," 21; Earl Caldwell, "'Fascism' Decried," 48; "Big Man" Howard, "Editorial Statement," *Black Panther,* July 26, 1969, 7.

36. Coordinating Committee of the Mexican Student Movement at Universidad Nacional Autónoma de México, a major university in Mexico, "Solidaridad al UFAF de Mexico," statement reprinted in *Black Panther,* July 26, 1969, 10; Tokyo Communist League, "Message to UFAF Conference from Japan," statement reproduced in *Black Panther,* July 26, 1969, 10; statement of support from Sweden, reproduced in *Black Panther,* August 2, 1969, 11; statement of support from Denmark, reproduced in *Black Panther,* August 9, 1969, 17.

37. Letters came in from Salt Lake City, Utah; Albany, New York; Las Vegas, Nevada; Toledo, Ohio; Sunflower, Mississippi; Keatchie, Louisiana; Erie, Pennsylvania; Richmond, Virginia; St. Louis, Missouri; and Austin, Texas, among other cities. "Part II, SF 157–1204," 15, folder: "David Hilliard's FBI trial," box 32, HPN Papers, cited in Robyn Ceanne Spencer, "Repression Breeds Resistance: The Rise and Fall of the Black Panther Party in Oakland, CA, 1966–1982" (PhD diss., Columbia University, 2001), 182.

38. Spencer, "Repression Breeds Resistance," 182.

39. "Black Panther Tells It Like It Is. U.F.A.F. Women's Panel: Roberta Alexander at Conference," transcript, *Black Panther* August 2, 1969, 7.

40. Ibid.

41. Marlene Dixon and Carol Henry in Caldwell, "3,000 Radicals, Mostly Whites," 43.

42. David Hilliard, conversation with Joshua Bloom, May 3, 2011.

43. Eldridge Cleaver, "Message to Sister Ericka Huggins of the Black Panther Party," *Black Panther,* July 5, 1969, 12.

44. Ibid.

45. Deborah Johnson [Akua Njeri], "Seize the Time, Off the Slime," *Black Panther,* December 13, 1969, 4.

46. Candi Robinson, "Message to Revolutionary Women," *Black Panther,* August 9, 1969, 23.

47. Adams quoted in Tracye Matthews, "No One Ever Asks a Woman What a Man's Place in the Revolution Is: Gender and Sexual Politics in the Black Panther Party" (PhD diss., University of Michigan, 1998), 293, 357.

48. Akua Njeri [Deborah Johnson], "Difficulties of Being a Single Mother in the Black Panther Party," in *My Life with the Black Panther Party* (Oakland: Burning Spear Publications, 1991), 45. Njeri also alludes to her differences with local leadership of the Party after Fred Hampton was killed, but the fact that local political tensions in Chicago may have exacerbated the situation for Njeri do not diminish the general point that the Party failed to systematically support Panther mothers with child care and other needs.

49. Huey P. Newton, "A Letter from Huey to the Revolutionary Brothers and Sisters about the Women's Liberation and Gay Liberation Movements," *Black Panther,* August 21, 1970, 5.

50. Ibid.

51. Ibid.

52. Ibid.

53. Bettye Collier-Thomas and V. P. Franklin, eds., *Sisters in the Struggle: African American Women in the Civil Rights-Black Power Movement* (New York: New York University Press, 2001); Anne McClintock, Aamir Mufti, and Ella Shohat, eds., *Dangerous Liaisons: Gender, Nation, and Postcolonial Perspectives* (Minneapolis: University of Minnesota Press, 1997); Anne McClintock, "Family Feuds: Gender, Nationalism, and the Family," *Feminist Review,* no. 44 (Summer 1993): 61–80.

54. Malika Adams, interview by Tracye Matthews, cited in Matthews, "No One Ever Asks a Woman," 269.

55. Angela Davis, interview by Tracye Matthews, ibid., 123.

56. Rosemari Meali, interview by Tracye Matthews, ibid., 266.

57. Janet Cyril, interview by Tracye Matthews, ibid., 271.

58. Ibid., 262.

59. Elaine Brown, *A Taste of Power: A Black Woman's Story* (New York: Pantheon Books, 1992), 194

60. Ericka Huggins, interview by Tracye Matthews, cited in Matthews, "No One Ever Asks a Woman," 127.

14. INTERNATIONAL ALLIANCE

1. Jean Tainturier, "A la Conférence de Montréal," *Le Monde,* December 3, 1968, 3.

2. Ibid.; Seale quote from Raymond Lewis, "Montreal: Bobby Seale—Panthers Take Control," *Black Panther,* December 21, 1968, 5.

3. Lewis, "Montreal," 5; Bobby Seale, "Complete Text of Bobby Seale's Address," *Black Panther,* December 21, 1968, 6.

4. Lewis, "Montreal," 5; David Hilliard, interview by Joshua Bloom, June 29, 2005.

5. "Intercommunalism: February 1971" (conversations with Erik Erick-

son at Yale), in *The Huey P. Newton Reader,* eds. David Hilliard and Donald Weise (New York: Seven Stories Press, 2002), 184. The conversations were originally printed in full in *In Search of Common Ground: Conversations with Eric H. Erickson and Huey P. Newton* (New York: Norton, 1973).

6. Eldridge Cleaver, "We Have Found It Here in Korea," *Black Panther,* November 1, 1969, 11. To make this point, Cleaver specifically invoked Kim Il Sung's concept of *Juche,* or self-reliance. Cleaver argued that the Korean experience supported the idea that a foreign ideology should not be adopted wholesale. For context, see Kathleen Neal Cleaver, "Back to Africa: The Evolution of the International Section of the Black Panther Party (1969–1972)," in *The Black Panther Party [Reconsidered],* ed. Charles E. Jones (Baltimore: Black Classic Press, 1998), 226. See also Eldridge Cleaver's later pamphlet *On the Ideology of the Black Panther Party,* circa 1970, which develops this line. Some have argued that the Black Panthers' emphasis on the lumpen proletariat was their downfall. But this line of argument is deeply flawed. While the black underclass was a core constituency of the Party, many members and most leaders were either working class or middle class with educated and professional families. No narrowly working-class Marxist revolutionary formation in the United States has had nearly as transformative a historical effect as the Black Panther Party.

7. The original Ten Point Program was first published in the *Black Panther* on May 15, 1967, 3; Huey P. Newton, "The Functional Definition of Politics," *Black Panther,* May 15, 1967, 4.

8. David Hilliard and Lewis Cole, *This Side of Glory: The Autobiography of David Hilliard and the Story of the Black Panther Party* (New York: Little, Brown, 1993), 223–26, also David Hilliard, conversation with Joshua Bloom, May 3, 2011, on Hilliard's view of Hewitt's key role in deepening the Party's engagement with Marx.

9. Ho Chi Minh on cover of *Black Panther,* March 3, 1969. To see the change in the Ten Point Program, compare the old version in the *Black Panther,* June 28, 1969, 21, to the new version in the newspaper on July 5, 1969, 22 [emphasis in original]. Ray "Masai" Hewitt is first listed as the minister of education in the *Black Panther,* July 12, 1969, 23, replacing George Murray; Hilliard and Cole, *This Side of Glory,* 223–26; on Chicago involvement, see also Clark Kissenger, *Guardian* Midwest Bureau, "Chicago Panthers Busted," reprinted in *Black Panther,* May 4, 1969, 6, and "Chicago Panthers Serve the People," *Black Panther,* May 31, 1969, 4.

10. This is not to say that the Party never took sides. To the contrary, in the Sino-Soviet split, the Party came down squarely on the side of China. See "Russia-U.S. Conspire to Trick China into War," *Black Panther,* March 23, 1969, 1, 10.

11. "Intercommunalism," *Huey P. Newton Reader,* 181–99. Newton here suggests four phases in the Party's ideological development, from black nationalism to revolutionary nationalism to internationalism to intercommunalism, a schema replicated by others. See Judson L. Jeffries, *Huey P. Newton: The Radical Theorist* (Jackson: University Press of Mississippi, 2002), 62–82. But these categories are ideal types, loosely reflecting the gradual trajectory of

change and accentuating differences in what remained basically black anti-imperialist thinking, rather than revealing any sharp categorical shifts in the Party's ideological history. In our view, the much sharper and more important shifts are the practical political ones around which we structure our book—rather than narrowly ideological ones.

12. See Penny Von Eschen, *Race against Empire: Black Americans and Anticolonialism 1937–1957* (Ithaca, NY: Cornell University Press, 1997); Joshua Bloom, "Black Insurgent Influence on Truman's Civil Rights Advocacy," unpublished, winner of the 2011 Reinhard Bendix Prize.

13. This treatment of the Black Panther solidarity activities in Scandinavia draws principally from the following articles in the *Black Panther*: "Bobby Seale in Sweden," March 31, 1969, ,14; "Chairman Seale & Masai Return to U.S.," March 31, 1969, 14; "Free Huey Demonstration in Scandinavia: Black Panther Spokesman Connie Matthews Speaks at Free Huey Rally in Sweden," June 21, 1969, 18; "Danish Left Wing Socialist Party," July 19, 1969, 9; Young Left League of Sweden, "From Sweden," August 2, 1969, 11; "Scandinavian Solidarity with the B.P.P.," September 13, 1969, 9; Klaus Pedersen, "Interview with Scandinavian Rep. of Black Panther Party: Connie Matthews," reprinted from *Land of Folk*, October 18, 1969, 9; Bobby Seale, "Bobby Speaks to Scandinavia," October 25, 1969, 10; Connie Matthews, "Connie Matthews at San Jose State on the Vietnam Moratorium," transcript, October 25, 1969, 11; Black Panther Party Solidarity Committee Stockholm, "People in Scandinavia Getting Hip to U.S. Fascism: Demand Release of Bobby Seale," October 25, 1969, 21; "Big Man" Howard, "Big Man Speaks to NLF in Stockholm, Sweden," transcript, November 18, 1969, 2; Sozialistischer Deutscher Studentenbund, "West German S.D.S. Supports Black Panthers and Black Liberation Movement," March 9, 1968, 13; "Black Panther Party Authorizes Leadership in Scandinavia," May 4, 1969, 10; Danish Left Wing Socialist Party, telegram, reproduced May 4, 1969, 10. Also see Kathleen Cleaver, "Back to Africa," 228.

14. According to Ruth Reitan, relations between the Panthers and the Cuban government were initially strong, and plans were in the works to develop a military training ground there for black revolutionaries; Reitan, *The Rise and Decline of an Alliance: Cuba and African American Leaders in the 1960s* (East Lansing: Michigan State University Press, 1999), especially 104–5. But by 1969, when Eldridge Cleaver sought to develop a training program, support had weakened. In an interview with Henry Louis Gates Jr. in 1975, Cleaver reported that the relationship with the Cuban government had been strained from the time of his arrival. The terms of asylum were that he would remain a private citizen and not engage in public activities. Eventually, Cleaver became dissatisfied with the arrangement because he could not promote Panther activities as he wished while remaining clandestine. This caused tensions with the Cuban government. Also, his wife, Kathleen, was pregnant, and there were difficulties getting her to Cuba. When an unconfirmed Reuters wire report appeared in May 1969 claiming that Cleaver was living in Havana, he made plans to leave for Algeria. He sent a message to Kathleen to meet him in Algiers through the writer Lee Lockwood, who was leaving Cuba one day

before Cleaver. Eldridge Cleaver, interview in Paris by Henry Louis Gates Jr., winter 1975, 28, 33, 56, transcript in Joshua Bloom's possession. Kathleen Cleaver, "Back to Africa," 216–17. In this chapter, Kathleen discusses the following international alliances: asylum from Algeria and Cuba; other diplomatic relations with North Korea, North Vietnam, China, and the People's Republic of the Congo; and alliances with independence movements from Angola, Mozambique, Guinea-Bissau, Palestine, as well as leftist revolutionary movements from Denmark, Sweden, the Netherlands, Belgium, Britain, and West Germany.

15. Mamadi quoted in Eric Pace, "Africans at Algiers Festival Denounce Concept of 'Negritude' as Outmoded," *New York Times*, July 28, 1969, 4.

16. Eldridge Cleaver, interview by Gates, 56–57.

17. Kathleen Cleaver, "Back to Africa," 213.

18. "Cleaver and Seale Accept Algiers Bid," *New York Times*, July 14, 1969. In his 1975 interview with Gates, Cleaver also said that the Panthers were placed on the invitation list independently by the Algerian government, but this and other sources imply that his decision to relocate in Algeria had much to with his desire to overcome the political restrictions inherent in exile in Cuba.

19. Eldridge Cleaver, interview by Gates, 61.

20. Sanche de Gramont, "Our Other Man in Algiers," *New York Times Magazine*, November 1, 1970, 228.

21. Kathleen Cleaver, "Back to Africa," 218.

22. "Cleaver Arrives for Algiers Fete," *New York Times*, July 16, 1969, 9. According to Cleaver, official status for the Black Panther delegation to Algeria was arranged by the National Liberation Front of Vietnam. When the Panthers arrived in Algiers, they met Charles Chikarema, an English-speaking representative of the Zimbabwe African People's Union. Chikarema introduced them to Elaine Klein, a vivacious woman from New York who had supported the Algerian Revolution as a student in New York and moved there immediately after independence, where she became a close friend of Frantz Fanon and served as press secretary to the first president, Ben Bella. At the time of the Pan-African Cultural Festival, she was working in the Ministry of Information there. She was on the committee to organize the festival and invited Cleaver and the Panthers to participate. She also introduced Cleaver to representatives of the NLF, who met with President Boumedienne the next day and arranged for the Panther delegation to have official status at the festival (Eldridge Cleaver, interview by Gates, 55–56; Kathleen Cleaver, "Back to Africa," 220).

23. Kathleen Cleaver, "Back to Africa," 220.

24. Ibid.

25. Eric Pace, "African Nations Open 12-Day Cultural Festival with Parade through Algiers," *New York Times*, July 22, 1969, 9; "Algerian Leader Opens Arts Festival," *New York Times*, July 22, 1969, A8.

26. Eldridge Cleaver, interview by Gates, 60; Kathleen Cleaver, "Back to Africa," 213.

27. See photo, *Black Panther*, August 9, 1969, 14; Kathleen Cleaver, "Back to Africa," 213.

28. Kathleen Cleaver, "Back to Africa," 220–21.

29. Ibid., 213, 221.

30. Eldridge Cleaver and Haitian representative at Pan-African Cultural Festival in "Black Panther Discussion with African and Haitian Liberation Fighters," transcript, *Black Panther* August 23, 1969, 16–17. The Tonton Macoutes were Duvalier's special paramilitary police force that maintained his control through brutality and terror.

31. Ibid.

32. J. Anthony Lukas, "Cleaver Is Said to Seek War Prisoner Trade for Jailed Panthers," *New York Times,* October 22, 1969, 18. See also Vietnam Moratorium Committee, "Panther Political Prisoners for U.S. Prisoners of War," *Black Panther,* November 22, 1969, 3. The negotiations were arranged with support from the Panthers' Chicago Eight allies. See also "Bobby Kidnapped, Under the Fugitive Slave Law," *Black Panther,* November 8, 1969, 4.

33. Committee on Internal Security of the House of Representatives, *Gun-Barrel Politics: The Black Panther Party, 1966–1971,* 92d Cong., 1st sess. (Washington, DC: Government Printing Office, 1971).

34. Kathleen Cleaver, "Back to Africa," 234.

35. Gramont, "Our Other Man in Algiers," 228.

36. Kathleen Cleaver, "Back to Africa," 228–30, Eldridge Cleaver, interview by Gates, 67.

37. Kathleen Cleaver, "Back to Africa," 232; Elaine Brown, *A Taste of Power: A Black Woman's Story* (New York: Pantheon Books, 1992), 232; Gramont, "Our Other Man in Algiers."

38. "An Inevitably Victorious Cause," quoted in "Cleaver and Black Panther Group Attend Hanoi Observance," *New York Times,* August 19, 1970, 13; Liberation News Service, "Message from Anti-Imperialist Delegation of American People While Still Enroute to D.P.R.K.," reprinted in *Black Panther,* August 8, 1970, 18; Gramont, "Our Other Man in Algiers." Kathleen Cleaver met up with the delegation in North Korea but was not part of the delegation and traveled separately; email, Cleaver to Waldo Martin, April 28, 2011.

39. "Anti-Imperialist Delegation of American People Here," *D.P.R.K. Pyongyang Times* (the North Korean government newspaper), reprinted in *Black Panther,* August 8, 1970, 18.

40. "Savage Repression against Black Panther Party of U.S.A. Must Be Stopped Immediately," *D.P.R.K. Pyongyang Times,* reprinted in *Black Panther,* August 8, 1970, 18.

41. Pham quoted in Eldridge Cleaver, *Gangster Cigarettes* (Stanford, CA: C.P. Times, 1984).

42. "An Inevitably Victorious Cause," quoted in "Cleaver and Black Panther Group Attend Hanoi Observance," 13.

43. Eldridge Cleaver, transcript of broadcast over Voice of Vietnam Radio, August 1970, *Black Panther,* September 26, 1970, 14; see also Kathleen Cleaver, "Back to Africa," 234.

44. Brown, *A Taste of Power,* 231; see also Eldridge Cleaver, "Cleaver Speaks," *New York Times,* November 1, 1970, 228.

45. Gramont, "Our Other Man in Algiers."

46. Ibid., 228.

15. RUPTURE

1. Wallace Turner, "More Than 100,000 on Coast Demonstrate in Moderate Vein," *New York Times,* November 16, 1969, 1; Daryl Lembke and Philip Hager, "Thousands Parade Quietly in S.F. to Show War Frustrations," *Los Angeles Times,* November 16, 1969, 1; Tom Wicker, "Dissent: Deepening Threat of a Sharply Divided Nation," *New York Times,* November 16, 1969, E1; John Herbers, "250,000 War Protesters Stage Peaceful Rally in Washington; A Record Throng," *New York Times,* November 16, 1969, 1; David Hilliard and Lewis Cole, *This Side of Glory: The Autobiography of David Hilliard and the Story of the Black Panther Party* (New York: Little, Brown, 1993), 260–65. The "moratorium" protests a month earlier were even more moderate.

2. Hilliard and Cole, *This Side of Glory,* 260–65. Video of Hilliard's speech and the crowd's reaction, in possession of David Hilliard. See also Turner, "More Than 100,000 on Coast Demonstrate in Moderate Vein"; Lembke and Hager, "Thousands Parade Quietly in S.F.," 1.

3. "3 Police on Coast Shot by Negroes," *New York Times,* November 20, 1968, 94; William Lee Brent, *Long Time Gone: A Black Panther's True-Life Story of His Hijacking and Twenty-Five Years in Cuba* (New York: Times Books, 1996), 17–124; "Central Committee, B.P.P. Press Conference," *Black Panther,* January 4, 1969, 6.

4. Huey P. Newton, "Executive Mandate No. 3," *Black Panther,* March 16, 1968, 1.

5. "Rules of the Black Panther Party, Central Headquarters—Oakland, California," *Black Panther,* September 7, 1968, 7. When these rules were first issued, Eldridge Cleaver and Bobby Seale were in charge of the Party, and David Hilliard was just emerging as the person most involved in managing the daily operations of the Party nationally. Kathleen Cleaver and Emory Douglas were also members of the Central Committee. Huey Newton had already been in jail for about a year, and it is hard to know whether he would have approved the rule about participation in the underground Black Liberation Army had he been directly in charge. The rule appears to run against his position in "The Correct Handling of the Revolution," although not his broader sensibilities. In any event, it is notable that the Party began to enforce strict rules and discipline member behavior in September 1968, the same month that the Panthers announced plans to launch their first Free Breakfast for Children Program. The initial rules and the initial announcement of the free breakfast program were published next to each other on the same page of the *Black Panther.* As the Party quickly grew and met with increasing repressive action from the state, and as both legitimate members and agent provocateurs engaged in unsupportable actions, the Party sought to groom its public image. Panther leaders likely saw both the purges and the community programs as ways to win broad support and burnish the Party's reputation.

6. "Central Committee, B.P.P. Press Conference," 6.

7. "Rules of the Black Panther Party," 20.

8. Bobby Seale quoted in "Panthers Deny Part in Berkeley Slaying," *San Francisco Examiner,* January 13, 1969, 16.

9. "Interview of Chief of Staff David Hilliard," *Black Panther*, April 20, 1969, 18.

10. "Interview of Chief of Staff David Hilliard," *Black Panther*, April 20, 1969, 18.

11. "Eldridge Cleaver Discusses Revolution—An Interview from Exile," *Black Panther*, October 11, 1969, 10–12.

12. "Last Statement by John Huggins," *Black Panther*, February 17, 1969, 8.

13. "Reactionaries from the East Oakland Chapter," *Black Panther*, March 23, 1969, 4; "Vallejo Chapter Expels Reactionaries," *Black Panther*, March 31, 1969, 17.

14. "Pig Conspiracy against Conn. Panthers," *Black Panther*, May 31, 1969, 5.

15. "Chicago Panthers Serve the People," *Black Panther*, May 31, 1969, 4.

16. Bert, "The Powells: Tools in the Hands of the Fascists," *Black Panther*, June 28, 1969, 11; "Harlem Branch Purges," *Black Panther*, June 14, 1969, 7.

17. "Boston Purge," *Black Panther*, July 19, 1969, 13.

18. "Denver Panthers' Statement to the Press," *Black Panther*, August 9, 1969, 22.

19. East Oakland Branch, Black Panther Party, "Renegers," *Black Panther*, February 7, 1970, 15; Illinois Chapter, Black Panther Party, "Expelled," *Black Panther*, February 7, 1970, 8; "No Longer Functioning with the B.P.P.," *Black Panther*, October 24, 1970, 9.

20. John W. Finney, "Democrats Back Vietnam Protest," *New York Times*, September 27, 1969, 1.

21. John W. Finney, "Lawmakers Back Antiwar Protest," *New York Times*, October 7, 1969, 8.

22. John W. Finney, "War Critics Plan to Force All-Night Session of House," *New York Times*, October 10, 1969, 1.

23. On Nixon's policy and for the statistics on troop levels and battle deaths, see Melvin Small, *Johnson, Nixon, and the Doves* (New Brunswick, NJ: Rutgers University Press, 1988), 131, 164, 179, 191, 195, 197, 203, 215.

24. SDS had split along ideological lines and lost much of its influence by the time of the large national protests in the fall of 1969. For a poll showing that the majority of respondents now believed that "War was a mistake," see Small, *Johnson, Nixon, and the Doves*, 130, 164. Draft induction statistics are from the Selective Service System, History and Records division, Washington, DC, www.sss.gov/induct.htm.

25. Committee on House Administration of the U.S. House of Representatives, *Black Americans in Congress: 1870–2007* (Washington, DC: U.S. House Office of History and Preservation, 2008).

26. Paul Frymer, *Uneasy Alliances: Race and Party Competition in America* (Princeton, NJ: Princeton University Press, 1999), 105–6.

27. Manning Marable, *Race, Reform, and Rebellion* (Jackson: University Press of Mississippi, 1991), 119–20.

28. Cedric Johnson, *Revolutionaries to Race Leaders* (Minneapolis: University of Minnesota Press, 2007), 129.

29. John Skrentny, *The Ironies of Affirmative Action: Politics, Culture, and Justice in America* (Chicago: University of Chicago Press, 1996), 186.

30. Ibid., 177–78.

31. Noliwe M. Rooks, *White Money/Black Power: The Surprising History of African American Studies and the Crisis of Race in Higher Education* (Boston: Beacon, 2006); Fabio Rojas, *From Black Power to Black Studies: How a Radical Social Movement Became an Academic Discipline* (Baltimore: Johns Hopkins Press, 2007). For statistics on the number of programs in doctoral universities, see ibid., 171.

32. "Chou [Zhou Enlai] Tells Americans Mao Made Decision to Invite U.S. Table Tennis Team," *New York Times,* October 7, 1971, 4.

33. Kathleen Neal Cleaver, "Back to Africa: The Evolution of the International Section of the Black Panther Party (1969–1972)," in *The Black Panther Party [Reconsidered],* ed. Charles E. Jones (Baltimore: Black Classic Press, 1998), 227, 253n; on the U.S.-Algerian diplomatic status, see U.S. Department of State, Office of the Historian, Historical Documents: Foreign Relations of the United States; Sanche de Gramont, "Our Other Man in Algiers," *New York Times Magazine,* November 1, 1970.

34. Ruth Reitan, "Cuba, the Black Panther Party, and the U.S. Black Movement in the 1960s: Issues of Security," in *Liberation, Imagination, and the Black Panther Party,* ed. Kathleen Cleaver and George Katsiaficas (New York: Routledge, 2001); Ruth Reitan, *The Rise and Decline of an Alliance: Cuba and African American Leaders in the 1960s* (East Lansing: Michigan State University Press, 1999). Reitan makes an interesting argument that ascendance of a pro-Soviet faction in the Castro government caused the Cubans to elevate concerns about Cuban security over interest in supporting the black insurgency in the United States.

35. Charlotte Curtis, "Black Panther Philosophy Is Debated at the Bernsteins," *New York Times,* January 15, 1971, 48. By this time, a liberal reverie was setting in. But the hypocrisy of Nixon's Cambodia campaign remobilized many student activists. The killings of students at Kent State and Jackson State in early May shattered the passivity that had been settling in among antiwar activists, and anti-imperialist mobilizations shut down college campuses throughout the country. In June, as the student mobilizations subsided, liberals sought to press their critique.

36. Tom Wolfe, "Radical Chic: That Party at Lenny's," *New York,* June 8, 1970; Tom Wolfe, *Radical Chic & Mau-Mauing the Flak Catchers* (New York: Farrar, Straus, & Giroux, 1970).

37. Edward Jay Epstein, "The Black Panthers and the Police: A Pattern of Genocide?" *New Yorker,* February 13, 1971, 6.

38. See, for example, Paul L. Montgomery, "Panthers' Allegation of Killings by Police Disputed in Magazine," *New York Times,* February 14, 1971, 51.

39. See Hilliard and Cole, *This Side of Glory,* 285.

40. In 1970, the *New York Times* published 1,217 articles containing the words *Black Panther* or *Black Panthers,* more than three per day on average and more than twice the number published any other year, according to a search on ProQuest Historical Newspapers, October 27, 2010. The second-

highest number of mentions was in 1971, with 553 stories, and then 1969, with 488 stories. Detailed reading of a systematic sampling of these articles shows that they contain little noise: almost all do discuss the Black Panther Party. But many mention the Party only in passing. A more conservative estimate of coverage, based on a narrower search for articles in which *Black Panther* or *Black Panther Party* appear in the citation or abstract, yielded 421 articles for 1970. Using either measure, the numbers are robust. In 1970, the Panthers received more than double the coverage they received in any other year. Moreover, this level of coverage is as high as the level of coverage devoted to leading civil rights organizations during their height, such as the Southern Christian Leadership Conference, the Student Nonviolent Coordinating Committee, and the Congress of Racial Equality. On the level of financial support the Panthers received, see Martin Kenner in Hilliard and Cole, *This Side of Glory,* 281.

41. "Huey Freed," *Newsweek,* August 17, 1970; photos in *Black Panther,* August 15, 1970, 14. In November, the Party set Newton up in a fancy, high-security, $650 per month penthouse overlooking Lake Merritt in Oakland and the Alameda County jail where he had been held in solitary confinement. Prompted by the FBI, the *San Francisco Examiner* published a smear article reporting the move and emphasizing the contrast between Newton's living conditions and those of many Panther members. As the FBI intended, the article generated outrage among some Panthers and supporters, who resented that Newton was living so lushly while they struggled. On the Party's acquisition of the penthouse, see Alex Hoffmann interview with Lewis Cole, transcript, 79, Black Thought and Culture collection, Alexander Street Press, http://solomon .bltc.alexanderstreet.com/cgi-bin/asp/philo/bltc/getdoc.pl?S15873-D001.

42. Alex Papillon described this rank-and-file reaction to Newton's release in a conversation with Joshua Bloom, November 18, 2005, Berkeley, California.

43. Huey P. Newton, "Repression Breeds Resistance," transcript, *Black Panther,* January 16, 1971, 10. Carlos Marighella (1911–1969) was a Brazilian Marxist revolutionary best known for his *Minimanual of the Urban Guerilla* (Berkeley: Berkeley Tribe, 1970, English edition).

44. "Let Us Hold High the Banner of Intercommunalism and the Invincible Thoughts of Huey P. Newton, Minister of Defense and Supreme Commander of the Black Panther Party," transcript of Newton speech at Boston College, *Black Panther,* January 23, 1971, supplement, B (emphasis ours). A January 9, 1971, article in the *Black Panther* by Gwen V. Hodges of Central Headquarters may be the first time the Party advanced the phrase "survival pending revolution": "The overthrow of one class by another must be carried out by revolutionary violence. Until this stage is achieved, we must concentrate on the immediate needs of the people in order to build a unified political force, based on the ideology of the Black Panther Party. Survival pending revolution is our immediate task and to do this we must meet the needs of the people. We have been doing this through our liberation schools, free breakfast programs, child care centers, bussing programs (people are able to visit members of their family in prison) and clothing programs. We will also move forward to institute a shoe shop" (3).

45. "Let Us Hold High the Banner," supplement, B (emphasis ours). Newton gave his first major speech after his release on September 5, 1970, in Philadelphia, at the plenary session of the People's Revolutionary Constitutional Convention. The speech was highly abstract and, by many secondary accounts, uninspiring. But in the speech, Newton did not take a clear position on immediate guerilla warfare. Raids and strip searches of Philadelphia Panthers by the police in the days before the convention also raised tensions. "Huey's Message to the Revolutionary People's Constitutional Convention Plenary Session September 5, 1970," transcript, *Black Panther,* September 12, 1970, 10. See photo on cover, *Black Panther,* September 5, 1970, 1, and coverage within. See also subsequent coverage in Rosemarie, "The People and the People Alone Were the Motive Force in the Making of History of the People's Revolutionary Constitutional Convention Plenary Session!" *Black Panther,* September 12, 1970, 3.

46. Martin Kenner, interview by Lewis Cole, transcript, 59–62, Black Thought and Culture collection, Alexander Street Press, http://solomon.bltc .alexanderstreet.com/cgi-bin/asp/philo/bltc/getdoc.pl?S15877-D001.

47. Ibid., 61.

48. Ibid.

49. Ibid., 63, 92, 96.

50. "Metropolitan," *Los Angeles Times,* August 19, 1970, 2; "Mrs. Sirhan Sues U.S. in Bid for Trip to Jordan," *Los Angeles Times,* September 12, 1970, 3.

51. Gaidi Faraj writes that Geronimo's focus while living underground from August to December 1970 was "on building guerilla cadres"; see Faraj, "Unearthing the Underground: A Study of Radical Activism in the Black Panther Party and the Black Liberation Army" (PhD diss., University of California, Berkeley, 2007), 148. Faraj provides the most thorough treatment available on the Black Panther underground.

52. "Shuns Court," *Los Angeles Times,* September 22, 1970, C5; "Southland," *Los Angeles Times,* September 22, 1970, B2.

53. "Press Statement to the Press on Elmer Pratt, Deputy Minister of Defense Southern California Chapter Black Panther Party," *Black Panther,* October 3, 1970, 5. See also Craig Williams, Southern California Chapter, "Reflections of Geronimo . . . The Essence of a Panther," *Black Panther,* August 29, 1970, 14.

54. Committee to Defend Abandoned Panthers, "Free Geronimo—The Urban Guerilla," *Right On!* April 3, 1971, 6.

55. "Metropolitan," *Los Angeles Times,* December 10, 1970, A2; "Metropolitan," *Los Angeles Times,* January 20, 1971, A2; Robert Finklea, "FBI Arrest Four Men Wanted in California," *Dallas Morning News,* December 9, 1970, 1.

56. Hilliard and Cole, *This Side of Glory,* 318.

57. Various authors claim that "Cotton" Smith was working as an agent provocateur. See Jo Durden-Smith, *Who Killed George Jackson?* (New York: Knopf, 1976), 125–57; Ward Churchill and Jim Vander Wall, *Agents of Repression* (Cambridge, MA: South End Press, 1990), 84–87; Louis Tackwood, *Glass House Tapes* (New York: Avon, 1973).

58. Don Cox, "Organizing Self-Defense Groups," *Black Panther,* Janu-

ary 16, 1971, 8. Cox dedicated the article to Jonathan Jackson and Carlos Marighella, for whom he named his son, Jonathan Carlos Cox.

59. Hilliard and Cole, *This Side of Glory*, 284.

60. Panther 21, "Open Letter to Weatherman Underground from Panther 21," *East Village Other*, January 19, 1971, 3.

61. Ibid. More pointedly, the New York Panthers also challenged Huey Newton's program of armed "self-defense" upon which the Party was founded and his idea of "revolutionary suicide": "We have had too many martyrs. We desperately need more revolutionists who are completely willing and ready at all times to KILL to change conditions. Just to be ready to die does not make a revolutionist—it just makes a martyr—'revolutionary suicide' and 'only those who die are proven revolutionaries'—are bullshit—a revolutionist accepts death as a natural phenomenon, but MUST be ready to KILL to change conditions."

62. "Metropolitan," *Los Angeles Times*, January 20, 1971, A2, records that Geronimo was still fighting extradition from Dallas to face charges in Los Angeles. In *Freedom, Humanity, Peace*, a pamphlet containing transcripts of interviews from prison, published by the Revolutionary Peoples Communication Network circa 1971, Geronimo Pratt asserted he was being closed out by Huey and the Central Committee (13). Pamphlet available in the Bancroft Library at the University of California, Berkeley.

63. Huey P. Newton, "On the Purge of Geronimo from the Black Panther Party," *Black Panther*, January 23, 1971, 7.

64. Pratt in *Freedom, Humanity, Peace*, 13. Once in court in Los Angeles on charges relating to the December 8, 1969, shoot-out at the L.A. Panther headquarters, Geronimo was also charged with the murder of a schoolteacher at a tennis court in Santa Monica in 1968. He had been secretly indicted for the crime on December 4, 1970, while he was in prison in Dallas fighting extradition. See Ron Einstoss, "Former Black Panther Aide Held for Murder," *Los Angeles Times*, February 17, 1971, D5. After many years in prison, Geronimo was released when it was proven that Julius Butler, whose testimony had led to Geronimo's conviction, was a paid FBI informant and thus not credible.

65. Rod Such, "Newton Expels 12 Panthers," *Guardian*, February 20, 1971, 4; Newton statement quoted in United Press International, "Panthers Oust Eleven," *Chicago Daily Defender*, February 11, 1971, 10; Edith Evans Asbury, "Newton Denounces 2 Missing Panthers," *New York Times*, February 10, 1971, 1.

66. Ibid. Newton statement quoted in UPI, "Panthers Oust Eleven," 10; Asbury, "Newton Denounces 2 Missing Panthers," 1. Through COINTELPRO, the FBI sent provocative letters in Matthews's name. Some have speculated that Matthews was working with the FBI, but we have not seen strong evidence to this effect. Matthews was an older and well-educated woman from the Caribbean who had proven quite capable. She organized early international support in Scandinavia, worked with Eldridge Cleaver in Algiers, and then was Newton's personal secretary. She absconded to Algiers just before the Cleavers' denunciation of Newton and Hilliard.

67. Richard Moore [Dhoruba Bin Wahad], "A Black Panther Speaks," *New York Times,* May 12, 1971, 43.

68. Asbury, "Newton Denounces 2 Missing Panthers," 1; Newton statement quoted in UPI, "Panthers Oust Eleven," 10; Such, "Newton Expels 12 Panthers," 4.

69. Central Committee, "Enemies of the People," *Black Panther,* February 13, 1971, 12.

70. Ibid.; Such, "Newton Expels 12 Panthers," 4.

71. "Black Panther Dispute," *Sun Reporter,* March 13, 1971, 2; Thomas A. Johnson, "Panthers Fear Growing Intraparty Strife," *New York Times,* April 10, 1971, 24.

72. Huey Newton quoted in Hilliard and Cole, *This Side of Glory,* 323. Hilliard provides extensive quotations from the discussion, which we believe are transcribed from a recording of the conversation. Hilliard once played the cassette for Joshua Bloom. He said that Cleaver secretly recorded the conversation and acted very cool while provoking Newton to anger. According to Hilliard, Cleaver then released the recording to a local Bay Area radio station, which is how the cassette eventually came into Hilliard's possession. We do not have a copy of the tape, or a full transcript, but Bloom believed the recoding to be genuine when he heard it, and the partial transcript reported in Hilliard's book appears consistent with the tenor of the conversation he heard.

73. "Black Panther Dispute," 2; see also Johnson, "Panthers Fear Growing Intraparty Strife," 24, which dates the release almost two weeks later: March 11, 1971. The *Sun Reporter* article is more proximate, so the dating is likely more credible. Also, by March 11, the *Black Panther* had published a lead article with a call to "Free Kathleen Cleaver" (March 6, 1971) and Robert Webb had been killed. The statements reported from the video appear to have been made before these events.

74. Elaine Brown, "Free Kathleen Cleaver," *Black Panther,* March 6, 1971, 1 and supplement; see also Johnson, "Panthers Fear Growing Intraparty Strife," 24; "Black Panther Dispute," 2.

75. Michael Knight, "Death Here Tied to Panther Feud," *New York Times,* March 10, 1971, 29.

76. United Press International, "Say N.Y. Panthers Balk in Death Probe," *Chicago Daily Defender,* March 13, 1971, 2.

77. "Black Panther Dispute," 2.

78. Curtis J. Austin, *Up against the Wall: Violence in the Making and Unmaking of the Black Panther Party* (Fayetteville: University of Arkansas Press, 2006), 314.

79. Knight, "Death Here Tied to Panther Feud," 29; "Black Panther Dispute," 2; UPI, "Say N.Y. Panthers Balk in Death Probe," 2; Johnson, "Panthers Fear Growing Intraparty Strife," 24.

80. Michael Knight, "A Black Panther Found Slain Here," *New York Times,* April 18, 1971, 1; "Murdered. . . . Sam Napier, Black Panther Party, Intercommunal News Service, Circulation Manager Murdered by Fascists, Revolutionary Service Scheduled for April 24," flier, April 17, 1971," copy in

Joshua Bloom's possession; Robert D. McFadden, "4 Panthers Admit Guilt in Slaying," *New York Times,* May 22, 1973, 1.

81. People close to these events describe the organizational rupture in very different terms. Three influential groups of Black Panthers—the Cleavers and their comrades, most of the New York 21, and Geronimo Pratt and his comrades—publicly broke from Huey Newton and the national leadership of the Black Panther Party. The large majority of Black Panther chapters and members at that time did not. Huey Newton called the organizational rupture a "defection," implying that those who broke from his leadership willfully joined forces with the U.S. government as counterrevolutionaries. Most did not. Conversely, some have argued that the Cleavers and comrades did not voluntarily leave the Party but were expelled from it. But this position obscures the basic organizational dynamic: Until early 1971, despite any underlying organizational tension, the Cleaver faction accepted the leadership of Huey Newton and the national Party and generally sought to maintain a unified public face. By March 1971, the Cleavers, Geronimo Pratt, and key members of the New York 21 had all publicly challenged the leadership of Huey Newton and the Central Committee in Oakland. We use the term *mutiny* to describe this organizational rebellion of smaller factions against the leadership of the national Party organization, and the term *split* to describe the eventual crystallization of two distinct ideological positions, one advocated by the national Party organization and the other advocated by the mutinous faction.

82. Central Committee, Black Panther Party, "Intercommunal Section Defects," *Black Panther,* March 20, 1971, 16. The announcement lists Eldridge, Kathleen, Donald Cox, "and all other members of the Intercommunal Section" as having "defected."

83. Emory Douglas, Masai Hewitt, "Big Man" Howard, Bob Rush, and Doug Miranda, "We Stand Rock Firm behind Our Beloved and Courageous Central Committee and Our Leader, Minister of Defense and Supreme Servant of the People, Huey P. Newton," *Black Panther,* March 20, 1971, 12.

84. Bobby Seale, "I Am the Chairman of Only One Party," *Black Panther,* April 3, 1971, 2.

85. San Quentin Branch, Black Panther Party, "TO Eldridge Cleaver and His Conspirators, FROM the San Quentin Branch of the Black Panther Party," *Black Panther,* March 20, 1971, 1; for Eldridge Cleaver on Jonathan Jackson, see Eldridge Cleaver, "On the Case of Angela Davis," *Black Panther,* January 23, 1971, 5.

86. "Survival Pending Revolution," *Black Panther,* March 20, 1971, back cover. Newton more fully articulated this position in June. In "Black Capitalism Re-Analyzed," *Black Panther,* June 5, 1971, A, Newton wrote, "All these programs satisfy the deep needs of the community but they are not solutions to our problems. That is why we call them survival programs, meaning survival pending revolution. . . . We say that the survival program of the Black Panther Party is like the survival kit of a sailor stranded on a raft. . . . The survival programs are not answers or solutions, but they will help us to organize the community."

87. *Black Panther,* March 27, 1971, 1, supplement, and throughout.

88. This tally includes both drawings and photographs. If a graphic image

included depictions of multiple weapons, we counted it only once. The specific tally of images depicting weapons, by date of issue, is as follows: January 2, 13 images; January 9, 22; January 16, 20; January 23, 14; January 30, 27; February 6, 21; February 13, 16; February 20, 24; February 27, 27; March 6, 11; March 13, 11; March 20, 19; March 27, 0; April 3, 0; April 10, 1; April 17, 0; May 1, 1; May 8, 0; May 15, 1; May 22, 1; May 29, 0; June 5, 0; June 12, 1; June 19, 0. Note that of the twelve issues through March 20, the issue with the least number of images of weapons contained 11 of them. Conversely, in the next twelve issues, the maximum number of images per issue was 1.

89. The last issue featuring the photos of Huey armed and the machine gun was March 6, 1971, 14. The following week, March 13, the photos were removed, but a cartoon of a machine gun retained. The week after, the cartoon of the machine gun disappeared, but the issue still bore the large-font bold caption "Survival Pending Revolution." The following week, the caption changed to "Serving the People Body and Soul," and that layout remained in subsequent issues.

90. Charles W. Hopkins, "The Deradicalization of the Black Panther Party: 1967–1973" (PhD, University of North Carolina at Chapel Hill, 1978), ch. 4.

91. *Right On!* April 3, 1971, quoted in *Sun Reporter,* April 24, 1971, 6.

92. Jack A. Smith, "Panther Rift Aired in Algiers," *Guardian,* April 17, 1971, 3. Kathleen Cleaver does not mention the fact, but Bobby Seale was also free until August 1969, and Huey Newton was released in August 1970.

93. Ibid.

94. Ibid.

95. Huey P. Newton, Minister of Defense of the Black Panther Party and Servant of the People, "On the Defection of Eldridge Cleaver from the Black Panther Party and the Defection of the Black Panther Party from the Black Community," *Black Panther,* April 17, 1971, 1 and supplement.

16. THE LIMITS OF HEROISM

1. "State to Open Its Case Today in Seale's Trial at New Haven," *New York Times,* March 18, 1971, 33; Earl Caldwell, "Newton Is on Trial Again for Slaying of a Policeman," *New York Times,* June 29, 1971, 14. In June, an Oakland jury found Hilliard guilty of two counts of assault on a police officer and sentenced him to two years to life in jail; see "Panther Chief of Staff Found Guilty," *Los Angeles Times,* June 13, 1971, B.

2. "Jersey City Police Seize 5 at Panther Offices," *New York Times,* April 3, 1971, 58.

3. "Black Panthers Jailed in Commune Slaying," *Chicago Daily Defender,* April 19, 1971, 4.

4. "Charred Remains of a Man Thought to Be Panther Found," *New York Times,* April 21, 1971, 36.

5. "3 Policemen Shot; 4 Held in Chicago: Panther Literature Is Found at South Side Building," *New York Times,* May 14, 1971, 21.

6. Martin Arnold, "Key Suspect Held in 2 Police Deaths," *New York Times,* May 25, 1971, 1.

7. "N.Y. Panthers Held in Police Shooting: Submachine Gun Used in Holdup Linked to Attack," *Los Angeles Times,* June 6, 1971, 1.

8. Roy Haynes, "Ex-Panther Tells of Plan to Blow Up L.A. Police Station," *Los Angeles Times,* July 24, 1971, A1; Roy Haynes, "Witness Says Gun Seized in Panther Raid Killed Three," *Los Angeles Times,* July 29, 1971, 3.

9. See, for example, Jo Durden-Smith, *Who Killed George Jackson?* (New York: Knopf, 1976), 125–57; Ward Churchill and Jim Vander Wall, *Agents of Repression* (Cambridge, MA: South End Press, 1990), 84–87; Louis Tackwood, *Glass House Tapes* (New York: Avon, 1973).

10. John Darnton, "7 Panthers Indicted in Slaying of a Party Official in Corona," *New York Times,* July 20, 1971, 30.

11. Earl Caldwell, "The Panthers: Dead or Regrouping," *New York Times,* March 1, 1971, 1.

12. Bobby Seale, interview by Ollie A. Johnson III, cited in Ollie A. Johnson III, "Explaining the Demise of the Black Panther Party," in *The Black Panther Party [Reconsidered],* ed. Charles E. Jones (Baltimore: Black Classic Press, 1998), 402.

13. Committee on Internal Security of the House of Representatives, *Gun-Barrel Politics: The Black Panther Party, 1966–1971,* 92d Cong., 1st sess. (Washington, DC: Government Printing Office, 1971), 143.

14. Wallace Turner, "Two Desperate Hours: How George Jackson Died," *New York Times,* September 3, 1971, 1.

15. George Jackson, *Soledad Brother: The Prison Letters of George Jackson* (New York: Coward-McCann, 1970).

16. For a biography by an ardent supporter, see Eric Mann, *Comrade George* (New York: Harper & Row, 1972).

17. "Political Assassination," *Black Panther,* January 25, 1969, 1.

18. *Black Panther,* January 25, 1969, graphics on 3, 24, 11, 16, 18, 9, 8, 6.

19. Randy, "Fred Hampton Murdered by Fascist Pigs," *Black Panther,* December 13, 1969, 2.

20. *Black Panther,* December 13, 1969, 1, 9–12, 16, 18–20.

21. Folsom Cadre of the Black Panther Party, "Open Letter to Mr. and Mrs. Jackson," excerpts, *Black Panther,* September 4, 1971, supplement, 1.

22. "Statement by Huey P. Newton, Minister of Defense of the Black Panther Party, at the Revolutionary Memorial Service for George Jackson," *Black Panther,* September 4, 1971, supplement, F.

23. *Black Panther,* September 4, 1971, supplement, A.

24. Jean Genet, *Black Panther,* September 4, 1971, supplement, L.

25. Tom Wicker, "4 Days of Attica Talks End in Failure," *New York Times,* September 14, 1971, 1.

26. Joseph Lelyveld, "A Hostage Says Threats Left Him 'Scared Silly'" *New York Times,* September 14, 1971, 1.

27. "Massacre at Attica," editorial, *New York Times,* September 14, 1971, 40.

28. Fred Ferretti, "Autopsies Show Shots Killed 9 Attica Hostages, Not Knives; State Official Admits Mistake," *New York Times,* September 15, 1971, 1.

29. James Clarity, "Observers Lay Killings to 'Official Intransigence,'" *New York Times,* September 19, 1971, 60.

30. *Black Panther,* September 18, 1971.

31. Clarity, "Observers Lay Killings to 'Official Intransigence,'" 60.

32. See *Black Panther,* January 22, 1972, 1.

33. The *Black Panther* featured statements of support by Chisholm and Dellums on the front covers of three issues in late April and early May—April 15, May 6, and May 13.

34. "Chairman Bobby Seale for Mayor!" *Black Panther,* May 20, 1972, 1.

35. See Huey P. Newton, "Oakland—A Base of Operation!" *Black Panther,* July 29, 1972, supplement, and long series of columns titled "Oakland—A Base of Operation!" which were published weekly thereafter.

36. Elaine Brown, October 26, 1972, quoted in "We're Talking about Winning in Oakland," *Black Panther,* November 9, 1972, 4.

37. Earl Caldwell, "Seale Puts Oakland Race into Runoff," *New York Times,* April 19, 1973, 27.

38. Bobby Rush, quoted in Hilliard and Cole, *This Side of Glory,* 327.

39. Huey Newton telephone conversation with David Hilliard in prison as recalled by David Hilliard. Joshua Bloom telephone conversation and email exchanges with David Hilliard, May 14 and May 28, 2012.

40. According to Newton's widow Fredrika Newton, and best friend David Hilliard. See David Hilliard with Keith and Kent Zimmerman, *Huey: Spirit of the Panther,* New York: Thunder's Mouth Press 2006, chapters 19 and 20. See also ibid., prologue, 6.

41. Elaine Brown, *A Taste of Power: A Black Woman's Story* (New York: Pantheon Books, 1992), 439.

42. Kate Coleman with Paul Avery, "The Party's Over," *New Times,* July 11, 1978.

43. Ibid., 34. A friend of Newton's who did not want to be named told us that Newton had beaten Callins but that Callins was actually a cocaine dealer and that the violence resulted from a drug deal gone sour.

44. Brown, *A Taste of Power,* 356.

45. "The Odyssey Of Huey Newton: Violence is never far from the Black Panthers' leader," *Time Magazine,* November 13, 1978, 38.

46. Flores A. Forbes, *Will You Die with Me?: My Life and the Black Panther Party* (New York: Atria Books, 2006).

47. Elaine Brown, foreword to Forbes, *Will You Die With Me?*

48. See Hilliard and Cole, "Prologue," in *This Side of Glory* for likely scenario of death. See "Huey Newton Killed; Was a Co-Founder of Black Panthers," *New York Times,* August 23, 1989, 1, for date of death.

49. Detractors such as David Horowitz, Peter Collier, and Kate Coleman, who made careers of vilifying the Panthers, advanced the public criminalization of the Party's entire history. These authors wrote extensively about the criminal activities of the miniscule and dying Black Panther Party and its leadership in the 1970s, and they retrospectively read the entire history of the national organization through this criminal lens, stripping the Party of its politics. Most large cities contain numerous organizations that engage in the kinds of criminal activities that some Panthers apparently did in the 1970s. The Panthers are interesting historically not because they were just like these

others but because they were a world apart from these petty criminal organizations in purpose and influence between 1968 and 1970. The detractors' accounts obscure rather than illuminate the historical import of the Black Panther Party. It is ironic that Horowitz took over *Ramparts* magazine, pushing out Robert Scheer, the leftist editor who helped the Black Panthers get their start, even as the Black Panther Party was unraveling. Horowitz established his credentials at *Ramparts* through collaboration with Newton, raising more than $100,000 and providing strong institutional support for Newton, turning a blind eye to his alleged criminality when many of his friends pointed it out. See Peter Richardson, *A Bomb in Every Issue: How the Short, Unruly Life of* Ramparts *Magazine Changed America* (New York: New Press, 2009), 187. Then, in the most cynical of personal politics, he made himself famous by denouncing Newton and by projecting the allegations about his criminal activities onto the entire legacy of the Black Panther Party.

50. See Brown, *A Taste of Power*, chs. 12–16.

51. For the dating of Elaine Brown's leadership, see "Leader of Panthers Booked in Assaults," *New York Times,* August 18, 1974, 31; and Robert Trumbull, "Newton Plans to Resume Control of Black Panthers," *New York Times,* June 28, 1977, 17.

52. See Robert O. Self, *American Babylon: Race and the Struggle for Postwar Oakland* (Princeton, NJ: Princeton University Press, 2003), 309–11; and Brown, *A Taste of Power*, ch. 17.

53. See Douglas Corbin, "The Oakland Black Panther Party School" (senior honors thesis, University of California, Berkeley, 2004); Daniel Willis, "A Critical Analysis of Mass Political Education and Community Organization as Utilized by the Black Panther Party" (EdD diss., University of Massachusetts, 1976); Brown, *A Taste of Power*, 391, 395.

54. William Endicott, "Black Panthers—Stalking on a Tamer Path," *Los Angeles Times,* August 25, 1977; Brown, *A Taste of Power*, ch. 20.

55. Brown, *A Taste of Power*, ch. 20; Self, *American Babylon*, 309–16; "Oakland Elects Judge as City's First Black Mayor," *Los Angeles Times,* May 18, 1977, A3.

56. Lionel Martin, "Newton Plans Return to U.S.," *Los Angeles Times,* June 25, 1977, 1.

57. Brown, *A Taste of Power*, ch. 21.

58. See Joshua Bloom, "Pathways of Insurgency: Black Liberation Struggle and the Second Reconstruction in the United States, 1945–1975," unpublished manuscript.

59. Huey P. Newton, "The Functional Definition of Politics," *Black Panther,* May 15, 1967, 4.

60. Assata Shakur, *Assata: An Autobiography* (Chicago: Lawrence Hill Books, 1987), 169.

61. Acoli in Akinyele Omowale Umoja, "Repression Breeds Resistance: The Black Liberation Army and the Radical Legacy of the Black Panther Party," in *Liberation, Imagination, and the Black Panther Party*, ed. Kathleen Cleaver and George Katsiaficas (New York: Routledge, 2001), 12.

62. Jalil Muntaqim, *On the Black Liberation Army,* pamphlet (1979; repr. Oakland, CA: Abraham Gullien Press, 2002), 3.

63. Coordinating Committee, Black Liberation Army, *Message to the Black Movement: A Political Statement from the Black Underground,* pamphlet (1975; repr. Oakland, CA: Abraham Gullien Press, 2002), 10–11.

64. Muntaqim, *On the Black Liberation Army,* 5–9.

65. Ibid., 12.

66. For the best overviews of the Black Liberation Army, see Umoja, "Repression Breeds Resistance"; Gaidi Faraj, "Unearthing the Underground: A Study of Radical Activism in the Black Panther Party and the Black Liberation Army" (PhD diss., University of California, Berkeley, 2007).

CONCLUSION

1. In 1970, the *New York Times* published 1,217 articles containing the text "Black Panther" or "Black Panthers," more than three per day on average, and more than twice the number published any other year, according to a search on ProQuest Historical Newspapers, October 27, 2010. The second-highest number of mentions was in 1971, with 553 stories, and then 1969, with 488 stories. Detailed reading of a systematic sampling of these articles shows that they contain little noise: almost all do discuss the Black Panther Party. But many mention the Party only in passing. A more conservative estimate of coverage, based on a narrower search for articles in which "Black Panther" or "Black Panther Party" appear in the citation or abstract, yields 421 articles for 1970. Using either measure, the proportions are robust. In 1970, the Panthers received more than double the coverage they received in any other year. Moreover, this level of coverage is as high as the level of coverage devoted to leading civil rights organizations during their height, such as the Southern Christian Leadership Conference, the Student Nonviolent Coordinating Committee, and the Congress of Racial Equality.

2. This budget figure is a conservative estimate based on data in the House Committee on Internal Security report *Gun-Barrel Politics: The Black Panther Party, 1966–1971,* part 470, 92d Cong., 1st sess. (Washington, DC: Government Printing Office, 1971), 84–87.

3. Interagency Committee on Intelligence (Ad Hoc), Special Report [Huston Report], June 1970, 9–10.

4. Some have suggested that revolution was "in the air" in the United States during the late 1960s and that it ceased to hold sway in the 1970s.While we generally agree, we do not especially favor the subtler implications of this formulation. Much like the "structuralism" of the political opportunity thesis, this view treats the question of whether revolution was "in the air" as exogenous to movement dynamics. In our view, the advent of effective revolutionary political practices itself makes revolutionary ideology more broadly appealing, putting revolution "in the air." Thus, while the broad political climate has a strong effect on the reception of a movement's political practices, it is itself contingent, and highly susceptible to change, often driven by the practices of movement activists themselves.

5. See, for example, the work of Martha Biondi, Jack Dougherty, Douglas Flamming, Jacqueline Dowd Hall, Patrick Jones, Matthew Lassiter, Annelise Orleck, Brian Purnell, and Clarence Taylor.

6. Thomas Sugrue, *Sweet Land of Liberty: The Forgotten Struggle for Civil Rights in the North* (New York: Random House, 2008).

7. Among these scholars of Black Power are Matthew Countryman, Judson Jeffries, Jeffery Ogbar, Kimberly Springer, Noliwe Rooks, Rhonda Williams, Yohuru Williams, and Komozi Woodard.

8. Peniel Joseph, *Waiting 'Til the Midnight Hour: A Narrative History of Black Power in America* (New York: Henry Holt, 2006).

9. See Harry Eckstein, "On the Etiology of Internal Wars," *History and Theory* 4, no. 2 (1965): 133–63; Ted Robert Gurr, "A Comparative Study of Civil Strife," *The History of Violence in America: Historical and Comparative Perspectives,* ed. Hugh D. Graham and Ted R. Gurr (New York: F.A. Praeger,1969), 572–632; or for a literary perspective, John Steinbeck, *Grapes of Wrath.*

10. See, for example, Douglas A. Hibbs, *Mass Political Violence: A Cross-National Causal Analysis* (New York: Wiley, 1973); Charles Tilly, *From Mobilization to Revolution* (Reading, MA: Addison-Wesley, 1978).

11. Ted Gurr writes, "The threat and severity of coercive violence used by a regime increases the anger of dissidents, thereby intensifying their opposition, up to some high threshold of government violence beyond which anger gives way to fear"; *Why Men Rebel* (Princeton, NJ: Princeton University Press, 1970), 238. See also Douglas P. Bwy, "Political Instability in Latin America: The Cross-Cultural Test of a Causal Model," *Latin American Research Review* 3, no. 2 (Summer 1968): 17–66.

12. The periodization is, of course, necessarily imprecise. The state's repressive actions did not all fail through December 1969 and then suddenly all work in January 1970. The political context shifted gradually during the period. The student mobilizations in May 1970 are a clear example of the limits of defining 1970 and 1971 as years in which the Panthers' anti-imperialist politics lost resilience, yet they are consistent with the general analysis. The student antiwar movement had been gradually moderating by the fall of 1969, and it continued to do so into 1970. But the hypocrisy of Nixon's Cambodia invasion after his promises of Vietnamization and the killing of students at Kent State in early May shattered the liberal reverie. The broad national student mobilization in insurgent anti-imperialist terms showed how fragile the moderation of the antiwar movement was and how important the full repeal of the draft and ending of the war would be to put the war protests to rest.

13. More recent scholarship has also sought to transcend the narrow debate about the relationship between repression and mobilization. Christian Davenport, Hank Johnston, and Carol McClurg Mueller, eds., *Repression and Mobilization* (Minneapolis: University of Minnesota, 2005) seek to further explore the divergence of outcomes, building on the classic works, introducing new variables such as the quality of repression, and accounting for lag effects. In a still-influential article, Mark Irving Lichbach argues that a rational actor model that accounts for the relative return to dissent can explain when repres-

sion deters mobilization and when it encourages it. See Lichbach, "Deterrence or Escalation?: The Puzzle of Aggregate Studies of Repression and Dissent," *Journal of Conflict Resolution* 31, no. 2 (June 1987): 266–97. We agree with the general point that activists' perceptions of the efficacy of a particular set of practices affects the level of mobilization. But Lichbach's model makes a number of simplifying assumptions that limit its ability to account for the Panther case. Most importantly, Lichbach does not account for the effects of the broader political context on efficacy. In our view, the receptivity of potential allies to a particular set of insurgent practices is crucial in determining the effects of repression.

14. See David S. Meyer, "Protest and Political Opportunities," *Annual Review of Sociology* 30 (2004): 125–45.

15. Doug McAdam, *Political Process and the Black Insurgency, 1930–1970* (Chicago: University of Chicago Press, 1982); Aldon Morris, *The Origins of the Civil Rights Movement: Black Communities Organizing for Change* (New York: Free Press, 1984).

16. For a full theorization, see Joshua Bloom, "Pathways of Insurgency: Black Liberation Struggle and the Second Reconstruction in the United States, 1945–1975," unpublished manuscript.

17. *Selections from the Prison Notebooks of Antonio Gramsci*, ed. Quintin Hoare and Geoffrey Nowell Smith (New York: International Publishers, 1971), 462.

18. Ibid., 125–26.

19. "The Modern Prince," in ibid., especially 180–82.

20. Winning allies allows the movement to make strides in what Gramsci calls the "War of Position"; see "The State and Civil Society," in ibid, 206–76.

21. Huey P. Newton, "Statement by Huey P. Newton, Minister of Defense of the Black Panther Party, Supreme Servant of the People at the Chicago Illinois Coliseum, February 21, 1971," *Black Panther*, April 10, 1971, 2. Note that the revolutionary ideology of the Party persisted beyond its wide political influence. At the time that Newton made this statement, the Party was beginning to collapse.

22. Our findings generally support the Michelsian "Iron Law of Oligarchy" argument advanced by Frances Fox Piven and Richard A. Cloward in *Poor People's Movements: Why They Succeed, How They Fail* (New York: Vintage, 1977), but with an important difference. Piven and Cloward argue that there is an inherent tension between the power of insurgency to advance poor people's interests and the tendency of organizations that claim to champion these interests to eschew disruption and become beholden to the elites who fund them. This tension was evident in the conflict between the increasing impetus for the national Panther organization to maintain its reputation among potential allies and the antiauthoritarianism of many Panther members. Our argument departs somewhat from Piven and Cloward's, however, in our assessment of the effect of social structure on insurgency. Piven and Cloward argue that social dislocation drives the emergence of insurgency. Insurgency, they write, is "always short-lived," and "those brief periods in which people are roused to indignation" soon subside as the social disloca-

tion resolves (xxi). This perspective, like the political opportunity thesis, gives undue weight to the independent role of structure and psychosocial discontent in determining mobilization. We revise Piven and Cloward's "Iron Law" argument by putting insurgent practices at the center. Structural dislocations may generate discontent and destabilize existing roles and relations, but they do not independently generate insurgency. Insurgency requires insurgent practices that effectively leverage political cleavages. Our analysis of Black Panther history shows why insurgency is short-lived. Concessions ameliorate the political divisions that feed the insurgency, undermining support for insurgent practices. Whereas the concessions to the Civil Rights Movement directly redressed the targets of insurgency and made civil rights organizations part of the establishment, the "Iron Law of Oligarchy" played out differently with the Panthers. Concessions redressed the interests of Panther allies rather than directly addressing those of the Panthers themselves. The costs of appeasing allies thus made continued insurgency impossible, and the national organization defanged itself, even as some insurgent members threw caution to the wind and fought until they were killed or jailed. We don't believe that indignation simply waned nor that the social structure restabilized so forcefully as to incapacitate all insurgency. To the contrary, in many historical moments, like the late 1960s United States, when revolutionary black nationalism erupted even as the insurgent Civil Rights Movement declined, new forms of insurgency emerge even as old forms are incapacitated.

Acknowledgments

Over more than a decade, many hundreds of people helped shape this book, contributing information, questions, and perspective. We wish we had the space to thank everyone by name here. If you spoke with us about this history, or worked with us to produce this book, whether or not your name is listed here, we offer our gratitude.

We benefited greatly from the assistance of dozens of graduate and undergraduate research assistants. Some of our graduate research assistants and advisees have gone on to complete dissertations, and several have published their own books on aspects of the Black Panther Party history, including Paul Alkebulan, Lauren Araiza, Lawrence David Barber, Gaidi Faraj, Jason Michael Ferreira, and Donna Murch. Undergraduate research assistants who wrote their theses on aspects of this history include Michael Brazeal, Douglas Corbin, Jason Luna Gavilan, Chris Hastings, Kambridge Hibrar, Keith Orejel, Patrick Sharma, and Felicia Viator. Research assistants who made special contributions to the project include Jason Curtis, Erica Flener, Grace Lee, and Maya Pandurangi. Other research assistants who made important contributions include Jacqueline Amparo, Dominique Alexis-Nechele Brown, Sharon Campbell, Colleen Dixon, Michael Eidelson, Monica Galindo Heim, Dominique Halliburton, Sherilyn Hanson, Karmela Herrera, Erica Hsu, Tiffany Huang, Linda Jordan, Valerie Kao, Cheryl Klatt, Lisa Knox, Nithya Krishnan, Jason LaBouyer, Donna Lee, Jade Leung, Jessica Liu, Jason Luna Gavilan, Ursula Manning, Suzanne Martindale, Steven McCarty-Snead, Kalin McKenna, Aisha Mohammed,

Felicia Moore-Jordan, Nancy Nguyen, Natalie Novoa, Sangmi Park, Alex Quintanilla, Martin Ricard, Jared Richmond, Justin Richmond, Sarah Slocum, Brittney Starling, Jennifer Tancredi, Trina Walker, Alexis Wilson, Alanna Wong, Nkauj Iab Yang, and Audrey Yap.

Several groups of people played key roles in the project's development and deserve special thanks. David Hilliard, Fredericka Newton, and Will Whalen collaborated with us to create the online archive of the *Black Panther* newspaper. Eddie Yuen, Ling-chi Wang, and Amanda Lashaw were our main partners in archiving the H. K. Yuen Collection. The Bancroft Library and the Ethnic Studies Library at the University of California, Berkeley, agreed to house parts of the evolving Yuen Collection. Librarians John Berry, Phyllis Bischoff, Lilian Castillo-Speed, Lincoln Cushing, Miki Goral, Gabriela Gray, Molly Molloy, and Teresa Salazar lent invaluable expertise at various phases of the project. The Institute for the Study of Social Change (ISSC) at UC Berkeley provided institutional and financial support at crucial stages. Former ISSC directors Troy Duster, Pegro Noguera, Michael Omi, and Rachel Moran as well as ISSC academic staff members David Minkus, Rivka Polatnick, and Christine Trost were true friends of the project. The Shepard Fund in the History Department and the URAP program at UC Berkeley; the Bunche Center and the Social Science Division at UCLA; the Center for Advanced Study at Stanford; and the Charles E. and Sue K. Young Award committee also provided invaluable support. Ruthie Gilmore, Gillian Hart, Percy Hintzen, Kim Voss, and Maurice Zeitlin each helped in crucial ways to develop the research proposal and framework. Several people provided especially close readings of and perceptive comments on the entire manuscript: Elaine Brown, Kathleen Cleaver, Max Elbaum, Raymond Gavins, David Hilliard, Darnell Hunt, Billy X Jennings, Leon Litwack, Doug McAdam, Michael Omi, Scott Saul, Bobby Seale, and Patricia Sullivan. Others provided especially helpful comments and information at various phases of the project, including Antwi Akom, Lauren Araiza, Curtis Austin, Rachel Bernard, Robert Blauner, Jeremy Brecher, Clayborne Carson, Joseph Duong, Troy Duster, Cathy Forman, Hardy Frye, Alex Garcia, Jeff Haas, Tom Hayden, Charles E. Jones, Naomi Klein, Harvey Lane, Kerima Lewis, Shelia Martin, David Matza, David Montejano, Joseph Orbock, Steven Pitts, Anthony Platt, Rachel Reinhard, Martha Saavedra, Ula Taylor, Felicia Viator, Richard Walker, Aaron Wilkinson, and Peter Zinoman. Thanks to Sophie Shalenberg, Kathy Bannerman, and especially Patrick Liem for their visual expertise, and to Shepard Fairey for his generosity. We were most fortunate to talk with and receive materials from many of the most important photographers of the Black Panther Party, including Jeffrey Blankfort, Alan Copeland, Roz Payne, and Stephen Shames, as well as the Pirkle Jones Foundation. Christopher Cook's editorial work at a key juncture helped make the manuscript sing. Michael Burawoy deepened the conversation with Gramsci. Tamara Kay showed the way. Christian Parenti pointed out a few simple things that proved very revealing in the end. Michael Mann helped us see the big picture. If you find the light of freedom shining in these pages, Douglas Corbin helped keep it burning. Gregory Morris went beyond the call. It is hard to convey the depth of our appreciation for William Roy, who has been there on the many occasions when we needed advice and support. Thanks to Marc Favreau for his grace. Niels Hooper has been our dream editor, expertly shepherding the project with a light touch. Thanks also to Adrienne Harris, Suzanne Knott, Kim Hogeland, Barbara Roos, and the rest of the University of California Press team.

We could not have kept sight of our purpose in this long journey without many dear comrades who helped us along the way, including Bhanica Adams, Kyle Arnone, Anita Bakshi, Jason Ball, Doyle Beasley, Gary Blasi, Edna Bonacich, Rose Braz, Lauren Bruce, Alex Caputo-Pearl, John Colon, Nadya Dabby, Alesandro Delfanti, Charlie Eaton, Max Elbaum, Erica Etelson, Che Patrice Lumumba Farmer, Stefania Galante, Pablo Gaston, Gia Grant, Arthur Hopkins, Raichele Jackson, Hazem Kandil, Elaine Kim, Misha Klein, Amanda Lashaw, Eric Lee, John Lew, Paul Liotsakis, Yingzhao Liu, Isaac Mankita, Ruth Milkman, Rachel Moran, Meley Mulughetta, Victor Narro, Mohammed Nuru, Satti Odeye, Peter Olney, Windy and Erin O'Malley, Caitlin Patler, Macquesta Pendleton, Cookie Polan, Pitch Pongsawat, Becca Prager, Ana-Christina Ramon, Arun Rasiah, Elisha Rochell, Tanay Rochell, Brynn Saito, Jono Shaffer, Harley Shaiken, Elina Shih, "Mama" Sylvia Simmons, Lola Smallwood-Cuevas, Terrell Smith, Forrest Stuart, Mayssoun Sukarieh, Iddo Tavory, Veronica Terriquez, Chris Tilly, Delvin Tobie, Tonya Tobie, Julia Tomassetti, Irvin Walker, Terri Weissman, Mario Wesson, Frank Wilderson III, Kent Wong, and Tse-Sung Wu. Thanks to Amy Cooper, Greg Hawkins, Judith Lassiter, and especially Donald Moyer for keeping us flexible.

Finally, we express our warm appreciation to the extended families that sustain each of us: Morgan Alber, Bonnie Bayuk, Ken Berg, Jon Blazer, Noah Bloom, Paul Bloom, Anna Bresnick, Bill and Gloria Broder, Tanya Broder, Janet Brodie, David Burbank, Semeon Chalbins, Katrina

Clark, Sally Connolly, Linda Drazen, Gail Eierweiss, David Forman, Debra Garlin and Michael Yellin, Jenn Garlin and Marcelo Guzman, Tom and Ilene Garlin, Liz Gersten, Karen Gersten-Rothenberg, Sara Gersten-Rothenberg and Josh Monaghan, Millie Grenough, Chris Heitmann, Aaron Hoffnung, Jeff Kilbreth, Cyra Levenson, Roberta Macklin, Robin Macklin, Stephen Macklin, Shelia Martin, Stephen Martin, April Martin, Avis Lester Martin, Sarah and Jay Moldenhauer-Salazar, Gilda Outremont, Vincenza Petrilli, Nina and Mark Pitts, Cookie, Maya, and Rosa Polan, Abby Reese, Alice Rosenthal, Peg Shalen, Eli Shalenberg, Bill Shields, Aaron Stark and Cecillia Chu, Maria Tupper and Fred Cervin, Corey Joseph Wade, Ted Wang, Yun Fen Wang, Crystal Martin White, Sedrick White, Seth Williams, Don Wunderlee, and especially to our mothers, Meg Bloom and Nettie Foxx Martin. Most especially, we thank Elizabeth and Catherine, who bring love, joy, and order to our lives.

Index

killings, 243; Sacramento gun law delegation (1967), 61

Chicanos. *See* Latinos/Chicanos

Chikarema, Charles, 469n22

child care: women responsible for, 193, 195, 306, 466n48. *See also* schools

Children's Institute/Intercommunal Youth Institute (IYI)/Oakland Community School, 3, 167*fig*, 169*fig*, 175*fig*, 192–93, 384

Chile, Allende of, 309

China: Black Panther allies, 1–2, 3, 319, 321, 338*fig*, 349–50, 467n10, 469n14; Black Panther trip, 319, 321, 383; Newton, 1–2, 3, 338*fig*, 349–50, 403n1; Nixon, 1–2, 350; "ping-pong diplomacy," 350; Red Guard ten-point program and, 290; revolution, 69, 290; Tiananmen Square rally, 2, 338*fig*; Robert F. Williams, 33; Zhou Enlai, 1–2, 338*fig*, 350. *See also* Mao Zedong

Chisholm, Shirley, 245

Churchill, Ward, 250

CIA (Central Intelligence Agency), 3, 204, 211–12, 392, 431n3

Cincinnati, rebellion, 88

Citizens for Creative Welfare, Los Angeles Black Congress, 141

citizenship rights: black insurgent mobilizations in North and West, 395; but still ghettoized, impoverished, and politically subordinated, 12, 27; Civil Rights Movement for, 2, 4, 11. *See also* civil rights; concessions; voting rights

citizenship schools, Civil Rights Movement, 191

City College of San Francisco, student strikes, 284–85

City University of New York, student strike, 265

Civil Air Patrol, Ford, 149

civil disobedience, Civil Rights Movement, 11, 42, 90, 113, 116, 121, 406n36

civil rights, 121, 395; *Brown v. Board*, 117; Civil Rights Act (1964), 11, 27, 117, 120, 138; Democratic Party and, 24–25, 26, 200, 203–4, 209, 442n24; Johnson administration and, 117; Kennedy administration and, 410n53; Newark police brutality cases, 83; New York Black Panthers and police, 156. *See also* citizenship rights; Civil Rights Movement; voting rights

Civil Rights Movement, 11, 32, 114, 121, 197, 405–6n36; Baker, 34; Belafonte,

131; Black Panther Party differences from, 2, 4, 395; black political organizations and, 116; Black Power activism and thought distinguished from, 395; and Black Power shift, 37; for citizenship rights, 2, 4, 11; citizenship schools, 191; civil disobedience, 11, 42, 90, 113, 116, 121, 406n36; and civil rights enforcement, 11; Eldridge Cleaver and, 74, 76; Comfort, 34; FBI monitoring, 200; freedom schools, 191–92; Gregory, 30, 125, 450n14; Hilliard view of, 183; insurgent movement, 11, 13, 65, 74, 114–22, 386n22, 406n36, 424nn3,14; legal costs, 74; limitations, 11–13, 23–27, 91, 390; Merritt College activists vs., 21; mobilization in South, 37; moderates, 11, 121; Murray, 269; NAACP foundational work for, 424n3; New Left growing out of, 127; *New York Times* coverage, 474n40; state concessions to, 11–13, 23–27, 76, 113–21, 138, 486n22; unraveled, 120, 124, 397, 406n36; urban rebellions and, 30, 90; victories, 11–13, 23–27, 76, 91, 113–21, 201, 392, 395, 406n36; women, 105–6; written accounts, 395. *See also* Congress of Racial Equality (CORE); integrationism; King, Martin Luther Jr.; nonviolence; Southern Christian Leadership Conference (SCLC); Student Nonviolent Coordinating Committee (SNCC)

Civil War, 3–4

Clark, Frank, 132

Clark, Mark, 238–43, 250–51, 325*fig*, 352, 375

Clark, Septima, 191

class struggle: Black Panthers emphasizing, 300, 313; black women, 303–4; global liberation, 317; Mao on American Negroes and, 409–10n53. *See also* middle class; working class

Clay, Cassius/Muhammad Ali, 23, 92, 93, 131–32, 407n16

Clay, William, 245

Cleage, Albert, 88

Cleaver, Eldridge, 48–49, 74–82, 107; Algeria, 3, 314–18, 321, 337*fig*, 350, 358, 360, 362, 368, 468–69nn14,18,22, 476n66; arrests, 61, 79, 118–19, 149; Asia trip, 319, 320–21; Berkeley lectures, 136–38, 173*fig*; and Beverly, 76–79; birth, 74; *Black Panther* newspaper beginnings, 56, 79, 416n1; Black